AF352561

The Legends of the Saints in Old Norse–Icelandic Prose

The Legends of the Saints in Old Norse–Icelandic Prose

KIRSTEN WOLF

UNIVERSITY OF TORONTO PRESS
Toronto Buffalo London

© University of Toronto Press 2013
Toronto Buffalo London
www.utppublishing.com
Printed in Canada

ISBN 978-1-4426-4621-6

Printed on acid-free, 100% post-consumer recycled paper with vegetable-based inks.

Library and Archives Canada Cataloguing in Publication

Wolf, Kirsten, 1959–
The legends of the saints in Old Norse – Icelandic prose / Kirsten Wolf.

(Toronto Old Norse and Icelandic studies)
Includes bibliographical references and index.
ISBN 978-1-4426-4621-6

1. Old Norse prose literature – Bibliography. 2. Christian saints – Legends –
Early works to 1800 – Bibliography. 3. Christian saints in literature –
Bibliography. I. Title. II. Series: Toronto Old Norse and Icelandic studies

Z2556.W64 2013   016.839630080382   C2013-901826-3

University of Toronto Press gratefully acknowledges the financial assistance of the
Centre for Medieval Studies, University of Toronto in the publication of this book.

University of Toronto Press acknowledges the financial assistance to its publishing
program of the Canada Council for the Arts and the Ontario Arts Council.

University of Toronto Press acknowledges the financial support of the Government
of Canada through the Canada Book Fund for its publishing activities.

Contents

Preface

Saints' legends form a substantial portion of Old Norse–Icelandic literature. The lives, passions, or miracles, in part or in full, of about 150 saints
have been preserved, and of some legends there are several versions. These
legends are extant in more than four hundred manuscripts or fragments of
manuscript dating from shortly before the twelfth century to two or three
centuries after the Reformation. Over the years, they have been the subject
of research by some three hundred scholars worldwide.

To students and scholars of Old Norse–Icelandic hagiographic literature, probably no one has provided a better service than C.R. Unger. In less
than a decade towards the end of the nineteenth century, he published an
edition of the legend and miracles of the Virgin Mary, a collection of various recensions of a dozen legends about the apostles, and a collection of
more than three dozen legends and lives of the saints. With his editions,
which were supplemented in 1893 by Gustav Morgenstern's edition of AM
655 4to III–VIII, AM 238 fol. II, and AM 921 4t5o IV, and in 1927 by
Finnur Jónsson's edition of AM 623 4to, Unger laid the foundation for
much of the ensuing research on hagiographic literature. Interest in Old
Norse–Icelandic hagiography was greatly invigorated in the decades following the mid-nineteenth century by Ole Widding's and Hans Bekker-
Nielsen's many articles on the topic, Peter Foote's study of Stock. Perg. fol.
no. 2, and Agnete Loth's edition of Stock. Perg. fol. no. 3. The last three or
four decades have witnessed a veritable outpouring of works on hagiography within the field of medieval studies in general, and the field of Old
Norse–Icelandic literature has been no exception. The legends of the saints
have enjoyed what can almost be called a renaissance: historians have
delved into the legends for what they reveal about the social, political, and
spiritual cultures that produced them; literary critics have examined the

theological and didactic agendas of their authors; and philologists have focused on the identification of sources for individual legends and provided new, scholarly editions of these texts.

An invaluable resource for scholars working on the Old Norse–Icelandic saints' legends in the last forty-eight years has been Hans Bekker-Nielsen, Ole Widding, and L.K. Shook's index, "The Lives of the Saints in Old Norse Prose: A Handlist," which was published in volume 25 of *Mediaeval Studies* in 1963. The handlist and the corpus of Old Norse–Icelandic saints' lives in general are described by Hans Bekker-Nielsen in "On a Handlist of Saints' Lives in Old Norse," published in volume 24 of *Mediaeval Studies* in 1962. With its list of saints along with the manuscripts preserving the individual legends and the editions in which the legends have been edited, the handlist is often the first publication to which scholars turn when in need of information about a particular saint's legend. However, because of the considerable amount of scholarship conducted within the field of Old Norse–Icelandic hagiography since the early 1960s, the handlist reads now as dated, though certainly most of the information contained in it remains unchanged.

It is the purpose of this volume to provide an updated version of the handlist. The volume follows the format of Bekker-Nielsen, Widding, and Shook's article (though I have noted the format of Marianne Kalinke and P.M. Mitchell's *Bibliography of Old Norse–Icelandic Romances*, published as volume 44 in the Islandica series by Cornell University Press in 1985).

This book is arranged according to the following principles:

1 Saints are listed alphabetically according to name, with their feast days indicated in each case.
2 Cross references to the *BHL* are provided whenever possible. Supplementary comments bearing on sources or other textual problems are sometimes added.
3 Arabic numerals followed by a title denote variant versions or redactions of the same life. Where possible, these are listed in chronological order. Epitomes and short tales of saints, such as those incorporated into the miracles of the Virgin Mary, are, however, listed at the end of an entry.
4 Manuscripts are listed in alphabetical order according to their location followed by the approximate date.
5 Editions of the individual lives are listed in alphabetical order by saint's name followed by references to Modern Icelandic language editions and translations.

6 The bibliographical material seeks to supplement that given in Bekker-Nielsen, Widding, and Shook's handlist, which is only selective. The present list does not presume to be exhaustive, but I hope that most books and mainstream journals within the field of Old Norse–Icelandic language and literature have been covered. The bibliography has a slight bias towards more recent publications and ones written in the Scandinavian languages, Icelandic, English, German, and French. The cut-off date for publications is the fall of 2011, when the manuscript was submitted to the University of Toronto Press. Icelandic names are alphabetized by given and not patronymic name.

7 The entries conclude with references to the handlist, which gives folio-numbers and also distinguishes between vellum and paper manuscripts.

The list of saints' legends is prefaced by a table of abbreviations and symbols used, a list of relevant published catalogues and bibliographies, a list of some of the main collections and anthologies of Old Norse–Icelandic saints' lives, a list of frequently cited general works, and a list of frequently cited essay collections, festschrifts, and conference proceedings.

My work on the volume was in the main conducted during a sabbatical leave from the University of Wisconsin–Madison in the spring of 2011. I am grateful to the Graduate School of the University of Wisconsin for a Kellett research award, which enabled me to spend time in the Arnamagnaean Collection in Copenhagen and to involve my able research assistants, Jackson Crawford and Natalie Van Deusen, in the project. Finally, I wish to thank the staff of the University of Toronto Press for its fine work and our pleasant collaboration.

Abbreviations and Symbols

ANF	*Arkiv för nordisk filologi*
APS	*Acta Philologica Scandinavica*
ASE	*Anglo-Saxon England*
Beiträge	*Beiträge zur Geschichte der deutschen Sprache und Literatur*
BHL	*Bibliotheca Hagiographica Latina*
CCI	Corpus Codicum Islandicorum Medii Aevi
CCN	Corpus Codicum Norvegicorum Medii Aevi
CM	*Collegium Medievale*
EIM	Early Icelandic Manuscripts in Facsimile
GR	*Germanic Review*
JEGP	*Journal of English and Germanic Philology*
KLNM	*Kulturhistorisk Leksikon for nordisk middelalder*
MLR	*Modern Language Review*
Mm	*Maal og minne*
MS	*Mediaeval Studies*
MScand	*Mediaeval Scandinavia*
Saga-Book	*Saga-Book of the Viking Society*
SI	*Scripta Islandica*
SS	*Scandinavian Studies*
STUAGNL	Samfund til Udgivelse af gammel nordisk Litteratur
*	Item not examined by the compiler
>>	Item's full bibliographical information can be found in "Collections and Anthologies," "General Works," or "Essay Collections, Festschrifts, and Conference Proceedings."

The Legends of the Saints in Old Norse–Icelandic Prose

I. Catalogues and Bibliographies

Arnamagnæanske Kommission, Den. *Ordbog over det norrøne prosasprog. Registre* (Odense: AiO, 1989).

Bibliotheca Hagiographica Latina Antiquae et Mediae Aetatis. Subsidia hagiographica 6 (Brussels: Société des Bollandistes, 1898–9. Rpt. 1992). *Supplementum*. Subsidia hagiographica 12 (Brussels: Société des Bollandistes, 1911). *Novum Supplementum*. Subsidia hagiographica 70 (Brussels: Société des Bollandistes, 1986).

British Library, The. *Catalogue of Additions to the Manuscripts 1756–1782. Additional Manuscripts 4101–5017* (London: British Museum Publications Ltd. for the British Library Board, 1973).

Carlsson, Thorsten. "Norrøn legendforskning – en kort presentation." *Scripta Islandica* 23 (1972): 31–58.

Fry, Donald K. *Norse Sagas Translated into English: A Bibliography* (New York: AMS Press, 1980).

Grímur M. Helgason and Lárus H. Blöndal. *Handritasafn Landsbókasafns. III. Aukabindi* (Reykjavík: Landsbókasafn Íslands, 1970).

Grímur M. Helgason and Ögmundur Helgason. *Handritasafn Landsbókasafns. IV. Aukabindi* (Reykjavík: Landsbókasafn Íslands – Háskólabókasafn, 1996).

Gödel, Vilhelm. *Katalog öfver Upsala Universitets Biblioteks fornisländska och fornnorska handskrifter* (Uppsala: Almqvist & Wiksell, 1892).

– *Katalog öfver Kongl. Bibliotekets fornisländska och fornnorska handskrifter* (Stockholm: Norstedt & Söner, 1897–1900).

Kålund, Kr. *Katalog over Den arnamagnæanske Håndskriftsamling*. 2 vols. (Copenhagen: Gyldendal, 1889–94).

– *Katalog over de oldnorsk-islandske Håndskrifter i Det store kongelige Bibliotek og i Universitetsbiblioteket (udenfor Den arnamagnæanske*

Samling samt den arnamagnæanske Samlings Tilvækst 1894–99)
(Copenhagen: Gyldendal, 1900).
Lárus H. Blöndal. *Handritasafn Landsbókasafns. II. Aukabindi. Viðauki.
Skrá um skinnblöð í Landsbókasafni Íslands eftir Jakob Benediktsson*
(Reykjavík: Félagsprintsmiðjan, 1959).
Páll Eggert Ólason. *Skrá um Handritasöfn Landsbókasafnsins.* 3 vols.
(Reykjavík: Gutenberg, 1918–37).
– *Handritasafn Landsbókasafns. I. Aukabindi* (Reykjavík: Félagsprintsmið-
jan, 1947).
Skulerud, Olai. *Catalogue of Norse Manuscripts in Edinburgh, Dublin and
Manchester* (Kristiania [Oslo]: Emil Moestue, 1918).
Þórhallur Þorgilsson. *Drög að skrá um ritverk á íslenzku að fornu og nýju
af latneskum eða rómönskum uppruna. I. Frakkland.* Bibliographiae
Latino-romanico-Islandicae Tentamen. Fasc. 1: Scripta e fontibus
gallicis (Reykjavík: Landsbókasafn Íslands, 1954).
– *Drög að skrá um ritverk á íslenzku að fornu og nýju af latneskum eða
rómönskum uppruna. II. Ítalía.* Bibliographiae Latino-romanico-
Islandicae Tentamen. Fasc. II: Scripta e fontibus gallicis (Reykjavík:
Landsbókasafn Íslands, 1958).
Widding, Ole, Hans Bekker-Nielsen, and L.K. Shook. "The Lives of the
Saints in Old Norse Prose: A Handlist." *Mediaeval Studies* 25 (1963):
294–337.

II. Collections and Anthologies

Carlé, Birte. *Skøger og jomfruer i den kristne fortællekunst* (Odense:
Odense Universitetsforlag, 1991).
Includes translations of *Agǫtu saga*, *Barbǫru saga*, *Maríu saga egipzku*,
and the legend of Thais in *Barlaams saga ok Jósafats*.
Clunies Ross, Margaret, ed. *Poetry on Christian Subjects*. 2 vols. *Skaldic
Poetry of the Scandinavian Middle Ages*. Vol. 7 (Turnhout: Brepols, 2007).
Includes editions of *Allra postula minnisvísur*, *Andréasdrápa*, *Brúðkaups-
vísur*, *Drápa af Máríugrát*, Gamli kanóki's *Jónsdrápa*, *Gyðingsvísur*,
Heilagra manna drápa, *Heilagra meyja drápa*, *Kátrínardrápa*, Kolbeinn
Tumason's *Jónsvísur*, *Máríuvísur I*, *Máríuvísur II*, *Máríuvísur III*,
Níkulás Bergsson's *Jónsdrápa*, *Pétrsdrápa*, *Plácítusdrápa*, and *Vitnisvísur
af Máríu*.
Einar Ól. Sveinsson, ed. *Leit eg suður til landa. Ævintýri og helgisögur frá
miðöldum* (Reykjavík: Heimskringla, 1944).
Includes modern Iceland language editions of *Niðrstigningar saga* as
well as extracts from *Barlaams saga ok Jósafats*, *Guðmundar saga*,
Jarteinabók Þorláks biskups in forna, *Jarteinabók Þorláks biskups ǫnnur*,
Jóns saga helga, and *Maríu jartegnir*.
Finnur Jónsson, ed. *AM 623, 4°: Helgensagaer*. Samfund til Udgivelse af
gammel nordisk Litteratur 52 (Copenhagen: Jørgensen, 1927).
Includes editions of *Alexíss saga*, *Blasíuss saga*, *XL riddara saga*, *Jóns
saga postola*, *Niðrstigningar saga*, and *Sjau sofanda saga*.
Foote, Peter, ed. *Lives of Saints. Perg. fol. nr. 2 in the Royal Library,
Stockholm*. Early Icelandic Manuscripts in Facsimile 4 (Copenhagen:
Rosenkilde and Bagger, 1962).
Facsimile editions of *Agǫtu saga*, *Agnesar saga*, *Ambrósiuss saga
biskups*, *Ágústínuss saga*, *Barbǫru saga*, *Benedikts saga*, *Blasíuss saga*,
Cecilíu saga, *Díónysíuss saga*, *Fídesar saga*, *Spesar ok Karítasar*,

*Gregors saga páfa, Katrínar saga, Kross saga (Flagellatio Crucis),
Lárentíuss saga erkidjákns, Lúcíu saga, Máritíuss saga, Maríu saga
egipzku, Marteins saga biskups, Máruss saga, Mǫrtu saga ok Maríu
Magðalenu, Nikúláss saga erkibiskups, Páls saga eremita, Silvesters
saga, Stefáns saga, Thómass saga erkibiskups,* and *Vincentíuss saga,*
along with facsimiles (extracts only) of *Díalógar (Viðrœður) Gregors
páfa, Hallvarðs saga, Jóns saga baptista,* and *Sebastíanuss saga.*

Gering, Hugo, ed. *Islendzk æventyri: Isländische Legenden Novellen und
Märchen.* 2 vols. (Halle a. S: Waisenhaus, 1882–4).
Includes editions and paraphrases of *Af biskupi ok púka, Af Celestíno
ok Bonifacío páfum, Af Dúnstano, Af frú Aglais, Af hinum helga
Thóma, Af Karlamagnúsi, Af Konstantíno kongi, Af Lanfranco, Af
Marcellíno páfa, Af Marínu munk, Af Remigío erkibiskupi, Af Sindulfo
ok hans frú,* and *Af tveimr munkum.*

Gudbrand Vigfusson and George W. Dasent, ed. and trans. *Icelandic
Sagas and Other Historical Documents Relating to the Settlements and
Descents of the Northmen on the British Isles.* 4 vols. Rolls Series 88
(London: Eyre & Spottiswoode, 1887–94; rpt. [Millwood]: Kraus, 1962).
Includes editions (and select translations) of *Af Beda presti, Dúnsta-
nuss saga, Játvarðar saga, Magnúss saga Eyjajarls lengri, Magnúss saga
Eyjajarls skemmri,* and *Orkneyinga saga.*

Guðni Jónsson, ed. *Byskupa sögur.* 3 vols. (Reykjavík: Íslendingasagnaútgáfan; Haukadalsútgáfan, 1948). Vol. 3, pp. 155–506.
Includes editions of *Guðmundar saga A, Guðmundar saga B, Guðmundar saga D, Jarteinabók Þorláks biskups in forna, Jarteinabók
Þorláks biskups ǫnnur, Jóns saga helga S, Jóns saga helga L, Jóns saga
helga H, Þorláks saga biskups A, Þorláks saga biskups B,* and *Þorláks
saga biskups C.*

Holtsmark, Anne, ed. *A Book of Miracles: MS No. 645 4to of the Arna-
Magnæan Collection in the University Library of Copenhagen.* Corpus
Codicum Islandicorum Medii Aevi 12 (Copenhagen: Einar Munks-
gaard, 1938).
Facsimile editions of *Andréss saga postola, Barthólómeuss saga postola,
Jakobs saga postola (ins eldra), Jarteinabók Þorláks biskups in forna,
Klements saga, Marteins saga biskups, Matheuss saga postola, Niðr-
stigningar saga, Páls saga postola,* and *Pétrs saga postola.*

Hreinn Benediktsson. *Early Icelandic Script As Illustrated in Vernacular
Texts from the Twelfth and Thirteenth Centuries.* Íslenzk handrit:
Icelandic Manuscripts, Series in Folio 2 (Reykjavík: The Manuscript
Institute of Iceland, 1965).

Includes facsimile and text editions (extracts only) of *Af Benedikt, Af Cuthberto, Af Gregor, Ambrósíuss saga biskups, Basilíuss saga, Díalógar (Viðrœður) Gregors páfa, Erasmuss saga, Jakobs saga postola (ins eldra), Jóns saga postola, Klements saga, Máritíuss saga, Maríu jartegnir, Marteins saga biskups, Matheuss saga postola, Niðrstigningar saga, Nikuláss saga erkibiskups, Óláfs saga helga en elsta, Páls saga postola, Pétrs saga postola, Silvesters saga, Stefáns saga,* and *Þorláks saga biskups B.*

Jón Helgason, ed. *Byskupa sǫgur. MS Perg. fol. No. 5 in the Royal Library of Stockholm.* Corpus Codicum Islandicorum Medii Aevi 19 (Copenhagen: Ejnar Munksgaard, 1950).

Facsimile editions of *Guðmunar saga D, Játvarðar saga, Jóns saga helga L,* and *Þorláks saga helga A.*

[Jón Sigurðsson and Guðbrandur Vigfússon, ed.] *Biskupa sögur.* 2 vols. (Copenhagen: Møller, 1858–78).

Includes editions of *Guðmundar saga A, Guðmundar saga B, Guðmundar saga D, Jarteinabók Þorláks biskups in forna, Jarteinabók Þorláks biskups ǫnnur, Jóns saga helga S, Jóns saga helga L, Jóns saga helga H, Þorláks saga biskups A, Þorláks saga biskups B, Þorláks saga biskups C,* and *Þorláks saga biskups D.*

Konráð Gíslason, ed. *Fire og fyrretyve for en stor Deel forhen utrykte Prøver af oldnordisk Sprog og Literatur* (Copenhagen: Gyldendal, 1860).

Includes editions of *Alexíss saga* and *Díalógar (Viðrœður) Gregors páfa.*

[Kålund, Kr.], ed. *Palæografisk Atlas: Oldnorsk-islandsk afdeling.* (Copenhagen and Christiania [Oslo]: Gyldendal, 1905).

Includes facsimile and text editions (extracts only) of *Blasíuss saga, Guðmundar saga A, Jarteinabók Þorláks biskups in forna, Magnúss saga Eyjajarls, Óláfs saga helga,* and *Thómass saga erkibiskups.*

– ed. *Palæografisk Atlas: Oldnorsk-islandsk afdeling. Ny serie. Oldnorsk-islandske skriftprøver c. 1300–1700* (Copenhagen and Kristiania [Oslo]: Gyldendal, 1907).

Includes facsimile and text editions (extracts only) of *Benedikts saga* and *Guðmundar saga D.*

Larsson, Ludvig, ed. *Isländska handskriften Nº 645 4º i Den Arnamagnæanske Samlingen på Universitetsbiblioteket i København: I. Handskriftens äldre del* (Lund: Gleerup, 1885).

Editions of *Andréss saga postola, Barthólómeuss saga postola, Jakobs saga postola (ins eldra), Jarteinabók Þorláks biskups in forna, Klements saga, Matheuss saga postola,* and *Pétrs saga postola.*

Loth, Agnete, ed. *Reykjahólabók: Islandske helgenlegender.* 2 vols.
Editiones Arnamagnæanæ, Ser. A, vols. 15–16 (Copenhagen: Munksgaard, 1969–70).
Editions of *Ágústínuss saga, Ambrósíuss saga biskups, Antóníuss saga,
Barlaams saga og Jósafats, Dóminíkuss saga, Erasmuss saga, Georgíuss
saga, Gregors saga biskups, Gregors saga páfa, Heilagra þriggja konunga
saga, Hendriks saga og Kúnigúndísar, Jerónimuss saga, Jóns saga
gullmunns, Kristófórs saga, Lárencíuss saga erkidjákns, Lazaruss saga,
Nikuláss saga af Tólentínó, Osvalds saga, Rokuss saga, Sebastíanuss
saga, Servasíuss saga, Silvesters saga, Sjau sofanda saga, Stefáns saga,*
and *Önnu saga og Maríu.*
Morgenstern, Gustav, ed. *Arnamagnæanische Fragmente (Cod. AM. 655
4to III–VIII, 238 fol. II, 921 4to IV 1.2): Ein Supplement zu den
Heilagra manna sögur* (Leipzig and Copenhagen: Møller, 1893).
Editions of *Basilíuss saga, Díalógar (Viðræður) Gregors páfa, Erasmuss
saga, Gregors saga páfa, Nikuláss saga erkibiskups,* and *Silvesters saga.*
Mundal, Else. *Legender frå mellomalderen. Soger om heilage kvinner og
menn* (Oslo: Det Norske Samlaget, 1995).
Includes translations of *Agnesar saga, Agǫtu saga, Benedikts saga,
Blasíuss saga, Cecilíu saga, Nikuláss saga erkibiskups, Óláfs saga helga,
Plácíduss saga,* and *Sunnivu saga.*
Ólafur Halldórsson, ed. *Sögur úr Skarðsbók* (Reykjavík: Almenna
bókafélagið, 1967).
Modern Icelandic language editions of *Andréss saga postola,
Barthólómeuss saga postola, Filippuss saga postola, Jakobs saga postola
(ins yngra), Matheuss saga postola, Mathíass saga postola, Páls saga
postola, Pétrs saga postola, Thómass saga postola, Tveggja postola saga
Jóns ok Jakobs (ins eldra),* and *Tveggja postola saga Símons ok Júdass.*
Slay, Desmond, ed. *Codex Scardensis.* Early Icelandic Manuscripts in
Facsimile 2 (Copenhagen: Rosenkilde and Bagger, 1960).
Facsimile editions of *Andréss saga postola, Barthólómeuss saga postola,
Filippuss saga postola, Jakobs saga postola (ins yngra), Matheuss saga
postola, Mathíass saga postola, Páls saga postola, Pétrs saga postola,
Thómass saga postola, Tveggja postola saga Jóns ok Jakobs (ins eldra),*
and *Tveggja postola saga Símons ok Júdass.*
Stefán Karlsson, ed. *Sagas of Icelandic Bishops. Fragments of Eight
Manuscripts.* Early Icelandic Manuscripts in Facsimile 7 (Copenhagen:
Rosenkilde and Bagger, 1967).
Includes facsimile editions (in full or extracts only) of *Ágústínuss saga,
Guðmundar saga A, Guðmundar saga D, Jóns saga helga S, Jóns saga*

helga L, *Magnúss saga Eyjajarls lengri*, *Maríu jartegnir*, *Jarteinabók Þorláks biskups in forna*, and *Þorláks saga biskups B*.

Sverrir Tómasson, Bragi Halldórsson, and Einar Sigurbjörnsson, ed. *Heilagra karla sögur*. Íslensk trúarrit 3 (Reykjavík: Bókmenntafræðistofnun Háskóla Íslands, 2007).

Modern Icelandic language editions of *Alexíss saga*, *Ágústínuss saga*, *Gregors saga biskups*, *Marteins saga biskups*, *Máruss saga*, *Níkuláss saga erkibiskups*, *Óláfs saga helga*, *Páls saga eremíta*, *Rokuss saga*, *Silvesters saga*, *Stefáns saga*, and *Vítuss saga*.

Þorsteinn Jónsson, ed. *Hér hefjast Tíu Sögur, af þeim enum heiløgu Guds Postulum og pínslar vottum* (Viðeyjarklaustur: Þ. Jónsson, 1836).

Editions of *Andréss saga postola*, *Barthólómeuss saga postola*, *Filippuss saga postola*, *Jakobs saga postola (ins eldra)*, *Jakobs saga postola (ins yngra)*, *Jóns saga postola*, *Matheuss saga postola*, *Mathíass saga postola*, *Pétrs saga postola*, *Thómass saga postola*, and *Tveggja postola saga Símons ok Júdass*.

Þorvaldur Bjarnarson. *Leifar fornra kristinna fræða íslenzkra: Codex Arna-Magnæanus 677 4to auk annara enna elztu brota af guðfræðisritum* (Copenhagen: Hagerup, 1878).

Includes editions of *Af Benedikt*, *Af Cuthberto*, *Af Gregor*, and *Díalógar (Viðræður) Gregors páfa*.

Unger, C.R., ed. *Mariu saga: Legender om Jomfru Maria og hendes jertegn* (Christiania [Oslo]: Brögger & Christie, 1871).

Editions of *Af Anselmo*, *Af Basilío*, *Af Beda*, *Af Bernardo*, *Af Bónifacío*, *Af Bonito*, *Af Dóminíco*, *Af Dúnstano*, *Af Eadmundo*, *Af Eusebío*, *Af Francisco*, *Af Fulberto*, *Af Gregorio*, *Af Heremanno*, *Af Húgo*, *Af Húgo ábóta*, *Af Hildifonso*, *Af Jóhanne elemosinario*, *Af Jóhanne Damasceno*, *Af Leó páfa*, *Af Maríu egipzku*, *Af Maríu de Oegines*, *Af Ódílo ábóta*, *Af Pétro Clarevallensis*, *Af Stephano*, *Af Thómasi erkibiskupi*, *Elizabetar leiðsla*, *Maríu jartegnir*, and *Maríu saga*.

– ed. *Postola sögur: Legendariske fortællinger om apostlernes liv, deres kamp for kristendommens udbredelse samt deres martyrdød* (Christiania [Oslo]: Bentzen, 1874).

Editions of *Andréss saga postola*, *Barthólómeuss saga postola*, *Filippuss saga postola*, *Klements saga*, *Jakobs saga postola (ins eldra)*, *Jakobs saga postola (ins yngra)*, *Jóns drápa postola*, *Jónsdrápa*, *Jóns saga baptista*, *Jóns saga postola*, *Jónsvísur*, *Matheuss saga postola*, *Mathíass saga postola*, *Páls saga postola*, *Pétrs saga postola*, *Thómass saga postola*, *Tveggja postola saga Jóns ok Jakobs (ins eldra)*, *Tveggja postola saga Pétrs ok Páls*, and *Tveggja postola saga Símons ok Júdass*.

– ed. *Heilagra manna søgur: Fortællinger og legender om hellige mænd og kvinder*. 2 vols. (Christiania [Oslo]: Bentzen, 1877).

Includes editions of *Agnesar saga, Ágústínuss saga, Agǫtu saga, Alexíss saga, Ambrósíuss saga biskups, Antóníuss saga, Barbǫru saga, Benedikts saga, Blasíuss saga, Brendanuss saga, Cecilíu saga, Díalógar (Viðræður) Gregors páfa, Díónysíuss saga, Dórótheu saga, Erasmuss saga, Fídesar saga, Spesar ok Karítasar, XL riddara saga, Gregors saga páfa, Hallvarðs saga, Katrínar saga, Kross saga, Lárentíuss saga erkidjákns, Lúcíu saga, Malkuss saga, Af Marcellíno páfa, Margrétar saga, Máritíuss saga, Maríu saga egipzku, Marteins saga biskups, Máruss saga, Mikjáls saga, Mǫrtu saga ok Maríu Magðalena, Niðrstigningar saga, Nikuláss saga erkibikups, Óláfs saga helga, Páls saga eremita, Plácíduss saga, Remigíuss saga, Sebastíanuss saga, Silvesters saga, Sjau sofanda saga, Stefáns saga, Theódórs saga, Thómass saga erkibiskups, Vincentíuss saga, Vitae Patrum (Heilagra feðra æfi)*, and *Vítuss saga*.

Wolf, Kirsten, ed. *Heilagra meyja sögur*. Íslensk trúarrit 1 (Reykjavík: Bókmenntafræðistofnun Háskola Íslands, 2003).

Modern Icelandic language editions of *Agnesar saga, Agǫtu saga, Barbǫru saga, Cecilíu saga, Dórótheu saga, Fídesar saga, Spesar ok Karítasar, Katrínar saga, Lúcíu saga, Margrétar saga, Marínu saga, Maríu saga egipzku*, and *Mǫrtu saga ok Maríu Magðalenu*.

– ed. *A Female Legendary from Iceland: "Kirkjubæjarbók" (AM 429 12mo) in The Arnamagnæan Collection, Copenhagen*. Manuscripta Nordica: Early Nordic Manuscripts in Digital Facsimile 3 (Copenhagen: Museum Tusculanum Press, 2011).

Includes facsimile and text editions of *Agnesar saga, Agǫtu saga, Barbǫru saga, Cecilíu saga, Dórótheu saga, Fídesar saga, Spesar ok Karítasar, Katrínar saga*, and *Margrétar saga*.

III. General Works

Bekker-Nielsen, Hans, Thorkil Damsgaard Olsen, and Ole Widding. *Norrøn fortællekunst. Kapitler af den norsk-islandske middelalderlitteraturs historie* ([Copenhagen]: Akademisk forlag, 1965).

Boyer, Régis. *La vie religieuse en Islande (1116–1264) d'après la* Sturlunga saga *et les* Sagas des Évêques (Paris: Fondation Singer-Polignac, 1979).

Böðvar Guðmundsson, Sverrir Tómasson, Torfi H. Tulinius, and Vésteinn Ólason, ed. *Íslensk bókmenntasaga 2* (Reykjavík: Mál og menning, 1993).

Carlé, Birte. *Jomfru-fortællingen: Et bidrag til genrehistorien* (Odense: Odense Universitetsforlag, 1985).

Clunies Ross, Margaret, ed. *Old Icelandic Literature and Society* (Cambridge: Cambridge University Press, 2000).

Cormack, Margaret. *The Saints in Iceland: Their Veneration from the Conversion to 1400*. Subsidia Hagiographica 78 (Brussels: Société des Bollandistes, 1994).

Finnur Jónsson. *Den oldnorske og oldislandske Litteraturs Historie*. 3 vols. (Copenhagen: Gad, 1898–1901; 2nd ed. 1920–4).

Guðrún Nordal, Sverrir Tómasson, and Vésteinn Ólason. *Íslensk bókmenntasaga 1* (Reykjavík: Mál og menning, 1992).

Holm-Olsen, Ludvig. "Middelalderens litteratur i Norge." In *Norges litteratur historie 1*. Ed. Edvard Beyer (Oslo: Cappelen, 1974). Pp. 18–342.

Jón Helgason. *Norrøn Litteraturhistorie* (Copenhagen: Levin and Munksgaard, 1934).

Jónas Kristjánsson. *Eddas and Sagas: Iceland's Medieval Literature*. Trans. Peter Foote (Reykjavík: Hið íslenska bókmenntafélag, 1988).

Kalinke, Marianne E. *The Book of Reykjahólar: The Last of the Great Medieval Legendaries* (Toronto: University of Toronto Press, 1996).

Kirby, Ian. *Biblical Quotation in Old Icelandic–Norwegian Religious Literature.* Vol. 1: *Text*; vol. 2: *Introduction* (Reykjavík: Stofnun Árna Magnússonar, 1976 and 1980).

Kulturhistorisk Leksikon for nordisk middelalder fra vikingetid til reformationstid. 22 vols. (Copenhagen: Rosenkilde & Bagger, 1956–78).

Lehmann, Paul. "Skandinaviens Anteil an der lateinischen Literatur und Wissenschaft des Mittelalters." *Sitzungsberichte der Bayrischen Akademie der Wissenschaften.* Philosophisch-historische Abteilung Jahrgang 1937, Heft 7 (Munich: Verlag der Bayerischen Akademie der Wissenschaften, 1937). Pp. 1–136.

Lönnroth, Lars. *European Sources of Icelandic Saga-Writing: An Essay Based on Previous Studies* (Stockholm: Aktiebolaget Thule, 1965).

McTurk, Rory, ed. *A Companion to Old Norse–Icelandic Literature and Culture* (Oxford: Blackwell, 2005).

Mogk, Eugen. *Geschichte der norwegisch-isländischen Literatur.* 2nd ed. (Strassburg: Trübner, 1904).

Paasche, Fredrik. *Norges og Islands litteratur inntil utgangen av middelalderen.* Rev. ed. by Anne Holtsmark (Oslo: Aschehoug, 1947).

Pulsiano, Phillip, and Kirsten Wolf, with Paul Acker and Donald K. Fry, ed. *Medieval Scandinavia: An Encyclopedia* (New York & London: Garland, 1993).

Schier, Kurt. *Sagaliteratur.* Sammlung Metzler M78 (Stuttgart: Metzler, 1970).

Seip, Didrik Arup. *Palæografi. Norge og Island.* Nordisk Kultur 28:B: Palæografi (Stockholm: Bonnier; Oslo: Aschehoug; Copenhagen: Schultz, 1954).

Sigurður Nordal. *Um íslenzkar fornsögur.* Trans. Árni Böðvarsson (Reykjavík: Mál og menning, 1968).

Turville-Petre, G. *Origins of Icelandic Literature* (Oxford: Clarendon Press, 1967).

Vries, Jan de. *Altnordische Literaturgeschichte.* 2 vols. 2nd ed. (Berlin: de Gruyter, 1964–7).

IV. Essay Collections, Festschrifts, and Conference Proceedings

Andersen, Peter, ed. *Pratiques de Traduction au Moyen Age: Actes du colloque de l'Université de Copenhague 25 et 26 octobre 2002. Medieval Translation Practices: Papers from the Symposium at the University of Copenhagen 25th and 26th October 2002* (Copenhagen: Museum Tusculanum Press, 2004).

Ásdís Egilsdóttir and Rudolf Simek, ed. *Sagnaheimur: Studies in Honour of Hermann Pálsson on His 80th Birthday, 26th May 2001* (Vienna: Fassbaender, 2001).

The Audience of the Sagas: The Eighth International Saga Conference, August 11–17, 1991, Gothenburg University. 2 vols. ([Gothenburg]: Göteborgs Universitet, 1991).

Barnes, Geraldine, and Margaret Clunies Ross, ed. *Old Norse Myths, Literature and Society: Proceedings of the 11th International Saga Conference 2–7 July 2000, University of Sydney* (Sydney: Centre for Medieval Studies, 2000).

Bekker-Nielsen, Hans, and Birte Carlé, ed. *Saints and Sagas: A Symposium* (Odense: Odense University Press, 1994).

Bekker-Nielsen, Hans, Peter Foote, and Olaf Olsen, ed. *Proceedings of the Eighth Viking Congress Århus 24–31 August 1977* (Odense: Odense University Press, 1981).

Boyer, Régis, ed. *Les Sagas de Chevaliers (Riddarasögur). Actes de la Ve Conférence Internationale sur les Sagas (Toulon, Juillet 1982).* Civilisations 10 (Paris: Presses de l'Université Paris-Sorbonne, 1985).

Brown, Arthur, and Peter Foote, ed. *Early English and Norse Studies Presented to Hugh Smith in Honour of His Sixtieth Birthday* (London: Methuen & Co., 1963).

Clemoes, Peter, ed. *The Anglo-Saxons: Studies in Some Aspects of Their History and Culture Presented to Bruce Dickens* (London: Bowes & Bowes, 1959).

Doane, A.N., and Kirsten Wolf, ed. *Beatus Vir: Studies in Early English and Norse Manuscripts in Memory of Phillip Pulsiano*. Medieval and Renaissance Texts and Studies 319 (Tempe, Ariz.: Arizona Center for Medieval and Renaissance Studies, 2006).

Dronke, Ursula, Guðrún P. Helgadóttir, Gerd Wolfgang Weber, and Hans Bekker-Nielsen, ed. *Specvlvm Norroenvm: Norse Studies in Memory of Gabriel Turville-Petre* (Odense: Odense University Press, 1981).

DuBois, Thomas, ed. *Sanctity in the North: Saints, Lives, and Cults in Medieval Scandinavia* (Toronto: University of Toronto Press, 2008).

Ekrem, Inger, Lars Boje Mortensen, and Karen Skovgaard-Petersen, ed. *Olavslegenden og den latinske historieskrivning i 1100-tallets Norge* (Copenhagen: Museum Tusculanum, 2000).

Foote, Peter, Hermann Pálsson, and Desmond Slay, ed. *Proceedings of the First International Saga Conference, University of Edinburgh 1971* (University College London: Viking Society for Northern Research, 1973). Pp. 1–27.

Gísli Sigurðsson, Guðrún Kvaran, and Sigurgeir Steingrímsson, ed. *Sagnaþing helgað Jónasi Kristjánssyni sjötugum 10. apríl 1994*. 2 vols. (Reykjavík: Hið íslenska bókmenntafélag, 1994). Vol. 1, pp. 87–96.

Guðni Kolbeinsson, ed. *Minjar og menntir: Afmælisrit helgað Kristjáni Eldjárn 6. desember 1976* (Reykjavík: Menningarsjóður, 1976).

Haki Antonsson and Ildar H. Garipzanov, ed. *Saints and Their Lives on the Periphery: Veneration of Saints in Scandinavia and Eastern Europe (c. 1000–1200)* (Turnhout: Brepols, 2010).

Hødnebø, Finn, et al., ed. *Eyvindarbók: Festskrift til Eyvind Fjeld Halvorsen 4. mai 1992* (Oslo: Drammen Grafisk AS, 1992).

Inga Huld Hákonardóttir, ed. *Konur og kristsmenn. Þættir úr kristnisögu Íslands* (Reykjavík: Háskólaútgáfan, 1996).

Johansson, Karl G., and Maria Arvidsson, ed. *Barlaam i nord: Legenden om Barlaam och Josaphat i den nordiska medeltidslitteraturen*. Bibliotheca Nordica 1 (Oslo: Novus, 2009).

Lindow, John, Lars Lönnroth, and Gerd Wolfgang Weber, ed. *Structure and Meaning in Old Norse Literature: New Approaches to Textual Analysis and Literary Criticism* (Odense: Odense University Press, 1986).

McKinnell, John, David Ashurst, and Donata Kick, ed. *The Fantastic in Old Norse/Icelandic Literature: Sagas and the British Isles. Preprint*

Papers of The 13th International Saga Conference, Durham and York, 6th–12th August, 2006. 2 vols. (Durham: The Centre for Medieval and Renaissance Studies, 2006).

Ney, Agneta, Henrik Williams, and Fredrik Charpentier Ljungqvist, ed. *Á austrvega: Sagas and East Scandinavia. Preprint Papers of the 14th International Saga Conference, Uppsala 9th–15th August 2009.* 2 vols. (Gävle: Gävle University Press, 2009).

Sagas and the Norwegian Experience / Sagaene og Noreg. 10th International Saga Conference, Trondheim, 3.–9. August 1977 (Trondheim: NTNU, 1997).

Samtíðarsögur. The Contemporary Sagas. Níunda Alþjóðlega Fornsagnaþingið. Akureyri 31.7–6.8.1994. 2 vols. ([Reykjavík]: Oddi, 1994).

Silja Aðalsteinsdóttir and Helgi Þorláksson, ed. *Forändringar i kvinnors villkor under medeltiden. Uppsatser framlagde vid ett kvinnohistoriskt symposium i Skálholt, Island, 22–25. juni 1981* (Reykjavík: Sagnfræðistofnun Háskóla Íslands, 1983).

Simek, Rudolf, Jónas Kristjánsson, and Hans Bekker-Nielsen, ed. *Sagnaskemmtun: Studies in Honour of Hermann Pálsson on His 65th Birthday, 26th May 1986* (Vienna: Böhlau, 1986).

Simek, Rudolf, and Judith Meurer, ed. *Scandinavia and Christian Europe in the Middle Ages. Papers of the 12th International Saga Conference Bonn/Germany, 28th July–2nd August 2003* (Bonn: Hausdruckerei der Universität Bonn, 2003).

The Sixth International Saga Conference 28/7–2/8 1985. Workshop Papers. 2 vols. ([Copenhagen]: Det arnamagnæanske Institut, 1985).

Wolf, Kirsten, and Johanna Denzin, ed. *Romance and Love in Late Medieval and Early Modern Iceland: Essays in Honor of Marianne Kalinke.* Islandica 54 (Ithaca: Cornell University Press, 2008).

V. Individual Legends

AGATHA   February 5

1. Agǫtu saga

A faithful though slightly abridged translation of a form of the common *passio*, *BHL* 133.

Manuscripts:
AM 429 12mo (ca. 1500) and Stock. Perg. fol. no. 2 (ca. 1425–45).
Editions:
Foote, Peter, ed. >> *Lives of Saints* (1962).
    Facsimile of Stock. Perg. fol. no. 2.
Unger, C.R. ed. >> *Heilagra manna søgur* (1877). Vol. 1, pp. 1–6.
    Edition of Stock. Perg. fol. no. 2.
Wolf, Kirsten, ed. >> *A Female Legendary from Iceland* (2011). Pp. 130–7.
    Facsimile and text edition of AM 429 12mo.
Modern Icelandic language edition:
Wolf, Kirsten, ed. >> *Heilagra meyja sögur* (2003). Pp. 11–17.
Danish translation:
Carlé, Birte. *Skøger og jomfruer i den kristne fortællekunst* (Odense:
    Odense Universitetsforlag, 1991). Pp. 98–103.
Norwegian translation:
Mundal, Else. *Legender frå mellomalderen. Soger om heilage kvinner og
    menn* (Oslo: Det Norske Samlaget, 1995). Pp. 17–25.
Literature:
Ásdís Egilsdóttir. "Kvendýrlingar og kvenímynd trúarlegra bókmennta á
    Íslandi." In Inga Huld Hákonardóttir, ed. >> *Konur og kristsmenn*
    (1996). Pp. 93–116, esp. pp. 93 and 99.

Bandlien, Bjørn. *Strategies of Passion: Love and Marriage in Medieval Iceland and Norway*. Trans. Betsy van der Hoeck (Turnhout: Brepols, 2005). Pp. 139–40.

Battista, Simonetta. "Interpretation of the Roman Pantheon in the Old Norse Hagiographic Saga." In Geraldine Barnes and Margaret Clunies Ross, ed. >> *Old Norse Myths, Literature and Society* (2000). Pp. 24–34, esp. p. 30.

Bekker-Nielsen, Hans, Thorkil Damsgaard Olsen, and Ole Widding. >> *Norrøn fortællekunst* (1965). P. 124.

Bruvoll, Kjersti. "The Good, the Bad and the Devil! On Rewriting a Religious Motif in Some Virgin Martyr Legends." In Agneta Ney, Henrik Williams, and Fredrik Charpentier Ljungqvist, ed. >> *Á austrvega: Sagas and East Scandinavia* (2009). Vol. 1, pp. 136–43, esp. p. 140.

Carlé, Birte. "Fra slægtssaga til kvindesaga." In Silja Aðalsteinsdóttir and Helgi Þorláksson, ed. >> *Forändringar i kvinnors villkor under medeltiden* (1983). Pp. 55–70, esp. pp. 56, 60–1, and 63.

– >> *Jomfru-fortællingen* (1985). Pp. 40–1, 43, 75, 79–80, 89–95, 98, 131, 133, and 137–8.

– "Some Observations Regarding Narrative Patterns in the Medieval Sagas of Holy Maids." In Régis Boyer, ed. >> *Les Sagas de Chevaliers (Riddarasögur)* (1985). Pp. 393–404, esp. pp. 395 and 397.

– "Men and Women in the Saints' Sagas of *Stock. 2, fol.*" In John Lindow, Lars Lönnroth, and Gerd Wolfgang Weber, ed. >> *Structure and Meaning in Old Norse Literature* (1986). Pp. 317–46, esp. pp. 319, 321, and 341–2.

Cormack, Margaret. >> *The Saints in Iceland* (1994). P. 74.

Jakob Benediktsson. "Helgener." *KLNM* 21 (1977). Cols. 194–5, esp. col. 194.

Jón Hnefill Aðalsteinsson. "Blot i forna skrifter." *SI* 47 (1996): 11–32, esp. pp. 26–7.

Jónas Kristjánsson. >> *Eddas and Sagas* (1988). P. 142.

Lehmann, Paul. >> "Skandinaviens Anteil an der lateinischen Literatur und Wissenschaft des Mittelalters" (1937). Pp. 43 and 47.

Lindow, John. "Norse Mythology and the Lives of the Saints." *SS* 73 (2001): 437–56, esp. pp. 447–50.

Magnús Már Lárusson. "Fornt helgidagaboð (AM. 696, 4to, fragm. XXIX)." *Skírnir* 125 (1951): 199–206, esp. p. 199.

Mogk, Eugen. >> *Geschichte der norwegisch-isländischen Literatur* (1904). P. 891.

Sverrir Tómasson. "Kristnar trúarbókmenntir í óbundnu máli." In

Guðrún Nordal, Sverrir Tómasson, and Vésteinn Ólason, ed. >>
Íslensk Bókmenntasaga 1 (1992). Pp. 419–79, esp. p. 436.

Þórhallur Þorgilsson. "Um þýðingar og endursagnir úr ítölskum miðaldaritum." *Landsbókasafn Íslands. Árbók* 1946–7 (1948): 212–24, esp.
p. 222.

Wolf, Kirsten. "The Severed Breast: A Topos in the Legends of Female
Virgin Martyr Saints." *ANF* 112 (1997): 97–112, esp. pp. 97 and 104.

– "Female Scribes at Work? A Consideration of Kirkjubæjarbók (Codex
AM 429 12mo)." In A.N. Doane and Kirsten Wolf, ed. >> *Beatus Vir*
(2006). Pp. 265–95, esp. pp. 270 and 278–9.

Handlist, p. 298.

2. Agǫtu saga

A translation of a form of the common *passio*, *BHL* 133, but not as
faithful a rendering as 1 and characterized by revision.

Manuscript:
AM 233a fol. (ca. 1350–75).
Edition:
Unger, C.R., ed. >> *Heilagra manna søgur* (1877). Vol. 1, pp. 7–13.
Literature:
Bandlien, Bjørn. *Strategies of Passion: Love and Marriage in Medieval
Iceland and Norway*. Trans. Betsy van der Hoeck (Turnhout: Brepols,
2005). Pp. 139–40.

Bruvoll, Kjersti. "The Good, the Bad and the Devil! On Rewriting a
Religious Motif in Some Virgin Martyr Legends." In Agneta Ney,
Henrik Williams, and Fredrik Charpentier Ljungqvist, ed. >> *Á
austrvega: Sagas and East Scandinavia* (2009). Vol. 1, pp. 136–43, esp.
pp. 136–41.

Carlé, Birte. >> *Jomfru-fortællingen* (1985). Pp. 35, 79–80.

Foote, Peter, ed. >> *Lives of Saints* (1962). P. 27.

Hallberg, Peter. "Imagery in Religious Old Norse Prose Literature: An
Outline." *ANF* 102 (1987): 120–70, esp. pp. 138–9.

Jakob Benediktsson. "Helgener." *KLNM* 21 (1977). Cols. 194–5, esp.
col. 194.

Lehmann, Paul. >> "Skandinaviens Anteil an der lateinischen Literatur
und Wissenschaft des Mittelalters" (1937). P. 43.

Mogk, Eugen. >> *Geschichte der norwegisch-isländischen Literatur* (1904).
P. 891.

Wolf, Kirsten, ed. >> *A Female Legendary from Iceland* (2011). Pp. 44–6.
Handlist, p. 298.

3. Agǫtu saga

A translation of a form of the common *passio*, *BHL* 133, related to 2, but revised in different ways.

Manuscript:
AM 238 fol. II (ca. 1300–50).
Edition:
Wolf, Kirsten. "*Agǫtu saga IV* and *V*." *Opuscula* 13. Bibliotheca
   Arnamagnæana.
   [Forthcoming.]
Literature:
Carlé, Birte. >> *Jomfru-fortællingen* (1985). Pp. 36, 79–80, and 94.
Foote, Peter, ed. >> *Lives of Saints* (1962). P. 27.
Jakob Benediktsson. "Helgener." *KLNM* 21 (1977). Cols. 194–5, esp.
   col. 194.
Wolf, Kirsten, ed. >> *A Female Legendary from Iceland* (2011).
   Pp. 46–7.
Handlist, p. 298.

4. Agǫtu saga

An independent, Norwegian translation of a form of the common *passio*, *BHL* 133.

Manuscript:
NRA 70 (ca. 1300–50).
Edition:
Unger, C.R., ed. >> *Heilagra manna søgur* (1877). Vol. 1, pp. 13.25–14.
Literature:
Foote, Peter, ed. >> *Lives of Saints* (1962). P. 27.
Jakob Benediktsson. "Helgener." *KLNM* 21 (1977). Cols. 194–5, esp.
   col. 194.
Lehmann, Paul. >> "Skandinaviens Anteil an der lateinischen Literatur
   und Wissenschaft des Mittelalters" (1937). Pp. 43 and 80.
Lindow, John. "Norse Mythology and the Lives of the Saints." *SS* 73
   (2001): 437–56, esp. pp. 451–2.

Mogk, Eugen. >> *Geschichte der norwegisch-isländischen Literatur* (1904).
P. 891.
Stefán Karlsson. "Islandsk bogeksport til Norge i middelalderen." *Mm*
(1979): 1–17, esp. p. 6. Rpt. in *Stafkrókar: Ritgerðir eftir Stefán
Karlsson gefnar út í tilefni af sjötugsafmæli hans 2. desember 1998*. Ed.
Guðvarður Már Gunnlaugsson (Reykjavík: Stofnun Árna Magnús-
sonar, 2000). Pp. 188–205, esp. p. 194.
Wolf, Kirsten, ed. >> *A Female Legendary from Iceland* (2011). P. 47.
Handlist, p. 298.

5. Agǫtu saga

An epitome possibly based on a common exemplar of AM 233a fol. (2)
and AM 238 fol. II (3).

Manuscript:
AM 672 4to (ca. 1400–1500).
Edition:
Wolf, Kirsten. "*Agǫtu saga IV* and *V*." *Opuscula* 13. Bibliotheca
Arnamagnæana.
[Forthcoming.]
Literature:
Carlé, Birte. >> *Jomfru-fortællingen* (1985). P. 41.
– "Men and Women in the Saints' Sagas of *Stock. 2, fol.*" In John Lindow,
Lars Lönnroth, and Gerd Wolfgang Weber, ed. >> *Structure and
Meaning in Old Norse Literature* (1986). Pp. 317–46, esp. pp. 319, 321,
and 341–2.
Foote, Peter, ed. >> *Lives of Saints* (1962). P. 27.
Jakob Benediktsson. "Helgener." *KLNM* 21 (1977). Cols. 194–5, esp.
col. 194.
Wolf, Kirsten, ed. >> *A Female Legendary from Iceland* (2011). P. 47.
Handlist, p. 298.

AGNES   January 21

1. Agnesar saga

A translation of the Pseudo-Ambrosian *passio*, *BHL* 156. The text is
slightly abridged, and the epilogue is omitted.

Manuscripts:
AM 235 fol. (ca. 1400, defective), AM 238 fol. I (ca. 1300), AM 238 fol. II
   (ca. 1300–50), AM 429 12mo (ca. 1500), and Stock. Perg. fol. no. 2
   (ca. 1425–45, defective).

Editions:
Foote, Peter, ed. >> *Lives of Saints* (1962).
   Facsimile of Stock. Perg. fol. no. 2.
Unger, C.R., ed. >> *Heilagra manna søgur* (1877). Vol. 1, pp. 15–22.
   Based on Stock. Perg. fol. no. 2 (pp. 15–19.18), AM 429 12mo
   (pp. 19.18–20.19 and 21.7–22.2), and AM 238 fol. I (pp. 20.29–21.7)
   with variants from AM 429 12mo (pp. 15–19.18 and 20.19– 21.7),
   AM 235 fol. (pp. 15–16.3), and AM 238 fol. I (pp. 18.29–19.26).
Wolf, Kirsten, ed. >> *A Female Legendary from Iceland* (2011).
   Pp. 122–9.
   Facsimile and text edition of AM 429 12mo.

Modern Icelandic language edition:
Wolf, Kirsten, ed. >> *Heilagra meyja sögur* (2003). Pp. 3–10.

Norwegian translation:
Mundal, Else. *Legender frå mellomalderen. Soger om heilage kvinner og
   menn* (Oslo: Det Norske Samlaget, 1995). Pp. 27–37.

Literature:
Ásdís Egilsdóttir. "Kvendýrlingar og kvenímynd trúarlegra bókmennta á
   Íslandi." In Inga Huld Hákonardóttir, ed. >> *Konur og kristsmenn*
   (1996). Pp. 93–116, esp. pp. 93, 95, and 99–100.
– "The Fantastic Reality: Hagiography, Miracles and Fantasy." In John
   McKinnell, David Ashurst, and Donata Kick, ed. >> *The Fantastic in
   Old Norse / Icelandic Literature* (2006). Vol. 1, pp. 63–70, esp. p. 64.
Bandlien, Bjørn. *Strategies of Passion: Love and Marriage in Medieval
   Iceland and Norway*. Trans. Betsy van der Hoeck (Turnhout: Brepols,
   2005). P. 139.
Battista, Simonetta. "Interpretation of the Roman Pantheon in the Old
   Norse Hagiographic Saga." In Geraldine Barnes and Margaret Clunies
   Ross, ed. >> *Old Norse Myths, Literature and Society* (2000). Pp. 24–34,
   esp. p. 31.
Bekker-Nielsen, Hans. "Kyrkofäderna ock kyrkolärarna. K. i vestnordisk
   litteratur." *KLNM* 9 (1964). Cols. 690–3, esp. col. 690.
– "Et par ord om de ældste norrøne helgensagaer." In Finn Hødnebø et
   al., ed. >> *Eyvindarbók* (1992). Pp. 29–33, esp. p. 32.
Bekker-Nielsen, Hans, Thorkil Damsgaard Olsen, and Ole Widding.
   >> *Norrøn fortællekunst* (1965). P. 124.

Carlé, Birte. "Fra slægtssaga til kvindesaga." In Silja Aðalsteinsdóttir and
Helgi Þorláksson, ed. >> *Forändringar i kvinnors villkor under medel-
tiden* (1983). Pp. 55–70, esp. pp. 56, 61, 63, and 65.
– >> *Jomfru-fortællingen* (1985). Pp. 34–7, 39–41, 43, 73, 75, 80, 109–15,
131, and 133.
– "Some Observations Regarding Narrative Patterns in the Medieval
Sagas of Holy Maids." In Régis Boyer, ed. >> *Les Sagas de Chevaliers
(Riddarasögur)* (1985). Pp. 393–404, esp. pp. 395 and 397.
– "Men and Women in the Saints' Sagas of *Stock. 2, fol.*" In John
Lindow, Lars Lönnroth, and Gerd Wolfgang Weber, ed. >> *Structure
and Meaning in Old Norse Literature* (1986). Pp. 317–46, esp. pp. 319,
321, and 341–2.
Cormack, Margaret. >> *The Saints in Iceland* (1994). P. 75.
Hallberg, Peter. "Imagery in Religious Old Norse Prose Literature: An
Outline." *ANF* 102 (1987): 120–70, esp. p. 159.
Lehmann, Paul. >> "Skandinaviens Anteil an der lateinischen Literatur
und Wissenschaft des Mittelalters" (1937). Pp. 43 and 47.
Mogk, Eugen. >> *Geschichte der norwegisch-isländischen Literatur* (1904).
P. 891.
Sverrir Tómasson. *Formálar íslenskra sagnaritara á miðöldum. Rannsókn
bókmenntahefðar* (Reykjavík: Stofnun Árna Magnússonar, 1988). P. 152.
– "Kristnar trúarbókmenntir í óbundnu máli." In Guðrún Nordal,
Sverrir Tómasson, and Vésteinn Ólason, ed. >> *Íslensk Bókmenntasaga*
1 (1992). Pp. 419–79, esp. pp. 436–7.
Wolf, Kirsten. "The Severed Breast: A Topos in the Legends of Female
Virgin Martyr Saints." *ANF* 112 (1997): 97–112, esp. pp. 105 and 110–11.
– "Female Scribes at Work? A Consideration of Kirkjubæjarbók (Codex
AM 429 12mo)." In A.N. Doane and Kirsten Wolf, ed. >> *Beatus Vir*
(2006). Pp. 265–95, esp. pp. 270 and 278.

2. Agnesar saga

A somewhat less faithful translation of *BHL* 156 than 1.

Manuscript:
AM 233a fol. (ca. 1350–75, defective).
Edition:
Unger, C.R., ed. >> *Heilagra manna søgur* (1877). Vol. 1, pp. 22.4–19.
Literature:
Bekker-Nielsen, Hans. "Kyrkofäderna ock kyrkolärarna. K. i vestnordisk
litteratur." *KLNM* 9 (1964). Cols. 690–3, esp. col. 690.

Bruvoll, Kjersti. "The Good, the Bad and the Devil! On Rewriting a
    Religious Motif in Some Virgin Martyr Legends." In Agneta Ney,
    Henrik Williams, and Fredrik Charpentier Ljungqvist, ed. >> *Á
    austrvega: Sagas and East Scandinavia* (2009). Vol. 1, pp. 136–43, esp.
    p. 136.
Carlé, Birte. >> *Jomfru-fortællingen* (1985). P. 35.
Cormack, Margaret. >> *The Saints in Iceland* (1994). P. 75.
Foote, Peter, ed. >> *Lives of Saints* (1962). Pp. 27–8.
Lehmann, Paul. >> "Skandinaviens Anteil an der lateinischen Literatur
    und Wissenschaft des Mittelalters" (1937). P. 43.
Mogk, Eugen. >> *Geschichte der norwegisch-isländischen Literatur* (1904).
    P. 891.
Wolf, Kirsten, ed. >> *A Female Legendary from Iceland* (2011). P. 42.
Handlist, p. 298.

3. Agnesar saga

A translation of *BHL* 156 different from 1 and 2 and much abridged.

Manuscript:
AM 238 fol. XV (ca. 1450–1500).
Edition:
Wolf, Kirsten, ed. >> *A Female Legendary from Iceland* (2011). P. 42.
Literature:
Bekker-Nielsen, Hans. "Kyrkofäderna ock kyrkolärarna. K. i vestnordisk
    litteratur." *KLNM* 9 (1964). Cols. 690–3, esp. col. 690.
Carlé, Birte. >> *Jomfru-fortællingen* (1985). P. 37.
Cormack, Margaret. >> *The Saints in Iceland* (1994). Pp. 37n45 and 75.
Foote, Peter, ed. >> *Lives of Saints* (1962). Pp. 27–8.
Lehmann, Paul. >> "Skandinaviens Anteil an der lateinischen Literatur
    und Wissenschaft des Mittelalters" (1937). P. 43.

ALEXIUS   July 17

Alexíss saga

A translation of *BHL* 288 and *BHL* 291.

Manuscript:
AM 623 4to (ca. 1325).

Editions:

Finnur Jónsson, ed. *AM 623, 4°: Helgensagaer.* STUAGNL 52 (Copenhagen: Jørgensen, 1927). Pp. 47.16–53.

Konráð Gíslason, ed. *Fire og fyrretyve for en stor Deel forhen utrykte Prøver af oldnordisk Sprog og Literatur* (Copenhagen: Gyldendal, 1860). Pp. 438–46.

Unger, C.R., ed. >> *Heilagra manna søgur* (1877). Vol. 1, pp. 23–7.

Modern Icelandic language edition:

Sverrir Tómasson, Bragi Halldórsson, and Einar Sigurbjörnsson, ed. >> *Heilagra karla sögur* (2007). Pp. 161–7.

Literature:

Jakob Benediktsson. "Helgener." *KLNM* 21 (1977). Cols. 194–5, esp. col. 194.

Kirby, Ian. >> *Biblical Quotation* (1980). Vol. 2, p. 38.

Konráð Gíslason. *Um frum-parta íslenzkrar túngu í fornöld* (Copenhagen: Trier, 1846). Pp. lv–lvi.

Lehmann, Paul. >> "Skandinaviens Anteil an der lateinischen Literatur und Wissenschaft des Mittelalters" (1937). P. 43.

Mogk, Eugen. >> *Geschichte der norwegisch-isländischen Literatur* (1904). P. 892.

Sverrir Tómasson. "Kristnar trúarbókmenntir í óbundnu máli." In Guðrún Nordal, Sverrir Tómasson, and Vésteinn Ólason, ed. >> *Íslensk Bókmenntasaga* 1 (1992). Pp. 419–79, esp. pp. 425, 467, and 473.

Turville-Petre, G. >> *Origins of Icelandic Literature* (1967). Pp. 126 and 179.

Þórhallur Þorgilsson. "Um þýðingar og endursagnir úr ítölskum miðaldaritum." *Landsbókasafn Íslands. Árbók* 1946–7 (1948): 212–24, esp. p. 222.

Handlist, p. 298.

AMBROSE   December 7

1. Ambrósíuss saga biskups

A translation of a version of *BHL* 377.

Manuscript:

AM 655 4to XXVIIIa (ca. 1250–1300).

Editions:

Hreinn Benediktsson. *Early Icelandic Script As Illustrated in Vernacular Texts from the Twelfth and Thirteenth Centuries.* Íslenzk handrit:

Icelandic Manuscripts, Series in Folio 2 (Reykjavík: The Manuscript
Institute of Iceland, 1965). Plate 70 and pp. xlviii–xlix.
Facsimile and text edition of fol. 2r.
Unger, C.R., ed. >> *Heilagra manna søgur* (1877). Vol. 1, pp. 52–4.

Literature:

Bekker-Nielsen, Hans. "Kyrkofäderna ock kyrkolärarna. K. i vestnordisk
litteratur." *KLNM* 9 (1964). Cols. 690–3, esp. col. 692.
– "Et par ord om de ældste norrøne helgensagaer." In Finn Hødnebø et
al., ed. >> *Eyvindarbók* (1992). Pp. 29–33, esp. p. 32.
Bekker-Nielsen, Hans, Thorkil Damsgaard Olsen, and Ole Widding.
>> *Norrøn fortællekunst* (1965). P. 125.
Bekker-Nielsen, Hans, and Ole Widding. "Religiøs prosalitteratur. Norge
og Island." *KLNM* 14 (1969). Cols. 42–4, esp. col. 43.
Boyer, Régis. >> *La vie religieuse en Islande* (1979). Pp. 161–2.
Ciklamini, Marlene. "Sainthood in the Making: The Arduous Path of
Guðmundr the Good, Iceland's Uncanonized Saint." *Alvíssmál* 11
(2004): 55–74, esp. pp. 56–7n4.
Cormack, Margaret. >> *The Saints in Iceland* (1994). Pp. 36 and 77.
Foote, Peter, ed. >> *Lives of Saints* (1962). P. 21.
Hallberg, Peter. "Imagery in Religious Old Norse Prose Literature: An
Outline." *ANF* 102 (1987): 120–70, esp. p. 155.
Jónas Kristjánsson. >> *Eddas and Sagas* (1988). P. 142.
Kirby, Ian. >> *Biblical Quotation* (1980). Vol. 2, pp. 38–9.
Lehmann, Paul. >> "Skandinaviens Anteil an der lateinischen Literatur
und Wissenschaft des Mittelalters" (1937). P. 43.
Mogk, Eugen. >> *Geschichte der norwegisch-isländischen Literatur* (1904).
P. 893.
Turville-Petre, G. *The Heroic Age of Scandinavia* (London: Brendon and
Sons, 1951). P. 183.
– >> *Origins of Icelandic Literature* (1967). P. 135.
Widding, Ole, and Hans Bekker-Nielsen. "En senmiddelalderlig legendesam-
ling." *Mm* (1960): 105–28, esp. pp. 119 and 126.
– "Low German Influence on Late Icelandic Hagiography." *GR* 37
(1962): 239–62, esp. pp. 241 and 251.
Handlist, p. 298.

2. Ambrósíuss saga biskups

A free and abridged rendering of a version of *BHL* 377 that lacks the
prologue and the epilogue and a short passage in chapter 7. It shares with
1 a common source.

Manuscripts:
AM 238 fol. X (ca. 1300–50) and Stock. Perg. fol. no. 2 (ca. 1425–45).
Editions:
Foote, Peter, ed. >> *Lives of Saints* (1962).
   Facsimile of Stock. Perg. fol. no. 2.
Unger, C.R., ed. >> *Heilagra manna søgur* (1877). Vol. 1, pp. 28–51.
   Based on Stock. Perg. fol. no. 2 with variants from AM 238 fol. X
   (pp. 34.12–39.20).
Literature:
Bekker-Nielsen, Hans. "Kyrkofäderna ock kyrkolärarna. K. i vestnordisk
   litteratur." *KLNM* 9 (1964). Cols. 690–3, esp. col. 692.
Bekker-Nielsen, Hans, and Ole Widding. "Legende. Norge og Island."
   KLNM 10 (1965). Cols. 421–3, esp. col. 421.
Bekker-Nielsen, Hans, Thorkil Damsgaard Olsen, and Ole Widding. .
   >> *Norrøn fortællekunst* (1965). P. 125.
Boyer, Régis. >> *La vie religieuse en Islande* (1979). Pp. 161–2.
Carlé, Birte. >> *Jomfru-fortællingen* (1985). Pp. 39–40, 56–7, 72–3, and 83.
– "Men and Women in the Saints' Sagas of *Stock. 2, fol.*" In John
   Lindow, Lars Lönnroth, and Gerd Wolfgang Weber, ed. >> *Structure
   and Meaning in Old Norse Literature* (1986). Pp. 317–46, esp. pp. 320,
   323, 325–6, and 335–8.
Ciklamini, Marlene. "Sainthood in the Making: The Arduous Path of
   Guðmundr the Good, Iceland's Uncanonized Saint." *Alvíssmál* 11
   (2004): 55–74, esp. p. 57n5.
Cormack, Margaret. >> *The Saints in Iceland* (1994). Pp. 36, 37n45,
   and 77.
Hofmann, Dietrich. *Die Legende von Sankt Clemens in den skandi-
   navischen Ländern im Mittelalter.* Beiträge zur Skandinavistik 13
   (Frankfurt am Main: Peter Lang, 1997). P. 136.
Jón Viðar Sigurðsson. "Utenlandske kvinnehelgener på Island i høymid-
   delalderen." In >> *Samtíðarsögur* (1994). Vol. 2, pp. 423–34, esp.
   pp. 429–30.
Jónas Kristjánsson. >> *Eddas and Saga* (1988). P. 142.
Kalinke, Marianne E. >> *The Book of Reykjahólar* (1996). Pp. 81, 86,
   93–5, 108, and 239.
Kirby, Ian. >> *Biblical Quotation* (1980). Vol. 2, pp. 38–9.
Lehmann, Paul. >> "Skandinaviens Anteil an der lateinischen Literatur
   und Wissenschaft des Mittelalters" (1937). P. 43.
Mogk, Eugen. >> *Geschichte der norwegisch-isländischen Literatur* (1904).
   P. 893.

Turville-Petre, G. >> *Origins of Icelandic Literature* (1967). P. 135.

Þórhallur Þorgilsson. "Um þýðingar og endursagnir úr ítölskum miðaldaritum." *Landsbókasafn Íslands. Árbók* 1946–7 (1948): 212–24, esp. p. 216.

Widding, Ole, and Hans Bekker-Nielsen. "En senmiddelalderlig
   legendesamling." *Mm* (1960): 105–28, esp. p. 119.

Handlist, p. 298.

3. Ambrósíuss saga biskups

A copy of an older Icelandic translation from Latin.

Manuscript:
Stock. Perg. fol. no. 3 (*Reykjahólabók*) (ca. 1530–40).

Edition:
Loth, Agnete, ed. >> *Reykjahólabók* (1969–70). Vol. 2, pp. 57–93.

Literature:
Bekker-Nielsen, Hans. "Kyrkofäderna ock kyrkolärarna. K. i vestnordisk
   litteratur." *KLNM* 9 (1964). Cols. 690–3, esp. col. 692.

Bekker-Nielsen, Hans, Thorkil Damsgaard Olsen, and Ole Widding.
   >> *Norrøn fortællekunst* (1965). Pp. 125 and 141.

Kalinke, Marianne E. "Reykjahólabók: A Legendary on the Eve of the
   Reformation." *Skáldskaparmál* 2 (1992): 239–69, esp. pp. 240, 251,
   and 264.

– >> *The Book of Reykjahólar* (1996). Pp. 28, 47, 56, 63, 80–1, 86, 93–4,
   108, 126, 137–8, 153, and 239.

Widding, Ole, and Hans Bekker-Nielsen. "En senmiddelalderlig
   legendesamling." *Mm* (1960): 105–28, esp. pp. 107, 119, and 127.

– "Low German Influence on Late Icelandic Hagiography." *GR* 37
   (1962): 239–62, esp. pp. 251 and 255.

Handlist, p. 299.

AMICUS AND AMELIUS   October 12

1. Amíkuss saga ok Amilíuss

A rendering of a version of *BHL* 387.

Manuscript:
Stock. Perg. 4to no. 6 (ca. 1400–25, defective).

Editions:
Kölbing, Eugen, ed. "Bruchstück einer Amícus ok Amilíus saga." *Germania* 19, NS 7 (1874): 184–9, esp. pp. 185–9.
– ed. *Elis saga ok Rosamundu. Mit Einleitung, deutscher Übersetzung und Anmerkungen zum ersten Mal herausgegeben* (Heilbronn: Henninger, 1881; rpt. Wiesbaden: Sändig, 1971). P. ix, n. 1.
Slay, Desmond, ed. *Romances. Perg. 4:o nr 6 in the Royal Library, Stockholm.* EIM 10 (Copenhagen: Rosenkilde and Bagger, 1972). Facsimile edition.

Literature:
Bekker-Nielsen, Hans, Thorkil Damsgaard Olsen, and Ole Widding. >> *Norrøn fortællekunst* (1965). Pp. 115 and 164.
Boyer, Régis. >> *La vie religieuse en Islande* (1979). Pp. 196 and 224.
Finnur Jónsson. >> *Den oldnorske og oldislandske Litteraturs Historie* (1920–4). Vol. 2, p. 975.
Halvorsen, E.F. *The Norse Version of the Chanson de Roland.* Bibliotheca Arnamagnæana 19 (Copenhagen: Ejnar Munksgaard, 1959). Pp. 21 and 30.
Hamer, Andrew. "Translation and Adaptation in *Amicus ok Amílius saga.*" In *Sources and Relations: Studies in Honour of J.E. Cross.* Ed. Marie Collins, Jocelyn Price, and Andrew Hamer. Leeds Studies in English, New Series 16 (1985): 246–58.
Henning, Sam. "Amicus och Amelius." *KLNM* 1 (1956). Cols. 127–9, esp. col. 128.
Holm-Olsen, Ludvig, and Kjell Heggelund. *Norges Litteratur Historie.* Ed. Edvard Beyer (Oslo: Cappelen, 1974). P. 142.
Hume, Kathryn. "Structure and Perspective: Romance and Hagiographic Features in the Amicus and Amelius Story." *JEGP* 69 (1970): 89–107, esp. pp. 89n2, 90, 94–6, and 100–7.
Kalinke, Marianne. "Norse Romance (*Riddarasögur*)." In *Old Norse–Icelandic Literature: A Critical Guide.* Ed. Carol J. Clover and John Lindow. Islandica 45 (Ithaca: Cornell University Press, 1985). Pp. 316–63, esp. pp. 322–3, 342, and 350.
Kalinke, Marianne, and P.M. Mitchell. *Bibliography of Old Norse–Icelandic Romances.* Islandica 44 (Ithaca and London: Cornell University Press, 1985). Pp. 23–4.
Krappe, A.H. "The Legend of Amicus and Amelius." *MLR* 18 (1923): 152–61, esp. p. 152n1.
Kölbing, Eugen. "Zur Ueberlieferung der Sage von Amicus und Amelius." *Beiträge* (1877): 271–314, esp. p. 273.

Leach, Henry Goddard. *Angevin Britain and Scandinavia*. Harvard Studies
in Comparative Literature (Cambridge, Mass.: Harvard University
Press, 1921). Pp. 167, 263, and 383.

Leach, MacEdward, ed. *Amis and Amiloun*. Early English Text Society,
Original Series 203 (London: Oxford University Press, 1937).
Pp. xiii–xiv.

Lehmann, Paul. >> "Skandinaviens Anteil an der lateinischen Literatur
und Wissenschaft des Mittelalters" (1937). P. 82.

Mogk, Eugen. >> *Geschichte der norwegisch-isländischen Literatur* (1904).
P. 866.

Slay, Desmond. "Order in AM 179 fol." *Opuscula* 9. Bibliotheca Arnamagnæana 39 (Copenhagen: Reitzel, 1991). Pp. 160–5, esp. pp. 160
and 163.

Torfi H. Tulinius. "Kynjasögur úr fortíð og framandi löndum." In Böðvar
Guðmundsson, Sverrir Tómasson, Torfi H. Tulinius, and Vésteinn
Ólason, ed. >> *Íslensk Bókmenntasaga* 2 (1993). Pp. 164–245, esp.
pp. 195–6.

Þórhallur Þorgilsson. "Um þýðingar og endursagnir úr ítölskum miðaldaritum." *Landsbókasafn Íslands. Árbók* 1946–7 (1948): 212–24, esp.
p. 224.

Wolf, Kirsten. "Amicus and Amileus." In Phillip Pulsiano and Kirsten
Wolf, with Paul Acker and Donald K. Fry, ed. >> *Medieval Scandinavia* (1993). Pp. 13–14.

Handlist, p. 299.

ANDREW THE APOSTLE   November 30

1. Andréss saga postola I

Based on a shortened and rearranged version of a text that combines the
passio (*BHL* 428) with Gregory of Tours' *Liber de miraculis s. Andreae
apostoli* (*BHL* 430).

Manuscripts:
AM 239 fol. (ca. 1350–1400, defective), AM 629 4to (1697), AM 630
4to (ca. 1650–1700), AM 645 4to (ca. 1220, defective), AM 652 4to
(ca. 1250–70, defective), AM 656 4to I (ca. 1325–50), AM 659a 4to
(ca. 1600–50, defective), JS fragm 8 A (ca. 1300–25), and Rask 69
(ca. 1800).

Editions:

Harty, Lenore. "An Edition of a Fourteenth-Century Version of *Andreas saga postola* and Its Sources." *MS* 39 (1977): 121–59, esp. pp. 131–59 (recto).
Edition of AM 239 fol.

Holtsmark, Anne, ed. *A Book of Miracles: MS No. 645 4to of the Arna-Magnæan Collection in the University Library of Copenhagen.* CCI 12 (Copenhagen: Einar Munksgaard, 1938).
Facsimile of AM 645 4to.

Larsson, Ludvig, ed. *Isländska handskriften Nº 645 4º i Den Arnamagnæan-ske Samlingen på Universitetsbiblioteket i København: I. Handskriftens äldre del* (Lund: Gleerup, 1885). Pp. 124.20–130.
Edition of AM 645 4to (older part only).

Þorsteinn Jónsson, ed. *Hér hefjast Tíu Sögur, af þeim enum heiløgu Guds Postulum og pínslar vottum* (Viðeyjarklaustur: Þ. Jónsson, 1836). Pp. 193–211.
Based on a manuscript descended from AM 630 4to.

Unger, C.R., ed. >> *Postola sögur* (1874). Pp. 318.29–353.
Edition of AM 630 4to (pp. 318.29–343.14) with variants from AM 239 fol. (pp. 324.27–343.14). Edition of AM 652 4to (pp. 343.16–345.16). Edition of AM 656 4to I (pp. 345.17–348). Edition of AM 645 4to (pp. 349–53). Edition of AM 630 4to (p. xx, extract only).

English translation:

Roughton, Philip G. "AM 645 4to and AM 652/630 4to: Study and Translation of Two Thirteenth-Century Icelandic Collections of Apostles' and Saints' Lives." PhD dissertation, University of Colorado, 2002. Pp. 600–54.

Literature:

Bekker-Nielsen, Hans. "Et par ord om de ældste norrøne helgensagaer." In Finn Hødnebø et al., ed. >> *Eyvindarbók* (1992). Pp. 29–33, esp. p. 32.

Bekker-Nielsen, Hans, Thorkil Damsgaard Olsen, and Ole Widding. >> *Norrøn fortællekunst* (1965). P. 122.

Cormack, Margaret. >> *The Saints in Iceland* (1994). Pp. 79 and 240.

Finnur Jónsson. >> *Den oldnorske og oldislandske Litteraturs Historie* (1920–4). Vol. 2, p. 870.

Foote, Peter. "Auðræði." In Arthur Brown and Peter Foote, ed. >> *Early English and Norse Studies* (1963). Pp. 62–76, esp. p. 65.

Hallberg, Peter. "Imagery in Religious Old Norse Prose Literature: An Outline." *ANF* 102 (1987): 120–70, esp. pp. 138 and 151.

Jón Ma. Ásgeirsson and Þórður Ingi Guðjónsson, ed. *Frá Sýrlandi til*

Íslands: Arfur Tómasar postula (Reykjavík: Háskólaútgáfan, 2007).
 Pp. 164–5 and 171.
Kirby, Ian. >> *Biblical Quotation* (1980). Vol. 2, pp. 26–7.
Louis-Jensen, Jonna. "To håndskrifter fra det nordvestlige Island."
 Opuscula 7. Bibliotheca Arnamagnæana 34 (Copenhagen: Reitzel,
 1979). Pp. 219–53, esp. p. 221.
McDougal, Ian, ed. "Anonymous, *Andréasdrápa* '*Drápa* about S. Andrew'."
 In Margaret Clunies Ross, ed. >> *Poetry on Christian Subjects* (2007).
 Vol. 2, pp. 845–51.
Mogk, Eugen. >> *Geschichte der norwegisch-isländischen Literatur* (1904).
 P. 888.
Ólafur Halldórsson, ed. *Mattheus saga postula* (Reykjavík: Stofnun Árna
 Magnússonar, 1994). Pp. xiii–xli, xlix–lvii, and lxxv–lxxxi.
Roughton, Philip. "Stylistics and Sources of the *Postola sögur* in AM 645
 4to and AM 652/630 4to." *Gripla* 16 (2005): 7–50.
– "'Þá syndi hann þeim mikinn skugga': Unmasking the Fantastic in the
 Postola sögur." In John McKinnell, David Ashurst, and Donata Kick,
 ed. >> *The Fantastic in Old Norse / Icelandic Literature* (2006). Vol. 2,
 pp. 846–55, esp. pp. 847, 849, and 852–3.
Sverrir Jakobsson. *Við og veröldin: Heimsmynd Íslendinga 1100–1400*
 (Reykjavík: Háskólaútgáfan, 2005). Pp. 105 and 138.
Sverrir Tómasson. *Formálar íslenskra sagnaritara á miðöldum. Rannsókn
 bókmenntahefðar* (Reykjavík: Stofnun Árna Magnússonar, 1988).
 Pp. 203 and 331–2.
Turville-Petre, G. >> *Origins of Icelandic Literature* (1967). P. 130.
Þórður Ingi Guðjónsson. "Apostlene i islandsk middelalderlitteratur." In
 Den nordiske renessansen i høymiddelalderen. Ed. Jón Viðar Sigurðsson
 and Preben Meulengracht Sørensen (Oslo: Historisk institutt, Universi-
 tetet i Oslo, 2000). Pp. 83–99, esp. pp. 93–4.
Handlist, p. 299.

2. Andréss saga postola II

A redaction different from 1 but based on the same source.

Manuscripts:
AM 238 fol. II (ca. 1300–50), AM 646 4to (ca. 1350–75, defective),
 AM 647 4to (ca. 1400–1500, defective), AM 667 4to VII (ca. 1500),
 and AM 696 4to XII (ca. 1400–1500).
Edition:
Unger, C.R., ed. >> *Postola sögur* (1874). Pp. 354–385.13.

Edition of AM 646 4to (pp. 354–370.1 and 371.27–383.5) and AM 647
4to (pp. 370.1–371.25) with variants from AM 647 4to (pp. 354–363.31,
365.18–370.1, and 376.8–383.5). To the saga proper is appended
a defective miracle involving Saint Andrew from AM 646 4to
(pp. 383.6–385.13).

Literature:
Bugge, Anders. "Andreas." *KLNM* 1 (1956). Cols. 133–8, esp. col. 135.
Carlé, Birte. >> *Jomfru-fortællingen* (1985). P. 36.
Cormack, Margaret. >> *The Saints in Iceland* (1994). Pp. 79 and 240.
Finnur Jónsson. >> *Den oldnorske og oldislandske Litteraturs Historie*
    (1920–4). Vol. 2, p. 870.
Harty, Lenore. "An Edition of a Fourteenth-Century Version of *Andreas
    saga postola* and Its Sources." *MS* 39 (1977): 121–59, esp. p. 121.
Kirby, Ian. >> *Biblical Quotation* (1980). Vol. 2, p. 27.
McDougal, Ian, ed. "Anonymous, *Andréasdrápa* 'Drápa about S. Andrew'."
    In Margaret Clunies Ross, ed. >> *Poetry on Christian Subjects* (2007).
    Vol. 2, pp. 845–51.
Mogk, Eugen. >> *Geschichte der norwegisch-isländischen Literatur* (1904).
    P. 888.
Overgaard, Mariane. "AM 244, 8vo: En islandsk schwank-samling."
    Opuscula 7. Bibliotheca Arnamagnæana 34 (Copenhagen: Reitzel,
    1979). Pp. 268–318, esp. p. 283.
Sverrir Tómasson. *Formálar íslenskra sagnaritara á miðöldum. Rannsókn
    bókmenntahefðar* (Reykjavík: Stofnun Árna Magnússonar, 1988).
    Pp. 50, 119, 131, 174, 203, 230, 237, 243, 245, 305, and 331–2.
Handlist, p. 299.

3. Andréss saga postola III

Based on a variant version of the *Legenda aurea* with use also of the Bible
and the sources of 1 and 2.

Manuscripts:
AM 628 4to (1711–12) and SÁM 1 fol. (*Codex Scardensis*) (ca. 1350–75).
Editions:
Slay, Desmond, ed. *Codex Scardensis*. EIM 2 (Copenhagen: Rosenkilde
    and Bagger, 1960).
    Facsimile of SÁM 1 fol.
Unger, C.R., ed. >> *Postola sögur* (1874). Pp. 389.8–404.7.
    Edition of AM 628 4to.

Modern Icelandic language edition:
Ólafur Halldórsson, ed. *Sögur úr Skarðsbók* (Reykjavík: Almenna
   bókafélagið, 1967). Pp. 70–9.
   Edition of SÁM 1 fol. (extracts only).
Literature:
Bekker-Nielsen, Hans, Thorkil Damsgaard Olsen, and Ole Widding.
   >> *Norrøn fortællekunst* (1965). P. 123.
Collings, Lucy Grace. "The Codex Scardensis: Studies in Icelandic
   Hagiography." PhD dissertation, Cornell University, 1969. Pp. 74–82
   and 237–48.
Cormack, Margaret. >> *The Saints in Iceland* (1994). Pp. 79 and 240.
– "Saints' Lives and Icelandic Literature in the Thirteenth and Four-
   teenth Centuries." In Hans Bekker-Nielsen and Birte Carlé, ed.
   >> *Saints and Sagas* (1994). Pp. 27–47, esp. p. 31.
Eiríkr Magnússon. "Kodex Skardensis af postulasögur." *ANF* 8 (1892):
   238–45, esp. p. 241.
Finnur Jónsson. >> *Den oldnorske og oldislandske Litteraturs Historie*
   (1920–4). Vol. 2, p. 870.
Jón Þorkelsson. "Islandske håndskrifter i England og Skotland." *ANF* 8
   (1892): 199–237, esp. pp. 235–6.
Kirby, Ian. >> *Biblical Quotation* (1980). Vol. 2, pp. 27–8.
McDougal, Ian, ed. "Anonymous, *Andréasdrápa* 'Drápa about S. Andrew'."
   In Margaret Clunies Ross, ed. >> *Poetry on Christian Subjects* (2007).
   Vol. 2, pp. 845–51.
Mogk, Eugen. >> *Geschichte der norwegisch-isländischen Literatur* (1904).
   P. 888.
Ólafur Halldórsson. *Helgafellsbækur fornar.* Studia Islandica 24 (Reykja-
   vík: Heimspekideild Háskóla Íslands and Menningarsjóður, 1966).
   Pp. 16–22 and 41–5.
Ólafur Halldórsson, ed. *Mattheus saga postula* (Reykjavík: Stofnun Árna
   Magnússonar, 1994). Pp. xli–xlix.
Sverrir Tómasson. *Formálar íslenskra sagnaritara á miðöldum. Rannsókn bók-
   menntahefðar* (Reykjavík: Stofnun Árna Magnússonar, 1988). Pp. 331–2.
Þórður Ingi Guðjónsson. "Apostlene i islandsk middelalderlitteratur." In
   Den nordiske renessansen i høymiddelalderen. Ed. Jón Viðar Sigurðsson
   and Preben Meulengracht Sørensen (Oslo: Historisk institutt, Universi-
   tetet i Oslo, 2000). Pp. 83–99, esp. p. 94.
Wolf, Kirsten. "Postola sögur." In Phillip Pulsiano and Kirsten Wolf,
   with Paul Acker and Donald K. Fry, ed. >> *Medieval Scandinavia*
   (1993). Pp. 511–12.

– "Skarðsbók." In Phillip Pulsiano and Kirsten Wolf, with Paul Acker
    and Donald K. Fry, ed. >> *Medieval Scandinavia* (1993). P. 596.
Handlist, p. 299.

4. Andréss saga postola IV

Derived from the same source(s) as 1 and 2.

Manuscripts:
AM 625 4to (ca. 1300–25) and AM 669a 4to (ca. 1700–1800).
Edition:
Unger, C.R., ed. >> *Postola sögur* (1874). Pp. 404.9–412.11.
    Edition of AM 625 4to.
Literature:
Cormack, Margaret. >> *The Saints in Iceland* (1994). P. 79.
Finnur Jónsson. >> *Den oldnorske og oldislandske Litteraturs Historie*
    (1920–4). Vol. 2, p. 870.
Foote, Peter. "Postulatal." In Guðni Kolbeinsson, ed. >> *Minjar og
    menntir* (1976). Pp. 152–73, esp. p. 159.
Hallberg, Peter. "Imagery in Religious Old Norse Prose Literature: An
    Outline." *ANF* 102 (1987): 120–70, esp. p. 141.
Jón Ma. Ásgeirsson and Þórður Ingi Guðjónsson, ed. *Frá Sýrlandi til
    Íslands: Arfur Tómasar postula* (Reykjavík: Háskólaútgáfan, 2007). P. 140.
Jónas Kristjánsson. *Um Fóstbræðra sögu* (Reykjavík: Stofnun Árna
    Magnússonar, 1972). P. 287.
Kirby, Ian. >> *Biblical Quotation* (1980). Vol. 2, p. 28.
Konráð Gíslason. *Um frum-parta íslenzkrar túngu í fornöld* (Copenhagen:
    Trier, 1846). Pp. lx–lxi.
McDougal, Ian, ed. "Anonymous, *Andréasdrápa* 'Drápa about S. Andrew'."
    In Margaret Clunies Ross, ed. >> *Poetry on Christian Subjects* (2007).
    Vol. 2, pp. 845–51.
Mogk, Eugen. >> *Geschichte der norwegisch-isländischen Literatur* (1904).
    P. 888.
Sverrir Tómasson. *Formálar íslenskra sagnaritara á miðöldum. Rannsókn
    bókmenntahefðar* (Reykjavík: Stofnun Árna Magnússonar, 1988).
    Pp. 331–2.
Handlist, p. 299.

5. Andréss saga postola

Translated from a Low German *Passionael*.

Manuscript:

AM 667 4to V (ca. 1525).

Literature:

Overgaard, Mariane, ed. *The History of the Cross-Tree Down to Christ's Passion: Icelandic Legend Versions.* Editiones Arnamagnæanæ, Ser. B, vol. 26 (Copenhagen: Munksgaard, 1968). Pp. xcix–cxix.

Sverrir Tómasson. *Formálar íslenskra sagnaritara á miðöldum. Rannsókn bókmenntahefðar* (Reykjavík: Stofnun Árna Magnússonar, 1988). Pp. 331–2.

Handlist, p. 299.

6. Af biskupi ok púka

The direct source of this miracle has not been established.

Manuscripts:

AM 646 4to (ca. 1350–75), AM 657a–b 4to (ca. 1350), AM 81 8vo (ca. 1600–1700), and AM 124 8vo (ca. 1600–1700).

Editions:

Gering, Hugo, ed. >> *Islendzk æventyri* (1882–3), Vol. 1, pp. 95–100. Based on AM 657a–b 4to with variants from AM 646 4to.

Unger, C.R., ed. >> *Postola sögur* (1874). Pp. 385.16–389.6 Edition of AM 657a–b 4to.

German paraphrase:

Gering, Hugo, ed. >> *Islendzk æventyri* (1882–3). Vol. 2, pp. 77–80.

Literature:

Cormack, Margaret. >> *The Saints in Iceland* (1994). Pp. 34n27 and 35.

Hallberg, Peter. *Stilsignalement och författarskap i norrön sagalitteratur: Synpunkter och exempel.* Nordistica Gothoburgensia 3 (Stockholm: Almqvist & Wiksell, 1968). P. 180.

Handlist, p. 300.

ANNE   July 26

1. Önnu saga

A translation of the Low German *De historie von der hilligen moder Anne* (known as the *St. Annen Büchlein*).

Manuscripts:

AM 238 fol. III (ca. 1525–50) and AM 82 8vo (ca. 1600–50, defective).

Edition:
Wolf, Kirsten, ed. *Saga heilagrar Önnu* (Reykjavík: Stofnun Árna
  Magnússonar, 2001). Pp. 3–163.
  Edition of AM 238 fol. III (pp. 151–63 recto) and AM 82 8vo
  (pp. 3–155 recto).
Literature:
Ásdís Egilsdóttir. "Kvendýrlingar og kvenímynd trúarlegra bókmennta á
  Íslandi." In Inga Huld Hákonardóttir, ed. >> *Konur og kristsmenn*
  (1996). Pp. 93–116, esp. p. 107.
Bekker-Nielsen, Hans. "En islandsk afladsbøn." *Opuscula* 2.1. Biblio-
  theca Arnamagnæana 25.1 (Copenhagen: Ejnar Munksgaard, 1961).
  Pp. 63–4.
– "St. Anna i islandsk senmiddelalder." *Fróðskaparrit* 13 (1964): 203–11.
Cormack, Margaret. "Christian Biography." In *A Companion to Old
  Norse–Icelandic Literature and Culture*. Ed. Rory McTurk (Oxford:
  Blackwell, 2005). Pp. 27–42, esp. p. 39.
Finnur Jónsson. >> *Den oldnorske og oldislandske Litteraturs Historie*
  (1920–4). Vol. 2, p. 873.
Gísli Baldur Róbertsson. "Heilög Anna birtist Árna Magnússyni undir
  andlátið." *Gripla* 16 (2005): 229–49.
Kalinke, Marianne E. >> *The Book of Reykjahólar* (1996), pp. 44 and
  67–9.
Þorbjörg Helgadóttir, ed. *Rómverja saga*. 2 vols. (Reykjavík: Stofnun
  Árna Magnússonar, 2010). Vol. 1, p. lx.
Widding, Ole, and Hans Bekker-Nielsen. "Low German Influence on
  Late Icelandic Hagiography." *GR* 37 (1962): 239–62, esp. p. 254.
Wolf, Kirsten. "The Cult of Saint Anne in Iceland." In >> *Samtíðarsögur*
  (1994). Vol. 2, pp. 863–77, esp. p. 868.
– "*Saga heilagrar Önnu* – en orientering." *ANF* 109 (1994): 101–39, esp.
  pp. 108 and 115–35.
Handlist, p. 300.

2. Önnu saga og Maríu

A translation of a now-lost Low German manuscript or imprint of a
legend of Saint Anne that also contained the Virgin Mary's *vita*.

Manuscript:
Stock. Perg. fol. no. 3 (*Reykjahólabók*) (ca. 1530–40).
Edition:
Loth, Agnete, ed. >> *Reykjahólabók* (1969–70). Vol. 2, pp. 305–468.

Literature:

Bekker-Nielsen, Hans, Thorkil Damsgaard Olsen, and Ole Widding.
    >> *Norrøn fortællekunst* (1965). P. 140.
Bekker-Nielsen, Hans, and Ole Widding. "Legende. Norge og Island."
    KLNM 10 (1965). Cols. 421–3, esp. col. 422.
Jónas Kristjánsson. >> *Eddas and Sagas* (1988). P. 145.
Kalinke, Marianne E. "Reykjahólabók: A Legendary on the Eve of the
    Reformation." *Skáldskaparmál* 2 (1992): 239–69, esp. pp. 240, 242, and
    245.
– "Maríu saga og Önnu." *ANF* 109 (1994): 43–99.
– >> *The Book of Reykjahólar* (1996), pp. 14–15, 28, 46, 67–76, 96,
    102–5, 110, 112–13, 126–8, 133–4, 136, 146–9, 161–3, 217–18, and 238.
Sverrir Tómasson. "Trúarbókmenntir í lausu máli á síðmiðöld." In
    Böðvar Guðmundsson, Sverrir Tómasson, Torfi H. Tulinius, and
    Vésteinn Ólason, ed. >> *Íslensk Bókmenntasaga* 2 (1993). Pp. 249–82,
    esp. pp. 278–9.
Vésteinn Ólason. "Kveðskapur frá síðmiðöldum: Trúarkvæði." In Böðvar
    Guðmundsson, Sverrir Tómasson, Torfi H. Tulinius, and Vésteinn
    Ólason, ed. >> *Íslensk Bókmenntasaga* 2 (1993). Pp. 283–378, esp.
    p. 310.
Widding, Ole, and Hans Bekker-Nielsen. "En senmiddelalderlig
    legendesamling." *Mm* (1960): 105–28, esp. pp. 108–9, 123–5, and
    127–8.
– "Low German Influence on Late Icelandic Hagiography." *GR* 37
    (1962): 239–62, esp. pp. 250 and 253–5.
Wolf, Kirsten. "The Cult of Saint Anne in Iceland." In >> *Samtíðarsögur*
    (1994). Vol. 2, pp. 863–77, esp. pp. 868–9.
Wolf, Kirsten, ed. *Saga heilagrar Önnu* (Reykjavík: Stofnun Árna
    Magnússonar, 2001). Pp. xli–xliii.
Handlist, p. 300.

ANSELM OF CANTERBURY   April 21

Tales of Saint Anselm of Canterbury incorporated into the miracles of
the Virgin Mary.

Af Anselmo

Manuscripts:
See Mary the Blessed Virgin 3 note (p. 245).

Edition:
Unger, C.R., ed. >> *Mariu saga* (1871). Pp. 174.27–180.5, 468.27–473.12, and 1142.25–1147.17.
Modern Icelandic language edition:
Einar Ól. Sveinsson, ed. *Leit eg suður til landa. Ævintýri og helgisögur frá miðöldum* (Reykjavík: Heimskringla, 1944). Pp. 174–7 (extract only).
Literature:
Heizmann, Wilhelm. "Arngríms Guðmundar saga, Maríu saga und Gregors Moralia in Iob." *Opuscula* 8. Bibliotheca Arnamagnæana 38 (Copenhagen: Reitzel, 1985). Pp. 189–98.
– "Liebe und Durst: Der Heilige Bernhard von Clairvaux in der altisländischen Mirakelüberlieferung." *Opuscula* 13. Bibliotheca Arnamagnæana 47 (Copenhagen: Museum Tusculanum Press, 2010). Pp. 55–118, esp. p. 109.
Widding, Ole. "Marialegender. Norge og Island." *KLNM* 11 (1966). Cols. 401–4, esp. col. 402.
– "Norrøne Marialegender på europæisk baggrund." *Opuscula* 10. Bibliotheca Arnamagnæana 40 (Copenhagen: Reitzel, 1996). Pp. 1–128, esp. pp. 11, 14, 17, 64, 79, and 86.
Handlist, pp. 300 and 323.

ANTHONY   January 17

1. Antóníuss saga

A translation of *BHL* 609.

Manuscript:
AM 234 fol. (ca. 1340, defective).
Edition:
Unger, C.R., ed. >> *Heilagra manna søgur* (1877). Vol. 1, pp. 55–121.
Literature:
Ásdís Egilsdóttir. "Jarteinir, líkami, sál og trúarlíf." In Ásdís Egilsdóttir and Rudolf Simek, ed. >> *Sagnaheimur* (2001). Pp. 13–19, esp. pp. 14–15.
Battista, Simonetta. "Interpretation of the Roman Pantheon in the Old Norse Hagiographic Saga." In Geraldine Barnes and Margaret Clunies

Ross, ed. >> *Old Norse Myths, Literature and Society* (2000). Pp. 24–34, esp. p. 33.

Bekker-Nielsen, Hans, Thorkil Damsgaard Olsen, and Ole Widding. >> *Norrøn fortællekunst* (1965). P. 125.

Foote, Peter. "Auðræði." In Arthur Brown and Peter Foote, ed. >> *Early English and Norse Studies* (1963). Pp. 62–76, esp. p. 67.

Hallberg, Peter. "Imagery in Religious Old Norse Prose Literature: An Outline." *ANF* 102 (1987): 120–70, esp. pp. 125, 131, 136, 148, 151, and 154.

Jakob Benediktsson. "Helgener." *KLNM* 21 (1977). Cols. 194–5, esp. col. 194.

Jónas Kristjánsson. *Um Fóstbrœðra sögu* (Reykjavík: Stofnun Árna Magnússonar, 1972). Pp. 281 and 289.

Kirby, Ian. >> *Biblical Quotation* (1980). Vol. 2, p. 39.

Lehmann, Paul. >> "Skandinaviens Anteil an der lateinischen Literatur und Wissenschaft des Mittelalters" (1937). Pp. 43–4 and 51.

Mogk, Eugen. >> *Geschichte der norwegisch-isländischen Literatur* (1904). P. 891.

Sverrir Tómasson. "Kristnar trúarbókmenntir í óbundnu máli." In Guðrún Nordal, Sverrir Tómasson, and Vésteinn Ólason, ed. >> *Íslensk Bókmenntasaga* 1 (1992). Pp. 419–79, esp. p. 467.

Sverrir Tómasson, Bragi Halldórsson, and Einar Sigurbjörnsson, ed. >> *Heilagra karla sögur* (2007). P. xxii.

Tveitane, Mattias. "Vitae Patrum." *KLNM* 20 (1976). Cols. 194–6, esp. col. 194.

Widding, Ole, and Hans Bekker-Nielsen. "Low German Influence on Late Icelandic Hagiography." *GR* 37 (1962): 239–62, esp. p. 247.

Handlist, p. 300.

2. Antóníuss saga

A version of the legend of Saint Anthony incorporated into the Old Norwegian *Barlaams saga ok Jósafats*.

Manuscripts:
See Barlaam ok Josaphat 1 note (p. 50).
Editions:
Keyser, R., and C.R. Unger, ed. *Barlaams ok Josaphats saga* (Christiania [Oslo]: Feilberg & Landmark, 1851). Pp. 52.11–55.2.

Rindal, Magnus, ed. *Barlaams ok Josaphats saga*. Norrøne tekster 4
(Oslo: Norsk historisk kjeldeskrift-institutt, 1981). Pp. 44.16–
46.33.

Literature:
Haugen, Odd Einar. "Exempla in Barlaams ok Josaphats saga." In
>> *Sagas and the Norwegian Experience* (1997). Pp. 227–36, esp. p. 232.
– "Forteljingane i forteljinga. Interpolasjonane i *Barlaams ok Josaphats
saga*." In Karl G. Johansson and Maria Arvidsson, ed. >> *Barlaam i
nord* (2009). Pp. 47–73, esp. pp. 58 and 67.
Jónas Kristjánsson. *Um Fóstbrœðra sögu* (Reykjavík: Stofnun Árna
Magnússonar, 1972). P. 289.
Tveitane, Mattias. "Vitae Patrum." *KLNM* 20 (1976). Cols. 194–6, esp.
col. 194.
Þórhallur Þorgilsson. "Um þýðingar og endursagnir úr ítölskum miðal-
daritum." *Landsbókasafn Íslands. Árbók* 1946–7 (1948): 212–24, esp.
p. 222.
Handlist, pp. 300 and 302.

3. Antóníuss saga

Translated from a now-lost Low German redaction that resembles the
source(s) of *Der Heiligen Leben*.

Manuscript:
Stock. Perg. fol. no. 3 (*Reykjahólabók*) (ca. 1530–40).
Edition:
Loth, Agnete, ed. >> *Reykjahólabók* (1969–70). Vol. 2, pp. 255–85.
Literature:
Bekker-Nielsen, Hans, Thorkil Damsgaard Olsen, and Ole Widding.
>> *Norrøn fortællekunst* (1965). P. 141.
Jakob Benediktsson. "Helgener." *KLNM* 21 (1977). Cols. 194–5, esp. col.
194.
Kalinke, Marianne E. "Reykjahólabók: A Legendary on the Eve of the
Reformation." *Skáldskaparmál* 2 (1992): 239–69, esp. p. 240.
– >> *The Book of Reykjahólar* (1996), pp. 28, 49–50, 99, and 191.
Widding, Ole, and Hans Bekker-Nielsen. "En senmiddelalderlig
legendesamling." *Mm* (1960): 105–28, esp. pp. 108 and 123.
– "Low German Influence on Late Icelandic Hagiography." *GR* 37
(1962): 239–62, esp. pp. 247 and 255.
Handlist, p. 300

AUGUSTINE   August 28

1. Ágústínuss saga

A translation ascribed to Runólfr Sigmundarson (d. 1307) of a text related to *BHL* 787, though the *incipit* follows that of *BHL* 789.

Manuscripts:
AM 221 fol. (ca. 1275–1300, defective), AM 234 fol. (ca. 1340), AM 235 fol. (ca. 1400), AM 627 4to (ca. 1700–1800), AM 648 4to (ca. 1700–1800), and Stock. Perg. fol. no. 2 (ca. 1425–45).

Editions:
Foote, Peter, ed. >> *Lives of Saints* (1962).
   Facsimile of Stock. Perg. fol. no. 2.
Stefán Karlsson, ed. *Sagas of Icelandic Bishops. Fragments of Eight Manuscripts.* EIM 7 (Copenhagen: Rosenkilde and Bagger, 1967).
   Facsimile of AM 221 fol.
Unger, C.R., ed. >> *Heilagra manna søgur* (1877). Vol. 1, pp. 122–52.
   Based on AM 234 fol. (pp. 122–142.15, 143.4–20, 144.14–145.1, 145.22–146.5, and 146.28–149.3) and Stock. Perg. fol. no. 2 (pp. 142.15–143.3, 143.21–144.13, 145.1–22, and 146.5–28) with variants from Stock. Perg. fol. no. 2 (pp. 122–142.15, 143.3–21, 144.13–145.1, and 145.22–146.5) and AM 235 fol. (pp. 122–149.3). Edition of AM 221 fol. (pp. 149.10–152).

Modern Icelandic language edition:
Sverrir Tómasson, Bragi Halldórsson, and Einar Sigurbjörnsson, ed.
   >> *Heilagra karla sögur* (2007). Pp. 231–64.

Literature:
Bekker-Nielsen, Hans. "Kyrkofäderna ock kyrkolärarna. K. i vestnordisk litteratur." *KLNM* 9 (1964). Cols. 690–3, esp. col. 692.
Bekker-Nielsen, Hans, and Ole Widding. "Legende. Norge og Island." *KLNM* 10 (1965). Cols. 421–3, esp. col. 421.
Bekker-Nielsen, Hans, Thorkil Damsgaard Olsen, and Ole Widding.
   >> *Norrøn fortællekunst* (1965). Pp. 145–6.
Boyer, Régis. >> *La vie religieuse en Islande* (1979). Pp. 146, 160, and 185.
Carlé, Birte. >> *Jomfru-fortællingen* (1985). Pp. 38–40, 60–1, 66–7, and 69–70.
– "Men and Women in the Saints' Sagas of *Stock. 2, fol.*" In John Lindow, Lars Lönnroth, and Gerd Wolfgang Weber, ed. >> *Structure and Meaning in Old Norse Literature* (1986). Pp. 317–46, esp. pp. 319–20, 322–3, 326–7, and 336.

Cormack, Margaret. >> *The Saints in Iceland* (1994). P. 82.

Finnur Jónsson. >> *Den oldnorske og oldislandske Litteraturs Historie* (1920–4). Vol. 2, pp. 873–4.

Hallberg, Peter. "Imagery in Religious Old Norse Prose Literature: An Outline." *ANF* 102 (1987): 120–70, esp. p. 141.

Jónas Kristjánsson. >> *Eddas and Sagas* (1988). P. 142.

Jørgensen, Jørgen Højgaard. "Hagiography and the Icelandic Bishop Sagas." *Peritia* 1 (1982): 1–16, esp. p. 4.

Kalinke, Marianne E. "*Augustinus saga*: A Learned and a Popular Version." In >> *Samtíðarsögur* (1994). Vol. 2, pp. 435–49.

– >> *The Book of Reykjahólar* (1996), pp. 34, 39, 47, 56–7, 60, 64–5, 67, 69, 80, 108, 116, 240, and 244.

Kirby, Ian. >> *Biblical Quotation* (1980). Vol. 2, p. 40.

Koppenberg, Peter. *Hagiographische Studien zu den Biskupa sögur: Unter besonderer Berücksichtigung der* Jóns Saga Helga. Scandia Wissenschaftliche Reihe 1 (Bochum: Scandia, 1980). Pp. 4–5 and 230.

Lehmann, Paul. >> "Skandinaviens Anteil an der lateinischen Literatur und Wissenschaft des Mittelalters" (1937). Pp. 31 and 44.

Louis-Jensen, Jonna. *Kongesagastudier: Kompilationen Hulda-Hrokkinskinna*. Bibliotheca Arnamagnæana 32 (Copenhagen: Reitzel, 1977). P. 19.

Magerøy, Hallvard. "Helgensoger." *KLNM* 6 (1961). Cols. 350–3, esp. col. 351.

Mogk, Eugen. >> *Geschichte der norwegisch-isländischen Literatur* (1904). P. 893.

Paasche, Fredrik. *Norges og Islands litteratur inntil utgangen av middelalderen*. Rev. ed. by Anne Holtsmark (Oslo: Aschehoug, 1947). P. 445.

Pizarro, Joaquín Martínez. "Conversion Narratives: Form and Utility." In >> *The Sixth International Saga Conference* (1985). Vol. 2, pp. 813–32, esp. p. 820.

Svanhildur Óskarsdóttir. "Universal History in Fourteenth-Century Iceland: Studies in AM 764 4to." PhD dissertation, University of London, 2000. Pp. 203 and 296.

Sverrir Tómasson. *Formálar íslenskra sagnaritara á miðöldum. Rannsókn bókmenntahefðar* (Reykjavík: Stofnun Árna Magnússonar, 1988). Pp. 7, 12, 34, 50, 128–9, 158, 183, 225, 241, and 254.

– "Er nýja textafræðin ný? Þankar um gamla fræðigrein." *Gripla* 13 (2002): 199–216, esp. p. 206. Rpt. in Sverrir Tómasson. *Tækileg vitni: Greinar um bókmenntir gefnar út í tilefni sjötugsafmælis hans 5. apríl 2011* (Reykjavík: Stofnun Árna Magnússonar and Hið íslenska bókmenntafélag, 2011). Pp. 231–50, esp. pp. 238–9.

Widding, Ole, and Hans Bekker-Nielsen. "En senmiddelalderlig
    legendesamling." *Mm* (1960): 105–28, esp. pp. 119–20
– "Low German Influence on Late Icelandic Hagiography." *GR* 37
    (1962): 239–62, esp. pp. 251 and 255.
Handlist, p. 300.

2. Ágústínuss saga

Translated from a now-lost Low German redaction that resembles the
source(s) of *Der Heiligen Leben.*

Manuscript:
Stock. Perg. fol. no. 3 (*Reykjahólabók*) (ca. 1530–40).
Edition:
Loth, Agnete, ed. >> *Reykjahólabók* (1969–70). Vol. 2, pp. 95–128.
Literature:
Bekker-Nielsen, Hans. "Kyrkofäderna ock kyrkolärarna. K. i vestnordisk
    litteratur." *KLNM* 9 (1964). Cols. 690–3, esp. cols. 692–3.
Bekker-Nielsen, Hans, Thorkil Damsgaard Olsen, and Ole Widding.
    >> *Norrøn fortællekunst* (1965). P. 141.
Kalinke, Marianne E. "Reykjahólabók: A Legendary on the Eve of the
    Reformation." *Skáldskaparmál* 2 (1992): 239–69, esp. pp. 240, 251,
    and 264.
– "*Augustinus saga*: A Learned and a Popular Version." In
    >> *Samtíðarsögur* (1994). Vol. 2, pp. 435–49, esp. pp. 438–49.
– >> *The Book of Reykjahólar* (1996), pp. 28, 34, 39, 47, 50, 56–9, 60,
    62–7, 69, 80, 98, 108, 116, 126, 141, 149–50, 153–8, 160, 240–1, 244,
    and 246.
Widding, Ole, and Hans Bekker-Nielsen. "En senmiddelalderlig
    legendesamling." *Mm* (1960): 105–28, esp. pp. 107, 119–20,
    and 126.
– "Low German Influence on Late Icelandic Hagiography." *GR* 37
    (1962): 239–62, esp. pp. 251–2.
Handlist, p. 301.

BARBARA   December 4

1. Barbǫru saga

A translation of *BHL* Suppl. 913a.

Manuscripts:
AM 429 12mo (ca. 1500) and Stock. Perg. fol. no. 2 (ca. 1425–45).
Editions:
Foote, Peter, ed. >> *Lives of Saints* (1962).
   Facsimile of Stock. Perg. fol. no. 2.
Unger, C.R., ed. >> *Heilagra manna søgur* (1877). Vol. 1, pp. 153–7.
   Based on Stock. Perg. fol. no. 2 with variants from AM 429 12mo.
Wolf, Kirsten, ed. *The Old Norse–Icelandic Legend of Saint Barbara.*
   Studies and Texts 134 (Toronto: Pontifical Institute of Mediaeval
   Studies, 2000). Pp. 134–43.
   Edition of Stock. Perg. fol. no. 2 and AM 429 12mo.
– ed. >> *A Female Legendary from Iceland* (2011). Pp. 137–41.
   Facsimile and text edition of AM 429 12mo.
Modern Icelandic language editions:
Sigurveig Guðmundsdóttir, ed. *Heilög Barbara* ([Reykjavík]: Barböru-
   sjóður, 1981).
Wolf, Kirsten, ed. >> *Heilagra meyja sögur* (2003). Pp. 142–7.
Danish translation:
Carlé, Birte. *Skøger og jomfruer i den kristne fortællekunst* (Odense:
   Odense Universitetsforlag, 1991). Pp. 115–18.
English translation:
Wolf, Kirsten, ed. *The Old Norse–Icelandic Legend of Saint Barbara.*
   Studies and Texts 134 (Toronto: Pontifical Institute of Mediaeval
   Studies, 2000). Pp. 144–55.
Literature:
Anna Sigurðardóttir. *Allt hafði annan róm áður í páfadóm. Nunnuklaus-
   trin tvö á miðöldum og brot úr kristnisögu.* Úr veröld kvenna 3 (Reykja-
   vík: Kvennasögusafn Íslands, 1988). Pp. 327–32.
Ásdís Egilsdóttir. "Kvendýrlingar og kvenímynd trúarlegra bókmennta á
   Íslandi." In Inga Huld Hákonardóttir, ed. >> *Konur og kristsmenn*
   (1996). Pp. 93–116, esp. p. 93.
Bekker-Nielsen, Hans, Thorkil Damsgaard Olsen, and Ole Widding.
   >> *Norrøn fortællekunst* (1965). P. 124.
Bruvoll, Kjersti. "The Good, the Bad and the Devil! On Rewriting a
   Religious Motif in Some Virgin Martyr Legends." In Agneta Ney,
   Henrik Williams, and Fredrik Charpentier Ljungqvist, ed. >> *Á
   austrvega: Sagas and East Scandinavia* (2009). Vol. 1, pp. 136–43, esp.
   p. 138.
Carlé, Birte. "Fra slægtssaga til kvindesaga." In Silja Aðalsteinsdóttir and
   Helgi Þorláksson, ed. >> *Forändringar i kvinnors villkor under medel-
   tiden* (1983). Pp. 55–70, esp. pp. 56, 60, and 64–5.

- >> *Jomfru-fortællingen* (1985). Pp. 40–1, 43, 75, 79–80, 100–3, 131, 133, and 137.
- "Some Observations Regarding Narrative Patterns in the Medieval Sagas of Holy Maids." In Régis Boyer, ed. >> *Les Sagas de Chevaliers (Riddarasögur)* (1985). Pp. 393–404, esp. pp. 395 and 397.
- "Men and Women in the Saints' Sagas of *Stock. 2, fol.*" In John Lindow, Lars Lönnroth, and Gerd Wolfgang Weber, ed. >> *Structure and Meaning in Old Norse Literature* (1986). Pp. 317–46, esp. pp. 319–20 and 341–2.

Cormack, Margaret. >> *The Saints in Iceland* (1994). P. 37n44.

Jakob Benediktsson. "Nödhjälparna." *KLNM* 21 (1977). Cols. 289–90, esp. col. 289.

Kirby, Ian. >> *Biblical Quotation* (1980). Vol. 2, pp. 40–1.

Lehmann, Paul. >> "Skandinaviens Anteil an der lateinischen Literatur und Wissenschaft des Mittelalters" (1937). P. 44.

Mogk, Eugen. >> *Geschichte der norwegisch-isländischen Literatur* (1904). P. 891.

Sverrir Tómasson. "Kristnar trúarbókmenntir í óbundnu máli." In Guðrún Nordal, Sverrir Tómasson, and Vésteinn Ólason, ed. >> *Íslensk Bókmenntasaga* 1 (1992). Pp. 419–79, esp. p. 436.

Þórhallur Þorgilsson. "Um þýðingar og endursagnir úr ítölskum miðaldaritum." *Landsbókasafn Íslands. Árbók* 1946–7 (1948): 212–24, esp. p. 222.

Wolf, Kirsten. "The Severed Breast: A Topos in the Legends of Female Virgin Martyr Saints." *ANF* 112 (1997): 97–112, esp. pp. 98 and 104.

- "Female Scribes at Work? A Consideration of Kirkjubæjarbók (Codex AM 429 12mo)." In A.N. Doane and Kirsten Wolf, ed. >> *Beatus Vir* (2006). Pp. 265–95, esp. pp. 270 and 279.

Handlist, p. 301.

2. Barbǫru saga

An epitome of the legend possibly based on 1.

Manuscript:
AM 672 4to (ca. 1400–1500).

Edition:
Wolf, Kirsten, ed. *The Old Norse–Icelandic Legend of Saint Barbara.* Studies and Texts 134 (Toronto: Pontifical Institute of Mediaeval Studies, 2000). P. 114.

Literature:
Carlé, Birte. >> *Jomfru-fortællingen* (1985). Pp. 41–2.
Foote, Peter, ed. >> *Lives of Saints* (1962). P. 26.
Louis-Jensen, Jonna. "'Seg Hallfríði góða nótt'." *Opuscula* 2.2. Bibliotheca
   Arnamagnæana 25.2 (Copenhagen: Reitzel, 1977). Pp. 149–53, esp. p. 150.
Handlist, p. 301.

BARLAAM AND JOSAPHAT   November 27

1. Barlaams saga ok Jósafats

A translation of a religious tale (cf. *BHL* 979) based upon legends of
the life of Buddha and believed to have been undertaken by King Hákon
Hákonarson (1232–57).

Manuscripts:
AM 230 fol. (ca. 1350–1400, defective), AM 231 fol. I (ca. 1400), AM
   231 fol. II (ca. 1300–50), AM 231 fol. III (ca. 1300–50), AM 231 fol.
   IV (ca. 1400–1500), AM 231 fol. V (ca. 1300–50), AM 231 fol. VI
   (ca. 1350), AM 231 fol. VII (ca. 1300–25), AM 231 fol. VIII (ca. 1400–
   1500), AM 231 fol. IX (ca. 1300–50), AM 231 fol. X (ca. 1400–1500),
   AM 232 fol. (ca. 1300, defective), AM 668 4to (ca. 1400–50, defect-
   ive), AM 696 4to XVIII (ca. 1400–1500), AM 233 8vo IV (ca. 1350),
   NRA 64 (ca. 1300–25), Stock. Papp. fol. no. 49 (1672), Stock. Perg.
   fol. no. 6 (ca. 1275, defective), Stock. Perg. fol. no. 12 V (ca. 1300–50),
   and Stock. Perg. fol. no. 12 VI (ca. 1300–50).
Editions:
Keyser, R., and C.R. Unger, ed. *Barlaams ok Josaphats saga* (Christiania
   [Oslo]: Feilberg & Landmark, 1851).
   Based on Stock. Perg. fol. no. 6 and filled in from AM 232 fol.
   (pp. 81.15–82.37, 143.34–145.30, 170.5–172.5, 179.24–181.14, 200.5–
   204.16, 212.17–29) and AM 230 fol. (pp. 1–9.22, 21.4–22.21) with
   variants from AM 231 fol. I, II, III, IV, V, VI, VII, VIII, IX, and X,
   NRA 64, and Stock. Perg. fol. no. 12 V and VI.
Kålund, Kr. "Nyfundet brudstykke af en gammelnorsk homilie." *ANF* 12
   (1896): 367–9, esp. pp. 368–9.
   Edition of AM 233 8vo IV.
[Kålund, Kr., ed.] *Palæografisk Atlas: Oldnorsk-islandsk afdeling* (Copenhagen and Christiania [Oslo]: Gyldendal, 1905). No. 21.
   Facsimile and text edition of Stock. Perg. fol. no. 6, fol. 44v.

Rindal, Magnus, ed. *Barlaams ok Josaphats saga. Manuscript no. 6 fol. in the Royal Library, Stockholm and the Norwegian Fragments.* CCN, Quarto Series 6 (Oslo: Society for the Publication of Old Norwegian Manuscripts, 1980).
   Facsimile of Stock. Perg. fol. no. 6.
– ed. *Barlaams ok Josaphats saga.* Norrøne tekster 4 (Oslo: Norsk historisk kjeldeskrift-institutt, 1981).
   Edition of Stock. Perg. fol. no. 6 (pp. 3–195), AM 230 fol. 1r–6v and 12r29–13r27 (pp. 199–209 and 212–13), AM 232 fol. 10vb32–11va14, 32rb19–33ra24, 41vb21–42va17, 44ra33–44vb13, 50va3–21, 50vb2–51vb31, 54rb18–37 (pp. 214–33), AM 321 fol. VI (pp. 237–41), AM 233 8vo IV (pp. 242–3), and NRA 64 (pp. 244–5).

Modern Icelandic language edition:
Einar Ól. Sveinsson, ed. *Leit eg suður til landa. Ævintýri og helgisögur frá miðöldum* (Reykjavík: Heimskringla, 1944). Pp. 94–5 and 199–202 (extracts only).

Norwegian translation:
Kinck, H.E. *Barlaam og Josaphat. En religiøs roman* (Christiania [Oslo]: Feilberg & Landmark, 1852).

Literature:
Astås, Reidar. "*Barlaams ok Josaphats saga* i nærlys." *Mm* (1990): 124–52.
– "Romantekst på vandring: 'Barlaams og Josaphats saga' fra India til Island." *Edda* 90 (1990): 3–13, esp. p. 11.
– "Spor av teologisk tenkning og refleksjon i norsk og islandsk høymiddelalder." *CM* 6 (1993): 133–67, esp. pp. 145–6 and 148–9.
– "Tekstkritikk til *Barlaams saga ok Jósafats*: Nokre merknader." *Mm* (2009): 20–36.
Bandlien, Bjørn. *Strategies of Passion: Love and Marriage in Medieval Iceland and Norway.* Trans. Betsy van der Hoeck (Turnhout: Brepols, 2005). Pp. 204 and 218.
Bekker-Nielsen, Hans. "Et brudstykke af Kongespejlet. Med bemærkninger om indholdet af AM 668, 4°." *Opuscula* 1. Bibliotheca Arnamagnæana 20 (Copenhagen: Munksgaard, 1960). Pp. 105–12, esp. pp. 109–10 and 112.
Bekker-Nielsen, Hans, Thorkil Damsgaard Olsen, and Ole Widding. >> *Norrøn fortællekunst* (1965). Pp. 78, 105–6, 111–12, 114, 135, and 164.
Bekker-Nielsen, Hans, and Ole Widding. "Religiøs prosalitteratur. Norge og Island." *KLNM* 14 (1969). Cols. 42–4, esp. col. 43.
Boyer, Régis. >> *La vie religieuse en Islande* (1979). Pp. 162, 197–8, and 224.
Cormack, Margaret. >> *The Saints in Iceland* (1994). Pp. 33n18 and 241.

Hallberg, Peter. "Imagery in Religious Old Norse Prose Literature: An Outline." *ANF* 102 (1987): 120–70, esp. pp. 126, 129, 137–8, 142, 144, 149–51, and 157.

Halvorsen, E.F. *The Norse Version of the Chanson de Roland*. Bibliotheca Arnamagnæana 19 (Copenhagen: Ejnar Munksgaard, 1959). Pp. 22 and 30.

Haugen, Odd Einar. "Om tidsforholdet mellom *Stjórn* og *Barlaams ok Josaphats saga*." *Mm* (1983): 18–28.

- "Buddha i Bjørgvin. Den norrøne soga om kongssonen Josaphat og munken Barlaam." *Syn og Segn* 92 (1986): 263–70.

- "Barlaam og Josaphat i ny utgåve." *Mm* (1991): 1–24.

- "Exempla in Barlaams ok Josaphats saga." In >> *Sagas and the Norwegian Experience* (1997). Pp. 227–36.

- "Forteljingane i forteljinga. Interpolasjonane i *Barlaams ok Josaphats saga*." In Karl G. Johansson and Maria Arvidsson, ed. >> *Barlaam i nord* (2009). Pp. 47–73.

Haugen, Odd Einar, and Karl J. Johansson. "De nordiske versjonene av Barlaam-legenden." In Karl G. Johansson and Maria Arvidsson, ed. >> *Barlaam i nord* (2009). Pp. 11–29, esp. pp. 15–20 and 26–9.

Holmboe, C.A. "En buddhistisk Legende, benyttet i et christeligt Opbyggelses-Skrift." *Forhandlinger i Videnskabs-Selskabet i Christiania Aar 1870* (Christiania: Brøgger & Christie, 1871). Pp. 340–51, esp. pp. 340 and 349–50.

Holm-Olsen, Ludvig. "Middelalderens litteratur i Norge." In *Norges litteratur historie* 1. Ed. Edvard Beyer (Oslo: Cappelen, 1974). Pp. 18–342, esp pp. 146–7.

* Johanterwage, Vera. "Die Barlaams ok Josaphats saga – eine höfische Legende am norwegischen Königshof." Doctoral dissertation, Westfällische Wilhelms-Universität zu Münster, 2007.

- "Kung Avennir i *Barlaams ok Josaphats saga* – en hövisk härskare?" In Karl G. Johansson and Maria Arvidsson, ed. >> *Barlaam i nord* (2009). Pp. 75–97.

Jónas Kristjánsson. *Um Fóstbrœðra sögu* (Reykjavík: Stofnun Árna Magnússonar, 1972). Pp. 236 and 259–60.

- "Learned Style or Saga Style?" In Ursula Dronke, Guðrún P. Helgadóttir, Gerd Wolfgang Weber, and Hans Bekker-Nielsen, ed. >> *Specvlvm Norroenvm* (1981). Pp. 260–92.

- >> *Eddas and Sagas* (1988). P. 143.

Kirby, Ian. >> *Biblical Quotation* (1980). Vol. 2, pp. 19, 78–9, 117, 123, and 127.

– *Bible Translation in Old Norse*. Université de Lausanne Publications de la faculté des lettres 27 (Geneva: Librairie Droz, 1986). Pp. 44–5, 62, 64n60, 66, 97, 112, 151, 159–62, and 166.

Kålund, Kr. "Tillægsbemærkning til gammel-norsk 'homilie'-brudstykke, Arkiv XII, 367–69." *ANF* 13 (1897): 100.

Leach, Henry Goddard. *Angevin Britain and Scandinavia*. Harvard Studies in Comparative Literature 6 (Cambridge, Mass.: Harvard University Press, 1921). Pp. 121, 154, and 383.

Lehmann, Paul. >> "Skandinaviens Anteil an der lateinischen Literatur und Wissenschaft des Mittelalters" (1937). P. 81.

Magerøy, Hallvard. "Barlaams ok Josaphats saga." *KLNM* 1 (1956). Cols. 342–4.

Mogk, Eugen. >> *Geschichte der norwegisch-isländischen Literatur* (1904). Pp 567, 858, and 871.

Naumann, Hans-Peter. "Hatte die *Barlaams saga ok Jósafats* eine mittel-hochdeutsche Vorlage?" *Alvíssmál* 10 (2001): 45–60.

Paasche, Fredrik. *Norges og Islands litteratur inntil utgangen av middelalder-en*. Rev. ed. by Anne Holtsmark (Oslo: Aschehoug, 1947). P. 473.

Rindal, Magnus. *Ortografi, fonologi og morfologi i Sth. perg. fol. nr. 6 (Barlaams ok Josaphats saga)* (Oslo: Novus: 1987).

– "Barlaams ok Josaphats saga." In Phillip Pulsiano and Kirsten Wolf, with Paul Acker and Donald K. Fry, ed. >> *Medieval Scandinavia* (1993). P. 36.

– "*Barlaams ok Josaphats saga* i det norske litterære miljøet." In Karl G. Johansson and Maria Arvidsson, ed. >> *Barlaam i nord* (2009). Pp. 31–45, esp. pp. 31–4 and 45.

Schier, Kurt. *Sagaliteratur*. Sammlung Metzler M78 (Stuttgart: Metzler, 1970). Pp. 98, 107–8, and 128.

Schnall, Jens Eike. "*Hǫmlubarði* – ein ruderloses Schiff, auf Grund gesetzt. Zu *Konungs skuggsjá, Barlaams saga ok Josaphats* und skandi-navischen Ortsnamen." In *Namenwelten. Orts- und Personennamen in historischer Sicht*. Ed. Astrid van Nahl, Lennart Elmevik, and Stefan Brink. Reallexikon der Germanischen Altertumskunde. Ergänzungs-bände 44 (Berlin: de Gruyter, 2004). Pp. 277–91.

– "Grundkedelig og lidet norsk? Om forholdet mellem *Barlaams ok Josaphats saga* og *Kongespejlet*." In Karl G. Johansson and Maria Arvidsson, ed. >> *Barlaam i nord* (2009). Pp. 99–130.

Simek, Rudolf. *Altnordische Kosmographie: Studien und Quellen zu Weltbild und Weltbeschreibung in Norwegen und Island vom 12. bis zum 14. Jahrhundert* (Berlin: de Gruyter, 1990). Pp. 101–2 and 252.

Stefán Karlsson. "Islandsk bogeksport til Norge i middelalderen." *Mm* (1979): 1–17, esp. pp. 6, 8, and 11. Rpt. in *Stafkrókar: Ritgerðir eftir Stefán Karlsson gefnar út í tilefni af sjötugsafmæli hans 2. desember 1998*. Ed. Guðvarður Már Gunnlaugsson (Reykjavík: Stofnun Árna Magnússonar, 2000). Pp. 188–205, esp. pp. 194, 197, and 201.

Storm, Gustav. "Om Tidsforholdet mellem Kongespeilet og Stjórn samt Barlaams og Josafats saga." *ANF* 3 (1886): 83–8.

Sverrir Tómasson. *Formálar íslenskra sagnaritara á miðöldum. Rannsókn bókmenntahefðar* (Reykjavík: Stofnun Árna Magnússonar, 1988). Pp. 222 and 246.

– "Trúarbókmenntir í lausu máli á síðmiðöld." In Böðvar Guðmundsson, Sverrir Tómasson, Torfi H. Tulinius, and Vésteinn Ólason, ed. >> *Íslensk Bókmenntasaga* 2 (1993). Pp. 249–82, esp. p. 275.

Vries, Jan de. >> *Altnordische Literaturgeschichte* (1964–7). Vol. 2, pp. 185–6.

Widding, Ole. "Et norsk fragment af Barlaams saga. Et bidrag til Barlaamsagaens tekstkritik." *Mm* (1963): 37–46.

– "Om fragmenter af Barlaams saga ok Josaphats. Holm 12 fol. V og NoRA 64." *Mm* (1972): 93–103.

Handlist, pp. 301–2.

NOTE:
In the saga, material about other saints is found, especially Anthony, Gregory Thaumaturgus, Pelagia the Penitent, and Thais. See the entries for the individual saints.

2. Barlaams saga og Jósafats

Translated from a now-lost Low German redaction that resembles the source(s) of *Der Heiligen Leben*.

Manuscript:
Stock. Perg. fol. no. 3 (*Reykjahólabók*) (ca. 1530–40).
Edition:
Loth, Agnete, ed. >> *Reykjahólabók* (1969–70). Vol. 1, pp. 97–131.
Literature:
Bekker-Nielsen, Hans, Thorkil Damsgaard Olsen, and Ole Widding. >> *Norrøn fortællekunst* (1965). P. 141.

Haugen, Odd Einar, and Karl J. Johansson. "De nordiske versjonene av Barlaam-legenden." In Karl G. Johansson and Maria Arvidsson, ed. >> *Barlaam i nord* (2009). Pp. 11–29, esp. pp. 24–9.

Kalinke, Marianne E. "Reykjahólabók: A Legendary on the Eve of
the Reformation." *Skáldskaparmál* 2 (1992): 239–69, esp. p. 240.
– >> *The Book of Reykjahólar* (1996). Pp. 28, 50, 192, and 240.
Rindal, Magnus. "Barlaams ok Josaphats saga." In Phillip Pulsiano and
Kirsten Wolf, with Paul Acker and Donald K. Fry, ed. >> *Medieval
Scandinavia* (1993). P. 36.
Widding, Ole, and Hans Bekker-Nielsen. "En senmiddelalderlig
legendesamling." *Mm* (1960): 105–28, esp. pp. 107 and 114.
– "Low German Influence on Late Icelandic Hagiography." *GR* 37
(1962): 239–62, esp. pp. 247 and 255.
Handlist, p. 302.

BARTHOLOMEW   August 24

1. Barthólómeuss saga postola I

Based on a version of *BHL* 1002 and possibly 1004.

Manuscripts:
AM 628 4to (1711–12), AM 629 4to (1697), AM 630 4to (ca. 1650–1700),
AM 645 4to (ca. 1220, defective), AM 652 4to (ca. 1250–70, defective),
AM 656 4to I (ca. 1600), Rask 69 (ca. 1800), and SÁM 1 fol. (*Codex
Scardensis*) (ca. 1350–75).

Editions:
Holtsmark, Anne, ed. *A Book of Miracles: MS No. 645 4to of the Arna-
Magnæan Collection in the University Library of Copenhagen*. CCI 12
(Copenhagen: Einar Munksgaard, 1938).
Facsimile of AM 645 4to.
Larsson, Ludvig, ed. *Isländska handskriften N° 645 4° i Den Ar-
namagnæanske Samlingen på Universitetsbiblioteket i København: I.
Handskriftens äldre del* (Lund: Gleerup, 1885). Pp. 99.25–108.4.
Edition of AM 645 4to.
Slay, Desmond, ed. *Codex Scardensis*. EIM 2 (Copenhagen: Rosenkilde
and Bagger, 1960).
Facsimile of SÁM 1 fol.
Þorsteinn Jónsson, ed. *Hér hefjast Tíu Sögur, af þeim enum heiløgu Guds
Postulum og pínslar vottum* (Viðeyjarklaustur: Þ. Jónsson, 1836). Pp. 136–53.
Based on a manuscript descended from AM 630 4to.
Unger, C.R., ed. >> *Postola sögur* (1874). Pp. 743.25–762.22.

Based on AM 630 4to (pp. 743.25–754.9), AM 652 4to (pp. 754.11–
757.2), and AM 645 4to (pp. 757.4–762.22) with variants from AM 628
4to (pp. 744.13–752.16).
Modern Icelandic language edition:
Ólafur Halldórsson, ed. *Sögur úr Skarðsbók* (Reykjavík: Almenna
bókafélagið, 1967). Pp. 174–85.
Edition of SÁM 1 fol.
English translation:
Roughton, Philip G. "AM 645 4to and AM 652/630 4to: Study and
Translation of Two Thirteenth-Century Icelandic Collections of
Apostles' and Saints' Lives." PhD dissertation, University of Colorado,
2002. Pp. 755–74.
Literature:
Battista, Simonetta. "Oversættelsesteknik i to *postola sögur*." In >> *Sagas
and the Norwegian Experience* (1997). Pp. 57–65.
– "Translation or Redaction in Old Norse Hagiography." In Peter
Andersen, ed. >> *Pratiques de Traduction au Moyen Age* (2004).
Pp. 100–10, esp. pp. 103–5.
– "The *Compilator* and Contemporary Literary Culture in Old Norse
Hagiography." *Viking and Medieval Scandinavia* 1 (2005): 1–13, esp.
pp. 5–6.
– "*Blámenn, djǫflar* and Other Representations of Evil in Old Norse
Literature." In John McKinnell, David Ashurst, and Donata Kick,
ed. >> *The Fantastic in Old Norse/Icelandic Literature* (2006). Vol. 1,
pp. 113–22, esp. pp. 113 and 117–18.
Bekker-Nielsen, Hans. "Et par ord om de ældste norrøne helgensagaer."
In Finn Hødnebø et al., ed. >> *Eyvindarbók* (1992). Pp. 29–33, esp.
p. 32.
Bekker-Nielsen, Hans, Thorkil Damsgaard Olsen, and Ole Widding.
>> *Norrøn fortællekunst* (1965). Pp. 122–3.
Bugge, Anders. "Bartholomæus." *KLNM* 1 (1956). Cols. 365–8, esp.
cols. 365–6.
Collings, Lucy Grace. "The Codex Scardensis: Studies in Icelandic
Hagiography." PhD dissertation, Cornell University, 1969. Pp. 18–21
and 171–85.
Cormack, Margaret. >> *The Saints in Iceland* (1994). Pp. 33n14 and 83.
Finnur Jónsson. >> *Den oldnorske og oldislandske Litteraturs Historie*
(1920–4). Vol. 2, p. 872.
Foote, Peter. "Postulatal." In Guðni Kolbeinsson, ed. >> *Minjar og
menntir* (1976). Pp. 152–73, esp. p. 165.

Hallberg, Peter. "Imagery in Religious Old Norse Prose Literature: An Outline." *ANF* 102 (1987): 120–70, esp. p. 150.

Helgi Guðmundsson. *Um haf innan. Vestrænir menn og íslenzk menning á miðöldum* (Reykjavík: Háskólaútgáfan, 1997). Pp. 110n20 and 313.

Jakob Benediktsson. "Traces of Latin Prose-Rhythm in Old Norse Literature." In *The Fifth Viking Congress, Tórshavn, July 1965*. Ed. Bjarni Niclasen (Tórshavn: Føroya Landsstýri, 1968. Pp. 17–24, esp. p. 23. Rpt. in Jakob Benediktsson. *Lærdómslistir. Afmælisrit 20. júlí 1987* (Reykjavík: Mál og menning, 1987). Pp. 153–60, esp. pp. 158–9.

Jón Hnefill Aðalsteinsson. "Blot i forna skrifter." *SI* 47 (1996): 11–32, esp. pp. 22–3.

Jón Ma. Ásgeirsson and Þórður Ingi Guðjónsson, ed. *Frá Sýrlandi til Íslands: Arfur Tómasar postula* (Reykjavík: Háskólaútgáfan, 2007). Pp. 164–5 and 175.

Jón Þorkelsson. "Islandske håndskrifter i England og Skotland." *ANF* 8 (1892): 199–237, esp. pp. 235–6.

Kirby, Ian. >> *Biblical Quotation* (1980). Vol. 2, pp. 33–4.

Kratz, Henry. "The Language of the Old Norse Saints' Lives." *Mm* (1988): 159–73.

Louis-Jensen, Jonna. "To håndskrifter fra det nordvestlige Island." *Opuscula* 7. Bibliotheca Arnamagnæana 34 (Copenhagen: Reitzel, 1979). Pp. 219–53, esp. p. 221.

McDougall, Ian, ed. "Anonymous, *Allra postula minnisvísur* 'Celebratory *Vísur* about All the Apostles'." In Margaret Clunies Ross, ed. >> *Poetry on Christian Subjects* (2007). Vol. 2, pp. 852–71, esp. p. 865.

Mogk, Eugen. >> *Geschichte der norwegisch-isländischen Literatur* (1904). P. 889.

Ólafur Halldórsson. *Helgafellsbækur fornar*. Studia Islandica 24 (Reykjavík: Heimspekideild Háskóla Íslands and Menningarsjóður, 1966). Pp. 16–22 and 41–5.

– "Rímbeglusmiður." *Opuscula* 2.2. Bibliotheca Arnamagnæana 25.2 (Copenhagen: Reitzel, 1977). Pp. 32–49, esp. p. 42. Rpt. in Ólafur Halldórsson. *Grettisfærsla: Safn ritgerða eftir Ólaf Halldórsson gefið út á sjötugsafmæli hans 18. apríl 1990* (Reykjavík: Stofnun Árna Magnússonar, 1990). Pp. 302–18, esp. p. 312.

Ólafur Halldórsson, ed. *Mattheus saga postula* (Reykjavík: Stofnun Árna Magnússonar, 1994). Pp. xiii–lvii and lxxv–lxxxi.

Roughton, Philip. "Stylistics and Sources of the *Postola sögur* in AM 645 4to and AM 652/630 4to." *Gripla* 16 (2005): 7–50.

– "'Þá syndi hann þeim mikinn skugga': Unmasking the Fantastic in the
  Postola sögur." In John McKinnell, David Ashurst, and Donata Kick,
  ed. >> *The Fantastic in Old Norse/Icelandic Literature* (2006). Vol. 2,
  pp. 846–55, esp. pp. 847–50.
Simek, Rudolf. *Altnordische Kosmographie: Studien und Quellen zu
  Weltbild und Weltbeschreibung in Norwegen und Island vom 12. bis zum
  14. Jahrhundert* (Berlin: de Gruyter, 1990). P. 157.
Sverrir Tómasson. *Formálar íslenskra sagnaritara á miðöldum. Rannsókn
  bókmenntahefðar* (Reykjavík: Stofnun Árna Magnússonar, 1988).
  Pp. 95, 189, 230, and 332.
Turville-Petre, G. >> *Origins of Icelandic Literature* (1967). P. 130.
Þórður Ingi Guðjónsson. "Apostlene i islandsk middelalderlitteratur." In
  Den nordiske renessansen i høymiddelalderen. Ed. Jón Viðar Sigurðsson
  and Preben Meulengracht Sørensen (Oslo: Historisk institutt, Universi-
  tetet i Oslo, 2000). Pp. 83–99, esp. pp. 93–4.
Wolf, Kirsten. "Postola sögur." In Phillip Pulsiano and Kirsten Wolf, with Paul
  Acker and Donald K. Fry, ed. >> *Medieval Scandinavia* (1993). Pp. 511–12.
– "Skarðsbók." In Phillip Pulsiano and Kirsten Wolf, with Paul Acker
  and Donald K. Fry, ed. >> *Medieval Scandinavia* (1993). P. 596.
Handlist, p. 302.

2. Barthólómeuss saga postola II

Based on a version of *BHL* 1002 and possibly 1004.

Manuscript:
AM 655 4to XII–XIII (ca. 1250–75).
Edition:
Unger, C.R., ed. >> *Postola sögur* (1874). Pp. 762.24–766.
Literature:
Battista, Simonetta. "Oversættelsesteknik i to *postola sögur*." In >> *Sagas
  and the Norwegian Experience* (1997). Pp. 57–65.
– "Translation or Redaction in Old Norse Hagiography." In Peter
  Andersen, ed. >> *Pratiques de Traduction au Moyen Age* (2004).
  Pp. 100–10, esp. pp. 102–4.
– "The *Compilator* and Contemporary Literary Culture in Old Norse
  Hagiography." *Viking and Medieval Scandinavia* 1 (2005): 1–13, esp.
  pp. 5–6.
– "*Blámenn, djǫflar* and Other Representations of Evil in Old Norse
  Literature." In John McKinnell, David Ashurst, and Donata Kick, ed.

>> *The Fantastic in Old Norse/Icelandic Literature* (2006). Vol. 1,
pp. 113–22, esp. pp. 113 and 117–18.

Cormack, Margaret. >> *The Saints in Iceland* (1994). P. 83.

Finnur Jónsson. >> *Den oldnorske og oldislandske Litteraturs Historie*
(1920–4). Vol. 2, p. 872.

Foote, Peter. "Postulatal." In Guðni Kolbeinsson, ed. >> *Minjar og
menntir* (1976). Pp. 152–73, esp. p. 165.

Jónas Kristjánsson. "Learned Style or Saga Style?" In Ursula Dronke,
Guðrún P. Helgadóttir, Gerd Wolfgang Weber, and Hans Bekker-
Nielsen, ed. >> *Specvlvm Norroenvm* (1981). Pp. 260–92.

Kirby, Ian. >> *Biblical Quotation* (1980). Vol. 2, p. 34.

Mogk, Eugen. >> *Geschichte der norwegisch-isländischen Literatur* (1904).
P. 889.

Ólafur Halldórsson, ed. *Mattheus saga postula* (Reykjavík: Stofnun Árna
Magnússonar, 1994). Pp. lxvi–lxxv.

Sverrir Tómasson. *Formálar íslenskra sagnaritara á miðöldum. Rannsókn
bókmenntahefðar* (Reykjavík: Stofnun Árna Magnússonar, 1988).
P. 332.

Þórður Ingi Guðjónsson. "Apostlene i islandsk middelalderlitteratur." In
Den nordiske renessansen i høymiddelalderen. Ed. Jón Viðar Sigurðsson
and Preben Meulengracht Sørensen (Oslo: Historisk institutt, Universitetet i Oslo, 2000). Pp. 83–99, esp. p. 94.

Handlist, p. 302.

3. Barthólómeuss saga postola

The source has not been identified.

Manuscript:
AM 237b fol. (ca. 1250, defective).

Edition:
Loth, Agnete. "Et gammelnorsk apostelsagafragment: AM 237b fol."
In *Afmælisrit Jóns Helgasonar 30. júní 1969*. Ed. Jakob Benediktsson
et al. (Reykjavík: Heimskringla, 1969). Pp. 219–34, esp. pp. 220–223.20
(text and facsimile).

Literature:
Cormack, Margaret. >> *The Saints in Iceland* (1994). P. 83.

Helgi Guðmundsson. *Um haf innan. Vestrænir menn og íslenzk menning á
miðöldum* (Reykjavík: Háskólaútgáfan, 1997). P. 110n20.

Kirby, Ian. >> *Biblical Quotation* (1980). Vol. 2, pp. 34 and 101.

Sverrir Tómasson. *Formálar íslenskra sagnaritara á miðöldum. Rannsókn bókmenntahefðar* (Reykjavík: Stofnun Árna Magnússonar, 1988). P. 332.
Handlist, p. 302.

4. Um Barthólómeus postola

An epitome based possibly on a version of 1.

Manuscript:
AM 672 4to (ca. 1400–1500).
Literature:
Carlé, Birte. >> *Jomfrufortællingen* (1985). P. 41.
– "Men and Women in the Saints' Sagas of *Stock. 2, fol.*" In John Lindow, Lars Lönnroth, and Gerd Wolfgang Weber, ed. >> *Structure and Meaning in Old Norse Literature* (1986). Pp. 317–46, esp. p. 319.
Handlist, p. 302.

BASIL THE GREAT   June 14

1. Basilíuss saga

A translation of *BHL* 1022.

Manuscript:
AM 655 4to VI (ca. 1200–25).
Editions:
Hreinn Benediktsson, ed. *Early Icelandic Script As Illustrated in Vernacular Texts from the Twelfth and Thirteenth Centuries.* Íslenzk handrit. Icelandic Manuscripts, Series in Folio 2 (Reykjavík: The Manuscript Institute of Iceland, 1965). Plate 21 and p. xvi.
Facsimile and text edition of fol. 2r.
Morgenstern, Gustav, ed. >> *Arnamagnæanische Fragmente* (1893). Pp. 24–5.
Literature:
Bekker-Nielsen, Hans, Thorkil Damsgaard Olsen, and Ole Widding. >> *Norrøn fortællekunst* (1965). P. 23.
Bekker-Nielsen, Hans, and Ole Widding. "Religiøs prosalitteratur. Norge og Island." *KLNM* 14 (1969). Cols. 42–4, esp. col. 43.
Boyer, Régis. >> *La vie religieuse en Islande* (1979). P. 162.

Cormack, Margaret. >> *The Saints in Iceland* (1994). P. 83.
Jónas Kristjánsson. "Learned Style or Saga Style?" In Ursula Dronke, Guðrún P. Helgadóttir, Gerd Wolfgang Weber, and Hans Bekker-Nielsen, ed. >> *Specvlvm Norroenvm* (1981). Pp. 260–92.
– >> *Eddas and Sagas* (1988). P. 148.
Mogk, Eugen. >> *Geschichte der norwegisch-isländischen Literatur* (1904). P. 893.
Morgenstern, Gustav. "Notizen." *ANF* 11 (1895): 95–7, esp. pp. 96–7.
Handlist, p. 303.

2. Basilíuss saga

A translation of a version of *BHL* 1022 with interpolations.

Manuscript:
AM 238 fol. II (ca. 1300–50).
Edition:
Morgenstern, Gustav, ed. >> *Arnamagnæanische Fragmente* (1893). Pp. 25–35.
Literature:
Boyer, Régis. >> *La vie religieuse en Islande* (1979). P. 162.
Carlé, Birte. >> *Jomfru-fortællingen* (1985). P. 36.
Cormack, Margaret. >> *The Saints in Iceland* (1994). P. 83.
Kirby, Ian. >> *Biblical Quotation* (1980). Vol. 2, p. 94.
Mogk, Eugen. >> *Geschichte der norwegisch-isländischen Literatur* (1904). P. 893.
Morgenstern, Gustav. "Notizen." *ANF* 11 (1895): 95–7, esp. pp. 96–7.
Handlist, p. 303

3. Af Basilío

A tale of Saint Basil incorporated into the miracles of the Virgin Mary.

Manuscripts:
See Mary the Blessed Virgin 3 note (p. 245).
Edition:
Unger, C.R., ed. >> *Mariu saga* (1871). Pp. 72.26–73.20 and 699.15–702.20.
Literature:
Boyer, Régis. >> *La vie religieuse en Islande* (1979). P. 162.

Cormack, Margaret. >> *The Saints in Iceland* (1994). P. 83.
Handlist, pp. 303 and 323.

BEDE THE VENERABLE   May 27

1. Af Beda presti

A short life of Bede the Venerable based possibly on an encyclopedic
work like the *Speculum historiale*.

Manuscript:
AM 764 4to (ca.1376–86).
Editions:
Gudbrand Vigfusson and George W. Dasent, ed. and trans. *Icelandic
   Sagas and Other Historical Documents Relating to the Settlements and
   Descents of the Northmen on the British Isles*. 4 vols. Rolls Series 88
   (London: Eyre & Spottiswoode, 1887–94; rpt. [Millwood]: Kraus,
   1962). Vol. 2, pp. 433–4.
Möbius, Th., ed. *Analecta Norræna. Auswahl aus der isländischen und
   norwegischen Litteratur des Mittelalters*. 2nd ed. (Leipzig: J.C.
   Hinrichs'sche Buchhandlung, 1877). P. 208.
Turville-Petre, Gabriel. "Legends of England in Icelandic Manuscripts."
   In Peter Clemoes, ed. >> *The Anglo-Saxons* (1959). Pp. 104–21,
   esp. pp. 106–7. Rpt. in Gabriel Turville-Petre. *Nine Norse Studies*
   (London: Viking Society for Northern Research, 1972). Pp. 59–78,
   esp. p. 62.
Literature:
Bekker-Nielsen, Hans, Thorkil Damsgaard Olsen, and Ole Widding. >>
   Norrøn fortællekunst (1965). P. 126.
Benedikz, Benedikt S. "Bede in the Uttermost North." In *Famulus Christi:
   Essays in Commemoration of the Thirteenth Centenary of the Birth of
   the Venerable Bede*. Ed. Gerald Bonner (London: SPCK, 1976).
   Pp. 334–43, esp. p. 341.
Boyer, Régis. >> *La vie religieuse en Islande* (1979). P. 181.
Cormack, Margaret. >> *The Saints in Iceland* (1994). P. 35.
Fell, Christine E. "Anglo-Saxon Saints in Old Norse Sources and Vice
   Versa." In Hans Bekker-Nielsen, Peter Foote, and Olaf Olsen, ed. >>
   Proceedings of the Eighth Viking Congress Århus (1981). Pp. 95–106,
   esp. pp. 97–100.

Fry, Donald K. "Bede." In Phillip Pulsiano and Kirsten Wolf, with Paul Acker and Donald K. Fry, ed. >> *Medieval Scandinavia* (1993). Pp. 36–7, esp. p. 37.

Svanhildur Óskarsdóttir. "Universal History in Fourteenth-Century Iceland: Studies in AM 764 4to." PhD dissertation, University of London, 2000. Pp. 58, 62, and 241.

Wolf, Kirsten, ed. >> *Heilagra meyja sögur* (2003). P. li.

Handlist, p. 303.

2. Af Beda

A tale of Bede the Venerable incorporated into the miracles of the Virgin Mary.

Manuscripts:
See Mary the Blessed Virgin 3 note (p. 245).
Edition:
Unger, C.R., ed. >> *Mariu saga* (1871). Pp. 650.12–652.5.
Literature:

Sverrir Tómasson. "Veraldleg sagnaritun 1120–1400." In Guðrún Nordal, Sverrir Tómasson, and Vésteinn Ólason, ed. >> *Íslensk Bókmenntasaga* 1 (1992). Pp. 263–418, esp. p. 303.

Turville-Petre, Gabriel. "Legends of England in Icelandic Manuscripts." In Peter Clemoes, ed. >> *The Anglo-Saxons* (1959). Pp. 104–21. Rpt. in Gabriel Turville-Petre. *Nine Norse Studies* (London: Viking Society for Northern Research, 1972). Pp. 59–78.

Widding, Ole. "Norrøne Marialegender på europæisk baggrund." *Opuscula* 10. Bibliotheca Arnamagnæana 40 (Copenhagen: Reitzel, 1996). Pp. 1–128, esp. pp. 25 and 71.

Handlist, pp. 303 and 323.

BENEDICT   March 21

1. Af Benedikt

A short passage about Saint Benedict to be read on his feast-day. The source has not been established.

Manuscript:
AM 655 4to XXI (ca. 1200–50).

Editions:

Hreinn Benediktsson. *Early Icelandic Script As Illustrated in Vernacular Texts from the Twelfth and Thirteenth Centuries.* Íslenzk handrit: Icelandic Manuscripts, Series in Folio 2 (Reykjavík: The Manuscript Institute of Iceland, 1965). Plate 45 and p. xxx.13–28.
   Facsimile and text edition of fol. 2r.

Þorvaldur Bjarnarson, ed. *Leifar fornra kristinna fræða íslenzkra: Codex Arna-Magnæanus 677 4to auk annara enna elztu brota af íslenzkum guðfræðisritum* (Copenhagen: Hagerup, 1878). Pp. 168.28–170.1.

Literature:

Bekker-Nielsen, Hans. "Homiletisk haandbog?" *Opuscula* 1. Bibliotheca Arnamagnæana 20 (Copenhagen: Munksgaard, 1960). Pp. 343–4.

Cormack, Margaret. >> *The Saints in Iceland* (1994). Pp. 37n45 and 240.

Konráð Gíslason. *Um frum-parta íslenzkrar túngu í fornöld* (Copenhagen: Trier, 1846). P. lxxxi.

2. Benedikts saga

A translation of the narrative parts (at times abridged) of Book II of the *Dialogi* of Gregory the Great. These are derived from the twelfth-century translation of the *Dialogi* made in Norway. The ultimate source is a version of *BHL* 1102.

Manuscript:

Stock. Perg. fol. no. 2 (ca. 1425–45).

Editions:

Foote, Peter, ed. >> *Lives of Saints* (1962).
   Facsimile.

Unger, C.R., ed. >> *Heilagra manna søgur* (1877). Vol. 1, pp. 158–179.2.

[Kålund, Kr., ed.] *Palæografisk Atlas: Oldnorsk-islandsk afdeling. Ny serie. Oldnorsk-islandske skriftprøver c. 1300–1700* (Copenhagen and Kristiania [Oslo]: Gyldendal, 1907). No. 28.
   Facsimile and text edition (extract only).

Norwegian translation:

Mundal, Else. *Legender frå mellomalderen. Soger om heilage kvinner og menn* (Oslo: Det Norske Samlaget, 1995). Pp. 129–55.

Literature:

Bekker-Nielsen, Hans. "Kyrkofäderna ock kyrkolärarna. K. i vestnordisk litteratur." *KLNM* 9 (1964). Cols. 690–3, esp. col. 691.

Boyer, Régis. >> *La vie religieuse en Islande* (1979). P. 164.

Carlé, Birte. >> *Jomfru-fortællingen* (1985). Pp. 39 and 64–71.

– "Men and Women in the Saints' Sagas of *Stock. 2, fol.*" In John Lindow, Lars Lönnroth, and Gerd Wolfgang Weber, ed. >> *Structure and Meaning in Old Norse Literature* (1986). Pp. 317–46, esp. pp. 320, 324, 331–2, and 334–6.

Cormack, Margaret. >> *The Saints in Iceland* (1994). P. 84.

Finnur Jónsson. >> *Den oldnorske og oldislandske Litteraturs Historie* (1920–4). Vol. 2, p. 874.

Hallberg, Peter. "Imagery in Religious Old Norse Prose Literature: An Outline." *ANF* 102 (1987): 120–70, esp. pp. 139 and 144.

Kalinke, Marianne E. >> *The Book of Reykjahólar* (1996). P. 30.

Lehmann, Paul. >> "Skandinaviens Anteil an der lateinischen Literatur und Wissenschaft des Mittelalters" (1937). P. 44.

Mogk, Eugen. >> *Geschichte der norwegisch-isländischen Literatur* (1904). P. 893.

Strömbäck, Dag. "Visionsdiktning." *KLNM* 20 (1976). Cols. 171–86, esp. col. 174.

Þórhallur Þorgilsson. "Um þýðingar og endursagnir úr ítölskum miðaldaritum." *Landsbókasafn Íslands. Árbók* 1946–7 (1948): 212–24, esp. p. 215.

Handlist, p. 303.

BERNARD OF CLAIRVAUX   August 20

Af Bernardo

A short *vita* of Saint Bernhard of Clairvaux incorporated into the miracles of the Virgin Mary. It is based on Wilhelm of St Thierry's *Vita prima* and Bernhard of Clairvaux's sermon *De aquaeductu*.

Manuscripts:
See Mary the Blessed Virgin 3 note (p. 245).

Editions:
Unger, C.R., ed. >> *Mariu saga* (1871). Pp. 193.6–198.4 and 489.2–493.19.

Heizmann, Wilhelm. "Liebe und Durst: Der Heilige Bernhard von Clairvaux in der altisländischen Mirakelüberlieferung." *Opuscula* 13. Bibliotheca Arnamagnæana 47 (Copenhagen: Museum Tusculanum Press, 2010). Pp. 55–118, esp. pp. 68–80 (verso).

Edition of AM 655 4to XXXII with variants from Stock. Perg. 4to no. 11, Stock. Perg. 4to no. 1, and AM 240 fol. IX.

German translation:

Heizmann, Wilhelm. "Liebe und Durst: Der Heilige Bernhard von Clairvaux in der altisländischen Mirakelüberlieferung." *Opuscula* 13. Bibliotheca Arnamagnæana 47 (Copenhagen: Museum Tusculanum Press, 2010). Pp. 55–118, esp. pp. 69–71 (recto).

Literature:

McGuire, Brian Patrick. *The Difficult Saint: Bernard of Clairvaux & His Tradition.* Cistercian Studies Series 126 (Kalamazoo: Cistercian Publications, 1991). Pp. 190 and 204–25.

Widding, Ole. "Marialegender. Norge og Island." *KLNM* 11 (1966). Cols. 401–4, esp. col. 402.

– "Norrøne Marialegender på europæisk baggrund." *Opuscula* 10. Bibliotheca Arnamagnæana 40 (Copenhagen: Reitzel, 1996). Pp. 1–128, esp. pp. 17–18, 79, and 87.

Handlist, pp. 303 and 323.

BLASE   February 3

1. Blasíuss saga

A Norwegian translation of a version of *BHL* 1377 that depends on the same original translation as 2.

Manuscripts:

AM 655 4to IX (ca. 1150–1200), Lbs 438 4to (ca. 1800–1900), and Steph 23 (ca. 1700–1800).

Editions:

[Kålund, Kr., ed.] *Palæografisk Atlas: Oldnorsk-islandsk afdeling.* (Copenhagen and Christiania [Oslo]: Gyldendal, 1905). No. 9.
Facsimile and text edition of AM 655 4to IX.

Unger, C.R., ed. >> *Heilagra manna søgur* (1877). Vol. 1, pp. 269.20–271.
Edition of AM 655 4to IX.

Literature:

Bekker-Nielsen, Hans. "Et par ord om de ældste norrøne helgensagaer." In Finn Hødnebø et al., ed. >> *Eyvindarbók* (1992). Pp. 29–33, esp. p. 32.

Bekker-Nielsen, Hans, Thorkil Damsgaard Olsen, and Ole Widding. >> *Norrøn fortællekunst* (1965). Pp. 17 and 123–4.

Bekker-Nielsen, Hans, and Ole Widding. "Legende. Norge og Island."
   KLNM 10 (1965). Cols. 421–3, esp. col. 422.
– "Religiøs prosalitteratur. Norge og Island." *KLNM* 14 (1969). Cols.
   42–4, esp. col. 42.
Boyer, Régis. >> *La vie religieuse en Islande* (1979). P. 224.
Cormack, Margaret. >> *The Saints in Iceland* (1994). Pp. 33 and 85.
Finnur Jónsson. >> *Den oldnorske og oldislandske Litteraturs Historie*
   (1920–4). Vol. 2, pp. 874 and 969.
Foote, Peter, ed. >> *Lives of Saints* (1962). P. 23.
Hallberg, Peter. "Imagery in Religious Old Norse Prose Literature: An
   Outline." *ANF* 102 (1987): 120–70, esp. p. 139.
Jakob Benediktsson. "Nödhjälparna." *KLNM* 21 (1977). Cols. 289–90,
   esp. col. 289.
Jónas Kristjánsson. "Learned Style or Saga Style?" In Ursula Dronke,
   Guðrún P. Helgadóttir, Gerd Wolfgang Weber, and Hans Bekker-
   Nielsen, ed. >> *Specvlvm Norroenvm* (1981). Pp. 260–92.
– >> *Eddas and Sagas* (1988). P. 148.
Jørgensen, Jørgen Højgaard. "Hagiography and the Icelandic Bishop
   Sagas." *Peritia* 1 (1982): 1–16, esp. p. 3.
Kirby, Ian. >> *Biblical Quotation* (1980). Vol. 2, p. 41.
– *Bible Translation in Old Norse*. Université de Lausanne Publications de
   la faculté des lettres 27 (Geneva: Librairie Droz, 1986). P. 34.
– "The Bible and Biblical Interpretation in Medieval Iceland." In
   Old Icelandic Literature and Society. Ed. Margaret Clunies Ross
   (Cambridge: Cambridge University Press, 2000). Pp. 287–301, esp.
   p. 295.
Lehmann, Paul. >> "Skandinaviens Anteil an der lateinischen Literatur
   und Wissenschaft des Mittelalters" (1937). P. 80.
Mogk, Eugen. >> *Geschichte der norwegisch-isländischen Literatur* (1904).
   Pp. 891–2.
Mundal, Else. "Legender, helgenkult og misjonsstrategi i kristningstida."
   In *Selja – heilag stad i 1000 år*. Ed. Magnus Rindal (Oslo: Universitets-
   forlaget, 1997). Pp. 77–101, esp. pp. 77–8.
Sverrir Tómasson. "Kristnar trúarbókmenntir í óbundnu máli." In
   Guðrún Nordal, Sverrir Tómasson, and Vésteinn Ólason, ed. >>
   Íslensk Bókmenntasaga 1 (1992). Pp. 419–79, esp. pp. 438–9.
Turville-Petre, G. >> *Origins of Icelandic Literature* (1967). Pp. 126 and
   132–3.
Widding, Ole, and Hans Bekker-Nielsen. "Low German Influence on
   Late Icelandic Hagiography." *GR* 37 (1962): 239–62, esp. p. 240.

Wolf, Kirsten. "The Severed Breast: A Topos in the Legends of
    Female Virgin Martyr Saints." *ANF* 112 (1997): 97–112, esp.
    p. 100.
Wolf, Kirsten, ed. "Anonymous, *Heilagra manna drápa* 'Drápa about
    Holy Men'." In Margaret Clunies Ross, ed. >> *Poetry on Christian
    Subjects* (2007). Vol. 2, pp. 872–90, esp. p. 883.
Handlist, p. 303.

2. Blasíuss saga

A translation of a version of *BHL* 1377 that depends on the same
original translation as 1.

Manuscripts:
AM 623 4to (ca. 1325, defective) and Stock. Perg. fol. no. 2 (ca. 1425–45).
Editions:
Finnur Jónsson, ed. *AM 623, 4°: Helgensagaer*. STUAGNL 52 (Copen-
    hagen: Jørgensen, 1927). Pp. 33.9–47.15.
    Edition of AM 623 4to.
Foote, Peter, ed. >> *Lives of Saints* (1962).
    Facsimile of Stock. Perg. fol. no. 2.
Unger, C.R., ed. >> *Heilagra manna søgur* (1877). Vol. 1, pp. 256–269.16.
    Based on AM 623 4to (pp. 256–264.8 and 265.29–269.16) and Stock.
    Perg. fol. no. 2 (pp. 264.9–265.29) with variants from Stock. Perg. fol.
    no. 2 (pp. 256–264.9 and 265.29–269.16).
Norwegian translation:
Mundal, Else. *Legender frå mellomalderen. Soger om heilage kvinner og
    menn* (Oslo: Det Norske Samlaget, 1995). Pp. 65–81.
Literature:
Carlé, Birte. >> *Jomfru-fortællingen* (1985). Pp. 39–40 and 61–2.
– "Men and Women in the Saints' Sagas of *Stock. 2, fol.*" In John
    Lindow, Lars Lönnroth, and Gerd Wolfgang Weber, ed. >> *Struc-
    ture and Meaning in Old Norse Literature* (1986). Pp. 317–46, esp.
    p. 320.
Cormack, Margaret. >> *The Saints in Iceland* (1994). P. 85.
Hallberg, Peter. "Imagery in Religious Old Norse Prose Literature: An
    Outline." *ANF* 102 (1987): 120–70, esp. p. 160.
Jakob Benediktsson. "Nödhjälparna." *KLNM* 21 (1977). Cols. 289–90,
    esp. col. 289.
Jørgensen, Jørgen Højgaard. "Hagiography and the Icelandic Bishop
    Sagas." *Peritia* 1 (1982): 1–16, esp. p. 3.

Konráð Gíslason. *Um frum-parta íslenzkrar túngu í fornöld* (Copenhagen: Trier, 1846). Pp. liv–lv.

Lehmann, Paul. >> "Skandinaviens Anteil an der lateinischen Literatur und Wissenschaft des Mittelalters" (1937). P. 44.

Mogk, Eugen. >> *Geschichte der norwegisch-isländischen Literatur* (1904). Pp. 891–2.

Widding, Ole, and Hans Bekker-Nielsen. "Low German Influence on Late Icelandic Hagiography." *GR* 37 (1962): 239–62, esp. p. 240.

Wolf, Kirsten. "The Severed Breast: A Topos in the Legends of Female Virgin Martyr Saints." *ANF* 112 (1997): 97–112, esp. p. 100.

Wolf, Kirsten, ed. "Anonymous, *Heilagra manna drápa* 'Drápa about Holy Men'." In Margaret Clunies Ross, ed. >> *Poetry on Christian Subjects* (2007). Vol. 2, pp. 872–90, esp. p. 883.

Handlist, p. 303.

3. Af Blasíus

An epitome of 2 closer to Stock. Perg. fol. no. 2 than to AM 623 4to.

Manuscript:
AM 672 4to (ca. 1400–1500).
Literature:

Carlé, Birte. >> *Jomfru-fortællingen* (1985). P. 42.

– "Men and Women in the Saints' Sagas of *Stock. 2, fol.*" In John Lindow, Lars Lönnroth, and Gerd Wolfgang Weber, ed. >> *Structure and Meaning in Old Norse Literature* (1986). Pp. 317–46, esp. p. 319.

Foote, Peter, ed. >> *Lives of Saints* (1962). P. 23.

Jakob Benediktsson. "Nödhjälparna." *KLNM* 21 (1977). Cols. 289–90, esp. col. 289.

Handlist, p. 303.

BONIFACE IV   May 8

Af Bónifacío

Tales of Saint Boniface IV incorporated into the miracles of the Virgin Mary.

Manuscripts:
See Mary the Blessed Virgin 3 note (p. 245).

Edition:
Unger, C.R., ed. >> *Mariu saga* (1871). Pp. 695.29–698.21.
Literature:
Kirby, Ian. >> *Biblical Quotation* (1980). Vol. 2, p. 45.
Handlist, pp. 304 and 323.

BONIFACE OF TARSUS   May 14

Af frú Aglais

Based on a version of *BHL* 1413.

Manuscript:
AM 657a–b 4to (ca. 1350).
Edition:
Gering, Hugo, ed. >> *Islendzk æventyri* (1882–3). Vol. 1, pp. 19–21.
German paraphrase:
Gering, Hugo, ed. >> *Islendzk æventyri* (1882–3). Vol. 2, pp. 9–11.
Literature:
Cormack, Margaret. >> *The Saints in Iceland* (1994). P. 35.
Wolf, Kirsten, ed. >> *Heilagra meyja sögur* (2003). P. lii.
Handlist, p. 304.

BONITUS   January 15

Af Bonito

A tale of Saint Bonitus incorporated into the miracles of the Virgin Mary.

Manuscripts:
See Mary the Blessed Virgin 3 note (p. 245).
Edition:
Unger, C.R., ed. >> *Mariu saga* (1871). Pp. 541.24–549.4 and
     1168.31–1171.6.
Literature:
Tveitane, Mattias. "'Bonus'. Et latinsk Maria-dikt i norrøn prosaversjon."
     Mm (1962): 107–21, esp. pp. 117–20.
Handlist, pp. 304 and 323.

BRENDAN THE VOYAGER   May 16

Brandanuss saga

A translation of *BHL* 1436. The text corresponds to chapters 6.56–11.35
in Carl Selmer, ed., *Navigatio Sancti Brendani Abbatis from Early Latin
Manuscripts*, The University of Notre Dame: Publications in Medieval
Studies 16 (Notre Dame: University of Notre Dame Press, 1959; Dublin:
Four Courts Press, 1989).

Manuscript:
NRA 68 (ca. 1200–1300).
Edition:
Unger, C.R., ed. >> *Heilagra manna søgur* (1877). Vol. 1, pp. 272.21–273.3,
    273.6–27, 273.31–274.19, 274.24–33, 274.24–275.9, and 275.14–24.
Literature:
Bekker-Nielsen, Hans, Thorkil Damsgaard Olsen, and Ole Widding.
    >> *Norrøn fortællekunst* (1965). P. 23.
Boyer, Régis. >> *La vie religieuse en Islande* (1979). P. 197.
Cormack, Margaret. >> *The Saints in Iceland* (1994). Pp. 36–7.
Halvorsen, E.F. "Brandanussaga." *KLNM* 2 (1957). Cols. 200–1.
Helgi Guðmundsson. *Um haf innan. Vestrænir menn og íslenzk menning á*
    miðöldum (Reykjavík: Háskólaútgáfan, 1997). P. 118.
Kalinke, Marianne E. >> *The Book of Reykjahólar* (1996). P. 144.
Lehmann, Paul. >> "Skandinaviens Anteil an der lateinischen Literatur
    und Wissenschaft des Mittelalters" (1937). P. 80.
Mogk, Eugen. >> *Geschichte der norwegisch-isländischen Literatur* (1904).
    P. 893.
Paasche, Fredrik. *Norges og Islands litteratur inntil utgangen av*
    middelalderen. Rev. ed. by Anne Holtsmark (Oslo: Aschehoug, 1947).
    Pp. 457–8.
Stefán Karlsson. "Islandsk bogeksport til Norge i middelalderen." *Mm*
    (1979): 1–17, esp. pp. 6 and 10. Rpt. in *Stafkrókar: Ritgerðir eftir*
    Stefán Karlsson gefnar út í tilefni af sjötugsafmæli hans 2. desember
    1998. Ed. Guðvarður Már Gunnlaugsson (Reykjavík: Stofnun Árna
    Magnússonar, 2000). Pp. 188–205, esp. pp. 194 and 200.
Sverrir Jakobsson. *Við og veröldin: Heimsmynd Íslendinga 1100–1400*
    (Reykjavík: Háskólaútgáfan, 2005). P. 264.
Sverrir Tómasson. "Trúarbókmenntir í lausu máli á síðmiðöld." In
    Böðvar Guðmundsson, Sverrir Tómasson, Torfi H. Tulinius, and

Vésteinn Ólason, ed. >> *Íslensk Bókmenntasaga* 2 (1993). Pp. 249–82, esp. p. 272.
– "Ferðir þessa heims og annars. Paradís – Ódáinsakur – Vínland í ferðalýsingum miðalda." *Gripla* 12 (2001): 23–40, esp. pp. 25n7 and 34–5. Rpt. in Sverrir Tómasson. *Tækileg vitni: Greinar um bókmenntir gefnar út í tilefni sjötugsafmælis hans 5. apríl 2011* (Reykjavík: Stofnun Árna Magnússonar and Hið íslenska bókmenntafélag, 2011). Pp. 359–78, esp. pp. 361n7 and 371.
Turville-Petre, G. *The Heroic Age of Scandinavia* (London: Brendon and Sons, 1951). Pp. 94–5.
Wellendorf, Jonas. "The Attraction of the Earliest Old Norse Vernacular Hagiography." In Haki Antonsson and Ildar H. Garipzanov, ed. >> *Saints and Their Lives on the Periphery* (2010). Pp. 241–58, esp. pp. 246.
Handlist, p. 304.

CANUTE OF DENMARK   January 19

The chapters on Saint Canute (d. 1086) in *Knýtlinga saga*, a secular work, cannot be regarded as a proper saint's legend. For an edition and discussion of the saga and its sources, see Bjarni Guðnason, ed., *Danakonunga sǫgur: Skjǫldunga saga, Knýtlinga saga, Ágrip af sǫgu Danakonunga*, Íslenzk fornrit 35 (Reykjavík: Hið íslenzka fornritafélag, 1982), pp. lxxi–cxciv and 91–321. For an English translation of *Knýtlinga saga*, see Hermann Pálsson and Paul Edwards, trans., *Knytlinga saga: The History of the Kings of Denmark* (Odense: Odense University Press, 1986).
Handlist, p. 304.

CANUTE LAVARD   January 7

The chapters on Saint Canute Lavard (d. 1131) in *Knýtlinga saga*, a secular work, cannot be regarded as a proper saint's legend. For an edition and discussion of the saga and its sources, see Bjarni Guðnason, ed., *Danakonunga sǫgur: Skjǫldunga saga, Knýtlinga saga, Ágrip af sǫgu Danakonunga*, Íslenzk fornrit 35 (Reykjavík: Hið íslenzka fornritafélag, 1982), pp. lxxi–cxciv and 91–321. For an English translation of *Knýtlinga saga*, see Hermann Pálsson and Paul Edwards, trans., *Knytlinga saga: The History of the Kings of Denmark* (Odense: Odense University Press, 1986).
Handlist, p. 304.

CATHERINE OF ALEXANDRIA   November 25

1. Katrínar saga

A translation based on *BHL* 1659 and 1600 with additional material from *BHL* 1657, 1663, 1667, and possibly 1661b.

Manuscripts:
AM 233a fol. (ca. 1350–75, defective), AM 238 fol. II (ca. 1300–50), AM
   667 4to II (ca. 1400–1500), AM 429 12mo (ca. 1500, defective), and
   Stock. Perg. fol. no. 2 (ca. 1425–45).
Editions:
Foote, Peter, ed. >> *Lives of Saints* (1962).
   Facsimile of Stock. Perg. fol. no. 2.
Unger, C.R., ed. >> *Heilagra manna søgur* (1877). Vol. 1, pp. 400–21.
   Based on AM 233a fol. (pp. 401.24–421) and Stock. Perg. fol. no. 2
   (pp. 400–401.24) with variants from AM 429 12mo (pp. 400–403.27
   and 411.29–421) and Stock. Perg. fol. nr. 2 (pp. 401.24– 421). One
   variant reading from AM 667 4to II is included (p. 404.28).
Wolf, Kirsten, ed. >> *A Female Legendary from Iceland* (2011).
   Pp. 79–91.
   Facsimile and text edition of AM 429 12mo.
Modern Icelandic language edition:
Wolf, Kirsten, ed. >> *Heilagra meyja sögur* (2003). Pp. 123–41.
Literature:
Ásdís Egilsdóttir. "Kvendýrlingar og kvenímynd trúarlegra bókmennta á
   Íslandi." In Inga Huld Hákonardóttir, ed. >> *Konur og kristsmenn*
   (1996). Pp. 93–116, esp. pp. 93 and 97.
Bekker-Nielsen, Hans, Thorkil Damsgaard Olsen, and Ole Widding.
   >> *Norrøn fortællekunst* (1965). P. 124.
Bekker-Nielsen, Hans, and Ole Widding. "Legende. Norge og Island."
   KLNM 10 (1965). Cols. 421–3, esp. col. 421.
Bruvoll, Kjersti. "The Good, the Bad and the Devil! On Rewriting
   a Religious Motif in Some Virgin Martyr Legends." In Agneta
   Ney, Henrik Williams, and Fredrik Charpentier Ljungqvist, ed.
   >> *Á austrvega: Sagas and East Scandinavia* (2009). Vol. 1,
   pp. 136–43, esp. pp. 136, 138–9, and 141.
Carlé, Birte. "Fra slægtssaga til kvindesaga." In Silja Aðalsteinsdóttir and
   Helgi Þorláksson, ed. >> *Forändringar i kvinnors villkor under medel-
   tiden* (1983). Pp. 55–70, esp. pp. 56 and 65–6.

- >> *Jomfru-fortællingen* (1985). Pp. 35–6, 40–1, 43, 75, 80, 105–9, 131, 133–4, and 136.
- "Some Observations Regarding Narrative Patterns in the Medieval Sagas of Holy Maids." In Régis Boyer, ed. >> *Les Sagas de Chevaliers (Riddarasögur)* (1985). Pp. 393–404, esp. p. 395.
- "Men and Women in the Saints' Sagas of *Stock. 2, fol.*" In John Lindow, Lars Lönnroth, and Gerd Wolfgang Weber, ed. >> *Structure and Meaning in Old Norse Literature* (1986). Pp. 317–46, esp. pp. 319–20 and 341–2.

Cormack, Margaret. >> *The Saints in Iceland* (1994). Pp. 87 and 241.

Gad, Tue. "Katarina af Alexandria." *KLNM* 8 (1963). Cols. 335–8, esp. cols. 336–7.

Jónas Kristjánsson. >> *Eddas and Sagas* (1988). P. 142.

Kirby, Ian. >> *Biblical Quotation* (1980). Vol. 2, pp. 42–3 and 107–8.

Lehmann, Paul. >> "Skandinaviens Anteil an der lateinischen Literatur und Wissenschaft des Mittelalters" (1937). Pp. 44 and 49.

Lindow, John. "Norse Mythology and the Lives of the Saints." *SS* 73 (2001): 437–56, esp. p. 447.

Mogk, Eugen. >> *Geschichte der norwegisch-isländischen Literatur* (1904). Pp. 719 and 891.

Ruggerinni, Maria Elena. "La ricezione dei *Disticha Catonis* nell'Islanda medievale." In *Cultura Classica e Cultura Germanica Settentrionale*. Ed. Pietro Janni, Diego Poli, and Carlo Santini (Macerata: Herder, 1985). Pp. 221–77, esp. pp. 232–4.

Svanhildur Óskarsdóttir. "Universal History in Fourteenth-Century Iceland: Studies in AM 764 4to." PhD dissertation, University of London, 2000. P. 203.

Sverrir Tómasson. "Kristnar trúarbókmenntir í óbundnu máli." In Guðrún Nordal, Sverrir Tómasson, and Vésteinn Ólason, ed. >> *Íslensk Bókmenntasaga* 1 (1992). Pp. 419–79, esp. pp. 438–9.

Tveitane, Mattias. "Interpretatio Norroena: Norrøne og antikke gudenavn i *Clemens saga*." In >> *The Sixth International Saga Conference* (1985). Vol. 2, pp. 1067–82, esp. pp. 1081–2.

Þórhallur Þorgilsson. "Um þýðingar og endursagnir úr ítölskum miðaldaritum." *Landsbókasafn Íslands. Árbók* 1946–7 (1948): 212–24, esp. p. 222.

Wolf, Kirsten. "The Severed Breast: A Topos in the Legends of Female Virgin Martyr Saints." *ANF* 112 (1997): 97–112, esp. p. 102.

- "Female Scribes at Work? A Consideration of Kirkjubæjarbók (Codex AM 429 12mo)." In A.N. Doane and Kirsten Wolf, ed. >> *Beatus Vir* (2006). Pp. 265–95, esp. pp. 270–1 and 276–7.

Wolf, Kirsten, ed. "Kálfr Hallsson, *Kátrínardrápa* '*Drápa* about S.
    Catharine'." In Margaret Clunies Ross, ed. >> *Poetry on Christian
    Subjects* (2007). Vol. 2, pp. 931–64.
Handlist, pp. 304–5.

2. Katrínar jartegnir

A translation of sections of the *Sanctae Catharinae Virginis et Martyris
Translatio et Miracula Rotomagensia* (*BHL* Supp. 1679 b).

Manuscript:
AM 180b fol. (ca. 1500, defective).
Editions:
Halvorsen, E.F., ed. *Karlamagnus saga and Some Religious Texts: AM
    180 a and b fol.* EIM 18 (Copenhagen: Rosenkilde and Bagger, 1989).
    Facsimile.
Wolf, Kirsten. "The *Translatio et Miracula Rotomagensia* in Icelandic
    Translation (AM 180b fol)." *Gripla* 19 (2008): 168–91, esp. pp. 171–81.
Literature:
Foote, Peter, ed. >> *Lives of Saints* (1962). P. 26.
Handlist, p. 305.

CECILIA   November 22

Ceciliu saga

A translation of a form of the longer recension of the *Passio Caecilia*
(*BHL* 1495) with chapters 1–2 omitted. Additional material (two Icelandic
miracles) in Stock. Perg. fol. no. 2.

Manuscripts:
AM 235 fol. (ca. 1400, defective), AM 429 12mo (ca. 1500), and Stock.
    Perg. fol. no. 2 (ca. 1425–45, defective).
Editions:
Foote, Peter, ed. >> *Lives of Saints* (1962).
    Facsimile of Stock. Perg. fol. no. 2.
Unger, C.R., ed. >> *Heilagra manna søgur* (1877). Vol. 1, pp. 276–97.
    Based on Stock. Perg. fol. no. 2 (pp. 276–279.20 and 289.20–297), AM
    235 fol. (pp. 279.20–287.1), and AM 429 12mo (pp. 287.1–289.10) with

variants from AM 235 fol. (pp. 276–279.20) and AM 429 12mo
(pp. 276–287.1 and 289.10–294.13).
Wolf, Kirsten, ed. >> *A Female Legendary from Iceland* (2011).
Pp. 92–108.
Facsimile and text edition of AM 429 12mo.
Modern Icelandic language edition:
Wolf, Kirsten, ed. >> *Heilagra meyja sögur* (2003). Pp. 101–22.
Norwegian translation:
Mundal, Else. *Legender frå mellomalderen. Soger om heilage kvinner og
menn* (Oslo: Det Norske Samlaget, 1995). Pp. 39–63.
Literature:

Anna Sigurðardóttir. *Allt hafði annan róm áður í páfadóm. Nunnuklaustrin
tvö á miðöldum og brot úr kristnisögu.* Úr veröld kvenna 3 (Reykjavík:
Kvennasögusafn Íslands, 1988). Pp. 333–41.
Ásdís Egilsdóttir. "Kvendýrlingar og kvenímynd trúarlegra bókmennta á
Íslandi." In Inga Huld Hákonardóttir, ed. >> *Konur og kristsmenn*
(1996). Pp. 93–116, esp. p. 93.
Astås, Reidar. "Spor av teologisk tenkning og refleksjon i norsk og
islandsk høymiddelalder." *CM* 6 (1993): 133–67, esp. pp. 139 and
144–6.
Battista, Simonetta. "Interpretation of the Roman Pantheon in the Old
Norse Hagiographic Saga." In Geraldine Barnes and Margaret Clunies
Ross, ed. >> *Old Norse Myths, Literature and Society* (2000). Pp. 24–
34, esp. p. 30.
Bekker-Nielsen, Hans, Thorkil Damsgaard Olsen, and Ole Widding.
>> *Norrøn fortællekunst* (1965). P. 124.
Bruvoll, Kjersti. "The Good, the Bad and the Devil! On Rewriting a
Religious Motif in Some Virgin Martyr Legends." In Agneta Ney,
Henrik Williams, and Fredrik Charpentier Ljungqvist, ed. >> *Á
austrvega: Sagas and East Scandinavia* (2009). Vol. 1, pp. 136–43, esp.
p. 138.
Carlé, Birte. "Fra slægtssaga til kvindesaga." In Silja Aðalsteinsdóttir and
Helgi Þorláksson, ed. >> *Forändringar i kvinnors villkor under medel-
tiden* (1983). Pp. 55–70, esp. pp. 56 and 61–2.
– >> *Jomfru-fortællingen* (1985). Pp. 38–41, 43, 75–6, 79–81, 115–21, 131,
and 135–9.
– "Some Observations Regarding Narrative Patterns in the Medieval
Sagas of Holy Maids." In Régis Boyer, ed. >> *Les Sagas de Chevaliers
(Riddarasögur)* (1985). Pp. 393–404, esp. pp. 395–6.

– "Men and Women in the Saints' Sagas of *Stock. 2, fol.*" In John Lindow, Lars Lönnroth, and Gerd Wolfgang Weber, ed. >> *Structure and Meaning in Old Norse Literature* (1986). Pp. 317–46, esp. pp. 319, 321, and 342–3.

Cormack, Margaret. >> *The Saints in Iceland* (1994). Pp. 21, 34, 55, 60, 65, 88–9.

– "Sagas of Saints." In *Old Icelandic Literature and Society*. Ed. Margaret Clunies Ross (Cambridge: Cambridge University Press, 2000). Pp. 302–25, esp. p. 314.

– "Christian Biography." In *A Companion to Old Norse–Icelandic Literature and Culture*. Ed. Rory McTurk (Oxford: Blackwell, 2005). Pp. 27–42, esp. pp. 30 and 39.

Finnur Jónsson. >> *Den oldnorske og oldislandske Litteraturs Historie* (1920–4). Vol. 2, p. 874.

Hallberg, Peter. "Imagery in Religious Old Norse Prose Literature: An Outline." *ANF* 102 (1987): 120–70, esp. p. 124.

Jakob Benediktsson. "Helgener." *KLNM* 21 (1977). Cols. 194–5, esp. col. 194.

Jón Hnefill Aðalsteinsson. "Blot i forna skrifter." *SI* 47 (1996): 11–32, esp. p. 27.

Jón Viðar Sigurðsson. "Utenlandske kvinnehelgener på Island i høymiddelalderen." In >> *Samtíðarsögur* (1994). Vol. 2, pp. 423–34, esp. pp. 431–2.

– *Den vennlige vikingen: Vennskapets makt i Norge og på Island ca. 900–1300* (Oslo: Pax Forlag, 2010). P. 119.

Jónas Kristjánsson. >> *Eddas and Sagas* (1988). P. 142.

Kirby, Ian. >> *Biblical Quotation* (1980). Vol. 2, p. 41.

Lehmann, Paul. >> "Skandinaviens Anteil an der lateinischen Literatur und Wissenschaft des Mittelalters" (1937). Pp. 44 and 47–8.

Lindow, John. "Norse Mythology and the Lives of the Saints." *SS* 73 (2001): 437–56, esp. pp. 452–4.

Mogk, Eugen. >> *Geschichte der norwegisch-isländischen Literatur* (1904). P. 891.

Mundal, Else. "Legender, helgenkult og misjonsstrategi i kristningstida." In *Selja – heilag stad i 1000 år*. Ed. Magnus Rindal (Oslo: Universitetsforlaget, 1997). Pp. 77–101, esp. pp. 93, 97, and 99.

Sverrir Tómasson. "Kristnar trúarbókmenntir í óbundnu máli." In Guðrún Nordal, Sverrir Tómasson, and Vésteinn Ólason, ed. >> *Íslensk Bókmenntasaga* 1 (1992). Pp. 419–79, esp. 436.

Þórhallur Þorgilsson. "Um þýðingar og endursagnir úr ítölskum miðaldaritum." *Landsbókasafn Íslands. Árbók* 1946–7 (1948): 212–24, esp.
p. 222.
Wolf, Kirsten. "The Severed Breast: A Topos in the Legends of Female
Virgin Martyr Saints." *ANF* 112 (1997): 97–112, esp. p. 105.
– "Female Scribes at Work? A Consideration of Kirkjubæjarbók (Codex
AM 429 12mo)." In A.N. Doane and Kirsten Wolf, ed. >> *Beatus Vir*
(2006). Pp. 265–95, esp. pp. 270 and 277.
Wolf, Kirsten, ed. "Anonymous, *Heilagra meyja drápa* 'Drápa about Holy
Maidens'." In Margaret Clunies Ross, ed. >> *Poetry on Christian
Subjects* (2007). Vol. 2, pp. 891–930, esp. p. 905.
Handlist, p. 305.
NOTE:
The saga includes the passion of Saints Tiburtius and Valerian. See the
entry for these two saints.

CHARLEMAGNE   January 28

The chapters on Charlemagne in *Karlamagnúss saga*, a secular work,
cannot be regarded as a proper saint's legend. For editions of the saga,
see C.R. Unger, ed., *Karlamagnus saga ok kappa hans: Fortællinger om
Keiser Karl Magnus og hans Jævninger i norsk Bearbeidelse fra det
trettende Aarhundrede* (Christiania [Oslo]: Jensen, 1860), and Agnete
Loth, ed., *Karlamagnús saga, Branches I, III, VII et IX. Edition bilingue
projetée par Knud Togeby et Pierre Halleux. Texte norrois édité par Agnete
Loth. Traduction française par Annette Patron-Godefroit. Avec une étude
par Povl Skårup* (Copenhagen: DSL., La Société pour l'étude de la langue
et de la littérature danoises; Reitzel, 1980). For a discussion of the sources
of the saga, see E.F. Halvorsen, *The Norse Version of the Chanson de
Roland*, Bibliotheca Arnamagnæana 19 (Copenhagen: Ejnar Munksgaard, 1959). For an English translation of the saga, see Constance B.
Hieatt, trans., *Karlamagnús saga: The Saga of Charlemagne and His
Heroes*, 3 vols, Mediaeval Sources in Translation 13, 17, 25 (Toronto:
Pontifical Institute of Mediaeval Studies, 1975–80). The tale *Af Karlamagnúsi* is a parallel to the saga (Unger, pp. 541–7). For an edition,
discussion, and German paraphrase of the tale, see Hugo Gering, ed.
>> *Islendzk æventyri* (1882–4), vol. 1, pp. 34–43, and vol. 2, pp. 23–8.
Handlist, p. 305.

CHRISTOPHER   July 25

1. Kristófórs saga

Translated from a now-lost Low German redaction that resembles the source(s) of *Der Heiligen Leben*.

Manuscript:
Stock. Perg. fol. no. 3 (*Reykjahólabók*) (ca. 1530–40).
Edition:
Loth, Agnete, ed. >> *Reykjahólabók* (1969–70). Vol. 1, pp. 273–96.
Literature:
Bekker-Nielsen, Hans, Thorkil Damsgaard Olsen, and Ole Widding. >> *Norrøn fortællekunst* (1965). P. 140.
Gad, Tue. "Kristoffer." *KLNM* 9 (1964). Cols. 355–61, esp. col. 359.
Jónas Kristjánsson. >> *Eddas and Sagas* (1988). P. 145.
Kalinke, Marianne E. "Reykjahólabók: A Legendary on the Eve of the Reformation." *Skáldskaparmál* 2 (1992): 239–69, esp. pp. 240, 246, and 259–69.
– >> *The Book of Reykjahólar* (1996), pp. 28, 50, 100–1, 158, 165–6, 169, 172–4, 198, and 200.
Rowe, Elizabeth Ashman. "Searching for the Highest King: St. Christopher and *Þáttr Sveins ok Finns*." *ANF* 105 (1990): 131–9, esp. p. 136.
Sverrir Tómasson. "Trúarbókmenntir í lausu máli á síðmiðöld." In Böðvar Guðmundsson, Sverrir Tómasson, Torfi H. Tulinius, and Vésteinn Ólason, ed >> *Íslensk Bókmenntasaga* 2 (1993). Pp. 249–82, esp. p. 279.
Widding, Ole, and Hans Bekker-Nielsen. "En senmiddelalderlig legendesamling." *Mm* (1960): 105–28, esp. pp. 107 and 117.
– "Low German Influence on Late Icelandic Hagiography." *GR* 37 (1962): 239–62, esp. pp. 249 and 255.
Handlist, p. 305.

CLEMENT I   November 23

1. Klements saga

A translation of the Pseudo-Clementine *Recognitiones* (*BHL* 6644) and a Latin *passio* ultimately derived from the work of Simeon Metaphrastes.

Manuscript:
AM 645 4to (ca. 1220, defective).
Editions:
Carron, Helen, ed. *Clemens saga: The Life of·St Clement of Rome.* Viking
   Society for Northern Research, Text Series 17 (University College
   London: Viking Society for Northern Research, 2005). Pp. 2–52
   (verso).
Hofmann, Dietrich. *Die Legende von Sankt Clemens in den skandi-
   navischen Ländern im Mittelalter.* Beiträge zur Skandinavistik 13
   (Frankfurt am Main: Peter Lang, 1997). Pp. 236–75.
Holtsmark, Anne, ed. *A Book of Miracles: MS No. 645 4ᵗᵒ of the Arna-
   Magnæan Collection in the University Library of Copenhagen.* CCI 12
   (Copenhagen: Einar Munksgaard, 1938).
   Facsimile.
Larsson, Ludvig, ed. *Isländska handskriften No 645 4° i Den Ar-
   namagnæanske Samlingen på Universitetsbiblioteket i København:
   I. Handskriftens äldre del* (Lund: Gleerup, 1885). Pp. 33.28–74.9.
Unger, C.R., ed. >> *Postola sögur* (1874). Pp. 126.19–151.11
English translations:
Carron, Helen, ed. *Clemens saga: The Life of St Clement of Rome.* Viking
   Society for Northern Research, Text Series 17 (University College
   London: Viking Society for Northern Research, 2005). Pp. 3–53 (recto).
Roughton, Philip G. "AM 645 4to and AM 652/630 4to: Study and
   Translation of Two Thirteenth-Century Icelandic Collections of
   Apostles' and Saints' Lives." PhD dissertation, University of Colorado,
   2002. Pp. 441–86.
German translation:
Hofmann, Dietrich. *Die Legende von Sankt Clemens in den skandi-
   navischen Ländern im Mittelalter.* Beiträge zur Skandinavistik 13
   (Frankfurt am Main: Peter Lang, 1997). Pp. 236–75.
Literature:
Battista, Simonetta. "Interpretations of the Roman Pantheon in the Old
   Norse Hagiographic Sagas." In Geraldine Barnes and Margaret
   Clunies Ross, ed. >> *Old Norse Myths, Literature and Society* (2000).
   Pp. 24–34, esp. pp. 25–8 and 32–3.
– "The *Compilator* and Contemporary Literary Culture in Old Norse
   Hagiography." *Viking and Medieval Scandinavia* 1 (2005): 1–13, esp.
   p. 8.
Bekker-Nielsen, Hans, Thorkil Damsgaard Olsen, and Ole Widding.
   >> *Norrøn fortællekunst* (1965). Pp. 23 and 122.

Boyer, Régis. >> *La vie religieuse en Islande* (1979). Pp. 162 and 228.

* Carron, H.C. "A Critical Edition of Pétrs saga Postola I, based on the Codex Scardensis." PhD dissertation, University of London, 1994.

Cormack, Margaret. >> *The Saints in Iceland* (1994). Pp. 90, 241, and 244.

Dillmann, François-Xavier. "Om hedningar och hundar. Kring den fornvästnordiska sammansättningen *hundheiðinn.*" *SI* 52 (2001): 17–33, esp. p. 30.

Foote, Peter, ed. *A Saga of St Peter the Apostle. Perg. 4:o nr 19 in the Royal Library, Stockholm.* EIM 19 (Copenhagen: Rosenkilde and Bagger, 1990). Pp. 12–13.

– "A Fragment of Text in AM 235 fol." In *Twenty-eight Papers Presented to Hans Bekker-Nielsen on the Occasion of His Sixtieth Birthday 28 April 1993* (Odense: Odense University Press, 1993). Pp. 237–55, esp. p. 243.

– "Saints' Lives and Sagas." In Hans Bekker-Nielsen and Birte Carlé, ed. >> *Saints and Sagas* (1994). Pp. 73–88, esp. pp. 83–5.

Hallberg, Peter. "Imagery in Religious Old Norse Prose Literature: An Outline." *ANF* 102 (1987): 120–70, esp. pp. 124–5 and 145.

Jónas Kristjánsson. >> *Eddas and Sagas* (1988). Pp. 137–8.

Kirby, Ian. >> *Biblical Quotation* (1980). Vol. 2, pp. 23–4.

Konráð Gíslason. *Um frum-parta íslenzkrar túngu í fornöld* (Copenhagen: Trier, 1846). P. lxiii.

Lassen, Annette. "Gud eller djævel? Kristningen af Odin." *ANF* 121 (2006): 121–38, esp. p. 126.

Lehmann, Paul. >> "Skandinaviens Anteil an der lateinischen Literatur und Wissenschaft des Mittelalters" (1937). P. 48.

Lindow, John. "Norse Mythology and the Lives of the Saints." *SS* 73 (2001): 437–56, esp. pp. 441–4.

Mogk, Eugen. >> *Geschichte der norwegisch-isländischen Literatur* (1904). P. 890.

Roughton, Philip. "Stylistics and Sources of the *Postola sögur* in AM 645 4to and AM 652/630 4to." *Gripla* 16 (2005): 7–50.

Sverrir Tómasson. "Kristnar trúarbókmenntir í óbundnu máli." In Guðrún Nordal, Sverrir Tómasson, and Vésteinn Ólason, ed. >> *Íslensk Bókmenntasaga* 1 (1992). Pp. 419–79, esp. pp. 425, 427, and 443–5.

Turville-Petre, G. >> *Origins of Icelandic Literature* (1967). Pp. 129–30.

Tveitane, Mattias. "Interpretatio norrœna. Norrøne og antikke gudenavn i *Clemens saga.*" >> *The Sixth International Saga Conference* (1985). Vol. 2, pp. 1067–82.

Þorbjörg Helgadóttir, ed. *Rómverja saga.* 2 vols. (Reykjavík: Stofnun
   Árna Magnússonar, 2010). Vol. 1, pp. lxxxvii–lxxxviii, cix, cxi–cxii, and
   cxxv.
Vries, Jan de. >> *Altnordische Literaturgeschichte* (1964–7). Vol. 2, p. 184.
Wellendorf, Jonas. "The Attraction of the Earliest Old Norse Vernacular
   Hagiography." In Haki Antonsson and Ildar H. Garipzanov, ed.
   >> *Saints and Their Lives on the Periphery* (2010). Pp. 241–58, esp.
   pp. 250–8.
Handlist, p. 305.

2. Klements saga

A fragment of the *passio* somewhat abridged in comparison to 1.

Manuscript:
AM 655 4to XXVIIIa 4to (ca. 1250–1300).
Editions:
* Carron, H.C. "A Critical Edition of Pétrs saga Postola I, based on
   the Codex Scardensis." PhD dissertation, University of London,
   1994.
Hofmann, Dietrich. *Die Legende von Sankt Clemens in den skandi-*
   navischen Ländern im Mittelalter. Beiträge zur Skandinavistik 13
   (Frankfurt am Main: Peter Lang, 1997). Pp. 277–82.
Hreinn Benediktsson. *Early Icelandic Script As Illustrated in Vernacular*
   Texts from the Twelfth and Thirteenth Centuries. Íslenzk handrit:
   Icelandic Manuscripts, Series in Folio 2 (Reykjavík: The Manuscript
   Institute of Iceland, 1965). Plate 69. Facsimile of 1v.
German translation:
Hofmann, Dietrich. *Die Legende von Sankt Clemens in den skandi-*
   navischen Ländern im Mittelalter. Beiträge zur Skandinavistik 13
   (Frankfurt am Main: Peter Lang, 1997). Pp. 277–82.
Literature:
Battista, Simonetta. "Interpretations of the Roman Pantheon in the Old
   Norse Hagiographic Sagas." In Geraldine Barnes and Margaret
   Clunies Ross, ed. >> *Old Norse Myths, Literature and Society* (2000).
   Pp. 24–34, esp. pp. 25–8 and 32–3.
– "The *Compilator* and Contemporary Literary Culture in Old Norse
   Hagiography." *Viking and Medieval Scandinavia* 1 (2005): 1–13, esp.
   p. 8.
Boyer, Régis. >> *La vie religieuse en Islande* (1979). Pp. 162 and 228.

Carron, Helen, ed. *Clemens saga: The Life of St Clement of Rome*. Viking Society for Northern Research, Text Series 17 (University College London: Viking Society for Northern Research, 2005). Pp. xxiii–xxiv.

Cormack, Margaret. >> *The Saints in Iceland* (1994). Pp. 77n12, 90, 241, and 244.

Foote, Peter, ed. *A Saga of St Peter the Apostle. Perg. 4:o nr 19 in the Royal Library, Stockholm*. EIM 19 (Copenhagen: Rosenkilde and Bagger, 1990). Pp. 12–13.

– "A Fragment of Text in AM 235 fol." In *Twenty-eight Papers Presented to Hans Bekker-Nielsen on the Occasion of His Sixtieth Birthday 28 April 1993* (Odense: Odense University Press, 1993). Pp. 237–55, esp. p. 243.

– "Saints' Lives and Sagas." In Hans Bekker-Nielsen and Birte Carlé, ed. >> *Saints and Sagas* (1994). Pp. 73–88, esp. pp. 83–5.

Lindow, John. "Norse Mythology and the Lives of the Saints." *SS* 73 (2001): 437–56, esp. pp. 443–4 and 446–7.

Mogk, Eugen. >> *Geschichte der norwegisch-isländischen Literatur* (1904). P. 890.

Wellendorf, Jonas. "The Attraction of the Earliest Old Norse Vernacular Hagiography." In Haki Antonsson and Ildar H. Garipzanov, ed. >> *Saints and Their Lives on the Periphery* (2010). Pp. 241–58, esp. pp. 250–8.

Handlist, p. 305.

NOTE:

Chapters 50–8 and 60–73 of *Pétrs saga postola I* depend on *Klements saga*.

CROSS, THE HOLY   September 14

I. KROSS SAGA: ORIGO CRUCIS

1. Origo Crucis

A close translation of Seth's journey to Paradise (cf. Hermann Suchier in *Denkmäler provenzalischer Literatur und Sprache* I [1883]: 165–200) followed by an abridged rendering of the story of King David and the growing together of the three rods to form a tree.

Manuscript:
AM 544 4to (*Hauksbók*) (ca. 1290–1334).

Editions:

Eiríkur Jónsson and Finnur Jónsson, ed. *Hauksbók udgiven efter de Arnamagnæanske håndskrifter no. 371, 544 og 675, 4° samt forskellige papirshåndskrifter af* Det *kongelige nordiske Oldskriftselskab* (Copenhagen: Thiele, 1892–6). Pp. 182.10–185.20.

Jón Helgason, ed. *Hauksbók. The Arna-Magnæan Manuscripts 371,4ᵗᵒ, 544,4ᵗᵒ, and 675, 4ᵗᵒ.* Manuscripta Islandica 5 (Copenhagen: Munksgaard, 1960). Facsimile.

Möbius, Th., ed. *Analecta Norræna. Auswahl aus der isländischen und norwegischen Litteratur des Mittelalters.* 2nd. ed. (Leipzig: J.C. Hinrichs'sche buchhandlung, 1877). Pp. 204–7.

Overgaard, Mariane, ed. *The History of the Cross-Tree Down to Christ's Passion: Icelandic Legend Versions.* Editiones Arnamagnæanæ, Ser. B, vol. 26 (Copenhagen: Munksgaard, 1968). Pp. 1–18 (upper text).

Unger, C.R., ed. >> *Heilagra manna søgur* (1877). Vol. 1, pp. 298–301.

Literature:

Boyer, Régis. >> *La vie religieuse en Islande* (1979). Pp. 224 and 278.

Cormack, Margaret. >> *The Saints in Iceland* (1994). Pp. 103–4.

Finnur Jónsson. >> *Den oldnorske og oldislandske Litteraturs Historie* (1920–4). Vol. 2, p. 931.

Jakob Benediktsson. "Kors. Island." *KLNM* 9 (1964). Cols. 181–2, esp. col. 182.

Lassen, Annette. "The God on the Tree." In *Greppaminni: Rit til heiðurs Vésteini Ólasyni sjötugum* (Reykjavík: Hið íslenska bókmenntafélag, 2009). Pp. 231–46, esp. pp. 235–6.

Lehmann, Paul. >> "Skandinaviens Anteil an der lateinischen Literatur und Wissenschaft des Mittelalters" (1937). P. 44.

Mogk, Eugen. >> *Geschichte der norwegisch-isländischen Literatur* (1904). P. 890.

Vésteinn Ólason. "Kveðskapur frá síðmiðöldum." In Böðvar Guðmundsson, Sverrir Tómasson, Torfi H. Tulinius, and Vésteinn Ólason, ed. >> *Íslensk Bókmenntasaga* 2 (1993). Pp. 283–378, esp. p. 304.

Handlist, p. 306.

2. Origo Crucis

A redaction closely related to 1. It differs by including a lengthy interpolation about the Queen of Sheba.

Manuscripts:
AM 65a 8vo (ca. 1600–1700), ÍBR 74 4to (ca. 1775, defective), Lbs 1057
   4to (1803), Lbs 2294 4to (1879–87), Lbs 714 8vo (ca. 1790), Lbs 841
   8vo (1780–1807), Lbs 1228 8vo (ca. 1780–1800, defective), Lbs 1977
   8vo (ca. 1820), NKS 1140 fol. (ca. 1775), and Stock. Papp. 8vo no. 4
   (1668).

Edition:
Overgaard, Mariane, ed. *The History of the Cross-Tree Down to
   Christ's Passion: Icelandic Legend Versions*. Editiones Arna-
   magnæanæ, Ser. B, vol. 26 (Copenhagen: Munksgaard, 1968).
   Pp. 1–18 (lower text).
   Based on AM 65a 8vo with variants from Lbs 1057 4to, Lbs 2294 4to,
   Lbs 841 8vo, Lbs 1228 8vo, Lbs 1977 8vo, Lbs 714 8vo, and Stock.
   Papp. 8to no. 4.

Literature:
Vésteinn Ólason. "Kveðskapur frá síðmiðöldum." In Böðvar Guðmundsson, Sverrir Tómasson, Torfi H. Tulinius, and Vésteinn Ólason,
   ed. >> *Íslensk Bókmenntasaga* 2 (1993). Pp. 283–378, esp. p. 304.
Handlist, p. 306.

3. Origo Crucis

A compilation based on a manuscript of 2, but with several interpolations containing material from a variety of sources.

Manuscripts:
ÍB 209 4to (1853), ÍB 214 8vo (1802), JS 201 4to (1849), Lbs 1057 4to
   (1803), Lbs 1218 4to (1856–9), Lbs 2122 4to (1888), Lbs 79 8vo (1831),
   Lbs 791 8vo (1888), Lbs 841 8vo (ca. 1780–1807), Lbs 1209 8vo (1837
   and 1853), and Lbs 2184 8vo (ca. 1850).

Edition:
Overgaard, Mariane, ed. *The History of the Cross-Tree Down to Christ's
   Passion: Icelandic Legend Versions*. Editiones Arnamagnæanæ, Ser. B,
   vol. 26 (Copenhagen: Munksgaard, 1968). Pp. 19–52.
   Based on Lbs 841 8vo with variants from ÍB 214 8vo, Lbs 1057 4to,
   Lbs 1218 4to, Lbs 791 8vo, and Lbs 1209 8vo.

4. Origo Crucis

A compilation based in part on the Low German *Passionael*.

Manuscript:
AM 667 4to V (ca. 1525).
Edition:
Overgaard, Mariane, ed. *The History of the Cross-Tree Down to Christ's
    Passion: Icelandic Legend Versions.* Editiones Arnamagnæanæ, Ser. B,
    vol. 26 (Copenhagen: Munksgaard, 1968). Pp. 53–58.6.
Literature:
Vésteinn Ólason. "Kveðskapur frá síðmiðöldum." In Böðvar Guð-
    mundsson, Sverrir Tómasson, Torfi H. Tulinius, and Vésteinn Ólason,
    ed. >> *Íslensk Bókmenntasaga* 2 (1993). Pp. 283–378, esp. p. 304.
Handlist, p. 306.

5. Origo Crucis

Derived from the same now-lost translation of the Latin legend as 6 but
presents a closer rendering than 6.

Manuscripts:
AM 727 4to II (1644), ÍB 35 fol. (ca. 1770–80), JS 404 8vo (1755), and JS
    510 8vo (ca. 1800–1900).
Edition:
Overgaard, Mariane, ed. *The History of the Cross-Tree Down to Christ's
    Passion: Icelandic Legend Versions.* Editiones Arnamagnæanæ, Ser. B,
    vol. 26 (Copenhagen: Munksgaard, 1968). Pp. 59–85 (pp. 60–84 upper
    text).
Edition of AM 727 4to II.
Literature:
Lassen, Annette. "The God on the Tree." In *Greppaminni: Rit til heiðurs
    Vésteini Ólasyni sjötugum* (Reykjavík: Hið íslenska bókmenntafélag,
    2009). Pp. 231–46, esp. p. 236.
Vésteinn Ólason. "Kveðskapur frá síðmiðöldum." In Böðvar Guð-
    mundsson, Sverrir Tómasson, Torfi H. Tulinius, and Vésteinn Ólason,
    ed. >> *Íslensk Bókmenntasaga* 2 (1993). Pp. 283–378, esp. p. 304.

6. Origo Crucis

Derived from the same now-lost translation of the Latin legend as 5. The
second half of the legend is somewhat abridged in comparison with the
Latin.

Manuscripts:
ÍB 205 8vo (1823), JS 394 8vo (1819), JS 397 8vo (ca. 1800), Kall 614 4to
    (ca. 1729–59), Lbs 575 4to (ca. 1850–80), Lbs 975 8vo (ca. 1800), and
    Lbs 1228 8vo (ca. 1780–1800, defective).
Edition:
Overgaard, Mariane, ed. *The History of the Cross-Tree Down to Christ's
    Passion: Icelandic Legend Versions*. Editiones Arnamagnæanæ,
    Ser. B, vol. 26 (Copenhagen: Munksgaard, 1968). Pp. 60–84 (lower
    text).
    Based on Kall 614 4to with variants from JS 394 8vo, Lbs 975 8vo, and
    Lbs. 1228 8vo.
Literature:
Vésteinn Ólason. "Kveðskapur frá síðmiðöldum." In Böðvar Guð-
    mundsson, Sverrir Tómasson, Torfi H. Tulinius, and Vésteinn Ólason,
    ed. >> *Íslensk Bókmenntasaga* 2 (1993). Pp. 283–378, esp. p. 304.
Handlist, p. 306.

7. Origo Crucis

Compiled from several sources, the main ones being *Sethskvæði*, *Krosskvæði*,
and a prose version of the Latin legend.

Manuscript:
ÍBR 113 8vo (ca. 1700–1800).
Edition:
Overgaard, Mariane, ed. *The History of the Cross-Tree Down to Christ's
    Passion: Icelandic Legend Versions*. Editiones Arnamagnæanæ, Ser. B,
    vol. 26 (Copenhagen: Munksgaard, 1968). Pp. 86–90.
Literature:
Vésteinn Ólason. "Kveðskapur frá síðmiðöldum." In Böðvar Guð-
    mundsson, Sverrir Tómasson, Torfi H. Tulinius, and Vésteinn
    Ólason, ed. >> *Íslensk Bókmenntasaga* 2 (1993). Pp. 283–378, esp.
    p. 304.

II. KROSS SAGA: INVENTIO CRUCIS

1. Inventio Crucis

An abbreviated translation of *BHL* 4169 with additional material.

Manuscripts:
AM 233a fol. (ca. 1350–60, defective), AM 238 fol. XI (ca. 1300–25), AM
  667 4to V (ca. 1525), and NRA 75 (ca. 1250–75).
Editions:
Overgaard, Mariane, ed. *The History of the Cross-Tree Down to Christ's
  Passion: Icelandic Legend Versions.* Editiones Arnamagnæanæ, Ser. B,
  vol. 26 (Copenhagen: Munksgaard, 1968). P. 58.7–14.
  Edition of AM 667 4to V.
Unger, C.R., ed. >> *Heilagra manna søgur* (1877). Vol. 1,
  pp. 301.19–308.13.
  Based on AM 238 fol. XI with variants from AM 233a fol.
Literature:
Bekker-Nielsen, Hans, and Ole Widding. "Legende. Norge og Island."
  KLNM 10 (1965). Cols. 421–3, esp. col. 421.
Boyer, Régis. >> *La vie religieuse en Islande* (1979). Pp. 224 and 278.
Carlé, Birte. >> *Jomfru-fortællingen* (1985). P. 35.
Cormack, Margaret. >> *The Saints in Iceland* (1994). Pp. 37n45, 103,
  240, and 242.
Finnur Jónsson. >> *Den oldnorske og oldislandske Litteraturs Historie*
  (1920–4). Vol. 2, p. 931.
Jakob Benediktsson. "Kors. Island." *KLNM* 9 (1964). Cols. 181–2, esp.
  col. 182.
Mogk, Eugen. >> *Geschichte der norwegisch-isländischen Literatur* (1904).
  P. 890.
Pizarro, Joaquín Martínez. "Conversion Narratives: Form and Utility."
  In >> *The Sixth International Saga Conference* (1985). Vol. 2, pp. 813–
  32, esp. p. 821.
Stefán Karlsson. "Inventio Crucis, cap 1, og Veraldar saga." In *Opuscula
  Septentrionalia: Festskrift til Ole Widding 10.10.1977* (Copenhagen:
  Reitzel, 1977). Pp. 116–33.
– "Islandsk bogeksport til Norge i middelalderen." *Mm* (1979): 1–17, esp.
  pp. 6 and 8. Rpt. in *Stafkrókar: Ritgerðir eftir Stefán Karlsson gefnar út í
  tilefni af sjötugsafmæli hans 2. desember 1998.* Ed. Guðvarður Már
  Gunnlaugsson (Reykjavík: Stofnun Árna Magnússonar, 2000). Pp. 188–
  205, esp. pp. 194 and 197.
Sverrir Tómasson. "Kristnar trúarbókmenntir í óbundnu máli." In
  Guðrún Nordal, Sverrir Tómasson, and Vésteinn Ólason, ed. >>
  Íslensk Bókmenntasaga 1 (1992). Pp. 419–79, esp. p. 421.
Vésteinn Ólason. "Kveðskapur frá síðmiðöldum." In Böðvar

Guðmundsson, Sverrir Tómasson, Torfi H. Tulinius, and Vésteinn
Ólason, ed. >> *Íslensk Bókmenntasaga* 2 (1993). Pp. 283–378, esp.
p. 304.
Handlist, p. 306.

2. Inventio Crucis

An epitome of the Latin legend.

Manuscript:
AM 764 4to (ca. 1376–86).
Edition:
Svanhildur Óskarsdóttir. "Universal History in Fourteenth-Century
Iceland: Studies in AM 764 4to." PhD dissertation, University of
London, 2000. Pp. 294–5.
Literature:
Cormack, Margaret. >> *The Saints in Iceland* (1994). Pp. 103 and 242.
Stefán Karlsson. "Inventio Crucis, cap 1, og Veraldar saga." In *Opuscula
Septentrionalia: Festskrift til Ole Widding 10.10.1977* (Copenhagen:
Reitzel, 1977). Pp. 116–33.

III. KROSS SAGA: FLAGELLATIO CRUCIS

Flagellatio Crucis

An abridged version derived from *BHL* 4230.

Manuscripts:
AM 235 fol. (ca. 1400) and Stock. Perg. fol. no. 2 (ca. 1425–45).
Editions:
Foote, Peter, ed. >> *Lives of Saints* (1962).
    Facsimile of Stock. Perg. fol. no. 2.
Unger, C.R., ed. >> *Heilagra manna søgur* (1877). Vol. 1, pp. 308.16–311.
    Based on Stock. Perg. fol. no. 2 with variants from AM 235 fol.
Literature:
Bekker-Nielsen, Hans, Thorkil Damsgaard Olsen, and Ole Widding. >>
    Norrøn fortællekunst (1965). P. 126.
Boyer, Régis. >> *La vie religieuse en Islande* (1979). Pp. 224 and 278.
Carlé, Birte. >> *Jomfru-fortællingen* (1985). Pp. 38 and 40–1.

– "Men and Women in the Saints' Sagas of *Stock. 2, fol.*" In John
  Lindow, Lars Lönnroth, and Gerd Wolfgang Weber, ed. >> *Structure
  and Meaning in Old Norse Literature* (1986). Pp. 317–46, esp. pp. 319
  and 321.

Cormack, Margaret. >> *The Saints in Iceland* (1994). P. 103.

Finnur Jónsson. >> *Den oldnorske og oldislandske Litteraturs Historie*
  (1920–4). Vol. 2, p. 931.

Hallberg, Peter. "Imagery in Religious Old Norse Prose Literature: An
  Outline." *ANF* 102 (1987): 120–70, esp. p. 142.

Jakob Benediktsson. "Kors. Island." *KLNM* 9 (1964). Cols. 181–2, esp.
  col. 182.

Mogk, Eugen. >> *Geschichte der norwegisch-isländischen Literatur* (1904).
  P. 890.

Sverrir Tómasson. "Kristnar trúarbókmenntir í óbundnu máli." In
  Guðrún Nordal, Sverrir Tómasson, and Vésteinn Ólason, ed. >>
  Íslensk Bókmenntasaga 1 (1992). Pp. 419–79, esp. p. 421.

Turville-Petre, G. >> *Origins of Icelandic Literature* (1967). Pp. 114 and
  131.

Handlist, pp. 306–7.

CUTHBERT   ·   March 20

1. Af Cuthberto

A short passage about Saint Cuthbert to be read on his feast-day. The
source has not been established.

Manuscript:
AM 655 4to XXI (ca. 1200–50).

Editions:
Hreinn Benediktsson. *Early Icelandic Script As Illustrated in Vernacular
  Texts from the Twelfth and Thirteenth Centuries.* Íslenzk handrit:
  Icelandic Manuscripts, Series in Folio 2 (Reykjavík: The Manuscript
  Institute of Iceland, 1965). Plate 45 and pp. xxx.10–12.
  Facsimile and edition of fol. 2r.

Þorvaldur Bjarnarson, ed. *Leifar fornra kristinna fræða íslenzkra:
  Codex Arna-Magnæanus 677 4to auk annara enna elztu brota
  af íslenzkum guðfræðisritum* (Copenhagen: Hagerup, 1878).
  P. 168.16–27.

Literature:
Bekker-Nielsen, Hans. "Homiletisk haandbog?" *Opuscula* 1. Bibliotheca
   Arnamagnæana 20 (Copenhagen: Munksgaard, 1960). Pp. 343–4.
Cormack, Margaret. >> *The Saints in Iceland* (1994). Pp. 37n45, 93, and
   240.
Konráð Gíslason. *Um frum-parta íslenzkrar túngu í fornöld* (Copenhagen:
   Trier, 1846). P. lxxxi.

2. Af Cuthberto

A short passage about Saint Cuthbert to be read on his feast-day. The
source has not been established.

Manuscript:
AM 686b 4to (ca. 1200–25, defective).
Edition:
Þorvaldur Bjarnarson, ed. *Leifar fornra kristinna fræða íslenzkra: Codex
   Arna-Magnæanus 677 4to auk annara enna elztu brota af íslenzkum
   guðfræðisritum* (Copenhagen: Hagerup, 1878). P. 168.5–13.
Literature:
Cormack, Margaret. >> *The Saints in Iceland* (1994). Pp. 37n45 and
   240.
Hreinn Benediktsson. *Early Icelandic Script As Illustrated in Vernacular
   Texts from the Twelfth and Thirteenth Centuries.* Íslenzk handrit:
   Icelandic Manuscripts, Series in Folio 2 (Reykjavík: The Manuscript
   Institute of Iceland, 1965). Pp. xi–xii.
Konráð Gíslason. *Um frum-parta íslenzkrar túngu í fornöld* (Copenhagen:
   Trier, 1846). P. c.

3. Af Cuthberto

A short passage about Saint Cuthbert based on an encyclopedic work like
the *Speculum historiale*.

Manuscript:
AM 764 4to (ca. 1376–86, defective).
Literature:
Cormack, Margaret. >> *The Saints in Iceland* (1994). Pp. 35 and 93.
Fell, Christine E. "Anglo-Saxon Saints in Old Norse Sources and Vice
   Versa." In Hans Bekker-Nielsen, Peter Foote, and Olaf Olsen, ed.

>> *Proceedings of the Eighth Viking Congress* (1981). Pp. 95–106, esp. pp. 98 and 100.

Svanhildur Óskarsdóttir. "Universal History in Fourteenth-Century Iceland: Studies in AM 764 4to." PhD dissertation, University of London, 2000. Pp. 62 and 241.

– "Arctic Garden of Delights: The Purpose of the Book of Reynistaður." In Kirsten Wolf and Johanna Denzin, ed. >> *Romance and Love in Late Medieval and Early Modern Iceland* (2008). Pp. 279–301, esp. p. 292.

Wolf, Kirsten, ed. >> *Heilagra meyja sögur* (2003). P. li.

Handlist, p. 307.

CYPRIAN AND JUSTINA   September 26

Exemplum af Sankti Sipríano þeim góða manni

A version of the well-known tale based possibly on an expanded version of Odo of Cheriton's *Parabolae*.

Manuscript:
AM 629 4to (1697).
Edition:
Wolf, Kirsten. "Two Exempla." *Gripla.*
   [Forthcoming.]
Literature:
Handlist, p. 307.

DIONYSIUS   October 9

Diónysíuss saga

Based in the main on *BHL* 2175, but with additional material from other sources.

Manuscripts:
AM 235 fol. (ca. 1400) and Stock. Perg. fol. no. 2 (ca. 1425–45).
Editions:
Foote, Peter, ed. >> *Lives of Saints* (1962).
   Facsimile of Stock. Perg. fol. no. 2.

Unger, C.R., ed. >> *Heilagra manna søgur* (1877). Vol. 1, pp. 312–322.3.
   Based on Stock. Perg. fol. no. 2 with variants from AM 235 fol.
Literature:
Bekker-Nielsen, Hans, Thorkil Damsgaard Olsen, and Ole Widding.
   >> *Norrøn fortællekunst* (1965). P. 124.
Boyer, Régis. >> *La vie religieuse en Islande* (1979). Pp. 183 and 186.
Carlé, Birte. >> *Jomfru-fortællingen* (1985). Pp. 38–40 and 57–8.
– "Men and Women in the Saints' Sagas of *Stock. 2, fol.*" In John Lindow,
   Lars Lönnroth, and Gerd Wolfgang Weber, ed. >> *Structure and Mean-
   ing in Old Norse Literature* (1986). Pp. 317–46, esp. pp. 319–20.
Cormack, Margaret. >> *The Saints in Iceland* (1994). P. 93.
Jakob Benediktsson. "Nödhjälparna." *KLNM* 21 (1977). Cols. 289–90,
   esp. col. 290.
Jón Hnefill Aðalsteinsson. "Blot i forna skrifter." *SI* 47 (1996): 11–32, esp. p. 27.
Kirby, Ian. >> *Biblical Quotation* (1980). Vol. 2, p. 42.
Lehmann, Paul. >> "Skandinaviens Anteil an der lateinischen Literatur
   und Wissenschaft des Mittelalters" (1937). Pp. 44 and 48–9.
Mogk, Eugen. >> *Geschichte der norwegisch-isländischen Literatur* (1904).
   P. 890.
Van Deusen, Natalie M. "Stitches in the Margins: The Embroidery
   Pattern in AM 235 fol." *Mm* (2011): 26–42, esp. pp. 28–9.
Wolf, Kirsten, ed. "Anonymous, *Heilagra manna drápa* 'Drápa about Holy
   Men'." In Margaret Clunies Ross, ed. >> *Poetry on Christian Subjects*
   (2007). Vol. 2, pp. 872–90, esp. pp. 880–2.
Handlist, p. 307.

DOMINIC   August 4

1. Dóminíkuss saga

Translated from a now-lost Low German redaction that resembles the
source(s) of *Der Heiligen Leben*.

Manuscript:
Stock. Perg. fol. no. 3 (*Reykjahólabók*) (ca. 1530–40, defective).
Edition:
Loth, Agnete, ed. >> *Reykjahólabók* (1969–70). Vol. 2, pp. 287–304.
Literature:
Bekker-Nielsen, Hans, Thorkil Damsgaard Olsen, and Ole Widding.
   >> *Norrøn fortællekunst* (1965). P. 307.

Kalinke, Marianne E. "Reykjahólabók: A Legendary on the Eve of the
    Reformation." *Skáldskaparmál* 2 (1992): 239–69, esp. pp. 240 and 245.
– >> *The Book of Reykjahólar* (1996). Pp. 28, 33, 50, 97, 99, 128–31,
    133–4, 158–9, 238, and 245.
Widding, Ole, and Hans Bekker-Nielsen. "En senmiddelalderlig
    legendesamling." *Mm* (1960): 105–28, esp. pp. 108, 123–4, and 127.
– "Low German Influence on Late Icelandic Hagiography." *GR* 37
    (1962): 239–62, esp. pp. 248 and 255.
Handlist, p. 307.

2. Af Dóminíco

Tales of Saint Dominic incorporated into the miracles of the Virgin Mary.

Manuscripts:
See Mary the Blessed Virgin 3 note (p. 245).
Edition:
Unger, C.R., ed. >> *Mariu saga* (1871). Pp. 811.23–812 and 813–816.10.
Literature:
Handlist, pp. 307 and 323.

DOROTHY   ·   February 6

1. Dórótheu saga

A translation of a text in the main identical with *BHL* 2324, but which
differs in regard to certain details, some of which are now found in *BHL*
2325d.

Manuscript:
AM 429 12mo (ca. 1500).
Editions:
Unger, C.R., ed. >> *Heilagra manna søgur* (1877). Vol. 1, pp. 322.6–328.
Wolf, Kirsten, ed. *The Icelandic Legend of Saint Dorothy.* Studies and
    Texts 130 (Toronto: Pontifical Institute of Mediaeval Studies, 1997).
    Pp. 89–103.
– ed. >> *A Female Legendary from Iceland* (2011). Pp. 111–19.
    Facsimile and text edition.
Modern Icelandic language edition:
Wolf, Kirsten, ed. >> *Heilagra meyja sögur* (2003). Pp. 18–24.

Literature:

Ásdís Egilsdóttir. "Kvendýrlingar og kvenímynd trúarlegra bókmennta á
   Íslandi." In Inga Huld Hákonardóttir, ed. >> *Konur og kristsmenn*
   (1996). Pp. 93–116, esp. p. 93.
Bekker-Nielsen, Hans, Thorkil Damsgaard Olsen, and Ole Widding.
   >> *Norrøn fortællekunst* (1965). P. 124.
Bekker-Nielsen, Hans, and Ole Widding. "Legende. Norge og Island."
   KLNM 10 (1965). Cols. 421–3, esp. col. 421.
Carlé, Birte. "Fra slægtssaga til kvindesaga." In Silja Aðalsteinsdóttir and
   Helgi Þorláksson, ed. >> *Forändringar i kvinnors villkor under medel-
   tiden* (1983). Pp. 55–70, esp. pp. 61 and 65.
– >> *Jomfru-fortællingen* (1985). Pp. 43 and 147–50.
– "Men and Women in the Saints' Sagas of *Stock. 2, fol.*" In John
   Lindow, Lars Lönnroth, and Gerd Wolfgang Weber, ed. >> *Structure
   and Meaning in Old Norse Literature* (1986). Pp. 317–46, esp. p. 319.
Hallberg, Peter. "Imagery in Religious Old Norse Prose Literature: An
   Outline." *ANF* 102 (1987): 120–70, esp. p. 163.
Jakob Benediktsson. "Nödhjälparna." *KLNM* 21 (1977). Cols. 289–90,
   esp. col. 290.
Jón Hnefill Aðalsteinsson. "Blot i forna skrifter." *SI* 47 (1996): 11–32,
   esp. pp. 27–8.
Lehmann, Paul. >> "Skandinaviens Anteil an der lateinischen Literatur
   und Wissenschaft des Mittelalters" (1937). P. 44.
Mogk, Eugen. >> *Geschichte der norwegisch-isländischen Literatur* (1904).
   P. 891.
Sverrir Tómasson. "Kristnar trúarbókmenntir í óbundnu máli." In Guðrún
   Nordal, Sverrir Tómasson, and Vésteinn Ólason, ed. >> *Íslensk Bók-
   menntasaga* 1 (1992). Pp. 419–79, esp. p. 436.
Þórhallur Þorgilsson. "Um þýðingar og endursagnir úr ítölskum miðalda-
   ritum." *Landsbókasafn Íslands. Árbók* 1946–7 (1948): 212–24, esp.
   p. 222.
Wolf, Kirsten. "The Legend of Saint Dorothy: Medieval Vernacular
   Renderings and Their Latin Source." *Analecta Bollandiana* 114 (1996):
   41–72, esp. pp. 64–6.
– "The Severed Breast: A Topos in the Legends of Female Virgin Martyr
   Saints." *ANF* 112 (1997): 97–112, esp. pp. 98 and 104.
– "Female Scribes at Work? A Consideration of Kirkjubæjarbók (Codex
   AM 429 12mo)." In A.N. Doane and Kirsten Wolf, ed. >> *Beatus Vir*
   (2006). Pp. 265–95, esp. p. 270.
Handlist, p. 307.

DUNSTAN   May 19

1. Dúnstanuss saga

A life of Saint Dunstan compiled by the monk Árni Laurentiusson (b. 1304) and based on *BHL* 2343, *BHL* 2346, *Speculum historiale*, and additional material.

Manuscripts:
AM 180b fol. (ca. 1500) and NKS 267 fol. (ca. 1700–1800).
Editions:
Fell, Christine Elizabeth, ed. *Dunstanus saga*. Editiones Arnamagnæanæ, Ser. B, vol. 5 (Copenhagen: Munksgaard, 1963).
Edition of AM 180b fol.
Gudbrand Vigfusson and George W. Dasent, ed. and trans. *Icelandic Sagas and Other Historical Documents Relating to the Settlements and Descents of the Northmen on the British Isles*. 4 vols. Rolls Series 88 (London: Eyre and Spottiswoode, 1887–94; rpt. Millwood: Kraus, 1964). Vol. 2, pp. 385–408.
Edition of AM 180b fol.
Halvorsen, E.F., ed. *Karlamagnus saga and Some Religious Texts: AM 180 a and b fol.* EIM 18 (Copenhagen: Rosenkilde and Bagger, 1989). Facsimile of AM 180b fol.
English translation:
Gudbrand Vigfusson and George W. Dasent, ed. and trans. *Icelandic Sagas and Other Historical Documents Relating to the Settlements and Descents of the Northmen on the British Isles*. 4 vols. Rolls Series 88 (London: Eyre and Spottiswoode, 1887–94; rpt. Millwood: Kraus, 1964). Vol. 4, pp. 397–420.
Literature:
Bekker-Nielsen, Hans. "Duen uden galde. Et forslag til en tekstrettelse i Dunstanus saga." *Opuscula* 1. Bibliotheca Arnamagnæana 20 (Copenhagen: Reitzel, 1960). Pp. 339–40.
Bekker-Nielsen, Hans, Thorkil Damsgaard Olsen, and Ole Widding. >> *Norrøn fortællekunst* (1965). Pp. 126 and 168.
Boyer, Régis. >> *La vie religieuse en Islande* (1979). P. 146.
Carron, Helen. "Dunstanus saga." In Phillip Pulsiano and Kirsten Wolf, with Paul Acker and Donald K. Fry, ed. >> *Medieval Scandinavia* (1993). Pp. 144–5.

Cormack, Margaret. >> *The Saints in Iceland* (1994). Pp. 33n18, 94, and 241.

– "Saints' Lives and Icelandic Literature in the Thirteenth and Fourteenth Centuries." In Hans Bekker-Nielsen and Birte Carlé, ed. >> *Saints and Sagas* (1994). Pp. 27–47, esp. pp. 31–2.

– "Christian Biography." In *A Companion to Old Norse–Icelandic Literature and Culture*. Ed. Rory McTurk (Oxford: Blackwell, 2005). Pp. 27–42, esp. pp. 32–3.

Fell, Christine E. "Anglo-Saxon Saints in Old Norse Sources and Vice Versa." In Hans Bekker-Nielsen, Peter Foote, and Olaf Olsen, ed. >> *Proceedings of the Eighth Viking Congress* (1981). Pp. 95–106, esp. pp. 97–8 and 100–5.

Finnur Jónsson. >> *Den oldnorske og oldislandske Litteraturs Historie* (1920–4). Vol. 3, p. 92.

Hallberg, Peter. "Om Magnúss saga helga." In *Einarsbók: Afmæliskveðja til Einars Ól. Sveinssonar 12. desember 1969*. Ed. Bjarni Guðnason, Halldór Halldórsson, and Jónas Kristjánsson ([Reykjavík]: Nokkrir vinir, 1969). Pp. 59–70, esp. p. 70.

– "Some Observations on the Language of *Dunstanus saga*, with an Appendix on the Bible Compilation *Stjórn*." *Saga-Book* 18 (1973): 324–53, esp. pp. 324–46.

– "Imagery in Religious Old Norse Prose Literature: An Outline." *ANF* 102 (1987): 120–70, esp. pp. 129, 133, 144, and 154–5.

Halvorsen, E.F. "Dunstanus saga." *KLNM* 2 (1957). Col. 370.

Harty, Lenore. "The Icelandic Life of St Dunstan." *Saga-Book* 15 (1957–9): 263–93.

Heizmann, Wilhelm. "Arngríms Guðmundar saga, Maríu saga und Gregors Moralia in Iob." *Opuscula* 8. Bibliotheca Arnamagnæana 38 (Copenhagen: Reitzel, 1985). Pp. 189–98, esp. p. 190.

Kirby, Ian. >> *Biblical Quotation* (1980). Vol. 2, pp. 20 and 100.

– *Bible Translation in Old Norse*. Université de Lausanne Publications de la faculté des lettres 27 (Geneva: Librairie Droz, 1986). P. 46.

Leach, Henry Goddard. *Angevin Britain and Scandinavia*. Harvard Studies in Comparative Literature (Cambridge, Mass.: Harvard University Press, 1921). P. 127.

Lehmann, Paul. >> "Skandinaviens Anteil an der lateinischen Literatur und Wissenschaft des Mittelalters" (1937). Pp. 51 and 53.

Magerøy, Hallvard. "Helgensoger." *KLNM* 6 (1961). Cols. 350–3, esp. cols. 351–2.

Mogk, Eugen. >> *Geschichte der norwegisch-isländischen Literatur* (1904).
P. 893.

O'Hare, Colman. "*Dunstanus Saga*: England and the Old Norse Church."
The American Benedictine Review 33 (1982): 394–422.

Schier, Kurt. *Sagaliteratur*. Sammlung Metzler M78 (Stuttgart: Metzler,
1970). Pp. 4, 67, 123, and 128.

Sverrir Tómasson. "Norðlenski Benediktínaskólinn." In >> *The Sixth
International Saga Conference* (1985). Vol. 2, pp. 1009–20, esp. p. 1009.
Rpt. in Sverrir Tómasson. *Tækileg vitni: Greinar um bókmenntir gefnar út í
tilefni sjötugsafmælis hans 5. apríl 2011* (Reykjavík: Stofnun Árna Magnússonar and Hið íslenska bókmenntafélag, 2011). Pp. 345–58, esp. p. 345.

– *Formálar íslenskra sagnaritara á miðöldum. Rannsókn bókmenntahefðar*
(Reykjavík: Stofnun Árna Magnússonar, 1988). Pp. 59–60, 65, 86, 90,
131, 162, 183–5, 311, and 334–5.

– "Trúarbókmenntir í lausu máli á síðmiðöld." In Böðvar Guðmundsson,
Sverrir Tómasson, Torfi H. Tulinius, and Vésteinn Ólason, ed. >>
Íslensk Bókmenntasaga 2 (1993). Pp. 249–82, esp. pp. 251, 253, and 263.

Vries, Jan de. >> *Altnordische Literaturgeschichte* (1964–7). Vol. 2, p. 528.

Handlist, p. 307.

2. Af Dúnstano

A tale about Saint Dunstan and a goldsmith. The direct source has not
been established.

Manuscripts:
AM 657a–b 4to (ca. 1350) and AM 238 fol. XXI (ca. 1500).
Edition:
Gering, Hugo, ed. >> *Islendzk æventyri* (1882–3), Vol. 1, pp. 46–7.
Based on AM 657a–b 4to with variants from AM 238 fol. XXI.
German paraphrase:
Gering, Hugo, ed. >> *Islendzk æventýri* (1882–3). Vol. 2, pp. 30–1.
Literature:
Cormack, Margaret. >> *The Saints in Iceland* (1994). Pp. 34n27 and 35.

Fell, Christine Elizabeth, ed. *Dunstanus saga*. Editiones Arnamagnæanæ,
Series B, vol. 5 (Copenhagen: Munksgaard, 1963). Pp. lxxxiii–lxxxiv.

Jorgensen, Peter A. "Four Æventýri." *Opuscula* 5. Bibliotheca Arnamagnæana 31 (Copenhagen: Munksgaard, 1975). Pp. 295–328, esp. p. 296.

Wolf, Kirsten, ed. >> *Heilagra meyja sögur* (2003). P. lii.

Handlist, p. 308.

3. Af Dúnstano

Tales of Saint Dunstan incorporated into the miracles of the Virgin Mary.

Manuscripts:
See Mary the Blessed Virgin 3 note (p. 245).
Edition:
Unger, C.R., ed. *Mariu saga* (1871). Pp. 716.29–722.24.
Literature:
Battista, Simonetta. "*Blámenn, djǫflar* and Other Representations of Evil
   in Old Norse Literature." In John McKinnell, David Ashurst, and
   Donata Kick, ed. >> *The Fantastic in Old Norse/Icelandic Literature*
   (2006). Vol. 1, pp. 113–22, esp. p. 119.
Widding, Ole. "Norrøne Marialegender på européisk baggrund."
   Opuscula 10. Bibliotheca Arnamagnæana 40 (Copenhagen: Reitzel,
   1996. Pp. 1–128, esp. p. 37.
Handlist, pp. 308 and 323.

EDMUND   November 20

In his *Íslendingabók* (chapter 1), Ari Þorgilsson (d. 1148) mentions a
"saga" of Saint Edmund. Opinions differ as to whether Ari refers to an
Icelandic legend or to Abbo of Fleury's *Passio Sancti Eadmundi*. For a
discussion and edition of *Íslendingabók*, see Jakob Benediktsson, ed.,
Íslendingabók. Landnámabók, Íslenzk fornrit 1 (Reykjavík: Hið íslenzka
fornritafélag, 1968), pp. v–xliv, esp. pp. xxii–xxiii, and 1–28. For an
English translation of *Íslendingabók*, see Halldór Hermannsson, ed.
and trans., *The Book of Icelanders (Íslendingabók) by Ari Thorgilsson*,
Islandica 20 (Ithaca: Cornell University Press; London: Milford; Oxford
University Press, 1930).
Handlist, p. 308.

EDMUND RICH   November 16

Af Eadmundo

Tales of Saint Edmund Rich incorporated into the miracles of the Virgin
Mary.

Manuscripts:
See Mary the Blessed Virgin 3 note (p. 245).
Edition:
Unger, C.R., ed. >> *Mariu saga* (1871). Pp. 725.26–728.22.
Literature:
Fell, Christine E. "Anglo-Saxon Saints in Old Norse Sources and Vice
    Versa." In Hans Bekker-Nielsen, Peter Foote, and Olaf Olsen, ed.
    >> *Proceedings of the Eighth Viking Congress* (1981). Pp. 95–106, esp.
    p. 98.
Widding, Ole. "Norrøne Marialegender på europæisk baggrund."
    Opuscula 10. Bibliotheca Arnamagnæana 40 (Copenhagen: Reitzel,
    1996). Pp. 1–128, esp. p. 76.
Handlist, pp. 308 and 323.

EDWARD THE CONFESSOR   October 13

1. Játvarðar saga

A compilation based on a variety of sources, including service books
containing lessons for Saint Edward's feast day (derived ultimately from
BHL 2422 and 2423), Vincent of Beauvais' *Speculum historiale*, the
Chronicon Laudunensis, and *Haralds saga Sigurðarsonar*.

Manuscripts:
AM 238 fol. XVI (ca. 1450–1500), AM 663a 4to (ca. 1675–1700),
    AM 663b 4to (ca. 1600–50), AM 663c 4to (ca. 1700), AM 950 4to
    (ca. 1700–1800), AM 237 8vo (ca. 1800), GKS 1005 fol. (*Flateyjarbók*)
    (ca. 1387–95), Kall 249 fol. (ca. 1700–1800), NKS 1148 fol. (ca.1700–
    1800), NKS 1733 4to (ca. 1700–1800), Rask 29 (ca. 1700–1800),
    Stock. Papp. fol. no. 55 (1688), and Stock. Perg. fol. no. 5
    (ca. 1350–65).
Editions:
Finnur Jónsson, ed. *Flateyjarbók (Codex Flateyensis): MS. No. 1005 fol.
    in the Old Royal Collection in the Royal Library of Copenhagen. CCI 1
    (Copenhagen: Levin & Munksgaard, 1930).
    Facsimile of GKS 1005 fol.
Gudbrand Vigfusson and George W. Dasent, ed. and trans. *Icelandic
    Sagas and Other Historical Documents Relating to the Settlements and*

Descents of the Northmen on the British Isles. 4 vols. Rolls Series 88 (London: Eyre and Spottiswoode, 1887–94; rpt. Millwood: Kraus, 1964). Vol. 1, pp. 388–400.

Based on GKS 1005 fol.

Guðbrandr Vigfússon and C.R. Unger, ed. *Flateyjarbók: En Samling af norske Konge-Sagaer med indskudte mindre Fortællinger om Begivenheder i og udenfor Norge samt Annaler.* 3 vols. (Christiania [Oslo]: Malling, 1860–8). Vol. 3, pp. 461–72.

Jón Helgason, ed. *Byskupa sǫgur. MS Perg. fol. No. 5 in the Royal Library of Stocholm.* CCI 19 (Copenhagen: Ejnar Munksgaard, 1950). Facsimile of Stock. Perg. fol. no. 5.

Rafn, C.C., and Jon Sigurdsson, ed. "Saga Játvarðar konúngs hins helga." *Annaler for nordisk Oldkyndighed og Historie* (1852). Pp. 3–43, esp. pp. 10–43.

Based on Stock. Perg. fol. no. 5 with variants from GKS 1005 fol.

Sigurður Nordal et al., ed. *Flateyjarbók.* 4 vols. (Akranes: Flateyjarútgáfan, 1944–5). Vol. 4, pp. 246–56.

Danish translation:

Rafn, C.C., and Jon Sigurdsson, ed. "Saga Játvarðar konúngs hins helga." *Annaler for nordisk Oldkyndighed og Historie* (1852). Pp. 3–43, esp. pp. 10–43.

English translation:

Gudbrand Vigfusson and George W. Dasent, ed. and trans. *Icelandic Sagas and Other Historical Documents Relating to the Settlements and Descents of the Northmen on the British Isles.* 4 vols. Rolls Series 88 (London: Eyre and Spottiswoode, 1887–94; rpt. Millwood: Kraus, 1964). Vol. 3, pp. 416–28.

Literature:

Ashdown, Margaret. "An Icelandic Account of the Survival of Harold Godwinson." In Peter Clemoes, ed. >> *The Anglo-Saxons* (1959). Pp. 122–36, esp. pp. 129–30.

Bekker-Nielsen, Hans, Thorkil Damsgaard Olsen, and Ole Widding. >> *Norrøn fortællekunst* (1965). P. 126.

Blalock, Martha Graham. "The *Vita Sancti Edwardi Regis et Confessoris* and the Vernacular Lives of Edward the Confessor." PhD dissertation, University of Wisconsin, Madison, 1983. Pp. 246–85.

Boyer, Régis. >> *La vie religieuse en Islande* (1979). Pp. 146 and 187.

Carron, Helen. "Játvarðar saga." In Phillip Pulsiano and Kirsten Wolf, with Paul Acker and Donald K. Fry, ed. >> *Medieval Scandinavia* (1993). P. 340.

Ciggaar, Krijnie N. "L'émigration anglaise a Byzance après 1066. Un nouveau texte en Latin sur les Varangues á Constantinople." *Revue des études Byzantines* 32 (1974): 301–42.

Cormack, Margaret. >> *The Saints in Iceland* (1994). Pp. 94 and 241.

– "Saints' Lives and Icelandic Literature in the Thirteenth and Fourteenth Centuries." In Hans Bekker-Nielsen and Birte Carlé, ed. >> *Saints and Sagas* (1994). Pp. 27–47, esp. pp. 31–2.

Fell, Christine E. "The Icelandic Saga of Edward the Confessor: The Hagiographic Sources." *ASE* 1 (1972): 247–58.

– "A Note on Pálsbók." *MScand* 6 (1973): 102–8.

– "The Icelandic Saga of Edward the Confessor: Its Version of the Anglo-Saxon Emigration to Byzantium." *ASE* 3 (1974): 179–96.

– "English History and Norman Legend in the Icelandic Saga of Edward the Confessor." *ASE* 6 (1977): 223–36.

– "Anglo-Saxon Saints in Old Norse Sources and Vice Versa." In Hans Bekker-Nielsen, Peter Foote, and Olaf Olsen, ed. >> *Proceedings of the Eighth Viking Congress* (1981). Pp. 95–106, esp. pp. 100–5.

Finnur Jónsson. >> *Den oldnorske og oldislandske Litteraturs Historie* (1920–4). Vol. 2, pp. 875–6.

Kirby, Ian. >> *Biblical Quotation* (1980). Vol. 2, p. 102.

– *Bible Translation in Old Norse.* Université de Lausanne Publications de la Faculté des Lettres 27 (Geneva: Librairie Droz, 1986). P. 47n67.

Leach, Henry Goddard. *Angevin Britain and Scandinavia.* Harvard Studies in Comparative Literature (Cambridge, Mass.: Harvard University Press, 1921). P. 127.

Lehmann, Paul. >> "Skandinaviens Anteil an der lateinischen Literatur und Wissenschaft des Mittelalters" (1937). P. 44.

Loth, Agnete. "Egidius saga hins helga. Fragmentet AM 238 XVI, fol." *Opuscula* 3. Bibliotheca Arnamagnæana 29 (Copenhagen: Munksgaard, 1967). Pp. 62–73, esp. pp. 62–5.

Louis-Jensen, Jonna. *Kongesagastudier. Kompilationen Hulda-Hrokkinskinna.* Bibliotheca Arnamagnæana 32 (Copenhagen: Reitzel, 1977). Pp. 129–35 and 144.

Lönnroth, Lars. "Det litterära porträttet i latinsk historiografi och isländsk sagaskrivning – en komparativ studie." *ANF* 27 (1969): 68–117, esp. p. 85.

Mogk, Eugen. >> *Geschichte der norwegisch-isländischen Literatur* (1904).
Pp. 893–4.

Powell, F.Y. "A Northern Legend of the English Conquest." *The English
Historical Review* 4 (1889): 87–9.

Rogers, H.L. "An Icelandic Life of St. Edward the Confessor." *Saga-
Book* 14 (1953–5): 249–72.

Rowe, Elizabeth Ashman. *The Development of Flateyjarbók: Iceland and
the Norwegian Dynastic Crisis of 1389* (Gylling: The University Press
of Southern Denmark, 2005). Pp. 12, 20, 207, 263, 280–3, 337, 340–2,
and 381–3.

Schier, Kurt. *Sagaliteratur*. Sammlung Metzler M78 (Stuttgart: Metzler,
1970). Pp. 124 and 129.

Simek, Rudolf. *Altnordische Kosmographie: Studien und Quellen zu
Weltbild und Weltbeschreibung in Norwegen und Island vom 12. bis zum
14. Jahrhundert* (Berlin: de Gruyter, 1990). Pp. 293–4.

Smith, A.H. "The Early Literary Relations of England and Scandinavia."
Saga-Book 11 (1936): 215–32, esp. pp. 227–30.

Vries, Jan de. >> *Altnordische Literaturgeschichte* (1964–7). Vol. 2, p. 561.

Wawn, Andrew. "Choking on a Morsel: *Saga Játvarðar konungs hins
helga* and the Nineteenth-Century Politics of Saga." In >> *The Audience of the Sagas* (1991). Vol. 2, pp. 331–40.

Handlist, p. 308.

2. Frá sýn Eðvarðs konungs

A short passage about Saint Edward.

Manuscript:
AM 764 4to (ca. 1376–86, defective).
Literature:

Cormack, Margaret. >> *The Saints in Iceland* (1994). Pp. 35 and 94.

Svanhildur Óskarsdóttir. "Universal History in Fourteenth-Century
Iceland: Studies in AM 764 4to." PhD dissertation, University of
London, 2000. P. 241.

– "Arctic Garden of Delights: The Purpose of the Book of Reynistaður."
In Kirsten Wolf and Johanna Denzin, ed. >> *Romance and Love in Late
Medieval and Early Modern Iceland* (2008). Pp. 279–301, esp. p. 292.

Wolf, Kirsten, ed. >> *Heilagra meyja sögur* (2003). P. li.

Handlist, p. 308.

ELIZABETH OF SCHÖNAU   June 18

1. Elisabetar leiðsla

A version of the story of Saint Elizabeth's visions included in *Guðmundar saga D*. The direct source has not been established.

Manuscripts:
See Guðmundr the Good 4 (p. 142).
Editions:
Guðni Jónsson, ed. *Byskupa sögur*. 3 vols. (Reykjavík: Íslendingasagnaútgáfan, Haukadalsútgáfan, 1948). Vol. 3, pp. 432–9.
Jón Helgason, ed. *Byskupa sǫgur. MS Perg. fol. No. 5 in the Royal Library of Stockholm*. CCI 19 (Copenhagen: Munksgaard, 1950). Facsimile edition.
[Jón Sigurðsson and Guðbrandur Vigfússon, ed.] *Biskupa sögur*. 2 vols. (Copenhagen: Møller, 1858–78). Vol. 2, pp. 151–5.
Stefán Karlsson. "Um handrit að Guðmundar sögu bróður Arngríms." *Opuscula* 1. Bibliotheca Arnamagnæana 20 (Copenhagen: Munksgaard, 1960). Pp. 179–89, esp. pp. 180–3.
Literature:
Ásdís Egilsdóttir. "Kvendýrlingar og kvenímynd trúarlegra bókmennta á Íslandi." In Inga Huld Hákonardóttir, ed. >> *Konur og kristsmenn* (1996). Pp. 93–116, esp. p. 105.
Astås, Reidar. "Spor av teologisk tenkning og refleksjon i norsk og islandsk høymiddelalder." *CM* 6 (1993): 133–67, esp. pp. 146–7n54.
Bekker-Nielsen, Hans, and Ole Widding. "Maria. Norge, Island." *KLNM* 11 (1966). Cols. 363–7, esp. col. 364.
Cormack, Margaret. >> *The Saints in Iceland* (1994). Pp. 34 and 128.
Finnur Jónsson. >> *Den oldnorske og oldislandske Litteraturs Historie* (1920–4). Vol. 3, pp. 65 and 67.
Lehmann, Paul. >> "Skandinaviens Anteil an der lateinischen Literatur und Wissenschaft des Mittelalters" (1937). Pp. 19 and 35.
Maurer, Konrad von. "Der Elizabeth von Schönau Visionen nach einar isländischen Quelle." In *Sitzungsberichte der Königlichen bayerischen Akademie der Wissenschaften: Philosophisch-Philologische Classe 1883* 3 (1883): 401–23.
Mogk, Eugen. >> *Geschichte der norwegisch-isländischen Literatur* (1904). P. 795.

Paasche, Fredrik. *Norges og Islands litteratur inntil utgangen av middelalder-en.* Rev. ed. by Anne Holtsmark (Oslo: Aschehoug, 1947). P. 309.

Svanhildur Óskarsdóttir. "Universal History in Fourteenth-Century Iceland: Studies in AM 764 4to." PhD dissertation, University of London, 2000. Pp. 184–8.

Sverrir Tómasson. "Kristnar trúarbókmenntir í óbundnu máli." In Guðrún Nordal, Sverrir Tómasson, and Vésteinn Ólason, ed. >> *Íslensk Bókmenntasaga* 1 (1992). Pp. 419–79, esp. p. 463.

Widding, Ole, and Hans Bekker-Nielsen. "Elisabeth of Schönau's Visions in an Old Icelandic Manuscript, AM 764, 4°." *Opuscula* 2.1. Bibliotheca Arnamagnæana 25.1 (Copenhagen: Munksgaard, 1961). Pp. 93–6, esp. pp. 94–6.

– "An Old Norse Translation of the 'Transitus Mariae'." *MS* 23 (1961): 324–9, esp. pp. 326–7.

Wolf, Kirsten, ed. >> *Heilagra meyja sögur* (2003). P. xln13.

Handlist, p. 309.

2. Elisabetar leiðsla

A version of the story of Saint Elizabeth's visions based possibly on the *Speculum historiale* incorporated into the miracles of the Virgin Mary.

Manuscripts:
See Mary the Blessed Virgin 3 note (p. 245).
Edition:
Unger, C.R., ed. >> *Mariu saga* (1871). Pp. 915.21–917.24.
Literature:

Bekker-Nielsen, Hans, and Ole Widding. "Maria. Norge, Island." *KLNM* 11 (1966). Cols. 363–7, esp. col. 364.

Cormack, Margaret. >> *The Saints in Iceland* (1994). P. 128.

Svanhildur Óskarsdóttir. "Universal History in Fourteenth-Century Iceland: Studies in AM 764 4to." PhD dissertation, University of London, 2000. P. 184.

Sverrir Tómasson. "Kristnar trúarbókmenntir í óbundnu máli." In Guðrún Nordal, Sverrir Tómasson, and Vésteinn Ólason, ed. >> *Íslensk Bókmenntasaga* 1 (1992). Pp. 419–79, esp. p. 463.

Widding, Ole, and Hans Bekker-Nielsen. "Elisabeth of Schönau's Visions in an Old Icelandic Manuscript, AM 764, 4°." *Opuscula* 2.1. Bibliotheca Arnamagnæana 25.1 (Copenhagen: Munksgaard, 1961). Pp. 93–6, esp. p. 93.

– "An Old Norse Translation of the 'Transitus Mariae'." *MS* 23 (1961): 324–9, esp. pp. 326–7.
Handlist, pp. 309 and 323.

3. Elisabetar leiðsla

A condensed version of the story of Saint Elizabeth's visions. The direct source has not been established, but it appears to be based on the same source as 1.

Manuscript:
AM 764 4to (ca. 1376–86).
Editions:
Svanhildur Óskarsdóttir. "Universal History in Fourteenth-Century Iceland: Studies in AM 764 4to." PhD dissertation, University of London, 2000. Pp. 282–3.
Widding, Ole, and Hans Bekker-Nielsen. "Elisabeth of Schönau's Visions in an Old Icelandic Manuscript, AM 764, 4°." *Opuscula* 2.1. Bibliotheca Arnamagnæana 25.1 (Copenhagen: Munksgaard, 1961). Pp. 93–6, esp. pp. 94–6.
Literature:
Bekker-Nielsen, Hans, and Ole Widding. "Maria. Norge, Island." *KLNM* 11 (1966). Cols. 363–7, esp. col. 364.
Boyer, Régis. >> *La vie religieuse en Islande* (1979). P. 183.
Cormack, Margaret. >> *The Saints in Iceland* (1994). Pp. 35 and 128.
Svanhildur Óskarsdóttir. "Arctic Garden of Delights: The Purpose of the Book of Reynistaður." In Kirsten Wolf and Johanna Denzin, ed. >> *Romance and Love in Late Medieval and Early Modern Iceland* (2008). Pp. 279–301, esp. p. 292.
Widding, Ole, and Hans Bekker-Nielsen. "An Old Norse Translation of the 'Transitus Mariae'." *MS* 23 (1961): 324–9, esp. pp. 326–7.
Wolf, Kirsten, ed. >> *Heilagra meyja sögur* (2003). Pp. li and lvi.
Handlist, p. 309.

ERASMUS   June 2

1. Erasmuss saga

Probably based on one of the recensions of the Latin *passio* (*BHL* 2578–82).

Manuscript:
AM 655 4to V (ca. 1200–25).
Editions:
Hreinn Benediktsson. *Early Icelandic Script As Illustrated in Vernacular Texts from the Twelfth and Thirteenth Centuries.* Íslenzk handrit: Icelandic Manuscripts, Series in Folio 2 (Reykjavík: The Manuscript Institute of Iceland, 1965). Plate 20. Facsimile of fol. 1v.

Morgenstern, Gustav, ed. >> *Arnamagnæanische Fragmente* (1893). Pp. 14.29–22.26.

Unger, C.R., ed. >> *Heilagra manna søgur* (1877). Vol. 1, pp. 363–8.
Literature:
Battista, Simonetta. "*Blámenn, djǫflar* and Other Representations of Evil in Old Norse Literature." In John McKinnell, David Ashurst, and Donata Kick, ed. >> *The Fantastic in Old Norse/Icelandic Literature* (2006). Vol. 1, pp. 113–22, esp. p. 120.

Bekker-Nielsen, Hans, Thorkil Damsgaard Olsen, and Ole Widding. >> *Norrøn fortællekunst* (1965). P. 23.

Cormack, Margaret. >> *The Saints in Iceland* (1994). P. 37.

Jónas Kristjánsson. "Learned Style or Saga Style?" In Ursula Dronke, Guðrún P. Helgadóttir, Gerd Wolfgang Weber, and Hans Bekker-Nielsen, ed. >> *Specvlvm Norroenvm* (1981). Pp. 260–92.

– >> *Eddas and Sagas* (1988). P. 148.

Lindow, John. "Norse Mythology and the Lives of the Saints." *SS* 73 (2001): 437–56, esp. pp. 439–41 and 447.

Mogk, Eugen. >> *Geschichte der norwegisch-isländischen Literatur* (1904). P. 891.

Þórhallur Þorgilsson. "Um þýðingar og endursagnir úr ítölskum miðaldaritum." *Landsbókasafn Íslands. Árbók* 1946–7 (1948): 212–24, esp. p. 222.

Handlist, p. 309.

2. Erasmuss saga

Translated from a now-lost Low German redaction that resembles the source(s) of *Der Heiligen Leben*.

Manuscript:
Stock. Perg. fol. no. 3 (*Reykjahólabók*) (ca. 1530–40).
Edition:
Loth, Agnete, ed. >> *Reykjahólabók* (1969–70). Vol. 2, pp. 129–48.

Literature:
Bekker-Nielsen, Hans, Thorkil Damsgaard Olsen, and Ole Widding.
  >> *Norrøn fortællekunst* (1965). P. 309.
Dillmann, François-Xavier. "Om hedningar och hundar. Kring den
  fornvästnordiska sammansättningen *hundheiðinn*." *SI* 52 (2001): 17–33,
  esp. pp. 20–1.
Kalinke, Marianne E. "Reykjahólabók: A Legendary on the Eve of the
  Reformation." *Skáldskaparmál* 2 (1992): 239–69, esp. pp. 240, 244,
  and 264.
– >> *The Book of Reykjahólar* (1996). Pp. 28, 50, and 114.
Widding, Ole, and Hans Bekker-Nielsen. "En senmiddelalderlig
  legendesamling." *Mm* (1960): 105–28, esp. pp. 107 and 120–1.
– "Low German Influence on Late Icelandic Hagiography." *GR* 37
  (1962): 239–62, esp. pp. 247 and 255.
Handlist, p. 309.

EUSEBIUS OF VERCELLI   December 16

Af Eusebío

A tale of Saint Eusebius of Vercelli incorporated into the miracles of the
Virgin Mary.

Manuscripts:
See Mary the Blessed Virgin 3 note (p. 245).
Edition:
Unger, C.R., ed. >> *Mariu saga* (1871). Pp. 698.23–699.13.
Literature:
Handlist, pp. 309 and 323.

EUSTACE   September 20

1. Plácíduss saga B

A translation of *BHL* 2760.

Manuscript:
AM 655 4to IX (ca. 1150–1200).

Editions:

Tucker, John, ed. *Plácidus saga. With an Edition of* Plácitus drápa *by Jonna Louis-Jensen*. Editiones Arnamagnæanæ, Ser. B, vol. 31 (Copenhagen: Reitzel, 1998). Pp. 8–22 verso.

Unger, C.R., ed. >> *Heilagra manna søgur* (1877). Vol. 2, pp. 207.24–209.13.

Literature:

Bekker-Nielsen, Hans. "Plácítus saga." *KLNM* 13 (1968). Col. 327.

– "Et par ord om de ældste norrøne helgensagaer." In Finn Hødnebø et al., ed. >> *Eyvindarbók* (1992). Pp. 29–33, esp. p. 32.

Bekker-Nielsen, Hans, Thorkil Damsgaard Olsen, and Ole Widding. >> *Norrøn fortællekunst* (1965). Pp. 17 and 123.

Bekker-Nielsen, Hans, and Ole Widding. "Legende. Norge og Island." *KLNM* 10 (1965). Cols. 421–3, esp. col. 422.

– "Religiøs prosalitteratur. Norge og Island." *KLNM* 14 (1969). Cols. 42–4, esp. col. 42.

Boyer, Régis. >> *La vie religieuse en Islande* (1979). Pp. 203 and 224.

Cormack, Margaret J. "Saints and Sinners: Reflections on Death in Some Icelandic Sagas." *Gripla* 8 (1993): 187–218, esp. p. 194.

– >> *The Saints in Iceland* (1994). P. 33.

– "Christian Biography." In *A Companion to Old Norse–Icelandic Literature and Culture*. Ed. Rory McTurk (Oxford: Blackwell, 2005). Pp. 27–42, esp. pp. 29–30.

Finnur Jónsson. >> *Den oldnorske og oldislandske Litteraturs Historie* (1920–4). Vol. 2, p. 874.

Jónas Kristjánsson. "Learned Style or Saga Style?" In Ursula Dronke, Guðrún P. Helgadóttir, Gerd Wolfgang Weber, and Hans Bekker-Nielsen, ed. >> *Specvlvm Norroenvm* (1981). Pp. 260–92.

– >> *Eddas and Sagas* (1988). P. 142.

Jørgensen, Jørgen Højgaard. "Hagiography and the Icelandic Bishop Sagas." *Peritia* 1 (1982): 1–16, esp. p. 3.

Kirby, Ian. >> *Biblical Quotation* (1980). Vol. 2, pp. 18 and 47–8.

– *Bible Translation in Old Norse*. Université de Lausanne Publications de la Faculté des Lettres 27 (Geneva: Librairie Droz, 1986). P. 34.

– "The Bible and Biblical Interpretation in Medieval Iceland." In *Old Icelandic Literature and Society*. Ed. Margaret Clunies Ross (Cambridge: Cambridge University Press, 2000). Pp. 287–301, esp. p. 295.

Lehmann, Paul. >> "Skandinaviens Anteil an der lateinischen Literatur und Wissenschaft des Mittelalters" (1937). Pp. 45 and 80.

Louis-Jensen, Jonna, and Tarrin Wills, ed. "Anonymous, *Plácitusdrápa* '*Drápa* about Plácitus'." In Margaret Clunies Ross, ed. >> *Poetry on Christian Subjects* (2007). Vol. 1, pp. 179–220, esp. p. 180.

Lönnroth, Lars. "Kroppen som själens spegel – ett motiv i de isländska sagorna." *Lychnos* (1963–4): 24–61, esp. p. 32.

– *Njáls saga: A Critical Introduction* (Berkeley: University of California Press, 1976). P. 122.

Mogk, Eugen. >> *Geschichte der norwegisch-isländischen Literatur* (1904). Pp. 712 and 890–1.

Ólafur Halldórsson, ed. *Mattheus saga postula* (Reykjavík: Stofnun Árna Magnússonar, 1994). Pp. lvii–lxvi.

Tucker, John. "St. Eustace in Iceland: On the Origins, Structure, and Possible Influence of the *Plácítus saga*." In Régis Boyer, ed. >> *Les Sagas de Chevaliers (Riddarasögur)* (1985). Pp. 327–39.

– "The Relation of the Plácítus drápa to the Plácítus saga." In >> *The Sixth International Saga Conference* (1985). Vol. 2, pp. 1057–66.

– "Plácítus saga." In Phillip Pulsiano and Kirsten Wolf, with Paul Acker and Donald K. Fry, ed. >> *Medieval Scandinavia* (1993). Pp. 504–5.

Turville-Petre, G. >> *Origins of Icelandic Literature* (1967). P. 131.

Þórhallur Þorgilsson. "Um þýðingar og endursagnir úr ítölskum miðal-daritum." *Landsbókasafn Íslands. Árbók* 1946–7 (1948): 212–24, esp. p. 222.

Vries, Jan de. >> *Altnordische Literaturgeschichte* (1964–7). Vol. 2, p. 184.

Widding, Ole, and Hans Bekker-Nielsen. "Low German Influence on Late Icelandic Hagiography." *GR* 37 (1962): 239–62, esp. pp. 240–1.

Handlist, p. 309.

2. Plácíduss saga A

A translation of *BHL* 2760 different from 1.

Manuscripts:
AM 655 4to X (ca. 1250–1300), ÍB 161 8vo (1845), ÍB 634 8vo (1743–7), Lbs 677 4to (1817), Lbs 1137 8vo (1878), Stock. Papp. 4to no. 31 (ca. 1650–1700, defective), and Stock. Papp. 8vo no. 8 (ca. 1650–60).

Editions:
Tucker, John, ed. *Plácidus saga. With an Edition of* Plácitus drápa *by Jonna Louis-Jensen*. Editiones Arnamagnæanæ, Ser. B, vol. 31 (Copenhagen: Reitzel, 1998). Pp. 2–71.

Edition of AM 655 4to X (pp. 2–8, 12–24, 28–36 verso) and Stock. Papp. 8vo no. 8 (pp. 3–71 recto) with variants from ÍB 634 8vo and Lbs 677 4to.

Unger, C.R., ed. >> *Heilagra manna søgur* (1877). Vol. 2, pp. 193–207.19.
Edition of Stock. Papp. 8vo no. 8 (pp. 193–203) and AM 655 4to X (pp. 204–207.19).

English translation:

Tucker, John, ed. *Plácidus saga. With an Edition of* Plácitus drápa *by Jonna Louis-Jensen.* Editiones Arnamagnæanæ, Ser. B, vol. 31 (Copenhagen: Reitzel, 1998). Pp. 73–86.

Norwegian translation:

Mundal, Else. *Legender frå mellomalderen. Soger om heilage kvinner og menn* (Oslo: Det Norske Samlaget, 1995). Pp. 83–98.

Literature:

Bekker-Nielsen, Hans. "Plácítus saga." *KLNM* 13 (1968). Col. 327.
Bekker-Nielsen, Hans, Thorkil Damsgaard Olsen, and Ole Widding. >> *Norrøn fortællekunst* (1965). P. 123.
Cormack, Margaret J. "Saints and Sinners: Reflections on Death in Some Icelandic Sagas." *Gripla* 8 (1993): 187–218, esp. p. 194.
– >> *The Saints in Iceland* (1994). P. 37n45.
– "Christian Biography." In *A Companion to Old Norse–Icelandic Literature and Culture.* Ed. Rory McTurk (Oxford: Blackwell, 2005). Pp. 27–42, esp. pp. 29–30.
Finnur Jónsson. >> *Den oldnorske og oldislandske Litteraturs Historie* (1920–4). Vol. 2, p. 874.
Hreinn Benediktsson. "Tvö handritsbrot." *Lingua Islandica – Íslenzk tunga* 5 (1964): 139–49, esp. pp. 140–4 and 147–8.
Jónas Kristjánsson. >> *Eddas and Sagas* (1988). P. 142.
Jørgensen, Jørgen Højgaard. "Hagiography and the Icelandic Bishop Sagas." *Peritia* 1 (1982): 1–16, esp. p. 3.
Kirby, Ian. >> *Biblical Quotation* (1980). Vol. 2, pp. 47–8.
Lehmann, Paul. >> "Skandinaviens Anteil an der lateinischen Literatur und Wissenschaft des Mittelalters" (1937). P. 45.
Louis-Jensen, Jonna, and Tarrin Wills, ed. "Anonymous, *Plácitusdrápa* 'Drápa about Plácitus'." In Margaret Clunies Ross, ed. >> *Poetry on Christian Subjects* (2007). Vol. 1, pp. 179–220, esp. pp. 180, 184–5, 187, 192, 194, 199–200, 207–8, 211–12, 215, 217, and 219.
Lönnroth, Lars. "Kroppen som själens spegel – ett motiv i de isländska sagorna." *Lychnos* (1963–4): 24–61, esp. p. 32.

– *Njáls saga: A Critical Introduction* (Berkeley: University of California Press, 1976). P. 122.
– "Saga and Jartegn: The Appeal of Mystery in Saga Texts." In *Die Aktualität der Saga: Festschrift für Hans Schottmann*. Ed. Stig Toftgaard Andersen (Berlin: de Gruyter, 1999). Pp. 111–23, esp. p. 115.
Mogk, Eugen. >> *Geschichte der norwegisch-isländischen Literatur* (1904). Pp. 712 and 890–1.
Tucker, John. "Scribal Hands in AM 655 4to X." *Opuscula* 6. Bibliotheca Arnamagnæana 33 (Copenhagen: Reitzel, 1979). Pp. 108–25.
– "The Relation of the Plácítus drápa to the Plácítus saga." In >> *The Sixth International Saga Conference* (1985). Vol. 2, pp. 1057–66.
– "St. Eustace in Iceland: On the Origins, Structure, and Possible Influence of the *Plácítus saga*." In Régis Boyer, ed. >> *Les Sagas de Chevaliers (Riddarasögur)* (1985). Pp. 327–39.
– "Plácítus saga." In Phillip Pulsiano and Kirsten Wolf, with Paul Acker and Donald K. Fry, ed. >> *Medieval Scandinavia* (1993). Pp. 504–5.
Turville-Petre, G. >> *Origins of Icelandic Literature* (1967). P. 131.
Þórhallur Þorgilsson. "Um þýðingar og endursagnir úr ítölskum miðaldaritum." *Landsbókasafn Íslands. Árbók* 1946–7 (1948): 212–24, esp. p. 222.
Widding, Ole. "Håndskriftanalyser. Én eller flere skrivere." *Opuscula* 1. Bibliotheca Arnamagnæana 20 (Copenhagen: Munksgaard, 1960). Pp. 81–96, esp. pp. 84–5.
Widding, Ole, and Hans Bekker-Nielsen. "Low German Influence on Late Icelandic Hagiography." *GR* 37 (1962): 239–62, esp. pp. 240–1.
Handlist, p. 309.

3. Plácíduss saga C

A version independent of 2 that freely reworks the Latin (*BHL* 2760).

Manuscripts:
ÍB 382 8vo (1845) and Lbs 1217 4to (1817).
Edition:
Tucker, John, ed. *Plácidus saga. With an Edition of* Plácitus drápa *by Jonna Louis-Jensen*. Editiones Arnamagnæanæ, Ser. B, vol. 31 (Copenhagen: Reitzel, 1998). Pp. 3–71 recto.
Based on Lbs 1217 4to, filled out where illegible from ÍB 382 8vo, and with variants from ÍB 382 8vo.

Literature:

Louis-Jensen, Jonna, and Tarrin Wills, ed. "Anonymous, *Plácitusdrápa* '*Drápa* about Plácitus'." In Margaret Clunies Ross, ed. >> *Poetry on Christian Subjects* (2007). Vol. 1, pp. 179–220, esp. pp. 180, 182, 184–6, 189–91, 194–5, 197, 200, 207–8, 211–12, 215, and 219.

Tucker, John. "The Relation of the Plácítus drápa to the Plácítus saga." In >> *The Sixth International Saga Conference* (1985). Vol. 2, pp. 1057–66.

– "St. Eustace in Iceland: On the Origins, Structure, and Possible Influence of the *Plácítus saga*." In Régis Boyer, ed. >> *Les Sagas de Chevaliers (Riddarasögur)* (1985). Pp. 327–39.

– "Plácítus saga." In Phillip Pulsiano and Kirsten Wolf, with Paul Acker and Donald K. Fry, ed. >> *Medieval Scandinavia* (1993). Pp. 504–5.

4. Plácíduss saga D

An abbreviated version, the source of which has not been determined.

Manuscript:
AM 696 4to III (ca. 1400).

Editions:

Tucker, John, ed. *Plácidus saga. With an Edition of* Plácitus drápa *by Jonna Louis-Jensen*. Editiones Arnamagnæanæ, Ser. B, vol. 31 (Copenhagen: Reitzel, 1998). Pp. 34–68 verso.

Unger, C.R., ed. >> *Heilagra manna søgur* (1877). Vol. 2, pp. 209.16–210.

Literature:

Bekker-Nielsen, Hans. "Plácítus saga." *KLNM* 13 (1968). Col. 327.

Bekker-Nielsen, Hans, Thorkil Damsgaard Olsen, and Ole Widding. >> *Norrøn fortællekunst* (1965). P. 123.

Cormack, Margaret J. "Saints and Sinners: Reflections on Death in Some Icelandic Sagas." *Gripla* 8 (1993): 187–218, esp. p. 194.

– "Christian Biography." In *A Companion to Old Norse–Icelandic Literature and Culture*. Ed. Rory McTurk (Oxford: Blackwell, 2005). Pp. 27–42, esp. pp. 29–30.

Dillmann, François-Xavier. "Om hedningar och hundar. Kring den fornvästnordiska sammansättningen *hundheiðinn*." *SI* 52 (2001): 17–33, esp. pp. 26–7.

Finnur Jónsson. >> *Den oldnorske og oldislandske Litteraturs Historie* (1920–4). Vol. 2, p. 874.

Jónas Kristjánsson. *Um Fóstbræðra sögu* (Reykjavík: Stofnun Árna
 Magnússonar, 1972). P. 274.
– >> *Eddas and Sagas* (1988). P. 142.
Kirby, Ian. >> *Biblical Quotation* (1980). Vol. 2, pp. 47–8.
Lönnroth, Lars. "Kroppen som själens spegel – ett motiv i de isländska
 sagorna." *Lychnos* (1963–4): 24–61, esp. p. 32.
– *Njáls saga: A Critical Introduction* (Berkeley: University of California
 Press, 1976). P. 122.
Mogk, Eugen. >> *Geschichte der norwegisch-isländischen Literatur* (1904).
 Pp. 712 and 890–1.
Tucker, John. "St. Eustace in Iceland: On the Origins, Structure, and
 Possible Influence of the *Plácítus saga*." In Régis Boyer, ed.
 >> *Les Sagas de Chevaliers (Riddarasögur)* (1985). Pp. 327–39.
– "Plácítus saga." In Phillip Pulsiano and Kirsten Wolf, with Paul Acker
 and Donald K. Fry, ed. >> *Medieval Scandinavia* (1993). Pp. 504–5.
Turville-Petre, G. >> *Origins of Icelandic Literature* (1967). P. 131.
Handlist, p. 309.

FIDES, SPES, AND CARITAS   August 1

1. Fídesar saga, Spesar ok Karítasar

A faithful translation of a version of the *passio* presented by *BHL* 2871.

Manuscripts:
AM 235 fol. (ca. 1400), AM 429 12mo (ca. 1500, defective), and Stock.
 Perg. fol. no. 2 (ca. 1425–45, defective).
Editions:
Foote, Peter, ed. >> *Lives of Saints* (1962).
 Facsimile of Stock. Perg. fol. no. 2.
Unger, C.R., ed. >> *Heilagra manna søgur* (1877). Vol. 1, pp. 372.15–
 376.
 Based on AM 235 fol. (pp. 372.15–23) and Stock. Perg. fol. no. 2
 (pp. 372.23–376) with variants from AM 235 fol. (pp. 372.23–376) and
 AM 429 12mo (pp. 372.15–28).
Wolf, Kirsten, ed. >> *A Female Legendary from Iceland* (2011).
 Pp. 142–5.
 Facsimile and text edition of AM 429 12mo.

– "Saga af Fídes, Spes ok Karítas." *Gripla* 22 (2011): 41–61, esp.
  pp. 46–55.
  Based on AM 235 fol. and Stock. Perg. fol. no. 2 with corrections and
  variant readings from AM 235 fol. and AM 429 12mo.
Modern Icelandic language edition:
Wolf, Kirsten, ed. >> *Heilagra meyja sögur* (2003). Pp. 93–100.
Literature:
Ásdís Egilsdóttir. "Kvendýrlingar og kvenímynd trúarlegra bókmennta
  á Íslandi." In Inga Huld Hákonardóttir, ed. >> *Konur og kristsmenn*
  (1996). Pp. 93–116, esp. p. 93.
Bekker-Nielsen, Hans, Thorkil Damsgaard Olsen, and Ole Widding.
  >> *Norrøn fortællekunst* (1965). Pp. 124–5.
Boyer, Régis. >> *La vie religieuse en Islande* (1979). P. 224.
Carlé, Birte. >> *Jomfru-fortællingen* (1985). Pp. 38–9, 41, 43, 75, 79–81,
  118, and 147–8.
– "Men and Women in the Saints' Sagas of *Stock. 2, fol.*" In John
  Lindow, Lars Lönnroth, and Gerd Wolfgang Weber, ed. >> *Structure
  and Meaning in Old Norse Literature* (1986). Pp. 317–46, esp. pp. 319,
  321, 341, and 343.
Cormack, Margaret. >> *The Saints in Iceland* (1994). Pp. 37–8.
Finnur Jónsson. >> *Den oldnorske og oldislandske Litteraturs Historie*
  (1920–4). Vol. 2, p. 931.
Lehmann, Paul. >> "Skandinaviens Anteil an der lateinischen Literatur
  und Wissenschaft des Mittelalters" (1937). P. 44.
Lindow, John. "Norse Mythology and the Lives of the Saints." *SS* 73
  (2001): 437–56, esp. p. 447.
Mogk, Eugen. >> *Geschichte der norwegisch-isländischen Literatur* (1904).
  P. 891.
Wellendorf, Jonas. "The Attraction of the Earliest Old Norse Vernacular
  Hagiography." In Haki Antonsson and Ildar H. Garipzanov, ed.
  >> *Saints and Their Lives on the Periphery* (2010). Pp. 241–58, esp.
  p. 253n34.
Wolf, Kirsten. "The Severed Breast: A Topos in the Legends of Female
  Virgin Martyr Saints." *ANF* 112 (1997): 97–112, esp. pp. 98–9
  and 104.
– "Female Scribes at Work? A Consideration of Kirkjubæjarbók (Codex
  AM 429 12mo)." In A.N. Doane and Kirsten Wolf, ed. >> *Beatus Vir*
  (2006). Pp. 265–95, esp. pp. 271 and 279.
– "On the Transmission of the Old Norse–Icelandic Legend of Saints

Faith, Hope, and Charity." In Kirsten Wolf and Johanna Denzin, ed.
>> *Romance and Love in Late Medieval and Early Modern Iceland*
(2008). Pp. 257–77.
Handlist, p. 310.

2. Fídesar saga, Spesar ok Karítasar

A translation characterized by editorial revisions of a version of the
passio presented by *BHL* 2871.

Manuscript:
AM 233a fol. (ca. 1350–75, defective).
Editions:
Unger, C.R., ed. >> *Heilagra manna søgur* (1877). Vol. 1, pp. 369–372.15.
Wolf, Kirsten. "Saga af Fídes, Spes ok Karítas." *Gripla* 22 (2011): 41–61,
esp. pp. 56–8.
Literature:
Ásdís Egilsdóttir. "Kvendýrlingar og kvenímynd trúarlegra bókmennta
á Íslandi." In Inga Huld Hákonardóttir, ed. >> *Konur og kristsmenn*
(1996). Pp. 93–116, esp. p. 93.
Bekker-Nielsen, Hans, Thorkil Damsgaard Olsen, and Ole Widding.
>> *Norrøn fortællekunst* (1965). Pp. 124–5.
Boyer, Régis. >> *La vie religieuse en Islande* (1979). P. 224.
Bruvoll, Kjersti. "The Good, the Bad and the Devil! On Rewriting a
Religious Motif in Some Virgin Martyr Legends." In Agneta Ney,
Henrik Williams, and Fredrik Charpentier Ljungqvist, ed.
>> *Á austrvega: Sagas and East Scandinavia* (2009). Vol. 1,
pp. 136–43, esp. p. 136.
Carlé, Birte. >> *Jomfru-fortællingen* (1985). Pp. 35–6 and 79–81.
Cormack, Margaret. >> *The Saints in Iceland* (1994). Pp. 37–8.
Finnur Jónsson. >> *Den oldnorske og oldislandske Litteraturs Historie*
(1920–4). Vol. 2, p. 931.
Lehmann, Paul. >> "Skandinaviens Anteil an der lateinischen Literatur
und Wissenschaft des Mittelalters" (1937). P. 44.
Lindow, John. "Norse Mythology and the Lives of the Saints." *SS* 73
(2001): 437–56, esp. p. 447.
Mogk, Eugen. >> *Geschichte der norwegisch-isländischen Literatur* (1904).
P. 891.
Tveitane, Mattias. "Interpretatio Norroena: Norrøne og antikke

gudenavn i *Clemens saga.*" In >> *The Sixth International Saga Confer-
ence* (1985). Vol. 2, pp. 1067–82, esp. p. 1080.
Wellendorf, Jonas. "The Attraction of the Earliest Old Norse Vernacu-
lar Hagiography." In Haki Antonsson and Ildar H. Garipzanov, ed.
>> *Saints and Their Lives on the Periphery* (2010). Pp. 241–58, esp.
p. 253n34.
Wolf, Kirsten. "The Severed Breast: A Topos in the Legends of Female
Virgin Martyr Saints." *ANF* 112 (1997): 97–112, esp. pp. 98–9 and 104.
– "On the Transmission of the Old Norse–Icelandic Legend of Saints
Faith, Hope, and Charity." In Kirsten Wolf and Johanna Denzin, ed.
>> *Romance and Love in Late Medieval and Early Modern Iceland*
(2008). Pp. 257–77.
Wolf, Kirsten, ed. >> *A Female Legendary from Iceland* (2011). Pp. 49–51.
Handlist, p. 310.

FORTY ARMENIAN MARTYRS   March 10

1. XL riddara saga

Based on a version of *BHL* 7539.

Manuscript:
AM 655 4to XXXIII (ca. 1250–1300).
Edition:
Unger, C.R., ed. >> *Heilagra manna søgur* (1877). Vol. 2, pp. 219.6–221.
Literature:
Bekker-Nielsen, Hans, Thorkil Damsgaard Olsen, and Ole Widding.
>> *Norrøn fortællekunst* (1965). P. 124.
Boyer, Régis. >> *La vie religieuse en Islande* (1979). P. 224.
Cormack, Margaret. >> *The Saints in Iceland* (1994). P. 37.
Finnur Jónsson. >> *Den oldnorske og oldislandske Litteraturs Historie*
(1920–4). Vol. 2, p. 874.
Hreinn Benediktsson. "Tvö handritsbrot." *Lingua Islandica – Íslenzk
tunga* 5 (1964): 139–49, esp. pp. 144–8.
Jakob Benediktsson. "Helgener." *KLNM* 21 (1977). Cols. 194–5.
Kirby, Ian. >> *Biblical Quotation* (1980). Vol. 2, p. 48.
Lehmann, Paul. >> "Skandinaviens Anteil an der lateinischen Literatur
und Wissenschaft des Mittelalters" (1937). P. 45.

Mogk, Eugen. >> *Geschichte der norwegisch-isländischen Literatur* (1904).
   P. 892.
Handlist, p. 310.

2. XL riddara saga

Based on a version of *BHL* 7539.

Manuscript:
AM 623 4to (ca. 1325, defective).
Editions:
Finnur Jónsson, ed. *AM 623, 4°: Helgensagaer*. STUAGNL 52 (Copen-
   hagen: Jørgensen, 1927). Pp. 25.7–33.8.
Unger, C.R., ed. >> *Heilagra manna søgur* (1877). Vol. 2, pp. 211–
   219.3.
Literature:
Bekker-Nielsen, Hans, Thorkil Damsgaard Olsen, and Ole Widding.
   >> *Norrøn fortællekunst* (1965). P. 124.
Boyer, Régis. >> *La vie religieuse en Islande* (1979). P. 224.
Cormack, Margaret. >> *The Saints in Iceland* (1994). P. 37.
Jakob Benediktsson. "Helgener." *KLNM* 21 (1977). Cols. 194–5.
Kirby, Ian. *Biblical Quotation* (1980). Vol. 2, p. 48.
Konráð Gíslason. *Um frum-parta íslenzkrar túngu í fornöld* (Copenhagen:
   Trier, 1846). P. liv.
Lehmann, Paul. >> "Skandinaviens Anteil an der lateinischen Literatur
   und Wissenschaft des Mittelalters" (1937). P. 45.
Mogk, Eugen. >> *Geschichte der norwegisch-isländischen Literatur* (1904).
   P. 892.
Handlist, p. 310.

FRANCIS OF ASSISI   October 4

Af Francisco

A tale of Saint Francis of Assisi incorporated into the miracles of the
Virgin Mary.

Manuscripts:
See Mary the Blessed Virgin 3 note (p. 245).

Edition:
Unger, C.R., ed. >> *Mariu saga* (1871). Pp. 811.23–812.
Literature:
Sverrir Tómasson. "Kristnar trúarbókmenntir í óbundnu máli." In
   Guðrún Nordal, Sverrir Tómasson, and Vésteinn Ólason, ed.
   >> *Íslensk Bókmenntasaga* 1 (1992). Pp. 419–79, esp. p. 432.
Handlist, pp. 310 and 323.

FULBERT OF CHARTRES   April 10

Af Fulberto

Tales of Saint Fulbert of Chartres incorporated into the miracles of the
Virgin Mary.

Manuscripts:
See Mary the Blessed Virgin 3 note (p. 245).
Edition:
Unger, C.R., ed. >> *Mariu saga* (1871). Pp. 549.6–554.2 and
   724.33–725.11.
Literature:
Widding, Ole. "Norrøne Marialegender på europæisk baggrund."
   Opuscula 10. Bibliotheca Arnamagnæana 40 (Copenhagen: Reitzel,
   1996). Pp. 1–128, esp. pp. 37 and 84.
Handlist, pp. 310 and 323.

GANGULPHUS   May 11

Af Sindulfo ok hans frú

A tale of Saint Gangulphus ultimately related to *BHL* 3328.

Manuscript:
AM 657a–b 4to (ca. 1350).
Edition:
Gering, Hugo, ed. >> *Islendzk æventyri* (1882–3). Vol. 1, pp. 28–30.
German paraphrase:
Gering, Hugo, ed. >> *Islendzk æventyri* (1882–3). Vol. 2, pp. 17–18.

Literature:
Cormack, Margaret. >> *The Saints in Iceland* (1994). P. 35.
Wolf, Kirsten, ed. >> *Heilagra meyja sögur* (2003). P. lii.
Handlist, p. 310.

GEORGE THE GREAT   April 23

1. Georgíuss saga

Translated from a now-lost Low German redaction that resembles the
source(s) of *Der Heiligen Leben*.

Manuscript:
Stock. Perg. fol. no. 3 (*Reykjahólabók*) (ca. 1530–40).
Edition:
Loth, Agnete, ed. >> *Reykjahólabók* (1969–70). Vol. 1, pp. 297–373.
Literature:
Bekker-Nielsen, Hans, Thorkil Damsgaard Olsen, and Ole Widding.
    >> *Norrøn fortællekunst* (1965). P. 140.
Jónas Kristjánsson. >> *Eddas and Sagas* (1988). P. 145.
Kalinke, Marianne E. "Reykjahólabók: A Legendary on the Eve of the
    Reformation." *Skáldskaparmál* 2 (1992): 239–69, esp. pp. 240, 246–7,
    and 261–4.
– >> *The Book of Reykjahólar* (1996). Pp. 28, 50, 95, 97, 99–101, 103,
    114, 165–6, 174–9, and 198–200.
Sverrir Tómasson. "Trúarbókmenntir í lausu máli á síðmiðöld." In Böðvar
    Guðmundsson, Sverrir Tómasson, Torfi H. Tulinius, and Vésteinn
    Ólason, ed. >> *Íslensk Bókmenntasaga* 2 (1993). Pp. 249–82, esp. p. 279.
Widding, Ole, and Hans Bekker-Nielsen. "En senmiddelalderlig
    legendesamling." *Mm* (1960): 105–28, esp. pp. 107 and 117.
– "Low German Influence on Late Icelandic Hagiography." *GR* 37
    (1962): 239–62, esp. pp. 249 and 255.
Handlist, p. 310.

GEREON   October 10

A passion of Saint Gereon based on *BHL* 3446 in a paraphrased and
abridged form included in *Máritíuss saga* 2.

Manuscripts:
See Maurice 2 note (p. 258).
Editions:
Foote, Peter, ed. >> *Lives of Saints* (1962).
  Facsimile of Stock. Perg. fol. no. 2.
Unger, C.R., ed. >> *Heilagra manna søgur* (1877). Vol. 1, pp. 643–644.20,
  645.2–11, 645.18–43, 646.22–26, 646.38–647.24, 651.22–653.13, and
  654.9–656.22.
Literature:
Cormack, Margaret. >> *The Saints in Iceland* (1994). P. 34.
Stefán Karlsson. "Inventio Crucis, cap 1, og Veraldar saga." In *Opuscula
  Septentrionalia: Festskrift til Ole Widding 10.10.1977* (Copenhagen:
  Reitzel, 1977). Pp. 116–33, esp. pp. 131–3.

GILES   September 1

Egidíuss saga

A translation of *BHL* 93.

Manuscript:
AM 238 fol. XVI (ca. 1450–1500).
Edition:
Loth, Agnete. "Egidius saga hins helga. Fragmentet AM 238 XVI, fol."
  Opuscula 3. Bibliotheca Arnamagnæana 29 (Copenhagen: Munks-
  gaard, 1967). Pp. 62–73, esp. pp. 66–73.
Literature:
Handlist, p. 310.

GREGORY THE GREAT   March 12

1. Af Gregor

A short passage about Saint Gregory to be read on his feast-day. The
source has not been established.

Manuscript:
AM 686b 4to (ca. 1200–25, defective).

Edition:
Þorvaldur Bjarnarson, ed. *Leifar fornra kristinna fræða íslenzkra: Codex Arna-Magnæanus 677 4to auk annara enna elztu brota af íslenzkum guðfræðisritum* (Copenhagen: Hagerup, 1878). Pp. 167.29–168.3.
Literature:
Cormack, Margaret.>> *The Saints in Iceland* (1994). Pp. 37n45 and 240.
Konráð Gíslason. *Um frum-parta íslenzkrar túngu í fornöld* (Copenhagen: Trier, 1846). P. c.

2. Gregors saga páfa

A translation based on *BHL* 3640 and augmented with material from *BHL* 3641.

Manuscripts:
AM 921 4to IV 2 (ca. 1250–75) and Stock. Perg. fol. no. 2 (ca. 1425–45, defective).
Editions:
Foote, Peter, ed. >> *Lives of Saints* (1962).
  Facsimile of Stock. Perg. fol. no. 2.
Hreinn Benediktsson, ed. *The Life of St. Gregory and His Dialogues. Fragments of an Icelandic Manuscript from the 13th Century*. Editiones Arnamagnæanæ, Ser. B, vol. 4 (Copenhagen: Munksgaard, 1963). Pp. 51–3.
  Edition of AM 921 4to IV 2.
Morgenstern, Gustav, ed. >> *Arnamagnæanische Fragmente* (1893), pp. 47–9.
  Edition of AM 921 4to IV 2.
Unger, C.R., ed. >> *Heilagra manna søgur* (1877). Vol. 1, pp. 377–395.18.
  Edition of Stock. Perg. fol. no. 2.
Literature:
Bekker-Nielsen, Hans. "Kyrkofäderna ock kyrkolärarna. K. i vestnordisk litteratur." *KLNM* 9 (1964). Cols. 690–3, esp. col. 693.
– "Et par ord om de ældste norrøne helgensagaer." In Finn Hødnebø et al., ed. >> *Eyvindarbók* (1992). Pp. 29–33, esp. p. 32.
Bekker-Nielsen, Hans, Thorkil Damsgaard Olsen, and Ole Widding. >> *Norrøn fortællekunst* (1965). P. 126.
Bekker-Nielsen, Hans, and Ole Widding. "Legende. Norge og Island." *KLNM* 10 (1965). Cols. 421–3, esp. col. 421.
Carlé, Birte. >> *Jomfru-fortællingen* (1985). Pp. 39, 59–60, and 74–5.

– "Men and Women in the Saints' Sagas of *Stock. 2, fol.*" In John
Lindow, Lars Lönnroth, and Gerd Wolfgang Weber, ed. >> *Structure
and Meaning in Old Norse Literature* (1986). Pp. 317–46, esp. pp. 320,
324, 327–8, and 334.

Cormack, Margaret. >> *The Saints in Iceland* (1994). Pp. 97 and 241.

Hofmann, Dietrich. *Die Legende von Sankt Clemens in den skandinavischen Ländern im Mittelalter*. Beiträge zur Skandinavistik 13
(Frankfurt am Main: Peter Lang, 1997). Pp. 116–18.

Jónas Kristjánsson. >> *Eddas and Sagas* (1988). P. 142.

Kalinke, Marianne E. >> *The Book of Reykjahólar* (1996). P. 39.

Lehmann, Paul. >> "Skandinaviens Anteil an der lateinischen Literatur
und Wissenschaft des Mittelalters" (1937). Pp. 44 and 80.

Mogk, Eugen. >> *Geschichte der norwegisch-isländischen Literatur* (1904).
P. 893.

Schier, Kurt. *Sagaliteratur*. Sammlung Metzler M78 (Stuttgart: Metzler,
1970). P. 129.

Svanhildur Óskarsdóttir. "Universal History in Fourteenth-Century
Iceland: Studies in AM 764 4to." PhD dissertation, University of
London, 2000. Pp. 196–7.

Widding, Ole, and Hans Bekker-Nielsen. "En senmiddelalderlig
legendesamling." *Mm* (1960): 105–28, esp. p. 118.

– "Low German Influence on Late Icelandic Hagiography." *GR* 37
(1962): 239–62, esp. p. 248.

Wolf, Kirsten. "Gregory's Influence on Old Norse–Icelandic Religious
Literature." In *Rome and the North: The Early Reception of Gregory the
Great in Germanic Europe*. Ed. Rolf H. Bremmer Jr, Kees Dekker, and
David F. Johnson (Paris: Peeters, 2001). Pp. 255–74, esp. pp. 271–2.

Handlist, p. 311.

3. Gregors saga páfa

A translation of *BHL* 3641.

Manuscripts:
AM 238 fol. X (ca. 1300–50) and NRA 71 (ca. 1250–75, defective).

Editions:
Hreinn Benediktsson, ed. *The Life of St. Gregory and His Dialogues.
Fragments of an Icelandic Manuscript from the 13th Century*. Editiones
Arnamagnæanæ, Ser. B, vol. 4 (Copenhagen: Munksgaard, 1963). P. 54.
Edition of NRA 71.

Unger, C.R., ed. >> *Heilagra manna søgur* (1877). Vol. 1, pp. 395.20–396.3.
Edition of NRA 71.
Wolf, Kirsten. "A Fragment of a *Gregorius saga* in AM 238 fol. X."
Opuscula 9. Bibliotheca Arnamagnæana 39 (Copenhagen: Reitzel,
1991). Pp. 100–7, esp. p. 103.
Edition of AM 238 fol. X.

Literature:
Bekker-Nielsen, Hans, and Ole Widding. "Legende. Norge og Island."
KLNM 10 (1965). Cols. 421–3, esp. col. 421.
Cormack, Margaret. >> *The Saints in Iceland* (1994). Pp. 37n45, 77n12,
97, and 241.
Foote, Peter, ed. *Lives of Saints* (1962). Pp. 22–3.
– "Auðræði." In Arthur Brown and Peter Foote, ed. >> *Early English and
Norse Studies* (1963). Pp. 62–76, esp. pp. 64–5.
Lönnroth, Lars. "Det litterära porträttet i latinsk historiografi och isländsk
sagaskrivning – en komparativ studie." *ANF* 27 (1969): 68–117, esp. p. 85.
Mogk, Eugen. >> *Geschichte der norwegisch-isländischen Literatur* (1904).
P. 893.
Stefán Karlsson. "Islandsk bogeksport til Norge i middelalderen." *Mm*
(1979): 1–17, esp. pp. 6 and 8. Rpt. in *Stafkrókar: Ritgerðir eftir Stefán
Karlsson gefnar út í tilefni af sjötugsafmæli hans 2. desember 1998*. Ed.
Guðvarður Már Gunnlaugsson (Reykjavík: Stofnun Árna Magnússo-
nar, 2000). Pp. 188–205, esp. pp. 194 and 197.
Svanhildur Óskarsdóttir. "Universal History in Fourteenth-Century
Iceland: Studies in AM 764 4to." PhD dissertation, University of
London, 2000. P. 197.
Widding, Ole, and Hans Bekker-Nielsen. "En senmiddelalderlig
legendesamling." *Mm* (1960): 105–28, esp. p. 118.
– "Low German Influence on Late Icelandic Hagiography." *GR* 37
(1962): 239–62, esp. p. 248.
Wolf, Kirsten. "Gregory's Influence on Old Norse–Icelandic Religious
Literature." In *Rome and the North: The Early Reception of Gregory the
Great in Germanic Europe*. Ed. Rolf H. Bremmer Jr, Kees Dekker, and
David F. Johnson (Paris: Peeters, 2001). Pp. 255–74, esp. pp. 271–2.
Handlist, p. 311.

4. Gregors saga páfa

Based ultimately on a version of the legend in Jacobus de Voragine's
Legenda aurea.

Manuscript:
AM 764 4to (ca. 1376–86).
Editions:
Svanhildur Óskarsdóttir. "Universal History in Fourteenth-Century
  Iceland: Studies in AM 764 4to." PhD dissertation, University of
  London, 2000. Pp. 288–90.
Wolf, Kirsten. "An Excerpt on Saint Gregory the Great in AM 764, 4to."
  In Ásdís Egilsdóttir and Rudolf Simek, ed. >> *Sagnaheimur* (2001).
  Pp. 287–94, esp. pp. 288–9.
Literature:
Bekker-Nielsen, Hans. "Kyrkofäderna ock kyrkolärarna. K. i vestnordisk
  litteratur." *KLNM* 9 (1964). Cols. 690–3, esp. col. 693.
Cormack, Margaret. >> *The Saints in Iceland* (1994). P. 35.
Tveitane, Mattias. *Den lærde stil. Oversetterprosa i den norrøne versjonen
  av Vitæ Patrum.* Årbok for Universitetet i Bergen, Humanistisk Serie
  1967, No. 2 (Bergen and Oslo: Norwegian Universities Press, 1968).
  P. 19.
Wolf, Kirsten. "Gregory's Influence on Old Norse–Icelandic Religious
  Literature." In *Rome and the North: The Early Reception of Gregory the
  Great in Germanic Europe.* Ed. Rolf H. Bremmer Jr, Kees Dekker, and
  David F. Johnson (Paris: Peeters, 2001). Pp. 255–74, esp. pp. 272–3.
Wolf, Kirsten, ed. >> *Heilagra meyja sögur* (2003). P. li.
Handlist, p. 311.

5. Gregors saga páfa

Translated from a now-lost Low German redaction that resembles the
source(s) of *Der Heiligen Leben.*

Manuscript:
Stock. Perg. fol. no. 3 (*Reykjahólabók*) (ca. 1530–40).
Edition:
Loth, Agnete, ed. >> *Reykjahólabók* (1969–70). Vol. 2, pp. 31–56.
Literature:
Bekker-Nielsen, Hans. "Kyrkofäderna ock kyrkolärarna. K. i vestnordisk
  litteratur." *KLNM* 9 (1964). Cols. 690–3, esp. col. 693.
Bekker-Nielsen, Hans, Thorkil Damsgaard Olsen, and Ole Widding.
  >> *Norrøn fortællekunst* (1965). Pp. 126 and 141.
Kalinke, Marianne E. "Reykjahólabók: A Legendary on the Eve of the
  Reformation." *Skáldskaparmál* 2 (1992): 239–69, esp. p. 240.

– "The Cowherd and the Saint: The Grateful Lion in Icelandic Folklore and Legend." *SS* 66 (1994): 1–22, esp. p. 10.
– >> *The Book of Reykjahólar* (1996). Pp. 28, 39, 50, 79, 108, and 160–1.
Widding, Ole, and Hans Bekker-Nielsen. "En senmiddelalderlig legendesamling." *Mm* (1960): 105–28, esp. pp. 107, 118–19, and 127.
– "Low German Influence on Late Icelandic Hagiography." *GR* 37 (1962): 239–62, esp. pp. 248, 255, and 259.
Wolf, Kirsten. "Gregory's Influence on Old Norse–Icelandic Religious Literature." In *Rome and the North: The Early Reception of Gregory the Great in Germanic Europe*. Ed. Rolf H. Bremmer Jr, Kees Dekker, and David F. Johnson (Paris: Peeters, 2001). Pp. 255–74, esp. pp. 272–3.
Handlist, p. 311.

6. Af Gregorio

A tale of Saint Gregory the Great incorporated into the miracles of the Virgin Mary.

Manuscripts:
See Mary the Blessed Virgin 3 note (p. 245).
Edition:
Unger, C.R., ed. >> *Mariu saga* (1871). Pp. 224.22–225 and 1172.23–1173.18.
Literature:
Bekker-Nielsen, Hans. "Kyrkofäderna ock kyrkolärarna. K. i vestnordisk litteratur." *KLNM* 9 (1964). Cols. 690–3, esp. col. 693.
Heizmann, Wilhelm. "Liebe und Durst: Der Heilige Bernhard von Clairvaux in der altisländischen Mirakelüberlieferung." *Opuscula* 13. Bibliotheca Arnamagnæana 47 (Copenhagen: Museum Tusculanum Press, 2010). Pp. 55–118, esp. p. 109.
Widding, Ole. "Norrøne Marialegender på europæisk baggrund." *Opuscula* 10. Bibliotheca Arnamagnæana 40 (Copenhagen: Reitzel, 1996. Pp. 1–128, esp. p. 33.
Handlist, pp. 311 and 323.

GREGORY'S DIALOGUES

Díalógar (Viðrœður) Gregors páfa

Old Norwegian and Old Icelandic translations of the *Dialogi* of Gregory the Great.

Manuscripts:
AM 239 fol. (ca. 1350–1400, defective), AM 629 4to (1697), AM 655 4to XV
(ca. 1250–1300), AM 667 4to XIV (ca. 1400), AM 677 4to (ca. 1200–25,
defective), AM 764 4to (ca. 1376–86), AM 921 4to IV 1 (ca. 1250–75),
NRA 71 (ca. 1250–75), NRA 72 & 76 (ca. 1250–75), NRA 72 B (ca.
1250–75), NRA 77 (ca. 1300–50), and Stock. Perg. fol. no. 2 (ca. 1425–45).

Editions:
Foote, Peter, ed.. *Lives of Saints* (1962).
 Facsimile of Stock. Perg. fol. no. 2.
Hreinn Benediktsson, ed. *The Life of St. Gregory and His Dialogues. Frag-
 ments of an Icelandic Manuscript from the 13th Century.* Editiones Ar-
 namagnæanæ, Ser. B, vol. 4 (Copenhagen: Munksgaard, 1963). Pp. 55–62.
 Edition of NRA 71 (p. 55.2–23), AM 921 4to IV 1 (pp. 55.26–57),
 NRA 72 & 76 (pp. 58–9), and NRA 72 B (p. 60).
– *Early Icelandic Script As Illustrated in Vernacular Texts from the
 Twelfth and Thirteenth Centuries.* Íslenzk handrit: Icelandic Manu-
 scripts, Series in Folio 2 (Reykjavík: The Manuscript Institute of
 Iceland, 1965). Plates 26 and 66 and p. xliv
 Facsimile of AM 677 4to fol. 39v and facsimile and edition of AM 655
 4to XV fol. 1v.
Konráð Gíslason, ed. *Fire og fyrretyve for en stor Deel forhen utrykte
 Prøver af oldnordisk Sprog og Literatur* (Copenhagen: Gyldendal,
 1860). Pp. 457–8.
 Edition of AM 677 4to (extract only).
Morgenstern, Gustav, ed. >> *Arnamagnæanische Fragmente* (1893). Pp. 44–7.
 Edition of AM 921 4to IV 1.
Seip, D.A., ed. *The Arna-Magnæan Manuscript 677, 4to: Pseudo-Cyprian
 Fragments, Prosper's Epigrams, Gregory's Homilies and Dialogues.* CCI
 18 (Copenhagen: Einar Munksgaard, 1949).
 Facsimile of AM 677 4to.
Unger, C.R., ed. >> *Heilagra manna søgur* (1877). Vol. 1, pp. 179.8–255.
 Based on AM 239 fol. (pp. 179.9–198.1), AM 677 4to (pp. 198.1–241.34
 and 242.26–250), NRA 72 (pp. 241.35–242.24), and NRA 77 (pp.
 188.32–40, 189.28–41, 190.30–41, 191.23–42, 192.28–41, 193.31–41,
 and 250.35–255) with variants from AM 239 fol. (pp. 198.1–211.13),
 NRA 77 (pp. 207.28–211.13), AM 655 4to XV (pp. 228.9–229.28), and
 NRA 71 (pp. 234.17–34).
Þorvaldur Bjarnarson, ed. *Leifar fornra kristinna fræða íslenzkra: Codex
 Arna-Magnæanus 677 4to auk annara enna elztu brota af íslenzkum
 guðfræðisritum* (Copenhagen: Thiele, 1878). Pp. 87–150.
 Edition of AM 677 4to.

Wolf, Kirsten. "Two Exempla." *Gripla.*
[Forthcoming.] Edition of the exemplum in AM 629 4to.
Literature:
Ashurst, David. "Imagining Paradise." In John McKinnell, David
   Ashurst, and Donata Kick, ed. >> *The Fantastic in Old Norse / Iceland-
   ic Literature* (2006). Vol. 1, pp. 71–80, esp. pp. 76–9.
Astås, Reidar. "Spor av teologisk tenkning og refleksjon i norsk og
   islandsk høymiddelalder." *CM* 6 (1993): 133–67, esp. pp. 137n19,
   138n22, and 147.
Bekker-Nielsen, Hans. "Kyrkofäderna ock kyrkolärarna. K. i vestnordisk
   litteratur." *KLNM* 9 (1964). Cols. 690–3, esp. col. 691.
Bekker-Nielsen, Hans, Thorkil Damsgaard Olsen, and Ole Widding.
   >> *Norrøn fortællekunst* (1965). Pp. 24 and 150.
Bekker-Nielsen, Hans, and Ole Widding. "Religiøs prosalitteratur. Norge
   og Island." *KLNM* 14 (1969). Cols. 42–4, esp. col. 43.
Boyer, Régis. "The Influence of Pope Gregory's *Dialogues* on Old Ice-
   landic Literature." In Peter Foote, Hermann Pálsson, and Desmond
   Slay, ed. >> *Proceedings of the First International Saga Conference*
   (1973). Pp. 1–27.
– >> *La vie religieuse en Islande* (1979). Pp. 163–76, 218, 224, and 384.
– "Gregory, St.: Dialogues." In Phillip Pulsiano and Kirsten Wolf, with Paul
   Acker and Donald K. Fry, ed. >> *Medieval Scandinavia* (1993). P. 241.
– "Les références expresses à la littérature dans les 'Sagas de contempor-
   ains'." In Gísli Sigurðsson, Guðrún Kvaran, and Sigurgeir Steingrímsson,
   ed. >> *Sagnaþing helgað Jónasi Kristjánssyni* (1994). Vol. 1, pp. 87–96.
Carlé, Birte. >> *Jomfru-fortællingen* (1985). P. 64.
Clunies Ross, Margaret. "The Art of Poetry and the Figure of the Poet in
   Egils saga." *Parergon* 22 (1978): 3–12, esp. p. 7. Rpt. in *Sagas of the
   Icelanders: A Book of Essays.* Ed. John Tucker (New York: Garland,
   1989). Pp. 126–45, esp. p. 140.
Cormack, Margaret J. "Saints and Sinners: Reflections on Death in Some
   Icelandic Sagas." *Gripla* 8 (1993): 187–218, esp. p. 189.
– >> *The Saints in Iceland* (1994). Pp. 84 and 97.
– "Saints' Lives and Icelandic Literature in the Thirteenth and Four-
   teenth Centuries." In Hans Bekker-Nielsen and Birte Carlé, ed.
   >> *Saints and Sagas* (1994). Pp. 27–47, esp. p. 39.
– "Sagas of Saints." In *Old Icelandic Literature and Society.* Ed. Mar-
   garet Clunies Ross (Cambridge: Cambridge University Press, 2000).
   Pp. 302–25, esp. pp. 304 and 306.
Crook, Eugene J. "Gregory's *Dialogi* and the Old Norse Sagas: *Njáls
   saga.*" In *Rome and the North: The Early Reception of Gregory the*

Great in Germanic Europe. Ed. Rolf H. Bremmer Jr, Kees Dekker, and David F. Johnson (Paris: Peeters, 2001) Pp. 275–85.

Einar Ól. Sveinsson. *Á Njálsbúð. Bók um mikið listaverk* (Reykjavík: Hið íslenzka bókmenntafélag, 1943). Pp. 10–11 and 171.

Falk, Oren. "Fragments of Fourteenth-Century Icelandic Folklore." In John McKinnell, David Ashurst, and Donata Kick, ed. >> *The Fantastic in Old Norse / Icelandic Literature* (2006). Vol. 1, pp. 231–40, esp. p. 235.

Finnur Jónsson. >> *Den oldnorske og oldislandske Litteraturs Historie* (1920–4). Vol. 2, p. 929.

Foote, Peter. "Saints' Lives and Sagas." In Hans Bekker-Nielsen and Birte Carlé, ed. >> *Saints and Sagas* (1994). Pp. 73–88, esp. p. 79.

Gísli Sigurðsson. *The Medieval Icelandic Saga and Oral Tradition*. Publications of the Milman Parry Collection of Oral Literature 2 (Cambridge, Mass.: Harvard University Press, 2004). Pp. 24–5.

Hallberg, Peter. "Imagery in Religious Old Norse Prose Literature: An Outline." *ANF* 102 (1987): 120–70, esp. pp. 129, 133, 144, and 154–5.

Harris, Joseph, and Thomas D. Hill. "Gestr's 'Prime Sign': Source and Signification in *Norna-Gests þáttr*." *ANF* 104 (1989): 103–22, esp. pp. 103–4 and 113–17.

Hill, Thomas D. "The Evisceration of Bróðir in 'Brennu-Njáls saga'." *Traditio* 37 (1981): 437–44, esp. p. 439.

Holm-Olsen, Ludvig. "Middelalderens litteratur i Norge." In *Norges litteratur historie* 1. Ed. Edvard Beyer (Oslo: Cappelen, 1974). Pp. 18–342, esp. pp. 53–4.

Jónas Kristjánsson. *Um Fóstbrœðra sögu* (Reykjavík: Stofnun Árna Magnússonar, 1972). P. 288.

– >> *Eddas and Sagas* (1988). P. 130.

Jørgensen, Jørgen Højgaard. "Hagiography and the Icelandic Bishop Sagas." *Peritia* 1 (1982): 1–16, esp. p. 4.

Kirby, Ian. >> *Biblical Quotation* (1980). Vol. 2, pp. 40–1 and 70–2.

– *Bible Translation in Old Norse*. Université de Lausanne Publications de la faculté des lettres 27 (Geneva: Librairie Droz, 1986). Pp. 35, 42, 92, 94–6, and 98.

Konráð Gíslason. *Um frum-parta íslenzkrar túngu í fornöld* (Copenhagen: Trier, 1846). Pp. xcv–xcviii.

Kratz, Henry. "The Language of the Old Norse Saints' Lives." *Mm* (1988): 159–73.

– "Saints' Lives. 2. Iceland and Norway." In Phillip Pulsiano and Kirsten Wolf, with Paul Acker and Donald K. Fry, ed. >> *Medieval Scandinavia* (1993). Pp. 562–4.

Lönnroth, Lars. *Njáls saga: A Critical Introduction* (Berkeley: University of California Press, 1976). Pp. 17, 38, 121–2, and 125.

McCreesh, Bernadine. "Elements of the Pagan Supernatural in the Bishops' Sagas." In John McKinnell, David Ashurst, and Donata Kick, ed. >> *The Fantastic in Old Norse/Icelandic Literature* (2006). Vol. 2, pp. 671–80, esp. p. 673.

Ólafur Halldórsson. "Rímbeglusmiður." *Opuscula* 2.2. Bibliotheca Arnamagnæana 25.2 (Copenhagen: Reitzel, 1977). Pp. 32–49, esp. p. 37n18. Rpt. in Ólafur Halldórsson. *Grettisfærsla: Safn ritgerða eftir Ólaf Halldórsson gefið út á sjötugsafmæli hans 18. april 1990* (Reykjavík: Stofnun Árna Magnússonar, 1990). Pp. 302–18, esp. p. 307n18.

Paasche, Fredrik. *Kristendom og kvad: En studie i norrøn middelalder* (Kristiania [Oslo]: Aschehoug, 1914). Pp. 67–8 and 166.

– *Norges og Islands litteratur inntil utgangen av middelalderen*. Rev. ed. by Anne Holtsmark (Oslo: Aschehoug, 1947). Pp. 297–8, 301, 307, 373, 429, 446, and 451.

Pizarro, Joaquín Martínez. "Conversion Narratives: Form and Utility." In >> *The Sixth International Saga Conference* (1985). Vol. 2, pp. 813–32, esp. p. 821.

Salvucci, Giovanna. "Between Heaven and Hell: The *Konungasǫgur* and the Emergence of the Idea of Purgatory." In John McKinnell, David Ashurst, and Donata Kick, ed. >> *The Fantastic in Old Norse/Icelandic Literature* (2006). Vol. 2, pp. 866–75, esp. pp. 866–7.

Seip, Didrik Arup. "Om oversettelsen av 'Gregors dialoger'." In Didrik Arup Seip. *Nye studier i norsk språkhistorie* (Oslo: Aschehoug, 1954). Pp. 92–100.

Stefán Karlsson. "Islandsk bogeksport til Norge i middelalderen." *Mm* (1979): 1–17, esp. pp. 6 and 8. Rpt. in *Stafkrókar: Ritgerðir eftir Stefán Karlsson gefnar út í tilefni af sjötugsafmæli hans 2. desember 1998*. Ed. Guðvarður Már Gunnlaugsson (Reykjavík: Stofnun Árna Magnússonar, 2000). Pp. 188–205, esp. pp. 194 and 197.

Strömbäck, Dag A. "Some Remarks on Learned and Novelistic Elements in the Icelandic Sagas." In *Nordica et Anglica: Studies in Honor of Stefán Einarsson*. Ed. Allan H. Orrick. Janua Linguarum, Series Maior 22 (The Hague: Mouton, 1968). Pp. 140–7.

– *The Conversion of Iceland: A Survey*. Trans. and annot. by Peter Foote (London: Viking Society for Northern Research, 1975). Pp. 94–109.

Strömbäck, Dag. "Visionsdiktning." *KLNM* 20 (1976). Cols. 171–86, esp. cols. 174 and 181.

Svanhildur Óskarsdóttir. "Universal History in Fourteenth-Century Iceland: Studies in AM 764 4to." PhD dissertation, University of London, 2000. Pp. 90, 144n157, and 240.

– "Prose of Christian Instruction." In *A Companion to Old Norse–Icelandic Literature*. Ed. Rory McTurk (Oxford: Blackwell, 2005). Pp. 338–53, esp. pp. 341–2 and 351.

Sverrir Tómasson. *Formálar íslenskra sagnaritara á miðöldum. Rannsókn bókmenntahefðar* (Reykjavík: Stofnun Árna Magnússonar, 1988). P. 199.

– "Erlendur vísdómur og forn fræði." In Guðrún Nordal, Sverrir Tómasson, and Vésteinn Ólason, ed. >> *Íslensk Bókmenntasaga* 1 (1992). Pp. 517–70, esp. pp. 547 and 549–51.

– "Trúarbókmenntir í lausu máli á síðmiðöld." In Böðvar Guðmundsson, Sverrir Tómasson, Torfi H. Tulinius, and Vésteinn Ólason, ed. >> *Íslensk Bókmenntasaga* 2 (1993). Pp. 249–82, esp. pp. 252, 270–1, and 275.

Turville-Petre, G. *The Heroic Age of Scandinavia* (London: Brendon and Sons, 1951). Pp. 134–5.

– >> *Origins of Icelandic Literature* (1967). Pp. 135–7.

Þórhallur Þorgilsson. "Um þýðingar og endursagnir úr ítölskum miðaldaritum." *Landsbókasafn Íslands. Árbók 1946–1947* (1948): 212–24, esp. pp. 214–16.

Vries, Jan de. >> *Altnordische Literaturgeschichte* (1964–7). Vol. 2, p. 182.

Wellendorf, Jonas. "Visions and the Fantastic." In John McKinnell, David Ashurst, and Donata Kick, ed. >> *The Fantastic in Old Norse/Icelandic Literature* (2006). Vol. 2, pp. 1025–33, esp. p. 1029.

Wolf, Kirsten. "Gregory's Influence on Old Norse–Icelandic Religious Literature." In *Rome and the North: The Early Reception of Gregory the Great in Germanic Europe*. Ed. Rolf H. Bremmer Jr, Kees Dekker, and David F. Johnson (Paris: Peeters, 2001). Pp. 255–74, esp. pp. 255 and 266–9.

Handlist, p. 311.

GREGORY ON THE STONE

Gregors saga biskups

Translated from a now-lost Low German redaction that resembles the source(s) of *Der Heiligen Leben*.

Manuscript:
Stock. Perg. fol. no. 3 (*Reykjahólabók*) (ca. 1530–40).
Edition:
Loth, Agnete, ed. >> *Reykjahólabók* (1969–70). Vol. 2, pp. 1–30.
Modern Icelandic language edition:
Sverrir Tómasson, Bragi Halldórsson, and Einar Sigurbjörnsson, ed.
   >> *Heilagra karla sögur* (2007). Pp. 317–51.
Literature:
Bekker-Nielsen, Hans, Thorkil Damsgaard Olsen, and Ole Widding.
   >> *Norrøn fortællekunst* (1965). P. 141.
Bekker-Nielsen, Hans, and Ole Widding. "Legende. Norge og Island."
   KLNM 10 (1965). Cols. 421–3, esp. col. 422.
Dillmann, François-Xavier. "Om hedningar och hundar. Kring den
   fornvästnordiska sammansättningen *hundheiðinn.*" *SI* 52 (2001): 17–33,
   esp. p. 21.
Jónas Kristjánsson. >> *Eddas and Sagas* (1988). Pp. 145–6.
Kalinke, Marianne E. "'Gregorius saga biskups' and 'Gregorius af dem
   Stein'." *Beiträge* 113 (1991): 67–88.
– "Reykjahólabók: A Legendary on the Eve of the Reformation."
   Skáldskaparmál 2 (1992): 239–69, esp. pp. 240, 265, and 268.
– "The Cowherd and the Saint: The Grateful Lion in Icelandic Folklore
   and Legend." *SS* 66 (1994): 1–22, esp. p. 7.
– >> *The Book of Reykjahólar* (1996). Pp. 28, 50, 79, 117, 121–3, 158,
   187, 201–11, 236, and 238.
Sverrir Tómasson. "Trúarbókmenntir í lausu máli á síðmiðöld." In Böðvar
   Guðmundsson, Sverrir Tómasson, Torfi H. Tulinius, and Vésteinn
   Ólason, ed. >> *Íslensk Bókmenntasaga* 2 (1993). Pp. 249–82, esp. p. 280.
Widding, Ole, and Hans Bekker-Nielsen. "En senmiddelalderlig
   legendesamling." *Mm* (1960): 105–28, esp. pp. 107, 118, and 127.
– "Low German Influence on Late Icelandic Hagiography." *GR* 37
   (1962): 239–62, esp. pp. 249–50.
Handlist, p. 311.

GREGORY THAUMATURGUS   November 17

Af Gregor Thaumarturgus

A version of the legend of Saint Gregory Thaumaturgus incorporated
into the Old Norwegian *Barlaams saga ok Jósafats.*

Manuscripts:
See Barlaam and Josaphat 1 note (p. 50).
Editions:
Keyser, R., and C.R. Unger, ed. *Barlaams ok Josaphats saga* (Christiania
    [Oslo]: Feilberg & Landmark, 1851). Pp. 63.31–67.10.
– ed. *Barlaams ok Josaphats saga.* Norrøne tekster 4 (Oslo: Norsk
    historisk kjeldeskrift-institutt, 1981). Pp. 55.3–58.11.
Literature:
Bekker-Nielsen, Hans, Thorkil Damsgaard Olsen, and Ole Widding.
    >> *Norrøn fortællekunst* (1965). P. 112.
Boyer, Régis. >> *La vie religieuse en Islande* (1979). P. 162.
Haugen, Odd Einar. "Exempla in Barlaams ok Josaphats saga." In
    >> *Sagas and the Norwegian Experience* (1997). Pp. 227–36, esp. p. 232.
– "Forteljingane i forteljinga. Interpolasjonane i *Barlaams ok Josaphats
    saga.*" In Karl G. Johansson and Maria Arvidsson, ed. >> *Barlaam i
    nord* (2009). Pp. 47–73, esp. pp. 58 and 69.
Handlist, pp. 302 and 312.

GUÐMUNDR THE GOOD   March 16

1. Guðmundar saga A

The so-called oldest saga of Bishop Guðmundr Arason, which is a
compilation of the *Prestssaga*, *Hrafns saga Sveinbjarnarsonar*, *Arons
saga Hjǫrleifssonar*, and annals.

Manuscripts:
AM 122b fol. (*Reykjarfjarðarbók*) (ca. 1375–1400, defective), AM 204 fol.
    (ca. 1650), AM 220 fol. II (ca. 1520–40), AM 394 4to (ca. 1575–1600,
    defective), AM 399 4to (*Codex Resenianus*) (ca. 1330–50, defective),
    AM 401 4to (ca. 1686–8, defective), AM 111 8vo (ca. 1575–1600,
    defective), Kall 256 fol. (1750–1800), and Stock. Papp. fol. no. 3 (1689).
Editions:
Guðni Jónsson, ed. *Byskupa sögur.* 3 vols. (Reykjavík: Íslendingasagnaút-
    gáfan; Haukadalsútgáfan, 1948). Vol. 2, pp. 179–410.
    Normalized text based on *Biskupa sögur.*
[Jón Sigurðsson and Guðbrandur Vigfússon, ed.] *Biskupa sögur.* 2 vols.
    (Copenhagen: Møller, 1858–78). Vol. 1, pp. 405–558.
    Based on AM 399 4to (pp. 407–412.7, 416.2–513.20, 527.24–547.26,

and 550.26–558) and AM 394 4to (pp. 412.8–416.2, 513.20–527.24, and
547.26–550.26) with select variants from AM 657c 4to.

Kålund, Kr. *Palæografisk atlas, oldnorsk-islandsk afdeling* (Copenhagen
and Christiania [Oslo]: Gyldendal, 1905). No. 40.
Facsimile and text edition of AM 399 4to, fol. 12r.

Stefán Karlsson, ed. *Sagas of Icelandic Bishops. Fragments of Eight
Manuscripts*. EIM 7 (Copenhagen: Rosenkilde and Bagger, 1967).
Facsimile of AM 220 fol. II.

– ed. *Guðmundar sögur Biskups I. Ævi Guðmundar biskups. Guðmundar
saga A*. Editiones Arnamagnæanæ, Ser. B, vol. 6 (Copenhagen: Reitzel,
1983). Pp. 15–262.
Based on AM 399 4to (pp. 17–24.15, 32.14–187, 208.22–237.26,
243.20–255) and AM 394 4to (pp. 24.15–32.13, 188–208.22, and
237.26–243.20) with variants from AM 122b fol. (pp. 92.10–99.11 and
115.17–117.4), AM 220 fol. II (pp. 21.13–29.12 and 46.6–58.4), AM
394 4to (pp. 17–24.15, 32.13–188, 208.22–237.26, and 243.20–255), AM
401 4to (pp. 17–24.15, 32.14–149.4, 149.25–187.1, 209.19–227.18,
228.17–237.26, and 243.20–255), and AM 204 fol. (pp. 96.1 and 97.3).
Edition of AM 111 8vo (pp. 256–62).

Modern Icelandic language edition:

Einar Ól. Sveinsson, ed. *Leit eg suður til landa. Ævintýri og helgisögur frá
miðöldum* (Reykjavík: Heimskringla, 1944). Pp. 240–3 and 265–91
(extracts only).

English translations:

Gudbrand Vigfusson and F. York Powell, ed. and trans. *Origines Islandicae.
A Collection of the More Important Sagas and Other Native Writings
Relating to the Settlement and Early History of Iceland*. 2 vols. (Oxford:
Clarendon, 1905; rpt. Millwood: Kraus, 1976). Vol. 1, pp. 606–13
(extract only).

Turville-Petre, G., and E.S. Olszewska, trans. *The Life of Gudmund the
Good, Bishop of Hólar* (Coventry: Viking Society for Northern Research, 1942). Pp. 2–110.

German translation:

Baetke, Walter, trans. *Islands Besiedlung und älteste Geschichte*. Neuausgabe
mit Nachwort von Rolf Heller. Thule: Altnordische Dichtung und
Prosa (Düsseldorf: Eugen Diederichs, 1967). Pp. 243–57 (extract
only).

Literature:

Ásdís Egilsdóttir. "Eru biskupasögur til?" *Skáldskaparmál* 2 (1992):
207–20, esp. pp. 208–9.

– "Biskupa sögur." In Phillip Pulsiano and Kirsten Wolf, with Paul Acker
   and Donald K. Fry, ed. >> *Medieval Scandinavia* (1993). Pp. 45–6.
– "Jarteinir, líkami, sál og trúarlíf." In Ásdís Egilsdóttir and Rudolf
   Simek, ed. >> *Sagnaheimur* (2001). Pp. 13–19, esp. p. 17.
Astås, Reidar. "Spor av teologisk tenkning og refleksjon i norsk og
   islandsk høymiddelalder." *CM* 6 (1993): 133–67, esp. p. 145.
Bekker-Nielsen, Hans, Thorkil Damsgaard Olsen, and Ole Widding.
   >> *Norrøn fortællekunst* (1965). Pp. 41 and 125.
Bekker-Nielsen, Hans, and Ole Widding. "Legende. Norge og Island."
   KLNM 10 (1965). Cols. 421–3, esp. col. 421.
Björn M. Ólsen. "Um Sturlungu." *Safn til sögu Íslands og íslenzkra
   bókmennta* 3 (1902): 193–510, esp. pp. 272–93 and 301–4.
Björn Sigfússon. "Guðmundar saga biskups Arasonar." *KLNM* 5 (1960).
   Cols. 542–3.
Boyer, Régis. "L'évéque Guðmundr Arason, témoin de son temps."
   Études Germaniques 3 (1967): 427–44, esp. pp. 428, 430, and 433.
– >> *La vie religieuse en Islande* (1979).
– "Les références expresses à la littérature dans les 'Sagas de contempor-
   ains'." In Gísli Sigurðsson, Guðrún Kvaran, and Sigurgeir Steingrímsson,
   ed. >> *Sagnaþing helgað Jónasi Kristjánssyni* (1994). Vol. 1, pp. 87–96.
Ciklamini, Marlene. "Sainthood in the Making: The Arduous Path of
   Guðmundr the Good, Iceland's Uncanonized Saint." *Alvíssmál* 11
   (2004): 55–74, esp. pp. 55, 57n7, and 59n9.
Cormack, Margaret. "'Fjǫlkunnigri kono scallatu í faðm sofa': Sex and
   the Supernatural in Icelandic Saints' Lives." *Skáldskaparmál* 2 (1992):
   221–8, esp. pp. 224–6.
– "Saints and Sinners: Reflections on Death in Some Icelandic Sagas."
   Gripla 8 (1993): 187–218, esp. pp. 201–2.
– >> *The Saints in Iceland* (1994). Pp. 12, 50, 60, 62, 64–5, 98–101, 106,
   112, 116, 121, 125, 137, 144, and 164.
– "Saints' Lives and Icelandic Literature in the Thirteenth and Four-
   teenth Centuries." In Hans Bekker-Nielsen and Birte Carlé, ed.
   >> *Saints and Sagas* (1994). Pp. 27–47, esp. p. 44.
– "Visions, Demons and Gender in the Sagas of Icelandic Saints." *CM* 7
   (1994): 185–209.
– "Women and Gender in the Sagas of Icelandic Saints." In >>
   Samtíðarsögur (1994). Vol. 1, pp. 188–93, esp. p. 191.
– "Sagas of Saints." In *Old Icelandic Literature and Society*. Ed. Margaret
   Clunies Ross (Cambridge: Cambridge University Press, 2000). Pp. 302–
   25, esp. pp. 308, 315, and 317–18.

– "Poetry, Paganism and the Sagas of Icelandic Bishops." In *Til heiðurs og hugbótar. Greinar um trúarkveðskap fyrri alda*. Ed. Svanhildur Óskarsdóttir and Anna Guðmundsdóttir (Reykholt: Snorrastofa, 2003). Pp. 33–51, esp. p. 49.

– "Christian Biography." In *A Companion to Old Norse–Icelandic Literature and Culture*. Ed. Rory McTurk (Oxford: Blackwell, 2005). Pp. 27–42, esp. pp. 37–8 and 40.

– "Holy Wells and National Identity in Iceland." In *Saints and Their Cults in the Atlantic World*. Ed. Margaret Cormack (Columbia, SC: University of South Carolina Press, 2007). Pp. 229–47, esp. pp. 231–6.

– "Catholic Saints in Lutheran Legend: Post-Reformation Ecclesiastical Folklore in Iceland." *SI* 59 (2008): 47–71, esp. pp. 52–3.

– "The Economics of Devotion: Vows and Indulgences in Medieval Iceland." *Viking and Medieval Scandinavia* 5 (2009): 41–63, esp. pp. 41–2.

Einar Ól. Sveinsson. "Jarteiknir." *Skírnir* 110 (1936): 23–48, esp. pp. 23–9, 33–4, and 36–7.

Finnur Jónsson. >> *Den oldnorske og oldislandske Litteraturs Historie* (1920–4). Vol. 2, pp. 763–4 and 932.

Foote, Peter. "Icelandic *sólarsteinn* and the Medieval Background." *Arv* 12 (1956): 26–40, esp. pp. 27 and 38. Rpt. in Peter Foote. *Aurvandilstá: Norse Studies* (Odense: Odense University Press, 1984). Pp. 140–54, esp. pp. 140 and 151.

– "Nafn guðs hit hæsta." In Ursula Dronke, Gerd Wolfgang Weber, and Hans Bekker-Nielsen, ed. >> *Specvlvm Norroenum* (1981). Pp. 139–54, esp. pp. 139–42, 146, and 151. Rpt. in Peter Foote. *Aurvandilstá: Norse Studies* (Odense: Odense University Press, 1984). Pp. 121–39, esp. pp. 121–5, 129, and 135.

Foote, Peter, ed. *Jóns saga Hólabyskups ens helga*. Editiones Arnamagnæanæ, Ser. A, vol. 14 (Copenhagen: Reitzel, 2003). Pp. 253–6.

Guðrún Nordal. *Tools of Literacy: The Role of Skaldic Verse in Icelandic Textual Culture of the Twelfth and Thirteenth Centuries* (Toronto: University of Toronto Press, 2001). Pp. 76, 100–14, 147, 154, 160, 163, 166, 175, 181, and 368.

Guðrún Nordal and Sverrir Tómasson. "Veraldleg sagnaritun 1120–1400." In Guðrún Nordal, Sverrir Tómasson, and Vésteinn Ólason, ed. >> *Íslensk Bókmenntasaga* 1 (1992). Pp. 263–418, esp. pp. 291, 345, 351–2, and 357.

Haki Antonsson. "Saints and Relics in Early Christian Scandinavia." *MScand* 15 (2005): 51–80, esp. p. 67.

Helga Kress. "'Grey þykir mér Freyja': Um konur, kristni og karlveldi í íslenskum fornbókmenntum." In Inga Huld Hákonardóttir, ed.
  >> *Konur og kristsmenn* (1996). Pp. 13–63, esp. p. 47. Rpt. in Helga Kress. *Fyrir dyrum fóstru: Konur og kynferði í íslenskum fornbókmenntum. Greinasafn* (Reykjavík: Háskóli Íslands, Rannsóknastofa í kvennafræðum, 1996). Pp. 167–219, esp. p. 214.

Hunt, Margaret Cushing. "A Study of Authorial Perspective in *Guðmundar saga A* and *Guðmundar saga D*: Hagiography and the Icelandic Bishop's Saga." PhD dissertation, Indiana University, 1985.

Jón Jóhannesson. "Tímatal Gerlands í íslenzkum ritum frá þjóðveldisöld." *Skírnir* 126 (1952): 76–93, esp. p. 87.

Jón Viðar Sigurðsson. "Utenlandske kvinnehelgener på Island i høymiddelalderen." In >> *Samtíðarsögur* (1994). Vol. 2, pp. 423–34, esp. p. 430.
  – *Den vennlige vikingen: Vennskapets makt i Norge og på Island ca. 900–1300* (Oslo: Pax Forlag, 2010). P. 117.

Jón Þorkelsson. *Skýringar á vísum í Guðmundar sögu Arasonar og Hrafns sögu Sveinbjarnarsonar* (Reykjavík: Einar Þórðarson, 1872). Pp. 3–18.

Jónas Kristjánsson. >> *Eddas and Sagas* (1988). Pp. 44 and 185.

Jørgensen, Jørgen Højgaard. *Bispesagaer – Laurentius saga: Studier i* Laurentius saga biskups, *indledt af overvejelser omkring* biskupa sǫgur *som litterær genre.* Udgivelsesudvalgets samling af studenterafhandlinger 12 (Odense: [n.p.], 1978). Pp. 21–4 and 29–30.

Kirby, Ian. >> *Biblical Quotation* (1980). Vol. 2, p. 80.

Koppenberg, Peter. *Hagiographische Studien zu den Biskupa sögur: Unter besonderer Berücksichtigung der* Jóns Saga Helga. Scandia Wissenschaftliche Reihe 1 (Bochum: Scandia, 1980). Pp. 3, 14, 143, and 200.

Larrington, Carolyne. "*Leizla Rannveigar*: Gender and Politics in the Otherworld Vision." *Medium Ævum* 64 (1995): 232–49.

Magerøy, Hallvard. "Guðmundr góði og Guðmundr ríki: Eit motivsamband." *Mm* (1959): 22–34, esp. pp. 22–3.

Magnús Jónsson. "Guðmundr biskup góði." *Eimreiðin* 27 (1921): 172–92.

Magnús Már Lárusson. "Helige Ande. Island." *KLNM* 6 (1961). Cols. 375–9, esp. col. 379.

McCreesh, Bernadine. "Prophetic Dreams and Visions in the Sagas of the Early Icelandic Saints." In *Verbal Encounters: Anglo-Saxon and Old Norse Studies for Roberta Frank*. Ed. Antonina Harbus and Russell Poole (Toronto: University of Toronto Press, 2005). Pp. 247–68, esp. pp. 251–2, 255–8, and 261–2.

– "Elements of the Pagan Supernatural in the Bishops' Sagas." In John McKinnell, David Ashurst, and Donata Kick, ed. >> *The Fantastic in Old Norse / Icelandic Literature* (2006). Vol. 2, pp. 671–80, esp. pp. 674 and 676–8.

Mogk, Eugen. >> *Geschichte der norwegisch-isländischen Literatur* (1904). P. 794.

Ólafur Lárusson. "Guðmundur góði í þjóðtrú Íslendinga." *Skírnir* 116 (1942): 113–39, esp. pp. 114, 116–17, 119, 126, and 137.

Paasche, Fredrik. *Norges og Islands litteratur inntil utgangen av middelalderen.* Rev. ed. by Anne Holtsmark (Oslo: Aschehoug, 1947). Pp. 403–4.

Schier, Kurt. *Sagaliteratur.* Sammlung Metzler M78 (Stuttgart: Metzler, 1970). P. 71.

Stefán Karlsson. "Resenshandrit." *Opuscula* 4. Bibliotheca Arnamagnæana 30 (Copenhagen: Munksgaard, 1970). Pp. 269–78, esp. pp. 271–2.

– "Ritun Reykjarfjarðarbókar. Excursus: Bókagerð bænda." *Opuscula* 4. Bibliotheca Arnamagnæana 30 (Copenhagen: Munksgaard, 1970). Pp. 120–40.

– "Misskilin orð og misrituð i Guðmundar sögum." *Gripla* 2 (1977): 121–31, esp. pp. 121–3.

– "Én biskop – flere biografer." *Selskab for Nordisk Filologi. Årsberetning for 1979–1980* (Copenhagen: B. Stougaard Jensen, 1981). Pp. 9–10.

– "Guðmundar sögur biskups: Authorial Viewpoints and Methods." In >> *The Sixth International Saga Conference* (1985). Vol. 2, pp. 983–1005. Rpt. in *Stafkrókar: Ritgerðir eftir Stefán Karlsson gefnar út í tilefni af sjötugsafmæli hans 2. desember 1998.* Ed. Guðvarður Már Gunnlaugsson (Reykjavík: Stofnun Árna Magnússonar, 2000). Pp. 153–71.

– "'*Bóklausir menn.*' A Note on Two Versions of *Guðmundar saga.*" In Rudolf Simek, Jónas Kristjánsson, and Hans Bekker-Nielsen, ed. >> *Sagnaskemmtun* (1986). Pp. 277–86, esp. pp. 277 and 279–81.

– "Guðmundar sögur biskups." In Phillip Pulsiano and Kirsten Wolf, with Paul Acker and Donald K. Fry, ed. >> *Medieval Scandinavia* (1993). Pp. 245–6.

Strömbäck, Dag. "Visionsdiktning." *KLNM* 20 (1976). Cols. 171–86, esp. cols. 182–3.

Svanhildur Óskarsdóttir. "Að kenna og rita tíða á millum. Um trúarviðhorf Guðmundar Arasonar." *Skáldskaparmál* 2 (1992): 229–38, esp. pp. 230–4 and 236.

– "Prose of Christian Instruction." In *A Companion to Old Norse–Icelandic Literature*. Ed. Rory McTurk (Oxford: Blackwell, 2005). Pp. 338–53, esp. p. 351.

Sverrir Tómasson. *Formálar íslenskra sagnaritara á miðöldum. Rannsókn bókmenntahefðar* (Reykjavík: Stofnun Árna Magnússonar, 1988). Pp. 20, 22, 29, 183, 192, 194, and 334–6.

– "Trúarbókmenntir í lausu máli á síðmiðöld." In Böðvar Guðmundsson, Sverrir Tómasson, Torfi H. Tulinius, and Vésteinn Ólason, ed. >> *Íslensk Bókmenntasaga* 2 (1993). Pp. 249–82, esp. pp. 258 and 270.

Turville-Petre, G. >> *Origins of Icelandic Literature* (1967). Pp. 122, 134, 197–8, and 209.

Vésteinn Ólason. "Kristileg trúarkvæði til loka 13. aldar." In Guðrún Nordal, Sverrir Tómasson, and Vésteinn Ólason, ed. >> *Íslensk Bókmenntasaga* 1 (1992). Pp. 481–515, esp. p. 506.

Whaley, Diana. "Miracles in the Sagas of Bishops: Icelandic Variations on an International Theme." *CM* 7 (1994): 155–84.

Widding, Ole. "Nogle problemer omkring sagaen om Gudmund den gode." *Mm* (1960): 13–26.

Wolf, Kirsten, ed. >> *Heilagra meyja sögur* (2003). Pp. lxv–lxvi.

Handlist, p. 312.

2. Guðmundar saga B

The so-called middle saga of Bishop Guðmundr Arason, which is a compilation of the *Prestssaga*, *Hrafns saga Sveinbjarnarsonar*, *Arons saga Hjǫrleifssonar*, and additional material.

Manuscripts:
AM 204 fol. (ca. 1650), AM 657c 4to (ca. 1340–90, defective), and Lbs fragm 5 (ca. 1330–70).

Editions:
Guðni Jónsson, ed. *Byskupa sögur*. 3 vols. (Reykjavík: Íslendingasagnaútgáfan; Haukadalsútgáfan, 1948). Vol. 2, pp. 413–519.
Normalized text based on *Biskupa sögur*.

Jakob Benediktsson. "Nokkur handritabrot." *Skírnir* 125 (1951): 182–98, esp. pp. 183–8.
Edition of Lbs fragm. 5.

[Jón Sigurðsson and Guðbrandur Vigfússon, ed.] *Biskupa sögur*. 2 vols. (Copenhagen: Møller, 1858–78). Vol. 1, pp. 559–618.

Based on AM 657c 4to (pp. 559–604.26 and 608.22–613.6) and AM
204 fol. (pp. 604.27–608.21 and 613.7–618).

English translation:
Turville-Petre, G., and E.S. Olszewska, trans. *The Life of Gudmund the
Good, Bishop of Hólar* (Coventry: Viking Society for Northern Re-
search, 1942). Pp. 110–12 (extract only).

Literature:
Ásdís Egilsdóttir. "Eru biskupasögur til?" *Skáldskaparmál* 2 (1992):
207–20, esp. pp. 208–9.
– "Biskupa sögur." In Phillip Pulsiano and Kirsten Wolf, with Paul Acker
and Donald K. Fry, ed. >> *Medieval Scandinavia* (1993). Pp. 45–6.
– "The Fantastic Reality: Hagiography, Miracles and Fantasy." In John
McKinnell, David Ashurst, and Donata Kick, ed. >> *The Fantastic
in Old Norse / Icelandic Literature: Sagas and the British Isles* (2006).
Vol. 1, pp. 63–70, esp. p. 65.
Bekker-Nielsen, Hans, Thorkil Damsgaard Olsen, and Ole Widding.
>> *Norrøn fortællekunst* (1965). Pp. 41 and 125.
Bekker-Nielsen, Hans, and Ole Widding. "Legende. Norge og Island."
KLNM 10 (1965). Cols. 421–3, esp. col. 421.
Björn M. Ólsen. "Um Sturlungu." *Safn til sögu Íslands og íslenzkra
bókmennta* 3 (1902): 193–510, esp. pp. 286–97 and 301–4.
Björn Sigfússon. "Guðmundar saga biskups Arasonar." *KLNM* 5 (1960).
Cols. 542–3.
Boyer, Régis. "L'évéque Guðmundr Arason, témoin de son temps."
Études Germaniques 3 (1967): 427–44, esp. p. 428.
– >> *La vie religieuse en Islande* (1979).
– "Les références expresses à la littérature dans les 'Sagas de contempor-
ains'." In Gísli Sigurðsson, Guðrún Kvaran, and Sigurgeir Steingríms-
son, ed. >> *Sagnaþing helgað Jónasi Kristjánssyni* (1994). Vol. 1,
pp. 87–96.
Cormack, Margaret. "'Fjǫlkunnigri kono scallatu í faðm sofa': Sex and
the Supernatural in Icelandic Saints' Lives." *Skáldskaparmál* 2 (1992):
221–8, esp. p. 227.
– >> *The Saints in Iceland* (1994). Pp. 12, 50, 54, 62, 65, 67, 98–101, 105,
107, and 144.
– "Visions, Demons and Gender in the Sagas of Icelandic Saints." *CM* 7
(1994): 185–209.
– "Sagas of Saints." In *Old Icelandic Literature and Society*. Ed. Margaret
Clunies Ross (Cambridge: Cambridge University Press, 2000). Pp. 302–
25, esp. pp. 308–9.

– "Poetry, Paganism and the Sagas of Icelandic Bishops." In *Til heiðurs og hugbótar. Greinar um trúarkveðskap fyrri alda*. Ed. Svanhildur Óskarsdóttir and Anna Guðmundsdóttir (Reykholt: Snorrastofa, 2003). Pp. 33–51, esp. p. 49.

– "Christian Biography." In *A Companion to Old Norse–Icelandic Literature and Culture*. Ed. Rory McTurk (Oxford: Blackwell, 2005). Pp. 27–42, esp. pp. 37–8.

– "Holy Wells and National Identity in Iceland." In *Saints and Their Cults in the Atlantic World*. Ed. Margaret Cormack (Columbia, SC: University of South Carolina Press, 2007). Pp. 229–47, esp. pp. 234–5 and 238.

– "Catholic Saints in Lutheran Legend: Post-Reformation Ecclesiastical Folklore in Iceland." *SI* 59 (2008): 47–71, esp. p. 53.

Einar Ól. Sveinsson. "Jarteiknir." *Skírnir* 110 (1936): 23–48, esp. pp. 33, 37–8, and 45.

Finnur Jónsson. >> *Den oldnorske og oldislandske Litteraturs Historie* (1920–4). Vol. 2, pp. 763–4 and 932.

Foote, Peter, ed. *Jóns saga Hólabyskups ens helga*. Editiones Arnamagnæanæ, Ser. A, vol. 14 (Copenhagen: Reitzel, 2003). P. 253.

Guðrún Nordal. *Tools of Literacy: The Role of Skaldic Verse in Icelandic Textual Culture of the Twelfth and Thirteenth Centuries* (Toronto: University of Toronto Press, 2001). Pp. 76, 100–1, 103–12, 147, 154–6, 160–3, 166–7, 175–6, 258, and 260.

Guðrún Nordal and Sverrir Tómasson. "Veraldleg sagnaritun 1120–1400." In Guðrún Nordal, Sverrir Tómasson, and Vésteinn Ólason, ed >> *Íslensk Bókmenntasaga* 1 (1992). Pp. 263–418, esp. p. 291.

Hallberg, Peter. "Imagery in Religious Old Norse Prose Literature: An Outline." *ANF* 102 (1987): 120–70, esp. pp. 120–1, 144, and 156.

Hunt, Margaret Cushing. "A Study of Authorial Perspective in *Guðmundar saga A* and *Guðmundar saga D*: Hagiography and the Icelandic Bishop's Saga." PhD dissertation, Indiana University, 1985. Pp. 6–7 and 16–19.

Jón Jóhannesson. "Tímatal Gerlands í íslenzkum ritum frá þjóðveldisöld." *Skírnir* 126 (1952): 76–93, esp. p. 93.

Jón Þorkelsson. *Skýringar á vísum í Guðmundar sögu Arasonar og Hrafns sögu Sveinbjarnarsonar* (Reykjavík: Einar Þórðarson, 1872). Pp. 18–25.

Jón Viðar Sigurðsson. "Utenlandske kvinnehelgener på Island i høymiddelalderen." In >> *Samtíðarsögur* (1994). Vol. 2, pp. 423–34, esp. p. 429.

Jónas Kristjánsson. >> *Eddas and Sagas* (1988). P. 185.

Jørgensen, Jørgen Højgaard. *Bispesagaer – Laurentius saga: Studier i*
Laurentius saga biskups, *indledt af overvejelser omkring* biskupa sǫgur
som litterær genre. Udgivelsesudvalgets samling af studenterafhand-
linger 12 (Odense: [n.p.], 1978). Pp. 21–4 and 29–30.

Kirby, Ian. >> *Biblical Quotation* (1980). Vol. 2, p. 80.

– "The Bible and Biblical Interpretation in Medieval Iceland." In *Old
Icelandic Literature and Society.* Ed. Margaret Clunies Ross (Cambridge: Cambridge University Press, 2000). Pp. 287–301, esp. p. 296.

Koppenberg, Peter. *Hagiographische Studien zu den Biskupa sögur: Unter
besonderer Berücksichtigung der* Jóns Saga Helga. Scandia Wissenschaftliche Reihe 1 (Bochum: Scandia, 1980). Pp. 106 and 200.

Larrington, Carolyne. "*Leizla Rannveigar*: Gender and Politics in the
Otherworld Vision." *Medium Ævum* 64 (1995): 232–49, esp. p. 232.

Magerøy, Hallvard. "Guðmundr góði og Guðmundr ríki: Eit motivsam-
band." *Mm* (1959): 22–34.

Magnús Már Lárusson. "Biskupa sögur." *KLNM* 1 (1956). Cols. 630–1.

Mogk, Eugen. >> *Geschichte der norwegisch-isländischen Literatur* (1904).
P. 794.

Ólafur Lárusson. "Guðmundur góði í þjóðtrú Íslendinga." *Skírnir* 116
(1942): 113–39, esp. pp. 115–17, 119, 121, 124–6, and 135.

Paasche, Fredrik. *Norges og Islands litteratur inntil utgangen av
middelalderen.* Rev. ed. by Anne Holtsmark (Oslo: Aschehoug, 1947).
Pp. 403–4.

Schier, Kurt. *Sagaliteratur.* Sammlung Metzler M78 (Stuttgart: Metzler,
1970). P. 71.

Stefán Karlsson. "Én biskop – flere biografer." *Selskab for Nordisk
Filologi. Årsberetning for 1979–1980* (Copenhagen: B. Stougaard
Jensen, 1981). Pp. 9–10.

– "Guðmundar sögur biskups: Authorial Viewpoints and Methods." In
>> *The Sixth International Saga Conference* (1985). Vol. 2, pp. 983–
1005. Rpt. in *Stafkrókar: Ritgerðir eftir Stefán Karlsson gefnar út í
tilefni af sjötugsafmæli hans 2. desember 1998.* Ed. Guðvarður Már
Gunnlaugsson (Reykjavík: Stofnun Árna Magnússonar, 2000).
Pp. 153–71.

– "'*Bóklausir menn.*' A Note on Two Versions of *Guðmundar saga.*" In
Rudolf Simek, Jónas Kristjánsson, and Hans Bekker-Nielsen, ed.
>> *Sagnaskemmtun* (1986). Pp. 277–86, esp. pp. 277, 280–2, and 286.

– "Guðmundar sögur biskups." In Phillip Pulsiano and Kirsten Wolf,
with Paul Acker and Donald K. Fry, ed. >> *Medieval Scandinavia*
(1993). Pp. 245–6.

Svanhildur Óskarsdóttir. "Að kenna og rita tíða á millum. Um
trúarviðhorf Guðmundar Arasonar." *Skáldskaparmál* 2 (1992):
229–38, esp. p. 231.

Sverrir Tómasson. *Formálar íslenskra sagnaritara á miðöldum. Rannsókn
bókmenntahefðar* (Reykjavík: Stofnun Árna Magnússonar, 1988).
Pp. 61–2, 67, 117, 119, 130–1, 167, 186–7, 194, 205, 207–8, 230, 232,
237–8, 255, 305, 311, and 335–6.

– "Trúarbókmenntir í lausu máli á síðmiðöld." In Böðvar Guðmundsson,
Sverrir Tómasson, Torfi H. Tulinius, and Vésteinn Ólason, ed.
>> *Íslensk Bókmenntasaga* 2 (1993). Pp. 249–82, esp. pp. 258–9 and 261.

Vésteinn Ólason. "Kristileg trúarkvæði til loka 13. aldar." In Guðrún
Nordal, Sverrir Tómasson, and Vésteinn Ólason, ed. >> *Íslensk
Bókmenntasaga* 1 (1992). Pp. 481–515, esp. pp. 496–7.

Whaley, Diana. "Miracles in the Sagas of Bishops: Icelandic Variations
on an International Theme." *CM* 7 (1994): 155–84.

Widding, Ole. "Nogle problemer omkring sagaen om Gudmund den
gode." *Mm* (1960): 13–26.

Handlist, p. 312.

3. Guðmundar saga C

Based on 2 and / or chiefly the same sources with some additional material.

Manuscripts:
AM 395 4to (ca. 1600–1700), AM 400 4to (ca. 1700, excerpts only),
Stock. Papp. fol. no. 3 (1689, defective), and Stock. Papp. 4to no. 4 (ca.
1600–50, defective).

Edition:
Foote, Peter. "Bishop Jörundr Þorsteinsson and the Relics of Guðmundr
inn góði Arason." In *Studia Centennalia in honorem memoriae Benedikt
S. Þórarinsson.* Ed. B.S. Benedikz (Reykjavík: Ísafold, 1961). Pp. 98–
114, esp. pp. 101–7.
Edition of an extract of Stock. Papp. 4to no. 4.

Literature:
Ásdís Egilsdóttir. "Eru biskupasögur til?" *Skáldskaparmál* 2 (1992):
207–20, esp. pp. 208–9.

– "Biskupa sögur." In Phillip Pulsiano and Kirsten Wolf, with Paul Acker
and Donald K. Fry, ed. >> *Medieval Scandinavia* (1993). Pp. 45–6.

– "Konur, draumar, dýrlingar." In *Bókmentaljós: Heiðursrit til Turið
Sigurðardóttur.* Ed. Malan Marnersdóttir, Leyvoy Joensen, and

Anfinnur Johansen (Tórshavn: Faroe University Press, 2006).
   Pp. 351–8, esp. p. 355.
Bekker-Nielsen, Hans, Thorkil Damsgaard Olsen, and Ole Widding.
   >> *Norrøn fortællekunst* (1965). Pp. 41 and 125.
Bekker-Nielsen, Hans, and Ole Widding. "Legende. Norge og Island."
   KLNM 10 (1965). Cols. 421–3, esp. col. 421.
Björn Sigfússon. "Guðmundar saga biskups Arasonar." *KLNM* 5 (1960).
   Cols. 542–3.
Ciklamini, Marlene. "Folklore and Hagiography in Arngrímr's *Guð-
   mundar saga Arasonar.*" In John McKinnell, David Ashurst, and
   Donata Kick, ed. >> *The Fantastic in Old Norse/Icelandic Literature*
   (2006). Vol. 1, pp. 171–9, esp. p. 177.
Cormack, Margaret. >> *The Saints in Iceland* (1994). Pp. 12, 50, 98–9,
   and 101.
– "Sagas of Saints." In *Old Icelandic Literature and Society.* Ed. Margaret
   Clunies Ross (Cambridge: Cambridge University Press, 2000). Pp. 302–
   25, esp. p. 308.
– "Poetry, Paganism and the Sagas of Icelandic Bishops." In *Til heiðurs
   og hugbótar. Greinar um trúarkveðskap fyrri alda.* Ed. Svanhildur
   Óskarsdóttir and Anna Guðmundsdóttir (Reykholt: Snorrastofa,
   2003). Pp. 33–51, esp. p. 49.
– "Christian Biography." In *A Companion to Old Norse–Icelandic
   Literature and Culture.* Ed. Rory McTurk (Oxford: Blackwell, 2005).
   Pp. 27–42, esp. pp. 37–8.
– "Catholic Saints in Lutheran Legend: Post-Reformation Ecclesiastical
   Folklore in Iceland." *SI* 59 (2008): 47–71, esp. p. 53.
Foote, Peter, ed. *Jóns saga Hólabyskups ens helga.* Editiones Ar-
   namagnæanæ, Ser. A, vol. 14 (Copenhagen: Reitzel, 2003). Pp. 253
   and 256.
Guðrún Nordal. *Tools of Literacy: The Role of Skaldic Verse in Icelandic
   Textual Culture of the Twelfth and Thirteenth Centuries* (Toronto:
   University of Toronto Press, 2001). Pp. 76, 100–1, 103–9, 111–12, 147,
   154, 160–1, 163, and 175–6.
Guðrún Nordal and Sverrir Tómasson. "Veraldleg sagnaritun 1120–1400."
   In Guðrún Nordal, Sverrir Tómasson, and Vésteinn Ólason, ed.
   >> *Íslensk Bókmenntasaga* 1 (1992). Pp. 263–418, esp. p. 291.
Hunt, Margaret Cushing. "A Study of Authorial Perspective in *Guð-
   mundar saga A* and *Guðmundar saga D*: Hagiography and the Icelandic
   Bishop's Saga." PhD dissertation, Indiana University, 1985. Pp. 6 and
   19–21.

Jónas Kristjánsson. >> *Eddas and Sagas* (1988). P. 185.

Jørgensen, Jørgen Højgaard. *Bispesagaer – Laurentius saga: Studier i* Laurentius saga biskups, *indledt af overvejelser omkring* biskupa sǫgur *som litterær genre.* Udgivelsesudvalgets samling af studenterafhandlinger 12 (Odense: [n.p.], 1978). Pp. 21–4, 29–30, 45, and 48–9.

Kirby, Ian. >> *Biblical Quotation* (1980). Vol. 2, p. 80.

Larrington, Carolyne. "*Leizla Rannveigar*: Gender and Politics in the Otherworld Vision." *Medium Ævum* 64 (1995): 232–49, esp. pp. 232–3 and 235.

Paasche, Fredrik. *Norges og Islands litteratur inntil utgangen av middelalderen.* Rev. ed. by Anne Holtsmark (Oslo: Aschehoug, 1947). Pp. 403–4.

Stefán Karlsson. "Misskilin orð og misrituð i Guðmundar sögum." *Gripla* 2 (1977): 121–31, esp. pp. 127–30.

– "Én biskop – flere biografer." *Selskab for Nordisk Filologi. Årsberetning for 1979–1980* (Copenhagen: B. Stougaard Jensen, 1981). Pp. 9–10.

– "Guðmundar sögur biskups: Authorial Viewpoints and Methods." In >> *The Sixth International Saga Conference* (1985). Vol. 2, pp. 983–1005. Rpt. in *Stafkrókar: Ritgerðir eftir Stefán Karlsson gefnar út í tilefni af sjötugsafmæli hans 2. desember 1998.* Ed. Guðvarður Már Gunnlaugsson (Reykjavík: Stofnun Árna Magnússonar, 2000). Pp. 153–71.

– "'*Bóklausir menn.*' A Note on Two Versions of *Guðmundar saga*." In Rudolf Simek, Jónas Kristjánsson, and Hans Bekker-Nielsen, ed. >> *Sagnaskemmtun* (1986). Pp. 277–86, esp. pp. 277–81 and 284–6.

– "Guðmundar sögur biskups." In Phillip Pulsiano and Kirsten Wolf, with Paul Acker and Donald K. Fry, ed. >> *Medieval Scandinavia* (1993). Pp. 245–6.

Svanhildur Óskarsdóttir. "Að kenna og rita tíða á millum. Um trúarviðhorf Guðmundar Arasonar." *Skáldskaparmál* 2 (1992): 229–38, esp. p. 231.

Sverrir Tómasson. "Norðlenski Benediktínaskólinn." In >> *The Sixth International Saga Conference* (1985). Vol. 2, pp. 1009–20, esp. p. 1012. Rpt. in Sverrir Tómasson. *Tækileg vitni: Greinar um bókmenntir gefnar út í tilefni sjötugsafmælis hans 5. apríl 2011* (Reykjavík: Stofnun Árna Magnússonar and Hið íslenska bókmenntafélag, 2011). Pp. 345–58, esp. p. 347.

– *Formálar íslenskra sagnaritara á miðöldum. Rannsókn bókmenntahefðar* (Reykjavík: Stofnun Árna Magnússonar, 1988). Pp. 335–6.

– "Trúarbókmenntir í lausu máli á síðmiðöld." In Böðvar Guðmundsson,
Sverrir Tómasson, Torfi H. Tulinius, and Vésteinn Ólason, ed. >>
Íslensk Bókmenntasaga 2 (1993). Pp. 249–82, esp. pp. 258 and 261.

4. Guðmundar saga D

A life of Bishop Guðmundr Arason written after 1343 by the monk
Arngrímr (Brandsson?) (d. 1361 or 1362). The principal source was 3.

Manuscripts:
AM 219 fol. (ca. 1370–80, defective), AM 220 fol. III (ca. 1450), AM 220
   fol. IV (ca. 1475–1525), AM 220 fol. V (ca. 1450–75), AM 394 4to (ca.
   1575–1600, extracts), AM 396 4to (ca. 1350–1400, defective), AM 397
   4to (ca. 1700, defective), AM 398 4to (ca. 1600–1700, defective), AM
   dipl. isl. fasc. LXX 7 (ca. 1400, defective), JS fragm 5 (ca. 1370–80), Lbs
   fragm. 6 (ca. 1370–80), SÁM 2 (ca. 1370–80), Stock. Papp. fol. no. 2
   (1689), Stock. Perg. fol. no. 5 (ca. 1350–65), and Þjms 176 (ca. 1370–90).
Editions:
Guðni Jónsson, ed. *Byskupa sögur*. 3 vols. (Reykjavík: Íslendingasagnaútgáfan; Haukadalsútgáfan, 1948). Vol. 3, pp. 155–506.
   Normalized text based on *Biskupa sögur*.
Jón Helgason, ed. *Byskupa sǫgur. MS Perg. fol. No. 5 in the Royal Library
   of Stockholm.* CCI 19 (Copenhagen: Ejnar Munksgaard, 1950).
   Facsimile of Stock. Perg. fol. no. 5.
[Jón Sigurðsson and Guðbrandur Vigfússon, ed.] *Biskupa sögur.* 2 vols.
   (Copenhagen: Møller, 1858–78). Vol. 2, pp. 3–187.10.
   Based on Stock. Perg. fol. no. 5 (pp. 3–184.14) and AM 398 4to
   (pp. 184.17–187.10) with variants from AM 219 fol. (pp. 42.29–177),
   AM 396 4to (pp. 1–20.20, 57.11–104.11, and 108.31–144.30), and AM
   398 4to (pp. 16.10–165.20).
Jón Þorkelsson, ed. *Nokkur blöð úr Hauksbók og brot úr Guðmundarsögu*
   (Reykjavík: E. Þórðarson, 1865). Pp. 43–7.
   Edition of Þjms 176.
[Kålund, Kr., ed.] *Palæografisk Atlas. Ny Serie. Oldnorsk-islandske
   skriftprøver c. 1300–1700* (Copenhagen and Kristiania [Oslo]:
   Gyldendal, 1907). No. 16.
   Facsimile and text edition of Stock. Perg. fol. no. 5, fol. 45v.
Möbius, Th., ed. *Analecta Norræna. Auswahl aus der isländischen und
   norwegischen Litteratur des Mittelalters.* 2nd ed. (Leipzig: J.C.
   Hinrichs'sche Buchhandlung, 1877). Pp. 146–7 (extract only).
   Based on *Biskupa sögur*.

Stefán Karlsson. "Um handrit að Guðmundar sögu bróður Arngríms." *Opuscula* 1. Bibliotheca Arnamagnæana 20 (Copenhagen: Ejnar Munksgaard, 1960). Pp. 179–89, esp. pp. 180.4–5 and 180.23–182. Edition of AM dipl. isl. fasc. LXX 7.

Stefán Karlsson, ed. *Sagas of Icelandic Bishops. Fragments of Eight Manuscripts*. EIM 7 (Copenhagen: Rosenkilde and Bagger, 1967). Facsimile of AM 219 fol., AM 220 fol. III, AM 220 fol. IV, and AM 220 fol. V.

Modern Icelandic language edition:

Einar Ól. Sveinsson, ed. *Leit eg suður til landa. Ævintýri og helgisögur frá miðöldum* (Reykjavík: Heimskringla, 1944). Pp. 264 and 292–9 (extracts only).

English translation:

Cormack, Margaret. "Better Off Dead: Approaches to Medieval Miracles." In Thomas A. DuBois, ed. >> *Sanctity in the North* (2008). Pp. 334–52, esp. pp. 334–5 and 344–5 (extracts only).

Literature:

Ásdís Egilsdóttir. "Eru biskupasögur til?" *Skáldskaparmál* 2 (1992): 207–20, esp. pp. 208–9.

– "Biskupa sögur." In Phillip Pulsiano and Kirsten Wolf, with Paul Acker and Donald K. Fry, ed. >> *Medieval Scandinavia* (1993). Pp. 45–6.

– "Kvendýrlingar og kvenímynd trúarlegra bókmennta á Íslandi." In Inga Huld Hákonardóttir, ed. >> *Konur og kristsmenn* (1996). Pp. 93–116, esp. pp. 105–7.

– "Jarteinir, líkami, sál og trúarlíf." In Ásdís Egilsdóttir and Rudolf Simek, ed. >> *Sagnaheimur* (2001). Pp. 13–19, esp. p. 17.

– "The Fantastic Reality: Hagiography, Miracles and Fantasy." In John McKinnell, David Ashurst, and Donata Kick, ed. >> *The Fantastic in Old Norse/Icelandic Literature* (2006). Vol. 1, pp. 63–70, esp. p. 66.

Battista, Simonetta. "*Blámenn, djǫflar* and Other Representations of Evil in Old Norse Literature." In John McKinnell, David Ashurst, and Donata Kick, ed. >> *The Fantastic in Old Norse/Icelandic Literature* (2006). Vol. 1, pp. 113–22, esp. p. 117.

Bekker-Nielsen, Hans. "Nova Historia Sancti Ambrosii. Et tabt rimofficium af Gunnlaugr Leifsson." *Mm* (1958): 8–14, esp. pp. 8–9.

Bekker-Nielsen, Hans, Thorkil Damsgaard Olsen, and Ole Widding. >> *Norrøn fortællekunst* (1965). Pp. 41, 105, 125, and 136.

Bekker-Nielsen, Hans, and Ole Widding. "Legende. Norge og Island." *KLNM* 10 (1965). Cols. 421–3, esp. col. 421.

Björn M. Ólsen. "Um Sturlungu." *Safn til sögu Íslands og íslenzkra bókmennta* 3 (1902): 193–510, esp. pp. 297–304.

Björn Sigfússon. "Guðmundar saga biskups Arasonar." *KLNM* 5 (1960).
Cols. 542–3.

Boyer, Régis. "L'évéque Guðmundr Arason, témoin de son temps."
Études Germaniques 3 (1967): 427–44, esp. p. 428.

– "Les références expresses à la littérature dans les 'Sagas de contem-
porains'." In Gísli Sigurðsson, Guðrún Kvaran, and Sigurgeir
Steingrímsson, ed. >> *Sagnaþing helgað Jónasi Kristjánssyni* (1994).
Vol. 1, pp. 87–96.

Ciklamini, Marlene. "The Hand of Revision: Abbot Arngrímr's Redaction of *Guðmundar saga biskups*." *Gripla* 8 (1993): 231–52.

– "Sainthood in the Making: The Arduous Path of Guðmundr the Good,
Iceland's Uncanonized Saint." *Alvíssmál* 11 (2004): 55–74, esp. p. 59n9.

– "Folklore and Hagiography in Arngrímr's *Guðmundar saga Arasonar*."
In John McKinnell, David Ashurst, and Donata Kick, ed. >> *The
Fantastic in Old Norse / Icelandic Literature* (2006). Vol. 1, pp. 171–9.

Cormack, Margaret. "'Fjǫlkunnigri kono scallatu í faðm sofa': Sex and
the Supernatural in Icelandic Saints' Lives." *Skáldskaparmál* 2 (1992):
221–8, esp. pp. 225–7.

– >> *The Saints in Iceland* (1994). Pp. 12, 42, 50, 60, 65, 77–8, 98–9,
106–7, and 120.

– "Saints' Lives and Icelandic Literature in the Thirteenth and Fourteenth Centuries." In Hans Bekker-Nielsen and Birte Carlé, ed. >>
Saints and Sagas (1994). Pp. 27–47, esp. p. 41–2.

– "Visions, Demons and Gender in the Sagas of Icelandic Saints." *CM* 7
(1994): 185–209.

– "Sagas of Saints." In *Old Icelandic Literature and Society*. Ed. Margaret
Clunies Ross (Cambridge: Cambridge University Press, 2000). Pp. 302–
25, esp. pp. 308 and 315.

– "Poetry, Paganism and the Sagas of Icelandic Bishops." In *Til heiðurs
og hugbótar. Greinar um trúarkveðskap fyrri alda*. Ed. Svanhildur
Óskarsdóttir and Anna Guðmundsdóttir (Reykholt: Snorrastofa,
2003). Pp. 33–51, esp. pp. 49–50.

– "Christian Biography." In *A Companion to Old Norse–Icelandic
Literature and Culture*. Ed. Rory McTurk (Oxford: Blackwell, 2005).
Pp. 27–42, esp. pp. 37–9.

– "Holy Wells and National Identity in Iceland." In *Saints and Their
Cults in the Atlantic World*. Ed. Margaret Cormack (Columbia, SC:
University of South Carolina Press, 2007). Pp. 229–47, esp. pp. 234–5.

– "Catholic Saints in Lutheran Legend: Post-Reformation Ecclesiastical
Folklore in Iceland." *SI* 59 (2008): 47–71, esp. p. 53.

Einar Ól. Sveinsson. "Jarteiknir." *Skírnir* 110 (1936): 23–48, esp. pp. 33–4, 42, 45, and 47–8.

Finnur Jónsson. >> *Den oldnorske og oldislandske Litteraturs Historie* (1920–4). Vol. 3, pp. 65–7.

Foote, Peter. "Icelandic *sólarsteinn* and the Medieval Background." *Arv* 12 (1956): 26–40, esp. pp. 27 and 38. Rpt. in Peter Foote. *Aurvandilstá: Norse Studies* (Odense: Odense University Press, 1984). Pp. 140–54, esp. pp. 141 and 151.

Foote, Peter, ed. *Jóns saga Hólabyskups ens helga*. Editiones Arnamagnæanæ, Ser. A, vol. 14 (Copenhagen: Reitzel, 2003). Pp. 253–9.

Guðrún Nordal. *Tools of Literacy: The Role of Skaldic Verse in Icelandic Textual Culture of the Twelfth and Thirteenth Centuries* (Toronto: University of Toronto Press, 2001). Pp. 76, 100, 103–9, 111–12, 114, 147, 155–6, 163, 175–6, 258, and 292.

Guðrún Nordal and Sverrir Tómasson. "Veraldleg sagnaritun 1120–1400." In Guðrún Nordal, Sverrir Tómasson, and Vésteinn Ólason, ed. >> *Íslensk Bókmenntasaga* 1 (1992). Pp. 263–418, esp. p. 291.

Gunnar F. Guðmundsson. "Latínusöngur leikra á miðöldum." In *Til heiðurs og hugbótar. Greinar um trúarkveðskap fyrri alda*. Ed. Svanhildur Óskarsdóttir and Anna Guðmundsdóttir (Reykholt: Snorrastofa, 2003). Pp. 93–112, esp. p. 101.

Haki Antonsson. *St. Magnús of Orkney: A Scandinavian Martyr-Cult in Context*. Northern World 29 (Leiden: Brill, 2007). P. 209.

Hallberg, Peter. *Stilsignalement och författarskap i norrön sagalitteratur: Synpunkter och exempel*. Nordistica Gothoburgensia 3 (Stockholm: Almqvist & Wiksell, 1968). Pp. 152–64, 174, 178, 181, and 185–9.

– "Some Observations on the Language of *Dunstanus saga*, with an Appendix on the Bible Compilation *Stjórn*." *Saga-Book* 18 (1973): 324–53, esp. pp. 326–32, 335–44, and 349–52.

– "Imagery in Religious Old Norse Prose Literature: An Outline." *ANF* 102 (1987): 120–70, esp. pp. 122, 130–2, 136–40, 144–6, 148–50, 159, 163, and 165.

– "Bergr Sokkason and Religious Icelandic Literature." In >> *Samtíðarsögur* (1994). Vol. 1, pp. 296–300, esp. pp. 297–300.

Heizmann, Wilhelm. "Arngríms Guðmundar saga, Maríu saga und Gregors Moralia in Iob." *Opuscula* 8. Bibliotheca Arnamagnæana 38 (Copenhagen: Reitzel, 1985). Pp. 189–98.

Helga Kress. "'Grey þykir mér Freyja': Um konur, kristni og karlveldi í íslenskum fornbókmenntum." In Inga Huld Hákonardóttir, *Konur og kristsmenn* (1996). Pp. 13–63, esp. pp. 39 and 55–6. Rpt. in Helga

Kress. *Fyrir dyrum fóstru: Konur og kynferði í íslenskum fornbók-menntum. Greinasafn* (Reykjavík: Háskóli Íslands, Rannsóknastofa í kvennafræðum, 1996). Pp. 167–219, esp. pp. 195 and 204–5.

Hunt, Margaret Cushing. "A Study of Authorial Perspective in *Guð-mundar saga A* and *Guðmundar saga D*: Hagiography and the Icelandic Bishop's Saga." PhD dissertation, Indiana University, 1985.

Jón Helgason. *Norrøn Litteraturhistorie* (Copenhagen: Levin and Munks-gaard, 1934). P. 194.

Jón Jóhannesson. "Tímatal Gerlands í íslenzkum ritum frá þjóðveldis-öld." *Skírnir* 126 (1952): 76–93, esp. p. 90.

Jón Þorkelsson. *Skýringar á vísum í Guðmundar sögu Arasonar og Hrafns sögu Sveinbjarnarsonar* (Reykjavík: Einar Þórðarson, 1872). Pp. 5–6.

Jónas Kristjánsson. *Um Fóstbræðra sögu* (Reykjavík: Stofnun Árna Magnússonar, 1972). Pp. 269, 283, and 305–7.

– >> *Eddas and Sagas* (1988). Pp. 143 and 185.

Jørgensen, Jørgen Højgaard. *Bispesagaer – Laurentius saga: Studier i* Laurentius saga biskups, *indledt af overvejelser omkring* biskupa sǫgur *som litterær genre*. Udgivelsesudvalgets samling af studenterafhand-linger 12 (Odense: [n.p.], 1978). Pp. 21–4, 29–30, 45, and 48–9.

Kirby, Ian. "The Bible and Biblical Interpretation in Medieval Iceland." In *Old Icelandic Literature and Society*. Ed. Margaret Clunies Ross (Cam-bridge: Cambridge University Press, 2000). Pp. 287–301, esp. p. 296.

Koppenberg, Peter. *Hagiographische Studien zu den Biskupa sögur: Unter besonderer Berücksichtigung der* Jóns Saga Helga. Scandia Wissen-schaftliche Reihe 1 (Bochum: Scandia, 1980). Pp. 6–7, 200–1, 235, and 244–6.

Larrington, Carolyne. "*Leizla Rannveigar*: Gender and Politics in the Otherworld Vision." *Medium Ævum* 64 (1995): 232–49, esp. pp. 232–3, 235–6, and 239.

Lehmann, Paul. >> "Skandinaviens Anteil an der lateinischen Literatur und Wissenschaft des Mittelalters" (1937). Pp. 23, 51, 53, and 59.

Lönnroth, Lars. "Det litterära porträttet i latinsk historiografi och isländsk sagaskrivning – en komparativ studie." *ANF* 27 (1969): 68–117, esp. p. 84.

Magnús Jónsson. "Guðmundr biskup góði." *Eimreiðin* 27 (1921): 172–92, esp. pp. 179 and 186–7.

Magnús Már Lárusson. "Biskupa sögur." *KLNM* 1 (1956). Cols. 630–1.

– "Helige Ande. Island." *KLNM* 6 (1961). Cols. 375–9, esp. cols. 378–9.

Magerøy, Hallvard. "Guðmundr góði og Guðmundr ríki: Eit motivsam-band." *Mm* (1959): 22–34, esp. pp. 22–3.

Mogk, Eugen. >> *Geschichte der norwegisch-isländischen Literatur* (1904). Pp. 715, 794–5, and 871.

Ólafur Lárusson. "Guðmundur góði í þjóðtrú Íslendinga." *Skírnir* 116 (1942): 113–39, esp. pp. 116–17, 119, 124–6, 128–9, and 135.

Paasche, Fredrik. *Norges og Islands litteratur inntil utgangen av middelalderen*. Rev. ed. by Anne Holtsmark (Oslo: Aschehoug, 1947). Pp. 403–4 and 532–3.

Schier, Kurt. *Sagaliteratur*. Sammlung Metzler M78 (Stuttgart: Metzler, 1970). Pp. 68, 70, 121, and 123.

Stefán Karlsson. "Icelandic Lives of Thomas a Becket: Questions of Authorship." In Peter Foote, Hermann Pálsson, and Desmond Slay, ed. >> *Proceedings of the First International Saga Conference* (1973). Pp. 212–43, esp. pp. 228–38. Rpt. in *Stafkrókar: Ritgerðir eftir Stefán Karlsson gefnar út í tilefni af sjötugsafmæli hans 2. desember 1998*. Ed. Guðvarður Már Gunnlaugsson (Reykjavík: Stofnun Árna Magnússonar, 2000). Pp. 135–52, esp. pp. 144–8.

– "Misskilin orð og misrituð i Guðmundar sögum." *Gripla* 2 (1977): 121–31, esp. pp. 123–30.

– "Én biskop – flere biografer." *Selskab for Nordisk Filologi. Årsberetning for 1979–1980* (Copenhagen: B. Stougaard Jensen, 1981). Pp. 9–10.

– "Guðmundar sögur biskups: Authorial Viewpoints and Methods." In >> *The Sixth International Saga Conference* (1985). Vol. 2, pp. 983–1005. Rpt. in *Stafkrókar: Ritgerðir eftir Stefán Karlsson gefnar út í tilefni af sjötugsafmæli hans 2. desember 1998*. Ed. Guðvarður Már Gunnlaugsson (Reykjavík: Stofnun Árna Magnússonar, 2000). Pp. 153–71.

– "'*Bóklausir menn*.' A Note on Two Versions of *Guðmundar saga*." In Rudolf Simek, Jónas Kristjánsson, and Hans Bekker-Nielsen, ed. >> *Sagnaskemmtun* (1986). Pp. 277–86, esp. pp. 277 and 280–6.

– "Guðmundar sögur biskups." In Phillip Pulsiano and Kirsten Wolf, with Paul Acker and Donald K. Fry, ed. >> *Medieval Scandinavia* (1993). Pp. 245–6.

Strömbäck, Dag. "Visionsdiktning." *KLNM* 20 (1976). Cols. 171–86, esp. cols. 182–4.

Svanhildur Óskarsdóttir. "Að kenna og rita tíða á millum. Um trúarviðhorf Guðmundar Arasonar." *Skáldskaparmál* 2 (1992): 229–38, esp. p. 231.

Sverrir Tómasson. "Norðlenski Benediktínaskólinn." In >> *The Sixth International Saga Conference* (1985). Vol. 2, pp. 1009–20, esp. pp. 1015 and 1018. Rpt. in Sverrir Tómasson. *Tækileg vitni: Greinar*

um bókmenntir gefnar út í tilefni sjötugsafmælis hans 5. apríl 2011
(Reykjavík: Stofnun Árna Magnússonar and Hið íslenska bók-
menntafélag, 2011). Pp. 345–58, esp. pp. 349–50 and 354.
– *Formálar íslenskra sagnaritara á miðöldum. Rannsókn bókmenntahefðar*
(Reykjavík: Stofnun Árna Magnússonar, 1988). Pp. 37, 50, 55–6, 87,
90, 118–19, 141, 194, 233, 334–6, and 342.
– "Kristnar trúarbókmenntir í óbundnu máli." In Guðrún Nordal,
Sverrir Tómasson, and Vésteinn Ólason, ed. >> *Íslensk Bókmenntasaga*
1 (1992). Pp. 419–79, esp. pp. 462–3 and 479.
– "Trúarbókmenntir í lausu máli á síðmiðöld." In Böðvar Guðmundsson,
Sverrir Tómasson, Torfi H. Tulinius, and Vésteinn Ólason, ed. >> *Íslensk
Bókmenntasaga* 2 (1993). Pp. 249–82, esp. pp. 251, 258, and 260–3.
Turville-Petre, G. >> *Origins of Icelandic Literature* (1967). Pp. 122–3,
135, and 197.
Van Deusen, Natalie M. "'Inn besti hlutr'? Martha of Bethany and
Women's Roles in Medieval Iceland." *ANF* 1265 (2011): 73–91, esp.
pp. 82–3.
Vries, Jan de. >> *Altnordische Literaturgeschichte* (1964–7). Vol. 2,
pp. 184, 189, 209, and 527.
Whaley, Diana. "Miracles in the Sagas of Bishops: Icelandic Variations
on an International Theme." *CM* 7 (1994): 155–84.
Widding, Ole, and Hans Bekker-Nielsen. "Low German Influence on
Late Icelandic Hagiography." *GR* 37 (1962): 239–62, esp. p. 242.
Handlist, p. 312.

5. Ævi Guðmundar biskups

A brief chronological summary of Bishop Guðmundr Arason's life.

Manuscript:
AM 555c 4to (ca. 1600–1700, defective).
Edition:
Stefán Karlsson, ed. *Guðmundar sögur Biskups I. Ævi Guðmundar
biskups. Guðmundar saga A*. Editiones Arnamagnæanæ, Ser. B, vol. 6
(Copenhagen: Reitzel, 1983). Pp. 3–13.
Literature:
Ásdís Egilsdóttir. "Eru biskupasögur til?" *Skáldskaparmál* 2 (1992):
207–20, esp. p. 209.
Foote, Peter, ed. *Jóns saga Hólabyskups ens helga*. Editiones Arna-
magnæanæ, Ser. A, vol. 14 (Copenhagen: Reitzel, 2003). P. 253.

Guðrún Nordal and Sverrir Tómasson. "Veraldleg sagnaritun 1120–
   1400." In Guðrún Nordal, Sverrir Tómasson, and Vésteinn Ólason, ed.
   >> *Íslensk Bókmenntasaga* 1 (1992). Pp. 263–418, esp. pp. 351–2.
Stefán Karlsson. "'*Bóklausir menn.*' A Note on Two Versions of *Guð-
   mundar saga.*" In Rudolf Simek, Jónas Kristjánsson, and Hans Bekker-
   Nielsen, ed. >> *Sagnaskemmtun* (1986). Pp. 277–86, esp. pp. 277n1
   and 281.
Sverrir Tómasson. *Formálar íslenskra sagnaritara á miðöldum. Rannsókn
   bókmenntahefðar* (Reykjavík: Stofnun Árna Magnússonar, 1988).
   Pp. 334–5.

HALLVARD   May 14

1. Hallvarðs saga

Possibly based on a now-lost, fuller version of *BHL* 3750.

Manuscripts:
AM 235 fol. (ca. 1400, defective), AM 238 fol. VIII (ca. 1425–50), and
   AM 670 1 4to (ca. 1700–1800, defective).
Editions:
Foote, Peter, ed. >> *Lives of Saints* (1962).
   Facsimile of AM 238 fol. VIII (1v).
Unger, C.R., ed. >> *Heilagra manna søgur* (1877). Vol. 1, p. 396.
   Edition of AM 238 fol. VIII (p. 396.7–15) and AM 235 fol.
   (p. 396.17–27).
Literature:
Bekker-Nielsen, Hans, and Ole Widding. "Legende. Norge og Island."
   KLNM 10 (1965). Cols. 421–3, esp. col. 421.
Benson, Adolph B. "Scandinavian Saints and Legends: A Résumé." *GR*
   31 (1956): 9–22, esp. p. 19.
Carlé, Birte. >> *Jomfru-fortællingen* (1985). Pp. 37–8.
Daae, Ludvig. *Norges helgener* (Christiania [Oslo]: Malling, 1879).
   Pp. 163–5.
Finnur Jónsson. >> *Den oldnorske og oldislandske Litteraturs Historie*
   (1920–4). Vol. 2, p. 875.
Gjerløw, Lilli. "Hallvard." *KLNM* 6 (1961). Cols. 63–6, esp. col. 64.
Haki Antonsson. "Saints and Relics in Early Christian Scandinavia."
   MScand 15 (2005): 51–80, esp. p. 70.

– *St. Magnús of Orkney: A Scandinavian Martyr-Cult in Context.*
Northern World 29 (Leiden: Brill, 2007). P. 122.

Holm-Olsen, Ludvig. "Middelalderens litteratur i Norge." In *Norges litteratur historie* 1. Ed. Edvard Beyer (Oslo: Cappelen, 1974). Pp. 18–342, esp. p. 68.

Kratz, Henry. "Saints' Lives. 2. Iceland and Norway." In Phillip Pulsiano and Kirsten Wolf, with Paul Acker and Donald K. Fry, ed. >> *Medieval Scandinavia* (1993). Pp. 562–4.

Lehmann, Paul. >> "Skandinaviens Anteil an der lateinischen Literatur und Wissenschaft des Mittelalters" (1937). P. 80.

Loth, Agnete. "Til Sebastianus saga." *Opuscula* 5. Bibliotheca Arnamagnæana 31 (Copenhagen: Munksgaard, 1975). Pp. 103–22, esp. pp. 119–20.

Mogk, Eugen. >> *Geschichte der norwegisch-isländischen Literatur* (1904). P. 895.

Phelpstead, Carl. *Holy Vikings: Saints' Lives in the Old Icelandic Kings' Sagas.* Medieval and Renaissance Texts and Studies 40 (Tempe, Ariz.: Arizona Center for Medieval and Renaissance Studies, 2007). P. 9.

Seierstad, Andr. "St. Hallvard-legenda." *Norsk teologisk tidsskrift* 46 (1945): 174–86.

Storm, Gustav. *Monumenta historia Norvegiæ: Latinske kildeskrifter til Norges historie i middelalderen* (Kristiania [Oslo]: Brøgger, 1880). Pp. xxxxiv–xxxxv.

Wolf, Kirsten, ed. "Anonymous, *Heilagra manna drápa* 'Drápa about Holy Men'." In Margaret Clunies Ross, ed. >> *Poetry on Christian Subjects* (2007). Vol. 2, pp. 872–90, esp. p. 888.

Handlist, p. 313.

HENRY AND CUNEGUND   July 15, March 3

Hendriks saga og Kúnigúndísar

Translated from a now-lost Low German redaction that resembles the source(s) of *Der Heiligen Leben*.

Manuscript:
Stock. Perg. fol. no. 3 (*Reykjahólabók*) (ca. 1530–40).

Edition:
Loth, Agnete, ed. >> *Reykjahólabók* (1969–70). Vol. 1, pp. 35–70.

English translation:
Kalinke, Marianne E. "*Hendreks saga og Kunegundis*: Marital Consent in the Legend of Henry and Cunegund." In Thomas A. DuBois, ed. >> *Sanctity in the North* (2008). Pp. 307–33, esp. pp. 322–31.

Literature:
Bekker-Nielsen, Hans, Thorkil Damsgaard Olsen, and Ole Widding. >> *Norrøn fortællekunst* (1965). P. 140.

Bekker-Nielsen, Hans, and Ole Widding. "Legende. Norge og Island." *KLNM* 10 (1965). Cols. 421–3, esp. col. 422.

Kalinke, Marianne E. "Reykjahólabók: A Legendary on the Eve of the Reformation." *Skáldskaparmál* 2 (1992): 239–69, esp. pp. 240, 244, 246, 250–1, and 256–9.

– >> *The Book of Reykjahólar* (1996). Pp. 28, 51–2, 112, 115–16, 138–41, 151, 158, 164, 211–23, 225–7, 236, and 245.

– "*Hendreks saga og Kunegundis* and Consensuality in Marriage." In Rudolf Simek and Judith Meurer, ed. >> *Scandinavia and Christian Europe in the Middle Ages* (2003). Pp. 294–302.

Mogk, Eugen. >> *Geschichte der norwegisch-isländischen Literatur* (1904). P. 895.

Widding, Ole, and Hans Bekker-Nielsen. "En senmiddelalderlig legendesamling." *Mm* (1960): 105–28, esp. pp. 107 and 113.

– "Low German Influence on Late Icelandic Hagiography." *GR* 37 (1962): 239–62, esp. pp. 249 and 255.

Handlist, p. 313.

HERMAN THE CRIPPLE   September 25

Af Heremanno

Tales of Saint Herman the Cripple incorporated into the miracles of the Virgin Mary.

Manuscripts:
See Mary the Blessed Virgin 3 note (p. 245).

Edition:
Unger, C.R., ed. >> *Mariu saga* (1871). Pp. 143.4–144, 1076.5–1079.5.

Literature:
Handlist, pp. 313 and 323.

HIPPOLYTUS   August 13

A legend of Saint Hippolytus based on *BHL* 3961 incorporated into
Lárentíuss saga erkidjákns 1.

Manuscripts:
See Laurence of Rome 1 note (p. 199).
Editions:
Foote, Peter, ed. >> *Lives of Saints* (1962).
Unger, C.R., ed. >> *Heilagra manna søgur* (1877). Vol. 1, pp. 430.14–
  432.
Literature:
Carlé, Birte. >> *Jomfru-fortællingen* (1985). Pp. 62–3 and 70.
Cormack, Margaret. >> *The Saints in Iceland* (1994). Pp. 34 and 118.
Mogk, Eugen. >> *Geschichte der norwegisch-isländischen Literatur* (1904).
  P. 891.
Sverrir Tómasson. "Kristnar trúarbókmenntir í óbundnu máli." In
  Guðrún Nordal, Sverrir Tómasson, and Vésteinn Ólason, ed.
  >> *Íslensk Bókmenntasaga* 1 (1992). Pp. 419–79, esp. p. 432.

HUGH OF BONNEVEAUX   April 1

Af Húgo

A tale of Saint Hugh of Bonneveaux incorporated into the miracles of
the Virgin Mary.

Manuscripts:
See Mary the Blessed Virgin 3 note (p. 245).
Edition:
Unger, C.R., ed. >> *Mariu saga* (1871). Pp. 483.27–488 and 1151.10–
  1152.25.
Literature:
Handlist, pp. 313 and 323.

HUGH THE GREAT OF CLUNY   April 29

Af Húgo ábóta

Tales of Saint Hugh the Great of Cluny incorporated into the miracles of the Virgin Mary.

Manuscripts:
See Mary the Blessed Virgin 3 note (p. 245).
Edition:
Unger, C.R., ed. >> *Mariu saga* (1871). Pp. 180.7–193.4, 473.14–483.25, 1024.7–33, and 1147.19–1151.7.
Literature:
Heizmann, Wilhelm. "Arngríms Guðmundar saga, Maríu saga und Gregors Moralia in Iob." *Opuscula* 8. Bibliotheca Arnamagnæana 38 (Copenhagen: Reitzel, 1985). Pp. 189–98.
– "Liebe und Durst: Der Heilige Bernhard von Clairvaux in der altisländischen Mirakelüberlieferung." *Opuscula* 13. Bibliotheca Arnamagnæana 47 (Copenhagen: Museum Tusculanum Press, 2010). Pp. 55–118, esp. pp. 56 and 109–10.
Widding, Ole. "Marialegender. Norge og Island." *KLNM* 11 (1966). Cols. 401–4, esp. col. 402.
– "Norrøne Marialegender på europæisk baggrund." *Opuscula* 10. Bibliotheca Arnamagnæana 40 (Copenhagen: Reitzel, 1996). Pp. 1–128, esp. pp. 11, 14, 17, 39, 42, 44, 79, and 85.
Handlist, pp. 313 and 323.

ILDEPHONSUS   January 23

Af Hildifonso

Tales of Saint Ildephonsus incorporated into the miracles of the Virgin Mary.

Manuscripts:
See Mary the Blessed Virgin 3 note (p. 245).
Edition:
Unger, C.R., ed. >> *Mariu saga* (1871). Pp. 78.4–80.2 and 704.13–708.25.

Literature:
Widding, Ole. "Norrøne Marialegender på europæisk baggrund."
   Opuscula 10. Bibliotheca Arnamagnæana 40 (Copenhagen: Reitzel,
   1996). Pp. 1–128, esp. pp. 22 and 36.
Handlist, pp. 313 and 323.

JAMES THE GREATER   July 25

1. Jakobs saga postola (ins eldra) I

Based on *BHL* 4057 with additional material from *Speculum Ecclesiae*.

Manuscripts:
AM 629 4to (1697), AM 630 4to (ca. 1650–1700), AM 645 4to (ca. 1220),
   AM 652 4to (ca. 1250–70, defective), AM 656 4to I (ca. 1600), AM
   659b 4to (ca. 1600–1700, defective), and Rask 69 (ca. 1800).

Editions:
Holtsmark, Anne, ed. *A Book of Miracles: MS No. 645 4to of the Arna-
   Magnæan Collection in the University Library of Copenhagen.* CCI 12
   (Copenhagen: Einar Munksgaard, 1938).
   Facsimile of AM 645 4to.
Larsson, Ludvig, ed. *Isländska handskriften No 645 4° i Den Arna-
   magnæanske Samlingen på Universitetsbiblioteket i København:
   I. Handskriftens äldre del* (Lund: Gleerup, 1885). Pp. 90.23–99.23.
   Edition of AM 645 4to.
Þorsteinn Jónsson, ed. *Hér hefjast Tíu Sögur, af þeim enum heiløgu Guds
   Postulum og pínslar vottum* (Viðeyjarklaustur: Þ. Jónsson, 1836).
   Pp. 103–36.
   Based on a manuscript descended from AM 630 4to.
Unger, C.R., ed. >> *Postola sögur* (1874). Pp. 513.32–529.
   Edition of AM 652 4to (pp. 521.29–523), AM 645 4to (pp. 524–529.25),
   and AM 630 4to (pp. 513.32–521.21).

English translation:
Roughton, Philip G. "AM 645 4to and AM 652/630 4to: Study and
   Translation of Two Thirteenth-Century Icelandic Collections of
   Apostles' and Saints' Lives." PhD dissertation, University of Colorado,
   2002. Pp. 698–715.
   Translation of AM 645 4to (pp. 698–709) and AM 630 4to and AM
   652 4to (pp. 710–15, extract only).

Literature:

Álfrún Gunnlaugsdóttir. "*Jakobs saga postola, Tveggia postola saga Jons ok Jakobs* og *Liber Sancti Jacobi*." *Gripla* 21 (2010): 235–80.

Battista, Simonetta. "Oversættelsesteknik i to *postola sögur*." In >> *Sagas and the Norwegian Experience* (1997). Pp. 57–65.

– "Translation or Redaction in Old Norse Hagiography." In Peter Andersen, ed. >> *Pratiques de Traduction au Moyen Age* (2004). Pp. 100–10, esp. pp. 101–3 and 105–6.

– "The *Compilator* and Contemporary Literary Culture in Old Norse Hagiography." *Viking and Medieval Scandinavia* 1 (2005): 1–13, esp. pp. 4–5.

Bekker-Nielsen, Hans. "Et par ord om de ældste norrøne helgensagaer." In Finn Hødnebø et al., ed. >> *Eyvindarbók* (1992). Pp. 29–33, esp. p. 32.

Bekker-Nielsen, Hans, Thorkil Damsgaard Olsen, and Ole Widding. >> *Norrøn fortællekunst* (1965). Pp. 122–3.

Cormack, Margaret. >> *The Saints in Iceland* (1994). Pp. 108 and 242.

Finnur Jónsson. >> *Den oldnorske og oldislandske Litteraturs Historie* (1920–4). Vol. 2, p. 871.

Foote, Peter G. *The Pseudo-Turpin Chronicle in Iceland: A Contribution to the Study of the Karlamagnús saga*. London Mediæval Studies: Monograph No. 4 (University College London: London Mediæval Studies, 1954). P. 49.

Hallberg, Peter. *Stilsignalement och författarskap i norrön sagalitteratur: Synpunkter och exempel*. Nordistica Gothoburgensia 3 (Stockholm: Almqvist & Wiksell, 1968). Pp. 120–3, 125, and 134–5.

Jón Ma. Ásgeirsson and Þórður Ingi Guðjónsson, ed. *Frá Sýrlandi til Íslands: Arfur Tómasar postula* (Reykjavík: Háskólaútgáfan, 2007). Pp. 164–5.

Jónas Kristjánsson. "Sagas and Saints' Lives." In *Cultura Classica e Cultura Germanica Settentrionale*. Ed. Pietro Janni, Diego Poli, and Carlo Santini (Macerata: Herder, 1985). Pp. 125–43.

Kirby, Ian. >> *Biblical Quotation* (1980). Vol. 2, p. 30.

– "The Bible and Biblical Interpretation in Medieval Iceland." In *Old Icelandic Literature and Society*. Ed. Margaret Clunies Ross (Cambridge: Cambridge University Press, 2000). Pp. 287–301, esp. p. 298.

Louis-Jensen, Jonna. "To håndskrifter fra det nordvestlige Island." *Opuscula* 7. Bibliotheca Arnamagnæana 34 (Copenhagen: Reitzel, 1979). Pp. 219–53, esp. p. 221.

Mogk, Eugen. >> *Geschichte der norwegisch-isländischen Literatur* (1904). P. 888.

Ólafur Halldórsson, ed. *Mattheus saga postula* (Reykjavík: Stofnun Árna
    Magnússonar, 1994). Pp. xiii–xli, xlix–lvii, and lxxv–lxxxi.
Roughton, Philip. "Stylistics and Sources of the *Postola sögur* in AM 645
    4to and AM 652/630 4to." *Gripla* 16 (2005): 7–50.
– "'Þá syndi hann þeim mikinn skugga': Unmasking the Fantastic in the
    Postola sögur." In John McKinnell, David Ashurst, and Donata Kick,
    ed. >> *The Fantastic in Old Norse/Icelandic Literature* (2006). Vol. 2,
    pp. 846–55, esp. pp. 847 and 850.
Turville-Petre, G. >> *Origins of Icelandic Literature* (1967). P. 130.
Þórður Ingi Guðjónsson. "Apostlene i islandsk middelalderlitteratur." In
    Den nordiske renessansen i høymiddelalderen. Ed. Jón Viðar Sigurðsson
    and Preben Meulengracht Sørensen (Oslo: Historisk institutt, Universi-
    tetet i Oslo, 2000). Pp. 83–99, esp. pp. 93–4.
Handlist, pp. 313–14.

2. Jakobs saga postola (ins eldra) II

An independent translation of the same source(s) as 1.

Manuscript:
AM 655 4to XII–XIII (ca. 1250–75).
Editions:
Hreinn Benediktsson. *Early Icelandic Script As Illustrated in Vernacular
    Texts from the Twelfth and Thirteenth Centuries.* Íslenzk handrit:
    Icelandic Manuscripts, Series in Folio 2 (Reykjavík: The Manuscript
    Institute of Iceland, 1965). Plate 36.
    Facsimile of fol. 2r.
Unger, C.R., ed. >> *Postola sögur* (1874). Pp. 529.27–533.
Literature:
Álfrún Gunnlaugsdóttir. "*Jakobs saga postola, Tveggia postola saga Jons
    ok Jakobs* og *Liber Sancti Jacobi.*" *Gripla* 21 (2010): 235–80.
Battista, Simonetta. "Oversættelsesteknik i to *postola sögur.*" In >> *Sagas
    and the Norwegian Experience* (1997). Pp. 57–65.
– "Translation or Redaction in Old Norse Hagiography." In Peter
    Andersen, ed. >> *Pratiques de Traduction au Moyen Age* (2004).
    Pp. 100–10, esp. pp. 102–3 and 106.
– "The *Compilator* and Contemporary Literary Culture in Old Norse
    Hagiography." *Viking and Medieval Scandinavia* 1 (2005): 1–13, esp.
    p. 5.
Cormack, Margaret. >> *The Saints in Iceland* (1994). Pp. 108 and 242.

Finnur Jónsson. >> *Den oldnorske og oldislandske Litteraturs Historie* (1920–4). Vol. 2, p. 871.

Foote, Peter G. *The Pseudo-Turpin Chronicle in Iceland: A Contribution to the Study of the Karlamagnús saga.* London Mediæval Studies: Monograph No. 4 (University College London: London Mediæval Studies, 1954). P. 49.

Hallberg, Peter. *Stilsignalement och författarskap i norrön sagalitteratur: Synpunkter och exempel.* Nordistica Gothoburgensia 3 (Stockholm: Almqvist & Wiksell, 1968). Pp. 120–3, 125, and 134–5.

Jónas Kristjánsson. "Learned Style or Saga Style?" In Ursula Dronke, Guðrún P. Helgadóttir, Gerd Wolfgang Weber, and Hans Bekker-Nielsen, ed. >> *Specvlvm Norroenvm* (1981). Pp. 260–92.

Kirby, Ian. >> *Biblical Quotation* (1980). Vol. 2, pp. 30–1.

– "The Bible and Biblical Interpretation in Medieval Iceland." In *Old Icelandic Literature and Society*. Ed. Margaret Clunies Ross (Cambridge: Cambridge University Press, 2000). Pp. 287–301, esp. p. 298.

Mogk, Eugen. >> *Geschichte der norwegisch-isländischen Literatur* (1904). P. 888.

Ólafur Halldórsson, ed. *Mattheus saga postula* (Reykjavík: Stofnun Árna Magnússonar, 1994). Pp. lxvi–lxxv.

Þórður Ingi Guðjónsson. "Apostlene i islandsk middelalderlitteratur." In *Den nordiske renessansen i høymiddelalderen*. Ed. Jón Viðar Sigurðsson and Preben Meulengracht Sørensen (Oslo: Historisk institutt, Universitetet i Oslo, 2000). Pp. 83–99, esp. p. 95.

Handlist, p. 314.

3. Jakobs saga postola (ins eldra) III

A translation of *BHL* 4057.

Manuscript:
AM 656 4to I (ca. 1325–50).
Edition:
Unger, C.R., ed. >> *Postola sögur* (1874). Pp. 534–5.
Literature:

Álfrún Gunnlaugsdóttir. "*Jakobs saga postola, Tveggia postola saga Jons ok Jakobs* og *Liber Sancti Jacobi.*" *Gripla* 21 (2010): 235–80.

Cormack, Margaret. >> *The Saints in Iceland* (1994). P. 108.

Finnur Jónsson. >> *Den oldnorske og oldislandske Litteraturs Historie* (1920–4). Vol. 2, p. 871.

Hallberg, Peter. *Stilsignalement och författarskap i norrön sagalitteratur:
Synpunkter och exempel.* Nordistica Gothoburgensia 3 (Stockholm:
Almqvist & Wiksell, 1968). Pp. 120–3, 125, and 134–5.
Kirby, Ian. >> *Biblical Quotation* (1980). Vol. 2, p. 31.
– "The Bible and Biblical Interpretation in Medieval Iceland." In *Old
Icelandic Literature and Society.* Ed. Margaret Clunies Ross (Cam-
bridge: Cambridge University Press, 2000). Pp. 287–301, esp. p. 298.
Louis-Jensen, Jonna. "To håndskrifter fra det nordvestlige Island."
Opuscula 7. Bibliotheca Arnamagnæana 34 (Copenhagen: Reitzel,
1979). Pp. 219–53, esp. p. 221.
Mogk, Eugen. >> *Geschichte der norwegisch-isländischen Literatur* (1904).
P. 888.
Ólafur Halldórsson, ed. *Mattheus saga postula* (Reykjavík: Stofnun Árna
Magnússonar, 1994). Pp. xlix–lvii.
Handlist, p. 314.

4. Jakobs saga postola (ins eldra)

Translated from a Low German *Passionael.*

Manuscripts:
AM 667 4to V (ca. 1525) and AM 667 4to XI (ca. 1525).
Literature:
Overgaard, Mariane, ed. *The History of the Cross-Tree Down to Christ's
Passion: Icelandic Legend Versions.* Editiones Arnamagnæanæ, Ser. B,
vol. 26 (Copenhagen: Munksgaard, 1968). Pp. xcix–cxix.
Handlist, p. 314.
NOTE:
See also John the Evangelist II.

JAMES THE LESS   May 1

1. Jakobs saga postola (ins yngra)

A translation of a variant of the *Passio Sancti Jacobi* of Pseudo-Abdias'
Historia Apostolorum (*BHL* 4089 and 4093–7).

Manuscripts:
AM 629 4to (1697), AM 630 4to (ca. 1650–1700), AM 659a 4to (ca.
1600–50), and Rask 69 (ca. 1800).

Editions:

Unger, C.R., ed. >> *Postola sögur* (1874). Pp. 737.50–740.21.
Edition of AM 630 4to.

Þorsteinn Jónsson, ed. *Hér hefjast Tíu Sögur, af þeim enum heiløgu Guds Postulum og pínslar vottum* (Viðeyjarklaustur: Þ. Jónsson, 1836).
Pp. 227–32.
Based on a manuscript descended from AM 630 4to.

English translation:

Roughton, Philip G. "AM 645 4to and AM 652/630 4to: Study and Translation of Two Thirteenth-Century Icelandic Collections of Apostles' and Saints' Lives." PhD dissertation, University of Colorado, 2002. Pp. 749–54.

Literature:

Astås, Reidar. "Spor av teologisk tenkning og refleksjon i norsk og islandsk høymiddelalder." *CM* 6 (1993): 133–67, esp. p. 139.

Collings, Lucy Grace. "The Codex Scardensis: Studies in Icelandic Hagiography." PhD dissertation, Cornell University, 1969. Pp. 70–3 and 233–6.

Cormack, Margaret. >> *The Saints in Iceland* (1994). Pp. 108 and 242.

Finnur Jónsson. >> *Den oldnorske og oldislandske Litteraturs Historie* (1920–4). Vol. 2, pp. 871–2.

Foote, Peter. "Postulatal." In Guðni Kolbeinsson, ed. >> *Minjar og menntir* (1976). Pp. 152–73, esp. p. 162.

Kirby, Ian. >> *Biblical Quotation* (1980). Vol. 2, p. 33.

Mogk, Eugen. >> *Geschichte der norwegisch-isländischen Literatur* (1904). P. 889.

Ólafur Halldórsson, ed. *Mattheus saga postula* (Reykjavík: Stofnun Árna Magnússonar, 1994). Pp. xxxvi–xli and lxxv–lxxxi.

Roughton, Philip. "Stylistics and Sources of the *Postola sögur* in AM 645 4to and AM 652/630 4to." *Gripla* 16 (2005): 7–50.

– "'Þá syndi hann þeim mikinn skugga': Unmasking the Fantastic in the *Postola sögur*." In John McKinnell, David Ashurst, and Donata Kick, ed. >> *The Fantastic in Old Norse/Icelandic Literature* (2006). Vol. 2, pp. 846–55, esp. pp. 847 and 849.

Sverrir Tómasson. *Formálar íslenskra sagnaritara á miðöldum. Rannsókn bókmenntahefðar* (Reykjavík: Stofnun Árna Magnússonar, 1988). Pp. 336–7.

Handlist, p. 314.

2. Jakobs saga postola (ins yngra)

A translation of the shortest recension (*BHL* 4093) of the *Passio Sancti Jacobi* of Pseudo-Abdias' *Historia Apostolorum*.

Manuscripts:
AM 238 fol. XI (ca. 1300–25), AM 628 4to (ca. 1711–12), and SÁM 1 fol.
(*Codex Scardensis*) (ca. 1350–75).

Editions:
Slay, Desmond, ed. *Codex Scardensis*. EIM 2 (Copenhagen: Rosenkilde
and Bagger, 1960).
Facsimile of SÁM 1 fol.
Unger, C.R., ed. >> *Postola sögur* (1874). Pp. 742.3–743.22.
Based on AM 628 4to with variants from AM 238 fol. XI.

Modern Icelandic language edition:
Ólafur Halldórsson, ed. *Sögur úr Skarðsbók* (Reykjavík: Almenna bókafé-
lagið, 1967). Pp. 172–3.
Edition of SÁM 1 fol.

Literature:
Bekker-Nielsen, Hans, Thorkil Damsgaard Olsen, and Ole Widding.
>> *Norrøn fortællekunst* (1965). P. 123.
Collings, Lucy Grace. "The Codex Scardensis: Studies in Icelandic Hagiog-
raphy." PhD dissertation, Cornell University, 1969. Pp. 70–3 and 227–36.
Cormack, Margaret. >> *The Saints in Iceland* (1994). Pp. 33n14, 37n45,
108, and 242.
Finnur Jónsson. >> *Den oldnorske og oldislandske Litteraturs Historie*
(1920–4). Vol. 2, pp. 871–2.
Foote, Peter. "Postulatal." In Guðni Kolbeinsson, ed. >> *Minjar og*
menntir (1976). Pp. 152–73, esp. p. 162.
Jón Þorkelsson. "Islandske håndskrifter i England og Skotland." *ANF* 8
(1892): 199–237, esp. pp. 235–6.
Kirby, Ian. >> *Biblical Quotation* (1980). Vol. 2, p. 33.
Mogk, Eugen. >> *Geschichte der norwegisch-isländischen Literatur* (1904).
P. 889.
Ólafur Halldórsson. *Helgafellsbækur fornar*. Studia Islandica 24 (Reykja-
vík: Heimspekideild Háskóla Íslands and Menningarsjóður, 1966).
Pp. 16–22 and 41–5.
Sverrir Tómasson. *Formálar íslenskra sagnaritara á miðöldum. Rannsókn*
bókmenntahefðar (Reykjavík: Stofnun Árna Magnússonar, 1988).
Pp. 336–7.
Þórður Ingi Guðjónsson. "Apostlene i islandsk middelalderlitteratur." In
Den nordiske renessansen i høymiddelalderen. Ed. Jón Viðar Sigurðsson
and Preben Meulengracht Sørensen (Oslo: Historisk institutt, Universi-
tetet i Oslo, 2000). Pp. 83–99, esp. p. 94.
Wolf, Kirsten. "Postola sögur." In Phillip Pulsiano and Kirsten Wolf, with
Paul Acker and Donald K. Fry, ed. >> *Medieval Scandinavia* (1993).

Pp. 511–12.
– "Skarðsbók." In Phillip Pulsiano and Kirsten Wolf, with Paul Acker
and Donald K. Fry, ed. >> *Medieval Scandinavia* (1993). P. 596.
Handlist, p. 314.

JEROME   September 30

Jerónimuss saga

Translated from a now-lost Low German redaction that resembles the
source(s) of *Der Heiligen Leben*.

Manuscript:
Stock. Perg. fol. no. 3 (*Reykjahólabók*) (ca. 1530–40).
Edition:
Loth, Agnete, ed. >> *Reykjahólabók* (1969–70). Vol. 2, pp. 211–53.
Literature:
Bekker-Nielsen, Hans. "Kyrkofäderna ock kyrkolärarna. K. i vestnordisk
    litteratur." *KLNM* 9 (1964). Cols. 690–3, esp. col. 693.
Bekker-Nielsen, Hans, Thorkil Damsgaard Olsen, and Ole Widding.
    >> *Norrøn fortællekunst* (1965). Pp. 126 and 141.
Bekker-Nielsen, Hans, and Ole Widding. "Legende. Norge og Island."
    KLNM 10 (1965). Cols. 421–3, esp. col. 421.
Boyer, Régis. >> *La vie religieuse en Islande* (1979). P. 160.
Kalinke, Marianne E. "Reykjahólabók: A Legendary on the Eve of the
    Reformation." *Skáldskaparmál* 2 (1992): 239–69, esp. p. 240.
– "The Cowherd and the Saint: The Grateful Lion in Icelandic Folklore
    and Legend." *SS* 66 (1994): 1–22, esp. pp. 8–22.
– >> *The Book of Reykjahólar* (1996). Pp. 28, 50, 54–6, 59, 65, 97–8,
    126, 137, 139, 152, 155–9, 161, 165–6, 174, 179–82, 184–5,
    and 198–9.
Sverrir Tómasson. "Trúarbókmenntir í lausu máli á síðmiðöld." In
    Böðvar Guðmundsson, Sverrir Tómasson, Torfi H. Tulinius, and
    Vésteinn Ólason, ed. >> *Íslensk Bókmenntasaga* 2 (1993). Pp. 249–82,
    esp. p. 279.
Widding, Ole, and Hans Bekker-Nielsen. "En senmiddelalderlig
    legendesamling." *Mm* (1960): 105–28, esp. pp. 108, 123, and 127.
– "Low German Influence on Late Icelandic Hagiography." *GR* 37
    (1962): 239–62, esp. pp. 247 and 255.
Handlist, p. 314.

JOHN THE ALMONER   January 23

Af Jóhanne elemosinario

A tale of Saint John the Almoner incorporated into the miracles of the
Virgin Mary.

Manuscripts:
See Mary the Blessed Virgin 3 note (p. 245).
Edition:
Unger, C.R., ed. >> *Mariu saga* (1871). Pp. 702.22–704.11.
Literature:
Handlist, pp. 315 and 323.

JOHN THE BAPTIST   June 24

1. Jóns saga baptista

A Norwegian translation of the legend of Saint John the Baptist. The
source has not been identified.

Manuscript:
AM 237b fol. (ca. 1250, defective).
Edition:
   Loth, Agnete. "Et gammelnorsk apostelsagafragment: AM 237 b fol."
   In *Afmælisrit Jóns Helgasonar 30. júní 1969*. Ed. Jakob Benediktsson et
   al. (Reykjavík: Heimskringla, 1969). Pp. 219–34, esp. pp. 223.21–224
   (text and facsimile).
Literature:
Cormack, Margaret. >> *The Saints in Iceland* (1994). P. 111.
Kirby, Ian. >> *Biblical Quotation* (1980). Vol. 2, p. 101.
Sverrir Tómasson. "Kristnar trúarbókmenntir í óbundnu máli." In
   Guðrún Nordal, Sverrir Tómasson, and Vésteinn Ólason, ed. >>
   Íslensk Bókmenntasaga 1 (1992). Pp. 419–79, esp. p. 448.
Handlist, p. 315.

2. Jóns saga baptista I

A legend of Saint John the Baptist based primarily on the biblical
accounts. The Latin source has not been identified.

Manuscripts:
AM 235 fol. (ca. 1400, defective), AM 238 fol. VIII (ca. 1425–50),
   AM 625 4to (ca. 1300–25, defective), and AM 669b 4to (ca.
   1700–25).
Editions:
Foote, Peter, ed. >> *Lives of Saints* (1962).
   Facsimile of AM 238 fol. VIII (2r–v).
Unger, C.R., ed. >> *Postola sögur* (1874). Pp. 842–849.5.
   Edition of AM 625 4to.
Literature:
Bekker-Nielsen, Hans, and Ole Widding. "Legende. Norge og Island."
   KLNM 10 (1965). Cols. 421–3, esp. col. 421.
Carlé, Birte. >> *Jomfru-fortællingen* (1985). Pp. 37–8.
Cormack, Margaret. >> *The Saints in Iceland* (1994). P. 111.
Finnur Jónsson. >> *Den oldnorske og oldislandske Litteraturs Historie*
   (1920–4). Vol. 2, p. 868.
Gjerløw, Lilli. "Johannes Baptista." *KLNM* 7 (1962). Cols. 593–4.
Holm-Olsen, Ludvig. "Apostelsagaer." *KLNM* 1 (1956). Cols. 177–8, esp.
   col. 178.
Kirby, Ian. >> *Biblical Quotation* (1980). Vol. 2, p. 37.
– *Bible Translation in Old Norse*. Université de Lausanne Publications
   de la faculté des lettres 27 (Geneva: Librairie Droz, 1986). Pp. 87 and
   95.
– "The Bible and Biblical Interpretation in Medieval Iceland." In
   Old Icelandic Literature and Society. Ed. Margaret Clunies Ross
   (Cambridge: Cambridge University Press, 2000). Pp. 287–301, esp.
   p. 298.
Loth, Agnete. "Til Sebastianus saga." *Opuscula* 5. Bibliotheca Arna-
   magnæana 31 (Copenhagen: Munksgaard, 1975). Pp. 103–22, esp.
   pp. 119–20.
Mogk, Eugen. >> *Geschichte der norwegisch-isländischen Literatur* (1904).
   P. 889.
Sverrir Tómasson. *Formálar íslenskra sagnaritara á miðöldum. Rannsókn*
   bókmenntahefðar (Reykjavík: Stofnun Árna Magnússonar, 1988).
   Pp. 275–6 and 337–8.
– "Kristnar trúarbókmenntir í óbundnu máli." In Guðrún Nordal, Sverrir
   Tómasson, and Vésteinn Ólason, ed. >> *Íslensk Bókmenntasaga* 1
   (1992). Pp. 419–79, esp. p. 448.
Widding, Ole, and Hans Bekker-Nielsen. "En senmiddelalderlig
   legendesamling." *Mm* (1960): 105–28, esp. p. 126.
Handlist, p. 315.

3. Jóns saga baptista II

A legend of Saint John the Baptist compiled by the priest Grímr
Hólmsteinsson (d. 1298) from various sources, including Vincent of
Beauvais' *Speculum historiale*, Peter Comestor's *Historia scholastica*, and
Ambrose's *Expositio Evangelii secundum Lucam*.

Manuscripts:
AM 232 fol. (ca. 1350), AM 233a fol. (ca. 1350–60, defective), AM 233b
    fol. (ca. 1700, prologue only), AM 236 fol. (ca. 1600, defective), AM
    238 fol. IX (ca. 1400), AM 239 fol. (ca. 1350–1400, defective), AM
    385 4to I (ca. 1375–1400), AM 637 4to (ca. 1700–25), AM 651 4to II
    (ca. 1375–1400), AM 667 4to IX (ca. 1350), and AM 667 4to XII
    (ca. 1400–1500).

Editions:
Agerschou, Agnes. "Et fragment af Jóns saga baptista." *Opuscula* 1.
    Bibliotheca Arnamagnæana 20 (Copenhagen: Munksgaard, 1960).
    Pp. 97–104, esp. pp. 101–4.
    Edition of AM 385 4to I.
Foote, Peter, ed. *A Saga of St Peter the Apostle. Perg. 4:o nr 19 in the
    Royal Library, Stockholm.* EIM 19 (Copenhagen: Rosenkilde and
    Bagger, 1990).
    Facsimile of AM 385 4to I, fol. 2r1–15.
Unger, C.R., ed. >> *Postola sögur* (1874). Pp. 849.8–931.
    Based on AM 233a fol. (pp. 849.8–850.19) and AM 232 fol. (pp. 850.20–
    931) with variants from AM 233a fol. (pp. 850.20–852.5, 873.2–885.6,
    and 925.10–931), AM 239 fol. (pp. 853.16–856.9, 861.6–863.31, 868.36–
    872.4, 888.25–891.7, 893.22–910.8, and 913.11–931), AM 236 fol.
    (pp. 903.1–919.9 and 926.34–931), and AM 651 4to II (pp. 924.14–
    925.28 and 928.19–929.30).

Literature:
Astås, Reidar. "Spor av teologisk tenkning og refleksjon i norsk og islandsk
    høymiddelalder." *CM* 6 (1993): 133–67, esp. pp. 138n23 and 139n25.
Battista, Simonette. "Translation or Redaction in Old Norse Hagiog-
    raphy." In Peter Andersen, ed. >> *Pratiques de Traduction au Moyen
    Age* (2004). Pp. 100–10, esp. p. 106.
– "The *Compilator* and Contemporary Literary Culture in Old Norse Hagi-
    ography." *Viking and Medieval Scandinavia* 1 (2005): 1–13, esp. pp. 6–7.
Bekker-Nielsen, Hans, Thorkil Damsgaard Olsen, and Ole Widding.
    >> *Norrøn fortællekunst* (1965). P. 136.

Bekker-Nielsen, Hans, and Ole Widding. "Legende. Norge og Island." *KLNM* 10 (1965). Cols. 421–3, esp. col. 421.

Boyer, Régis. >> *La vie religieuse en Islande* (1979). P. 146.

Carlé, Birte. >> *Jomfru-fortællingen* (1985). Pp. 35–6.

Cormack, Margaret. >> *The Saints in Iceland* (1994). Pp. 33 and 111.

– "Saints' Lives and Icelandic Literature in the Thirteenth and Fourteenth Centuries." In Hans Bekker-Nielsen and Birte Carlé, ed. >> *Saints and Sagas* (1994). Pp. 27–47, esp. pp. 33–6.

– "Sagas of Saints." In *Old Icelandic Literature and Society*. Ed. Margaret Clunies Ross (Cambridge: Cambridge University Press, 2000). Pp. 302–25, esp. p. 305.

– "Christian Biography." In *A Companion to Old Norse–Icelandic Literature and Culture*. Ed. Rory McTurk (Oxford: Blackwell, 2005). Pp. 27–42, esp. p. 33.

Finnur Jónsson. >> *Den oldnorske og oldislandske Litteraturs Historie* (1920–4). Vol. 2, p. 868.

Gjerløw, Lilli. "Johannes Baptista." *KLNM* 7 (1962). Cols. 593–4.

Hallberg, Peter. "Imagery in Religious Old Norse Prose Literature: An Outline." *ANF* 102 (1987): 120–70, esp. pp. 121, 125, 141–5, 150, 160, and 165–6.

Holm-Olsen, Ludvig. "Apostelsagaer." *KLNM* 1 (1956). Cols. 177–8, esp. col. 178.

Johannessen, Ole-Jörgen. "Litt om kildene til Jóns saga baptista II." *Opuscula Septentrionalia. Festskrift til Ole Widding 10.10.1977* (Copenhagen: Reitzel, 1977). Pp. 110–15.

Jón Helgason. *Norrøn Litteraturhistorie* (Copenhagen: Levin and Munksgaard, 1934). P. 103..

Jónas Kristjánsson. *Um Fóstbræðra sögu* (Reykjavík: Stofnun Árna Magnússonar, 1972). Pp. 261, 264, 269, 303, and 307.

– >> *Eddas and Sagas* (1988). Pp. 139 and 232.

Kirby, Ian. >> *Biblical Quotation* (1980). Vol. 2, pp. 37–8.

– *Bible Translation in Old Norse*. Université de Lausanne Publications de la faculté des lettres 27 (Geneva: Librairie Droz, 1986). Pp. 6, 46, 87, 89, 100–1, 110, and 117.

– "The Bible and Biblical Interpretation in Medieval Iceland." In *Old Icelandic Literature and Society*. Ed. Margaret Clunies Ross (Cambridge: Cambridge University Press, 2000). Pp. 287–301, esp. p. 291.

Kratz, Henry. "Saints' Lives. 2. Iceland and Norway." In Phillip Pulsiano and Kirsten Wolf, with Paul Acker and Donald K. Fry, ed. >> *Medieval Scandinavia* (1993). Pp. 562–4.

Magerøy, Hallvard. "Helgensoger." *KLNM* 6 (1961). Cols. 350–3, esp. col. 351.

Mogk, Eugen. >> *Geschichte der norwegisch-isländischen Literatur* (1904). P. 889.

Paasche, Fredrik. *Norges og Islands litteratur inntil utgangen av middelalderen.* Rev. ed. by Anne Holtsmark (Oslo: Aschehoug, 1947). Pp. 445–6.

Svanhildur Óskarsdóttir. "Prose of Christian Instruction." In *A Companion to Old Norse–Icelandic Literature.* Ed. Rory McTurk (Oxford: Blackwell, 2005). Pp. 338–53, esp. p. 346.

Sverrir Tómasson. *Formálar íslenskra sagnaritara á miðöldum. Rannsókn bókmenntahefðar* (Reykjavík: Stofnun Árna Magnússonar, 1988). Pp. 17, 54, 85, 87, 90, 95, 97, 99, 117–18, 126, 132–3, 145, 152–4, 184–5, 251, 254, 307, 310–12, 325, 329, 337–8, 358, and 394.

– "Kristnar trúarbókmenntir í óbundnu máli." In Guðrún Nordal, Sverrir Tómasson, and Vésteinn Ólason, ed. >> *Íslensk Bókmenntasaga* 1 (1992). Pp. 419–79, esp. pp. 447–51.

– "Trúarbókmenntir í lausu máli á síðmiðöld." In Böðvar Guðmundsson, Sverrir Tómasson, Torfi H. Tulinius, and Vésteinn Ólason, ed. >> *Íslensk Bókmenntasaga* 2 (1993). Pp. 249–82, esp. p. 264.

– "Er nýja textafræðin ný? Þankar um gamla fræðigrein." *Gripla* 13 (2002): 199–216, esp. p. 207. Rpt. in Sverrir Tómasson. *Tækileg vitni: Greinar um bókmenntir gefnar út í tilefni sjötugsafmælis hans 5. apríl 2011* (Reykjavík: Stofnun Árna Magnússonar and Hið íslenska bókmenntafélag, 2011). Pp. 231–50, esp. p. 239.

Vries, Jan de. >> *Altnordische Literaturgeschichte* (1964–7). Vol. 2, p. 183.

Widding, Ole, and Hans Bekker-Nielsen. "En senmiddelalderlig legendesamling." *Mm* (1960): 105–28, esp. p. 126.

– "Low German Influence on Late Icelandic Hagiography." *GR* 37 (1962): 239–62, esp. p. 242.

Handlist, p. 315.

JOHN CHRYSOSTOM   January 27

Jóns saga gullmunns

Translated from a now-lost Low German redaction that resembles the source(s) of *Der Heiligen Leben*.

Manuscript:
Stock. Perg. fol. no. 3 (*Reykjahólabók*) (ca. 1530–40).

Edition:
Loth, Agnete, ed. >> *Reykjahólabók* (1969–70). Vol. 2, pp. 167–91.
Modern Icelandic language edition:
Kalinke, Marianne E. "*Jóhannes saga gullmunns*: The Icelandic Legend of
the Hairy Anchorite." In A.N. Doane and Kirsten Wolf, ed. >> *Beatus
Vir* (2006). Pp. 176–227, esp. pp. 186–225 (verso).
English translation:
Kalinke, Marianne E. "*Jóhannes saga gullmunns*: The Icelandic Legend of
the Hairy Anchorite." In A.N. Doane and Kirsten Wolf, ed. >> *Beatus
Vir* (2006). Pp. 176–227, esp. pp. 186–225 (recto).
Literature:
Bekker-Nielsen, Hans, Thorkil Damsgaard Olsen, and Ole Widding.
>> *Norrøn fortællekunst* (1965). P. 141.
Kalinke, Marianne E. "Reykjahólabók: A Legendary on the Eve of the
Reformation." *Skáldskaparmál* 2 (1992): 239–69, esp. p. 240.
– "The Cowherd and the Saint: The Grateful Lion in Icelandic Folklore
and Legend." *SS* 66 (1994): 1–22, esp. pp. 7–8.
– "The Icelandic Legend of the Hairy Anchorite." In Gísli Sigurðsson,
Guðrún Kvaran, and Sigurgeir Steingrímsson, ed. >> *Sagnaþing helgað
Jónasi Kristjánssyni* (1994). Vol. 2, pp. 485–95.
– >> *The Book of Reykjahólar* (1996). Pp. 28, 50, 99, 127–8, 136–7, 140,
144–5, 158, 165–6, 185–98, 201–2, and 211.
Sverrir Tómasson. "Trúarbókmenntir í lausu máli á síðmiðöld." In
Böðvar Guðmundsson, Sverrir Tómasson, Torfi H. Tulinius, and
Vésteinn Ólason, ed. >> *Íslensk Bókmenntasaga* 2 (1993). Pp. 249–82,
esp. p. 279.
Widding, Ole, and Hans Bekker-Nielsen. "En senmiddelalderlig
legendesamling." *Mm* (1960): 105–28, esp. pp. 107 and 121.
– "Low German Influence on Late Icelandic Hagiography." *GR* 37
(1962): 239–62, esp. p. 250.
Handlist, p. 315.

JOHN DAMASCENE   March 27

Af Jóhanne Damasceno

Tales of Saint John Damascene incorporated into the miracles of the
Virgin Mary.

Manuscripts:
See Mary the Blessed Virgin 3 note (p. 245).
Edition:
Unger, C.R., ed. >> *Mariu saga* (1871). Pp. 438.30–444.26 and
1116.29–1126.2.
Literature:
Boyer, Régis. >> *La vie religieuse en Islande* (1979). P. 162.
Widding, Ole. "Norrøne Marialegender på europæisk baggrund."
Opuscula 10. Bibliotheca Arnamagnæana 40 (Copenhagen: Reitzel,
1996). Pp. 1–128, esp. pp. 39–40 and 66.
Handlist, pp. 315 and 323.

JOHN THE EVANGELIST   December 27

I.

1. Jóns saga postola I

A legend of Saint John the Evangelist based on a variety of sources,
including *BHL* 4316, 4320, and 4324.

Manuscripts:
AM 629 4to (1697), AM 630 4to (ca. 1650–1700), AM 652 4to (ca. 1250–70,
defective), AM 659b 4to (ca. 1600–1700, defective), NRA 67 (ca. 1300–
25), and Rask 69 (ca. 1800).
Editions:
Hreinn Benediktsson. *Early Icelandic Script As Illustrated in Vernacular
Texts from the Twelfth and Thirteenth Centuries.* Íslenzk handrit:
Icelandic Manuscripts, Series in Folio 2 (Reykjavík: The Manuscript
Institute of Iceland, 1965). Plate 64.
Facsimile of AM 652 4to fol. 3v.
Þorsteinn Jónsson, ed. *Hér hefjast Tíu Sögur, af þeim enum heiløgu Guds
Postulum og pínslar vottum* (Viðeyjarklaustur: Þ. Jónsson, 1836).
Pp. 62–102.
Based on a manuscript descended from AM 630 4to.
Unger, C.R., ed. >> *Postola sögur* (1874). Pp. 412.14–445.17.
Editions of AM 630 4to (pp. 412.14–436.3), AM 652 4to (pp. 436.6–
443.5), and NRA 67e (pp. 443.15–445.17). Edition of AM 629 4to
(pp. viii–ix, extract only).

English translation:
Roughton, Philip G. "AM 645 4to and AM 652/630 4to: Study and
  Translation of Two Thirteenth-Century Icelandic Collections of
  Apostles' and Saints' Lives." PhD dissertation, University of Colorado,
  2002. Pp. 654–97.

Literature:
Battista, Simonetta. "Old Norse Hagiography and the Question of the
  Latin Sources." In Rudolf Simek and Judith Meurer, ed. >> *Scandi-
  navia and Christian Europe in the Middle Ages* (2003). Pp. 26–33, esp.
  pp. 28–31.
Bekker-Nielsen, Hans, Thorkil Damsgaard Olsen, and Ole Widding.
  >> *Norrøn fortællekunst* (1965). P. 122.
Cormack, Margaret. >> *The Saints in Iceland* (1994). Pp. 113 and 242.
Finnur Jónsson. >> *Den oldnorske og oldislandske Litteraturs Historie*
  (1920–4). Vol. 2, pp. 870–1.
Hallberg, Peter. *Stilsignalement och författarskap i norrön sagalitteratur:
  Synpunkter och exempel.* Nordistica Gothoburgensia 3 (Stockholm:
  Almqvist & Wiksell, 1968). Pp. 120–37, 139–41, 147, 149–50, 161–4,
  and 185–9.
– "Imagery in Religious Old Norse Prose Literature: An Outline." *ANF*
  102 (1987): 120–70, esp. pp. 122 and 146.
Jón Ma. Ásgeirsson and Þórður Ingi Guðjónsson, ed. *Frá Sýrlandi til
  Íslands: Arfur Tómasar postula* (Reykjavík: Háskólaútgáfan, 2007). P. 165.
Jónas Kristjánsson. *Um Fóstbrǿðra sögu* (Reykjavík: Stofnun Árna
  Magnússonar, 1972). P. 281.
Kirby, Ian. >> *Biblical Quotation* (1980). Vol. 2, p. 28.
Lange, Wolfgang. *Studien zur christlichen Dichtung der Nordgermanen
  1000–1200.* Palaestra 222 (Göttingen: Vandenhoeck & Ruprecht, 1958).
  Pp. 78 and 85.
Mogk, Eugen. >> *Geschichte der norwegisch-isländischen Literatur* (1904).
  P. 888.
Ólafur Halldórsson, ed. *Mattheus saga postula* (Reykjavík: Stofnun Árna
  Magnússonar, 1994). Pp. xxix–xli.
Paasche, Fredrik. *Norges og Islands litteratur inntil utgangen av
  middelalderen.* Rev. ed. by Anne Holtsmark (Oslo: Aschehoug, 1947).
  P. 446.
Roughton, Philip. "Stylistics and Sources of the *Postola sögur* in AM 645
  4to and AM 652/630 4to." *Gripla* 16 (2005): 7–50.
– "'Þá syndi hann þeim mikinn skugga': Unmasking the Fantastic in the
  Postola sögur." In John McKinnell, David Ashurst, and Donata Kick,

ed >> *The Fantastic in Old Norse/Icelandic Literature* (2006). Vol. 2, pp. 846–55, esp. pp. 847 and 850–2.

Stefán Karlsson. "Islandsk bogeksport til Norge i middelalderen." *Mm* (1979): 1–17, esp. p. 6. Rpt. in *Stafkrókar: Ritgerðir eftir Stefán Karlsson gefnar út í tilefni af sjötugsafmæli hans 2. desember 1998*. Ed. Guðvarður Már Gunnlaugsson (Reykjavík: Stofnun Árna Magnússonar, 2000). Pp. 188–205, esp. p. 194.

Sverrir Tómasson. "Kristnar trúarbókmenntir í óbundnu máli." In Guðrún Nordal, Sverrir Tómasson, and Vésteinn Ólason, ed. >> *Íslensk Bókmenntasaga* 1 (1992). Pp. 419–79, esp. pp. 425 and 444.

Þórður Ingi Guðjónsson. "Apostlene i islandsk middelalderlitteratur." In *Den nordiske renessansen i høymiddelalderen*. Ed. Jón Viðar Sigurðsson and Preben Meulengracht Sørensen (Oslo: Historisk institutt, Universitetet i Oslo, 2000). Pp. 83–99, esp. p. 93.

Vries, Jan de. >> *Altnordische Literaturgeschichte* (1964–7). Vol. 2, p. 183.

Handlist, p. 316.

2. Jóns saga postola II

A legend of Saint John the Evangelist based on a version of *BHL* 4320 (and 4324).

Manuscript:
AM 656 4to I (ca. 1325–50).
Edition:
Unger, C.R., ed. >> *Postola sögur* (1874). Pp. 445.25–454.
Literature:
Battista, Simonetta. "Old Norse Hagiography and the Question of the Latin Sources." In Rudolf Simek and Judith Meurer, ed. >> *Scandinavia and Christian Europe in the Middle Ages* (2003). Pp. 26–33, esp. pp. 28–31.

Cormack, Margaret. >> *The Saints in Iceland* (1994). P. 113.

Finnur Jónsson. >> *Den oldnorske og oldislandske Litteraturs Historie* (1920–4). Vol. 2, pp. 870–1.

Foote, Peter. "Postulatal." In Guðni Kolbeinsson, ed. >> *Minjar og menntir* (1976). Pp. 152–73, esp. pp. 160–1.

Hallberg, Peter. *Stilsignalement och författarskap i norrön sagalitteratur: Synpunkter och exempel*. Nordistica Gothoburgensia 3 (Stockholm: Almqvist & Wiksell, 1968). Pp. 120–37, 139–41, 147, 149–50, 161–4, and 185–9.

- "Imagery in Religious Old Norse Prose Literature: An Outline." *ANF* 102 (1987): 120–70, esp. pp. 122 and 140.

Jón Ma. Ásgeirsson and Þórður Ingi Guðjónsson, ed. *Frá Sýrlandi til Íslands: Arfur Tómasar postula* (Reykjavík: Háskólaútgáfan, 2007). P. 165.

Kirby, Ian. >> *Biblical Quotation* (1980). Vol. 2, p. 29.

Lange, Wolfgang. *Studien zur christlichen Dichtung der Nordgermanen 1000–1200.* Palaestra 222 (Göttingen: Vandenhoeck & Ruprecht, 1958). P. 85.

Louis-Jensen, Jonna. "To håndskrifter fra det nordvestlige Island." *Opuscula* 7. Bibliotheca Arnamagnæana 34 (Copenhagen: Reitzel, 1979). Pp. 219–53, esp. p. 221.

Mogk, Eugen. >> *Geschichte der norwegisch-isländischen Literatur* (1904). P. 888.

Ólafur Halldórsson, ed. *Mattheus saga postula* (Reykjavík: Stofnun Árna Magnússonar, 1994). Pp. xlix–lvii.

Paasche, Fredrik. *Norges og Islands litteratur inntil utgangen av middelalderen.* Rev. ed. by Anne Holtsmark (Oslo: Aschehoug, 1947). P. 446.

Þórður Ingi Guðjónsson. "Apostlene i islandsk middelalderlitteratur." In *Den nordiske renessansen i høymiddelalderen.* Ed. Jón Viðar Sigurðsson and Preben Meulengracht Sørensen (Oslo: Historisk institutt, Universitetet i Oslo, 2000). Pp. 83–99, esp. p. 94.

Vries, Jan de. >> *Altnordische Literaturgeschichte* (1964–7). Vol. 2, p. 183.

Handlist, p. 316.

3. Jóns saga postola III

A legend of Saint John the Evangelist based on a version of *BHL* 4316 and 4320.

Manuscript:
AM 623 4to (ca. 1325).

Editions:
Finnur Jónsson, ed. *AM 623, 4°: Helgensagaer.* STUAGNL 52 (Copenhagen: Jørgensen, 1927). Pp. 9.19–25.6.

Hreinn Benediktsson. *Early Icelandic Script As Illustrated in Vernacular Texts from the Twelfth and Thirteenth Centuries.* Íslenzk handrit: Icelandic Manuscripts, Series in Folio 2 (Reykjavík: The Manuscript Institute of Iceland, 1965). Plate 56 and pp. xxxvii–xxxviii. Facsimile and text edition of fol. 12v.

Unger, C.R., ed. >> *Postola sögur* (1874). Pp. 455–65.

Literature:

Battista, Simonetta. "Old Norse Hagiography and the Question of the Latin Sources." In Rudolf Simek and Judith Meurer, ed. >> *Scandinavia and Christian Europe in the Middle Ages* (2003). Pp. 26–33, esp. pp. 28–31.

Cormack, Margaret. >> *The Saints in Iceland* (1994). Pp. 242–3.

Finnur Jónsson. >> *Den oldnorske og oldislandske Litteraturs Historie* (1920–4). Vol. 2, pp. 870–1.

Foote, Peter. "Postulatal." In Guðni Kolbeinsson, ed. >> *Minjar og menntir* (1976). Pp. 152–73, esp. p. 161.

Hallberg, Peter. *Stilsignalement och författarskap i norrön sagalitteratur: Synpunkter och exempel.* Nordistica Gothoburgensia 3 (Stockholm: Almqvist & Wiksell, 1968). Pp. 120–37, 139–41, 147, 149–50, 161–4, and 185–9.

Kirby, Ian. >> *Biblical Quotation* (1980). Vol. 2, p. 29.

Lange, Wolfgang. *Studien zur christlichen Dichtung der Nordgermanen 1000–1200.* Palaestra 222 (Göttingen: Vandenhoeck & Ruprecht, 1958). P. 85.

Mogk, Eugen. >> *Geschichte der norwegisch-isländischen Literatur* (1904). P. 888.

Paasche, Fredrik. *Norges og Islands litteratur inntil utgangen av middelalderen.* Rev. ed. by Anne Holtsmark (Oslo: Aschehoug, 1947). P. 446.

Vries, Jan de. >> *Altnordische Literaturgeschichte* (1964–7). Vol. 2, p. 183.

Handlist, p. 316.

4. Jóns saga postola IV

A revised recension of 1–3 with additional material, including the story of Saint Marcellinus. It incorporates writings of Peter Damian, Pope Leo the Great, and Gregory the Great.

Manuscripts:

AM 649a 4to (ca. 1350–1400 and 1500–1600) and AM 649b 4to (ca. 1700–25, extracts).

Edition:

Unger, C.R., ed. >> *Postola sögur* (1874). Pp. 466–513.22.
   Edition of AM 649a 4to.

Literature:

Astås, Reidar. "Spor av teologisk tenkning og refleksjon i norsk og islandsk høymiddelalder." *CM* 6 (1993): 133–67, esp. p. 139.

Battista, Simonetta. "Old Norse Hagiography and the Question of the Latin Sources." In Rudolf Simek and Judith Meurer, ed. >> *Scandinavia and Christian Europe in the Middle Ages* (2003). Pp. 26–33, esp. pp. 28–31.

Cormack, Margaret. >> *The Saints in Iceland* (1994). Pp. 34, 41, 114, and 243.

– "Saints' Lives and Icelandic Literature in the Thirteenth and Fourteenth Centuries." In Hans Bekker-Nielsen and Birte Carlé, ed. >> *Saints and Sagas* (1994). Pp. 27–47, esp. p. 33.

Dillmann, François-Xavier. "Om hedningar och hundar. Kring den fornvästnordiska sammansättningen *hundheiðinn*." *SI* 52 (2001): 17–33, esp. pp. 21 and 24.

Finnur Jónsson. >> *Den oldnorske og oldislandske Litteraturs Historie* (1920–4). Vol. 2, pp. 870–1.

Foote, Peter. "Postulatal." In Guðni Kolbeinsson, ed. >> *Minjar og menntir* (1976). Pp. 152–73, esp. p. 161.

Guðrún Nordal. *Tools of Literacy: The Role of Skaldic Verse in Icelandic Textual Culture of the Twelfth and Thirteenth Centuries* (Toronto: University of Toronto Press, 2001). Pp. 76, 89, 101, 114, 141, 175–6, 294, and 388.

Hallberg, Peter. *Stilsignalement och författarskap i norrön sagalitteratur: Synpunkter och exempel.* Nordistica Gothoburgensia 3 (Stockholm: Almqvist & Wiksell, 1968). Pp. 120–37, 139–41, 147, 149–50, 161–4, and 185–9.

– "Imagery in Religious Old Norse Prose Literature: An Outline." *ANF* 102 (1987): 120–70, esp. pp. 136, 140, 142, 146–7, 154, 156–7, 160, and 165.

Holm-Olsen, Ludvig. "Apostelsagaer." *KLNM* 1 (1956). Cols. 177–8, esp. col. 178.

Jakob Benediktsson. "Cursus hos Bergr Sokkason." In *Festskrift til Ludvig Holm-Olsen på hans 70-årsdag den 9. juni 1984* (Øvre Ervik: Alvheim & Eide, 1984). Pp. 34–40, esp. pp. 36–7. Rpt. in Jakob Benediktsson. *Lærdómslistir. Afmælisrit 20. júlí 1987* (Reykjavík: Mál og menning, 1987). Pp. 262–9, esp. p. 265.

Jónas Kristjánsson. *Um Fóstbræðra sögu* (Reykjavík: Stofnun Árna Magnússonar, 1972). Pp. 268, 290, and 305.

Kirby, Ian. >> *Biblical Quotation* (1980). Vol. 2, p. 29.

La Farge, Beatrice, ed. "Gamli kanóki, *Jónsdrápa* 'Drápa about S. John'." In Margaret Clunies Ross, ed. >> *Poetry on Christian Subjects* (2007). Vol. 1, pp. 133–6.

– ed. "Kolbeinn Tumason, *Jónsvísur* '*Vísur* about S. John'." In Margaret Clunies Ross, ed. >> *Poetry on Christian Subjects* (2007). Vol. 1, pp. 223–7.

– ed. "Níkulás Bergsson, *Jónsdrápa* '*Drápa* about S. John'." In Margaret Clunies Ross, ed. >> *Poetry on Christian Subjects* (2007). Vol. 1, pp. 66–9.

Lange, Wolfgang. *Studien zur christlichen Dichtung der Nordgermanen 1000–1200.* Palaestra 222 (Göttingen: Vandenhoeck & Ruprecht, 1958). Pp. 81, 83, 85, and 101–2.

Lehmann, Paul. >> "Skandinaviens Anteil an der lateinischen Literatur und Wissenschaft des Mittelalters" (1937). P. 20.

Mogk, Eugen. >> *Geschichte der norwegisch-isländischen Literatur* (1904). P. 888.

Paasche, Fredrik. *Norges og Islands litteratur inntil utgangen av middelalderen.* Rev. ed. by Anne Holtsmark (Oslo: Aschehoug, 1947). P. 446.

Simek, Rudolf. *Altnordische Kosmographie: Studien und Quellen zu Weltbild und Weltbeschreibung in Norwegen und Island vom 12. bis zum 14. Jahrhundert* (Berlin: de Gruyter, 1990). P. 265.

Sverrir Jakobsson. *Við og veröldin: Heimsmynd Íslendinga 1100–1400* (Reykjavík: Háskólaútgáfan, 2005). Pp. 164–5.

Sverrir Tómasson. "Norðlenski Benediktínaskólinn." In >> *The Sixth International Saga Conference* (1985). Vol. 2, pp. 1009–20, esp. pp. 1009, 1013, and 1015. Rpt. in Sverrir Tómasson. *Tækileg vitni: Greinar um bókmenntir gefnar út í tilefni sjötugsafmælis hans 5. apríl 2011* (Reykjavík: Stofnun Árna Magnússonar and Hið íslenska bókmenntafélag, 2011). Pp. 345–58, esp. pp. 345, 349–50, and 356.

– *Formálar íslenskra sagnaritara á miðöldum. Rannsókn bókmenntahefðar* (Reykjavík: Stofnun Árna Magnússonar, 1988). Pp. 118, 150, and 153.

– "Kristnar trúarbókmenntir í óbundnu máli." In Guðrún Nordal, Sverrir Tómasson, and Vésteinn Ólason, ed. >> *Íslensk Bókmenntasaga* 1 (1992). Pp. 419–79, esp. pp. 444 and 446.

– "Trúarbókmenntir í lausu máli á síðmiðöld." In Böðvar Guðmundsson, Sverrir Tómasson, Torfi H. Tulinius, and Vésteinn Ólason, ed. >> *Íslensk Bókmenntasaga* 2 (1993). Pp. 249–82, esp. p. 251.

Vries, Jan de. >> *Altnordische Literaturgeschichte* (1964–7). Vol. 2, p. 183.

Handlist, p. 316.

NOTE:

The saga includes a story of Saint Marcellinus. See the entry for this saint.

5. Jóns saga postola

An abridged version of 1–3.

Manuscript:
AM 238 fol. IV (ca. 1500).
Literature:
Battista, Simonetta. "Old Norse Hagiography and the Question of the
Latin Sources." In Rudolf Simek and Judith Meurer, ed. >> *Scandi-
navia and Christian Europe in the Middle Ages* (2003). Pp. 26–33,
esp. p. 28.
Handlist, p. 316.

6. Jóns saga postola

An abridged version of 1(–3).

Manuscript:
AM 655 4to XIV (ca. 1250–75).
Literature:
Battista, Simonetta. "Old Norse Hagiography and the Question of the
Latin Sources." In Rudolf Simek and Judith Meurer, ed. >> *Scandi-
navia and Christian Europe in the Middle Ages* (2003). Pp. 26–33,
esp. p. 28.
Cormack, Margaret. >> *The Saints in Iceland* (1994). Pp. 41 and 114.
Handlist, p. 316.

II.

Tveggja postola saga Jóns ok Jakobs (ins eldra)

A composite text based on *BHL* 4320 and 4057 with material added from
the *Pseudo-Turpin Chronicle*, Vincent of Beauvais's *Speculum historiale*,
Eusebius of Caesarea's *Historia Ecclesiastica*, a commentary on the
Gospel of John, a commentary on John's Apocalypse, and other sources.

Manuscripts:
AM 236 fol. (ca. 1600, defective), AM 239 fol. (ca. 1360–70, defective),
AM 632 4to (ca. 1700–25), AM 636 4to (ca. 1700–25), AM 650a 4to
(ca. 1400, defective), AM 651 4to I (ca. 1375–1400), AM 653a 4to

(ca. 1350–75, defective), AM 653b 4to I (ca. 1300–1400), AM 653b 4to II (ca. 1350–1400), JS fragm 7 (ca. 1350–75), Lbs 2454 8vo (ca. 1350–1400), and SÁM 1 fol. (*Codex Scardensis*) (ca. 1350–75).

Editions:

Foote, Peter, ed. *A Saga of St Peter the Apostle. Perg. 4:o nr 19 in the Royal Library, Stockholm.* EIM 19 (Copenhagen: Rosenkilde and Bagger, 1990).

Facsimile of AM 651 4to I, fol. 49v.

Slay, Desmond, ed. *Codex Scardensis.* EIM 2 (Copenhagen: Rosenkilde and Bagger, 1960).

Facsimile of SÁM 1 fol.

Unger, C.R., ed. >> *Postola sögur* (1874). Pp. 536–711.

Based on AM 636 4to (pp. 536–639.14 and 643.11–711), AM 651 4to I (pp. 642.5–643.11), and AM 650a 4to (pp. 639.14–642.5) with variants from AM 239 fol. (pp. 536–540.21, 547.25–554.16, 557.24–604.30, 649.35–677.25, 680.24–691.28, and 694.24–699.35), AM 651 4to I (pp. 536–694.25), AM 650a 4to (pp. 639.7–648.16), AM 653b 4to I (pp. 536–538.10 and 543.12–546.7), AM 653b 4to II (pp. 536–538.14), AM 653a 4to (pp. 562.24–565.28, 574.27–576.17, 584.1–589.31, 598.23–601.15, 663.30–670.3, 694.12–697.18, 700.19–703.17), and AM 236 fol. (pp. 536–567.12, 582.20–600.4, 602.17–672.2). A section of AM 236 fol. is also printed pp. 672.4–673 (lower text).

Modern Icelandic language edition:

Ólafur Halldórsson, ed. *Sögur úr Skarðsbók* (Reykjavík: Almenna bókafélagið, 1967). Pp. 80–150.

Edition of SÁM 1 fol. (extracts only)

Literature:

Álfrún Gunnlaugsdóttir. "*Jakobs saga postola, Tveggia postola saga Jons ok Jakobs* og *Liber Sancti Jacobi*." *Gripla* 21 (2010): 235–80.

Ásdís Egilsdóttir. "Kvendýrlingar og kvenímynd trúarlegra bókmennta á Íslandi." In Inga Huld Hákonardóttir, ed. >> *Konur og kristsmenn* (1996). Pp. 93–116, esp. pp. 111–12.

Astås, Reidar. "Spor av teologisk tenkning og refleksjon i norsk og islandsk høymiddelalder." *CM* 6 (1993): 133–67, esp. p. 139.

Battista, Simonetta. "Old Norse Hagiography and the Question of the Latin Sources." In Rudolf Simek and Judith Meurer, ed. >> *Scandinavia and Christian Europe in the Middle Ages* (2003). Pp. 26–33, esp. pp. 30–1.

Bekker-Nielsen, Hans, Thorkil Damsgaard Olsen, and Ole Widding. >> *Norrøn fortællekunst* (1965). Pp. 123, 136, and 168.

Boyer, Régis. >> *La vie religieuse en Islande* (1979). Pp. 183 and 194.

Collings, Lucy Grace. "The Codex Scardensis: Studies in Icelandic
   Hagiography." PhD dissertation, Cornell University, 1969. Pp. 113–38
   and 270–90.
Cormack, Margaret. >> *The Saints in Iceland* (1994). Pp. 108, 113, and 242.
– "Saints' Lives and Icelandic Literature in the Thirteenth and Four-
   teenth Centuries." In Hans Bekker-Nielsen and Birte Carlé, ed.
   >> *Saints and Sagas* (1994). Pp. 27–47, esp. p. 31.
– "Christian Biography." In *A Companion to Old Norse–Icelandic
   Literature and Culture*. Ed. Rory McTurk (Oxford: Blackwell, 2005).
   Pp. 27–42, esp. p. 34.
Dillmann, François-Xavier. "Om hedningar och hundar. Kring den
   fornvästnordiska sammansättningen *hundheiðinn*." *SI* 52 (2001): 17–33,
   esp. pp. 21 and 24.
Eiríkr Magnússon. "Kodex Skardensis af postulasögur." *ANF* 8 (1892):
   238–45, esp. p. 241.
Finnur Jónsson. >> *Den oldnorske og oldislandske Litteraturs Historie*
   (1920–4). Vol. 2, p. 871.
Foote, Peter G. *The Pseudo-Turpin Chronicle in Iceland: A Contribution to
   the Study of the Karlamagnús saga*. London Mediæval Studies: Mono-
   graph No. 4 (University College London: London Mediæval Studies,
   1954). Pp. 6, 9–22, and 52–6.
– "A Note on the Source of the Icelandic Translation of the Pseudo-
   Turpin Chronicle." *Neophilologus* 43 (1959): 137–42.
– "Pseudo-Turpin in the North – Forty Years On." In *International
   Scandinavian and Medieval Studies in Memory of Gerd Wolfgang
   Weber*. Ed. Michael Dallapiazza, Olaf Hansen, Preben Meulengracht
   Sørensen, and Yvolle S. Bonnetain (Trieste: Edizioni Parnaso, 2000).
   Pp. 187–97, esp. p. 189. Rpt. in Peter Foote. *Kreddur: Select Studies in
   Early Icelandic Law and Literature* (Reykjavík: Hið íslenska bók-
   menntafélag, 2004). Pp. 182–95, esp. p. 184.
Hallberg, Peter. *Stilsignalement och författarskap i norrön sagalitteratur:
   Synpunkter och exempel*. Nordistica Gothoburgensia 3 (Stockholm:
   Almqvist & Wiksell, 1968). Pp. 120–37, 139–41, 147, 149, 157–8, 161–4,
   167, 181, and 185–9.
– "Imagery in Religious Old Norse Prose Literature: An Outline." *ANF*
   102 (1987): 120–70, esp. pp. 122, 125–6, 142, 144–5, 147–54, 156–8,
   160–2, and 165.
Halvorsen, E.F. *The Norse Version of the Chanson de Roland*. Bibliotheca
   Arnamagnæana 19 (Copenhagen: Ejnar Munksgaard, 1959). Pp. 38–9,
   40–3, 47–8, and 66.

– "Karlamagnús saga." *KLNM* 8 (1963). Cols. 286–90, esp. col. 288.

Holm-Olsen, Ludvig. "Apostelsagaer." *KLNM* 1 (1956). Cols. 177–8, esp. col. 178.

Jakob Benediktsson. "Cursus hos Bergr Sokkason." In *Festskrift til Ludvig Holm-Olsen på hans 70-årsdag den 9. juni 1984* (Øvre Ervik: Alvheim & Eide, 1984). Pp. 34–40, esp. pp. 36–7. Rpt. in Jakob Benediktsson. *Lærdómslistir. Afmælisrit 20. júlí 1987* (Reykjavík: Mál og menning, 1987). Pp. 262–9, esp. pp. 264–5.

Jón Þorkelsson. "Islandske håndskrifter i England og Skotland." *ANF* 8 (1892): 199–237, esp. pp. 235–6.

Jónas Kristjánsson. *Um Fóstbræðra sögu* (Reykjavík: Stofnun Árna Magnússonar, 1972). Pp. 269 and 303–5.

– >> *Eddas and Sagas* (1988). P. 142.

Kirby, Ian. >> *Biblical Quotation* (1980). Vol. 2, pp. 19 and 31–2.

– "The Bible and Biblical Interpretation in Medieval Iceland." In *Old Icelandic Literature and Society*. Ed. Margaret Clunies Ross (Cambridge: Cambridge University Press, 2000). Pp. 287–301, esp. p. 298.

Lehmann, Paul. >> "Skandinaviens Anteil an der lateinischen Literatur und Wissenschaft des Mittelalters" (1937). P. 53.

McDougall, Ian, ed. "Anonymous, *Allra postula minnisvísur* 'Celebratory *Vísur* about all the Apostles'." In Margaret Clunies Ross, ed. >> *Poetry on Christian Subjects* (2007). Vol. 2, pp. 852–71, esp. pp. 859–60.

Mogk, Eugen. >> *Geschichte der norwegisch-isländischen Literatur* (1904). P. 888.

Ólafur Halldórsson. *Helgafellsbækur fornar*. Studia Islandica 24 (Reykjavík: Heimspekideild Háskóla Íslands and Menningarsjóður, 1966). Pp. 16–22 and 41–5.

– "Rímbeglusmíður." *Opuscula* 2.2. Bibliotheca Arnamagnæana 25.2 (Copenhagen: Reitzel, 1977). Pp. 32–49, esp. p. 41.

– "Rimnaerindi í postulasögum." *Gripla* 2 (1977): 194–5. Rpt. In Ólafur Halldórsson. *Grettisfærsla: Safn ritgerða eftir Ólaf Halldórsson gefið út á sjötugsafmæli hans 18. april 1990* (Reykjavík: Stofnun Árna Magnússonar, 1990). Pp. 371–2.

Ólafur Halldórsson, ed. *Mattheus saga postula* (Reykjavík: Stofnun Árna Magnússonar, 1994). Pp. xli–xlviii.

Seip, Didrik Arup. "Jærtegnsamlinger." *KLNM* 8 (1963). Cols. 65–8, esp. col. 66.

Svanhildur Óskarsdóttir. "Dómsdagalýsing í AM 764 4to." *Opuscula* 10. Bibliotheca Arnamagæana 40 (Copenhagen: Reitzel, 1996). Pp. 186–93.

– "Universal History in Fourteenth-Century Iceland: Studies in AM 764 4to." PhD dissertation, University of London, 2000. Pp. 71, 172, 190, 200, 206, and 212–17.

– "The World and Its Ages: The Organisation of an 'Encyclopaedic' Narrative in MS AM 764 4to." In *Sagas, Saints and Settlements*. Ed. Gareth Williams and Paul Bibire. The Northern World 2 (Leiden: Brill, 2004). Pp. 1–11, esp. p. 10.

Sverrir Jakobsson. *Við og veröldin: Heimsmynd Íslendinga 1100–1400* (Reykjavík: Háskólaútgáfan, 2005). Pp. 106, 137, 152–3, and 169.

Sverrir Tómasson. "Norðlenski Benediktínaskólinn." In >> *The Sixth International Saga Conference* (1985). Vol. 2, pp. 1009–20, esp. pp. 1009 and 1014. Rpt. in Sverrir Tómasson. *Tækileg vitni: Greinar um bókmenntir gefnar út í tilefni sjötugsafmælis hans 5. apríl 2011* (Reykjavík: Stofnun Árna Magnússonar and Hið íslenska bókmenntafélag, 2011). Pp. 345–58, esp. pp. 345 and 349.

– *Formálar íslenskra sagnaritara á miðöldum. Rannsókn bókmenntahefðar* (Reykjavík: Stofnun Árna Magnússonar, 1988). Pp. 97, 117, 126, 131, 145, 171, 174, 177, 183, 225, 232, 234, 252, 343–4, and 362.

– "Erlendur vísdómur og forn fræði." In Guðrún Nordal, Sverrir Tómasson, and Vésteinn Ólason, ed. >> *Íslensk Bókmenntasaga* 1 (1992). Pp. 517–71, esp. p. 532.

– "Kristnar trúarbókmenntir í óbundnu máli." In Guðrún Nordal, Sverrir Tómasson, and Vésteinn Ólason, ed. >> *Íslensk Bókmenntasaga* 1 (1992). Pp. 419–79, esp. pp. 441–2, 446, and 464.

– "Trúarbókmenntir í lausu máli á síðmiðöld." In Böðvar Guðmundsson, Sverrir Tómasson, Torfi H. Tulinius, and Vésteinn Ólason, ed. >> *Íslensk Bókmenntasaga* 2 (1993). Pp. 249–82, esp. pp. 251 and 253.

Sverrir Tómasson, Bragi Halldórsson, and Einar Sigurbjörnsson, ed. >> *Heilagra karla sögur* (2007). Pp. xxvii, xxxix–xlii, l, and liii.

Þorbjörg Helgadóttir, ed. *Rómverja saga*. 2 vols. (Reykjavík: Stofnun Árna Magnússonar, 2010). Vol. 1, p. cxci.

Þórður Ingi Guðjónsson. "Apostlene i islandsk middelalderlitteratur." In *Den nordiske renessansen i høymiddelalderen*. Ed. Jón Viðar Sigurðsson and Preben Meulengracht Sørensen (Oslo: Historisk institutt, Universitetet i Oslo, 2000). Pp. 83–99, esp. p. 94.

Vries, Jan de. >> *Altnordische Literaturgeschichte* (1964–7). Vol. 2, pp. 183 and 198.

Widding, Ole, and Hans Bekker-Nielsen. "Low German Influence on Late Icelandic Hagiography." *GR* 37 (1962): 239–62, esp. p. 242.

Wolf, Kirsten. "Postola sögur." In Phillip Pulsiano and Kirsten Wolf,
    with Paul Acker and Donald K. Fry, ed. >> *Medieval Scandinavia*
    (1993). Pp. 511–12.
– "Skarðsbók." In Phillip Pulsiano and Kirsten Wolf, with Paul Acker and
    Donald K. Fry, ed. >> *Medieval Scandinavia* (1993). P. 596.
Handlist, pp. 316–17.

JÓN OF HÓLAR   April 23

1. Jóns saga helga S

The so-called oldest saga of Bishop Jón Ǫgmundarson written probably
in association with Gunnlaugr Leifsson's Latin *vita* commissioned by
Guðmundr Arason. The saga may be classified as an abridged descendant
from this *vita*.

Manuscripts:
AM 221 fol. (ca. 1275–1300, defective), AM 222 fol. (ca. 1700), AM
    234 fol. (ca. 1340), AM 235 fol. (ca. 1400, defective), AM 391 4to
    (ca. 1690), AM 393 4to (ca. 1700), BLAdd 4867 (ca. 1675–1700),
    BLAdd 5313 (ca. 1750–1800), Kall 616 4to (ca. 1700–1800), Kall
    618 4to (ca. 1725–50), Kall 619 4to (ca. 1750–1800), Lbs 839 4to
    (ca. 1750–75), Lbs 1442 4to (ca. 1725), Lbs 2243 4to (ca. 1840–50),
    NBO 367 4to (ca. 1700–1800), NKS 1201 fol. (ca. 1700–1800), NRA
    57 (ca. 1330), Rask 30 (ca. 1800), TCD 1028 (ca. 1750), and Thott
    1770 4to (ca. 1750–1800, defective).

Editions:
Foote, Peter, ed. *Jóns saga Hólabyskups ens helga*. Editiones Ar-
    namagnæanæ, Ser. A, vol. 14 (Copenhagen: Reitzel, 2003). Pp. 3–54.
    Based on AM 221 fol. (pp. 34.25–44.21 and 51.13–54) and AM 234
    fol. (pp. 3–34.25 and 44.21–51.13) with variants from AM 234 fol.
    (pp. 34.25–44.21 and 51.13–54), NRA 57 (pp. 5.7–9.19) and AM 235
    fol. (pp. 3–15.8).
Gudbrand Vigfusson and F. York Powell, ed. and trans. *Origines
    Islandicae: A Collection of the More Important Sagas and Other
    Native Writings Relating to the Settlement and Early History of
    Iceland*. 2 vols. (Oxford: Clarendon, 1905; rpt. Millwood: Kraus,
    1976). Vol. 1, pp. 534–67.
    Based on *Biskupa sögur*, pp. 151–77.

Guðni Jónsson, ed. *Byskupa sögur*. 3 vols. (Reykjavík: Íslendingasagnaút-
gáfan; Haukadalsútgáfan, 1948). Vol. 2, pp. 81–156.
Normalized text based on *Biskupa sögur*.
[Jón Sigurðsson and Guðbrandur Vigfússon, ed.] *Biskupa sögur*. 2 vols.
(Copenhagen: Møller, 1858–78). Vol. 1, pp. 151–202.
Based on AM 234 fol. with variants from AM 221 fol. (pp. 182.10–
192.31 and 199.26–202) and AM 235 fol. (pp. 151–161.9).
Sigurgeir Steingrímsson, Ólafur Halldórsson, and Peter Foote, ed.
*Biskupa sögur I: Kristni saga, Kristni þættir, Þorvalds þáttr víðförla I,
Þorvalds þáttr víðförla II, Stefnis þáttr Þorgilssonar, Af Þangbrandi, Af
Þiðranda ok dísunum, Kristniboð Þangbrands, Þrír þættir, Kristnitakan,
Jóns saga ins helga, Gísls þáttr Illugasonar, Sæmundar þáttr*. Vol. 1:
Fræði, Vol. 2: *Sögutextar*. Íslenzk fornrit 15 (Reykjavík: Hið íslenzka
fornritafélag, 2003). Vol. 2, pp. 175–343.
Based on 1, but with material omitted or abridged in this recension
supplemented from 2 and 3.
Stefán Karlsson, ed. *Sagas of Icelandic Bishops: Fragments of Eight
Manuscripts*. EIM 7 (Copenhagen: Rosenkilde and Bagger, 1967).
Facsimile of AM 221 fol.

Modern Icelandic language edition:

Einar Ól. Sveinsson, ed. *Leit eg suður til landa. Ævintýri og helgisögur frá
miðöldum* (Reykjavík: Heimskringla, 1944). Pp. 228–36 (extracts only).

English translation:

Gudbrand Vigfusson and F. York Powell, ed. and trans. *Origines Islandicae:
A Collection of the More Important Sagas and Other Native Writings
Relating to the Settlement and Early History of Iceland*. 2 vols. (Oxford:
Clarendon, 1905; rpt. Millwood: Kraus, 1976). Vol. 1, pp. 534–67.

Literature:

Ásdís Egilsdóttir. "Biskupa sögur." In Phillip Pulsiano and Kirsten Wolf,
with Paul Acker and Donald K. Fry, ed. >> *Medieval Scandinavia: An
Encyclopedia* (1993). Pp. 45–6.
– "Jarteinir, líkami, sál og trúarlíf." In Ásdís Egilsdóttir and Rudolf
Simek, ed. >> *Sagnaheimur* (2001). Pp. 13–19, esp. p. 16.
– "Konur, draumar, dýrlingar." In *Bókmentaljós: Heiðursrit til Turið
Sigurðardóttur*. Ed. Malan Marnersdóttir, Leyvoy Joensen, and
Anfinnur Johansen (Tórshavn: Faroe University Press, 2006).
Pp. 351–8.
Bandlien, Bjørn. *Strategies of Passion: Love and Marriage in Medieval
Iceland and Norway*. Trans. Betsy van der Hoeck (Turnhout: Brepols,
2005). Pp. 141–2 and 173.

Bekker-Nielsen, Hans, Thorkil Damsgaard Olsen, and Ole Widding.
>> *Norrøn fortællekunst* (1965). Pp. 40–1, 119, 125, and 153.

Bekker-Nielsen, Hans, and Ole Widding. "Legende. Norge og Island."
KLNM 10 (1965). Cols. 421–3, esp. col. 421.

Bjarni Aðalbjarnarson. *Om de norske kongers sagaer*. Skrifter utgitt. av
Det Norske Videnskaps-Akademi i Oslo, II. Hist.-filos. Kl., 1936, 4
(Oslo: Dybwad, 1937). Pp. 76–9 and 89–90.

Boyer, Régis. "Paganism and Literature: The So-Called 'Pagan Survivals'
in the Samtíðarsögur." *Gripla* 1 (1975): 135–67, esp. pp. 146, 149, 151,
155, 158, 161, and 163.

– >> *La vie religieuse en Islande* (1979).

– "Les références expresses à la littérature dans les 'Sagas de contem-
porains'." In Gísli Sigurðsson, Guðrún Kvaran, and Sigurgeir
Steingrímsson, ed. >> *Sagnaþing helgað Jónasi Kristjánssyni* (1994).
Vol. 1, pp. 87–96.

Carlé, Birte. >> *Jomfru-fortællingen* (1985). P. 38.

– "Men and Women in the Saints' Sagas of *Stock. 2, fol.*" In John
Lindow, Lars Lönnroth, and Gerd Wolfgang Weber, ed. >> *Structure
and Meaning in Old Norse Literature* (1986). Pp. 317–46, esp. p. 318.

Cormack, Margaret. "'Fjǫlkunnigri kono scallatu í faðm sofa': Sex and
the Supernatural in Icelandic Saints' Lives." *Skáldskaparmál* 2 (1992):
221–8, esp. pp. 223–6.

– >> *The Saints in Iceland* (1994). Pp. 49–50, 53–5, 57, 62, 66, 103n146,
106, 115– 16, and 125.

– "Saints' Lives and Icelandic Literature in the Thirteenth and Fourteenth Centuries." In Hans Bekker-Nielsen and Birte Carlé, ed.
>> *Saints and Sagas* (1994). Pp. 27–47, esp. pp. 41–2.

– "Visions, Demons and Gender in the Sagas of Icelandic Saints." *CM* 7
(1994): 185–209.

– "Women and Gender in the Sagas of Icelandic Saints." In
>> *Samtíðarsögur* (1994). Vol. 1, pp. 188–93, esp. p. 191.

– "Sagas of Saints." In *Old Icelandic Literature and Society*. Ed. Margaret
Clunies Ross (Cambridge: Cambridge University Press, 2000). Pp. 302–
25, esp. pp. 308, 310, and 315–17.

– "Christian Biography." In *A Companion to Old Norse–Icelandic
Literature and Culture*. Ed. Rory McTurk (Oxford: Blackwell, 2005).
Pp. 27–42, esp. pp. 30–2 and 35–6.

Einar Ól. Sveinsson. *Dating the Icelandic Sagas: An Essay in Method*
(University College London: Viking Society for Northern Research,
1958). Pp. 60 and 109n1.

Finnur Jónsson. >> *Den oldnorske og oldislandske Litteraturs Historie* (1920–4). Vol. 2, pp. 395–7.

Foote, Peter. "Latnesk þýðing eftir Árna Magnússon?" *Landsbókasafn Íslands. Árbók 1953–1954* (1955): 137–41.

– "Auðræði." In Arthur Brown and Peter Foote, ed. >> *Early English and Norse Studies* (1963). Pp. 62–76, esp. p. 64.

– "Aachen, Lund, Hólar." *Les relations littéraires franco-scandinaves au Moyen Age. Colloque de Liège (avril 1972)*. Bibliothèque de la Faculté de Philosophie et Lettres de l'Université de Liège 208 (1975): 53–73, esp. pp. 54, 61, 64, and 68. Rpt. in Peter Foote. *Aurvandilstá: Norse Studies* (Odense: Odense University Press, 1984). Pp. 101–20, esp. pp. 102, 106–8, 111, and 114–15.

– "Jóns saga ens helga." In Phillip Pulsiano and Kirsten Wolf, with Paul Acker and Donald K. Fry, ed. >> *Medieval Scandinavia* (1993). P. 345.

Gottskálk Þ. Jensson. "The Latin Fragments of *Þorláks saga helga* and Their Classical Context." In Rudolf Simek and Judith Meurer, ed. >> *Scandinavia and Christian Europe in the Middle Ages* (2003). Pp. 257–67, esp. p. 264.

G. Hjaltason. "Islands første helgen. Bishop Jón Ögmundsson." *For Kirke og Kultur* 15 (1908): 420–31.

Guðrún Nordal. *Tools of Literacy: The Role of Skaldic Verse in Icelandic Textual Culture of the Twelfth and Thirteenth Centuries* (Toronto: University of Toronto Press, 2001). Pp. 21, 37–8, 48, and 168.

Guðrún Nordal and Sverrir Tómasson. "Veraldleg sagnaritun 1120–1400." In Guðrún Nordal, Sverrir Tómasson, and Vésteinn Ólason, ed. >> *Íslensk Bókmenntasaga* 1 (1992). Pp. 263–418, esp. pp. 285, 345, and 392.

Gunnar F. Guðmundsson. "Latínusöngur leikra á miðöldum." In *Til heiðurs og hugbótar. Greinar um trúarkveðskap fyrri alda*. Ed. Svanhildur Óskarsdóttir and Anna Guðmundsdóttir (Reykholt: Snorrastofa, 2003). Pp. 93–112, esp. pp. 94 and 102.

Haki Antonsson. "Saints and Relics in Early Christian Scandinavia." *MScand* 15 (2005): 51–80, esp. p. 67.

Hallberg, Peter. "Jóns saga helga." In *Afmælisrit Jóns Helgasonar 30. júní 1969*. Ed. Jakob Benediktsson et al. (Reykjavík: Heimskringla, 1969). Pp. 59–79, esp. pp. 59–68.

– "Imagery in Religious Old Norse Prose Literature: An Outline." *ANF* 102 (1987): 120–70, esp. pp. 121–2.

Hunt, Margaret Cushing. "A Study of Authorial Perspective in *Guðmundar saga A* and *Guðmundar saga D*: Hagiography and the Icelandic Bishop's Saga." PhD dissertation, Indiana University, 1985. Pp. 58–63.

Jón Helgason. *Norrøn Litteraturhistorie* (Copenhagen: Levin and Munksgaard, 1934). Pp. 89, 144, and 192.

Jón Jóhannesson. "Tímatal Gerlands í íslenzkum ritum frá þjóðveldisöld." *Skírnir* 126 (1952): 76–93, esp. pp. 86–7.

Jón Viðar Sigurðsson. "Utenlandske kvinnehelgener på Island i høymiddelalderen." In >> *Samtíðarsögur* (1994). Vol. 2, pp. 423–34, esp. pp. 433–4.

Jónas Kristjánsson. >> *Eddas and Sagas* (1988). Pp. 120, 179, 181–2, and 193.

Jørgensen, Jørgen Højgaard. *Bispesagaer – Laurentius saga: Studier i* Laurentius saga biskups, *indledt af overvejelser omkring* biskupa sǫgur *som litterær genre.* Udgivelsesudvalgets samling af studenterafhandlinger 12 (Odense: [n.p.], 1978). Pp. 20–1, 29–30, 38–9, and 48.

Kirby, Ian. >> *Biblical Quotation* (1980). Vol. 2, p. 80.

– "The Bible and Biblical Interpretation in Medieval Iceland." In *Old Icelandic Literature and Society.* Ed. Margaret Clunies Ross (Cambridge: Cambridge University Press, 2000). Pp. 287–301, esp. p. 296.

Koppenberg, Peter. *Hagiographische Studien zu den Biskupa sögur: Unter besonderer Berücksichtigung der* Jóns Saga Helga. Scandia Wissenschaftliche Reihe 1 (Bochum: Scandia, 1980). Pp. 1–21, 47–108, 122–43, 149–227, 232–3, and 236–8.

Kuttner, Stephan. "St. Jón of Hólar: Canon Law and Hagiography in Medieval Iceland." *Analecta Cracoviensia* 7 (1975): 367–75, esp. pp. 369–70 and 374–5.

Lehmann, Paul. >> "Skandinaviens Anteil an der lateinischen Literatur und Wissenschaft des Mittelalters" (1937). P. 13.

Louis-Jensen, Jonna. *Kongesagastudier: Kompilationen Hulda-Hrokkinskinna.* Bibliotheca Arnamagnæana 32 (Copenhagen: Reitzel, 1977). Pp. 19, 111–17, 119–21, 122n46, and 144.

Magnús Már Lárusson. "Biskupa sögur." *KLNM* 1 (1956). Cols. 630–1.

– "Jóns saga helga." *KLNM* 7 (1962). Cols. 617–18.

Martin, John Stanley. "The Function of Bishops in the Early Icelandic Church." In >> *Samtíðarsögur* (1994). Vol. 2, pp. 561–76.

McCreesh, Bernadine. "Elements of the Pagan Supernatural in the Bishops' Sagas." In John McKinnell, David Ashurst, and Donata Kick, ed. >> *The Fantastic in Old Norse/Icelandic Literature* (2006). Vol. 2, pp. 671–80, esp. pp. 671 and 679.

McDougall, Ian. "Foreigners and Foreign Languages in Medieval Iceland." *Saga-Book* 22 (1986–9): 180–233, esp. p. 191.

Mogk, Eugen. >> *Geschichte der norwegisch-isländischen Literatur* (1904). P. 793.

Orri Vésteinsson. *The Christianization of Iceland: Priests, Power, and Social Change 1000–1300* (Oxford: Oxford University Press, 2000). Pp. 34–5, 59–65, 133–4, 144–5, 234, and 292.

Paasche, Fredrik. *Norges og Islands litteratur inntil utgangen av middelalderen.* Rev. ed. by Anne Holtsmark (Oslo: Aschehoug, 1947). Pp. 302, 381–2, and 507.

Paul, Fritz. "Historiographische und hagiographische Tendenzen in isländischen Bischofsviten des 12. und 13. Jahrhunderts." *Skandinavistik* 9 (1979): 36–46.

Samuelson, David Robert. "The Operation of the Bishop's Legend in Early Medieval England and Iceland." PhD dissertation, University of Michigan, 1977. Pp. 203–12.

Schach, Paul. *Icelandic Sagas.* Twayne's World Author Series (Boston: Twayne, 1984). Pp. 11, 66–8, 71, and 98.

Schier, Kurt. *Sagaliteratur.* Sammlung Metzler M78 (Stuttgart: Metzler, 1970). Pp. 4, 68, 70, 121, 123, and 129.

Sigurður Nordal. *Um íslenzkar fornsögur.* Trans. Árni Böðvarsson (Reykjavík: Mál og menning, 1968). Pp. 71–3.

Sigurður Pétursson. "Ovid in Iceland." In *Cultura Classica e Cultura Germanica Settentrionale.* Ed. Pietro Janni, Diego Poli, and Carlo Santini (Macerata: Herder, 1985). Pp. 53–63, esp. pp. 55–6.

Sigurgeir Steingrímsson, Ólafur Halldórsson, and Peter Foote, ed. *Biskupa sögur I: Kristni saga, Kristni þættir, Þorvalds þáttr víðförla I, Þorvalds þáttr víðförla II, Stefnis þáttr Þorgilssonar, Af Þangbrandi, Af Þiðranda ok dísunum, Kristniboð Þangbrands, Þrír þættir, Kristnitakan, Jóns saga ins helga, Gísls þáttr Illugasonar, Sæmundar þáttr.* Vol. 1: *Fræði,* Vol. 2: *Sögutextar.* Íslenzk fornrit 15 (Reykjavík: Hið íslenzka fornritafélag, 2003). Vol. 1, pp. ccxiii–cccxxi.

Stefán Karlsson. "Islandsk bogeksport til Norge i middelalderen." *Mm* (1979): 1–17, esp. p. 6. Rpt. in *Stafkrókar: Ritgerðir eftir Stefán Karlsson gefnar út í tilefni af sjötugsafmæli hans 2. desember 1998.* Ed. Guðvarður Már Gunnlaugsson (Reykjavík: Stofnun Árna Magnússonar, 2000). Pp. 188–205, esp. p. 194.

Steingrímur Matthíasson. "Jón helgi. Æðsti prestur í þessu lífi og landlæknir í öðru lífi." *Eimreiðin* 28 (1922): 65–80.

Sverrir Tómasson. "Helgisögur, mælskufræði og forn frásagnarlist." *Skírnir* 157 (1983): 130–62, esp. pp. 141–7.

– *Formálar íslenskra sagnaritara á miðöldum. Rannsókn bókmenntahefðar* (Reykjavík: Stofnun Árna Magnússonar, 1988). Pp. 17, 19, 20, 24–6, 37, 67, 170, 232, 240–3, and 339–43.

- "Erlendur vísdómur og forn fræði." In Guðrún Nordal, Sverrir Tómasson, and Vésteinn Ólason, ed. >> *Íslensk Bókmenntasaga* 1 (1992). Pp. 517–71, esp. p. 543.
- "Kristnar trúarbókmenntir í óbundnu máli." In Guðrún Nordal, Sverrir Tómasson, and Vésteinn Ólason, ed. >> *Íslensk Bókmenntasaga* 1 (1992). Pp. 419–79, esp. pp. 425, 467, 473–4, and 479.

Turville-Petre, G. >> *Origins of Icelandic Literature* (1967). Pp. 110, 133, and 197–8.

Vries, Jan de. >> *Altnordische Literaturgeschichte* (1964–7). Vol. 2, pp. 246 and 363.

Whaley, Diana. "Miracles in the Sagas of Bishops: Icelandic Variations on an International Theme." *CM* 7 (1994): 155–84.

Widding, Ole. "Ave Maria eller Maríuvers i norrøn litteratur." *Mm* (1958): 1–7, esp. pp. 3–6.

Handlist, p. 317.

2. Jóns saga helga L

An early fourteenth-century revision based on a text like 1 but one that closely resembles 3.

Manuscripts:
AM 205 fol. (1644), AM 210 fol. (ca. 1600–1700), AM 219 fol. (ca. 1370–80, defective), AM 396 fol. (1676), AM 392 4to (ca. 1600–1700), Don. var. 1 vol. XII (ca. 1700), JS 21 fol. (1841), JS 629 4to (ca. 1825–50), Lbs 140 4to (ca. 1750–90), Lbs 671 4to (1846–8), Lbs 795 4to (ca. 1700–1800), Lbs 1402 4to (ca. 1852), Lbs 1573 4to (ca. 1820–30), NKS 1202 fol. (1768), NRA 57 (ca. 1330), Stock. Papp. fol. no. 2 (1689), Stock. Papp. 4to no. 4 (ca. 1600–50), Stock. Perg. fol. no. 5 (ca.1350–65), and Thott 1748 4to (ca. 1760–70).

Editions:
Foote, Peter, ed. *Jóns saga Hólabyskups ens helga*. Editiones Arnamagnæanæ, Ser. A, vol. 14 (Copenhagen: Reitzel, 2003). Pp. 57–108. Based on AM 219 fol. (pp. 102.9–108) and Stock. Perg. fol. no. 5 (pp. 57–102.8) with variants from AM 219 fol. (pp. 61.34–66.17 and 75.24–79.15), NRA 57 (pp. 73.3–74.5), Stock. Papp 4to no. 4 (pp. 63.5–74.2) and AM 392 4to (pp. 63.5–74.2).

Guðni Jónsson, ed. *Byskupa sögur*. 3 vols. (Reykjavík: Íslendingasagnaútgáfan; Haukadalsútgáfan, 1948). Vol. 2, pp. 1–77. Normalized text based on *Biskupa sögur*.

Gudbrand Vigfusson and F. York Powell, ed. and trans. *Origines Islandicae: A Collection of the More Important Sagas and Other Native Writings Relating to the Settlement and Early History of Iceland*. 2 vols. (Oxford: Clarendon, 1905; rpt. Millwood: Kraus, 1976). Vol. 1, pp. 593–4.
   Based on *Biskupa sögur*, pp. 215, 235, and 239–41.
Jón Helgason, ed. *Byskupa sǫgur. MS Perg. fol. No. 5 in the Royal Library of Stockholm*. CCI 19 (Copenhagen: Ejnar Munksgaard, 1950). Facsimile of Stock. Perg. fol. no. 5.
[Jón Sigurðsson and Guðbrandur Vigfússon, ed.] *Biskupa sögur*. 2 vols. (Copenhagen: Møller, 1858–78). Vol. 1, pp. 215–60.
   Based on Stock. Perg. fol. no 5 (pp. 215–254.22) and AM 219 fol. (pp. 254.23–260) with variants from AM 219 fol. (pp. 220.8–223.30 and 229.36–232.36).
Möbius, Th., ed. *Analecta Norrœna. Auswahl aus der isländischen und norwegischen Litteratur des Mittelalters*. 2nd. ed. (Leipzig: J.C. Hinrichs'sche Buchhandlung, 1877). Pp. 141–6 (extract only).
   Based on *Biskupa sögur*.
Sigurgeir Steingrímsson, Ólafur Halldórsson, and Peter Foote, ed. *Biskupa sögur I: Kristni saga, Kristni þættir, Þorvalds þáttr víðförla I, Þorvalds þáttr víðförla II, Stefnis þáttr Þorgilssonar, Af Þangbrandi, Af Þiðranda ok dísunum, Kristniboð Þangbrands, Þrír þættir, Kristnitakan, Jóns saga ins helga, Gísls þáttr Illugasonar, Sæmundar þáttr*. Vol. 1: *Fræði*, Vol. 2: *Sögutextar*. Íslenzk fornrit 15 (Reykjavík: Hið íslenzka fornritafélag, 2003). Vol. 2, pp. 175–343.
   Based on 1, but with material omitted or abridged in this recension supplemented from 2 and 3.
Stefán Karlsson, ed. *Sagas of Icelandic Bishops: Fragments of Eight Manuscripts*. EIM 7 (Copenhagen: Rosenkilde and Bagger, 1967). Facsimile of AM 219 fol.
English translations:
Gudbrand Vigfusson and F. York Powell, ed. and trans. *Origines Islandicae: A Collection of the More Important Sagas and Other Native Writings Relating to the Settlement and Early History of Iceland*. 2 vols. (Oxford: Clarendon, 1905; rpt. Millwood: Kraus, 1976). Vol. 1, pp. 593–4 (extracts only).
Simpson, Jacqueline, trans. *The Northmen Talk: A Choice of Tales from Iceland* (London: Phoenix House; Madison: University of Wisconsin Press, 1965). Pp. 65–76 (extracts only).

Norwegian translation:
Venås, Kjell. "Soga om Jon den heilage." In *Den norrøne litteraturen.* VI:
   Dikt og prosa (Oslo: Det Norske Samlaget, 1963). Pp. 72–110.
Literature:
Ásdís Egilsdóttir. "Biskupa sögur." In Phillip Pulsiano and Kirsten Wolf,
   with Paul Acker and Donald K. Fry, ed. >> *Medieval Scandinavia*
   (1993). Pp. 45–6.
– "Kvendýrlingar og kvenímynd trúarlegra bókmennta á Íslandi." In
   Inga Huld Hákonardóttir, ed. >> *Konur og kristsmenn* (1996). Pp. 93–
   116, esp. pp. 113–14.
– "Jarteinir, líkami, sál og trúarlíf." In Ásdís Egilsdóttir and Rudolf
   Simek, ed. >> *Sagnaheimur* (2001). Pp. 13–19, esp. p. 16.
– "Konur, draumar, dýrlingar." In *Bókmentaljós: Heiðursrit til Turið
   Sigurðardóttur.* Ed. Malan Marnersdóttir, Leyvoy Joensen, and
   Anfinnur Johansen (Tórshavn: Faroe University Press, 2006).
   Pp. 351–8.
Bekker-Nielsen, Hans, Thorkil Damsgaard Olsen, and Ole Widding.
   >> *Norrøn fortællekunst* (1965). Pp. 37, 40–1, 119, 125, and 153.
Bekker-Nielsen, Hans, and Ole Widding. "Legende. Norge og Island."
   KLNM 10 (1965). Cols. 421–3, esp. col. 421.
Bjarni Aðalbjarnarson. *Om de norske kongers sagaer.* Skrifter utgitt. av
   Det Norske Videnskaps-Akademi i Oslo, II. Hist.-filos. Kl., 1936, 4
   (Oslo: Dybwad, 1937). Pp. 76–9 and 89–90.
– "Bemerkninger om de eldste bispesagaer." *Studia Islandica* 17 (Reykja-
   vík: Heimspekideild Háskóla Íslands; Menningarsjóður, 1959): 27–37,
   esp. p. 36.
Boyer, Régis. >> *La vie religieuse en Islande* (1979).
– "Les références expresses à la littérature dans les 'Sagas de contempor-
   ains'." In Gísli Sigurðsson, Guðrún Kvaran, and Sigurgeir Steingríms-
   son, ed. >> *Sagnaþing helgað Jónasi Kristjánssyni* (1994). Vol. 1,
   pp. 87–96.
Carlé, Birte. "Eneboersken Hild: En norrøn jomfrufortælling." In >> *The
   Sixth International Saga Conference* (1985). Vol. 2, pp. 103–14.
Cormack, Margaret. "'Fjǫlkunnigri kono scallatu í faðm sofa': Sex and
   the Supernatural in Icelandic Saints' Lives." *Skáldskaparmál* 2 (1992):
   221–8, esp. p. 223.
– >> *The Saints in Iceland* (1994). Pp. 11, 49–50, 53, 56, 115, and 125.
– "Saints' Lives and Icelandic Literature in the Thirteenth and Four-
   teenth Centuries." In Hans Bekker-Nielsen and Birte Carlé, ed.
   >> *Saints and Sagas* (1994). Pp. 27–47, esp. p. 42.

– "Visions, Demons and Gender in the Sagas of Icelandic Saints." *CM* 7 (1994): 185–209.
– "Women and Gender in the Sagas of Icelandic Saints." In >> *Samtíðarsögur* (1994). Vol. 1, pp. 188–93, esp. p. 191.
– "Sagas of Saints." In *Old Icelandic Literature and Society*. Ed. Margaret Clunies Ross (Cambridge: Cambridge University Press, 2000). Pp. 302–25, esp. pp. 308, 310, 314, and 317.
– "Poetry, Paganism and the Sagas of Icelandic Bishops." In *Til heiðurs og hugbótar. Greinar um trúarkveðskap fyrri alda*. Ed. Svanhildur Óskarsdóttir and Anna Guðmundsdóttir (Reykholt: Snorrastofa, 2003). Pp. 33–51, esp. p. 42.
– "Christian Biography." In *A Companion to Old Norse–Icelandic Literature and Culture*. Ed. Rory McTurk (Oxford: Blackwell, 2005). Pp. 27–42, esp. pp. 32, 35–6, and 39.
– "The Economics of Devotion: Vows and Indulgences in Medieval Iceland." *Viking and Medieval Scandinavia* 5 (2009): 41–63, esp. pp. 44 and 48–9.
Einar Ól. Sveinsson. *Dating the Icelandic Sagas: An Essay in Method* (University College London: Viking Society for Northern Research, 1958). Pp. 60 and 109n1.
Finnur Jónsson. >> *Den oldnorske og oldislandske Litteraturs Historie* (1920–4). Vol. 2, pp. 395–7.
Foote, Peter. "Latnesk þýðing eftir Árna Magnússon?" *Landsbókasafn Íslands. Árbók 1953–1954* (1955): 137–41.
– "Auðræði." In Arthur Brown and Peter Foote, ed. >> *Early English and Norse Studies* (1963). Pp. 62–76, esp. p. 64.
– "Aachen, Lund, Hólar." *Les relations littéraires franco-scandinaves au Moyen Age. Colloque de Liège (avril 1972)*. Bibliothèque de la Faculté de Philosophie et Lettres de l'Université de Liège 208 (1975): 53–73, esp. pp. 54, 55, 61, 64, and 68. Rpt. in Peter Foote. *Aurvandilstá: Norse Studies* (Odense: Odense University Press, 1984). Pp. 101–20, esp. pp. 102–3, 106–8, 111, and 114–15.
– "Jóns saga ens helga." In Phillip Pulsiano and Kirsten Wolf, with Paul Acker and Donald K. Fry, ed. >> *Medieval Scandinavia* (1993). P. 345.
– "The B Version of Jóns saga helga: Two Benedictine Associations." In Gísli Sigurðsson, Guðrún Kvaran, and Sigurgeir Steingrímsson, ed. >> *Sagnaþing helgað Jónasi Kristjánssyni* (1994). Vol. 1, pp. 181–7.
G. Hjaltason. "Islands første helgen. Bishop Jón Ögmundsson." *For Kirke og Kultur* 15 (1908): 420–31.

Guðrún Nordal. *Tools of Literacy: The Role of Skaldic Verse in Icelandic Textual Culture of the Twelfth and Thirteenth Centuries* (Toronto: University of Toronto Press, 2001). Pp. 168 and 275.

Guðrún Nordal and Sverrir Tómasson. "Veraldleg sagnaritun 1120–1400." In Guðrún Nordal, Sverrir Tómasson, and Vésteinn Ólason, ed. >> *Íslensk Bókmenntasaga* 1 (1992). Pp. 263–418, esp. pp. 268, 345, and 392.

Gunnar F. Guðmundsson. "Latínusöngur leikra á miðöldum." In *Til heiðurs og hugbótar. Greinar um trúarkveðskap fyrri alda*. Ed. Svanhildur Óskarsdóttir and Anna Guðmundsdóttir (Reykholt: Snorrastofa, 2003). Pp. 93–112, esp. pp. 94–5.

Hallberg, Peter. "Jóns saga helga." In *Afmælisrit Jóns Helgasonar 30. júní 1969*. Ed. Jakob Benediktsson et al. (Reykjavík: Heimskringla, 1969). Pp. 59–79.

– "Some Observations on the Language of *Dunstanus saga*, with an Appendix on the Bible Compilation *Stjórn*." *Saga-Book* 18 (1973): 324–53, esp. pp. 332–51.

– "Imagery in Religious Old Norse Prose Literature: An Outline." *ANF* 102 (1987): 120–70, esp. pp. 130, 136, 141, 146, 152, and 154–5.

Helga Kress. *Máttugar meyjar: Íslensk fornbókmenntasaga* (Reykjavík: Háskólaútgáfan, 1993). Pp. 17–19, 21, and 115.

– "'Grey þykir mér Freyja': Um konur, kristni og karlveldi í íslenskum fornbókmenntum." In Inga Huld Hákonardóttir, ed. >> *Konur og kristsmenn* (1996). Pp. 13–63, esp. pp. 45–6 and 58. Rpt. in Helga Kress. *Fyrir dyrum fóstru: Konur og kynferði í íslenskum fornbókmenntum. Greinasafn* (Reykjavík: Háskóli Íslands, Rannsóknastofa í kvennafræðum, 1996). Pp. 167–219, esp. pp. 122–3 and 217.

Hunt, Margaret Cushing. "A Study of Authorial Perspective in *Guðmundar saga A* and *Guðmundar saga D*: Hagiography and the Icelandic Bishop's Saga." PhD dissertation. Indiana University, 1985. Pp. 63–5.

Jakob Benediktsson. "Cursus hos Bergr Sokkason." In *Festskrift til Ludvig Holm-Olsen på hans 70-årsdag den 9. juni 1984* (Øvre Ervik: Alvheim & Eide, 1984). Pp. 34–40, esp. pp. 38–9. Rpt. in Jakob Benediktsson. *Lærdómslistir. Afmælisrit 20. júlí 1987* (Reykjavík: Mál og menning, 1987). Pp. 262–9, esp. p. 267.

Jón Jóhannesson. "Tímatal Gerlands í íslenzkum ritum frá þjóðveldisöld." *Skírnir* 126 (1952): 76–93, esp. pp. 86–7.

Jón Viðar Sigurðsson. "Utenlandske kvinnehelgener på Island i høymiddelalderen." In >> *Samtíðarsögur* (1994). Vol. 2, pp. 423–34, esp. pp. 433–4.

Jónas Kristjánsson. *Um Fóstbrœðra sögu* (Reykjavík: Stofnun Árna
    Magnússonar, 1972). Pp. 265, 269, and 305.
– >> *Eddas and Sagas* (1988). Pp. 116, 179, 181–2, and 193.
Jørgensen, Jørgen Højgaard. *Bispesagaer – Laurentius saga: Studier i*
    Laurentius saga biskups, *indledt af overvejelser omkring* biskupa sǫgur
    som litterær genre. Udgivelsesudvalgets samling af studenterafhand-
    linger 12 (Odense: [n.p.], 1978). Pp. 20–1, 29–30, 38–9, and 48.
Kirby, Ian. >> *Biblical Quotation* (1980). Vol. 2, p. 80.
– "The Bible and Biblical Interpretation in Medieval Iceland." In *Old
    Icelandic Literature and Society.* Ed. Margaret Clunies Ross (Cam-
    bridge: Cambridge University Press, 2000). Pp. 287–301, esp. p. 296.
Koppenberg, Peter. *Hagiographische Studien zu den Biskupa sögur: Unter
    besonderer Berücksichtigung der* Jóns Saga Helga. Scandia Wissen-
    schaftliche Reihe 1 (Bochum: Scandia, 1980). Pp. 1–21, 62, 73–7,
    99–100, 105, 121, 143, 159, and 200–58.
Kuttner, Stephan. "St. Jón of Hólar: Canon Law and Hagiography in
    Medieval Iceland." *Analecta Cracoviensia* 7 (1975): 367–75, esp. pp. 369–
    70 and 374–5.
Lassen, Annette. "The God on the Tree." In *Greppaminni: Rit til heiðurs
    Vésteini Ólasyni sjötugum* (Reykjavík: Hið íslenska bókmenntafélag,
    2009). Pp. 231–46, esp. pp. 242–3.
Lehmann, Paul. >> "Skandinaviens Anteil an der lateinischen Literatur
    und Wissenschaft des Mittelalters" (1937). P. 13.
Louis-Jensen, Jonna. *Kongesagastudier: Kompilationen Hulda-
    Hrokkinskinna.* Bibliotheca Arnamagnæana 32 (Copenhagen: Reitzel,
    1977). Pp. 111–17, 119–21, 122n46, 144, and 149.
Magnús Már Lárusson. "Biskupa sögur." *KLNM* 1 (1956). Cols. 630–1.
– "Jóns saga helga." *KLNM* 7 (1962). Cols. 617–18.
McCreesh, Bernadine. "Prophetic Dreams and Visions in the Sagas of the
    Early Icelandic Saints." In *Verbal Encounters: Anglo-Saxon and Old
    Norse Studies for Roberta Frank.* Ed. Antonina Harbus and Russell
    Poole (Toronto: University of Toronto Press, 2005). Pp. 247–68, esp.
    pp. 251–3, 259–62, and 266.
– "Elements of the Pagan Supernatural in the Bishops' Sagas." In John
    McKinnell, David Ashurst, and Donata Kick, ed. >> *The Fantastic in Old
    Norse/Icelandic Literature* (2006). Vol. 2, pp. 671–80, esp. pp. 674 and 679.
McDougall, Ian. "Foreigners and Foreign Languages in Medieval
    Iceland." *Saga-Book* 22 (1986–9): 180–233, esp. pp. 185 and 191.
Mogk, Eugen. >> *Geschichte der norwegisch-isländischen Literatur* (1904).
    P. 793.

Orri Vésteinsson. *The Christianization of Iceland: Priests, Power, and Social Change 1000–1300* (Oxford: Oxford University Press, 2000). Pp. 34–5, 58–65, 133–4, 144–5, 234, and 292.

Paasche, Fredrik. *Norges og Islands litteratur inntil utgangen av middelalderen*. Rev. ed. by Anne Holtsmark (Oslo: Aschehoug, 1947). Pp. 302, 381–2, and 507.

Paul, Fritz. "Historiographische und hagiographische Tendenzen in isländischen Bischofsviten des 12. und 13. Jahrhunderts." *Skandinavistik* 9 (1979): 36–46.

Power, Rosemary. "Cursing the King: An Irish Conversation in *Jóns saga helga*." *Saga-Book* 25 (2000): 310–13.

Schach, Paul. *Icelandic Sagas*. Twayne's World Author Series (Boston: Twayne, 1984). Pp. 11, 66–8, 71, and 98.

Schier, Kurt. *Sagaliteratur*. Sammlung Metzler M78 (Stuttgart: Metzler, 1970). Pp. 4, 68, 70, 121, 123, and 129.

Sigurður Nordal. *Um íslenzkar fornsögur*. Trans. Árni Böðvarsson (Reykjavík: Mál og menning, 1968). Pp. 71–3.

Sigurður Pétursson. "Ovid in Iceland." In *Cultura Classica e Cultura Germanica Settentrionale*. Ed. Pietro Janni, Diego Poli, and Carlo Santini (Macerata: Herder, 1985). Pp. 53–63, esp. pp. 55–6.

Sigurgeir Steingrímsson, Ólafur Halldórsson, and Peter Foote, ed. *Biskupa sögur I: Kristni saga, Kristni þættir, Þorvalds þáttr víðförla I, Þorvalds þáttr víðförla II, Stefnis þáttr Þorgilssonar, Af Þangbrandi, Af Þiðranda ok dísunum, Kristniboð Þangbrands, Þrír þættir, Kristnitakan, Jóns saga ins helga, Gísls þáttr Illugasonar, Sæmundar þáttr*. Vol. 1: *Fræði*, Vol. 2: *Sögutextar*. Íslenzk fornrit 15 (Reykjavík: Hið íslenzka fornritafélag, 2003). Vol. 1, pp. ccxiii–ccxxi.

Steingrímur Matthíasson. "Jón helgi. Æðsti prestur í þessu lífi og landlæknir í öðru lífi." *Eimreiðin* 28 (1922): 65–80.

Sverrir Tómasson. "Helgisögur, mælskufræði og forn frásagnarlist." *Skírnir* 157 (1983): 130–62, esp. pp. 141–4 and 146–7.

– "Norðlenski Benediktínaskólinn." In >> *The Sixth International Saga Conference* (1985). Vol. 2, pp. 1009–20, esp. pp. 1009, 1015, and 1018. Rpt. in Sverrir Tómasson. *Tækileg vitni: Greinar um bókmenntir gefnar út í tilefni sjötugsafmælis hans 5. apríl 2011* (Reykjavík: Stofnun Árna Magnússonar and Hið íslenska bókmenntafélag, 2011). Pp. 345–58, esp. pp. 345, 350, and 354.

– *Formálar íslenskra sagnaritara á miðöldum. Rannsókn bókmenntahefðar* (Reykjavík: Stofnun Árna Magnússonar, 1988). Pp. 17, 19–20, 24–6, 28,

37, 50, 54, 67, 84–5, 87, 89–90, 96–7, 112–14, 118, 126, 128, 143–6, 148,
161, 164–5, 172, 175–7, 184, 200–1, 222, 226, 229–30, 232–3, 235,
242–3, 305, 311, 314, 339–43, and 355.
– "Erlendur vísdómur og forn fræði." In Guðrún Nordal, Sverrir Tómas-
son, and Vésteinn Ólason, ed. >> *Íslensk Bókmenntasaga* 1 (1992).
Pp. 517–71, esp. p. 566.
– "Kristnar trúarbókmenntir í óbundnu máli." In Guðrún Nordal,
Sverrir Tómasson, and Vésteinn Ólason, ed. >> *Íslensk Bókmenntasaga*
1 (1992). Pp. 419–79, esp. pp. 467, 473–4, and 479.
– "Trúarbókmenntir í lausu máli á síðmiðöld." In Böðvar Guðmundsson,
Sverrir Tómasson, Torfi H. Tulinius, and Vésteinn Ólason, ed. >>
Íslensk Bókmenntasaga 2 (1993). Pp. 249–82, esp. pp. 251 and 266.
– "Er nýja textafræðin ný? Þankar um gamla fræðigrein." *Gripla* 13
(2002): 199–216, esp. pp. 208–9. Rpt. in Sverrir Tómasson. *Tækileg
vitni: Greinar um bókmenntir gefnar út í tilefni sjötugsafmælis hans 5.
apríl 2011* (Reykjavík: Stofnun Árna Magnússonar and Hið íslenska
bókmenntafélag, 2011). Pp. 231–50, esp. p. 241.
Turville-Petre, G. >> *Origins of Icelandic Literature* (1967). Pp. 110,
113–15, 131, 133, 135, and 197–9.
Þóra Kristjánsdóttir. "Margrét hin oddhaga, hreinferðuga júngfrú og
allar hinar." In *Kvennaslóðir: Rit til heiðurs Sigríði Erlendsdóttur
sagnfræðingi*. Ed. Anna Agnarsdóttir et al. (Reykjavík: Kvennasögusafn Íslands, 2001). Pp. 89–98, esp. p. 92.
Vries, Jan de. >> *Altnordische Literaturgeschichte* (1964–7). Vol. 2, pp. 96,
188, and 246.
Whaley, Diana. "Miracles in the Sagas of Bishops: Icelandic Variations
on an International Theme." *CM* 7 (1994): 155–84.
Widding, Ole. "Ave Maria eller Maríuvers i norrøn litteratur." *Mm* (1958):
1–7, esp. pp. 3–6.
Widding, Ole, and Hans Bekker-Nielsen. "Low German Influence on
Late Icelandic Hagiography." *GR* 37 (1962): 239–62, esp. p. 242.
Handlist, p. 317.

3. Jóns saga helga H

A fuller account than 1 with more miracles included.

Manuscripts:
AM 392 4to (ca. 1600–1700) and Stock. Papp. 4to no. 4 (ca. 1600–50).

Editions:

Foote, Peter, ed. *Jóns saga Hólabyskups ens helga*. Editiones Arnamagnæanæ, Ser. A, vol. 14 (Copenhagen: Reitzel, 2003). Pp. 111–70. Based on Stock. Papp. 4to no. 4 with variants from AM 392 4to.

Guðni Jónsson, ed. *Byskupa sögur*. 3 vols. (Reykjavík: Íslendingasagnaútgáfan; Haukadalsútgáfan, 1948). Vol. 2, pp. 159–75. Normalized text based on *Biskupa sögur*.

[Jón Sigurðsson and Guðbrandur Vigfússon, ed.] *Biskupa sögur.* 2 vols. (Copenhagen: Møller, 1858–78). Vol. 1, pp. 203–12. Edition of AM 392 4to. Only miracles are included. Readings from AM 392 4to are given as footnotes to 1 (pp. 151–202).

Sigurgeir Steingrímsson, Ólafur Halldórsson, and Peter Foote, ed. *Biskupa sögur I: Kristni saga, Kristni þættir, Þorvalds þáttr víðförla I, Þorvalds þáttr víðförla II, Stefnis þáttr Þorgilssonar, Af Þangbrandi, Af Þiðranda ok dísunum, Kristniboð Þangbrands, Þrír þættir, Kristnitakan, Jóns saga ins helga, Gísls þáttr Illugasonar, Sæmundar þáttr.* Vol. 1: *Fræði*, Vol. 2: *Sögutextar*. Íslenzk fornrit 15 (Reykjavík: Hið íslenzka fornritafélag, 2003). Vol. 2, pp. 175–343. Based on 1, but with material omitted or abridged in this recension supplemented from 2 or 3.

Danish translation:

Carlé, Birte. *Skøger og jomfruer i den kristne fortællekunst* (Odense: Odense Universitetsforlag, 1991). Pp. 120–2 (extract only).

Literature:

Ásdís Egilsdóttir. "Biskupa sögur." In Phillip Pulsiano and Kirsten Wolf, with Paul Acker and Donald K. Fry, ed. >> *Medieval Scandinavia* (1993). Pp. 45–6.

– "Kvendýrlingar og kvenímynd trúarlegra bókmennta á Íslandi." In Inga Huld Hákonardóttir, ed. >> *Konur og kristsmenn* (1996). Pp. 93–116, esp. pp. 106–7.

– "Konur, draumar, dýrlingar." In *Bókmentaljós: Heiðursrit til Turið Sigurðardóttur.* Ed. Malan Marnersdóttir, Leyvoy Joensen, and Anfinnur Johansen (Tórshavn: Faroe University Press, 2006). Pp. 351–8.

Bekker-Nielsen, Hans, Thorkil Damsgaard Olsen, and Ole Widding. >> *Norrøn fortællekunst* (1965). Pp. 40, 119, and 125.

Bekker-Nielsen, Hans, and Ole Widding. "Legende. Norge og Island." *KLNM* 10 (1965). Cols. 421–3, esp. col. 421.

Bjarni Aðalbjarnarson. *Om de norske kongers sagaer*. Skrifter utgitt. av Det Norske Videnskaps-Akademi i Oslo, II. Hist.-filos. Kl., 1936, 4 (Oslo: Dybwad, 1937). Pp. 76–9 and 89–90.

Boyer, Régis. >> *La vie religieuse en Islande* (1979).

– "Les références expresses à la littérature dans les 'Sagas de contemporains'." In Gísli Sigurðsson, Guðrún Kvaran, and Sigurgeir Steingrímsson, ed. >> *Sagnaþing helgað Jónasi Kristjánssyni* (1994). Vol. 1, pp. 87–96.

Carlé, Birte. "Eneboersken Hild: En norrøn jomfrufortælling." In >> *The Sixth International Saga Conference* (1985). Vol. 2, pp. 103–14.

Cormack, Margaret. >> *The Saints in Iceland* (1994). Pp.11, 49–50, 106, and 115.

– "Saints' Lives and Icelandic Literature in the Thirteenth and Fourteenth Centuries." In Hans Bekker-Nielsen and Birte Carlé, ed. >> *Saints and Sagas* (1994). Pp. 27–47, esp. p. 42.

– "Visions, Demons and Gender in the Sagas of Icelandic Saints." *CM* 7 (1994): 185–209, esp. pp. 187 and 199–201.

– "Women and Gender in the Sagas of Icelandic Saints." In >> *Samtíðarsögur* (1994). Vol. 1, pp. 188–93, esp. p. 191.

– "Sagas of Saints." In *Old Icelandic Literature and Society*. Ed. Margaret Clunies Ross (Cambridge: Cambridge University Press, 2000). Pp. 302–25, esp. pp. 308, 310, and 317.

Finnur Jónsson. >> *Den oldnorske og oldislandske Litteraturs Historie* (1920–4). Vol. 2, pp. 395–7.

Foote, Peter. "Latnesk þýðing eftir Árna Magnússon?" *Landsbókasafn Íslands. Árbók 1953–1954* (1955): 137–41.

– "Aachen, Lund, Hólar." *Les relations littéraires franco-scandinaves au Moyen Age. Colloque de Liège (avril 1972)*. Bibliothèque de la Faculté de Philosophie et Lettres de l'Université de Liège 208 (1975): 208 (1975): 53–73, esp. p. 54. Rpt. in Peter Foote. *Aurvandilstá: Norse Studies* (Odense: Odense University Press, 1984). Pp. 101–20, esp. p. 102.

– "Jóns saga ens helga." In Phillip Pulsiano and Kirsten Wolf, with Paul Acker and Donald K. Fry, ed. >> *Medieval Scandinavia* (1993). P. 345.

Guðrún Nordal and Sverrir Tómasson. "Veraldleg sagnaritun 1120–1400." In Guðrún Nordal, Sverrir Tómasson, and Vésteinn Ólason, ed. >> *Íslensk Bókmenntasaga* 1 (1992). Pp. 263–418, esp. pp. 345 and 392.

Hallberg, Peter. "Imagery in Religious Old Norse Prose Literature: An Outline." *ANF* 102 (1987): 120–70, esp. p. 126.

Jón Viðar Sigurðsson. "Utenlandske kvinnehelgener på Island i høymiddelalderen." In >> *Samtíðarsögur* (1994). Vol. 2, pp. 423–34, esp. p. 433.

Jónas Kristjánsson. >> *Eddas and Sagas* (1988). Pp. 179, 181–2, and 193.

Jørgensen, Jørgen Højgaard. *Bispesagaer – Laurentius saga: Studier i* Laurentius saga biskups, *indledt af overvejelser omkring* biskupa sǫgur *som litterær genre.* Udgivelsesudvalgets samling af studenterafhandlinger 12 (Odense: [n.p.], 1978). Pp. 20–1, 29–30, 38–9, and 48.

Kirby, Ian. >> *Biblical Quotation* (1980). Vol. 2, p. 80.

– "The Bible and Biblical Interpretation in Medieval Iceland." In *Old Icelandic Literature and Society*. Ed. Margaret Clunies Ross (Cambridge: Cambridge University Press, 2000). Pp. 287–301, esp. p. 296.

Koppenberg, Peter. *Hagiographische Studien zu den Biskupa sögur: Unter besonderer Berücksichtigung der* Jóns Saga Helga. Scandia Wissenschaftliche Reihe 1 (Bochum: Scandia, 1980). Pp. 1–4, 7–19, and 239.

Louis-Jensen, Jonna. *Kongesagastudier: Kompilationen Hulda-Hrokkinskinna.* Bibliotheca Arnamagnæana 32 (Copenhagen: Reitzel, 1977). Pp. 111–17, 119–21, 122n46, 144, and 149.

Magnús Már Lárusson. "Biskupa sögur." *KLNM* 1 (1956). Cols. 630–1.

– "Helige Ande. Island." *KLNM* 6 (1961). Cols. 375–9, esp. col. 377.

– "Jóns saga helga." *KLNM* 7 (1962). Cols. 617–18.

Mogk, Eugen. >> *Geschichte der norwegisch-isländischen Literatur* (1904). P. 793.

Orri Vésteinsson. *The Christianization of Iceland: Priests, Power, and Social Change 1000–1300* (Oxford: Oxford University Press, 2000). Pp. 35 and 65.

Paasche, Fredrik. *Kristendom og kvad: En studie i norrøn middelalder* (Kristiania [Oslo]: Aschehoug, 1914). Pp. 32–3.

– *Norges og Islands litteratur inntil utgangen av middelalderen.* Rev. ed. by Anne Holtsmark (Oslo: Aschehoug, 1947). Pp. 302, 381–2, and 507.

Paul, Fritz. "Historiographische und hagiographische Tendenzen in isländischen Bischofsviten des 12. und 13. Jahrhunderts." *Skandinavistik* 9 (1979): 36–46.

Schach, Paul. *Icelandic Sagas.* Twayne's World Author Series (Boston: Twayne, 1984). Pp. 11, 66–8, 71, and 98.

Schier, Kurt. *Sagaliteratur.* Sammlung Metzler M78 (Stuttgart: Metzler, 1970). Pp. 4, 68, 70, 121, 123, and 129.

Sigurður Nordal. *Um íslenzkar fornsögur.* Trans. Árni Böðvarsson (Reykjavík: Mál og menning, 1968). Pp. 71–3.

Sigurður Pétursson. "Ovid in Iceland." In *Cultura Classica e Cultura Germanica Settentrionale*. Ed. Pietro Janni, Diego Poli, and Carlo Santini (Macerata: Herder, 1985). Pp. 53–63, esp. pp. 55–6.

Sigurgeir Steingrímsson, Ólafur Halldórsson, and Peter Foote, ed. *Biskupa sögur I: Kristni saga, Kristni þættir, Þorvalds þáttr víðförla I, Þorvalds þáttr víðförla II, Stefnis þáttr Þorgilssonar, Af Þangbrandi, Af Þiðranda ok dísunum, Kristniboð Þangbrands, Þrír þættir, Kristnitakan, Jóns saga ins helga, Gísls þáttr Illugasonar, Sæmundar þáttr.* Vol. 1: *Fræði,* Vol. 2: *Sögutextar.* Íslenzk fornrit 15 (Reykjavík: Hið íslenzka fornritafélag, 2003). Vol. 1, pp. ccxiii–cccxxi.

Steingrímur Matthíasson. "Jón helgi. Æðsti prestur í þessu lífi og land-læknir í öðru lífi." *Eimreiðin* 28 (1922): 65–80.

Sverrir Tómasson. "Helgisögur, mælskufræði og forn frásagnarlist." *Skírnir* 157 (1983): 130–62, esp. pp. 141–3.

– *Formálar íslenskra sagnaritara á miðöldum. Rannsókn bókmenntahefðar* (Reykjavík: Stofnun Árna Magnússonar, 1988). Pp. 19–20, 24, 37, 67, and 339–43.

– "Kristnar trúarbókmenntir í óbundnu máli." In Guðrún Nordal, Sverrir Tómasson, and Vésteinn Ólason, ed. >> *Íslensk Bókmenntasaga* 1 (1992). Pp. 419–79, esp. pp. 467, 473–4, and 479.

Turville-Petre, G. >> *Origins of Icelandic Literature* (1967). Pp. 110 and 197–8.

Whaley, Diana. "Miracles in the Sagas of Bishops: Icelandic Variations on an International Theme." *CM* 7 (1994): 155–84.

Widding, Ole. "Ave Maria eller Maríuvers i norrøn litteratur." *Mm* (1958): 1–7, esp. p. 3.

Wolf, Kirsten, ed. >> *Heilagra meyja sögur* (2003). Pp. lxiv–lxvi.

Handlist, p. 317.

LANFRANC OF CANTERBURY   May 28

Af Lanfranco

Based on various sections of *Speculum historiale.*

Manuscript:
AM 657a–b 4to (ca. 1350, defective).
Edition:
Gering, Hugo, ed. >> *Islendzk æventyri* (1882–3). Vol. 1, pp. 298–305.
German paraphrase:
Gering, Hugo, ed. >> *Islendzk æventyri* (1882–3). Vol. 2, pp. 231–9.

Literature:
Boyer, Régis. >> *La vie religieuse en Islande* (1979). P. 186.
Fell, Christine E. "Anglo-Saxon Saints in Old Norse Sources and Vice Versa."
   In Hans Bekker-Nielsen, Peter Foote, and Olaf Olsen, ed. >> *Proceedings of the Eighth Viking Congress* (1981). Pp. 95–106, esp. pp. 97–8.
Handlist, p. 318.

LAURENCE OF ROME   August 10

1. Lárentíuss saga erkidjákns

Chapters 1–3 based on *BHL* 7802, chapters 4–7 on *BHL* 4754, and
chapter 8 on *BHL* 3961. The Icelandic text is somewhat abridged.

Manuscripts:
AM 235 fol. (ca. 1400) and Stock. Perg. fol. no. 2 (ca. 1425–45).
Editions:
Foote, Peter, ed. >> *Lives of Saints* (1962).
   Facsimile of Stock. Perg. fol. no. 2.
Unger, C.R., ed. >> *Heilagra manna søgur* (1877). Vol. 1, pp. 422–32.
   Based on Stock. Perg. fol. no. 2 with variants from AM 235 fol.
Literature:
Battista, Simonetta. "Interpretations of the Roman Pantheon in the Old
   Norse Hagiographic Sagas." In Geraldine Barnes and Margaret
   Clunies Ross, ed. >> *Old Norse Myths, Literature and Society* (2000).
   Pp. 24–34, esp. pp. 33–4.
Bekker-Nielsen, Hans, Thorkil Damsgaard Olsen, and Ole Widding.
   >> *Norrøn fortællekunst* (1965). P. 124.
Bekker-Nielsen, Hans, and Ole Widding. "Legende. Norge og Island."
   KLNM 10 (1965). Cols. 421–3, esp. col. 421.
Carlé, Birte. >> *Jomfru-fortællingen* (1985). Pp. 38–9, 41, 62–3, 70–1,
   and 83.
– "Men and Women in the Saints' Sagas of *Stock. 2, fol.*" In John
   Lindow, Lars Lönnroth, and Gerd Wolfgang Weber, ed. >> *Structure
   and Meaning in Old Norse Literature* (1986). Pp. 317–46, esp. pp. 319–
   20, 322, 324, 328, 330–1, and 334–6.
Cormack, Margaret. >> *The Saints in Iceland* (1994). Pp. 34 and 118.
Jón Hnefill Aðalsteinsson. "Blot i forna skrifter." *SI* 47 (1996): 11–32,
   esp. p. 28.

Kalinke, Marianne E. "Reykjahólabók: A Legendary on the Eve of the Reformation." *Skáldskaparmál* 2 (1992): 239–69, esp. p. 252.

– "'Þa kom þar þessi forbrende Lavrencivs': Two Versions of *Laurencius saga*." *Mm* (1994): 113–34.

– >> *The Book of Reykjahólar* (1996). Pp. 47, 83–6, 95, 110, and 119–21.

Lehmann, Paul. >> "Skandinaviens Anteil an der lateinischen Literatur und Wissenschaft des Mittelalters" (1937). Pp. 44 and 49.

Mogk, Eugen. >> *Geschichte der norwegisch-isländischen Literatur* (1904). P. 891.

Sverrir Tómasson. "Trúarbókmenntir í lausu máli á síðmiðöld." In Böðvar Guðmundsson, Sverrir Tómasson, Torfi H. Tulinius, and Vésteinn Ólason, ed. >> *Íslensk Bókmenntasaga* 2 (1993). Pp. 249–82, esp. p. 279.

Þórhallur Þorgilsson. "Um þýðingar og endursagnir úr ítölskum miðaldaritum." *Landsbókasafn Íslands. Árbók* 1946–7 (1948): 212–24, esp. p. 222.

Widding, Ole, and Hans Bekker-Nielsen. "En senmiddelalderlig legendesamling." *Mm* (1960): 105–28, esp. pp. 116–17.

– "Low German Influence on Late Icelandic Hagiography." *GR* 37 (1962): 239–62, esp. p. 252.

Handlist, p. 318.

NOTE:

In the saga, material about Saints Hippolytus and Sixtus II is found. See the entries for the individual saints.

2. Lárencíuss saga erkidjákns

A copy of an Icelandic translation from the Latin.

Manuscript:
Stock. Perg. fol. no. 3 (*Reykjahólabók*) (ca. 1530–40).

Edition:
Loth, Agnete, ed. >> *Reykjahólabók* (1969–70). Vol. 1, pp. 247–72.

Literature:

Bekker-Nielsen, Hans, Thorkil Damsgaard Olsen, and Ole Widding. >> *Norrøn fortællekunst* (1965). P. 124.

Kalinke, Marianne E. "Reykjahólabók: A Legendary on the Eve of the Reformation." *Skáldskaparmál* 2 (1992): 239–69, esp. pp. 240 and 251–2.

– "'Þa kom þar þessi forbrende Lavrencivs': Two Versions of *Laurencius saga*." *Mm* (1994): 113–34.

– >> *The Book of Reykjahólar* (1996). Pp. 28, 47, 56, 63, 80, 82–6, 93, 95, 110–13, 117–21, 131–3, 139, 141, 165, and 239.

Sverrir Tómasson. "Trúarbókmenntir í lausu máli á síðmiðöld." In
   Böðvar Guðmundsson, Sverrir Tómasson, Torfi H. Tulinius, and
   Vésteinn Ólason, ed. >> *Íslensk Bókmenntasaga* 2 (1993). Pp. 249–82,
   esp. p. 279.
Widding, Ole, and Hans Bekker-Nielsen. "En senmiddelalderlig
   legendesamling." *Mm* (1960): 105–28, esp. pp. 107, 116–17, and 127.
– "Low German Influence on Late Icelandic Hagiography." *GR* 37
   (1962): 239–62, esp. pp. 252 and 255.
Handlist, p. 318.

LAZARUS   December 17

Lazaruss saga

Translated from a now-lost Low German redaction that resembles the
source(s) of *Der Heiligen Leben*.

Manuscript:
Stock. Perg. fol. no. 3 (*Reykjahólabók*) (ca. 1530–40).
Edition:
Loth, Agnete, ed. >> *Reykjahólabók* (1969–70). Vol. 1, pp. 167–90.
Literature:
Bekker-Nielsen, Hans. "Marta fra Betania. Norge og Island." *KLNM* 11
   (1966). Col. 472.
Kalinke, Marianne E. "Reykjahólabók: A Legendary on the Eve of the
   Reformation." *Skáldskaparmál* 2 (1992): 239–69, esp. p. 240.
– >> *The Book of Reykjahólar* (1996). Pp. 28, 50, 109, 114, and 126–7.
Widding, Ole, and Hans Bekker-Nielsen. "En senmiddelalderlig
   legendesamling." *Mm* (1960): 105–28, esp. pp. 107, 115, and 128.
– "Low German Influence on Late Icelandic Hagiography." *GR* 37 (1962):
   239–62, esp. p. 249.
Handlist, p. 318.

LEO THE GREAT   April 11

Af Leó páfa

A tale of Saint Leo the Great incorporated into the miracles of the Virgin
Mary.

Manuscripts:
See Mary the Blessed Virgin 3 note (p. 245).
Edition:
Unger, C.R., ed. >> *Mariu saga* (1871). Pp. 694.13–695.27.
Literature:
Boyer, Régis. >> *La vie religieuse en Islande* (1979). P. 162.
Widding, Ole. "Norrøne Marialegender på europæisk baggrund."
   Opuscula 10. Bibliotheca Arnamagnæana 40 (Copenhagen: Reitzel,
   1996). Pp. 1–128, esp. p. 64.
Handlist, pp. 318 and 323.

LEONARD OF NOBLAC   November 6

A short legend (*BHL* 4862) of Saint Leonard of Noblac included in a
prayer to Saint Margaret of Antioch.

Manuscripts:
AM 431 12mo (ca. 1550) and AM 433c 12mo (1525–50).
Editions:
Bekker-Nielsen, Hans. "En god bøn." *Opuscula* 2.1. Bibliotheca Arna-
   magnæana 25.1 (Copenhagen: Ejnar Munksgaard, 1961). Pp. 52–8, esp.
   pp. 55–8.
   Edition of AM 431 12mo and AM 433c 12mo.
Kålund, Kr., ed. *Alfræði íslenzk: Islandsk encyklopædisk litteratur III.*
   Landalýsingar m. fl. STUAGNL 45 (Copenhagen: Møller, 1917–18).
   Pp. 86.15–88.10.
   Edition of AM 431 12mo.
Literature:
Bekker-Nielsen, Hans. "Margareta (af Antiochia). Norge og Island."
   KLNM 11 (1966). Cols. 347–8, esp. col. 348.
Handlist, p. 318.

LUCY OF SYRACUSE   December 13

1. Lúcíu saga

A translation of the common form of the *passio*, *BHL* 4992, in a
version closer to that given by Surius than to any of the other printed
versions.

Manuscript:
AM 921 4to V (ca. 1400; this manuscript has been demonstrated to belong
  to AM 235 fol.).
Edition:
Loth, Agnete. "'Roted fragmentum membraneum, um Sanctam Luciam
  og Agatham': AM 921, V, 4°." In *Festskrift til Ludvig Holm-Olsen på
  hans 70-årsdag den 9. juni 1984* (Øvre Ervik: Alvheim & Eide, 1984).
  Pp. 221–35, esp. pp. 226.8–229.18.
Literature:
Foote, Peter, ed. >> *Lives of Saints* (1962). P. 26.
Van Deusen, Natalie M. "Stitches in the Margins: The Embroidery
  Pattern in AM 235 fol." *Mm* (2011–12): 26–42, esp. p. 28.
Handlist, p. 319.

2. Lúcíu saga

A version different from 1. Both appear to be independently derived from
the same original.

Manuscript:
Stock. Perg. fol. no. 2 (ca. 1425–45).
Editions:
Foote, Peter, ed. >> *Lives of Saints* (1962).
    Facsimile.
Unger, C.R., ed. >> *Heilagra manna søgur* (1877). Vol. 1, pp. 433–6.
Modern Icelandic language edition:
Wolf, Kirsten, ed. >> *Heilagra meyja sögur* (2003). Pp. 148–51.
Literature:
Ásdís Egilsdóttir. "Kvendýrlingar og kvenímynd trúarlegra bókmennta á
  Íslandi." In Inga Huld Hákonardóttir, ed. >> *Konur og kristsmenn*
  (1996). Pp. 93–116, esp. p. 93.
Bekker-Nielsen, Hans, Thorkil Damsgaard Olsen, and Ole Widding.
  >> *Norrøn fortællekunst* (1965). P. 124.
Carlé, Birte. "Fra slægtssaga til kvindesaga." In Silja Aðalsteinsdóttir and
  Helgi Þorláksson, ed. >> *Forändringar i kvinnors villkor under medel-
  tiden* (1983). Pp. 55–70, esp. pp. 56, 58, 60–1, 63, and 65.
– >> *Jomfru-fortællingen* (1985). Pp. 40–1, 75, 79–80, 95–100, 133, and 145.
– "Some Observations Regarding Narrative Patterns in the Medieval
  Sagas of Holy Maids." In Régis Boyer, ed. >> *Les Sagas de Chevaliers
  (Riddarasögur)* (1985). Pp. 393–404, esp. pp. 395 and 399.

– "Men and Women in the Saints' Sagas of *Stock. 2, fol.*" In John
Lindow, Lars Lönnroth, and Gerd Wolfgang Weber, ed. >> *Structure
and Meaning in Old Norse Literature* (1986). Pp. 317–46, esp. pp. 320
and 241–2.

Cormack, Margaret. >> *The Saints in Iceland* (1994). P. 119.

Celander, Hilding. "Lucia." *KLNM* 10 (1965). Cols. 704–9, esp, col. 705.

Kirby, Ian. >> *Biblical Quotation* (1980). Vol. 2, p. 43.

Mogk, Eugen. >> *Geschichte der norwegisch-isländischen Literatur* (1904).
P. 891.

Sverrir Tómasson. "Kristnar trúarbókmenntir í óbundnu máli." In
Guðrún Nordal, Sverrir Tómasson, and Vésteinn Ólason, ed.
>> *Íslensk Bókmenntasaga* 1 (1992). Pp. 419–79, esp. 436.

Þórhallur Þorgilsson. "Um þýðingar og endursagnir úr ítölskum miðaldaritum." *Landsbókasafn Íslands. Árbók* 1946–7 (1948): 212–24, esp. p. 222.

Handlist, p. 319.

MAGNUS   April 6

1. Magnúss saga Eyjajarls

A life and miracles of Saint Magnus, earl of Orkney (d. ca. 1117), incorporated into *Orkneyinga saga* (chapters 33, 39–40, 44–52, and 57).

Manuscripts:
AM 325 4to I (ca. 1300), AM 325α 4to III (ca. 1300–50), AM 325β 4to
III (ca. 1300), AM 332 4to (ca. 1700), AM 762 4to (ca. 1600–50), GKS
1005 fol. (*Flateyjarbók*) (ca. 1387–95), GKS 1013 fol. (ca. 1575–1600),
and Upps UB R 702 4to (ca. 1600–50).

Editions:
Finnbogi Guðmundsson, ed. *Orkneyinga saga. Legenda de Sancto Magno.*
Magnúss saga skemmri. Magnúss saga lengri. Helga þáttr ok Úlfs.
Íslenzk fornrit 34 (Reykjavík: Hið íslenzka fornritafélag, 1965).
Pp. 1–300.

Finnur Jónsson, ed. *Flateyjarbók (Codex Flateyensis): MS. No. 1005 fol.*
in the Old Royal Collection in the Royal Library of Copenhagen. CCI 1
(Copenhagen: Levin & Munksgaard, 1930).
Facsimile of GKS 1005 fol.

Gudbrand Vigfusson and George W. Dasent, ed. and trans. *Icelandic*
Sagas and Other Historical Documents Relating to the Settlements and

Descents of the Northmen on the British Isles. 4 vols. Rolls Series 88
(London: Eyre and Spottiswoode, 1887–94; rpt. Millwood: Kraus,
1964). Vol. 1, pp. 1–221.
 Based on AM 332 4to (pp. 3.29–10.7, 27.5–40.30, 179.14–185.17, and
 197.9–203.21), AM 324 4to I (pp. 49.27–51.1, 81.11–113.11, 154.15–
 162.19, 178.1–179.14, 185.17–197.9, and 197.9–200.14), GKS 1005 fol.
 (pp. 1–3.29, 10.7–27.5, 40.30–49.27, 54.32–69.28, 73.13–81.11, 113.11–
 154.15, 162.19–178.1, and 203.21–221), and Upps UB R 702 4to
 (pp. 51.1–54.32 and 69.28–73.13) with variants from GKS 1005 fol.
Guðbrandr Vigfusson and C.R. Unger, ed. *Flateyjarbók: En Samling af
 norske Konge-Sagaer med indskudte mindre Fortællinger om Begivenheder i og udenfor Norge samt Annaler*. 3 vols. (Christiania [Oslo]: Malling, 1860–8). Vol. 2, pp. 176–82 and 404–519.
 Edition of GKS 1005 fol.
[Kålund, Kr., ed.] *Palæografisk Atlas: Oldnorsk-islandsk afdeling* (Copenhagen and Christiania [Oslo]: Gyldendal, 1905). No. 32.
 Facsimile and text edition of AM 235 4to I, fol. 15v.
Sigurður Nordal, ed. *Orkneyinga saga*. STUAGNL 40 (Copenhagen:
 Møller, 1913–16).
 Based on GKS 1005 fol. (pp. 1–4.18, 14.1–26.20, 61.11–73.1, 82.4–
 102.11, 105.7–18, 107.20–120.4, 168.17–223.5, 236.4–257.11, 297.19–
 331), AM 332 4to (pp. 4.19–14.1, 40.5–51.16, 61.1–11, 293.2–297.19),
 AM 325 4to I (pp. 73.1–78.13, 120.4–168.17, 223.5–236.4, 257.11–
 293.1), AM 325a 4to III (pp. 78.13–82.4, 102.11–105.7, 105.18–107.20),
 AM 325b 4to III (pp. 51.16–61.1), and Upps UB R 702 (pp. 220.3–30
 and 221.7–33) with variants from AM 332 4to and GKS 1005 fol.
Sigurður Nordal et al, ed. *Flateyjarbók*. 4 vols. (Akranes: Flateyjarútgáfan, 1944–5). Vol. 2, pp. 42–5 and vol. 3, pp. 1–130.
 Edition of GKS 1005 fol.

Danish translations:

Møller, Asger, trans. *Orkney-Sagaer* (Aarhus: Aros, 1956) (extracts only).
Ægidius, Jens Peter, trans. *Orknøboernes saga*. Odense University Studies
 in Scandinavian Language and Literature 49 (Odense: Odense Universitetsforlag, 2002).

English translations:

Gudbrand Vigfusson and George W. Dasent, ed. and trans. *Icelandic
 Sagas and Other Historical Documents Relating to the Settlements and
 Descents of the Northmen on the British Isles*. 4 vols. Rolls Series 88
 (London: Eyre and Spottiswoode, 1887–94; rpt. Millwood: Kraus,
 1964). Vol. 3, pp. 1–224.

Hermann Pálsson and Paul Edwards, trans. *Orkneyinga saga: The History of the Earls of Orkney* (London: Hogarth, 1978; rpt. Harmondsworth: Penguin, 1981).

Jon A. Hjaltalin and Gilbert Goudie, trans., Joseph Anderson, ed. *The Orkneyinga Saga* (Edinburgh: Edmonston and Douglas, 1873).

Taylor, Alexander Burt, trans. *The Orkneyinga Saga: A New Translation with Introduction and Notes* (Edinburgh and London: Oliver and Boyd, 1938).

Tomany, Maria-Claudia. "Sacred Non-Violence, Cowardice Profaned: St Magnus of Orkney in Nordic Hagiography and History." In Thomas A. DuBois, ed. >> *Sanctity in the North* (2008). Pp. 128–53, esp. pp. 129–37.

German translation:

Baetke, Walter, trans. *Die Geschichte von den Orkaden, Dänemark und der Jomsburg*. Neuausgabe mit Nachwort von Dr. Rolf Heller. Thule: Altnordische Dichtung und Prosa 19 (Düsseldorf: Eugen Diederichs, 1966). Pp. 21–219.

Norwegian translations:

Holtsmark, Anne, trans. *Orknøyingenes saga* (Oslo: Aschehoug, 1970).

Indrebø, Gustav, trans. *Orknøyingasoga*. Norrøne bokverk 25 (Oslo: Det Norske Samlaget, 1929).

Literature:

Ásdís Egilsdóttir. "Hrafn Sveinbjarnarson, Pilgrim and Martyr." In *Sagas, Saints and Settlements*. Ed. Gareth Williams and Paul Bibire. The Northern World 2 (Leiden: Brill, 2004). Pp. 29–39, esp. p. 34.

Bekker-Nielsen, Hans, Thorkil Damsgaard Olsen, and Ole Widding. >> *Norrøn fortællekunst* (1965). P. 47.

Bibire, Paul. "The Poetry of Earl Rǫgnvaldr's Court." In *St Magnus Cathedral and Orkney's Twelfth-Century Renaissance*. Ed. Barbara E. Crawford (Aberdeen: Aberdeen University Press, 1988). Pp. 208–40, esp. pp. 208–9, 212–15, 218, 223, and 235.

– "Magnúss saga helga eyjajarls." In Phillip Pulsiano and Kirsten Wolf, with Paul Acker and Donald K. Fry, ed. >> *Medieval Scandinavia* (1993). P. 401.

Chesnutt, Michael. "Orkneyinga saga." In Phillip Pulsiano and Kirsten Wolf, with Paul Acker and Donald K. Fry, ed. >> *Medieval Scandinavia* (1993). Pp. 456–7.

Cormack, Margaret J. "Saints and Sinners: Reflections on Death in Some Icelandic Sagas." *Gripla* 8 (1993): 187–218, esp. pp. 191–3.

– >> *The Saints in Iceland* (1994). Pp. 120 and 243.

Einar Ól. Sveinsson. *Sagnaritun Oddaverja: nokkrar athuganir*. Studia Islandica 1 (Reykjavík: Ísafold, 1937). Pp. 16–39.

Ellehøj, Svend. *Studier over den ældste norrøne historieskrivning.* Bibliotheca Arnamagnæana 26 (Copenhagen: Munksgaard, 1965). Pp. 97,
104–7, 163–5, 167, and 169–70.

Finnbogi Guðmundsson. "Orkneyinga saga." *KLNM* 12 (1967). Cols.
699–702.

Foote, Peter. "Observations on *Orkneyinga saga.*" In *St Magnus Cath-
edral and Orkney's Twelfth-Century Renaissance.* Ed. Barbara E.
Crawford (Aberdeen: Aberdeen University Press, 1988). Pp. 192–207.
Rpt. in Peter Foote. *Kreddur: Select Studies in Early Icelandic Law
and Literature* (Reykjavík: Hið íslenska bókmenntafélag, 2004).
Pp. 107–27.

– "Master Robert's Prologue in Magnúss saga lengri." In *Festskrift til
Finn Hødnebø 29. desember 1989.* Ed. Bjørn Eithun, Eyvind Fjeld
Halvorsen, Magnus Rindal, and Erik Simensen (Oslo: Novus, 1989).
Pp. 65–81, esp. p. 67.

– "Saints' Lives and Sagas." In Hans Bekker-Nielsen and Birte Carlé, ed.
>> *Saints and Sagas* (1994). Pp. 73–88, esp. p. 79.

Haki Antonsson: "Two Twelfth-Century Martyrs: St Thomas of Canterbury and St Magnús of Orkney." In *Sagas, Saints and Settlements.* Ed.
Gareth Williams and Paul Bibire. The Northern World 2 (Leiden: Brill,
2004). Pp. 41–64.

– "The Kings of Norway and the Earls of Orkney: The Case of *Orkneyinga saga.*" *MScand* 15 (2005): 81–100.

– "Saints and Relics in Early Christian Scandinavia." *MScand* 15 (2005):
51–80, esp. p. 73.

– *St. Magnús of Orkney: A Scandinavian Martyr-Cult in Context.* Northern World 29 (Leiden: Brill, 2007). Pp. 5–102.

Halvorsen, E.F. "Magnúss saga." *KLNM* 11 (1966). Cols. 238–9.

Helgi Guðmundsson. *Um haf innan. Vestrænir menn og íslenzk menning á
miðöldum* (Reykjavík: Háskólaútgáfan, 1997). Pp. 12–13, 17, 19, 22,
24–31, 33, 45, 50, 53, 56, 66, 68, 70–1, 77–8, 82, 87, 108, 116, 120,
133–5, 146, 157–9, 163, 170, 176, 179, 184, 189, 191, 200–15, 217–36,
238–55, 257–79, 282, 284, 286–90, 292–301, 306, 308–10, 313–14, 317,
320, 324, and 326.

Jakob Benediktsson. "Cursus hos Bergr Sokkason." In *Festskrift til
Ludvig Holm-Olsen på hans 70-årsdag den 9. juni 1984* (Øvre Ervik:
Alvheim & Eide, 1984). Pp. 34–40, esp. p. 36. Rpt. in Jakob Benediktsson. *Lærdómslistir. Afmælisrit 20. júlí 1987* (Reykjavík: Mál og menning, 1987). Pp. 262–9, esp. pp. 265–6.

Jesch, Judith. "Narrating *Orkneyinga saga.*" *SS* 64 (1992): 336–55.

Kratz, Henry. "Saints' Lives. 2. Iceland and Norway." In Phillip Pulsiano and Kirsten Wolf, with Paul Acker and Donald K. Fry, ed. >> *Medieval Scandinavia* (1993). Pp. 562–4.

Louis-Jensen, Jonna. *Kongesagastudier: Kompilationen Hulda-Hrokkinskinna.* Bibliotheca Arnamagnæana 32 (Copenhagen: Reitzel, 1977). Pp. 48, 63, 65, 80–2, 95–6, 122, 124–7, and 144.

Magnús Már Lárusson. "Sct. Magnus Orcadensis Comes." *Saga* 3 (1960–3): 470–503, esp. pp. 477, 485–6, 488, 490–3, 495–7, and 500–2.

Mogk, Eugen. >> *Geschichte der norwegisch-isländischen Literatur* (1904). Pp. 695, 814, 817–18, and 831.

Mooney, John. *St. Magnus – Earl of Orkney* (Kirkwall: Mackintosh, 1935).

Owen, Olwyn, ed. *The World of Orkneyinga Saga: "The Broad-Cloth Viking Trip"* (Kirkwall: The Orcadian Limited, 2005).

Paasche, Fredrik. *Norges og Islands litteratur inntil utgangen av middelalderen.* Rev. ed. by Anne Holtsmark (Oslo: Aschehoug, 1947). Pp. 388, 396, 419, 455, and 493.

Phelpstead, Carl. "Masculinity and Sexuality in Sagas of Scandinavian Royal Saints." In Rudolf Simek and Judith Meurer, ed. >> *Scandinavia and Christian Europe in the Middle Ages* (2003). Pp. 421–8, esp. pp. 421–4.

– *Holy Vikings: Saints' Lives in the Old Icelandic Kings' Sagas.* Medieval and Renaissance Texts and Studies 40 (Tempe, Ariz.: Arizona Center for Medieval and Renaissance Studies, 2007). Pp. 2, 10–16, 21, 32, 33–5, 37, 39, 42, 45, 47, 52, 54, 74–115, 137, 155, 159, 191, 197, 202, 206–10, 212–14, 216, and 225.

Piebenga, Gryt Anne. "Miracles, Collections of." In Phillip Pulsiano and Kirsten Wolf, with Paul Acker and Donald K. Fry, ed. >> *Medieval Scandinavia* (1993). Pp. 413–14.

Rowe, Elizabeth Ashman. *The Development of Flateyjarbók: Iceland and the Norwegian Dynastic Crisis of 1389* (Gylling: The University Press of Southern Denmark, 2005). Pp. 20, 23, 36–7, 48, 101, 205–6, 317, 320, 322, 336, 339, 344, 359, 361–2, 370, 372, and 410.

Seip, Didrik Arup. "Jærtegnsamlinger." *KLNM* 8 (1963). Cols. 65–8, esp. col. 67.

– "Some Remarks on the Language of the Magnus Legend in the *Orkneyinga saga.*" In *Nordica et Anglica: Studies in Honor of Stefán Einarsson.* Ed. Allan H. Orrick. Janua Linguarum Series Maior 22 (The Hague and Paris: Mouton, 1968). Pp. 93–6.

Taylor, A.B. "Orkneyinga saga – Patronage and Authorship." In Peter
Foote, Hermann Pálsson, and Desmond Slay, ed. >> *Proceedings of
the First International Saga Conference* (1973). Pp. 396–410.

Turville-Petre, G. >> *Origins of Icelandic Literature* (1967). P. 216.

Vries, Jan de. >> *Altnordische Literaturgeschichte* (1964–7). Vol. 1, pp. 297
and 318, and vol. 2, pp. 24–5, 27–8, 33, 212, 262–3, 287, 289, 397, and
400.

Waugh, Robin. "Saint Magnús's Fame in *Orkneyinga Saga.*" *JEGP* 102
(2003): 163–87.

Handlist, p. 319.

2. Magnúss saga Eyjajarls skemmri

A shorter version of the life and miracles of Saint Magnus, earl of
Orkney, closely related to and possibly derived from *Orkneyinga saga*.

Manuscript:
AM 235 fol. (ca. 1400).

Editions:
Finnbogi Guðmundsson, ed. *Orkneyinga saga. Legenda de Sancto Magno.
Magnúss saga skemmri. Magnúss saga lengri. Helga þáttr ok Úlfs.* Íslenzk
fornrit 34 (Reykjavík: Hið íslenzka fornritafélag, 1965). Pp. 309–32.

Gudbrand Vigfusson and George W. Dasent, ed. and trans. *Icelandic
Sagas and Other Historical Documents Relating to the Settlements and
Descents of the Northmen on the British Isles.* 4 vols. Rolls Series 88
(London: Eyre and Spottiswoode, 1887–94; rpt. Millwood: Kraus,
1964). Vol. 3, pp. 281–98.

English translations:
Gudbrand Vigfusson and George W. Dasent, ed. and trans. *Icelandic
Sagas and Other Historical Documents Relating to the Settlements and
Descents of the Northmen on the British Isles.* 4 vols. Rolls Series 88
(London: Eyre and Spottiswoode, 1887–94; rpt. Millwood: Kraus,
1964). Vol. 3, pp. 281–301.

Hermann Pálsson and Paul Edwards, trans. *Magnus' Saga: The Life of
St Magnus Earl of Orkney 1075–1116* (Oxford: Perpetua Press, 1987).
Pp. 21–43.

Literature:
Ásdís Egilsdóttir. "Hrafn Sveinbjarnarson, Pilgrim and Martyr." In
Sagas, Saints and Settlements. Ed. Gareth Williams and Paul Bibire.
The Northern World 2 (Leiden: Brill, 2004). Pp. 29–39, esp. p. 34.

Bekker-Nielsen, Hans, and Ole Widding. "Legende. Norge og Island."
     KLNM 10 (1965). Cols. 421–3, esp. col. 421.
Bibire, Paul. "Magnúss saga helga eyjajarls." In Phillip Pulsiano and
     Kirsten Wolf, with Paul Acker and Donald K. Fry, ed. >> *Medieval
     Scandinavia* (1993). P. 401.
Carlé, Birte. >> *Jomfru-fortællingen* (1985). P. 38.
– "Men and Women in the Saints' Sagas of *Stock. 2, fol.*" In John
     Lindow, Lars Lönnroth, and Gerd Wolfgang Weber, ed. >> *Structure
     and Meaning in Old Norse Literature* (1986). Pp. 317–46, esp. p. 318.
Cormack, Margaret J. "Saints and Sinners: Reflections on Death in Some
     Icelandic Sagas." *Gripla* 8 (1993): 187–218, esp. pp. 191–3.
– >> *The Saints in Iceland* (1994). Pp. 67, 120, and 243.
– "Christian Biography." In *A Companion to Old Norse–Icelandic
     Literature and Culture*. Ed. Rory McTurk (Oxford: Blackwell, 2005).
     Pp. 27–42, esp. p. 30.
Einar Ól. Sveinsson. *Sagnaritun Oddaverja: nokkrar athuganir*. Studia
     Islandica 1 (Reykjavík: Ísafold, 1937). Pp. 22–9.
Finnur Jónsson. >> *Den oldnorske og oldislandske Litteraturs Historie*
     (1920–4). Vol. 2, pp. 651–2.
Haki Antonsson: "Two Twelfth-Century Martyrs: St Thomas of Canter-
     bury and St Magnús of Orkney." In *Sagas, Saints and Settlements*. Ed.
     Gareth Williams and Paul Bibire. The Northern World 2 (Leiden: Brill,
     2004). Pp. 41–64.
– "St Magnús of Orkney: Aspects of His Cult from a European Perspec-
     tive." In *The World of Orkneyinga Saga: "The Broad-Cloth Viking Trip"*
     (Kirkwall: The Orcadian Limited, 2005). Pp. 145–59, esp. pp. 149 and
     151–3.
– *St. Magnús of Orkney: A Scandinavian Martyr-Cult in Context*.
     Northern World 29 (Leiden: Brill, 2007). Pp. 5–102.
Hallberg, Peter. "Imagery in Religious Old Norse Prose Literature: An
     Outline." *ANF* 102 (1987): 120–70, esp. pp. 122–3.
Halvorsen, E.F. "Magnúss saga." *KLNM* 11 (1966). Cols. 238–9.
Helgi Guðmundsson. *Um haf innan. Vestrænir menn og íslenzk menning á
     miðöldum* (Reykjavík: Háskólaútgáfan, 1997). Pp. 54, 201, 222, 284,
     and 287.
Jakob Benediktsson. "Cursus hos Bergr Sokkason." In *Festskrift til
     Ludvig Holm-Olsen på hans 70-årsdag den 9. juni 1984* (Øvre Ervik:
     Alvheim & Eide, 1984). Pp. 34–40, esp. p. 37. Rpt. in Jakob Benedikts-
     son. *Lærdómslistir. Afmælisrit 20. júlí 1987* (Reykjavík: Mál og men-
     ning, 1987). Pp. 262–9, esp. pp. 265–6.

Jesch, Judith. "Literature in Medieval Orkney." In *The World of Orkney-inga Saga: "The Broad-Cloth Viking Trip"* (Kirkwall: The Orcadian Limited, 2005). Pp. 11–24, esp. p. 14.

Jesch, Judith, and Theya Molleson. "The Death of Magnus Erlendsson and the Relics of St Magnus." In *The World of Orkneyinga Saga: "The Broad-Cloth Viking Trip"* (Kirkwall: The Orcadian Limited, 2005). Pp. 127–43, esp. p. 132.

Kratz, Henry. "Saints' Lives. 2. Iceland and Norway." In Phillip Pulsiano and Kirsten Wolf, with Paul Acker and Donald K. Fry, ed. >> *Medieval Scandinavia* (1993). Pp. 562–4.

Lamb, Raymond, and Judith Robertson. "Kirkwall: Saga, History, Archaeology." In *The World of Orkneyinga Saga: "The Broad-Cloth Viking Trip"* (Kirkwall: The Orcadian Limited, 2005). Pp. 161–91, esp. pp. 161, 164–7, and 174.

Louis-Jensen, Jonna. *Kongesagastudier: Kompilationen Hulda-Hrokkin-skinna*. Bibliotheca Arnamagnæana 32 (Copenhagen: Reitzel, 1977). P. 127.

Magnús Már Lárusson. "Sct. Magnus Orcadensis Comes." *Saga* 3 (1960–3): 470–503, esp. pp. 477, 485–91, 495–7, and 503.

– "Magnús." *KLNM* 11 (1966). Cols. 221–2, esp. col. 222.

Mogk, Eugen. >> *Geschichte der norwegisch-isländischen Literatur* (1904). P. 817.

Mooney, John. *St. Magnus – Earl of Orkney* (Kirkwall: Mackintosh, 1935).

Paasche, Fredrik. *Norges og Islands litteratur inntil utgangen av middelalderen*. Rev. ed. by Anne Holtsmark (Oslo: Aschehoug, 1947). P. 455.

Phelpstead, Carl. "Masculinity and Sexuality in Sagas of Scandinavian Royal Saints." In Rudolf Simek and Judith Meurer, ed. >> *Scandinavia and Christian Europe in the Middle Ages* (2003). Pp. 421–8, esp. pp. 421 and 423.

– *Holy Vikings: Saints' Lives in the Old Icelandic Kings' Sagas*. Medieval and Renaissance Texts and Studies 40 (Tempe, Ariz.: Arizona Center for Medieval and Renaissance Studies, 2007). Pp. 15, 46–7, 52, 77–9, 84, 88, 91, 94, 100, 207–10, and 215.

Sverrir Tómasson. *Formálar íslenskra sagnaritara á miðöldum. Rannsókn bókmenntahefðar* (Reykjavík: Stofnun Árna Magnússonar, 1988). P. 344.

– "Kristnar trúarbókmenntir í óbundnu máli." In Guðrún Nordal, Sverrir Tómasson, and Vésteinn Ólason, ed. >> *Íslensk Bókmenntasaga* 1 (1992). Pp. 419–79, esp. pp. 451 and 457–8.

Tomany, Maria-Claudia. "Sacred Non-Violence, Cowardice Profaned:
St Magnus of Orkney in Nordic Hagiography and History." In Thomas
A. DuBois, ed. >> *Sanctity in the North* (2008). Pp. 128–53, esp. pp. 131–3.
Vries, Jan de. >> *Altnordische Literaturgeschichte* (1964–7). Vol. 2, p. 263.
Waugh, Robin. "Saint Magnús's Fame in *Orkneyinga Saga.*" *JEGP* 102
(2003): 163–87, esp. pp. 163, 175, 178, and 185.
Handlist, p. 319.

3. Magnúss saga Eyjajarls lengri

A longer version of the life and miracles of Saint Magnus, earl of Orkney,
based upon a text of *Orkneyinga saga* close to GKS 1005 fol. and a
now-lost life of Saint Magnus composed by Master Rodbert of Cricklade.

Manuscripts:
AM 350 4to (ca. 1700), AM 351 4to (ca. 1700), AM 352 4to (ca. 1675–
1700), Kall 263 fol. (1750–1800), NKS 1218 fol. (1750–1800), and NKS
1786 4to (1750–1800).

Editions:
Finnbogi Guðmundsson, ed. *Orkneyinga saga. Legenda de Sancto
Magno. Magnúss saga skemmri. Magnúss saga lengri. Helga þáttr ok
Úlfs.* Íslenzk fornrit 34 (Reykjavík: Hið íslenzka fornritafélag, 1965).
Pp. 333–83.
Gudbrand Vigfusson and George W. Dasent, ed. and trans. *Icelandic
Sagas and Other Historical Documents Relating to the Settlements and
Descents of the Northmen on the British Isles.* 4 vols. Rolls Series 88
(London: Eyre and Spottiswoode, 1887–94; rpt. Millwood: Kraus,
1964). Vol. 1, pp. 237–80.
Edition of AM 350 4to.
Stefán Karlsson, ed. *Sagas of Icelandic Bishops: Fragments of Eight
Manuscripts.* EIM 7 (Copenhagen: Rosenkilde and Bagger, 1967).
Facsimile of AM 350 fol. (extract only).
English translations:
Gudbrand Vigfusson and George W. Dasent, ed. and trans. *Icelandic
Sagas and Other Historical Documents Relating to the Settlements and
Descents of the Northmen on the British Isles.* 4 vols. Rolls Series 88
(London: Eyre and Spottiswoode, 1887–94; rpt. Millwood: Kraus,
1964). Vol. 3, pp. 239–80.
Tomany, Maria-Claudia. "Sacred Non-Violence, Cowardice Profaned:
St Magnus of Orkney in Nordic Hagiography and History." In Thomas

A. DuBois, ed. >> *Sanctity in the North* (2008). Pp. 128–53, esp.
pp. 140–53 (extract only).

Literature:
Ásdís Egilsdóttir. "Hrafn Sveinbjarnarson, Pilgrim and Martyr." In
Sagas, Saints and Settlements. Ed. Gareth Williams and Paul Bibire.
The Northern World 2 (Leiden: Brill, 2004). Pp. 29–39, esp. p. 34.
Bekker-Nielsen, Hans, Thorkil Damsgaard Olsen, and Ole Widding.
>> *Norrøn fortællekunst* (1965). Pp. 46–7.
Bekker-Nielsen, Hans, and Ole Widding. "Legende. Norge og Island."
KLNM 10 (1965). Cols. 421–3, esp. col. 421.
Bibire, Paul. "Magnúss saga helga eyjajarls." In Phillip Pulsiano and
Kirsten Wolf, with Paul Acker and Donald K. Fry, ed. >> *Medieval
Scandinavia* (1993). P. 401.
Cormack, Margaret J. "Saints and Sinners: Reflections on Death in Some
Icelandic Sagas." *Gripla* 8 (1993): 187–218, esp. pp. 191–3.
– >> *The Saints in Iceland* (1994). Pp. 120 and 243.
– "Christian Biography." In *A Companion to Old Norse–Icelandic
Literature and Culture*. Ed. Rory McTurk (Oxford: Blackwell, 2005).
Pp. 27–42, esp. p. 30.
Einar Ól. Sveinsson. *Sagnaritun Oddaverja: nokkrar athuganir*. Studia
Islandica 1 (Reykjavík: Ísafold, 1937). Pp. 19–34.
Finnur Jónsson. >> *Den oldnorske og oldislandske Litteraturs Historie*
(1920–4). Vol. 2, pp. 651–2.
Foote, Peter. "Observations on *Orkneyinga saga*." In *St Magnus Cath-
edral and Orkney's Twelfth-Century Renaissance*. Ed. Barbara E.
Crawford (Aberdeen: Aberdeen University Press, 1988). Pp. 192–207,
esp. pp. 202 and 204. Rpt. in Peter Foote. *Kreddur: Select Studies in
Early Icelandic Law and Literature* (Reykjavík: Hið íslenska bók-
menntafélag, 2004). Pp. 107–27, esp. pp. 118 and 125.
– "Master Robert's Prologue in Magnúss saga lengri." In *Festskrift til Finn
Hødnebø 29. desember 1989*. Ed. Bjørn Eithun, Eyvind Fjeld Halvorsen,
Magnus Rindal, and Erik Simensen (Oslo: Novus, 1989). Pp. 65–81.
Haki Antonsson: "Two Twelfth-Century Martyrs: St Thomas of Canter-
bury and St Magnús of Orkney." In *Sagas, Saints and Settlements*. Ed.
Gareth Williams and Paul Bibire. The Northern World 2 (Leiden: Brill,
2004). Pp. 41–64.
– "The Kings of Norway and the Earls of Orkney: The Case of *Orkney-
inga saga*." *MScand* 15 (2005): 81–100, esp. pp. 82, 84, and 91.
– "St Magnús of Orkney: Aspects of His Cult from a European
Perspective." In *The World of Orkneyinga Saga: "The Broad-Cloth*

Viking Trip" (Kirkwall: The Orcadian Limited, 2005). Pp. 145–59, esp. pp. 149 and 151–3.
– *St. Magnús of Orkney: A Scandinavian Martyr-Cult in Context.* Northern World 29 (Leiden: Brill, 2007). Pp. 5–102.
Hallberg, Peter. "Om Magnúss saga helga." In *Einarsbók. Afmæliskveðja til Einars Ól. Sveinssonar 12. desember 1969.* Ed. Bjarni Guðnason, Halldór Halldórsson, and Jónas Kristjánsson (Reykjavík: Nokkrir vinir, 1969). Pp. 59–70.
– "Imagery in Religious Old Norse Prose Literature: An Outline." *ANF* 102 (1987): 120–70, esp. pp. 122–3, 130, 133, 148–9, and 152–4.
Halvorsen, E.F. "Magnúss saga." *KLNM* 11 (1966). Cols. 238–9.
Helgi Guðmundsson. *Um haf innan. Vestrænir menn og íslenzk menning á miðöldum* (Reykjavík: Háskólaútgáfan, 1997). Pp. 56, 201, 284–5, and 287.
Jakob Benediktsson. "Cursus hos Bergr Sokkason." In *Festskrift til Ludvig Holm-Olsen på hans 70-årsdag den 9. juni 1984* (Øvre Ervik: Alvheim & Eide, 1984). Pp. 34–40, esp. p. 37. Rpt. in Jakob Benediktsson. *Lærdómslistir. Afmælisrit 20. júlí 1987* (Reykjavík: Mál og menning, 1987). Pp. 262–9, esp. pp. 265–6.
Jesch, Judith. "Literature in Medieval Orkney." In *The World of Orkneyinga Saga: "The Broad-Cloth Viking Trip"* (Kirkwall: The Orcadian Limited, 2005). Pp. 11–24, esp. p. 14.
Jesch, Judith, and Theya Molleson. "The Death of Magnus Erlendsson and the Relics of St Magnus." In *The World of Orkneyinga Saga: "The Broad-Cloth Viking Trip"* (Kirkwall: The Orcadian Limited, 2005). Pp. 127–43, esp. pp. 132–3 and 137.
Jónas Kristjánsson. *Um Fóstbræðra sögu* (Reykjavík: Stofnun Árna Magnússonar, 1972). P. 305.
Kratz, Henry. "Saints' Lives. 2. Iceland and Norway." In Phillip Pulsiano and Kirsten Wolf, with Paul Acker and Donald K. Fry, ed. >> *Medieval Scandinavia* (1993). Pp. 562–4.
Lamb, Raymond, and Judith Robertson. "Kirkwall: Saga, History, Archaeology." In *The World of Orkneyinga Saga: "The Broad-Cloth Viking Trip"* (Kirkwall: The Orcadian Limited, 2005). Pp. 161–91, esp. p. 161.
Lehmann, Paul. >> "Skandinaviens Anteil an der lateinischen Literatur und Wissenschaft des Mittelalters" (1937). P. 51.
Louis-Jensen, Jonna. *Kongesagastudier: Kompilationen Hulda-Hrokkinskinna.* Bibliotheca Arnamagnæana 32 (Copenhagen: Reitzel, 1977). Pp. 126–7.

Magnús Már Lárusson. "Sct. Magnus Orcadensis Comes." *Saga* 3
(1960–3): 470–503, esp. pp. 485–93, 495–7, and 502.
– "Magnús." *KLNM* 11 (1966). Cols. 221–2, esp. col. 222.
Mogk, Eugen. >> *Geschichte der norwegisch-isländischen Literatur* (1904).
P. 817.
Mooney, John. *St Magnus – Earl of Orkney* (Kirkwall: Mackintosh, 1935).
Paasche, Fredrik. *Norges og Islands litteratur inntil utgangen av middelalder-*
en. Rev. ed. by Anne Holtsmark (Oslo: Aschehoug, 1947). P. 455.
Phelpstead, Carl. "Masculinity and Sexuality in Sagas of Scandinavian
Royal Saints." In Rudolf Simek and Judith Meurer, ed. >> *Scandinavia*
and Christian Europe in the Middle Ages (2003). Pp. 421–8, esp. pp. 421–4.
– *Holy Vikings: Saints' Lives in the Old Icelandic Kings' Sagas.* Medieval
and Renaissance Texts and Studies 40 (Tempe, Ariz.: Arizona Center
for Medieval and Renaissance Studies, 2007). Pp. 1, 11, 15–16, 36–7,
46–7, 52, 77–95, 100, 114, 207–10, and 215.
Sverrir Tómasson. "Norðlenski Benediktínaskólinn." In >> *The Sixth*
International Saga Conference (1985). Vol. 2, pp. 1009–20, esp.
pp. 1009, 1013, and 1015. Rpt. in Sverrir Tómasson. *Tækileg vitni:*
Greinar um bókmenntir gefnar út í tilefni sjötugsafmælis hans 5. apríl
2011 (Reykjavík: Stofnun Árna Magnússonar and Hið íslenska bók-
menntafélag, 2011). Pp. 345–58, esp. pp. 345 and 348–50.
– *Formálar íslenskra sagnaritara á miðöldum. Rannsókn bókmenntahefðar*
(Reykjavík: Stofnun Árna Magnússonar, 1988). Pp. 116–18, 122, 178,
234–5, 305, 307, 310, 325, and 344.
– "Kristnar trúarbókmenntir í óbundnu máli." In Guðrún Nordal,
Sverrir Tómasson, and Vésteinn Ólason, ed. >> *Íslensk Bókmenntasaga*
1 (1992). Pp. 419–79, esp. pp. 451 and 457–8.
– "Trúarbókmenntir í lausu máli á síðmiðöld." In Böðvar Guðmundsson,
Sverrir Tómasson, Torfi H. Tulinius, and Vésteinn Ólason, ed.
>> *Íslensk Bókmenntasaga* 2 (1993). Pp. 249–82, esp. p. 251.
– "Er nýja textafræðin ný? Þankar um gamla fræðigrein." *Gripla* 13
(2002): 199–216, esp. p. 206. Rpt. in Sverrir Tómasson. *Tækileg vitni:*
Greinar um bókmenntir gefnar út í tilefni sjötugsafmælis hans 5. apríl
2011 (Reykjavík: Stofnun Árna Magnússonar and Hið íslenska bók-
menntafélag, 2011). Pp. 231–50, esp. p. 239.
Vries, Jan de. >> *Altnordische Literaturgeschichte* (1964–7). Vol. 2, p. 263.
Waugh, Robin. "Saint Magnús's Fame in *Orkneyinga Saga*." *JEGP* 102
(2003): 163–87, esp. pp. 163, 175, and 185.
Handlist, p. 319.

MALCHUS   October 21

Malkuss saga

Based on a version of *BHL* 5190.

Manuscript:
AM 764 4to (ca. 1376–86).
Edition:
Unger, C.R., ed. >> *Heilagra manna søgur* (1877). Vol. 1, pp. 437–446.25.
Literature:
Bekker-Nielsen, Hans. "Kyrkofäderna ock kyrkolärarna. K. i vestnordisk
    litteratur." *KLNM* 9 (1964). Cols. 690–3, esp. col. 692.
Bekker-Nielsen, Hans, Thorkil Damsgaard Olsen, and Ole Widding.
    >> *Norrøn fortællekunst* (1965). P. 125.
Boyer, Régis. >> *La vie religieuse en Islande* (1979). P. 160.
Cormack, Margaret. >> *The Saints in Iceland* (1994). P. 35.
Jónas Kristjánsson. *Um Fóstbræðra sögu* (Reykjavík: Stofnun Árna
    Magnússonar, 1972). P. 274.
Lehmann, Paul. >> "Skandinaviens Anteil an der lateinischen Literatur
    und Wissenschaft des Mittelalters" (1937). P. 44.
Svanhildur Óskarsdóttir. "Universal History in Fourteenth-Century
    Iceland: Studies in AM 764 4to." PhD dissertation, University of
    London, 2000. Pp. 14–15, 58, and 240.
– "Arctic Garden of Delights: The Purpose of the Book of Reynistaður."
    In Kirsten Wolf and Johanna Denzin, ed. >> *Romance and Love in
    Late Medieval and Early Modern Iceland* (2008). Pp. 279–301, esp.
    pp. 292–5.
Sverrir Tómasson. "Er nýja textafræðin ný? Þankar um gamla fræði-
    grein." *Gripla* 13 (2002): 199–216, esp. p. 205. Rpt. in Sverrir Tómasson.
    *Tækileg vitni: Greinar um bókmenntir gefnar út í tilefni sjötugsafmælis
    hans 5. apríl 2011* (Reykjavík: Stofnun Árna Magnússonar and Hið
    íslenska bókmenntafélag, 2011). Pp. 231–50, esp. p. 238.
Tveitane, Mattias. *Den lærde stil. Oversetterprosa i den norrøne versjonen
    av Vitæ Patrum.* Årbok for Universitetet i Bergen, Humanistisk Serie
    1967, No. 2 (Bergen and Oslo: Norwegian Universities Press, 1968).
    Pp. 11 and 18.
Wolf, Kirsten, ed. >> *Heilagra meyja sögur* (2003). P. li.
Handlist, p. 319.

MARCELLINUS   April 26

1. Af Marcellíno páfa

Based on a version resembling the legend in Jacobus de Voragine's
Legenda aurea.

Manuscript:
AM 657a–b 4to (ca. 1350).
Editions:
Gering, Hugo, ed. >> *Islendzk æventyri* (1882–4). Vol. 1, pp. 16–19.
Unger, C.R., ed. >> *Heilagra manna søgur* (1877). Vol. 1, pp. 714–16.
German paraphrase:
Gering, Hugo, ed. >> *Islendzk æventyri* (1882–4). Vol. 2, pp. 8–9.
Literature:
Cormack, Margaret. >> *The Saints in Iceland* (1994). Pp. 34n27 and 35.
Finnur Jónsson. >> *Den oldnorske og oldislandske Litteraturs Historie*
    (1920–4). Vol. 2, p. 874.
Hallberg, Peter. *Stilsignalement och författarskap i norrön sagalitteratur:*
    Synpunkter och exempel. Nordistica Gothoburgensia 3 (Stockholm:
    Almqvist & Wiksell, 1968). Pp. 136–7 and 179.
Kirby, Ian. >> *Biblical Quotation* (1980). Vol. 2, p. 45.
Wolf, Kirsten, ed. >> *Heilagra meyja sögur* (2003). P. li.
Handlist, p. 319.

2. Af Marcellíno páfa

A separate recension based on a version of *BHL* 5223 incorporated into
the legend of John the Evangelist 4.

Manuscripts:
See John the Evangelist 4 note (p. 174).
Edition:
Unger, C.R., ed. >> *Postola sögur* (1874). Pp. 467.36–469.16.
Literature:
Cormack, Margaret. >> *The Saints in Iceland* (1994). Pp. 34n27 and 243.
Hallberg, Peter. *Stilsignalement och författarskap i norrön sagalitteratur:*
    Synpunkter och exempel. Nordistica Gothoburgensia 3 (Stockholm:
    Almqvist & Wiksell, 1968). Pp. 136–7.

Kirby, Ian. >> *Biblical Quotation* (1980). Vol. 2, pp. 29 and 45.
Handlist, p. 319.

MARGARET OF ANTIOCH   July 20

1. Margrétar saga

A translation of the *passio* in *BHL* 1503, which has been occasionally
supplemented from 3 below.

Manuscripts:
AM 233a fol. (ca. 1350–75, defective), AM 235 fol. (ca. 1400), AM 277
  8vo (ca. 1800–50), AM 428b 12mo (ca. 1400, defective), AM 433c
  12mo (ca. 1525–50), BLAdd 4889 (ca. 1700–1800), ÍB 34 8vo
  (ca. 1800–1900), ÍB 255 8vo (ca. 1700–1900), ÍBR 3 8vo (ca. 1750),
  ÍBR 32 8vo (ca. 1700–1900), ÍBR 64 8vo (ca. 1700–1900), JS 640 4to
  (ca. 1600–1900), JS 392 8vo (1747–52), JS 396 8vo (ca. 1700–1900), JS
  484 8vo (ca. 1700–1900), Lbs 650 fol. (1958), Lbs 726 4to (ca. 1800–
  20), Lbs 1276 4to (1862–70), Lbs 39 8vo (ca. 1780), Lbs 404 8vo
  (ca. 1700–1900), Lbs 405 8vo (ca. 1850), Lbs 1077 8vo (1783), Lbs 1197
  8vo (1773), Lbs 1228 8vo (ca. 1780–1800), Lbs 1812b 8vo (ca. 1700–
  1900), Lbs 2098 8vo (ca. 1895), Lbs 2285 4to (1892–5), Lbs 2532 8vo
  (1854), Lbs 2856 8vo (ca. 1860), Lbs 3386 8vo (1806–ca. 1850),
  Lbs 3929 8vo (1872), and NKS 1265 fol. II 1 (ca. 1500–50).[1]

Editions:
Haugen, Odd Einar, ed. "Margrétar saga." In *Norrøne tekster i utval*. Ed.
  Odd Einar Haugen (Oslo: Ad Notam Gyldendal, 1994). Pp. 266–77.
Normalized text based on Unger's edition.
Rasmussen, Peter. "Tekstforholdene i *Margrétar saga*." 3 vols. Specialeaf-
  handling til magisterkonferens i nordisk filologi, University of Copen-
  hagen (1977). Vol. 3, pp. 1–10.
Transcription of AM 235 fol. and a section of AM 233a fol.
Unger, C.R., ed. >> *Heilagra manna søgur* (1877). Vol. 1, pp. 474–81.

---

1 Additional manuscripts could exist. Peter Rasmussen, "Tekstforholdene i *Margrétar*
  saga," 3 vols., Specialeafhandling til magisterkonferens i nordisk filologi, University of
  Copenhagen (1977), refers in vol. 1, pp. 26 and 66, to a so-called Höfn-manuscript and a
  so-called Köldukinn-manuscript, both in private possession.

Based on AM 235 fol. with variants from AM 233a fol. (pp. 474–6).
The latter part of AM 233a fol. (chapter 5), which differs considerably
from AM 235 fol., is printed in the footnote text (p. 477).

Modern Icelandic language edition:
Wolf, Kirsten, ed. >> *Heilagra meyja sögur* (2003). Pp. 42–9.

Norwegian translation:
Mundal, Else. "Soga om Margreta." In *Norrøne tekster i utval.* Ed. Odd
Einar Haugen (Oslo: Ad Notam Gyldendal, 1994). Pp. 266–77.

Literature:
* Ásdís Egilsdóttir. "Um Margrétar sögu meyjar." *Merki krossins* 2
(1990): 1–16.
– "Kvendýrlingar og kvenímynd trúarlegra bókmennta á Íslandi." In
Inga Huld Hákonardóttir, ed. >> *Konur og kristsmenn* (1996). Pp. 93–
116, esp. pp. 93 and 97.
– "Drekar, slöngur og heilög Margrét." In *Heiðin minni. Greinar um fornar
bókmenntir.* Ed. Haraldur Bessason and Baldur Hafstað (Reykjavík:
Heimskringla, 1999). Pp. 241–56, esp. pp. 241–3 and 252.
Bekker-Nielsen, Hans. "Margareta (af Antiochia). Norge og Island."
KLNM 11 (1966). Cols. 347–8, esp. col. 347–8.
Bekker-Nielsen, Hans, Thorkil Damsgaard Olsen, and Ole Widding.
>> *Norrøn fortællekunst* (1965). P. 124.
Bruvoll, Kersti. "An Old Norse Version of the Legend of St. Margaret of
Antioch." In Rudolf Simek and Judith Meurer, ed. >> *Scandinavia and
Christian Europe in the Middle Ages* (2003). Pp. 45–55.
– "The Good, the Bad and the Devil! On Rewriting a Religious Motif in
Some Virgin Martyr Legends." In Agneta Ney, Henrik Williams, and
Fredrik Charpentier Ljungqvist, ed. >> *Á austrvega: Sagas and East
Scandinavia* (2009). Vol. 1, pp. 136–43, esp. pp. 136–8 and 142–3.
Carlé, Birte. "Fra slægtssaga til kvindesaga." In Silja Aðalsteinsdóttir and
Helgi Þorláksson, ed. >> *Forändringar i kvinnors villkor under medel-
tiden* (1983). Pp. 55–70, esp. pp. 56, 60, and 63.
– >> *Jomfru-fortællingen* (1985). Pp. 35, 38, 48, and 149–50.
– "Some Observations Regarding Narrative Patterns in the Medieval
Sagas of Holy Maids." In Régis Boyer, ed. >> *Les Sagas de Chevaliers
(Riddarasögur)* (1985). Pp. 393–404, esp. pp. 395 and 396–8.
– "Men and Women in the Saints' Sagas of *Stock. 2, fol.*" In John
Lindow, Lars Lönnroth, and Gerd Wolfgang Weber, ed. >> *Struc-
ture and Meaning in Old Norse Literature* (1986). Pp. 317–46, esp.
p. 318.
Cormack, Margaret. >> *The Saints in Iceland* (1994). P. 122.

Foote, Peter. "Auðræði." In Arthur Brown and Peter Foote, ed. >> *Early English and Norse Studies* (1963). Pp. 62–76, esp. p. 67.

Helga Kress. *Máttugar meyjar: Íslensk fornbókmenntasaga* (Reykjavík: Háskólaútgáfan, 1993). Pp. 139 and 198.

Jón Hnefill Aðalsteinsson. "Blot i forna skrifter." *SI* 47 (1996): 11–32, esp. pp. 28–9.

Jón Steffensen. "*Margrétar saga* and Its History in Iceland." *Saga-Book* 16 (1965): 273–82.

– "Margrétar saga og ferill hennar á Íslandi." *Menning og meinsemdir. Ritgerðasafn um mótunarsögu íslenzkrar þjóðar og baráttu hennar við hungur og sóttir* (Reykjavík: Ísafold, 1975): 208–15.

Jón Viðar Sigurðsson. "Utenlandske kvinnehelgener på Island i høymiddelalderen." In >> *Samtíðarsögur* (1994). Vol. 2, pp. 423–34, esp. p. 432.

Jónas Kristjánsson. >> *Eddas and Sagas* (1988). P. 142.

Lehmann, Paul. >> "Skandinaviens Anteil an der lateinischen Literatur und Wissenschaft des Mittelalters" (1937). P. 44.

Mogk, Eugen. >> *Geschichte der norwegisch-isländischen Literatur* (1904). P. 891.

Stefán Karlsson. "Kvennahandrit í karlahöndum." In *Stafkrókar: Ritgerðir eftir Stefán Karlsson gefnar út í tilefni af sjötugsafmæli hans 2. desember 1998.* Ed. Guðvarður Már Gunnlaugsson (Reykjavík: Stofnun Árna Magnússonar, 2000). Pp. 378–82.

Sverrir Tómasson. *Formálar íslenskra sagnaritara á miðöldum. Rannsókn bókmenntahefðar* (Reykjavík: Stofnun Árna Magnússonar, 1988). Pp. 11, 189, and 305.

– "Kristnar trúarbókmenntir í óbundnu máli." In Guðrún Nordal, Sverrir Tómasson and Vésteinn Ólason, ed. >> *Íslensk Bókmenntasaga* 1 (1992). Pp. 419–79, esp. p. 436.

Þórhallur Þorgilsson. "Um þýðingar og endursagnir úr ítölskum miðaldaritum." *Landsbókasafn Íslands. Árbók* 1946–7 (1948): 212–24, esp. p. 222.

Van Deusen, Natalie M. "Stitches in the Margins: The Embroidery Pattern in AM 235 fol." *Mm* (2011): 26–42, esp. p. 27.

Wolf, Kirsten. "The Severed Breast: A Topos in the Legends of Female Virgin Martyr Saints." *ANF* 112 (1997): 97–112, esp. p. 98.

– "Female Scribes at Work? A Consideration of Kirkjubæjarbók (Codex AM 429 12mo)." In A.N. Doane and Kirsten Wolf, ed. >> *Beatus Vir* (2006). Pp. 265–95, esp. pp. 270 and 276.

Wolf, Kirsten, ed. >> *A Female Legendary from Iceland* (2011). P. 32.

Handlist, p. 320.

2. Margrétar saga

A separate and more faithful translation of *BHL* 5303 that omits the introductory section and shows some abridgment.

Manuscripts:
AM 428a 12mo (ca. 1300–1400), AM 429 12mo (ca. 1500), and AM 433c 12mo, fols. 17v8–24r14 (ca. 1525–50).

Editions:
Rasmussen, Peter. "Tekstforholdene i *Margrétar saga.*" 3 vols. Specialeafhandling til magisterkonferens i nordisk filologi, University of Copenhagen (1977). Vol. 3, pp. 19–27.
  Transcription of AM 429 12mo and a section of AM 428a 12mo.
Wolf, Kirsten, ed. >> *A Female Legendary from Iceland* (2011). Pp. 67–78.
  Facsimile and text edition of AM 429 12mo.
– ed. "*Margrétar saga II.*" *Gripla* 21 (2010): 61–104, esp. pp. 68–78 and 80–3.
  Edition of AM 428a 12mo and AM 433c 12mo.

Literature:
Bekker-Nielsen, Hans. "En god bøn." *Opuscula* 2. Bibliotheca Arnamagnæana 25.1 (Copenhagen: Reitzel, 1961), pp. 52–8, esp. pp. 52–4.
– "Margareta (af Antiochia). Norge og Island." *KLNM* 11 (1966). Cols. 347–8, esp. col. 348.
Bruvoll, Kjersti. "The Good, the Bad and the Devil! On Rewriting a Religious Motif in Some Virgin Martyr Legends." In Agneta Ney, Henrik Williams, and Fredrik Charpentier Ljungqvist, ed. >> *Á austrvega: Sagas and East Scandinavia* (2009). Vol. 1, pp. 136–43, esp. pp. 142–3.
Carlé, Birte. >> *Jomfru-fortællingen* (1985). Pp. 43, 48, and 149.
– "Men and Women in the Saints' Sagas of *Stock. 2, fol.*" In John Lindow, Lars Lönnroth, and Gerd Wolfgang Weber, ed. >> *Structure and Meaning in Old Norse Literature* (1986). Pp. 317–46, esp. p. 319.
Helga Kress. *Máttugar meyjar: Íslensk fornbókmenntasaga* (Reykjavík: Háskólaútgáfan, 1993). Pp. 139 and 198.
Jón Steffensen. "*Margrétar saga* and Its History in Iceland." *Saga-Book* 16 (1965): 273–82.
– "Margrétar saga og ferill hennar á Íslandi." *Menning og meinsemdir. Ritgerðasafn um mótunarsögu íslenzkrar þjóðar og baráttu hennar við hungur og sóttir* (Reykjavík: Ísafold, 1975): 208–15.
Stefán Karlsson. "Kvennahandrit í karlahöndum." In *Stafkrókar: Ritgerðir eftir Stefán Karlsson gefnar út í tilefni af sjötugsafmæli hans

2. desember 1998. Ed. Guðvarður Már Gunnlaugsson (Reykjavík: Stofnun Árna Magnússonar, 2000). Pp. 378–82.

Van Deusen, Natalie M. "Stitches in the Margins: The Embroidery Pattern in AM 235 fol." *Mm* (2011): 26–42, esp. pp. 36–7.

Handlist, p. 320.

3. Margrétar saga

The source is *BHL* 5303 with interpolations from *BHL* 5308.

Manuscripts:
AM 667 4to I (ca. 1300–1400), AM 667 4to VIII (ca. 1600–1700), AM 430 12mo (ca. 1400–1500, defective), AM 431 12mo (ca. 1550), AM 432 12mo (ca. 1400–1500, defective), AM 433a 12mo (ca. 1500, defective), AM 433b 12mo (ca. 1500), AM 433d 12mo (ca. 1500–25), JS 43 4to (ca. 1660–80), Lbs 2294 4to (1879–87) Lbs 2435 4to (1930), Lbs 412 8vo (ca. 1759–1825), and Lbs 738 8vo (1774).

Edition:
Rasmussen, Peter. "Tekstforholdene i *Margrétar saga.*" 3 vols. Specialeafhandling til magisterkonferens i nordisk filologi, University of Copenhagen (1977). Vol. 3, pp. 29–48.

Transcription of AM 433a 12mo and a section of AM 433b 12mo.

Literature:
Ásdís Egilsdóttir. "Drekar, slöngur og heilög Margrét." In *Heiðin minni. Greinar um fornar bókmenntir.* Ed. Haraldur Bessason and Baldur Hafstað (Reykjavík: Heimskringla, 1999). Pp. 241–56, esp. p. 241.

Bekker-Nielsen, Hans. "En god bøn." *Opuscula* 2. Bibliotheca Arnamagnæana 25.1 (Copenhagen: Reitzel, 1961), pp. 52–8, esp. pp. 53–4.

– "Margareta (af Antiochia). Norge og Island." *KLNM* 11 (1966). Cols. 347–8, esp. col. 348.

Carlé, Birte. >> *Jomfrufortællingen* (1985). Pp. 48 and 149.

Helga Kress. *Máttugar meyjar: Íslensk fornbókmenntasaga* (Reykjavík: Háskólaútgáfan, 1993). Pp. 139 and 198.

Jón Steffensen. "*Margrétar saga* and Its History in Iceland." *Saga-Book* 16 (1965): 273–82.

– "Margrétar saga og ferill hennar á Íslandi." *Menning og meinsemdir. Ritgerðasafn um mótunarsögu íslenzkrar þjóðar og baráttu hennar við hungur og sóttir* (Reykjavík: Ísafold, 1975): 208–15.

Wolf, Kirsten, ed. >> *A Female Legendary from Iceland* (2011). P. 32.

Handlist, p. 320.

MARINA   July 17

Af Marínu munk

Based on a text, which resembles the account in Honorius Augustodunensis' *Speculum Ecclesiae*.

Manuscript:
AM 657a–b 4to (ca. 1350).
Edition:
Gering, Hugo, ed. >> *Islendzk æventyri* (1882–4). Vol. 1, pp. 149–51.
Modern Icelandic language edition:
Wolf, Kirsten, ed. >> *Heilagra meyja sögur* (2003). Pp. 40–1.
German paraphrase:
Gering, Hugo, ed. >> *Islendzk æventyri* (1882–4). Vol. 2, pp. 125–7.
Literature:
Cormack, Margaret. >> *The Saints in Iceland* (1994). Pp. 34n27 and 35.
Tveitane, Mattias. *Den lærde stil. Oversetterprosa i den norrøne versjonen
    av Vitæ Patrum.* Årbok for Universitetet i Bergen, Humanistisk Serie
    1967, No. 2 (Bergen and Oslo: Norwegian Universities Press, 1968).
    P. 19.
Vrátný, Karel. "Zu 'Islendzk Æventyri'." *Arkiv för nordisk filologi* 38
    (1922): 176–89, esp. pp. 177–83.
Wolf, Kirsten. "Klæðskiptingar í Íslendingasögunum." *Skírnir* 171 (1997):
    381–400, esp. p. 383.
– "The Severed Breast: A Topos in the Legends of Female Virgin Martyr
    Saints." *ANF* 112 (1997): 97–112, esp. p. 108.

MARK   April 25

Translated from a Low German *Passionael*.

Manuscript:
AM 667 4to V (ca. 1525).
Literature:
Overgaard, Mariane, ed. *The History of the Cross-Tree Down to Christ's
    Passion: Icelandic Legend Versions.* Editiones Arnamagnæanæ, Ser. B,
    vol. 26 (Copenhagen: Munksgaard, 1968). Pp. xcix–cxix.
Handlist, p. 320.

MARTHA AND MARY MAGDALEN   July 29, 22

1. Mǫrtu saga ok Maríu Magðalenu

Based in the main on Vincent of Beauvais' *Speculum historiale* with additional material from Peter Comestor, Gregory the Great, Innocent III, Augustine, Honorius Augustodunensis, and Bede. The miracles at the end correspond to *BHL* 5481, 5489–90, 5462–3, 5465, 5474–6, 5482, 5484, and 5483.

Manuscripts:
AM 233a fol. (ca. 1350–75, defective), AM 235 fol. (ca. 1400), NRA 79 (ca. 1350, defective), and Stock. Perg. fol. no. 2 (ca. 1425–45, defective).

Editions:
Foote, Peter, ed. >> *Lives of Saints* (1962).
  Facsimile of Stock. Perg. fol. no. 2.
Unger, C.R., ed. >> *Heilagra manna søgur* (1877). Vol. 1, pp. 513–53.
  Based on AM 233a fol. (pp. 513–550.23) and Stock. Perg. fol. no. 2 (pp. 550.24–553) with variants from Stock. Perg. fol. no. 2 (pp. 513–522.27, 527.7–535.27, and 539.31–550.23) and AM 235 fol. (pp. 513–53). The text of AM 233a fol. is printed in the footnote text (pp. 550–1).

Modern Icelandic language edition:
Wolf, Kirsten, ed. >> *Heilagra meyja sögur* (2003). Pp. 50–92.

Literature:
Ásdís Egilsdóttir. "Kvendýrlingar og kvenímynd trúarlegra bókmennta á Íslandi." In Inga Huld Hákonardóttir, ed. >> *Konur og kristsmenn* (1996). Pp. 93–116, esp. pp. 104–5.
– "Drekar, slöngur og heilög Margrét." In *Heiðin minni. Greinar um fornar bókmenntir*. Ed. Haraldur Bessason and Baldur Hafstað (Reykjavík: Heimskringla, 1999). Pp. 241–56, esp. pp. 247–9.
Bekker-Nielsen, Hans. "Maria Magdalena. Norge og Island." *KLNM* 11 (1966). Cols. 410–11, esp. col. 410.
– "Marta fra Betania. Norge og Island." *KLNM* 11 (1966). Col. 472.
– "The French Influence on Ecclesiastical Literature in Old Norse." *Les relations littéraires franco-scandinaves au Moyen Age. Colloque de Liège (avril 1972)*. Bibliothèque de la Faculté de Philosophie et Lettres de l'Université de Liège 208 (1975): 137–47, esp. p. 142.
Boyer, Régis. >> *La vie religieuse en Islande* (1979). Pp. 160, 164, 181, and 183.

Carlé, Birte. "Fra slægtssaga til kvindesaga." In Silja Aðalsteinsdóttir and Helgi Þorláksson, ed. >> *Forändringar i kvinnors villkor under medeltiden* (1983). Pp. 55–70, esp. pp. 56 and 66.

– >> *Jomfru-fortællingen* (1985). Pp. 35–6, 38, 40–1, and 75–8.

– "Some Observations Regarding Narrative Patterns in the Medieval Sagas of Holy Maids." In Régis Boyer, ed. >> *Les Sagas de Chevaliers (Riddarasögur)* (1985). Pp. 393–404, esp. p. 395.

– "Men and Women in the Saints' Sagas of *Stock. 2, fol.*" In John Lindow, Lars Lönnroth, and Gerd Wolfgang Weber, ed. >> *Structure and Meaning in Old Norse Literature* (1986). Pp. 317–46, esp. pp. 318, 320, 322, and 338–40.

Cormack, Margaret. >> *The Saints in Iceland* (1994). P. 130.

Finnur Jónsson. >> *Den oldnorske og oldislandske Litteraturs Historie* (1920–4). Vol. 2, p. 874.

Foote, Peter, ed. *Jóns saga Hólabyskups ens helga*. Editiones Arnamagnæanæ, Ser. A, vol. 14 (Copenhagen: Reitzel, 2003). Pp. 76 and 78.

Hallberg, Peter. "Imagery in Religious Old Norse Prose Literature: An Outline." *ANF* 102 (1987): 120–70, esp. pp. 131, 140, 145–6, and 148–9.

Hofmann, Dietrich. *Die Legende von Sankt Clemens in den skandinavischen Ländern im Mittelalter*. Beiträge zur Skandinavistik 13 (Frankfurt am Main: Peter Lang, 1997). P. 128.

Jón Viðar Sigurðsson. *Den vennlige vikingen: Vennskapets makt i Norge og på Island ca. 900–1300* (Oslo: Pax Forlag, 2010). P. 119.

Kirby, Ian. >> *Biblical Quotation* (1980). Vol. 2, pp. 13, 19, and 43–4.

– *Bible Translation in Old Norse*. Université de Lausanne Publications de la faculté des lettres 27 (Geneva: Librairie Droz, 1986). Pp. 6, 47, 86, and 95.

Lehmann, Paul. >> "Skandinaviens Anteil an der lateinischen Literatur und Wissenschaft des Mittelalters" (1937). P. 45.

Mogk, Eugen. >> *Geschichte der norwegisch-isländischen Literatur* (1904). P. 890.

Svanhildur Óskarsdóttir. "Universal History in Fourteenth-Century Iceland: Studies in AM 764 4to." PhD dissertation, University of London, 2000. P. 71.

Þórhallur Þorgilsson. "Um þýðingar og endursagnir úr ítölskum miðaldaritum." *Landsbókasafn Íslands. Árbók* 1946–7 (1948): 212–24, esp. p. 219.

Van Deusen, Natalie M. "'Inn besti hlutr'? Martha of Bethany and Women's Roles in Medieval Iceland." *ANF* 126 (2011): 73–91.

– "Stitches in the Margins: The Embroidery Pattern in AM 235 fol." *Mm* (2011): 26–42, esp. pp. 27–8.

Wolf, Kirsten. "Mary Magdalen's Precious Ointment." *Opuscula* 11. Bibliotheca Arnamagnæana 42 (Copenhagen: Reitzel, 2003). Pp. 182–6.

Wolf, Kirsten, ed. "Anonymous, *Heilagra meyja drápa* 'Drápa about Holy
   Maidens'." In Margaret Clunies Ross, ed. >> *Poetry on Christian
   Subjects* (2007). Vol. 2, pp. 891–930, esp. p. 899.
Handlist, pp. 320–1.

2. Mǫrtu saga

An extract of 1, chapters 15 and 26.

Manuscript:
AM 764 4to (ca. 1376–86).
Edition:
Svanhildur Óskarsdóttir. "Universal History in Fourteenth-Century Iceland:
   Studies in AM 764 4to." PhD dissertation, University of London, 2000.
   Pp. 281–2.
Literature:
Bekker-Nielsen, Hans. "Marta fra Betania. Norge og Island." *KLNM* 11
   (1966). Col. 472.
Svanhildur Óskarsdóttir. "The Book of Judith: A Medieval Icelandic
   Translation." *Gripla* 11 (2000): 79–123, esp. p. 84.
– "Arctic Garden of Delights: The Purpose of the Book of Reynistaður."
   In Kirsten Wolf and Johanna Denzin, ed. >> *Romance and Love in
   Late Medieval and Early Modern Iceland* (2008). Pp. 279–301, esp.
   p. 288.
Handlist, p. 321.

MARTIN OF TOURS   November 11

1. Marteins saga biskups I

Based on *BHL* 5610 with additional material from *BHL* 5611, 5615,
and 5616.

Manuscript:
AM 645 4to (ca. 1225–50, defective).
Editions:
Holtsmark, Anne, ed. *A Book of Miracles: MS No. 645 4ᵗᵒ of the Arna-
   Magnæan Collection in the University Library of Copenhagen.* CCI 12
   (Copenhagen: Einar Munksgaard, 1938).
   Facsimile.

Hreinn Benediktsson. *Early Icelandic Script As Illustrated in Vernacular Texts from the Twelfth and Thirteenth Centuries*. Íslenzk handrit: Icelandic Manuscripts, Series in Folio 2 (Reykjavík: The Manuscript Institute of Iceland, 1965). Plate 28.
Facsimile of fol. 55v.
Unger, C.R., ed. >> *Heilagra manna søgur* (1877). Vol. 1, pp. 554–74.
English translation:
Roughton, Philip G. "AM 645 4to and AM 652/630 4to: Study and Translation of Two Thirteenth-Century Icelandic Collections of Apostles' and Saints' Lives." PhD dissertation, University of Colorado, 2002. Pp. 831–71.
Literature:
Battista, Simonetta. "Interpretations of the Roman Pantheon in the Old Norse Hagiographic Sagas." In Geraldine Barnes and Margaret Clunies Ross, ed. >> *Old Norse Myths, Literature and Society* (2000). Pp. 24–34, esp. p. 30.
– "*Blámenn, djøflar* and Other Representations of Evil in Old Norse Literature." In John McKinnell, David Ashurst, and Donata Kick, ed. >> *The Fantastic in Old Norse/Icelandic Literature* (2006). Vol. 1, pp. 113–22, esp. pp. 113 and 118.
Bekker-Nielsen, Hans. "Et par ord om de ældste norrøne helgensager." In Finn Hødnebø et al., ed. >> *Eyvindarbók* (1992). Pp. 29–33, esp. p. 32.
Bekker-Nielsen, Hans, Thorkil Damsgaard Olsen, and Ole Widding. >> *Norrøn fortællekunst* (1965). Pp. 23 and 125.
Bekker-Nielsen, Hans, and Ole Widding. "Legende. Norge og Island." *KLNM* 10 (1965). Cols. 421–3, esp. cols. 421–2.
– "Religiøs prosalitteratur. Norge og Island." *KLNM* 14 (1969). Cols. 42–4, esp. col. 43.
Boyer, Régis. "An Attempt to Define the Typology of Medieval Hagiography." In *Hagiography and Medieval Literature: A Symposium*. Ed. Hans Bekker-Nielsen, Peter Foote, Jørgen Højgaard-Jørgensen, and Tore Nyberg (Odense: Odense University Press, 1981). Pp. 27–36, esp. pp. 28–30 and 33–4.
Cormack, Margaret. >> *The Saints in Iceland* (1994). P. 124.
Finnur Jónsson. >> *Den oldnorske og oldislandske Litteraturs Historie* (1920–4). Vol. 2, p. 874.
Foote, Peter, ed. >> *Lives of Saints* (1962). P. 20.
Gad, Tue. "Martinus." *KLNM* 11 (1966). Cols. 472–4, esp. col. 473.
Kirby, Ian. >> *Biblical Quotation* (1980). Vol. 2, p. 44.

Konráð Gíslason. *Um frum-parta íslenzkrar túngu í fornöld* (Copenhagen: Trier, 1846). P. lxvi.

Kratz, Henry. "The Language of the Old Norse Saints' Lives." *Mm* (1988): 159–73.

Lehmann, Paul. >> "Skandinaviens Anteil an der lateinischen Literatur und Wissenschaft des Mittelalters" (1937). P. 45.

Lindow, John. "Norse Mythology and the Lives of the Saints." *SS* 73 (2001): 437–56, esp. pp. 444–6.

Mogk, Eugen. >> *Geschichte der norwegisch-isländischen Literatur* (1904). P. 893.

Roughton, Philip. "Stylistics and Sources of the *Postola sögur* in AM 645 4to and AM 652/630 4to." *Gripla* 16 (2005): 7–50.

– "'Þá syndi hann þeim mikinn skugga': Unmasking the Fantastic in the *Postola sögur*." In John McKinnell, David Ashurst, and Donata Kick, ed. >> *The Fantastic in Old Norse/Icelandic Literature* (2006). Vol. 2, pp. 846–55, esp. p. 852.

Sverrir Tómasson. "Kristnar trúarbókmenntir í óbundnu máli." In Guðrún Nordal, Sverrir Tómasson, and Vésteinn Ólason, ed. >> *Íslensk Bókmenntasaga* 1 (1992). Pp. 419–79, esp. pp. 424 and 470.

Sverrir Tómasson, Bragi Halldórsson, and Einar Sigurbjörnsson, ed. >> *Heilagra karla sögur* (2007). Pp. xxiii and 316.

Turville-Petre, G. >> *Origins of Icelandic Literature* (1967). Pp. 133 and 179.

Wellendorf, Jonas. "The Attraction of the Earliest Old Norse Vernacular Hagiography." In Haki Antonsson and Ildar H. Garipzanov, ed. >> *Saints and Their Lives on the Periphery* (2010). Pp. 241–58, esp. p. 253.

Widding, Ole, and Hans Bekker-Nielsen. "En senmiddelalderlig legendesamling." *Mm* (1960): 105–28, esp. p. 126.

– "Low German Influence on Late Icelandic Hagiography." *GR* 37 (1962): 239–62, esp. p. 241.

Handlist, p. 321.

2. Marteins saga biskups II

Based on the same material as 1, but supplemented from *BHL* 5612, 5613, 5619, 5621, 5622, and 5623.

Manuscript:
AM 235 fol. (ca. 1400).

Edition:
Unger, C.R., ed. >> *Heilagra manna søgur* (1877). Vol. 1, pp. 575–607.20.
Modern Icelandic language edition:
Sverrir Tómasson, Bragi Halldórsson, and Einar Sigurbjörnsson, ed.
   >> *Heilagra karla sögur* (2007). Pp. 267–315.
Literature:
Bekker-Nielsen, Hans, Thorkil Damsgaard Olsen, and Ole Widding.
   >> *Norrøn fortællekunst* (1965). P.125.
Bekker-Nielsen, Hans, and Ole Widding. "Legende. Norge og Island."
   KLNM 10 (1965). Cols. 421–3, esp. col. 421.
Boyer, Régis. "An Attempt to Define the Typology of Medieval Hagiog-
   raphy." In *Hagiography and Medieval Literature: A Symposium*. Ed.
   Hans Bekker-Nielsen, Peter Foote, Jørgen Højgaard-Jørgensen, and
   Tore Nyberg (Odense: Odense University Press, 1981). Pp. 27–36, esp.
   pp. 28–30 and 33–4.
Carlé, Birte. >> *Jomfru-fortællingen* (1985). P. 38.
– "Men and Women in the Saints' Sagas of *Stock. 2, fol.*" In John Lindow,
   Lars Lönnroth, and Gerd Wolfgang Weber, ed. >> *Structure and
   Meaning in Old Norse Literature* (1986). Pp. 317–46, esp. p. 319.
Cormack, Margaret. >> *The Saints in Iceland* (1994). Pp. 65n98
   and 124.
Finnur Jónsson. >> *Den oldnorske og oldislandske Litteraturs Historie*
   (1920–4). Vol. 2, p. 874.
Foote, Peter, ed. >> *Lives of Saints* (1962). P. 20.
Gad, Tue. "Martinus." *KLNM* 11 (1966). Cols. 472–4, esp. col. 473.
Kirby, Ian. >> *Biblical Quotation* (1980). Vol. 2, p. 44.
Lehmann, Paul. >> "Skandinaviens Anteil an der lateinischen Literatur
   und Wissenschaft des Mittelalters" (1937). P. 45.
Mogk, Eugen. >> *Geschichte der norwegisch-isländischen Literatur* (1904).
   P. 893.
Sverrir Tómasson. "Kristnar trúarbókmenntir í óbundnu máli." In
   Guðrún Nordal, Sverrir Tómasson, and Vésteinn Ólason, ed. >>
   Íslensk Bókmenntasaga 1 (1992). Pp. 419–79, esp. pp. 424, 431, and 470.
Turville-Petre, G. >> *Origins of Icelandic Literature* (1967). Pp. 133
   and 179.
Handlist, p. 321.

3. Marteins saga biskups III

Based on the same sources as 2, but with additional material.

Manuscript:
Stock. Perg. fol. no. 2 (ca. 1425–45).
Editions:
Foote, Peter, ed. >> *Lives of Saints* (1962).
   Facsimile.
Unger, C.R., ed. >> *Heilagra manna søgur* (1877). Vol. 1, pp. 607:24–
   642.
Literature:
Battista, Simonetta. "Interpretations of the Roman Pantheon in the Old
   Norse Hagiographic Sagas." In Geraldine Barnes and Margaret
   Clunies Ross, ed. >> *Old Norse Myths, Literature and Society* (2000).
   Pp. 24–34, esp. p. 30.
Bekker-Nielsen, Hans, Thorkil Damsgaard Olsen, and Ole Widding.
   >> *Norrøn fortællekunst* (1965). P.125.
Boyer, Régis. "An Attempt to Define the Typology of Medieval Hagiog-
   raphy." In *Hagiography and Medieval Literature: A Symposium*. Ed.
   Hans Bekker-Nielsen, Peter Foote, Jørgen Højgaard-Jørgensen, and
   Tore Nyberg (Odense: Odense University Press, 1981). Pp. 27–36, esp.
   pp. 28–30 and 33–4.
Carlé, Birte. >> *Jomfru-fortællingen* (1985). Pp. 39–40 and 55.
– "Men and Women in the Saints' Sagas of *Stock. 2, fol.*" In John
   Lindow, Lars Lönnroth, and Gerd Wolfgang Weber, ed. >> *Structure
   and Meaning in Old Norse Literature* (1986). Pp. 317–46, esp. pp. 320,
   323, 325, 327, 334, 336, and 338.
Cormack, Margaret. >> *The Saints in Iceland* (1994). P. 124.
Finnur Jónsson. >> *Den oldnorske og oldislandske Litteraturs Historie*
   (1920–4). Vol. 2, p. 874.
Gad, Tue. "Martinus." *KLNM* 11 (1966). Cols. 472–4, esp. col. 473.
Hallberg, Peter. "Imagery in Religious Old Norse Prose Literature: An
   Outline." *ANF* 102 (1987): 120–70, esp. p. 140.
Kirby, Ian. >> *Biblical Quotation* (1980). Vol. 2, p. 44.
Lehmann, Paul. >> "Skandinaviens Anteil an der lateinischen Literatur
   und Wissenschaft des Mittelalters" (1937). P. 45.
Lindow, John. "Norse Mythology and the Lives of the Saints." *SS* 73
   (2001): 437–56, esp. pp. 445–6.
Mogk, Eugen. >> *Geschichte der norwegisch-isländischen Literatur* (1904).
   P. 893.
Svanhildur Óskarsdóttir. "Universal History in Fourteenth-Century
   Iceland: Studies in AM 764 4to." PhD dissertation, University of
   London, 2000. P. 203.

Sverrir Tómasson. "Kristnar trúarbókmenntir í óbundnu máli." In
   Guðrún Nordal, Sverrir Tómasson, and Vésteinn Ólason, ed.
   >> *Íslensk Bókmenntasaga* 1 (1992). Pp. 419–79, esp. pp. 424 and 470.
Sverrir Tómasson, Bragi Halldórsson, and Einar Sigurbjörnsson, ed.
   >> *Heilagra karla sögur* (2007). P. 316.
Turville-Petre, G. >> *Origins of Icelandic Literature* (1967). Pp. 133
   and 179.
Handlist, p. 321.

4. Marteins saga biskups

Fols. 1–2 are based on *BHL* 5615 and the text stands nearest that of 1.
Fol. 3 is based on *BHL* 5653.

Manuscript:
AM 655 4to XXXI (ca. 1300–25).
Literature:
Bekker-Nielsen, Hans, Thorkil Damsgaard Olsen, and Ole Widding.
   >> *Norrøn fortællekunst* (1965). P. 125.
Boyer, Régis. "An Attempt to Define the Typology of Medieval Hagiog-
   raphy." In *Hagiography and Medieval Literature: A Symposium*. Ed.
   Hans Bekker-Nielsen, Peter Foote, Jørgen Højgaard-Jørgensen, and
   Tore Nyberg (Odense: Odense University Press, 1981). Pp. 27–36, esp.
   pp. 28–30 and 33–4.
Cormack, Margaret. >> *The Saints in Iceland* (1994). P. 124.
Foote, Peter, ed. >> *Lives of Saints* (1962). P. 20.
Gad, Tue. "Martinus." *KLNM* 11 (1966). Cols. 472–4, esp. col. 473.
Mogk, Eugen. >> *Geschichte der norwegisch-isländischen Literatur* (1904).
   P. 893.
Svanhildur Óskarsdóttir. "Universal History in Fourteenth-Century
   Iceland: Studies in AM 764 4to." PhD dissertation, University of
   London, 2000. P. 204.
Sverrir Tómasson. "Kristnar trúarbókmenntir í óbundnu máli." In
   Guðrún Nordal, Sverrir Tómasson, and Vésteinn Ólason, ed.
   >> *Íslensk Bókmenntasaga* 1 (1992). Pp. 419–79, esp. p. 424.
Sverrir Tómasson, Bragi Halldórsson, and Einar Sigurbjörnsson, ed.
   >> *Heilagra karla sögur* (2007). P. 316
Turville-Petre, G. >> *Origins of Icelandic Literature* (1967). Pp. 133
   and 179.
Handlist, p. 321.

MARY THE BLESSED VIRGIN   August 15

1. Maríu saga

A life of the Virgin Mary based on the apocryphal gospels *Liber de ortu beatae Mariae et infantia salvatoris* and *De nativitate Mariae*, the canonical gospels of Matthew and Luke, the *Trinubium Annae*, Flavius Josephus' *Antiquitates Judaicae*, and various works of the church fathers Jerome, Gregory the Great, Augustine, and John Chrysostom. It has been attributed to the priest Kygri-Bjǫrn Hjaltason (d. 1237 or 1238).

Manuscripts:
AM 232 fol. (ca. 1350), AM 233a fol. (ca. 1350–60, defective), AM 234 fol. (ca. 1340), AM 235 fol. (ca. 1400, extract), AM 240 fol. I (ca. 1375–1400), AM 240 fol. II (ca. 1300), AM 240 fol. IX (ca. 1350–1400), AM 240 fol. X (ca. 1400), AM 240 fol. XI (ca. 1275–1300), AM 240 fol. XIII (ca. 1400–1500 and ca. 1500), AM 240 fol. XIV (ca. 1300), AM 633 4to (ca. 1700–25), AM 634 4to (ca. 1700–25), AM 635 4to (ca. 1700–25), AM 656 4to I (ca. 1325–50), NRA 78 (ca. 1250–1300), NRA 79 (ca. 1350), Stock. Perg. 4to no. 1 (ca. 1450–1500), Stock. Perg. 4to no. 11 (ca. 1325–75), and Stock. Perg. 8vo no. 5 (ca. 1325–50, extracts).

Editions:
Heizmann, Wilhelm. "Das altisländische Marienleben. 1. Historisch-philologische Studien; 2. Edition der drei Redaktionen nach den Handschriften AM 234 fol., Holm 11 4to und Holm 1 4to." Habilitationsschrift, Georg-August-Universität Göttingen, 1993.
  Edition of AM 234 fol. (pp. 75–119), Stock Perg 4to no. 1 (pp. 222–83), and Stock. Perg. 4to no. 11 (pp. 120–221).
Unger, C.R., ed. >> *Mariu saga* (1871). Pp. 1–62 and 332–401.8.
  I. Based on Stock. Perg. 4to no. 11 with variants from AM 232 fol., AM 633 4to, AM 634–635 4to (pp. 1–22.14 and 51.26–62), and Stock. Perg. 4to no. 1.
  II. Based on AM 234 fol. (pp. 339.14–401.8) and AM 240 fol. IX (pp. 332–339.11) with variants from AM 240 fol. I (pp. 360.27–366.20), AM 240 fol. II (pp. 393.18–398.18), AM 240 fol. X (pp. 343.9–351.4 and 362.28–367.24), AM 240 fol. XI (pp. 377.25–380.20), AM 240 fol. XIV (pp. 393.7–396.14), and Stock. Perg. 4to no. 1 (pp. 332–401.8).
  Edition of AM 232 fol. (pp. xii–xiii, beginning only).

Modern Icelandic language edition:
Ásdís Egilsdóttir, Gunnar Harðarson, and Svanhildur Óskarsdóttir, ed.
   Maríukver. Sögur og kvæði af heilagri guðsmóður frá fyrri tíð (Reykja-
   vík: Hið íslenska bókmenntafélag, 1996). Pp. 3–66.

Literature:
Ásdís Egilsdóttir. "Kvendýrlingar og kvenímynd trúarlegra bókmennta á
   Íslandi." In Inga Huld Hákonardóttir, ed >> *Konur og kristsmenn*
   (1996). Pp. 93–116, esp. pp. 94–5, and 108.
Astås, Reidar. "Spor av teologisk tenkning og refleksjon i norsk og
   islandsk høymiddelalder." *CM* 6 (1993): 133–67, esp. p. 146.
Bekker-Nielsen, Hans. "Kyrkofäderna ock kyrkolärarna. K. i vestnordisk
   litteratur." *KLNM* 9 (1964). Cols. 690–3, esp. col. 692.
Bekker-Nielsen, Hans, Thorkil Damsgaard Olsen, and Ole Widding.
   >> *Norrøn fortællekunst* (1965). Pp. 121–2, 127–32, and 168–9.
Bekker-Nielsen, Hans, and Ole Widding. "Legende. Norge og Island."
   KLNM 10 (1965). Cols. 421–3, esp. col. 421.
– "Maria. Norge, Island." *KLNM* 11 (1966). Cols. 363–7, esp.
   cols. 364–5.
– "Religiøs prosalitteratur. Norge og Island." *KLNM* 14 (1969). Cols.
   42–4, esp. col. 43.
Boyer, Régis. >> *La vie religieuse en Islande* (1979). Pp. 146, 153, 158,
   160–1, 164, 193, 214, 219, 224, 285, 301, and 386.
Carlé, Birte. "Men and Women in the Saints' Sagas of *Stock. 2, fol.*" In
   John Lindow, Lars Lönnroth, and Gerd Wolfgang Weber, ed. >>
   Structure and Meaning in Old Norse Literature (1986). Pp. 317–46, esp.
   p. 319.
Cormack, Margaret. >> *The Saints in Iceland* (1994). Pp. 34, 55n22,
   and 127.
– "Sagas of Saints." In *Old Icelandic Literature and Society.* Ed.
   Margaret Clunies Ross (Cambridge: Cambridge University Press,
   2000). Pp. 302–25, esp. p. 303.
– "Christian Biography." In *A Companion to Old Norse–Icelandic
   Literature and Culture.* Ed. Rory McTurk (Oxford: Blackwell, 2005).
   Pp. 27–42, esp. pp. 30 and 32.
Einar Sigurbjörnsson. "Maríukveðskapur á mótum kaþólsku og lúther-
   sku." In *Til heiðurs og hugbótar. Greinar um trúarkveðskap fyrri alda.*
   Ed. Svanhildur Óskarsdóttir and Anna Guðmundsdóttir (Reykholt:
   Snorrastofa, 2003). Pp. 113–29, esp. pp. 123–5.
Finnur Jónsson. >> *Den oldnorske og oldislandske Litteraturs Historie*
   (1920–4). Vol. 2, pp. 868–9.

Foote, Peter. "Auðræði." In Arthur Brown and Peter Foote, ed. >> *Early English and Norse Studies* (1963). Pp. 62–76, esp. p. 65.

Gunnar F. Guðmundsson. "Latínusöngur leikra á miðöldum." In *Til heiðurs og hugbótar. Greinar um trúarkveðskap fyrri alda.* Ed. Svanhildur Óskarsdóttir and Anna Guðmundsdóttir (Reykholt: Snorrastofa, 2003). Pp. 93–112, esp. pp. 97–8.

Hallberg, Peter. "Imagery in Religious Old Norse Prose Literature: An Outline." *ANF* 102 (1987): 120–70, esp. pp. 129, 133, 139, 144–5, 149, and 150.

Halldór Laxness. "Ávarp vegna Maríusögu." *Skírnir* 155 (1981): 142–6.

Heizmann, Wilhelm. "Zur typologischen Interpretation des Magnificat in Maríu saga." In >> *The Sixth International Saga Conference* (1985). Vol. 1, pp. 469–82.

– "Maríu saga." In Phillip Pulsiano and Kirsten Wolf, with Paul Acker and Donald K. Fry, ed. >> *Medieval Scandinavia* (1993). Pp. 407–8.

– "Liebe und Durst: Der Heilige Bernhard von Clairvaux in der altisländischen Mirakelüberlieferung." *Opuscula* 13. Bibliotheca Arnamagnæana 47 (Copenhagen: Museum Tusculanum Press, 2010). Pp. 55–118, esp. pp. 56–60.

Holm-Olsen, Ludvig. "Middelalderens litteratur i Norge." In *Norges litteratur historie* 1. Ed. Edvard Beyer (Oslo: Cappelen, 1974). Pp. 18–342, esp. p. 61.

Jón Helgason. *Norrøn Litteraturhistorie* (Copenhagen: Levin and Munksgaard, 1934). P. 103.

Jón Hnefill Aðalsteinsson. "Blot i forna skrifter." *SI* 47 (1996): 11–32, esp. p. 25.

Jón Jóhannesson. "Tímatal Gerlands í íslenzkum ritum frá þjóðveldisöld." *Skírnir* 126 (1952): 76–93, esp. p. 90.

Jónas Kristjánsson. >> *Eddas and Sagas* (1988). P. 142 and 148.

Jørgensen, Jørgen Højgaard. "Hagiography and the Icelandic Bishop Sagas." *Peritia* 1 (1982): 1–16, esp. p. 4.

Kirby, Ian. >> *Biblical Quotation* (1980). Vol. 2, pp. 18–19, 52–3, 58, 71, 74–5, and 101.

– *Bible Translation in Old Norse.* Université de Lausanne Publications de la faculté des lettres 27 (Geneva: Librairie Droz, 1986). Pp. 35, 45, 131, 155–6, 162, and 167.

Magerøy, Hallvard. "Helgensoger." *KLNM* 6 (1961). Cols. 350–3, esp. col. 351.

Mogk, Eugen. >> *Geschichte der norwegisch-isländischen Literatur* (1904). P. 886.

Ólafur Halldórsson. "Rímbeglusmiður." *Opuscula* 2.2. Bibliotheca
Arnamagnæana 25.2 (Copenhagen: Reitzel, 1977). Pp. 32–49, esp.
p. 41. Rpt. in Ólafur Halldórsson. *Grettisfærsla: Safn ritgerða eftir Ólaf
Halldórsson gefið út á sjötugsafmæli hans 18. april 1990* (Reykjavík:
Stofnun Árna Magnússonar, 1990). Pp. 302–18, esp. p. 311.

Paasche, Fredrik. *Norges og Islands litteratur inntil utgangen av
middelalderen*. Rev. ed. by Anne Holtsmark (Oslo: Aschehoug, 1947).
Pp. 295–6, 301–2, 308, and 525.

Schier, Kurt. *Sagaliteratur*. Sammlung Metzler M78 (Stuttgart: Metzler,
1970). Pp. 123–4 and 128–9.

Stefán Karlsson. "Islandsk bogeksport til Norge i middelalderen." *Mm*
(1979): 1–17, esp. p. 6. Rpt. in *Stafkrókar: Ritgerðir eftir Stefán
Karlsson gefnar út í tilefni af sjötugsafmæli hans 2. desember 1998*. Ed.
Guðvarður Már Gunnlaugsson (Reykjavík: Stofnun Árna Magnússonar, 2000). Pp. 188–205, esp. p. 194.

Svanhildur Óskarsdóttir. "Universal History in Fourteenth-Century
Iceland: Studies in AM 764 4to." PhD dissertation, University of
London, 2000. P. 212.

Sverrir Jakobsson. *Við og veröldin: Heimsmynd Íslendinga 1100–1400*
(Reykjavík: Háskólaútgáfan, 2005). P. 95.

Sverrir Tómasson. *Formálar íslenskra sagnaritara á miðöldum. Rannsókn
bókmenntahefðar* (Reykjavík: Stofnun Árna Magnússonar, 1988).
Pp. 12, 29, 45, 67, 87, 119–21, 125, 142–3, 178, 183, 196, 198, 206,
222–3, 230, 234, 241, 307, 309, and 345–6.

– "Kristnar trúarbókmenntir í óbundnu máli." In Guðrún Nordal,
Sverrir Tómasson, and Vésteinn Ólason, ed. >> *Íslensk Bókmenntasaga*
1 (1992). Pp. 419–79, esp. pp. 459–65.

– "Trúarbókmenntir í lausu máli á síðmiðöld." In Böðvar Guðmundsson,
Sverrir Tómasson, Torfi H. Tulinius, and Vésteinn Ólason, ed.
>> *Íslensk Bókmenntasaga* 2 (1993). Pp. 249–82, esp. p. 257.

Tomassini, Laura. "Attempts at Biblical Exegesis in Old Norse: Some
Examples from *Maríu saga*." *Opuscula* 10. Bibliotheca Arnamagnæana
40 (Copenhagen: Reitzel, 1996). Pp. 129–35.

Turville-Petre, G. "The Old Norse Homily on the Assumption and the Maríu
saga." *MS* 9 (1947): 131–40. Rpt. in Gabriel Turville-Petre. *Nine Norse
Studies* (London: Viking Society for Northern Research, 1972). Pp. 102–17.

– >> *Origins of Icelandic Literature* (1967). Pp. 120–5.

Vésteinn Ólason. "Kveðskapur frá síðmiðöldum: Trúarkvæði." In
Böðvar Guðmundsson, Sverrir Tómasson, Torfi H. Tulinius, and
Vésteinn Ólason, ed. >> *Íslensk Bókmenntasaga* 2 (1993). Pp. 283–
378, esp. pp. 309–11.

Vrátný, Karel. "Enthält das Stockholmer Homilienbuch durchweg Übersetzungen?" *ANF* 32 (1916): 31–49, esp. p. 42.

Vries, Jan de. >> *Altnordische Literaturgeschichte* (1964–7). Vol. 2, pp. 184–5 and 194.

Widding, Ole. "Conscientia i norrøne oversættelser." *Opuscula* 2.1. Bibliotheca Arnamagnæana 25.1 (Copenhagen: Ejnar Munksgaard, 1961). Pp. 48–51, esp. pp. 48 and 51.

– "Marialegender. Norge og Island." *KLNM* 11 (1966). Cols. 401–4, esp. cols. 401–2.

– "Norrøne Marialegender på europæisk baggrund." *Opuscula* 10. Bibliotheca Arnamagnæana 40 (Copenhagen: Reitzel, 1996). Pp. 1–128, esp. pp. 2–3, 33, 60, and 78.

Widding, Ole, and Hans Bekker-Nielsen. "The Fifteen Steps of the Temple: A Problem in the Maríu Saga." *Opuscula* 2.1. Bibliotheca Arnamagnæana 25.1 (Copenhagen: Ejnar Munksgaard, 1961). Pp. 80– 91.

– "An Old Norse Translation of the 'Transitus Mariae'." *MS* 23 (1961): 324–33, esp. pp. 325–7.

– "Low German Influence on Late Icelandic Hagiography." *GR* 37 (1962): 239–62, esp. p. 243, 248, and 256–7.

Wolf, Kirsten. "The Cult of Saint Anne in Iceland." In >> *Samtíðarsögur* (1994). Vol. 2, pp. 863–77, esp. pp. 870–1.

Handlist, pp. 321–2.

2. Framfǫr Maríu

A translation of *BHL* 5350.

Manuscript:
AM 232 fol. (ca. 1400–1500).

Edition:
Widding, Ole, and Hans Bekker-Nielsen. "An Old Norse Translation of the 'Transitus Mariae'." *MS* 23 (1961): 324–33, esp. pp. 329–33.

Modern Icelandic language edition:
Ásdís Egilsdóttir, Gunnar Harðarson, and Svanhildur Óskarsdóttir, ed. *Maríukver. Sögur og kvæði af heilagri guðsmóður frá fyrri tíð* (Reykjavík: Hið íslenska bókmenntafélag, 1996). Pp. 101–8.

Literature:
Astås, Reidar. "Spor av teologisk tenkning og refleksjon i norsk og islandsk høymiddelalder." *CM* 6 (1993): 133–67, esp. p. 146n54.

Bekker-Nielsen, Hans, Thorkil Damsgaard Olsen, and Ole Widding. >> *Norrøn fortællekunst* (1965). P. 129.

Bekker-Nielsen, Hans, and Ole Widding. "Legende. Norge og Island." *KLNM* 10 (1965). Cols. 421–3, esp. col. 421.
– "Maria. Norge, Island." *KLNM* 11 (1966). Cols. 363–7, esp. cols. 363–4.
– "Religiøs prosalitteratur. Norge og Island." *KLNM* 14 (1969). Cols. 42–4, esp. col. 43.
Boyer, Régis. >> *La vie religieuse en Islande* (1979). Pp. 224–5 and 301.
Kirby, Ian. >> *Biblical Quotation* (1980). Vol. 2, p. 107.
Widding, Ole. "Marialegender. Norge og Island." *KLNM* 11 (1966). Cols. 401–4, esp. col. 402.
Handlist, p. 322.

3. Maríu jartegnir

Based primarily on Latin versions.

Manuscripts:
AM 232 fol. (ca. 1350), AM 233a fol. (ca. 1350–60 and ca. 1300–1400), AM 234 fol. (ca. 1340), AM 235 fol. (ca. 1400), AM 238 fol. VI (ca. 1400), AM 238 fol. XIII (ca. 1500), AM 238 fol. XXIII (ca. 1400–1500), AM 240 fol. II (ca. 1300), AM 240 fol. III (ca. 1300–1400), AM 240 fol. IV (ca. 1350), AM 240 fol. V (ca. 1330–70), AM 240 fol. VI (ca. 1400), AM 240 fol. VII (ca. 1300–1400), AM 240 fol. VIII (ca. 1350–1400), AM 240 fol. IX (ca. 1350–1400), AM 240 fol. XI (ca. 1275–1300), AM 240 fol. XII (ca. 1300), AM 240 fol. XIII (ca. 1400–1500 and ca. 1500), AM 633 4to (ca. 1700–25), AM 634 4to (ca. 1700–25), AM 635 4to (ca. 1700–25), AM 655 4to II (ca. 1200–25), AM 655 4to XIX (ca. 1225–50), AM 655 4to XXIV (ca. 1300–1400), AM 655 4to XXXII (ca. 1300–1400), AM 656 4to I (ca. 1325–50), AM 656 4to II (ca. 1250), AM 657a–b 4to (ca. 1350), AM 662b 4to (ca. 1350–1400), AM 666a 4to (ca. 1350–1400), AM 667 4to III (ca. 1300–50), AM 667 4to XIII (ca. 1400–1500), AM 681a 4to (ca. 1450), AM 720a 4to VIII (ca. 1400–50), AM 764 4to (ca. 1376–86), AM 433c 12mo (ca. 1525–50), BLAdd 11.242 (ca. 1540–90), Lbs fragm 3 (ca. 1300–50), Lbs fragm. 4 (ca. 1350–1400), NRA 78 (ca. 1250–1300), Stock. Perg. 4to no. 1 (ca. 1450–1500), Stock. Perg. 4to no. 11 (ca. 1325–75 and ca. 1400–50), and Stock. Perg. 8vo no. 1 (ca. 1325–50).

Editions:
Dasent, George Webbe. *Theophilus in Icelandic, Low German and Other Tongues from MSS. in the Royal Library Stockholm* (London: William Pickering, 1845). Pp. 1–28 (extracts only).

Edition of Stock. Perg. 4to no. 11 (pp. 1–10) and Stock. Perg. 4to no. 1 (pp. 11–28).

Gering, Hugo, ed. >> *Islendzk æventyri* (1882–84). Vol. 1, pp. 147–9.
Edition of part of AM 657a–b 4to.

Hreinn Benediktsson. *Early Icelandic Script As Illustrated in Vernacular Texts from the Twelfth and Thirteenth Centuries.* Íslenzk handrit: Icelandic Manuscripts, Series in Folio 2 (Reykjavík: The Manuscript Institute of Iceland, 1965). Plates 17, 37, and 63, and p. xii.
Facsimile and edition of AM 655 4to II, fol. 1v; facsimile of AM 655 4to XIX, fol. 2v; and facsimile of AM 656 4to II, fol. 1v.

Jakob Benediktsson. "Nokkur handritabrot." *Skírnir* 125 (1951): 182–98, esp. pp. 191–6.
Edition of Lbs fragm. 4.

Jakobsen, Alfred. "Et bruddstykke av en Maria-legende." *Opuscula* 1. Bibliotheca Arnamagnæana 20 (Copenhagen: Ejnar Munksgaard, 1960). Pp. 267–70, esp. p. 268.
Edition of AM 657a–b 4to, fol. 91v.18–33.

Jensen, Helle. "En Marialegende uden Maria." *Opuscula* 3. Bibliotheca Arnamagnæana 29 (Copenhagen: Munksgaard, 1967). Pp. 272–7, esp. pp. 273–4.
Edition of AM 720a 4to VIII.

Stefán Karlsson, ed. *Sagas of Icelandic Bishops: Fragments of Eight Manuscripts.* EIM 7 (Copenhagen: Rosenkilde and Bagger, 1967).
Facsimile of AM 240 fol. V (extract only).

Unger, C.R., ed. >> *Mariu saga* (1871). Pp. 63–331 and 401–1204.
I. Based on AM 232 fol. (pp. 65.4–152), AM 233a fol. (pp. 243.4–249.11, 266.14–268.21, 275.22–276, 291.29–297, and 302.16–306.17), AM 234 fol. (pp. 153.3–157.20), and Stock. Perg. 4to no. 11 (pp. 63–65.2, 157.23–243.2, 249.13–266.12, 268.23–275.20, 277.2–291.27, 298.2–302.15, and 306.19–331).
II. Based on AM 233a fol. (pp. 444.28–445.14 and 521.11–527.13, 533.10–534.10, 554.13–555.27, 598.18–599.16, and 1160.6–1161.1), AM 234 fol. (pp. 1022.26–1023.19), AM 240 fol. II (pp. 633.16–634.21), AM 240 fol. IV (pp. 509.2–23, 916.2–920, 946.8–947.5, 947.21–948.19, 949.4–9, 1107.17–1108.15, 1108.25–1109.21, 1109.30–1110.27, 1111.4–1112.5, and 1157.33–1158.17), AM 240 fol. V (pp. 409.12–411.3, 411.23–412.28, 450.25–453.29, 472.6–482.32, and 502.21–508.28), AM 240 fol. VII (pp. 1177.2–1178.4), AM 240 fol. VIII (pp. 1174.28–1175.28), AM 240 fol. IX (pp. 417.23–424.25, 436.6–439.22, 468.27–472.6, 482.34–487.22, 501.11–502.20, 796.1–801.17, 802.9–805.28, 861.23–869.10, 871.2–27, 890.4–893.10, 895.25–896.27, 913.6–916.2, and 1182.11–

1185.16), AM 240 fol. XII (pp. 1076.5–1077.13), AM 655 4to XXXII
(pp. 430.20–436.6, 445.14–450.25, 457.21–468.25, 487.22–499.10,
572.4–577.10, 577.17–583.18, 599.25–604.34, 608–613 lower text,
614.6–619.21, and 623.19–629.8), AM 634 4to (pp. 691.31–694.11,
695.29–698.21, 699.15–707.7, 708.27–711.18, 711.33–724.5, 724.33–
725.11, 740.2–748.21, 749.12–763.4, 764.7–770.17, 770.32–783.11,
786.5–788.9, 789.19–796.1, 805.28–806, 813.2–832.16, 835.2–836.25,
839.22–842.12, 845.2–848.10, 851.7–861.23, 879.7–887.3, 888.9–890.2,
893.12–894.11, 1023.21–1025, 1090.24–1104.14, 1116.29–1121.30,
1142.25–1145.5, 1147.19–1157.31, 1161.1–11, 1162.18–1171.6,
1172.23–1173.18, 1178.4–1182.11, and 1191.16–1192.20), AM 635 4to
(pp. 588.12–594.25, 649.22–6, 654.12–681.23, 690.8–691.29, 694.13–
695.27, 727.21–728.22, 736.4–739, 783.12–786.3, 807.2–812, 832.18–
834, 836.27–839.20, 842.14–844, 848.12–851.5, 871.27–872.4, 872.26–
879.5, 896.27–913.6, 921.2–942.29, 945.24–946.8, 947.5–17,
949.11–950.10, 951.12–987.11, 989.33–990.9, 993.12–994.5, 996.11–
1002.5, 1026.2–1031.21, 1032.17–1058.23, 1064.8–1070.2, 1072.8–27,
1073.31–1076.3, 1104.16–1107.17, 1108.15–25, 1109.21–30, 1110.27–
1111.4, 1112.5–25, 1126.4–1133.28, 1141.24–1142.23, 1158.20–1160.4,
1171.8–1172.21, 1173.20–1174.26, 1175.28–1176, 1185.18–1190.26,
and 1193.23–1204), Stock. Perg. 4to no. 1 (pp. 401.10–409.12, 411.3–
23, 412.29–417.23, 424.25–430.20, 439.22–444.26, 453.29–457.21,
499.10–501.10, 508.28–509.2, 509.24–521.9, 527.15–533.8, 534.15–
554.2, 555.32–566.9, 566.20–571, 583.18–588.10, 594.25–7, 595.2–
598.16, 604.34–608.13, 608.21–614.6 (608–13 upper text), 619.21–
622.29, 623.5–19, 629.8–633.16, 634.21–635.28, 635.33–639.5,
639.10–649.22, 649.26–654.10, 681.24–690.6, 698.23–699.13, 725.13–
727.20, 728.24–736.2, 887.5–888.7, 894.13–895.23, 947.17–20, 948.19–
949.4, 987.13–988, 999.11–993.10, 994.7–995.12, and 1002.7–1022.24),
Stock. Perg. 4to no. 11 (pp. 707.9–708.25, 711.20–31, 724.7–31,
748.23–749.10, 763.6–764.5, 770.19–30, 788.11–789.17, 801.19–802.7,
869.12–870, 872.6–24, 942.31–945.22, 950.12–951.10, 989.2–31,
995.14–996.9, 1031.23–1032.15, 1058.25–1064.6, 1070.4–30, 1071.29–
1072.6, 1072.29–1073.29, 1077.15–1090.22, and 1192.22–1193.21), and
Stock. Perg. 8vo no. 1 (pp. 1112.27–1116.27, 1121.32–1126.2, 1133.30–
1141.22, 1145.7–1147.17, and 1161.13–1162.16).
Editions of AM 240 fol. XI (pp. xxiv, extract only), AM 655 4to II
(pp. xxxii–xxxviii), AM 655 4to XIX (pp. xxxi–xxxii), AM 656 4to II
(pp. xxxix–xl), AM 667 4to III (pp. xv–xviii), and NRA 78 (pp. xxi–xxii,
prologue and Latin prayer).

Modern Icelandic language editions:
Ásdís Egilsdóttir, Gunnar Harðarson, and Svanhildur Óskarsdóttir,
  ed. *Maríukver. Sögur og kvæði af heilagri guðsmóður frá fyrri tíð*
  (Reykjavík: Hið íslenska bókmenntafélag, 1996). Pp. 69–98 (extracts
  only).
Einar Ól. Sveinsson, ed. *Leit eg suður til landa. Ævintýri og helgisögur
  frá miðöldum.* (Reykjavík: Heimskringla, 1944). Pp. 152–98 (extracts
  only).
English translation:
Cormack, Margaret. "Better Off Dead: Approaches to Medieval Miracles."
  In Thomas A. DuBois, ed. >> *Sanctity in the North* (2008). Pp. 334–52,
  esp. pp. 346–9 (extracts only).
German paraphrase:
Gering, Hugo, ed. >> *Islendzk æventyri* (1882–4). Vol. 2, pp. 122–3. The
  miracle *Af tveimr munkum* only.
Literature:
Astås, Reidar. "Spor av teologisk tenkning og refleksjon i norsk og
  islandsk høymiddelalder." *CM* 6 (1993): 133–67, esp. pp. 141 and 147.
Attwood, Katrina, ed. "Anonymous, *Gyðingsvísur 'Vísur* about a Jew'."
  In Margaret Clunies Ross, ed. >> *Poetry on Christian Subjects* (2007).
  Vol. 2, p. 516.
Battista, Simonetta. "*Blámenn, djǫflar* and Other Representations of Evil
  in Old Norse Literature." In John McKinnell, David Ashurst, and
  Donata Kick, ed. >> *The Fantastic in Old Norse/Icelandic Literature*
  (2006). Vol. 1, pp. 113–22, esp. pp. 116 and 188–9.
Bekker-Nielsen, Hans. "Kyrkofäderna ock kyrkolärarna. K. i vestnordisk
  litteratur." *KLNM* 9 (1964). Cols. 690–3, esp. col. 693.
– "Mariadigtning. Island (og Norge)." *KLNM* 11 (1966). Cols. 379–80,
  esp. col. 380.
– "The Victorines and Their Influence on Old Norse Literature." In *The
  Fifth Viking Congress, Tórshavn, July 1965.* Ed. Bjarni Niclasen
  (Tórshavn: Føroya Landsstýri, 1968). Pp. 32–6, esp. pp. 35–6.
Bekker-Nielsen, Hans, Thorkil Damsgaard Olsen, and Ole Widding.
  >> *Norrøn fortællekunst* (1965). Pp. 107, 119, 121–2, 128–33, 136, 139,
  and 168–9.
Bekker-Nielsen, Hans, and Ole Widding. "Legende. Norge og Island."
  KLNM 10 (1965). Cols. 421–3, esp. cols. 421–2.
– "Maria. Norge, Island." *KLNM* 11 (1966). Cols. 363–7, esp. col. 364.
– "Religiøs prosalitteratur. Norge og Island." *KLNM* 14 (1969). Cols.
  42–4, esp. col. 43.

Boyer, Régis. >> *La vie religieuse en Islande* (1979). Pp. 183, 214, 219, and 224.

Clunies Ross, Margaret. "Love in a Cold Climate – with the Virgin Mary." In Kirsten Wolf and Johanna Denzin, ed. >> *Romance and Love in Late Medieval and Early Modern Iceland* (2008). Pp. 303–17, esp. pp. 303, 307, 310, 311n16, and 313.

Cormack, Margaret. >> *The Saints in Iceland* (1994). Pp. 55n22, 127, and 137n352.

– "Sagas of Saints." In *Old Icelandic Literature and Society*. Ed. Margaret Clunies Ross (Cambridge: Cambridge University Press, 2000). Pp. 302–25, esp. p. 303.

– "Christian Biography." In *A Companion to Old Norse–Icelandic Literature and Culture*. Ed. Rory McTurk (Oxford: Blackwell, 2005). Pp. 27–42, esp. p. 30.

Finnur Jónsson. >> *Den oldnorske og oldislandske Litteraturs Historie* (1920–4). Vol. 2, pp. 931–2.

Foote, Peter. "Auðræði." In Arthur Brown and Peter Foote, ed. >> *Early English and Norse Studies* (1963). Pp. 62–76, esp. pp. 66–7.

– "A Question of Conscience." *Opuscula* 2.2. Bibliotheca Arnamagnæana 25.2 (Copenhagen: Reitzel, 1977). Pp. 11–18, esp. pp. 11–15.

Gade, Kari Ellen, ed. "Anonymous, *Drápa af Máriugrát* 'Drápa about the Lament of Mary'." In Margaret Clunies Ross, ed. >> *Poetry on Christian Subjects* (2007). Vol. 2, pp. 758–9.

– ed. "Anonymous, *Máriuvísur I* 'Vísur about Mary I'." In Margaret Clunies Ross, ed. >> *Poetry on Christian Subjects* (2007). Vol. 2, pp. 678–9.

– ed. "Anonymous, *Máriuvísur II* 'Vísur about Mary II'." In Margaret Clunies Ross, ed. >> *Poetry on Christian Subjects* (2007). Vol. 2, pp. 701–2.

– ed. "Anonymous, *Máriuvísur III* 'Vísur about Mary III'." In Margaret Clunies Ross, ed. >> *Poetry on Christian Subjects* (2007). Vol. 2, p. 718.

– ed. "Anonymous, *Vitnisvísur af Máriu* 'Testimonial *Vísur* about Mary'." In Margaret Clunies Ross, ed. >> *Poetry on Christian Subjects* (2007). Vol. 2, p. 740.

Hallberg, Peter. *Stilsignalement och författarskap i norrön sagalitteratur: Synpunkter och exempel*. Nordistica Gothoburgensia 3 (Stockholm: Almqvist & Wiksell, 1968). Pp. 138–47, 149, 157–64, 181, 185–9.

– "Imagery in Religious Old Norse Prose Literature: An Outline." *ANF* 102 (1987): 120–70, esp. pp. 123, 126, 130–6, 138, 140, 142–50, 152–5, 157–8, 160, and 163–6.

Halvorsen, E.F. *The Norse Version of the Chanson de Roland*. Bibliotheca Arnamagnæana 19 (Copenhagen: Ejnar Munksgaard, 1959). Pp. 47–8.

Heizmann, Wilhelm. "Arngríms Guðmundar saga, Maríu saga und Gregors Moralia in Iob." *Opuscula* 8. Bibliotheca Arnamagnæana 38 (Copenhagen: Reitzel, 1985). Pp. 189–98.

– "Das altisländische Marienleben. 1. Historisch-philologische Studien; 2. Edition der drei Redaktionen nach den Handschriften AM 234 fol., Holm 11 4to und Holm 1 4to." Habilitationsschrift, Georg-August-Universität Göttingen, 1993. Pp. 5–70.

– "Maríu saga." In Phillip Pulsiano and Kirsten Wolf, with Paul Acker and Donald K. Fry, ed. >> *Medieval Scandinavia* (1993). Pp. 407–8.

– "Liebe und Durst: Der Heilige Bernhard von Clairvaux in der altisländischen Mirakelüberlieferung." *Opuscula* 13. Bibliotheca Arnamagnæana 47 (Copenhagen: Museum Tusculanum Press, 2010). Pp. 55–118.

Holm-Olsen, Ludvig. "Middelalderens litteratur i Norge." In *Norges litteratur historie* 1. Ed. Edvard Beyer (Oslo: Cappelen, 1974). Pp. 18–342, esp. pp. 61 and 321.

Jakob Benediktsson. "Cursus hos Bergr Sokkason." In *Festskrift til Ludvig Holm-Olsen på hans 70-årsdag den 9. juni 1984* (Øvre Ervik: Alvheim & Eide, 1984). Pp. 34–40, esp. p. 38. Rpt. in Jakob Benediktsson. *Lærdómslistir. Afmælisrit 20. júlí 1987* (Reykjavík: Mál og menning, 1987). Pp. 262–9, esp. pp. 266–7.

Jón Hnefill Aðalsteinsson. "Blot i forna skrifter." *SI* 47 (1996): 11–32, esp. p. 26.

Jón Viðar Sigurðsson. *Den vennlige vikingen: Vennskapets makt i Norge og på Island ca. 900–1300* (Oslo: Pax Forlag, 2010). P. 120.

Jónas Kristjánsson. *Um Fóstbræðra sögu* (Reykjavík: Stofnun Árna Magnússonar, 1972). Pp. 258–9, 268, 272–3, 280–1, 287, 289–90, and 304–5.

– "Learned Style or Saga Style?" In Ursula Dronke, Guðrún P. Helgadóttir, Gerd Wolfgang Weber, and Hans Bekker-Nielsen, ed. >> *Specvlvm Norroenvm* (1981). Pp. 260–92.

– >> *Eddas and Sagas* (1988). Pp. 142–3.

Jorgensen, Peter A. "Four Literary Styles in Three Centuries: The Old Icelandic Theophilus Legend." In >> *Samtíðarsögur* (1994). Vol. 1, pp. 395–402.

Kirby, Ian. >> *Biblical Quotation* (1980). Vol. 2, pp. 43n12, 45, 74–7, and 117–18.

Lehmann, Paul. >> "Skandinaviens Anteil an der lateinischen Literatur und Wissenschaft des Mittelalters" (1937). Pp. 24, 56, and 81.

Mogk, Eugen. >> *Geschichte der norwegisch-isländischen Literatur* (1904). Pp. 886–7.

Paasche, Fredrik. *Norges og Islands litteratur inntil utgangen av middelalderen*. Rev. ed. by Anne Holtsmark (Oslo: Aschehoug, 1947). Pp. 296–7, 489–90, and 505.

Piebenga, Gryt Anne. "Om den norrøne oversettelsen av noen fragmenter av *Vita Mariae Oigniacensis*." *Mm* (1988): 174–84.

– "Om Marialegenden 'Vor fru frelsti brodur fra iðtni'." *Mm* (1988): 13–22.

– "'Heyrðu hjálpin skæra', an Icelandic Miracle Poem and Its Antecedents." In *Atti del 12° Congresso Internazionale di Studi Sull' Alto Medioevo Studi, 4–10 settembre 1988* (Spoleto: Presso la Sede del Centro Studi, 1990). Pp. 609–17, esp. pp. 610, 612, and 615.

– "Den norsk-islandske bearbeidelsen av Beatricelegenden." *Mm* (1991): 97–106.

– "Miracles, Collections of." In Phillip Pulsiano and Kirsten Wolf, with Paul Acker and Donald K. Fry, ed. >> *Medieval Scandinavia* (1993). Pp. 413–14.

Seip, Didrik Arup. "Jærtegnsamlinger." *KLNM* 8 (1963). Cols. 65–8, esp. col. 66.

Simek, Rudolf. *Altnordische Kosmographie: Studien und Quellen zu Weltbild und Weltbeschreibung in Norwegen und Island vom 12. bis zum 14. Jahrhundert* (Berlin: de Gruyter, 1990). P. 200.

Sprenger, Ulrike. "Gefrorensein und Schmelzen als Metapher im Altnordischen: Ghv. 20, 7/8, Sg. 8,3 und Maríu saga." *Opuscula* 8. Bibliotheca Arnamagnæana 38 (Copenhagen: Reitzel, 1985). Pp. 162–88, esp. pp. 171–88.

Stefán Karlsson. "Islandsk bogeksport til Norge i middelalderen." *Mm* (1979): 1–17, esp. p. 6. Rpt. in *Stafkrókar: Ritgerðir eftir Stefán Karlsson gefnar út í tilefni af sjötugsafmæli hans 2. desember 1998*. Ed. Guðvarður Már Gunnlaugsson (Reykjavík: Stofnun Árna Magnússonar, 2000). Pp. 188–205, esp. p. 194.

Strömbäck, Dag. "Visionsdiktning." *KLNM* 20 (1976). Cols. 171–86, esp. col. 177.

Svanhildur Óskarsdóttir. "Universal History in Fourteenth-Century Iceland: Studies in AM 764 4to." PhD dissertation, University of London, 2000. Pp. 140, 198, 210–1, and 240–1.

– "The World and Its Ages: The Organisation of an 'Encyclopaedic' Narrative in MS AM 764 4to." In *Sagas, Saints and Settlements*. Ed. Gareth Williams and Paul Bibire. The Northern World 2 (Leiden: Brill, 2004). Pp. 1–11, esp. p. 2.

Sverrir Jakobsson. *Við og veröldin: Heimsmynd Íslendinga 1100–1400* (Reykjavík: Háskólaútgáfan, 2005). Pp. 145 and 149.

Sverrir Tómasson. "Norðlenski Benediktínaskólinn." In >> *The Sixth International Saga Conference* (1985). Vol. 2, pp. 1009–20, esp. p. 1012. Rpt. in Sverrir Tómasson. *Tækileg vitni: Greinar um bókmenntir gefnar út í tilefni sjötugsafmælis hans 5. apríl 2011* (Reykjavík: Stofnun Árna Magnússonar and Hið íslenska bókmenntafélag, 2011). Pp. 345–58, esp. p. 348.

– *Formálar íslenskra sagnaritara á miðöldum. Rannsókn bókmenntahefðar* (Reykjavík: Stofnun Árna Magnússonar, 1988). Pp. 45, 87, 120, 125–6, 129, 178, 206, 248, and 309.

– "Erlendur vísdómur og forn fræði." In Guðrún Nordal, Sverrir Tómasson, and Vésteinn Ólason, ed. >> *Íslensk Bókmenntasaga* 1 (1992). Pp. 517–71, esp. p. 560.

– "Kristnar trúarbókmenntir í óbundnu máli." In Guðrún Nordal, Sverrir Tómasson, and Vésteinn Ólason, ed. >> *Íslensk Bókmenntasaga* 1 (1992). Pp. 419–79, esp. pp. 428, 432, 464–6, and 472.

– "Er nýja textafræðin ný? Þankar um gamla fræðigrein." *Gripla* 13 (2002): 199–216, esp. p. 206. Rpt. in Sverrir Tómasson. *Tækileg vitni: Greinar um bókmenntir gefnar út í tilefni sjötugsafmælis hans 5. apríl 2011* (Reykjavík: Stofnun Árna Magnússonar and Hið íslenska bókmenntafélag, 2011). Pp. 231–50, esp. pp. 238–9.

Sverrir Tómasson, Bragi Halldórsson, and Einar Sigurbjörnsson, ed. >> *Heilagra karla sögur* (2007). Pp. xliv–xlv.

Toorn-Piebenga, Gryte van der. "Comments and Questions on the Old Norse Miracles of Mary." In >> *The Sixth International Saga Conference* (1985). Vol. 2, pp. 1051–6.

Turville-Petre, Gabriel. "Legends of England in Icelandic Manuscripts." In Peter Clemoes, ed. >> *The Anglo-Saxons* (1959). Pp. 104–21. Rpt. in Gabriel Turville-Petre. *Nine Norse Studies* (London: Viking Society for Northern Research, 1972). Pp. 59–78.

Tveitane, Mattias. "'Bonus'. Et latinsk Maria-dikt i norrøn prosaversjon." *Mm* (1962): 109–21, esp. pp. 117–20.

Valgerður Erna Þorvaldsdóttir, ed. "Anonymous, *Brúðkaupsvísur* 'Vísur about a Wedding'." In Margaret Clunies Ross, ed. >> *Poetry on Christian Subjects* (2007). Vol. 2, p. 527.

Wellendorf, Jonas. "Visions and the Fantastic." In John McKinnell, David Ashurst, and Donata Kick, ed. >> *The Fantastic in Old Norse / Icelandic Literature* (2006). Vol. 2, pp. 1025–33, esp. pp. 1028–9 and 1031.

– "The Attraction of the Earliest Old Norse Vernacular Hagiography." In Haki Antonsson and Ildar H. Garipzanov, ed. >> *Saints and Their Lives on the Periphery* (2010). Pp. 241–58, esp. p. 255.

Widding, Ole. "Conscientia i norrøne oversættelser." *Opuscula* 2.1. Bibliotheca Arnamagnæana 25.1 (Copenhagen: Ejnar Munksgaard, 1961). Pp. 48–51, esp. pp. 48 and 51.

– "Om de norrøne Marialegender." *Opuscula* 2.1. Bibliotheca Arnamagnæana 25.1 (Copenhagen: Ejnar Munksgaard, 1961). Pp. 1–9.

– "A Preliminary Note on an Anecdote in the Maríu saga." *Opuscula* 2.1. Bibliotheca Arnamagnæana 25.1 (Copenhagen: Ejnar Munksgaard, 1961). P. 92.

– "Marialegender. Norge og Island." *KLNM* 11 (1966). Cols. 401–4, esp. cols. 402–4.

– "Norrøne Marialegender med Rhinegnene som hjemsted." *Arv* 23 (1967): 143–58.

– "Nogle norske Marialegender." *Mm* (1969): 51–9.

– "To norrøne varianter af legenden om Leuricus." *Mm* (1982): 41–8.

– "Norrøne Marialegender på europæisk baggrund." *Opuscula* 10. Bibliotheca Arnamagnæana 40 (Copenhagen: Reitzel, 1996). Pp. 1–128.

Widding, Ole, and Hans Bekker-Nielsen. "The Virgin Bares Her Breast: An Icelandic Version of a Miracle of the Blessed Virgin." *Opuscula* 2.1. Bibliotheca Arnamagnæana 25.1 (Copenhagen: Munksgaard, 1961). Pp. 76–9.

Wrightson, Kellinde. "Changing Attitudes to Old Norse Marian Poetry." In *Old Norse Studies in the New World: A Collection of Essays to Celebrate the Jubilee of the Teaching of Old Norse at the University of Sydney 1943–1993*. Ed. Geraldine Barnes, Margaret Clunies Ross, and Judy Quinn (Sydney: Department of English, University of Sydney, 1994). Pp. 138–53.

– "Marian Miracles in Old Icelandic Skaldic Poetry." In *Treasures of the Elder Tongue: Fifty Years of Old Norse in Melbourne. The Proceedings of the Symposium to Celebrate the Golden Jubilee of Old Norse at the University of Melbourne 14th May 1994*. Ed. Katrina Burge and John Stanley Martin (Melbourne: Department of Germanic and Russian Studies, University of Melbourne, 1995). Pp. 87–99, esp. p. 89.

- "*Drápa af Maríugrát*, the Joys and Sorrows of the Virgin and Christ, and the Dominican Rosary." *Saga-Book* 24 (1997): 283–92, esp. p. 283.
- "The Jilted Fiancée: The Old Icelandic Miracle Poem *Vitnisvísur af Maríu* and Its Modern English Translation." *Parergon* 15 (1997): 117–36, esp. pp. 118n4 and 122–7.

Handlist, pp. 322–4.

NOTE:

The miracles of the Virgin Mary include hagiographical material dealing with several other saints. The following have received special prominence: Anselm of Canterbury, Basil the Great, Bede the Venerable, Bernhard of Clairvaux, Boniface IV, Bonitus, Dominic, Dunstan, Edmund Rich, Elizabeth of Schönau, Eusebius of Vercelli, Francis of Assisi, Fulbert of Chartres, Gregory the Great, Herman the Cripple, Hugh of Bonneveaux, Hugh the Great of Cluny, Ildephonsus, John the Almoner, John Damascene, Leo the Great, Mary of Egypt, Mary of Oignies, Odilo of Cluny, Peter Monoculus, Stephen of Grandmont, and Thomas Becket. See the entries for the individual saints.

MARY OF EGYPT   April 2

1. Maríu saga egipzku II

A translation of a form of the *vita*, *BHL* Suppl. 5417d, which is considered to be an extract of *BHL* 5417, with some use also of *BHL* 5415. Generally the text is closer to the Latin than 3.

Manuscripts:
AM 655 4to XXXIII (ca. 1250–1300) and AM 657c 4to (ca. 1340–90).
Edition:
Unger, C.R., ed. >> *Heilagra manna søgur* (1877). Vol. 1, pp. 495–509
   Based on AM 657c 4to with variants from AM 655 4to XXXIII
   (pp. 495.5–21, 504.20–505.31, 506.11–507.32).
Literature:
Finnur Jónsson. >> *Den oldnorske og oldislandske Litteraturs Historie* (1920–4). Vol. 2, p. 874.
Foote, Peter, ed. >> *Lives of Saints* (1962). P. 25.
Hreinn Benediktsson. "Tvö handritsbrot." *Lingua Islandica – Íslenzk tunga* 5 (1964): 139–49, esp. pp. 144–8.
Jakob Benediktsson. "Helgener." *KLNM* 21 (1977). Cols. 194–5, esp. col. 194.

Lehmann, Paul. >> "Skandinaviens Anteil an der lateinischen Literatur und Wissenschaft des Mittelalters" (1937). Pp. 44–5.

Mogk, Eugen. >> *Geschichte der norwegisch-isländischen Literatur* (1904). P. 892.

Orchard, Andy. "Hot Lust in a Cold Climate: Comparison and Contrast in the Old Norse Version of the Life of Mary of Egypt." In *The Legend of Mary of Egypt in Medieval Insular Hagiography*. Ed. Erich Poppe and Bianca Ross (Dublin: Four Courts Press, 1996). Pp. 175–204.

Wolf, Kirsten, ed. "Anonymous, *Heilagra meyja drápa* 'Drápa about Holy Maidens'." In Margaret Clunies Ross, ed. >> *Poetry on Christian Subjects* (2007). Vol. 2, pp. 891–930, esp. p. 902.

Handlist, p. 324.

2. Maríu saga egipzku

A translation of a form of the *vita*, *BHL* Suppl. 5417d, which is considered to be an extract of *BHL* 5417, with some use also of *BHL* 5415. The legend is related to 1 and 3, but seems to have independent textual value.

Manuscript:
AM 238 fol. I (ca. 1300).
Edition:
Unger, C.R., ed. >> *Heilagra manna søgur* (1877). Vol. 1, pp. 510–12.
Literature:

Carlé, Birte. >> *Jomfru-fortællingen* (1985). P. 34.

Foote, Peter, ed. >> *Lives of Saints* (1962). P. 25.

Jakob Benediktsson. "Helgener." *KLNM* 21 (1977). Cols. 194–5, esp. col. 194.

Lehmann, Paul. >> "Skandinaviens Anteil an der lateinischen Literatur und Wissenschaft des Mittelalters" (1937). Pp. 44–5.

Mogk, Eugen. >> *Geschichte der norwegisch-isländischen Literatur* (1904). P. 892.

Orchard, Andy. "Hot Lust in a Cold Climate: Comparison and Contrast in the Old Norse Version of the Life of Mary of Egypt." In *The Legend of Mary of Egypt in Medieval Insular Hagiography*. Ed. Erich Poppe and Bianca Ross (Dublin: Four Courts Press, 1996). Pp. 175–204.

Wolf, Kirsten, ed. "Anonymous, *Heilagra meyja drápa* 'Drápa about Holy Maidens'." In Margaret Clunies Ross, ed. >> *Poetry on Christian Subjects* (2007). Vol. 2, pp. 891–930, esp. p. 902.

Handlist, p. 324.

3. Maríu saga egipzku I

A translation of a form of the *vita*, *BHL* Suppl. 5417d, which is
considered to be an extract of *BHL* 5417, with some use also of
BHL 5415. It is not as close to the Latin as 1, but it sometimes has a
better text.

Manuscripts:
AM 235 fol. (ca. 1400, defective) and Stock. Perg. fol. no. 2 (ca. 1425–45).
Editions:
Foote, Peter, ed. >> *Lives of Saints* (1962).
   Facsimile of Stock. Perg. fol. no. 2.
Unger, C.R., ed. >> *Heilagra manna søgur* (1877). Vol. 1, pp. 482–95.
   Based on Stock. Perg. fol. no. 2 with variants from AM 235 fol. (pp. 487.25–
   495.2).
Modern Icelandic language edition:
Wolf, Kirsten, ed. >> *Heilagra meyja sögur* (2003). Pp. 25–39.
Danish translation:
Carlé, Birte. *Skøger og jomfruer i den kristne fortællekunst* (Odense: Odense
   Universitetsforlag, 1991). Pp. 56–69.
Literature:
Ásdís Egilsdóttir. "Kvendýrlingar og kvenímynd trúarlegra bókmennta á
   Íslandi." In Inga Huld Hákonardóttir, ed. >> *Konur og kristsmenn*
   (1996). Pp. 93–116, esp. pp. 100–2.
Carlé, Birte. "Fra slægtssaga til kvindesaga." In Silja Aðalsteinsdóttir and
   Helgi Þorláksson, ed. >> *Forändringar i kvinnors villkor under medel-
   tiden* (1983). Pp. 55–70, esp. pp. 56, 62, and 66–7.
– >> *Jomfru-fortællingen* (1985). Pp. 38, 40–1, 75, and 78–9.
– "Some Observations Regarding Narrative Patterns in the Medieval
   Sagas of Holy Maids." In Régis Boyer, ed. >> *Les Sagas de Chevaliers
   (Riddarasögur)* (1985). Pp. 393–404, esp. p. 395.
– "Men and Women in the Saints' Sagas of *Stock. 2, fol.*" In John
   Lindow, Lars Lönnroth, and Gerd Wolfgang Weber, ed. >> *Structure
   and Meaning in Old Norse Literature* (1986). Pp. 317–46, esp. pp. 318,
   320, 322, 338, and 340–1.
Finnur Jónsson. >> *Den oldnorske og oldislandske Litteraturs Historie*
   (1920–4). Vol. 2, p. 874.
Jakob Benediktsson. "Helgener." *KLNM* 21 (1977). Cols. 194–5, esp.
   col. 194.

Jón Viðar Sigurðsson. "Utenlandske kvinnehelgener på Island i høymiddelalderen." In >> *Samtíðarsögur* (1994). Vol. 2, pp. 423–34, esp. pp. 431–2.

– *Den vennlige vikingen: Vennskapets makt i Norge og på Island ca. 900–1300* (Oslo: Pax Forlag, 2010). P. 119.

Kirby, Ian. >> *Biblical Quotation* (1980). Vol. 2, p. 43.

Lehmann, Paul. >> "Skandinaviens Anteil an der lateinischen Literatur und Wissenschaft des Mittelalters" (1937). Pp. 44–5.

Mogk, Eugen. >> *Geschichte der norwegisch-isländischen Literatur* (1904). P. 892.

Orchard, Andy. "Hot Lust in a Cold Climate: Comparison and Contrast in the Old Norse Version of the Life of Mary of Egypt." In *The Legend of Mary of Egypt in Medieval Insular Hagiography*. Ed. Erich Poppe and Bianca Ross (Dublin: Four Courts Press, 1996). Pp. 175–204.

Sverrir Jakobsson. *Við og veröldin: Heimsmynd Íslendinga 1100–1400* (Reykjavík: Háskólaútgáfan, 2005). P. 146.

Sverrir Tómasson. "Kristnar trúarbókmenntir í óbundnu máli." In Guðrún Nordal, Sverrir Tómasson, and Vésteinn Ólason, ed. >> *Íslensk Bókmenntasaga* 1 (1992). Pp. 419–79, esp. pp. 466–9.

Wolf, Kirsten, ed. "Anonymous, *Heilagra meyja drápa* 'Drápa about Holy Maidens'." In Margaret Clunies Ross, ed. >> *Poetry on Christian Subjects* (2007). Vol. 2, pp. 891–930, esp. pp. 901–2.

Handlist, p. 324.

4. Af Maríu egipzku

A tale of Saint Mary of Egypt incorporated into the miracles of the Virgin Mary.

Manuscripts:
See Mary the Blessed Virgin 3 note (p. 245).
Edition:
Unger, C.R., ed. >> *Mariu saga* (1871). Pp. 895.25–900.24.
Literature:
Jakob Benediktsson. "Helgener." *KLNM* 21 (1977). Cols. 194–5, esp. col. 194.

Kirby, Ian. >> *Biblical Quotation* (1980). Vol. 2, pp. 43n12 and 77.

Handlist, p. 324.

MARY OF OIGNIES   June 23

Af Maríu de Oegines

A tale of Saint Mary of Oignies incorporated into the miracles of the
Virgin Mary. The source appears to be a condensed version of *BHL* 5516.

Manuscripts:
See Mary the Blessed Virgin 3 note (p. 245).
Edition:
Unger, C.R., ed. >> *Mariu saga* (1871). Pp. 917.26–920.
Literature:
Piebenga, Gryt Anne. "Om den norrøne oversettelsen av noen fragmenter
    av *Vita Mariae Oigniacensis*." *Mm* (1988): 174–84.
Wolf, Kirsten, ed. >> *Heilagra meyja sögur* (2003). Pp. xlii–xliv and lvi.
Handlist, p. 324.

MATERNUS   September 14

1. Um Maternus

A short tale of Saint Maternus included in *Máritíuss saga* 1.

Manuscripts:
See Maurice note (p. 257).
Edition:
Unger, C.R., ed. >> *Heilagra manna søgur* (1877). Vol. 1,
    pp. 654.34–655.2.
Literature:
Foote, Peter. "A Fragment of Text in AM 235 fol." In *Twenty-eight Papers
    Presented to Hans Bekker-Nielsen on the Occasion of His Sixtieth
    Birthday 28 April 1993* (Odense: Odense University Press, 1993).
    Pp. 237–55, esp. pp. 248–9.

2. Um Maternus

A short tale of Saint Maternus derived from Honorius Augustodunensis'
Speculum Ecclesiae incorporated into *Pétrs saga postula I*.

Manuscripts:
See Peter the Apostle 5 note (p. 317).
Edition:
Unger, C.R., ed. >> *Postola sögur* (1874). P. 83.4–17.
Literature:
Foote, Peter, ed. >> *Lives of Saints* (1962). P. 28.
– "A Fragment of Text in AM 235 fol." In *Twenty-eight Papers Presented to Hans Bekker-Nielsen on the Occasion of His Sixtieth Birthday 28 April 1993* (Odense: Odense University Press, 1993). Pp. 237–55, esp. pp. 248–9.

MATTHEW   September 21

Matheuss saga postola

A translation of a version of *BHL* 5690.

Manuscripts:
AM 628 4to (1711–12), AM 629 4to (1697), AM 630 4to (ca. 1650–1700), AM 645 4to (ca. 1220), AM 652 4to (ca. 1250–70, defective), AM 655 4to IX (ca. 1150–1200), AM 655 4to XII–XIII (ca. 1250–75), AM 656 4to I (ca. 1325–50), Rask 69 (ca. 1800), and SÁM 1 fol. (*Codex Scardensis*) (ca. 1350–75).

Editions:

Holtsmark, Anne, ed. *A Book of Miracles: MS No. 645 4ᵗᵒ of the Arna-Magnæan Collection in the University Library of Copenhagen.* CCI 12 (Copenhagen: Einar Munksgaard, 1938).
Facsimile of AM 645 4to.

Hreinn Benediktsson. *Early Icelandic Script As Illustrated in Vernacular Texts from the Twelfth and Thirteenth Centuries.* Íslenzk handrit: Icelandic Manuscripts, Series in Folio 2 (Reykjavík: The Manuscript Institute of Iceland, 1965). Plate 27.
Facsimile of AM 645 4to fol. 38r.

Larsson, Ludvig, ed. *Isländska handskriften Nᵒ 645 4ᵒ i Den Ar-namagnæanske Samlingen på Universitetsbiblioteket i København: I. Handskriftens äldre del* (Lund: Gleerup, 1885). Pp. 108.6–124.18.
Edition of AM 645 4to.

Ólafur Halldórsson, ed. *Mattheus saga postula* (Reykjavík: Stofnun Árna Magnússonar, 1994). Pp. 4–83.

Diplomatic edition based on AM 645 4to with variants from AM 652
4to, AM 655 4to IX, AM 656 I 4to, and SÁM 1 fol., and also AM 630
4to (where there are lacunae in AM 652 4to) and AM 628 4to (where
SÁM is damaged) on pp. 4–68 (recto). Reconstructed, normalized text
on pp. 5–69 (verso). Edition of AM 655 4to XII–XIII (pp. 73–83).
Slay, Desmond, ed. *Codex Scardensis*. EIM 2 (Copenhagen: Rosenkilde
and Bagger, 1960).
Facsimile of SÁM 1 fol.
Þorsteinn Jónsson, ed. *Hér hefjast Tíu Sögur, af þeim enum heiløgu Guds
Postulum og pínslar vottum* (Viðeyjarklaustur: Þ. Jónsson, 1836).
Pp. 211–26.
Based on a manuscript descended from AM 630 4to.
Unger, C.R., ed. >> *Postola sögur* (1874). Pp. 797–841.
Edition of AM 630 4to with variants from AM 628 4to (pp. 797.24–
807.5). Edition of AM 652 4to (pp. 807.7–813.5). Edition of AM 645
4to (pp. 813.8–823.8). Edition of AM 655 4to IX (pp. 823.10–825.5).
Edition of AM 656 4to I (pp. 825.7–834.6). Edition of AM 655 4to
XII–XIII (pp. 834.8–641).
Modern Icelandic language edition:
Ólafur Halldórsson, ed. *Sögur úr Skarðsbók* (Reykjavík: Almenna
bókafélagið, 1967). Pp. 207–20.
Edition of SÁM 1 fol.
English translation:
Roughton, Philip G. "AM 645 4to and AM 652/630 4to: Study and
Translation of Two Thirteenth-Century Icelandic Collections of
Apostles' and Saints' Lives." PhD dissertation, University of Colorado,
2002. Pp. 811–30.
Literature:
Battista, Simonetta. "Old Norse Hagiography and the Question of the
Latin Sources." In Rudolf Simek and Judith Meurer, ed. >> *Scandi-
navia and Christian Europe in the Middle Ages* (2003). Pp. 26–33, esp.
pp. 27–8.
– "The *Compilator* and Contemporary Literary Culture in Old Norse
Hagiography." *Viking and Medieval Scandinavia* 1 (2005): 1–13, esp.
pp. 3–4, and 6.
Bekker-Nielsen, Hans. "Et par ord om de ældste norrøne helgensagaer."
In Finn Hødnebø et al., ed. >> *Eyvindarbók* (1992). Pp. 29–33, esp.
p. 32.
Bekker-Nielsen, Hans, Thorkil Damsgaard Olsen, and Ole Widding.
>> *Norrøn fortællekunst* (1965). Pp. 17 and 122–3.

Bekker-Nielsen, Hans, and Ole Widding. "Legende. Norge og Island."
    KLNM 10 (1965). Cols. 421–3, esp. col. 422.
– "Religiøs prosalitteratur. Norge og Island." *KLNM* 14 (1969). Cols.
    42–4, esp. col. 42.
Boyer, Régis. >> *La vie religieuse en Islande* (1979). P. 224.
Collings, Lucy Grace. "The Codex Scardensis: Studies in Icelandic
    Hagiography." PhD dissertation, Cornell University, 1969. Pp. 28–30
    and 199–207.
Cormack, Margaret. >> *The Saints in Iceland* (1994). Pp. 33, 131,
    and 243.
Eiríkr Magnússon. "Kodex Skardensis af postulasögur." *ANF* 8 (1892):
    238–45, esp. p. 241.
Finnur Jónsson. >> *Den oldnorske og oldislandske Litteraturs Historie*
    (1920–4). Vol. 2, pp. 872–3.
Foote, Peter. "Postulatal." In Guðni Kolbeinsson, ed. >> *Minjar og
    menntir* (1976). Pp. 152–73, esp. p. 169.
Hallberg, Peter. "Imagery in Religious Old Norse Prose Literature: An
    Outline." *ANF* 102 (1987): 120–70, esp. p. 130.
Holm-Olsen, Ludvig. "Apostelsagaer." *KLNM* 1 (1956). Cols. 177–8, esp.
    col. 178.
Jón Hnefill Aðalsteinsson. "Blot i forna skrifter." *SI* 47 (1996): 11–32,
    esp. pp. 20–1.
Jón Ma. Ásgeirsson and Þórður Ingi Guðjónsson, ed. *Frá Sýrlandi til
    Íslands: Arfur Tómasar postula* (Reykjavík: Háskólaútgáfan, 2007).
    Pp. 164–5, 174–5, and 189.
Jón Þorkelsson. "Islandske håndskrifter i England og Skotland." *ANF* 8
    (1892): 199–237, esp. pp. 235–6.
Jónas Kristjánsson. "Learned Style or Saga Style?" In Ursula Dronke,
    Guðrún P. Helgadóttir, Gerd Wolfgang Weber, and Hans Bekker-
    Nielsen, ed. >> *Specvlvm Norroenvm* (1981). Pp. 260–92.
– >> *Eddas and Sagas* (1988). Pp. 140 and 148.
Jørgensen, Jørgen Højgaard. "Hagiography and the Icelandic Bishop
    Sagas." *Peritia* 1 (1982): 1–16, esp. p. 3.
Kirby, Ian. >> *Biblical Quotation* (1980). Vol. 2, pp. 17–19 and 35–6.
– *Bible Translation in Old Norse*. Université de Lausanne Publications de
    la faculté des lettres 27 (Geneva: Librairie Droz, 1986). P. 34
– "The Bible and Biblical Interpretation in Medieval Iceland." In *Old
    Icelandic Literature and Society*. Ed. Margaret Clunies Ross (Cam-
    bridge: Cambridge University Press, 2000). Pp. 287–301, esp. p. 295.
Lehmann, Paul. >> "Skandinaviens Anteil an der lateinischen Literatur
    und Wissenschaft des Mittelalters" (1937). P. 80.

Louis-Jensen, Jonna. "To håndskrifter fra det nordvestlige Island." *Opuscula* 7. Bibliotheca Arnamagnæana 34 (Copenhagen: Reitzel, 1979). Pp. 219–53, esp. p. 221.

Mogk, Eugen. >> *Geschichte der norwegisch-isländischen Literatur* (1904). P. 889.

Ólafur Halldórsson. *Helgafellsbækur fornar*. Studia Islandica 24 (Reykjavík: Heimspekideild Háskóla Íslands and Menningarsjóður, 1966). Pp. 16–22 and 41–5.

Poli, Diego. "Linearizzazione sintattica, flessione degli antroponimi e formule liturgiche nella *Matheus saga postola*." In *Cultura Classica e Cultura Germanica Settentrionale*. Ed. Pietro Janni, Diego Poli, and Carlo Santini (Macerata: Herder, 1985). Pp. 425–49.

Roughton, Philip. "Stylistics and Sources of the *Postola sögur* in AM 645 4to and AM 652/630 4to." *Gripla* 16 (2005): 7–50.

– "'Þá syndi hann þeim mikinn skugga': Unmasking the Fantastic in the *Postola sögur*." In John McKinnell, David Ashurst, and Donata Kick, ed. >> *The Fantastic in Old Norse/Icelandic Literature* (2006). Vol. 2, pp. 846–55, esp. p. 847.

Sverrir Jakobsson. *Við og veröldin: Heimsmynd Íslendinga 1100–1400* (Reykjavík: Háskólaútgáfan, 2005). P. 288.

Turville-Petre, G. >> *Origins of Icelandic Literature* (1967). Pp. 130–1.

Þórður Ingi Guðjónsson. "Apostlene i islandsk middelalderlitteratur." In *Den nordiske renessansen i høymiddelalderen*. Ed. Jón Viðar Sigurðsson and Preben Meulengracht Sørensen (Oslo: Historisk institutt, Universitetet i Oslo, 2000). Pp. 83–99, esp. pp. 93–5.

Vries, Jan de. >> *Altnordische Literaturgeschichte* (1964–7). Vol. 2, p. 183.

Widding, Ole, and Hans Bekker-Nielsen. "Low German Influence on Late Icelandic Hagiography." *GR* 37 (1962): 239–62, esp. p. 240.

Wolf, Kirsten. "Postola sögur." In Phillip Pulsiano, Kirsten Wolf, Paul Acker, and Donald K. Fry, ed. >> *Medieval Scandinavia* (1993). Pp. 511–2.

– "Skarðsbók." In Phillip Pulsiano and Kirsten Wolf, with Paul Acker and Donald K. Fry, ed. >> *Medieval Scandinavia* (1993). P. 596.

Handlist, pp. 324–5.

MATTHIAS   February 24

1. Mathíass saga postola I

A homiletic version based on the source of the *vita* composed by Lambertus Parvus a Legio (*BHL* 5698).

Manuscripts:
AM 629 4to (1697), AM 630 4to (ca. 1650–1700), AM 659a 4to (ca. 1600–
50, defective), and Rask 69 (ca. 1800, defective).

Editions:
Þorsteinn Jónsson, ed. *Hér hefjast Tíu Sögur, af þeim enum heiløgu Guds
Postulum og pínslar vottum* (Viðeyjarklaustur: Þ. Jónsson, 1836).
Pp. 237–53.
Based on a manuscript descended from AM 630 4to.
Unger, C.R., ed. >> *Postola sögur* (1874). Pp. 767–775.3.
Edition of AM 630 4to.

English translation:
Roughton, Philip G. "AM 645 4to and AM 652/630 4to: Study and
Translation of Two Thirteenth-Century Icelandic Collections of
Apostles' and Saints' Lives." PhD dissertation, University of Colo-
rado, 2002. Pp. 775–90.

Literature:
Collings, Lucy. "A Legend from Trier in Old Norse Postola Sögur." *MScand*
6 (1973): 109–21.
Cormack, Margaret. >> *The Saints in Iceland* (1994). Pp. 33, 131, and 243.
Finnur Jónsson. >> *Den oldnorske og oldislandske Litteraturs Historie*
(1920–4). Vol. 2, p. 872.
Kirby, Ian. >> *Biblical Quotation* (1980). Vol. 2, p. 34.
Lehmann, Paul. >> "Skandinaviens Anteil an der lateinischen Literatur
und Wissenschaft des Mittelalters" (1937). P. 19.
Mogk, Eugen. >> *Geschichte der norwegisch-isländischen Literatur* (1904).
P. 889.
Ólafur Halldórsson, ed. *Mattheus saga postula* (Reykjavík: Stofnun Árna
Magnússonar, 1994). Pp. xxxvi–xli and lxxv–lxxxi.
Roughton, Philip. "Stylistics and Sources of the *Postola sögur* in AM 645
4to and AM 652/630 4to." *Gripla* 16 (2005): 7–50.
Sverrir Tómasson. *Formálar íslenskra sagnaritara á miðöldum. Rannsókn
bókmenntahefðar* (Reykjavík: Stofnun Árna Magnússonar, 1988). P. 346.
Wolf, Kirsten. "Postola sögur." In Phillip Pulsiano and Kirsten Wolf, with Paul
Acker and Donald K. Fry, ed. >> *Medieval Scandinavia* (1993). Pp. 511–12.
Handlist, p. 325.

2. Mathíass saga postola II

Based on the source of the *vita* composed by Lambertus Parvus a Legio
(*BHL* 5698) but abbreviated and reworked in a fashion different from 1.

Manuscripts:
AM 238 fol. X (ca. 1300–50), AM 628 4to (1711–12), and SÁM 1 fol.
   (*Codex Scardensis*) (ca. 1350–75).

Editions:
Slay, Desmond, ed. *Codex Scardensis*. EIM 2 (Copenhagen: Rosenkilde
   and Bagger, 1960).
   Facsimile of SÁM 1 fol.
Unger, C.R., ed. >> *Postola sögur* (1874). Pp. 775.5–778.
   Edition of AM 628 4to with variants from AM 238 fol. X (pp.
   775.15–778.16).

Modern Icelandic language edition:
Ólafur Halldórsson, ed. *Sögur úr Skarðsbók* (Reykjavík: Almenna bókafé-
   lagið, 1967). Pp. 186–91.
   Edition of SÁM 1 fol.

Literature:
Bekker-Nielsen, Hans, Thorkil Damsgaard Olsen, and Ole Widding.
   >> *Norrøn fortællekunst* (1965). P. 123.
Collings, Lucy Grace. "The Codex Scardensis: Studies in Icelandic
   Hagiography." PhD dissertation, Cornell University, 1969. Pp. 53–62
   and 213–22.
– "A Legend from Trier in Old Norse Postola Sögur." *MScand* 6 (1973):
   109–21.
Cormack, Margaret. >> *The Saints in Iceland* (1994). Pp. 37n45, 77n12,
   131, and 243.
Eiríkr Magnússon. "Kodex Skardensis af postulasögur." *ANF* 8 (1892):
   238–45, esp. p. 241.
Finnur Jónsson. >> *Den oldnorske og oldislandske Litteraturs Historie*
   (1920–4). Vol. 2, p. 872.
Jón Þorkelsson. "Islandske håndskrifter i England og Skotland." *ANF* 8
   (1892): 199–237, esp. pp. 235–6.
Kirby, Ian. >> *Biblical Quotation* (1980). Vol. 2, p. 35.
Mogk, Eugen. >> *Geschichte der norwegisch-isländischen Literatur* (1904).
   P. 889.
Ólafur Halldórsson. *Helgafellsbækur fornar*. Studia Islandica 24 (Reykjavík:
   Heimspekideild Háskóla Íslands and Menningarsjóður, 1966). Pp. 16–
   22 and 41– 5.
Ólafur Halldórsson, ed. *Mattheus saga postula* (Reykjavík: Stofnun Árna
   Magnússonar, 1994). P. xlix.
Sverrir Tómasson. *Formálar íslenskra sagnaritara á miðöldum. Rannsókn
   bókmenntahefðar* (Reykjavík: Stofnun Árna Magnússonar, 1988). P. 346.

Wolf, Kirsten. "Postola sögur." In Phillip Pulsiano and Kirsten Wolf, with Paul
    Acker and Donald K. Fry, ed. >> *Medieval Scandinavia* (1993). Pp. 511–12.
– "Skarðsbók." In Phillip Pulsiano and Kirsten Wolf, with Paul Acker
    and Donald K. Fry, ed. >> *Medieval Scandinavia* (1993). P. 596.
Handlist, p. 325.

MAURICE   September 22

1. Máritíuss saga

A translation of *BHL* 5740–7. The text followed is closest to *BHL* 5746.

Manuscript:
AM 655 4to X (ca. 1250–1300).
Editions:
Hreinn Benediktsson. *Early Icelandic Script As Illustrated in Vernacular
    Texts from the Twelfth and Thirteenth Centuries.* Íslenzk handrit:
    Icelandic Manuscripts, Series in Folio 2 (Reykjavík: The Manuscript
    Institute of Iceland, 1965). Plate 65 and pp. xliii–xliv.
    Facsimile and text edition of fol. 1r.
Unger, C.R., ed. >> *Heilagra manna søgur* (1877). Vol. 1, pp. 656.25–658.
Literature:
Bekker-Nielsen, Hans, Thorkil Damsgaard Olsen, and Ole Widding.
    >> *Norrøn fortællekunst* (1965). P.124.
Cormack, Margaret. >> *The Saints in Iceland* (1994). Pp. 34, 37n45, 132,
    and 243.
Finnur Jónsson. >> *Den oldnorske og oldislandske Litteraturs Historie*
    (1920–4). Vol. 2, p. 874.
Foote, Peter, ed. >> *Lives of Saints* (1962). P. 28.
· Hreinn Benediktsson. "Tvö handritsbrot." *Lingua Islandica – Íslenzk
    tunga* 5 (1964): 139–49, esp. pp. 140–4 and 147–8.
Kirby, Ian. >> *Biblical Quotation* (1980). Vol. 2, p. 44.
Mogk, Eugen. >> *Geschichte der norwegisch-isländischen Literatur* (1904).
    P. 891.
Tucker, John J. "Scribal Hands in AM 655 4to X." *Opuscula* 6. Biblioth-
    eca Arnamagnæana 33 (Copenhagen: Reitzel, 1979). Pp. 108–25.
Widding, Ole. "Håndskriftanalyser." *Opuscula* 1. Bibliotheca
    Arnamagnæana 20 (Copenhagen: Munksgaard, 1960). Pp. 81–96,
    esp. pp. 84–5.

Wolf, Kirsten, ed. "Anonymous, *Heilagra manna drápa* 'Drápa' about Holy Men." In Margaret Clunies Ross, ed. >> *Poetry on Christian Subjects* (2007). Vol. 2, pp. 872–90, esp. p. 890.
Handlist, p. 325.
NOTE:
The saga includes a short tale of Saint Maternus. See the entry for this saint.

2. Máritíuss saga

An adaptation and conflation of 1 and a free translation of *BHL* 3446.

Manuscripts:
AM 235 fol. (ca. 1400) and Stock. Perg. fol. no. 2 (ca. 1425–45, defective).
Editions:
Foote, Peter, ed. >> *Lives of Saints* (1962).
    Facsimile of Stock. Perg. fol. no. 2.
Unger, C.R., ed. >> *Heilagra manna søgur* (1877). Vol. 1, pp. 643–656.22. Based on AM 235 fol. with variants from Stock. Perg. fol. no. 2 (pp. 644.22–645.21).
Literature:
Bekker-Nielsen, Hans, Thorkil Damsgaard Olsen, and Ole Widding. >> *Norrøn fortællekunst* (1965). Pp. 124 and 126.
Carlé, Birte. >> *Jomfru-fortællingen* (1985). Pp. 38–41.
– "Men and Women in the Saints' Sagas of *Stock. 2, fol.*" In John Lindow, Lars Lönnroth, and Gerd Wolfgang Weber, ed. >> *Structure and Meaning in Old Norse Literature* (1986). Pp. 317–46, esp. pp. 319 and 321.
Cormack, Margaret. >> *The Saints in Iceland* (1994). Pp. 34, 132, and 243.
Finnur Jónsson. >> *Den oldnorske og oldislandske Litteraturs Historie* (1920–4). Vol. 2, p. 874.
Kirby, Ian. >> *Biblical Quotation* (1980). Vol. 2, p. 44.
Mogk, Eugen. >> *Geschichte der norwegisch-isländischen Literatur* (1904). P. 891.
Stefán Karlsson. "Inventio Crucis, cap 1, og Veraldar saga." In *Opuscula Septentrionalia: Festskrift til Ole Widding 10.10.1977* (Copenhagen: Reitzél, 1977). Pp. 116–33, esp. pp. 130–3.
Van Deusen, Natalie M. "Stitches in the Margins: The Embroidery Pattern in AM 235 fol." *Mm* (2011–12): 26–42, esp. p. 29.

Wolf, Kirsten, ed. "Anonymous, *Heilagra manna drápa* 'Drápa' about Holy Men." In Margaret Clunies Ross, ed. >> *Poetry on Christian Subjects* (2007). Vol. 2, pp. 872–90, esp. p. 890.
Handlist, p. 325.
NOTE:
The saga includes the passion of Saint Gereon. See the entry for this saint.

MAURUS   January 15

Máruss saga

Based on *BHL* 5773 with the introductory epistle and the prologue omitted.

Manuscript:
Stock. Perg. fol. no. 2 (ca. 1425–45).
Editions:
Foote, Peter, ed. >> *Lives of Saints* (1962).
   Facsimile.
Unger, C.R., ed. >> *Heilagra manna søgur* (1877). Vol. 1, pp. 659–75.
Modern Icelandic language edition:
Sverrir Tómasson, Bragi Halldórsson, and Einar Sigurbjörnsson, ed.
   >> *Heilagra karla sögur* (2007). Pp. 111–33.
Literature:
Carlé, Birte. >> *Jomfru-fortællingen* (1985). Pp. 40 and 66.
– "Men and Women in the Saints' Sagas of *Stock. 2, fol.*" In John Lindow, Lars Lönnroth, and Gerd Wolfgang Weber, ed. >> *Structure and Meaning in Old Norse Literature* (1986). Pp. 317–46, esp. p. 320.
Jakob Benediktsson. "Helgener." *KLNM* 21 (1977). Cols. 194–5, esp. col. 194.
Kirby, Ian. >> *Biblical Quotation* (1980). Vol. 2, p. 45.
Magerøy, Hallvard. "In dedicatione ecclesiæ sermo. Om overleveringa av Stavkyrkjepreika." *Opuscula* 8. Bibliotheca Arnamagnæana 38 (Copenhagen: Reitzel, 1985). Pp. 96–122, esp. p. 114.
Mogk, Eugen. >> *Geschichte der norwegisch-isländischen Literatur* (1904). P. 893.
Handlist, p. 325.

MICHAEL THE ARCHANGEL   September 29

Mikjáls saga

A compilation ascribed to Abbot Bergr Sokkason (d. ca. 1370) from
a variety of sources.

Manuscripts:
AM 657a–b 4to (ca. 1350), AM 657c 4to (ca. 1340–90, defective), and
  Stock. Perg. 8vo no. 10 V (ca. 1400).
Edition:
Unger, C.R., ed. >> *Heilagra manna søgur* (1877). Vol. 1, pp. 676–713.
  Based on AM 657a–b 4to with variants from AM 657c 4to (pp.
  707.29–713).
Literature:
Battista, Simonetta. "*Blámenn, djǫflar* and Other Representations of Evil
  in Old Norse Literature." In John McKinnell, David Ashurst, and
  Donata Kick, ed. >> *The Fantastic in Old Norse/Icelandic Literature*
  (2006). Vol. 1, pp. 113–22, esp. p. 115.
Boyer, Régis. >> *La vie religieuse en Islande* (1979). Pp. 146 and 283.
Cormack, Margaret. >> *The Saints in Iceland* (1994). Pp. 32, 72, and 133.
– "Saints' Lives and Icelandic Literature in the Thirteenth and Four-
  teenth Centuries." In Hans Bekker-Nielsen and Birte Carlé, ed.
  >> *Saints and Sagas* (1994). Pp. 27–47, esp. pp. 32–3.
– "Sagas of Saints." In *Old Icelandic Literature and Society*. Ed.
  Margaret Clunies Ross (Cambridge: Cambridge University Press,
  2000). Pp. 302–25, esp. pp. 302–3 and 310.
– "Christian Biography." In *A Companion to Old Norse–Icelandic
  Literature and Culture*. Ed. Rory McTurk (Oxford: Blackwell, 2005).
  Pp. 27–42, esp. pp. 32 and 38.
Fell, Christine. "Bergr Sokkason's *Michaels saga* and Its Sources."
  Saga-Book 16 (1962–5): 354–71.
Foote, Peter G. *The Pseudo-Turpin Chronicle in Iceland: A Contribution to
  the Study of the Karlamagnús saga*. London Mediæval Studies: Mono-
  graph No. 4 (University College London: London Mediæval Studies,
  1954). Pp. 22–4.
Gad, Tue. "Mikael." *KLNM* 11 (1966). Cols. 616–20, esp. col. 619.
Hallberg, Peter. *Stilsignalement och författarskap i norrön sagalitteratur:
  Synpunkter och exempel*. Nordistica Gothoburgensia 3 (Stockholm:

Almqvist & Wiksell, 1968). Pp. 128–37, 140, 149, 161–6, 181, 188–9, 231, and 232.

– "Jóns saga helga." In *Afmælisrit Jóns Helgasonar 30. júní 1969*. Ed. Jakob Benediktsson et al. (Reykjavík: Heimskringla, 1969). Pp. 59–79, esp. pp. 63 and 73–9.

– "Om Magnúss saga helga." In *Einarsbók: Afmæliskveðja til Einars Ól. Sveinssonar 12. desember 1969*. Ed. Bjarni Guðnason, Halldór Halldórsson, and Jónas Kristjánsson ([Reykjavík]: Nokkrir vinir, 1969). Pp. 59–70, esp. p. 59.

– "Some Observations on the Language of *Dunstanus saga*, with an Appendix on the Bible Compilation *Stjórn*." *Saga-Book* 18 (1973): 324–53, esp. pp. 324–32, 335–44, and 349–52.

– "Imagery in Religious Old Norse Prose Literature: An Outline." *ANF* 102 (1987): 120–70, esp. pp. 122, 126, 131–2, 136, 140, and 146–51.

– "Bergr Sokkason and Religious Icelandic Literature." In >> *Samtíðarsögur* (1994). Vol. 1, pp. 396–300, esp. p. 296.

Halvorsen, E.F. *The Norse Version of the Chanson de Roland*. Bibliotheca Arnamagnæana 19 (Copenhagen: Ejnar Munksgaard, 1959). Pp. 46, 48–9, and 75.

Jakob Benediktsson. "Cursus hos Bergr Sokkason." In *Festskrift til Ludvig Holm-Olsen på hans 70-årsdag den 9. juni 1984* (Øvre Ervik: Alvheim & Eide, 1984). Pp. 34–40. Rpt. in Jakob Benediktsson. *Lærdómslistir. Afmælisrit 20. júlí 1987* (Reykjavík: Mál og menning, 1987). Pp. 262–9.

Jón Ma. Ásgeirsson and Þórður Ingi Guðjónsson, ed. *Frá Sýrlandi til Íslands: Arfur Tómasar postula* (Reykjavík: Háskólaútgáfan, 2007). P. 140.

Jónas Kristjánsson. *Um Fóstbræðra sögu* (Reykjavík: Stofnun Árna Magnússonar, 1972). Pp. 261, 268, 290, and 304–6.

Kalinke, Marianne E. >> *The Book of Reykjahólar* (1996). P. 38.

Kirby, Ian. >> *Biblical Quotation* (1980). Vol. 2, p. 45.

– *Bible Translation in Old Norse*. Université de Lausanne Publications de la faculté des lettres 27 (Geneva: Librairie Droz, 1986). Pp. 6 and 46.

Lehmann, Paul. >> "Skandinaviens Anteil an der lateinischen Literatur und Wissenschaft des Mittelalters" (1937). P. 45.

Louis-Jensen, Jonna. "Nogle ævintýri." *Opuscula* 5. Bibliotheca Arnamagnæana 31 (Copenhagen: Munksgaard, 1975). Pp. 263–77, esp. p. 263.

Mogk, Eugen. >> *Geschichte der norwegisch-isländischen Literatur* (1904). P. 890.

Mundal, Else. "Legender, helgenkult og misjonsstrategi i kristningstida."
In *Selja – heilag stad i 1000 år*. Ed. Magnus Rindal (Oslo: Universitetsforlaget, 1997). Pp. 77–101, esp. pp. 84–5 and 99.

* Musset, Lucien. "La saga de Saint-Michel par Bergr Sokkason, abbé
de Munkathverâ." *Millénaire monastique du Mont Saint-Michel* 2
(Paris: Lethielleux, 1967). Pp. 435–8.

Stefán Karlsson. "Icelandic Lives of Thomas a Becket: Questions of
Authorship." In Peter Foote, Hermann Pálsson, and Desmond Slay, ed.
>> *Proceedings of the First International Saga Conference* (1973).
Pp. 212–43, esp. p. 237. Rpt. in *Stafkrókar: Ritgerðir eftir Stefán
Karlsson gefnar út í tilefni af sjötugsafmæli hans 2. desember 1998*. Ed.
Guðvarður Már Gunnlaugsson (Reykjavík: Stofnun Árna Magnússo-
nar, 2000). Pp. 135–52, esp. p. 147.

Sverrir Tómasson. "Norðlenski Benediktínaskólinn." In >> *The Sixth
International Saga Conference* (1985). Vol. 2, pp. 1009–20, esp. p. 1012.
Rpt. in Sverrir Tómasson. *Tækileg vitni: Greinar um bókmenntir gefnar
út í tilefni sjötugsafmælis hans 5. apríl 2011* (Reykjavík: Stofnun Árna
Magnússonar and Hið íslenska bókmenntafélag, 2011). Pp. 345–58,
esp. pp. 347–8

– *Formálar íslenskra sagnaritara á miðöldum. Rannsókn bókmenntahefðar*
(Reykjavík: Stofnun Árna Magnússonar, 1988). Pp. 67, 95, 109, 130,
132, 233, 276, 307, 311, 333, and 346.

– "Kristnar trúarbókmenntir í óbundnu máli." In Guðrún Nordal,
Sverrir Tómasson, and Vésteinn Ólason, ed. >> *Íslensk Bókmenntasaga*
1 (1992). Pp. 419–79, esp. p. 422.

– "Trúarbókmenntir í lausu máli á síðmiðöld." In Böðvar Guðmundsson,
Sverrir Tómasson, Torfi H. Tulinius, and Vésteinn Ólason, ed.
>> *Íslensk Bókmenntasaga* 2 (1993). Pp. 249–82, esp. pp. 249–50,
252–3, and 255–7.

Sverrir Tómasson, Bragi Halldórsson, and Einar Sigurbjörnsson, ed.
>> *Heilagra karla sögur* (2007). P. xxii.

Tveitane, Mattias. "'Bonus'. Et latinsk Maria-dikt i norrøn prosaversjon."
Mm (1962): 109–21.

– "Visio Paulo og den norrøne Michaels saga." *Mm* (1963): 106–11.

– *Den lærde stil. Oversetterprosa i den norrøne versjonen av Vitæ Patrum*.
Årbok for Universitetet i Bergen, Humanistisk Serie 1967, No. 2
(Bergen and Oslo: Norwegian Universities Press, 1968). Pp. 21–3, 26,
and 129.

– "*Nocifer*, a Medieval Latin Word-Play." *Symbolae Osloensis* 44 (1969):
160–9.

Van Deusen, Natalie M. "'Inn besti hlutr'? Martha of Bethany and
Women's Roles in Medieval Iceland." *ANF* 126 (2011): 73–91, esp.
p. 88n23.
Widding, Ole. "St Michele at Gargano: As Seen from Iceland." *Analecta
Romana. Institvti-Danici* 13 (1984): 77–83, esp. pp. 81–2.
Handlist, p. 326.

NICHOLAS   December 6

1. Nikuláss saga erkibiskups

The direct sources have not been established.

Manuscripts:
AM 642a 4to II (ca. 1400), AM 655 4to III (ca. 1200), and AM 921 4to V
(ca. 1400; this manuscript has been demonstrated to belong to AM 235
fol.).

Editions:
Hreinn Benediktsson. *Early Icelandic Script As Illustrated in Vernacular
Texts from the Twelfth and Thirteenth Centuries.* Íslenzk handrit:
Icelandic Manuscripts, Series in Folio 2 (Reykjavík: The Manuscript
Institute of Iceland, 1965). Plate 18.
Facsimile of AM 655 4to fol. III, fol. 2r.
Loth, Agnete. "'Roted fragmentum membraneum, um Sanctam Luciam
og Agatham': AM 921, V, 4°." In *Festskrift til Ludvig Holm-Olsen på
hans 70-årsdag den 9. juni 1984* (Øvre Ervik: Alvheim & Eide, 1984).
Pp. 221–35, esp. pp. 224–226.7.
Edition of AM 921 4to V.
Morgenstern, Gustav, ed. >> *Arnamagnæanische Fragmente* (1893).
Pp. 1–7.
Edition of AM 655 4to III.
Unger, C.R., ed. >> *Heilagra manna søgur* (1877). Vol. 2, pp. 41.17–46.9.
Edition of AM 655 4to III.

Literature:
Bekker-Nielsen, Hans. "Et par ord om de ældste norrøne helgensagaer."
In Finn Hødnebø et al., ed. >> *Eyvindarbók* (1992). Pp. 29–33, esp.
p. 32.
Bekker-Nielsen, Hans, Thorkil Damsgaard Olsen, and Ole Widding.
>> *Norrøn fortællekunst* (1965). Pp. 23, 125, and 135.

Bekker-Nielsen, Hans, and Ole Widding. "Legende. Norge og Island."
    KLNM 10 (1965). Cols. 421–3, esp. col. 421.
– "Religiøs prosalitteratur. Norge og Island." *KLNM* 14 (1969). Cols.
    42–4, esp. col. 43.
Boyer, Régis. >> *La vie religieuse en Islande* (1979). P. 224.
Cormack, Margaret. >> *The Saints in Iceland* (1994). Pp. 33 and 137.
Foote, Peter, ed. >> *Lives of Saints* (1962). P. 21.
Gad, Tue. "Nicolaus af Myra." *KLNM* 12 (1967). Cols. 288–91, esp.
    col. 289.
Hallberg, Peter. *Stilsignalement och författarskap i norrön sagalitteratur:
    Synpunkter och exempel.* Nordistica Gothoburgensia 3 (Stockholm:
    Almqvist & Wiksell, 1968). Pp. 130–5 and 231–2.
– "Imagery in Religious Old Norse Prose Literature: An Outline." *ANF*
    102 (1987): 120–70, esp. p. 122.
– "Bergr Sokkason and Religious Icelandic Literature." In >>
    Samtíðarsögur (1994). Vol. 1, pp. 296–300, esp. p. 297.
Jónas Kristjánsson. "Learned Style or Saga Style?" In Ursula Dronke,
    Guðrún P. Helgadóttir, Gerd Wolfgang Weber, and Hans Bekker-
    Nielsen, ed. >> *Specvlvm Norroenvm* (1981). Pp. 260–92.
– >> *Eddas and Sagas* (1988). P. 139.
Mogk, Eugen. >> *Geschichte der norwegisch-isländischen Literatur* (1904).
    P. 892.
Sigfús Blöndal. "St. Nikulás og dýrkun hans, sérstaklega á Íslandi."
    Skírnir 123 (1949): 69–97, esp. p. 81.
Sverrir Tómasson. "Íslenskar Nikulás sögur." In *Helgastaðabók. Nikulás
    saga. Perg. 4to nr. 16 Konungsbókhlöðu í Stokkhólmi.* Introduction by
    Selma Jónsdóttir, Stefán Karlsson, and Sverrir Tómasson. Íslensk
    miðaldahandrit: Manuscripta Islandica medii aevi 2 (Reykjavík: Lög-
    berg, 1982). Pp. 11–41, esp. pp. 23–4 and 33–4. Rpt. in Sverrir Tómas-
    son. *Tækileg vitni: Greinar um bókmenntir gefnar út í tilefni sjötug-
    safmælis hans 5. apríl 2011* (Reykjavík: Stofnun Árna Magnússonar and
    Hið íslenska bókmenntafélag, 2011). Pp. 311–44, esp. pp. 323–4 and 333.
Sverrir Tómasson, Bragi Halldórsson, and Einar Sigurbjörnsson, ed.
    >> *Heilagra karla sögur* (2007). P. 31.
Turville-Petre, G. >> *Origins of Icelandic Literature* (1967). P. 133.
Van Deusen, Natalie M. "Stitches in the Margins: The Embroidery
    Pattern in AM 235 fol." *Mm* (2011): 26–42, esp. p. 28.
Wellendorf, Jonas. "The Attraction of the Earliest Old Norse Vernacular
    Hagiography." In Haki Antonsson and Ildar H. Garipzanov, ed.
    >> *Saints and Their Lives on the Periphery* (2010). Pp. 241–58, esp. p. 256.

Widding, Ole. "AM 655, 4° fragment III. Et brudstykke af Nicolaus saga." *Opuscula* 2.1. Bibliotheca Arnamagnæana 25 (Copenhagen: Munksgaard, 1961). Pp. 27–33.

– "Kilderne til den norrøne Nicolaus saga." *Opuscula* 2.1. Bibliotheca Arnamagnæana 25 (Copenhagen: Munksgaard, 1961). Pp. 17–26, esp. pp. 18 and 21.

Widding, Ole, and Hans Bekker-Nielsen. "En senmiddelalderlig legendesamling." *Mm* (1960): 105–28, esp. p. 126.

– "Low German Influence on Late Icelandic Hagiography." *GR* 37 (1962): 239–62, esp. pp. 241–2.

Handlist, p. 326.

2. Nikuláss saga erkibiskups I

The direct sources have not been established.

Manuscript:
Stock. Perg. fol. no. 2 (ca. 1425–45).
Editions:
Foote, Peter, ed. >> *Lives of Saints* (1962).
   Facsimile.
Unger, C.R., ed. >> *Heilagra manna søgur* (1877). Vol. 2, pp. 21–41.13.
Modern Icelandic language edition:
Sverrir Tómasson, Bragi Halldórsson, and Einar Sigurbjörnsson, ed.
   >> *Heilagra karla sögur* (2007). Pp. 3–30.
Norwegian translation:
Mundal, Else. *Legender frå mellomalderen. Soger om heilage kvinner og menn* (Oslo: Det Norske Samlaget, 1995). Pp. 99–127.
Literature:
Battista, Simonetta. "Interpretations of the Roman Pantheon in the Old Norse Hagiographic Sagas." In Geraldine Barnes and Margaret Clunies Ross, ed. >> *Old Norse Myths, Literature and Society* (2000). Pp. 24–34, esp. p. 31.

Bekker-Nielsen, Hans, Thorkil Damsgaard Olsen, and Ole Widding. >> *Norrøn fortællekunst* (1965). P. 125.

Bekker-Nielsen, Hans, and Ole Widding. "Legende. Norge og Island." *KLNM* 10 (1965). Cols. 421–3, esp. col. 421.

Carlé, Birte. >> *Jomfru-fortællingen* (1985). Pp. 39–40, 55–6, 67, and 73.

– "Men and Women in the Saints' Sagas of *Stock. 2, fol.*" In John Lindow, Lars Lönnroth, and Gerd Wolfgang Weber, ed. >> *Structure and Meaning in Old Norse Literature* (1986). Pp. 317–46, esp. pp. 320, 322, 324, 328–9, and 338.

Finnur Jónsson. >> *Den oldnorske og oldislandske Litteraturs Historie* (1920–4). Vol. 2, p. 874.

Hallberg, Peter. "Imagery in Religious Old Norse Prose Literature: An Outline." *ANF* 102 (1987): 120–70, esp. p. 159.

– "Bergr Sokkason and Religious Icelandic Literature." In >> *Samtíðarsögur* (1994). Vol. 1, pp. 296–300, esp. p. 297.

Mogk, Eugen. >> *Geschichte der norwegisch-isländischen Literatur* (1904). P. 892.

Selma Jónsdóttir. *Illumination in a Manuscript of Stjórn.* Trans. Peter G. Foote (Reykjavík: Almenna bókafélagið, 1971). P. 66.

Sigfús Blöndal. "St. Nikulás og dýrkun hans, sérstaklega á Íslandi." *Skírnir* 123 (1949): 69–97, esp. p. 81.

Sverrir Tómasson. "Íslenskar Nikulás sögur." In *Helgastaðabók. Nikulás saga. Perg. 4to nr. 16 Konungsbókhlöðu í Stokkhólmi.* Introduction by Selma Jónsdóttir, Stefán Karlsson, and Sverrir Tómasson. Íslensk miðaldahandrit: Manuscripta Islandica medii aevi 2 (Reykjavík: Lögberg, 1982). Pp. 11–41, esp. pp. 24, 29–31, 33–4, and 38. Rpt. in Sverrir Tómasson. *Tækileg vitni: Greinar um bókmenntir gefnar út í tilefni sjötugsafmælis hans 5. apríl 2011* (Reykjavík: Stofnun Árna Magnússonar and Hið íslenska bókmenntafélag, 2011). Pp. 311–44, esp. pp. 324, 329–30, 333, and 337–8.

– "Norðlenski Benediktínaskólinn." In >> *The Sixth International Saga Conference* (1985). Vol. 2, pp. 1009–20, esp. pp. 1014. Rpt. in Sverrir Tómasson. *Tækileg vitni: Greinar um bókmenntir gefnar út í tilefni sjötugsafmælis hans 5. apríl 2011* (Reykjavík: Stofnun Árna Magnússonar and Hið íslenska bókmenntafélag, 2011). Pp. 345–58, esp. p. 350.

– "Trúarbókmenntir í lausu máli á síðmiðöld." In Böðvar Guðmundsson, Sverrir Tómasson, Torfi H. Tulinius, and Vésteinn Ólason, ed. >> *Íslensk Bókmenntasaga* 2 (1993). Pp. 249–82, esp. p. 267.

Turville-Petre, G. > *Origins of Icelandic Literature* (1967). P. 133.

Widding, Ole. "Kilderne til den norrøne Nicolaus saga." *Opuscula* 2.1. Bibliotheca Arnamagnæana 25 (Copenhagen: Munksgaard, 1961). Pp. 17–26.

Handlist, p. 326.

3. Nikuláss saga erkibiskups

The direct sources have not been established.

Manuscript:
NRA 69 (ca. 1330).
Edition:
Unger, C.R., ed. >> *Heilagra manna søgur* (1877). Vol. 2, pp. 46.12–
49.8.
Literature:
Bekker-Nielsen, Hans, Thorkil Damsgaard Olsen, and Ole Widding.
    >> *Norrøn fortællekunst* (1965). P. 125.
Bekker-Nielsen, Hans, ånd Ole Widding. "Legende. Norge og Island."
    KLNM 10 (1965). Cols. 421–3, esp. col. 421.
Cormack, Margaret. >> *The Saints in Iceland* (1994). P.137.
Finnur Jónsson. >> *Den oldnorske og oldislandske Litteraturs Historie*
    (1920–4). Vol. 2, p. 874.
Foote, Peter, ed. >> *Lives of Saints* (1962). P. 20.
Mogk, Eugen. >> *Geschichte der norwegisch-isländischen Literatur* (1904).
    P. 892.
Sigfús Blöndal. "St. Nikulás og dýrkun hans, sérstaklega á Íslandi."
    Skírnir 123 (1949): 69–97, esp. p. 81.
Stefán Karlsson. "Islandsk bogeksport til Norge i middelalderen." *Mm*
    (1979): 1–17, esp. p. 6. Rpt. in *Stafkrókar: Ritgerðir eftir Stefán
    Karlsson gefnar út í tilefni af sjötugsafmæli hans 2. desember 1998*. Ed.
    Guðvarður Már Gunnlaugsson (Reykjavík: Stofnun Árna Magnús-
    sonar, 2000). Pp. 188–205, esp. p. 194.
Sverrir Tómasson. "Íslenskar Nikulás sögur." In *Helgastaðabók. Nikulás
    saga. Perg. 4to nr. 16 Konungsbókhlöðu í Stokkhólmi*. Introduction by
    Selma Jónsdóttir, Stefán Karlsson, and Sverrir Tómasson. Íslensk
    miðaldahandrit: Manuscripta Islandica medii aevi 2 (Reykjavík:
    Lögberg, 1982). Pp. 11–41, esp. p. 25. Rpt. in Sverrir Tómasson.
    *Tækileg vitni: Greinar um bókmenntir gefnar út í tilefni sjötugsafmælis
    hans 5. apríl 2011* (Reykjavík: Stofnun Árna Magnússonar and Hið
    íslenska bókmenntafélag, 2011). Pp. 311–44, esp. p. 324.
Sverrir Tómasson, Bragi Halldórsson, and Einar Sigurbjörnsson, ed.
    >> *Heilagra karla sögur* (2007). Pp. 31–2.
Turville-Petre, G. >> *Origins of Icelandic Literature* (1967). P. 133.
Handlist, p. 326.

4. Nikuláss saga erkibiskups II

A compilation by Abbot Bergr Sokkason (d. ca. 1370) based on a variety
of sources, which have not been established.

Manuscripts:

AM 638 4to (ca. 1700–25), AM 640 4to (ca. 1450–1500), AM 641 4to
(ca. 1430–1500, defective), AM 642a 4to I α (ca. 1350–1400), AM
642a 4to I ß (ca. 1375–1425), AM 642a 4to I γ (ca. 1340–90), AM
642a 4to I δ (ca. 1330–70), AM 642a 4to II (ca. 1400), AM 642b 4to
(ca. 1375–1425, defective), AM 643 4to (ca. 1400–1500, defective),
AM 644 4to (ca. 1700–1800), NKS 1222 fol. (ca. 1700–1800),
NKS 1789 4to 1 (ca. 1700–1800), and Stock. Perg. 4to no. 16
(*Helgastaðabók*) (ca. 1375–1400).

Editions:

*Helgastaðabók. Nikulás saga. Perg. 4to nr. 16 Konungsbókhlöðu í Stok-
khólmi.* Introduction by Selma Jónsdóttir, Stefán Karlsson, and Sverrir
Tómasson. Íslensk miðaldahandrit: Manuscripta Islandica medii aevi 2
(Reykjavík: Lögberg, 1982).
Facsimile of Stock. Perg. 4to no. 16.

Unger, C.R., ed. >> *Heilagra manna søgur* (1877). Vol. 2, pp. 49.14–158.
An eclectic text based primarily on AM 638 4to.

Modern Icelandic language edition:

*Helgastaðabók. Nikulás saga. Perg. 4to nr. 16 Konungsbókhlöðu í Stokk-
hólmi.* Introduction by Selma Jónsdóttir, Stefán Karlsson, and Sverrir
Tómasson. Íslensk miðaldahandrit: Manuscripta Islandica medii aevi 2
(Reykjavík: Lögberg, 1982). A specimen of chapters based on Stock.
Perg. 4to no. 16 (with emendations from AM 638 4to, AM 640 4to, and
AM 643 4to listed pp. 143–6) corresponding to C.R. Unger, ed.,
>> *Heilagra manna søgur* (1877), vol. 2, pp. 65.12–6622, 68.23–71.23,
72.26–74.22, 79.20–80.12, 95.40–97.12, 110.8–133.10, 122.38–125.9,
and 229.28–133.24.

English paraphrase and extract:

*Helgastaðabók. Nikulás saga. Perg. 4to nr. 16 Konungsbókhlöðu í Stokk-
hólmi.* Introduction by Selma Jónsdóttir, Stefán Karlsson, and Sverrir
Tómasson. Íslensk miðaldahandrit: Manuscripta Islandica medii aevi 2
(Reykjavík: Lögberg, 1982). Pp. 229–32.

Literature:

Astås, Reidar. "Spor av teologisk tenkning og refleksjon i norsk og
islandsk høymiddelalder." *CM* 6 (1993): 133–67, esp. p. 141.

Bekker-Nielsen, Hans, Thorkil Damsgaard Olsen, and Ole Widding.
>> *Norrøn fortællekunst* (1965). Pp. 135–6, 125, and 171.

Bekker-Nielsen, Hans, and Ole Widding. "Legende. Norge og Island."
KLNM 10 (1965). Cols. 421–3, esp. col. 421.

Boyer, Régis. >> *La vie religieuse en Islande* (1979). P. 146.

Cormack, Margaret. >> *The Saints in Iceland* (1994). Pp. 137 and 244.
– "Saints' Lives and Icelandic Literature in the Thirteenth and Four-
teenth Centuries." In Hans Bekker-Nielsen and Birte Carlé, ed.
>> *Saints and Sagas* (1994). Pp. 27–47, esp. p. 33.
– "Christian Biography." In *A Companion to Old Norse–Icelandic
Literature and Culture*. Ed. Rory McTurk (Oxford: Blackwell, 2005).
Pp. 27–42, esp. p. 34.
Dillmann, François-Xavier. "Om hedningar och hundar. Kring den
fornvästnordiska sammansättningen *hundheiðinn*." *SI* 52 (2001): 17–33,
esp. pp. 21–2 and 24.
Finnur Jónsson. >> *Den oldnorske og oldislandske Litteraturs Historie*
(1920–4). Vol. 2, p. 874, and vol. 3, p. 91.
Foote, Peter G. *The Pseudo-Turpin Chronicle in Iceland: A Contribution to
the Study of the Karlamagnús saga*. London Mediæval Studies: Mono-
graph No. 4 (University College London: London Mediæval Studies,
1954). Pp. 24–5.
Foote, Peter G., ed. >> *Lives of Saints* (1962). Pp. 20–1.
Gad, Tue. "Nicolaus af Myra." *KLNM* 12 (1967). Cols. 288–91, esp.
col. 289.
Hallberg, Peter. *Stilsignalement och författarskap i norrön sagalitteratur:
Synpunkter och exempel*. Nordistica Gothoburgensia 3 (Stockholm:
Almqvist & Wiksell, 1968). Pp. 130–6, 161–6, and 188–9.
– "Jóns saga helga." In *Afmælisrit Jóns Helgasonar 30. júní 1969*.
Ed. Jakob Benediktsson et al. (Reykjavík: Heimskringla, 1969).
Pp. 59–79.
– "Om Magnúss saga helga." In *Einarsbók: Afmæliskveðja til Einars Ól.
Sveinssonar 12. desember 1969*. Ed. Bjarni Guðnason, Halldór Hall-
dórsson, and Jónas Kristjánsson ([Reykjavík]: Nokkrir vinir, 1969).
Pp. 59–70.
– "Some Observations on the Language of *Dunstanus saga*, with an
Appendix on the Bible Compilation *Stjórn*." *Saga-Book* 18 (1973):
324–53, esp. pp. 324–32, 336–44, and 350–3.
– "A Group of Icelandic 'Riddarasögur' from the Middle of the Four-
teenth Century." In Régis Boyer, ed. >> *Les Sagas de Chevaliers
(Riddarasögur)* (1985). Pp. 7–53, esp. pp. 13, 15–20, and 26–53.
– "Imagery in Religious Old Norse Prose Literature: An Outline." *ANF*
102 (1987): 120–70, esp. pp. 122, 130–1, 138, 141, 144, 146–50, 152–3,
155, and 158– 9.
– "Bergr Sokkason and Religious Icelandic Literature." In >>
Samtíðarsögur (1994). Vol. 1, pp. 296–300, esp. pp. 296 and 299–300.

Jakob Benediktsson. "Cursus hos Bergr Sokkason." In *Festskrift til Ludvig Holm-Olsen på hans 70-årsdag den 9. juni 1984* (Øvre Ervik: Alvheim & Eide, 1984). Pp. 34–40. Rpt. in Jakob Benediktsson. *Lærdómslistir. Afmælisrit 20. júlí 1987* (Reykjavík: Mál og menning, 1987). Pp. 262–9.

– "Stjórn og Nikulás saga." *Gripla* 6 (1984): 7–11.

Jónas Kristjánsson. *Um Fóstbræðra sögu* (Reykjavík: Stofnun Árna Magnússonar, 1972). Pp. 259, 261, 273, 289, and 305.

– "The Court Style." In Régis Boyer, ed. >> *Les Sagas de Chevaliers (Riddarasögur)* (1985). Pp. 431–40, esp. pp. 433, 436, and 438.

– "Sagas and Saints' Lives." In *Cultura Classica e Cultura Germanica Settentrionale*. Ed. Pietro Janni, Diego Poli, and Carlo Santini (Macerata: Herder, 1985). Pp. 125–43, esp. p. 133.

– >> *Eddas and Sagas* (1988). Pp. 139–40.

Kirby, Ian. >> *Biblical Quotation*. Vol. 2, pp. 45n14, 46–7, and 51n18.

– *Bible Translation in Old Norse*. Université de Lausanne Publications de la faculté des lettres 27 (Geneva: Librairie Droz, 1986). Pp. 46 and 53n10.

Lehmann, Paul. >> "Skandinaviens Anteil an der lateinischen Literatur und Wissenschaft des Mittelalters" (1937). P. 59.

Magerøy, Hallvard. "Helgensoger." *KLNM* 6 (1961). Cols. 350–3, esp. col. 351.

Mogk, Eugen. >> *Geschichte der norwegisch-isländischen Literatur* (1904). Pp. 719 and 892.

Selma Jónsdóttir. *Illumination in a Manuscript of Stjórn*. Trans. Peter G. Foote (Reykjavík: Almenna bókafélagið, 1971). Pp. 65–71.

Sigfús Blöndal. "St. Nikulás og dýrkun hans, sérstaklega á Íslandi." *Skírnir* 123 (1949): 69–97, esp. p. 81.

Simek, Rudolf. *Altnordische Kosmographie: Studien und Quellen zu Weltbild und Weltbeschreibung in Norwegen und Island vom 12. bis zum 14. Jahrhundert* (Berlin: de Gruyter, 1990). Pp. 162, 169, 183, 199, 234, 256, 331–41, 344, 365, 374, and 393.

– "Enzyklopädisches Schrifttum als Quelle von Bergr Sokkasons Nikulás saga." *Gripla* 8 (1993): 219–30.

Stefán Karlsson. "Icelandic Lives of Thomas a Becket: Questions of Authorship." In Peter Foote, Hermann Pálsson, and Desmond Slay, ed. >> *Proceedings of the First International Saga Conference* (1973). Pp. 212–43, esp. pp. 237–8. Rpt. in *Stafkrókar: Ritgerðir eftir Stefán Karlsson gefnar út í tilefni af sjötugsafmæli hans 2. desember 1998*. Ed. Guðvarður Már Gunnlaugsson (Reykjavík: Stofnun Árna Magnússonar, 2000). Pp. 135–52, esp. pp. 147–8.

– "Guðmundar sögur biskups: Authorial Viewpoints and Methods." In
>> *The Sixth International Saga Conference* (1985). Vol. 2, pp. 983–
1005, esp. pp. 999–1001. Rpt. in *Stafkrókar: Ritgerðir eftir Stefán
Karlsson gefnar út í tilefni af sjötugsafmæli hans 2. desember 1998*. Ed.
Guðvarður Már Gunnlaugsson (Reykjavík: Stofnun Árna Magnússonar, 2000). Pp. 153–71, esp. pp. 165–7.

Svanhildur Óskarsdóttir. "Universal History in Fourteenth-Century
Iceland: Studies in AM 764 4to." PhD dissertation, University of
London, 2000. Pp. 69–71 and 240.

– "The World and Its Ages: The Organisation of an 'Encyclopaedic'
Narrative in MS AM 764 4to." In *Sagas, Saints and Settlements*. Ed.
Gareth Williams and Paul Bibire. The Northern World 2 (Leiden: Brill,
2004). Pp. 1–11, esp. pp. 8–10.

Sverrir Jakobsson. *Við og veröldin: Heimsmynd Íslendinga 1100–1400*
(Reykjavík: Háskólaútgáfan, 2005). Pp. 81 and 149.

Sverrir Tómasson. "Norðlenski Benediktínaskólinn." In >> *The Sixth
International Saga Conference* (1985). Vol. 2, pp. 1009–20, esp.
pp. 1009, 1012, and 1014–19. Rpt. In Sverrir Tómasson. *Tækileg vitni:
Greinar um bókmenntir gefnar út í tilefni sjötugsafmælis hans 5. apríl
2011* (Reykjavík: Stofnun Árna Magnússonar and Hið íslenska bókmenntafélag, 2011). Pp. 345–58, esp. pp. 347–55.

– *Formálar íslenskra sagnaritara á miðöldum. Rannsókn bókmenntahefðar*
(Reykjavík: Stofnun Árna Magnússonar, 1988). Pp. 55–6, 59, 67, 86,
90, 92, 97, 109, 120, 132, 144–5, 149, 152, 154–5, 164, 184–6, 234,
303–4, 306, 329, 346–7, and 357.

– "Kristnar trúarbókmenntir í óbundnu máli." In Guðrún Nordal,
Sverrir Tómasson, and Vésteinn Ólason, ed. >> *Íslensk Bókmenntasaga*
1 (1992). Pp. 419–79, esp. pp. 471–3.

– "Trúarbókmenntir í lausu máli á síðmiðöld." In Böðvar Guðmundsson,
Sverrir Tómasson, Torfi H. Tulinius, and Vésteinn Ólason, ed.
>> *Íslensk Bókmenntasaga* 2 (1993). Pp. 249–82, esp. pp. 249–54, 257,
261, 263, and 266–7.

– "'Nikulám skulu vér heiðra hér ...': Spjall um Annan málfræðinginn,
kveðskap og músik." In *Til heiðurs og hugbótar. Greinar um trúarkveðskap fyrri alda*. Ed. Svanhildur Óskarsdóttir and Anna Guðmundsdóttir (Reykholt: Snorrastofa, 2003). Pp. 79–92, esp. pp. 88–90.

– "Bergur Sokkason og íslenskar Nikulás sögur." In Sverrir Tómasson.
*Tækileg vitni: Greinar um bókmenntir gefnar út í tilefni sjötugsafmælis
hans 5. apríl 2011* (Reykjavík: Stofnun Árna Magnússonar and Hið
íslenska bókmenntafélag, 2011). Pp. 311–44.

Sverrir Tómasson, Bragi Halldórsson, and Einar Sigurbjörnsson, ed.
     >> *Heilagra karla sögur* (2007). Pp. 31–2.
Turville-Petre, Gabriel. "Legends of England in Icelandic Manuscripts."
     In Peter Clemoes, ed. >> *The Anglo-Saxons* (1959). Pp. 104–21, esp.
     pp. 115–19. Rpt. in Gabriel Turville-Petre. *Nine Norse Studies* (London:
     Viking Society for Northern Research, 1972). Pp. 59–78, esp. pp. 71–6.
– >> *Origins of Icelandic Literature* (1967). P. 133.
Þórhallur Þorgilsson. "Um þýðingar og endursagnir úr ítölskum miðal-
     daritum." *Landsbókasafn Íslands. Árbók* 1946–7 (1948): 212–24, esp.
     pp. 215 and 217.
Vésteinn Ólason. "Kveðskapur frá síðmiðöldum." In Böðvar Guð-
     mundsson, Sverrir Tómasson, Torfi H. Tulinius, and Vésteinn Ólason,
     ed. >> *Íslensk Bókmenntasaga* 2 (1993). Pp. 283–378, esp. p. 317.
Wellendorf, Jonas. "The Attraction of the Earliest Old Norse Vernacular
     Hagiography." In Haki Antonsson and Ildar H. Garipzanov, ed.
     >> *Saints and Their Lives on the Periphery* (2010). Pp. 241–58, esp. p. 257.
Widding, Ole. "Ave Maria aller Maríuvers i norrøn litteratur." *Mm* (1958):
     1–7, esp. pp. 4–5.
– "Kilderne til den norrøne Nicolaus saga." *Opuscula* 2.1. Bibliotheca
     Arnamagnæana 25 (Copenhagen: Munksgaard, 1961). Pp. 17–26, esp.
     pp. 18 and 21–5.
Widding, Ole, and Hans Bekker-Nielsen. "Low German Influence on
     Late Icelandic Hagiography." *GR* 37 (1962): 239–62, esp. pp. 241–2.
Handlist, p. 326.

5. Af Nikulás

An extract of the legend of Saint Nicholas. The direct source has not
been established.

Manuscript:
AM 764 4to (ca. 1376–86).
Literature:
Svanhildur Óskarsdóttir. "Universal History in Fourteenth-Century
     Iceland: Studies in AM 764 4to." PhD dissertation, University of
     London, 2000. Pp. 69–70 and 240.
– "The World and Its Ages: The Organisation of an 'Encyclopaedic'
     Narrative in MS AM 764 4to." In *Sagas, Saints and Settlements*. Ed.
     Gareth Williams and Paul Bibire. The Northern World 2 (Leiden: Brill,
     2004). Pp. 1–11, esp. pp. 8–10.

Sverrir Tómasson, "Íslenskar Nikulás sögur." In *Helgastaðabók. Nikulás saga. Perg. 4to nr. 16 Konungsbókhlöðu í Stokkhólmi.* Introduction by Selma Jónsdóttir, Stefán Karlsson, and Sverrir Tómasson. Íslensk miðaldahandrit: Manuscripta Islandica medii aevi 2 (Reykjavík: Lögberg, 1982). Pp. 11–41, esp. p. 27n17.
Handlist, p. 326.

6. Af Nikulás

An epitome of the legend of Saint Nicholas based on a text like Stock. Perg. fol. no. 2.

Manuscript:
AM 672 4to (ca. 1400–1500).
Literature:
Carlé, Birte. >> *Jomfru-fortællingen* (1985). Pp. 39–40, 55–6, 67, and 73.
– "Men and Women in the Saints' Sagas of *Stock. 2, fol.*" In John Lindow, Lars Lönnroth, and Gerd Wolfgang Weber, ed. >> *Structure and Meaning in Old Norse Literature* (1986). Pp. 317–46, esp. p. 319.
Foote, Peter, ed. >> *Lives of Saints* (1962). P. 21.
Kirby, Ian. >> *Biblical Quotation.* Vol. 2, p. 96.
Handlist, p. 327.

NICHOLAS OF TOLENTINO   September 10

Nikuláss saga af Tólentínó

Translated from a now-lost Low German redaction that resembles the source(s) of *Der Heiligen Leben.*

Manuscript:
Stock. Perg. fol. no. 3 (*Reykjahólabók*) (ca. 1530–40).
Edition:
Loth, Agnete, ed. >> *Reykjahólabók* (1969–70). Vol. 2, pp. 149–66.
Literature:
Bekker-Nielsen, Hans, Thorkil Damsgaard Olsen, and Ole Widding. >> *Norrøn fortællekunst* (1965). P. 140.
Kalinke, Marianne E. "Reykjahólabók: A Legendary on the Eve of the Reformation." *Skáldskaparmál* 2 (1992): 239–69, esp. pp. 240, 247–8, and 268.

– >> *The Book of Reykjahólar* (1996), pp. 28, 33, 50, 103–4, 127, 138, 142–4, 186, 238–9, 240–2, and 244–5.
Salvucci, Giovanna. "Between Heaven and Hell: The *Konungasǫgur* and the Emergence of the Idea of Purgatory." In John McKinnell, David Ashurst, and Donata Kick, ed. >> *The Fantastic in Old Norse/Icelandic Literature* (2006). Vol. 2, pp. 866–75, esp. p. 868.
Sverrir Tómasson. "Trúarbókmenntir í lausu máli á síðmiðöld." In Böðvar Guðmundsson, Sverrir Tómasson, Torfi H. Tulinius, and Vésteinn Ólason, ed. >> *Íslensk Bókmenntasaga* 2 (1993). Pp. 249–82, esp. p. 279.
Widding, Ole, and Hans Bekker-Nielsen. "En senmiddelalderlig legendesamling." *Mm* (1960): 105–28, esp. pp. 107 and 121.
– "Low German Influence on Late Icelandic Hagiography." *GR* 37 (1962): 239–62, esp. pp. 248 and 255.
Handlist, p. 327.

NICODEMUS, GOSPEL OF

1. Niðrstigningar saga

A translation of the *Descensus Christi ad inferos* based on the A-group of texts in Constantinus Tischendorf, ed., *Evangelia apocrypha*, 2nd ed. (Leipzig: Mendelssohn, 1876). Versions 1, 2, and 3 probably have a common ancestor.

Manuscript:
AM 645 4to (ca. 1225–50).
Editions:
Haugen, Odd Einar. "Stamtre og tekstlandskap: Studiar i resensjons-metodikk med grunnlag i *Niðrstigningar saga*." 2 vols. Dr. philos-dissertation, University of Bergen, 1992. Vol. 2, pp. 17–28.
Haugen, Odd Einar, ed. "Niðrstigningar saga." In *Norrøne tekster i utval*. Ed. Odd Einar Haugen (Oslo: Ad Notam Gyldendal, 1994). Pp. 250–65.
Normalized edition based on AM 645 4to.
Holtsmark, Anne, ed. *A Book of Miracles: Ms No. 645 4to of the Arna-Magnæan Collection in the University Library of Copenhagen*. CCI 12 (Copenhagen: Einar Munksgaard, 1938).
Facsimile of AM 645 4to.

Hreinn Benediktsson. *Early Icelandic Script As Illustrated in Vernacular Texts from the Twelfth and Thirteenth Centuries.* Íslenzk handrit: Icelandic Manuscripts, Series in Folio 2 (Reykjavík: The Manuscript Institute of Iceland, 1965). Plate 28.
Facsimile of AM 645 4to fol. 55v.
Unger, C.R., ed.>> *Heilagra manna søgur* (1877). Vol. 2, pp. 1–8.
Modern Icelandic language edition:
Einar Ól. Sveinsson, ed. *Leit eg suður til landa. Ævintýri og helgisögur frá miðöldum* (Reykjavík: Heimskringla, 1944). Pp. 141–51.
English translation:
Roughton, Philip G. "AM 645 4to and AM 652/630 4to: Study and Translation of Two Thirteenth-Century Icelandic Collections of Apostles' and Saints' Lives." PhD dissertation, University of Colorado, 2002. Pp. 872–86.
Norwegian translation:
Haugen, Odd Einar. "Soga om nedstigninga i dødsriket." In *Norrøne tekster i utval.* Ed. Odd Einar Haugen (Oslo: Ad Notam Gyldendal, 1994). Pp. 250–65.
Literature:
Aho, Gary L. "A Comparison of Old English and Old Norse Treatments of Christ's Harrowing of Hell." PhD dissertation, University of Oregon, 1966. Pp. 152–8, 160–83, and 198–242.
– "*Niðrstigningarsaga*: An Old Norse Version of Christ's Harrowing of Hell." *SS* 41 (1969): 150–9.
Battista, Simonetta. "*Blámenn, djǫflar* and Other Representations of Evil in Old Norse Literature." In John McKinnell, David Ashurst, and Donata Kick, ed. >> *The Fantastic in Old Norse / Icelandic Literature* (2006). Vol. 1, pp. 113–22, esp. pp. 117 and 119–20.
Bekker-Nielsen, Hans. "Nikodemusevangeliet." *KLNM* 12 (1967). Cols. 308–10, esp. cols. 308–9.
Bekker-Nielsen, Hans, Thorkil Damsgaard Olsen, and Ole Widding. >> *Norrøn fortællekunst* (1965). P.123.
Bekker-Nielsen, Hans, and Ole Widding. "Legende. Norge og Island." *KLNM* 10 (1965). Cols. 421–3, esp. cols. 421–2.
Boyer, Régis. >> *La vie religieuse en Islande* (1979). Pp. 159, 164, and 224.
Finnur Jónsson. >> *Den oldnorske og oldislandske Litteraturs Historie* (1920–4). Vol. 2, p. 929.
Gschwantler, Otto. "Christus, Thor und die Midgardschlange." In *Festschrift für Otto Höfler zum 65. Geburtstag.* Ed. Helmut Birkhan,

Otto Gschwantler, and Irmgard Hansberger-Wilflinger. 2 vols. (Vienna: Notring, 1968). Vol. 1, pp. 145–68, esp. pp. 151–6, 158, 161–2, and 167.

Hallberg, Peter. "Imagery in Religious Old Norse Prose Literature: An Outline." *ANF* 102 (1987): 120–70, esp. p. 125. ·

Haugen, Odd Einar. "The Evaluation of Stemmatic Evidence: Recension and Revision of *Niðrstigningar saga*." In >> *The Sixth International Saga Conference* (1985). Vol. 1, pp. 423–50, esp. pp. 424–38.

– "Between Graphonomy and Phonology: Deciding on Scribes in AM 645 4°." In *Papers from the Tenth Scandinavian Conference of Linguistics, Bergen, June 11–13, 1987*. Ed. Victoria Rosén. 2 vols. (Bergen: Institutt for fonetikk og lingvistikk, 1988). Vol. 1, pp. 254–72.

– "Mål og metodar i tekstkritikken." In *Den filologiske vitenskap*. Ed. Odd Einar Haugen and Einar Thomassen (Oslo: Solum, 1990). Pp. 128–80, esp. pp. 131 and 157–60.

– "Nicodemus, Gospel of." In Phillip Pulsiano and Kirsten Wolf, with Paul Acker and Donald K. Fry, ed. >> *Medieval Scandinavia* (1993). Pp. 430–2.

Jón Helgason. *Norrøn Litteraturhistorie* (Copenhagen: Levin and Munksgaard, 1934). P. 103.

Jónas Kristjánsson. *Um Fóstbræðra sögu* (Reykjavík: Stofnun Árna Magnússonar, 1972). Pp. 267 and 271.

Kirby, Ian. >> *Biblical Quotation* (1980). Vol. 2, p. 46.

– *Bible Translation in Old Norse*. Université de Lausanne Publications de la Faculté des Lettres 27 (Geneva: Librairie Droz, 1986). P. 35.

Konráð Gíslason. *Um frum-parta íslenzkrar túngu í fornöld* (Copenhagen: Trier, 1846). Pp. lxv–lxvi.

Kratz, Henry. "The Language of the Old Norse Saints' Lives." *Mm* (1988): 159–73.

Magnús Már Lárusson. "Um Niðurstigningarsögu." *Skírnir* 129 (1955): 159–68, esp. pp. 159–65.

Marchand, James W. "Leviathan and the Mousetrap in the *Niðrstigningarsaga*." *SS* 47 (1975): 328–38.

Mogk, Eugen. >> *Geschichte der norwegisch-isländischen Literatur* (1904). P. 890.

Overgaard, Mariane, ed. *The History of the Cross-Tree down to Christ's Passion: Icelandic Legend Versions*. Editiones Arnamagnæanæ, Series B, vol. 26 (Copenhagen: Munksgaard, 1968). Pp. cxx–cxxi.

Paasche, Fredrik. *Norges og Islands litteratur inntil utgangen av middelalderen*. Rev. ed. by Anne Holtsmark (Oslo: Aschehoug, 1947). Pp. 298–9, 334, and 535.

Roughton, Philip. "Stylistics and Sources of the *Postola sögur* in AM 645 4to and AM 652/630 4to." *Gripla* 16 (2005): 7–50.

Strömbäck, Dag. "Visionsdiktning." *KLNM* 20 (1976). Cols. 171–86, esp. col. 181.

Svanhildur Óskarsdóttir. "Prose of Christian Instruction." In *A Companion to Old Norse–Icelandic Literature.* Ed. Rory McTurk (Oxford: Blackwell, 2005). Pp. 338–53, esp. p. 351.

Sverrir Tómasson. *Formálar íslenskra sagnaritara á miðöldum. Rannsókn bókmenntahefðar* (Reykjavík: Stofnun Árna Magnússonar, 1988). Pp. 57–8, 189, and 255.

– "Kristnar trúarbókmenntir í óbundnu máli." In Guðrún Nordal, Sverrir Tómasson, and Vésteinn Ólason, ed. >> *Íslensk Bókmenntasaga* 1 (1992). Pp. 419–79, esp. pp. 421 and 425.

– "Trúarbókmenntir í lausu máli á síðmiðöld." In Böðvar Guðmundsson, Sverrir Tómasson, Torfi H. Tulinius, and Vésteinn Ólason, ed. >> *Íslensk Bókmenntasaga* 2 (1993). Pp. 249–82, esp. pp. 269–70 and 306.

– "Ferðir þessa heims og annars. Paradís – Ódáinsakur – Vínland í ferðalýsingum miðalda." *Gripla* 12 (2001): 23–40, esp. p. 25. Rpt. in Sverrir Tómasson. *Tækileg vitni: Greinar um bókmenntir gefnar út í tilefni sjötugsafmælis hans 5. apríl 2011* (Reykjavík: Stofnun Árna Magnússonar and Hið íslenska bókmenntafélag, 2011). Pp. 259–78, esp. p. 361.

Turville-Petre, G. >> *Origins of Icelandic Literature* (1967). Pp. 126–8.

Vries, Jan de. >> *Altnordische Literaturgeschichte* (1964–7). Vol. 2, pp. 182–3.

Wolf, Kirsten. "Om en 'tabt' islandsk oversættelse af Nikodemusevangeliet." *ANF* 107 (1992): 167–79, esp. pp. 170–2.

– "The Influence of the *Evangelium Nicodemi* on Norse Literature: A Survey." *MS* 55 (1993): 219–42, esp. pp. 219–31, 233, 242. Rpt. in *The Medieval* Gospel of Nicodemus. *Texts, Intertexts, and Contexts in Western Europe.* Ed. Zbigniew Izydorczyk. Medieval and Renaissance Texts and Studies 158 (Tempe, Ariz.: Medieval and Renaissance Texts and Studies, 1997). Pp. 261–86, esp. pp. 262–74, 276, 286.

Handlist, p. 327.

2. Niðrstigningar saga

A translation of the *Descensus Christi ad inferos* based on the A-group of texts in Constantinus Tischendorf, ed., *Evangelia apocrypha*, 2nd ed. (Leipzig: Mendelssohn, 1876). Versions 1, 2, and 3 probably have a common ancestor.

Manuscript:
AM 623 4to (ca. 1325, defective).
Editions:
Finnur Jónsson, ed. *AM 623, 4°: Helgensagaer*. STUAGNL 52 (Copenhagen: Jørgensen, 1927). Pp. 1–9.17.

Haugen, Odd Einar. "Stamtre og tekstlandskap: Studiar i resensjonsmetodikk med grunnlag i *Niðrstigningar saga*." 2 vols. Dr. philosdissertation, University of Bergen, 1992. Vol. 2, pp. 29–36.

Unger, C.R., ed. >> *Heilagra manna søgur* (1877). Vol. 2, pp. 9–14.19.
Literature:
Aho, Gary L. "A Comparison of Old English and Old Norse Treatments of Christ's Harrowing of Hell." PhD dissertation, University of Oregon, 1966. Pp. 152–8, 160–83.

– "*Niðrstigningarsaga*: An Old Norse Version of Christ's Harrowing of Hell." *SS* 41 (1969): 150–9.

Battista, Simonetta. "*Blámenn, djǫflar* and Other Representations of Evil in Old Norse Literature." In John McKinnell, David Ashurst, and Donata Kick, ed. >> *The Fantastic in Old Norse/Icelandic Literature* (2006). Vol. 1, pp. 113–22, esp. p. 114.

Bekker-Nielsen, Hans. "Nikodemusevangeliet." *KLNM* 12 (1967). Cols. 308–10, esp. cols. 308–9.

Bekker-Nielsen, Hans, Thorkil Damsgaard Olsen, and Ole Widding. >> *Norrøn fortællekunst* (1965). P.123.

Bekker-Nielsen, Hans, and Ole Widding. "Legende. Norge og Island." *KLNM* 10 (1965). Cols. 421–3, esp. col. 421.

Boyer, Régis. >> *La vie religieuse en Islande* (1979). Pp. 159, 164, and 224.

Finnur Jónsson. >> *Den oldnorske og oldislandske Litteraturs Historie* (1920–4). Vol. 2, p. 929.

Gschwantler, Otto. "Christus, Thor und die Midgardschlange." In *Festschrift für Otto Höfler zum 65. Geburtstag*. Ed. Helmut Birkhan, Otto Gschwantler, and Irmgard Hansberger-Wilflinger. 2 vols. (Vienna: Notring, 1968). Vol. 1 p. 145–68, esp. pp. 151–2, 155–6, 158, 161–2, and 167.

Haugen, Odd Einar. "The Evaluation of Stemmatic Evidence: Recension and Revision of *Niðrstigningar saga*." In >> *The Sixth International Saga Conference* (1985). Vol. 1, pp. 423–50, esp. pp. 424–38.

– "Mål og metodar i tekstkritikken." In *Den filologiske vitenskap*. Ed. Odd Einar Haugen and Einar Thomassen (Oslo: Solum, 1990). Pp. 128–80, esp. pp. 131 and 157–60.

– "Nicodemus, Gospel of." In Phillip Pulsiano and Kirsten Wolf, with Paul Acker and Donald K. Fry, ed. >> *Medieval Scandinavia* (1993). Pp. 430–2.

Kirby, Ian. >> *Biblical Quotation* (1980). Vol. 2, p. 46.

Konráð Gíslason. *Um frum-parta íslenzkrar túngu í fornöld* (Copenhagen: Trier, 1846). P. lii.

Magnús Már Lárusson. "Um Niðurstigningarsögu." *Skírnir* 129 (1955): 159–68, esp. pp. 159–65.

Marchand, James W. "Leviathan and the Mousetrap in the *Niðrstigningarsaga*." *SS* 47 (1975): 328–38.

Mogk, Eugen. >> *Geschichte der norwegisch-isländischen Literatur* (1904). P. 890.

Overgaard, Mariane, ed. *The History of the Cross-Tree down to Christ's Passion: Icelandic Legend Versions*. Editiones Arnamagnæanæ, Series B, vol. 26 (Copenhagen: Munksgaard, 1968). Pp. cxx–cxxi and cxxxviii.

Paasche, Fredrik. *Norges og Islands litteratur inntil utgangen av middelalderen*. Rev. ed. by Anne Holtsmark (Oslo: Aschehoug, 1947). Pp. 298–9, 334, and 535.

Strömbäck, Dag. "Visionsdiktning." *KLNM* 20 (1976). Cols. 171–86, esp. col. 181.

Svanhildur Óskarsdóttir. "Prose of Christian Instruction." In *A Companion to Old Norse–Icelandic Literature*. Ed. Rory McTurk (Oxford: Blackwell, 2005). Pp. 338–53, esp. p. 351.

Sverrir Tómasson. "Kristnar trúarbókmenntir í óbundnu máli." In Guðrún Nordal. Sverrir Tómasson, and Vésteinn Ólason, ed. >> *Íslensk Bókmenntasaga* 1 (1992). Pp. 419–79, esp. pp. 421 and 425.

– "Trúarbókmenntir í lausu máli á síðmiðöld." In Böðvar Guðmundsson, Sverrir Tómasson, Torfi H. Tulinius, and Vésteinn Ólason, ed. >> *Íslensk Bókmenntasaga* 2 (1993). Pp. 249–82, esp. pp. 269–70.

– "Ferðir þessa heims og annars. Paradís – Ódáinsakur – Vínland í ferðalýsingum miðalda." *Gripla* 12 (2001): 23–40, esp. p. 25. Rpt. in Sverrir Tómasson. *Tækileg vitni: Greinar um bókmenntir gefnar út í tilefni sjötugsafmælis hans 5. apríl 2011* (Reykjavík: Stofnun Árna Magnússonar and Hið íslenska bókmenntafélag, 2011). Pp. 359–78, esp. p. 361.

Turville-Petre, G. >> *Origins of Icelandic Literature* (1967). Pp. 126–8.

Vries, Jan de. >> *Altnordische Literaturgeschichte* (1964–7). Vol. 2, pp. 182–3.

Wolf, Kirsten. "Om en 'tabt' islandsk oversættelse af Nikodemusevangeliet." *ANF* 107 (1992): 167–79, esp. pp. 170–2.

– "The Influence of the *Evangelium Nicodemi* on Norse Literature: A Survey." *MS* 55 (1993): 219–42, esp. pp. 219–31, 233, 242. Rpt. in *The Medieval* Gospel of Nicodemus. *Texts, Intertexts, and Contexts in*

Western Europe. Ed. Zbigniew Izydorczyk. Medieval and Renaissance
Texts and Studies 158 (Tempe, Ariz.: Medieval and Renaissance Texts
and Studies, 1997). Pp. 261–86, esp. pp. 262–74, 276, 286.
Handlist, p. 327.

3. Niðrstigningar saga

A translation of the *Descensus Christi ad inferos* based on the A-group
of texts in Constantinus Tischendorf, ed., *Evangelia apocrypha*, 2nd ed.
(Leipzig: Mendelssohn, 1876). Versions 1, 2, and 3 probably have a
common ancestor.

Manuscript:
AM 233a fol. (ca. 1350–60, defective).
Editions:
Haugen, Odd Einar. "Stamtre og tekstlandskap: Studiar i resensjons-
metodikk med grunnlag i *Niðrstigningar saga*." 2 vols. Dr. philos-
dissertation, University of Bergen, 1992. Vol. 2, pp. 37–40.
Unger, C.R., ed. >> *Heilagra manna søgur* (1877). Vol. 2,
pp. 14.22–17.18.
Literature:
Aho, Gary L. "A Comparison of Old English and Old Norse Treatments
of Christ's Harrowing of Hell." PhD dissertation, University of
Oregon, 1966. Pp. 152–8 and 160–83.
– "*Niðrstigningarsaga*: An Old Norse Version of Christ's Harrowing of
Hell." *SS* 41 (1969): 150–9.
Bekker-Nielsen, Hans. "Nikodemusevangeliet." *KLNM* 12 (1967). Cols.
308–10, esp. cols. 308–9.
Bekker-Nielsen, Hans, Thorkil Damsgaard Olsen, and Ole Widding.
>> *Norrøn fortællekunst* (1965). P.123.
Bekker-Nielsen, Hans, and Ole Widding. "Legende. Norge og Island."
KLNM 10 (1965). Cols. 421–3, esp. col. 421.
Boyer, Régis. >> *La vie religieuse en Islande* (1979). Pp. 159, 164, and 224.
Finnur Jónsson. >> *Den oldnorske og oldislandske Litteraturs Historie*
(1920–4). Vol. 2, p. 929.
Gschwantler, Otto. "Christus, Thor und die Midgardschlange." In
Festschrift für Otto Höfler zum 65. Geburtstag. Ed. Helmut Birkhan,
Otto Gschwantler, and Irmgard Hansberger-Wilflinger. 2 vols. (Vienna:
Notring, 1968). Vol. 1, pp. 145–68, esp. pp. 151–2, 156, 158, 161–2,
and 167.

Haugen, Odd Einar. "The Evaluation of Stemmatic Evidence: Recension and Revision of *Niðrstigningar saga*." In >> *The Sixth International Saga Conference* (1985). Vol. 1, pp. 423–50, esp. pp. 424–38.

– "Mål og metodar i tekstkritikken." In *Den filologiske vitenskap*. Ed. Odd Einar Haugen and Einar Thomassen (Oslo: Solum, 1990). Pp. 128–80, esp. pp. 131 and 157–60.

– "Nicodemus, Gospel of." In Phillip Pulsiano and Kirsten Wolf, with Paul Acker and Donald K. Fry, ed. >> *Medieval Scandinavia* (1993). Pp. 430–2.

Kirby, Ian. >> *Biblical Quotation* (1980). Vol. 2, p. 46.

Magnús Már Lárusson. "Um Niðurstigningarsögu." *Skírnir* 129 (1955): 159–68, esp. pp. 159–65.

Marchand, James W. "Leviathan and the Mousetrap in the *Niðrstigning-arsaga*." *SS* 47 (1975): 328–38.

Mogk, Eugen. >> *Geschichte der norwegisch-isländischen Literatur* (1904). P. 890.

Overgaard, Mariane, ed. *The History of the Cross-Tree down to Christ's Passion: Icelandic Legend Versions*. Editiones Arnamagnæanæ, Series B, vol. 26 (Copenhagen: Munksgaard, 1968). Pp. cxx–cxxi.

Paasche, Fredrik. *Norges og Islands litteratur inntil utgangen av middelalderen*. Rev. ed. by Anne Holtsmark (Oslo: Aschehoug, 1947). Pp. 298–9, 334, and 535.

Strömbäck, Dag. "Visionsdiktning." *KLNM* 20 (1976). Cols. 171–86, esp. col. 181.

Svanhildur Óskarsdóttir. "Prose of Christian Instruction." In *A Companion to Old Norse–Icelandic Literature*. Ed. Rory McTurk (Oxford: Blackwell, 2005). Pp. 338–53, esp. p. 351.

Sverrir Tómasson. "Kristnar trúarbókmenntir í óbundnu máli." In Guðrún Nordal, Sverrir Tómasson, and Vésteinn Ólason, ed. >> *Íslensk Bókmenntasaga* 1 (1992). Pp. 419–79, esp. p. 421.

– "Trúarbókmenntir í lausu máli á síðmiðöld." In Böðvar Guðmundsson, Sverrir Tómasson, Torfi H. Tulinius, and Vésteinn Ólason, ed. >> *Íslensk Bókmenntasaga* 2 (1993). Pp. 249–82, esp. pp. 269–70

– "Ferðir þessa heims og annars. Paradís – Ódáinsakur – Vínland í ferðalýsingum miðalda." *Gripla* 12 (2001): 23–40, esp. p. 25. Rpt. in Sverrir Tómasson. *Tækileg vitni: Greinar um bókmenntir gefnar út í tilefni sjötugsafmælis hans 5. apríl 2011* (Reykjavík: Stofnun Árna Magnússonar and Hið íslenska bókmenntafélag, 2011). Pp. 359–78, esp. p. 361.

Turville-Petre, G. >> *Origins of Icelandic Literature* (1967). Pp. 126–8.

Vries, Jan de. >> *Altnordische Literaturgeschichte* (1964–7). Vol. 2, pp. 182–3.

Wolf, Kirsten. "Om en 'tabt' islandsk oversættelse af Nikodemusevan-
geliet." *ANF* 107 (1992): 167–79, esp. pp. 170–2.
– "The Influence of the *Evangelium Nicodemi* on Norse Literature: A
Survey." *MS* 55 (1993): 219–42, esp. pp. 219–31, 233, 242. Rpt. in *The
Medieval* Gospel of Nicodemus. *Texts, Intertexts, and Contexts in
Western Europe*. Ed. Zbigniew Izydorczyk. Medieval and Renaissance
Texts and Studies 158 (Tempe, Ariz.: Medieval and Renaissance Texts
and Studies, 1997). Pp. 261–86, esp. pp. 262–74, 276, 286.
Handlist, p. 327.

4. Niðstigningar saga

A revision of the older recension (versions 1, 2, and 3) based on the Latin
source text.

Manuscript:
AM 238 fol. V (ca. 1400–1500).
Editions:
Haugen, Odd Einar. "Stamtre og tekstlandskap: Studiar i resensjons-
metodikk med grunnlag i *Niðrstigningar saga*." 2 vols. Dr. philos-
dissertation, University of Bergen, 1992. Vol. 2, pp. 41–5.
Unger, C.R., ed. >> *Heilagra manna søgur* (1877). Vol. 2, pp. 17.21–20.
Literature:
Aho, Gary L. "A Comparison of Old English and Old Norse Treatments
of Christ's Harrowing of Hell." PhD dissertation, University of
Oregon, 1966. Pp. 152–8 and 160–83.
– "*Niðrstigningarsaga*: An Old Norse Version of Christ's Harrowing of
Hell." *SS* 41 (1969): 150–9.
Bekker-Nielsen, Hans. "Nikodemusevangeliet." *KLNM* 12 (1967). Cols.
308–10, esp. cols. 308–9.
Bekker-Nielsen, Hans, Thorkil Damsgaard Olsen, and Ole Widding.
>> *Norrøn fortællekunst* (1965). P.123.
Bekker-Nielsen, Hans, and Ole Widding. "Legende. Norge og Island."
KLNM 10 (1965). Cols. 421–3, esp. col. 421.
Boyer, Régis. >> *La vie religieuse en Islande* (1979). Pp. 159, 164, and 224.
Finnur Jónsson. >> *Den oldnorske og oldislandske Litteraturs Historie*
(1920–4). Vol. 2, p. 929.
Gschwantler, Otto. "Christus, Thor und die Midgardschlange." In
Festschrift für Otto Höfler zum 65. Geburtstag. Ed. Helmut Birkhan,
Otto Gschwantler, and Irmgard Hansberger-Wilflinger. 2 vols.

(Vienna: Notring, 1968). Vol. 1, pp. 145–68, esp. pp. 151–2, 156, 158, 161–2, and 167.

Hallberg, Peter. "Imagery in Religious Old Norse Prose Literature: An Outline." *ANF* 102 (1987): 120–70, esp. pp. 125 and 150.

Haugen, Odd Einar. "The Evaluation of Stemmatic Evidence: Recension and Revision of *Niðrstigningar saga*." >> *The Sixth International Saga Conference* (1985). Vol. 1, pp. 423–50, esp. pp. 424–38.

– "Nicodemus, Gospel of." In Phillip Pulsiano and Kirsten Wolf, with Paul Acker and Donald K. Fry, ed. >> *Medieval Scandinavia* (1993). Pp. 430–2.

Kirby, Ian. >> *Biblical Quotation* (1980). Vol. 2, p. 46.

Magnús Már Lárusson. "Um Niðurstigningarsögu." *Skírnir* 129 (1955): 159–68, esp. pp. 159–65.

Marchand, James W. "Leviathan and the Mousetrap in the *Niðrstigningarsaga*." *SS* 47 (1975): 328–38.

Mogk, Eugen. >> *Geschichte der norwegisch-isländischen Literatur* (1904). P. 890.

Overgaard, Mariane, ed. *The History of the Cross-Tree down to Christ's Passion: Icelandic Legend Versions*. Editiones Arnamagnæanæ, Series B, vol. 26 (Copenhagen: Munksgaard, 1968). Pp. cxx–cxxi.

Paasche, Fredrik. *Norges og Islands litteratur inntil utgangen av middelalderen*. Rev. ed. by Anne Holtsmark (Oslo: Aschehoug, 1947). Pp. 298–9, 334, and 535.

Strömbäck, Dag. "Visionsdiktning." *KLNM* 20 (1976). Cols. 171–86, esp. col. 181.

Svanhildur Óskarsdóttir. "Prose of Christian Instruction." In *A Companion to Old Norse–Icelandic Literature*. Ed. Rory McTurk (Oxford: Blackwell, 2005). Pp. 338–53, esp. p. 351.

Sverrir Tómasson. "Kristnar trúarbókmenntir í óbundnu máli." In Guðrún Nordal, Sverrir Tómasson, and Vésteinn Ólason, ed. >> *Íslensk Bókmenntasaga* 1 (1992). Pp. 419–79, esp. p. 421.

– "Trúarbókmenntir í lausu máli á síðmiðöld." In Böðvar Guðmundsson, Sverrir Tómasson, Torfi H. Tulinius, and Vésteinn Ólason, ed. >> *Íslensk Bókmenntasaga* 2 (1993). Pp. 249–82, esp. pp. 269–70.

Turville-Petre, G. >> *Origins of Icelandic Literature* (1967). Pp. 126–8.

Vries, Jan de. >> *Altnordische Literaturgeschichte* (1964–7). Vol. 2, pp. 182–3.

Wolf, Kirsten. "Om en 'tabt' islandsk oversættelse af Nikodemusevangeliet." *ANF* 107 (1992): 167–79, esp. pp. 170–2.

– "The Influence of the *Evangelium Nicodemi* on Norse Literature: A Survey." *MS* 55 (1993): 219–42, esp. pp. 219–31, 233, 242. Rpt. in *The

Medieval Gospel of Nicodemus. *Texts, Intertexts, and Contexts in Western Europe*. Ed. Zbigniew Izydorczyk. Medieval and Renaissance Texts and Studies 158 (Tempe, Ariz.: Medieval and Renaissance Texts and Studies, 1997). Pp. 261–86, esp. pp. 262–74, 276, 286.
Handlist, p. 327.

5. Niðrstigningar saga

A copy of a medieval manuscript made by Ólafur Jónsson in Arney. The manuscript has been demonstrated to have independent textual value.

Manuscript:
JS 405 8vo (1780).
Edition:
Haugen, Odd Einar. "Stamtre og tekstlandskap: Studiar i resensjons-metodikk med grunnlag i *Niðrstigningar saga*." 2 vols. Dr. philos-dissertation, University of Bergen, 1992. Vol. 2, pp. 46–59.
Literature:
Haugen, Odd Einar. "Nicodemus, Gospel of." In Phillip Pulsiano and Kirsten Wolf, with Paul Acker and Donald K. Fry, ed. >> *Medieval Scandinavia* (1993). Pp. 430–2.
Magnús Már Lárusson. "Um Niðurstigningarsögu." *Skírnir* 129 (1955): 159–68, esp. pp. 167–8.
Wolf, Kirsten. "Om en 'tabt' islandsk oversættelse af Nikodemusevan-geliet." *ANF* 107 (1992): 167–79, esp. pp. 170–2.
– "The Influence of the *Evangelium Nicodemi* on Norse Literature: A Survey." *MS* 55 (1993): 219–42, esp. pp. 219–31, 233, 242. Rpt. in *The Medieval* Gospel of Nicodemus. *Texts, Intertexts, and Contexts in Western Europe*. Ed. Zbigniew Izydorczyk. Medieval and Renais-sance Texts and Studies 158 (Tempe, Ariz.: Medieval and Renais-sance Texts and Studies, 1997). Pp. 261–86, esp. pp. 262–74, 276, and 286.

ODILO OF CLUNY   January 1

Af Ódílo ábóta

A tale of Saint Odilo of Cluny incorporated into the miracles of the Virgin Mary.

Manuscripts:
See Mary the Blessed Virgin 3 note (p. 245).
Edition:
Unger, C.R., ed. >> *Mariu saga* (1871). Pp. 783.15–786.3.
Literature:
Widding, Ole. "Norrøne Marialegender på europæisk baggrund."
    Opuscula 10. Bibliotheca Arnamagnæana 40 (Copenhagen: Reitzel,
    1996). Pp. 1–128, esp. pp. 11 and 47.
Handlist, pp. 324 and 327.

OLAV OF NORWAY   July 29

1. In die sancti Olaui regis et martiris

A sermon and a collection of the miracles of King Óláfr Haraldsson
(d. 1030).

Manuscript:
AM 619 4to (ca. 1200–25).
Editions:
Flom, George T., ed. *Codex AM 619 Quarto. Old Norwegian Book of
    Homilies Containing* The Miracles of Saint Olaf *and Alcuin's* De
    virtutibus et vitiis. University of Illinois Studies in Language
    and Literature 14 no. 4 (Urbana: University of Illinois, 1929).
    Pp. 159.10–177.13.
Indrebø, Gustav, ed. *Gamal Norsk Homiliebok.* Norsk historisk
    kjeldeskrift-institutt, Skrifter 54 (Oslo: Dybwad, 1931; rpt. Oslo:
    Universitetsforlaget, 1966). Pp. 108.13–127.5 and 129.10–24.
Knudsen, Trygve, ed. *Gammelnorsk homiliebok etter AM 619 qv.* CCN,
    Series in Quarto 1 (Oslo: Selskapet til utgivelse av gamle norske
    håndskrifter, 1952).
    Facsimile.
Unger, Carl R., ed. *Gammel norsk homiliebog (codex Arn. Magn. 619 qv).*
    Norsk oldskriftselskabs samlinger 1.5 (Christiania [Oslo]: Brøgger &
    Christie, 1862–4). Pp. 146–166.3 and 167.34–168.15.
Norwegian translation:
Salvesen, Astrid, trans. *Gammelnorsk Homilibok.* Introduction and
    commentary by Erik Gunnes (Oslo: Universitetsforlaget, 1971).
    Pp. 141–156.27 and 158.16–29.

Literature:

Bekker-Nielsen, Hans, Thorkil Damsgaard Olsen, and Ole Widding.
>> *Norrøn fortællekunst* (1965). Pp. 21 and 60.

Boyer, Régis. >> *La vie religieuse en Islande* (1979). P. 224.

Cormack, Margaret. >> *The Saints in Iceland* (1994). P. 141.

Daae, Ludvig. *Norges helgener* (Christiania [Oslo]: Malling, 1879).
Pp. 116–17.

Dillmann, François-Xavier. "Om hedningar och hundar. Kring den
fornvästnordiska sammansättningen *hundheiðinn*." *SI* 52 (2001): 17–33,
esp. p. 28.

Ekrem, Inger. "Om *Passio Olavis* tilblivelse og eventuelle forbindelse med
Historia Norwegie." In Inger Ekrem, Lars Boje Mortensen, and Karen
Skovgaard- Petersen, ed. >> *Olavslegenden* (2000). Pp. 108–56, esp.
pp. 115–17, 120, 124, and 127–8.

Heinrichs, Anne. "Óláfs saga helga." In Phillip Pulsiano and Kirsten
Wolf, with Paul Acker and Donald K. Fry, ed. >> *Medieval Scandinavia* (1993). Pp. 447–8.

Holm-Olsen, Ludvig. "Middelalderens litteratur i Norge." In *Norges
litteratur historie* 1. Ed. Edvard Beyer (Oslo: Cappelen, 1974). Pp. 18–
342, esp. pp. 54–9 and 62–4.

Holtsmark, Anne. "Sankt Olavs liv og mirakler." In *Festskrift til Francis
Bull på 50 årsdagen* (Oslo: Gyldendal, 1937). Pp. 121–33. Rpt. in
Anne Holtsmark. *Studier i norrøn diktning* (Oslo: Gyldendal, 1956).
Pp. 15–24.

– "Olavslegenden." *KLNM* 12 (1967). Cols. 584–8, esp. col. 586.

Jakob Benediktsson. "Traces of Latin Prose-Rhythm in Old Norse
Literature." In *The Fifth Viking Congress, Tórshavn, July 1965*. Ed.
Bjarni Niclasen (Tórshavn: Føroya Landsstýri, 1968). Pp. 17–24, esp.
pp. 20–1. Rpt. in Jakob Benediktsson. *Lærdómslistir. Afmælisrit 20.
júlí 1987* (Reykjavík: Mál og menning, 1987). Pp. 153–60, esp.
pp. 156–7.

Jónas Kristjánsson. >> *Eddas and Sagas* (1988). Pp. 159 and 282.

Jørgensen, Jon Gunnar. "Passio Olavi og Snorre." In Inger Ekrem, Lars
Boje Mortensen, and Karen Skovgaard-Petersen, ed. >> *Olavslegenden*
(2000). Pp. 157–69, esp. pp. 159–62.

Kirby, Ian. >> *Biblical Quotation* (1980). Vol. 2, pp. 62, 67, 103, and 108.

Kunin, Devra, trans. *A History of Norway and The Passion and Miracles
of the Blessed Óláfr*. Edited with an Introduction and Notes by Carl
Phelpstead. London: Viking Society for Northern Research, 2001).
Pp. xxviii, xxix, xxxiv–xxxvi, xxxix–xli, and xlv.

Lindow, John. "St Olaf and the Skalds." In Thomas A. DuBois, ed.
   >> *Sanctity in the North* (2008). Pp. 103–27, esp. p. 104.
* McDougall, David. "Studies in the Prose Style of the Old Icelandic
   and Old Norwegian Homily Books." PhD dissertation. University of
   London, 1983.
– "Homilies (West Norse)." In Phillip Pulsiano and Kirsten Wolf, with Paul
   Acker and Donald K. Fry, ed. >> *Medieval Scandinavia* (1993). Pp. 290–2.
Mogk, Eugen. >> *Geschichte der norwegisch-isländischen Literatur* (1904).
   P. 807.
Mortensen, Lars Boje. "Olav den Helliges mirakler i det 12. årh.: streng
   tekstkontrol eller fri fabuleren?" In Inger Ekrem, Lars Boje Mortensen,
   and Karen Skovgaard- Petersen, ed. >> *Olavslegenden* (2000). Pp. 89–
   107, esp. p. 96.
Mortensen, Lars Boje, and Else Mundal. "Erkebispesetet i Nidaros
   – arnestad og verkstad for Olavs litteraturen." In *Ecclesia Nidrosiensis
   1153–1537: Søkelys på Nidaroskirskens og Nidarosprovinsens historie.*
   Ed. Steinar Imsen (Trondheim: Tapir Akademisk Forlag, 2003).
   Pp. 353–84, esp. pp. 360, 363–4, and 374.
Phelpstead, Carl. *Holy Vikings: Saints' Lives in the Old Icelandic Kings'
   Sagas.* Medieval and Renaissance Texts and Studies 40 (Tempe, Ariz.:
   Arizona Center for Medieval and Renaissance Studies, 2007). Pp. 20,
   45, and 152.
Røthe, Gunnhild. "Fortellinger om Olav den helliges fødsel og dåp i sagalit-
   teraturen." In Inger Ekrem, Lars Boje Mortensen, and Karen Skovgaard-
   Petersen, ed. >> *Olavslegenden* (2000). Pp. 170–85, esp. p. 174.
Sandnes, Jørn. "Olav den hellige – myter og virkelighet." In *Helgonet i
   Nidaros: Olavskult och kristnande i Norden.* Ed. Lars Rumar (Jyväsky-
   lä: Gummerus, 1997). Pp. 13–25, esp. p. 23.
Seip, Didrik Arup. "Jærtegnsamlinger." *KLNM* 8 (1963). Cols. 65–8, esp.
   col. 66.
Sverrir Tómasson, Bragi Halldórsson, and Einar Sigurbjörnsson, ed.
   >> *Heilagra karla sögur* (2007). P. 203.
Whaley, Diana. "Heimskringla and Its Sources: The Miracles of Óláfr
   helgi." In >> *The Sixth International Saga Conference* (1985). Vol. 2,
   pp. 1083–1103.
Handlist, p. 327.

2. Óláfs saga helga en elsta

Fragments of the first full-scale saga rendition of the history of King
Óláfr Haraldsson known as the "oldest saga."

Manuscript:
NRA 52 (ca. 1225).

Editions:

Guðni Jónsson, ed. *Konunga sögur*. 3 vols. ([Reykjavík]: Íslendingasagnaútgáfan, 1957). Vol. 1, pp. 403–26.

Hreinn Benediktsson. *Early Icelandic Script As Illustrated in Vernacular
Texts from the Twelfth and Thirteenth Centuries*. Íslenzk handrit:
Icelandic Manuscripts, Series in Folio 2 (Reykjavík: The Manuscript
Institute of Iceland, 1965). Plate 32 and p. xxii.
Facsimile and edition of fol. 2r.

Keyser, R., and C.R. Unger, ed. *Óláfs saga hins helga* (Christiania [Oslo]:
Feilberg & Landmark, 1849). Pp. 90–5.

Storm, Gustav, ed. *Otte Brudstykker af den ældste Saga om Olav den Hellige*
(Christiania [Oslo]: Grøndahl & Søn, 1893). Pp. 2–12.2.
Facsimile and text edition.

Literature:

Andersson, Theodore M. "Kings' Sagas (*Konungasögur*)." In *Old Norse–
Icelandic Literature: A Critical Guide*. Ed. Carol J. Clover and John
Lindow. Islandica 45 (Ithaca: Cornell University Press, 1985). Pp. 197–
238, esp. pp. 204, 212–14, 216–18, 222–3, 226, and 229.

– "The First Icelandic King's Saga: Oddr Snorrason's *Óláfs saga Tryggvasonar* or *The Oldest Saga of Saint Olaf?*" *JEGP* 103 (2004): 139–55.

– *The Growth of the Medieval Icelandic Sagas* (Ithaca: Cornell University
Press, 2006). Pp. 1–2, 14, 25, 46–8, 51–5, 59, 61, 64, 69–70, 84, 86–7, 98,
and 205.

– "The Oral Sources of *Óláfs saga helga* in *Heimskringla*." *Saga-Book* 32
(2008): 5–38, esp. pp. 30 and 34–5.

– "The Formation of the Kings' Sagas." *SI* 60 (2009): 77–87, esp. p. 81.

Ármann Jakobsson. "Royal Biography." In *A Companion to Old Norse–
Icelandic Literature*. Ed. Rory McTurk (Oxford: Blackwell, 2005).
Pp. 388–402, esp. p. 394.

Bagge, Sverre. "St. Óláfr and His Enemies in the Saga Tradition." In
Agneta Ney, Henrik Williams, and Fredrik Charpentier Ljungqvist, ed.
>> *Á austrvega: Sagas and East Scandinavia* (2009). Vol. 1, pp. 71–7,
esp. pp. 71–2 and 76.

– "Warrior, King, and Saint: The Medieval Histories about St. Óláfr
Haraldsson." *JEGP* 109 (2010): 281–321, esp. pp. 285, 287, 306, and 320.

Bekker-Nielsen, Hans, Thorkil Damsgaard Olsen, and Ole Widding.
>> *Norrøn fortællekunst* (1965). Pp. 62, 64, and 66.

Bekker-Nielsen, Hans, and Ole Widding. "Legende. Norge og Island."
KLNM 10 (1965). Cols. 421–3, esp. col. 422.

Cormack, Margaret. >> *The Saints in Iceland* (1994). P. 141.

Finnur Jónsson. >> *Den oldnorske og oldislandske Litteraturs Historie* (1920–4). Vol. 2, pp. 605–11.

Foote, Peter. "Saints' Lives and Sagas." In Hans Bekker-Nielsen and Birte Carlé, ed. >> *Saints and Sagas* (1994). Pp. 73–88, esp. p. 79.

Heinrichs, Anne. *Der Óláfs þáttr Geirstaðaálfs: Eine Variantenstudie* (Heidelberg: Carl Winter, 1989). Pp. 11, 22, 113, 123, 135, and 139.

– "Óláfs saga helga." In Phillip Pulsiano and Kirsten Wolf, with Paul Acker and Donald K. Fry, ed. >> *Medieval Scandinavia* (1993). Pp. 447–8.

– "Wenn ein König liebeskrank wird: Der Fall Óláfr Haraldsson." In *Die Aktualität der Saga: Festschrift für Hans Schottmann.* Ed. Stig Toftegaard Andersen (Berlin: de Gruyter, 1999). Pp. 27–51, esp. pp. 35n12, 44, 46, and 48n28.

Holm-Olsen, Ludvig. "Middelalderens litteratur i Norge." In *Norges litteratur historie* 1. Ed. Edvard Beyer (Oslo: Cappelen, 1974). Pp. 18–342, esp pp. 114–15.

Holtsmark, Anne. "Óláfs saga helga." *KLNM* 12 (1967). Cols. 546–50, esp. cols. 546–7.

– "Olavslegenden." *KLNM* 12 (1967). Cols. 584–8, esp. col. 586.

Johnsen, Oscar Albert. "Olavssagaens genesis." *Edda* 6 (1916): 209–24, esp. pp. 212–17.

Jón Helgason. *Norrøn Litteraturhistorie* (Copenhagen: Levin and Munksgaard, 1934). P. 140.

Jónas Kristjánsson. *Um Fóstbrœðra sögu* (Reykjavík: Stofnun Árna Magnússonar, 1972). Pp. 87, 91, 101–3, 108, 110–20, 129, 151–8, 160–87, 190–1, 196–9, 210–17, 220–3, 239, and 250.

– "The Legendary Saga." In Guðni Kolbeinsson, ed. >> *Minjar og menntir* (1976). Pp. 281–93.

– "Sagas and Saints' Lives." In *Cultura Classica e Cultura Germanica Settentrionale.* Ed. Pietro Janni, Diego Poli, and Carlo Santini (Macerata: Herder, 1985). Pp. 125–43, esp. p. 129.

– >> *Eddas and Sagas* (1988). Pp. 149, 157, 159–61, and 299.

Jørgensen, Jon Gunnar. "Passio Olavi og Snorre." In Inger Ekrem, Lars Boje Mortensen, and Karen Skovgaard-Petersen, ed. >> *Olavslegenden* (2000). Pp. 157–69, esp. p. 160.

Jørgensen, Jørgen Højgaard. "Hagiography and the Icelandic Bishop Sagas." *Peritia* 1 (1982): 1–16, esp. p. 5.

Kunin, Devra, trans. *A History of Norway and The Passion and Miracles of the Blessed Óláfr*. Edited with an Introduction and Notes by Carl Phelpstead. London: Viking Society for Northern Research, 2001). Pp. xxxiii and xxxix.

Lindow, John. "St Olaf and the Skalds." In Thomas A. DuBois, ed.
>> *Sanctity in the North* (2008). Pp. 103–27, esp. p. 103.

Louis-Jensen, Jonna. "'Syvende og ottende brudstykke': Fragmentet AM
325 α 4to IV." *Opuscula* 4. Bibliotheca Arnamagnæana 30 (Copenhagen: Munksgaard, 1970). Pp. 31–60, esp. pp. 45–60.

Lönnroth, Lars. "Det litterära porträttet i latinsk historiografi och
isländsk sagaskrivning – en komparativ studie." *ANF* 27 (1969):
68–117, esp. p. 74.

– "The Baptist and the Saint: Odd Snorrason's View of the Two King
Olavs." In *International Scandinavian and Medieval Studies in Memory
of Gerd Wolfgang Weber*. Ed. Michael Dallapiazza, Olaf Hansen,
Preben Meulengracht Sørensen, and Yvonne S. Bonnetain (Trieste:
Edizioni Parnaso, 2000). Pp. 257–64, esp. pp. 258–9 and 263.

Mogk, Eugen. >> *Geschichte der norwegisch-isländischen Literatur* (1904).
Pp. 806 and 810.

Mortensen, Lars Boje. "Olav den Helliges mirakler i det 12. årh.: streng
tekstkontrol eller fri fabuleren?" In Inger Ekrem, Lars Boje Mortensen,
and Karen Skovgaard-Petersen, ed. >> *Olavslegenden* (2000). Pp. 89–
107, esp. p. 95.

Mortensen, Lars Boje, and Else Mundal. "Erkebispesetet i Nidaros
– arnestad og verkstad for Olavs litteraturen." In *Ecclesia Nidrosiensis
1153–1537: Søkelys på Nidaroskirkens og Nidarosprovinsens historie*.
Ed. Steinar Imsen (Trondheim: Tapir Akademisk Forlag, 2003).
Pp. 353–84, esp. pp. 272–6.

Paasche, Fredrik. *Norges og Islands litteratur inntil utgangen av
middelalderen*. Rev. ed. by Anne Holtsmark (Oslo: Aschehoug, 1947).
P. 379.

Phelpstead, Carl. "In Honour of St Óláfr: The Miracle Stories in Snorri
Sturluson's *Óláfs saga helga*." *Saga-Book* 25 (2000): 292–306, esp.
p. 296.

– *Holy Vikings: Saints' Lives in the Old Icelandic Kings' Sagas*. Medieval
and Renaissance Texts and Studies 40 (Tempe, Ariz.: Arizona Center
for Medieval and Renaissance Studies, 2007). Pp. 21–2, 45, 197,
and 200.

Sandnes, Jørn. "Olav den hellige – myter og virkelighet." In *Helgonet i
Nidaros: Olavskult och kristnande i Norden*. Ed. Lars Rumar (Jyväskylä:
Gummerus, 1997). Pp. 13–25, esp. p. 23.

Schach, Paul. *Icelandic Sagas*. Twayne's World Author Series (Boston:
Twayne, 1984). Pp. 48–50, 55–6, 63, and 71.

Schier, Kurt. *Sagaliteratur*. Sammlung Metzler M78 (Stuttgart: Metzler,
1970). Pp. 12, 16–19, 23, 96, and 121.

Schreiner, Johan. *Tradisjon og saga om Olav den hellige.* Skrifter utgitt av
Det Norske Videnskaps-Akademi i Oslo, Hist.-Filos. Klasse 1926,
No. 1 (Oslo: Dybwad, 1926).
– "Studier i Olav den Helliges saga." *ANF* 43 (1927): 1–18.
Seip, Didrik Arup. *Den legendariske Olavssaga og Fagrskinna.* Avhand-
linger utgitt av Det Norske Videnskaps-Akademi i Oslo, II. Hist.-Filos.
Klasse 1929, No. 2 (Oslo: Dybwad, 1929). Pp. 3 and 6–7.
Sigurður Nordal. *Om Olaf den helliges saga: En kritisk undersøgelse*
(Copenhagen: Gad, 1914).
– *Um íslenzkar fornsögur.* Trans. Árni Böðvarsson (Reykjavík: Mál og
menning, 1968). Pp. 57 and 60–1.
Stefán Karlsson. "Islandsk bogeksport til Norge i middelalderen." *Mm*
(1979): 1–17, esp. p. 4. Rpt. in *Stafkrókar: Ritgerðir eftir Stefán
Karlsson gefnar út í tilefni af sjötugsafmæli hans 2. desember 1998.* Ed.
Guðvarður Már Gunnlaugsson (Reykjavík: Stofnun Árna Magnússonar,
2000). Pp. 188–205, esp. p. 192.
Sverrir Tómasson. *Formálar íslenskra sagnaritara á miðöldum. Rannsókn
bókmenntahefðar* (Reykjavík: Stofnun Árna Magnússonar, 1988).
Pp. 219 and 236.
– "Kristnar trúarbókmenntir í óbundnu máli." In Guðrún Nordal,
Sverrir Tómasson, and Vésteinn Ólason, ed. >> *Íslensk Bókmenntasaga*
1 (1992). Pp. 419–79, esp. p. 452.
– "The Hagiography of Snorri Sturluson Especially in the Great Saga of
St Olaf." In Hans Bekker-Nielsen and Birte Carlé, ed. >> *Saints and
Sagas* (1994). Pp. 49–71, esp. pp. 56–7.
Sverrir Tómasson, Bragi Halldórsson, and Einar Sigurbjörnsson, ed.
>> *Heilagra karla sögur* (2007). Pp. 203–4.
Turville-Petre, G. >> *Origins of Icelandic Literature* (1967). Pp. 175–6,
178–80, 182–3, 189–91, 194, 220, and 222.
Vries, Jan de. >> *Altnordische Literaturgeschichte* (1964–7). Vol. 1, p. 238,
and vol. 2, pp. 240, 243, 278, 285, and 387.
Handlist, p. 327.

3. Óláfs saga helga

A fragment of a separate collection of the miracles of King Óláfr
Haraldsson.

Manuscripts:
AM 325 α 4to IV (ca. 1250), NKS 1019c fol. (ca. 1750–1800), and NKS

1602 4to (ca. 1700–1800).

Editions:

Louis-Jensen, Jonna. "'Syvende og ottende brudstykke': Fragmentet AM
325 α 4to IV." *Opuscula* 4. Bibliotheca Arnamagnæana 30 (Copenhagen: Munksgaard, 1970). Pp. 31–60, esp. pp. 35–9.
Edition of AM 325 α 4to IV.

Storm, Gustav, ed. *Otte Brudstykker af den ældste Saga om Olav
den Hellige* (Christiania [Oslo]: Grøndahl & Søn, 1893).
Pp. 12.10–16.
Facsimile and text edition of AM 325 α 4to IV.

Literature:

Andersson, Theodore M. "Kings' Sagas (*Konungasögur*)." In *Old Norse–
Icelandic Literature: A Critical Guide*. Ed. Carol J. Clover and John
Lindow. Islandica 45 (Ithaca: Cornell University Press, 1985). Pp. 197–
238, esp. pp. 212–13.

Cormack, Margaret. >> *The Saints in Iceland* (1994). P. 141.

Finnur Jónsson. >> *Den oldnorske og oldislandske Litteraturs Historie*
(1920–4). Vol. 2, pp. 605–11.

Heinrichs, Anne. "Óláfs saga helga." In Phillip Pulsiano and Kirsten
Wolf, with Paul Acker and Donald K. Fry, ed. >> *Medieval Scandinavia* (1993). Pp. 447–8.

Holm-Olsen, Ludvig, and Kjell Heggelund. *Norges Litteratur Historie*.
Ed. Edvard Beyer (Oslo: Cappelen,1974). Pp. 114–16.

Holtsmark, Anne. "Óláfs saga helga." *KLNM* 12 (1967). Cols. 546–50,
esp. cols. 546–7.

– "Olavslegenden." *KLNM* 12 (1967). Cols. 584–8, esp. col. 586.

Johnsen, Oscar Albert. "Olavssagaens genesis." *Edda* 6 (1916): 209–24,
esp. pp. 212–17.

Jónas Kristjánsson. "The Legendary Saga." In Guðni Kolbeinsson, ed.
>> *Minjar og menntir* (1976). Pp. 281–93.

– >> *Eddas and Sagas* (1988). P. 157.

Jørgensen, Jon Gunnar. "Passio Olavi og Snorre." In Inger Ekrem, Lars
Boje Mortensen, and Karen Skovgaard-Petersen, ed. >> *Olavslegenden*
(2000). Pp. 157–69, esp. pp. 160–2.

Jørgensen, Jørgen Højgaard. "Hagiography and the Icelandic Bishop
Sagas." *Peritia* 1 (1982): 1–16, esp. p. 5.

Kunin, Devra, trans. *A History of Norway and The Passion and Miracles
of the Blessed Óláfr*. Edited with an Introduction and Notes by Carl
Phelpstead. London: Viking Society for Northern Research, 2001).
Pp. xxxiii–xxxiv, xxxix, and xli.

Lindow, John. "St Olaf and the Skalds." In Thomas A. DuBois, ed.
>> *Sanctity in the North* (2008). Pp. 103–27, esp. p. 103.

Mogk, Eugen. >> *Geschichte der norwegisch-isländischen Literatur* (1904).
Pp. 806 and 810.

Mortensen, Lars Boje. "Olav den Helliges mirakler i det 12. årh.: streng
tekstkontrol eller fri fabuleren?" In Inger Ekrem, Lars Boje Mortensen,
and Karen Skovgaard-Petersen, ed. >> *Olavslegenden* (2000). Pp. 89–
107, esp. p. 95.

Mortensen, Lars Boje, and Else Mundal. "Erkebispesetet i Nidaros
– arnestad og verkstad for olavs litteraturen." In *Ecclesia Nidrosiensis
1153–1537: Søkelys på Nidaroskirkens og Nidarosprovinsens historie*.
Ed. Steinar Imsen (Trondheim: Tapir Akademisk Forlag, 2003).
Pp. 353–84, esp. pp. 360 and 364–5.

Paasche, Fredrik. *Norges og Islands litteratur inntil utgangen av middelalderen*. Rev. ed. by Anne Holtsmark (Oslo: Aschehoug, 1947). P. 379.

Phelpstead, Carl. *Holy Vikings: Saints' Lives in the Old Icelandic Kings'
Sagas*. Medieval and Renaissance Texts and Studies 40 (Tempe, Ariz.:
Arizona Center for Medieval and Renaissance Studies, 2007). Pp. 45,
197, and 200.

Sandnes, Jørn. "Olav den hellige – myter og virkelighet." In *Helgonet i
Nidaros: Olavskult och kristnande i Norden*. Ed. Lars Rumar (Jyväskylä:
Gummerus, 1997). Pp. 13–25, esp. p. 23.

Schier, Kurt. *Sagaliteratur*. Sammlung Metzler M78 (Stuttgart: Metzler,
1970). Pp. 12, 16–19, 23, 96, and 121.

Schreiner, Johan. *Tradisjon og saga om Olav den hellige*. Skrifter utgitt
av Det Norske Videnskaps-Akademi i Oslo, Hist.-Filos. Klasse 1926,
No. 1 (Oslo: Dybwad, 1926).

– "Studier i Olav den Helliges saga." *ANF* 43 (1927): 1–18.

Seip, Didrik Arup. *Den legendariske Olavssaga og Fagrskinna*. Avhandlinger utgitt av Det Norske Videnskaps-Akademi i Oslo, II. Hist.-Filos.
Klasse 1929, No. 2 (Oslo: Dybwad, 1929). Pp. 3 and 6–7.

Sigurður Nordal. *Om Olaf den helliges saga: En kritisk undersøgelse*
(Copenhagen: Gad, 1914).

– *Um íslenzkar fornsögur*. Trans. Árni Böðvarsson (Reykjavík: Mál og
menning, 1968). Pp. 57 and 60–1.

Sverrir Tómasson. "The Hagiography of Snorri Sturluson Especially in
the Great Saga of St Olaf." In Hans Bekker-Nielsen and Birte Carlé,
ed. >> *Saints and Sagas* (1994). Pp. 49–71, esp. pp. 56–7.

– "Kristnar trúarbókmenntir í óbundnu máli." In Guðrún Nordal, Sverrir
Tómasson, and Vésteinn Ólason, ed. >> *Íslensk Bókmenntasaga 1*

(1992). Pp. 419–79, esp. p. 452.

Sverrir Tómasson, Bragi Halldórsson, and Einar Sigurbjörnsson, ed.
>> *Heilagra karla sögur* (2007). Pp. 203–4.

Turville-Petre, G. >> *Origins of Icelandic Literature* (1967). Pp. 175–7,
179–80, 182–3, 189–91, 194, 220, and 222.

Vries, Jan de. >> *Altnordische Literaturgeschichte* (1964–7). Vol. 2,
pp. 240, 243, 278, 285, and 387.

Whaley, Diana. "Heimskringla and Its Sources: The Miracles of Óláfr
helgi." In >> *The Sixth International Saga Conference* (1985). Vol. 2,
pp. 1083–1103.

Handlist, p. 327.

4. Óláfs saga helga (Helgisaga)

A Norwegian revision known as the "legendary saga" of the *Óláfs saga
helga en elsta*.

Manuscript:
DG 8 fol. (ca. 1225–50).
Editions:
Guðni Jónsson, ed. *Konunga sögur*. 3 vols. ([Reykjavík]: Íslendinga-
sagnaútgáfan, 1957). Vol. 1, pp. 201–400.

Heinrichs, Anne, Doris Janshen, Elke Radicke, and Hartmut Röhn, ed.
and trans. *Olafs saga hins helga: Die "Legendarische Saga" über Olaf
den Heiligen (Hs. Delagard. saml. nr. 8^{II})* (Heidelberg: Winter, 1982).
Pp. 30–236 (verso).

Holtsmark, Anne, ed. *Legendarisk Olavssaga etter Uppsala Universitets-
biblioteks Delagardieska Samlingen nr. 8 II*. CNN, Quarto serie 2 (Oslo:
Dreyer, 1956).
Facsimile.

Johnsen, Oscar Albert, ed. *Óláfs saga hins helga: Efter pergamentshaand-
skrift i Uppsala Universitetsbibliotek, Delagardieske Samling nr. 8^{II}*.
Det norske historiske kildeskriftfonds skrifter 47 (Christiania [Oslo]:
Dybwad, 1922. Pp. 1–108.

[Kålund, Kr., ed.] *Palæografisk Atlas: Oldnorsk-islandsk afdeling* (Copenhagen and Christiania [Oslo]: Gyldendal, 1905). No. 20.
Facsimile and text edition of fol. 82r.

Keyser, R., and C.R. Unger, ed. *Óláfs saga hins helga* (Christiania [Oslo]:
Feilberg & Landmark, 1849). Pp. 1–89.

Möbius, Th., ed. *Analecta Norræna. Auswahl aus der isländischen und norwegischen Litteratur des Mittelalters.* 2nd. ed. (Leipzig: J.C. Hinrichs'sche Buchhandlung, 1877). Pp. 42–9 (extract only).

English translation:

Lindow, John. "St Olaf and the Skalds." In Thomas A. DuBois, ed. >> *Sanctity in the North* (2008). Pp. 103–27, esp. pp. 121–3 (extracts only).

German translation:

Heinrichs, Anne, Doris Janshen, Elke Radicke, and Hartmut Röhn, ed. and trans. *Olafs saga hins helga: Die "Legendarische Saga" über Olaf den Heiligen (Hs. Delagard. saml. nr. 8^{II})* (Heidelberg: Winter, 1982). Pp. 31–237 (recto).

Literature:

Andersson, Theodore M. "Kings' Sagas (*Konungasögur*)." In *Old Norse–Icelandic Literature: A Critical Guide.* Ed. Carol J. Clover and John Lindow. Islandica 45 (Ithaca: Cornell University Press, 1985). Pp. 197–238, esp. pp. 204, 212–13, 221, 223–4, and 228–9.

– "Lore and Literature in a Scandinavian Conversion Episode." In *Idee-Gestalt-Geschichte. Festschrift Klaus von See. Studien zur europäischen Kulturtradition. Studies in European Cultural Tradition.* Ed. Gerd Wolfgang Weber (Odense: Odense University Press, 1988). Pp. 261–84.

– "The First Icelandic King's Saga: Oddr Snorrason's *Óláfs saga Tryggvasonar* or *The Oldest Saga of Saint Olaf?*" *JEGP* 103 (2004): 139–55.

– *The Growth of the Medieval Icelandic Sagas* (Ithaca: Cornell University Press, 2006). Pp. 1–2, 13–15, 20, 43–59, 64–5, 70, 84, 87–8, 93, 98, and 120.

– "The Oral Sources of *Óláfs saga helga* in *Heimskringla.*" *Saga-Book* 32 (2008): 5–38, esp. pp. 22, 30, and 34–5.

– "The Formation of the Kings' Sagas." *SI* 60 (2009): 77–87, esp. p. 81.

Ármann Jakobsson. "Royal Biography." In *A Companion to Old Norse–Icelandic Literature.* Ed. Rory McTurk (Oxford: Blackwell, 2005). Pp. 388–402, esp. p. 394.

Bagge, Sverre. "St. Óláfr and his Enemies in the Saga Tradition." In Agneta Ney, Henrik Williams, and Fredrik Charpentier Ljungqvist, ed. >> *Á austrvega: Sagas and East Scandinavia* (2009). Vol. 1, pp. 71–7.

– "Warrior, King, and Saint: The Medieval Histories about St. Óláfr Haraldsson." *JEGP* 109 (2010): 281–321.

Bekker-Nielsen, Hans, Thorkil Damsgaard Olsen, and Ole Widding. >> *Norrøn fortællekunst* (1965). Pp. 64 and 67–8.

Bekker-Nielsen, Hans, and Ole Widding. "Religiøs prosalitteratur. Norge og Island." *KLNM* 14 (1969). Cols. 42–4, esp. col. 42.

Clover, Carol J. *The Medieval Saga* (Ithaca: Cornell University Press, 1982). Pp. 99–100, 161–4, 172, 174, 179, and 182–4.

Cormack, Margaret. >> *The Saints in Iceland* (1994). P. 141.

Daae, Ludvig. *Norges helgener* (Christiania [Oslo]: Malling, 1879). Pp. 23, 27, 39, 41, 52, 57, 60, 117, and 127.

Dillmann, François-Xavier. "Om hedningar och hundar. Kring den fornvästnordiska sammansättningen *hundheiðinn*." *SI* 52 (2001): 17–33, esp. p. 28.

Ellehøj, Svend. *Studier over den ældste norrøne historieskrivning*. Bibliotheca Arnamagnæana 26 (Copenhagen: Munksgaard, 1965). Pp. 172–4.

Finnur Jónsson. >> *Den oldnorske og oldislandske Litteraturs Historie* (1920–4). Vol. 2, pp. 605–11.

Foote, Peter. "Auðræði." In Arthur Brown and Peter Foote, ed. >> *Early English and Norse Studies* (1963). Pp. 62–76, esp. p. 63.

Frankis, John. "An Old English Source for the Guðbrandsdal Episode in *Óláfs saga helga*." In *The Third International Saga Conference, Oslo, July 26th–31st, 1976* (Oslo, 1976). [Preprints distributed to participants.]

Haki Antonsson. *St. Magnús of Orkney: A Scandinavian Martyr-Cult in Context*. Northern World 29 (Leiden: Brill, 2007). Pp. 107–8.

Hallberg, Peter. "Direct Speech and Dialogue in Three Versions of *Óláfs saga helga*." *ANF* 93 (1978): 116–37.

Heinrichs, Anne. "Episoden als Strukturelemente in der Legendarischen Saga und ihre Varianten in anderen Olafssaga." In *The Third International Saga Conference, Oslo, July 26th–31st, 1976* (Oslo, 1976). [Preprints distributed to participants.]

– "'Intertexture' and Its Function in Early Written Sagas: A Stylistic Observation of *Heiðarvíga saga*, *Reykdæla saga* and the *Legendary Olafssaga*." *SS* 48 (1976): 127–45.

– "Christliche Überformung traditioneller Erzählstoffe in der 'Legendarischen Olafssaga'." In >> *The Sixth International Saga Conference* (1985). Vol. 1, pp. 451–67.

– *Der Óláfs þáttr Geirstaðaálfs: Eine Variantenstudie* (Heidelberg: Carl Winter, 1989). Pp. 11–12, 16, 18, 22, 26, 28, 39, 43, 48–51, 60, 62–3, 65–9, 73–6, 95, 99, 104–6, 108, 111, 113–14, 118, 121–3, 134–5, 139, 152, and 154.

– "Óláfs saga helga." In Phillip Pulsiano and Kirsten Wolf, with Paul Acker and Donald K. Fry, ed. >> *Medieval Scandinavia* (1993). Pp. 447–8.

– "Wenn ein König liebeskrank wird: Der Fall Óláfr Haraldsson." In *Die Aktualität der Saga: Festschrift für Hans Schottmann*. Ed. Stig Toftegaard Andersen (Berlin: de Gruyter, 1999). Pp. 27–51.

Heller, Rolf. "Olaf vor der Küste Irlands. (Leg.) Óláfs saga hins helga und Laxdæla saga." *ANF* 83 (1968): 23–34.

Holm-Olsen, Ludvig. "Middelalderens litteratur i Norge." In *Norges litteratur historie* 1. Ed. Edvard Beyer (Oslo: Cappelen, 1974). Pp. 18–342, esp pp. 116–17.

Holtsmark, Anne. "Sankt Olavs liv og mirakler." In *Festskrift til Francis Bull på 50 årsdagen* (Oslo: Gyldendal, 1937). Pp. 121–33, esp. pp. 121 and 127. Rpt. in Anne Holtsmark. *Studier i norrøn diktning* (Oslo: Gyldendal, 1956). Pp. 15–24, esp. pp. 15 and 20.

– "Olav den hellige og 'seiersskjorten'." *Mm* (1954): 104–8. Rpt. in Anne Holtsmark, *Studier i norrøn diktning* (Oslo: Gyldendal, 1956). Pp. 172–5.

– "Óláfs saga helga." *KLNM* 12 (1967). Cols. 546–50, esp. cols. 547–8.

– "Olavslegenden." *KLNM* 12 (1967). Cols. 584–8, esp. cols. 585–7.

Johnsen, Oscar Albert. "Olavssagaens genesis." *Edda* 6 (1916): 209–24, esp. pp. 215–17.

Jón Helgason. *Norrøn Litteraturhistorie* (Copenhagen: Levin and Munksgaard, 1934). P. 141.

Jónas Kristjánsson. *Um Fóstbrœðra sögu* (Reykjavík: Stofnun Árna Magnússonar, 1972). Pp. 87–8, 90–1, 94–6, 100–3, 108, 114, 118, 120–1, 126, 128, 130, 144–5, 149, 151–64, 166–88, 190–1, 193, 196–221, 223, 229, 239–40, 250, 273, and 296.

– "The Legendary Saga." In Guðni Kolbeinsson, ed. >> *Minjar og menntir* (1976). Pp. 281–93.

– >> *Eddas and Sagas* (1988). Pp. 159, 170, 172, 211, 280–1, and 299.

Jørgensen, Jon Gunnar. "Passio Olavi og Snorre." In Inger Ekrem, Lars Boje Mortensen, and Karen Skovgaard-Petersen, ed. >> *Olavslegenden* (2000). Pp. 157–69, esp. pp. 159–63.

Kirby, Ian. >> *Biblical Quotation* (1980). Vol. 2, pp. 67 and 103–4.

Kunin, Devra, trans. *A History of Norway and The Passion and Miracles of the Blessed Óláfr*. Edited with an Introduction and Notes by Carl Phelpstead. London: Viking Society for Northern Research, 2001). Pp. xxix, xxxix, xl, and xliv.

Louis-Jensen, Jonna. "'Syvende og ottende brudstykke': Fragmentet AM 325 α 4to IV." *Opuscula* 4. Bibliotheca Arnamagnæana 30 (Copenhagen: Munksgaard, 1970). Pp. 31–60, esp. pp. 46–60.

Lönnroth, Lars. "Det litterära porträttet i latinsk historiografi och isländsk sagaskrivning – en komparativ studie." *ANF* 27 (1969): 68–117, esp. pp. 74, 86, and 90.

– "The Baptist and the Saint: Odd Snorrason's view of the Two King Olavs." In *International Scandinavian and Medieval Studies in Memory of Gerd Wolfgang Weber*. Ed. Michael Dallapiazza, Olaf Hansen, Preben Meulengracht Sørensen, and Yvonne S. Bonnetain (Trieste: Edizioni Parnaso, 2000). Pp. 257–64, esp. pp. 258–9 and 263–4.

Mogk, Eugen. >> *Geschichte der norwegisch-isländischen Literatur* (1904). Pp. 687 and 807.

Mortensen, Lars Boje, and Else Mundal. "Erkebispesetet i Nidaros – arnestad og verkstad for Olavs litteraturen." In *Ecclesia Nidrosiensis 1153–1537: Søkelys på Nidaroskirkens og Nidarosprovinsens historie.* Ed. Steinar Imsen (Trondheim: Tapir Akademisk Forlag, 2003). Pp. 353–84, esp. pp. 372 and 374–6.

Ólafur Halldórsson. "Þingamanna þáttur." In Gísli Sigurðsson, Guðrún Kvaran, and Sigurgeir Steingrímsson, ed. >> *Sagnaþing helgað Jónasi Kristjánssyni* (1994). Vol. 2, pp. 617–40.

Paasche, Fredrik. *Norges og Islands litteratur inntil utgangen av middelalderen*. Rev. ed. by Anne Holtsmark (Oslo: Aschehoug, 1947). Pp. 268, 379, and 526.

Phelpstead, Carl. "In Honour of St Óláfr: The Miracle Stories in Snorri Sturluson's *Óláfs saga helga.*" *Saga-Book* 25 (2000): 292–306, esp. pp. 296–7.

– *Holy Vikings: Saints' Lives in the Old Icelandic Kings' Sagas*. Medieval and Renaissance Texts and Studies 40 (Tempe, Ariz.: Arizona Center for Medieval and Renaissance Studies, 2007). Pp. 22, 45, 125, 128–30, 132, 135–6, 138, 152, 154, 202, 212, and 215.

Reinskou, Finn. "Olav den helliges vimpel?" *Mm* (1922): 32–6.

Røthe, Gunnhild. "Fortellinger om Olav den helliges fødsel og dåp i sagalitteraturen." In Inger Ekrem, Lars Boje Mortensen, and Karen Skovgaard-Petersen, ed. >> *Olavslegenden* (2000). Pp. 170–85, esp. pp. 173, 175, and 177–80.

Sandnes, Jørn. "Olav den hellige – myter og virkelighet." In *Helgonet i Nidaros: Olavskult och kristnande i Norden*. Ed. Lars Rumar (Jyväskylä: Gummerus, 1997). Pp. 13–25, esp. p. 23.

Schach, Paul. *Icelandic Sagas*. Twayne's World Author Series (Boston: Twayne, 1984). Pp. 15, 50–1, 56–7, 59, 71–2, 77, 79, 82, 99, and 124.

Schier, Kurt. *Sagaliteratur*. Sammlung Metzler M78 (Stuttgart: Metzler, 1970). Pp. 3–4, 13, 16, 19, 23, and 121.

Schreiner, Johan. *Tradisjon og saga om Olav den hellige*. Skrifter utgitt av Det Norske Videnskaps-Akademi i Oslo, Hist.-Filos. Klasse 1926, No. 1 (Oslo: Dybwad, 1926).

– "Studier i Olav den Helliges saga." *ANF* 43 (1927): 1–18.

Seip, Didrik Arup. *Den legendariske Olavssaga og Fagrskinna*. Avhandlinger utgitt av Det Norske Videnskaps-Akademi i Oslo, II. Hist.-Filos. Klasse 1929, No. 2 (Oslo: Dybwad, 1929).

Sigurður Nordal. *Om Olaf den helliges saga: En kritisk undersøgelse* (Copenhagen: Gad, 1914).

– *Um íslenzkar fornsögur*. Trans. Árni Böðvarsson (Reykjavík: Mál og menning, 1968). Pp. 60–1.

Stefán Karlsson. "Islandsk bogeksport til Norge i middelalderen." *Mm* (1979): 1–17, esp. p. 4. Rpt. in *Stafkrókar: Ritgerðir eftir Stefán Karlsson gefnar út í tilefni af sjötugsafmæli hans 2. desember 1998*. Ed. Guðvarður Már Gunnlaugsson (Reykjavík: Stofnun Árna Magnússonar, 2000). Pp. 188–205, esp. p. 192.

Storm, Gustav, ed. *Otte Brudstykker af den ældste Saga om Olav den Hellige* (Christiania [Oslo]: Grøndahl & Søn, 1893). Pp. 10–22.

Sverrir Tómasson. *Formálar íslenskra sagnaritara á miðöldum. Rannsókn bókmenntahefðar* (Reykjavík: Stofnun Árna Magnússonar, 1988). Pp. 269–70.

– "The Hagiography of Snorri Sturluson Especially in the Great Saga of St Olaf." In Hans Bekker-Nielsen and Birte Carlé, ed. >> *Saints and Sagas* (1994). Pp. 49–71, esp. pp. 56–7.

– "Kristnar trúarbókmenntir í óbundnu máli." In Guðrún Nordal, Sverrir Tómasson, and Vésteinn Ólason, ed. >> *Íslensk Bókmenntasaga* 1 (1992). Pp. 419–79, esp. pp. 451, 453, 421, and 452–3.

Sverrir Tómasson, Bragi Halldórsson, and Einar Sigurbjörnsson, ed. >> *Heilagra karla sögur* (2007). P. 204.

Turville-Petre, G. >> *Origins of Icelandic Literature* (1967). Pp. 136, 176–8, 183–8, 194, 220, and 222.

Vries, Jan de. >> *Altnordische Literaturgeschichte* (1964–7). Vol. 2, pp. 240, 257, and 278.

Weber, Gerd Wolfgang. *Studien zur europäischen Kulturtradition. Studies in European Cultural Tradition* (Odense: Odense University Press, 1968). Pp. 261–84.

Wellendorf, Jonas. "Ideologi og trosforestillinger i Óláfs saga Geirstaðaálfs: Om jordfundne genstande og rituelle højbrud." *Nordica Bergensia* 29 (2003): 147–69

– "The Attraction of the Earliest Old Norse Vernacular Hagiography." In Haki Antonsson and Ildar H. Garipzanov, ed. >> *Saints and Their Lives on the Periphery* (2010). Pp. 241–58, esp. pp. 255–6.

Whaley, Diana. "Heimskringla and Its Sources: The Miracles of Óláfr

helgi." In >> *The Sixth International Saga Conference* (1985). Vol. 2,
pp. 1083–1103.
Handlist, p. 327–8.

5. Óláfs saga helga

A short separate saga including material from 1–4.

Manuscript:
AM 235 fol. (ca. 1400).
Edition:
Unger, C.R., ed. >> *Heilagra manna søgur* (1877). Vol. 2, pp. 159–82.
Modern Icelandic language edition:
Sverrir Tómasson, Bragi Halldórsson, and Einar Sigurbjörnsson, ed.
    >> *Heilagra karla sögur* (2007). Pp. 169–202.
Norwegian translation:
Mundal, Else. *Legender frå mellomalderen. Soger om heilage kvinner og
    menn* (Oslo: Det Norske Samlaget, 1995). Pp. 157–91.
Literature:
Carlé, Birte. >> *Jomfru-fortællingen* (1985). P. 38.
– "Men and Women in the Saints' Sagas of *Stock. 2, fol.*" In John
    Lindow, Lars Lönnroth, and Gerd Wolfgang Weber, ed. >> *Structure
    and Meaning in Old Norse Literature* (1986). Pp. 317–46, esp. p. 319.
Daae, Ludvig. *Norges helgener* (Christiania [Oslo]: Malling, 1879).
    Pp. 27–8, 40, 44, 52, 60, and 117.
Dillmann, François-Xavier. "Om hedningar och hundar. Kring den
    fornvästnordiska sammansättningen *hundheiðinn.*" *SI* 52 (2001): 17–33,
    esp. pp. 22 and 24.
Hallberg, Peter. "Imagery in Religious Old Norse Prose Literature: An
    Outline." *ANF* 102 (1987): 120–70, esp. p. 139.
Jónas Kristjánsson. >> *Eddas and Sagas* (1988). P. 157.
Sverrir Tómasson. "Kristnar trúarbókmenntir í óbundnu máli." In Guðrún
    Nordal, Sverrir Tómasson, and Vésteinn Ólason, ed. >> *Íslensk Bók-
    menntasaga* 1 (1992). Pp. 419–79, esp. pp. 421, 451, and 453–4.
Handlist, p. 328
NOTE:
Episodes and miracles related in 1–5 can also be found in the secular
sagas of King Óláfr Haraldsson (not listed here). These include *Óláfs
saga helga en mesta* and *Óláfs saga helga* in *Heimskringla.*

OSWALD   August 5

Osvalds saga

Translated from a now-lost Low German redaction that resembles the source(s) of *Der Heiligen Leben.*

Manuscript:
Stock. Perg. fol. no. 3 (*Reykjahólabók*) (ca. 1530–40).
Editions:
Jón Sigurðsson, ed. "Saga Ósvalds konúngs hins helga." *Annaler for nordisk Oldkyndighed og Historie* (1854): 3–91, esp. pp. 24–91.
Kalinke, Marianne E., ed. *St. Oswald of Northumbria: Continental Metamorphoses. With an Edition and Translation of* Ósvalds saga *and* Van sunte Oswaldo deme konninghe. Medieval and Renaissance Texts and Studies 27 (Tempe, Ariz.: Arizona Center for Medieval and Renaissance Studies, 2005). Pp. 110–17 (verso).
Loth, Agnete, ed. >> *Reykjahólabók* (1969–70). Vol. 1, pp. 71–95.
Danish translation:
Repp, Thorleif Gudm. "Saga Ósvalds konúngs hins helga." *Annaler for nordisk Oldkyndighed og Historie* (1854): 3–91, esp. pp. 24–91.
English translation:
Kalinke, Marianne E., ed. *St. Oswald of Northumbria: Continental Metamorphoses. With an Edition and Translation of* Ósvalds saga *and* Van sunte Oswaldo deme konninghe. Medieval and Renaissance Texts and Studies 27 (Tempe, Ariz.: Arizona Center for Medieval and Renaissance Studies, 2005). Pp. 110–17 (recto).
Literature:
Baesecke, Georg, ed. *Der Münchener Oswald. Text und Abhandlung* (Breslau: Marcus, 1709; rpt. Hildesheim: Olms, 1977). P. 221.
Bekker-Nielsen, Hans, Thorkil Damsgaard Olsen, and Ole Widding. >> *Norrøn fortællekunst* (1965). P. 126.
Bekker-Nielsen, Hans, and Ole Widding. "Legende. Norge og Island." *KLNM* 10 (1965). Cols. 421–3, esp. col. 421.
Benati, Chiara. "The Fantastic and the Supernatural in the *Saga Ósvalds konúngs hins helga.*" In John McKinnell, David Ashurst, and Donata Kick, ed. >> *The Fantastic in Old Norse/Icelandic Literature* (2006). Vol. 1, pp. 130–9.
Edzardi, Anton. *Untersuchungen über das Gedicht von St. Oswald* (Hannover: Carl Rümpler, 1876). Pp. 3–10.

Finnur Jónsson. >> *Den oldnorske og oldislandske Litteraturs Historie* (1920–4). Vol. 3, p. 141.

Kalinke, Marianne E. "*Osvalds saga konungs.*" In >> *The Audience of the Sagas* (1991). Vol. 1, pp. 268–77.

– "Reykjahólabók: A Legendary on the Eve of the Reformation." *Skáldskaparmál* 2 (1992): 239–69, esp. p. 240.

– "The Cowherd and the Saint: The Grateful Lion in Icelandic Folklore and Legend." *SS* 66 (1994): 1–22, esp. p. 7.

– >> *The Book of Reykjahólar* (1996). Pp. 28, 45–6, 50, 116–17, 211, and 222–36.

– "The Genesis of Fiction in the North." In John McKinnell, David Ashurst, and Donata Kick, ed. >> *The Fantastic in Old Norse / Icelandic Literature* (2006). Vol. 1, pp. 464–78, esp. pp. 473–4.

Klockhoff, Oskar. "Om Osvalds saga." In *Små Bidrag till nordiska Literaturhistorien under Medeltiden* (Uppsala: E. Edquist, 1880). Pp. 1–22.

Leach, Henry Goddard. *Angevin Britain and Scandinavia.* Harvard Studies in Comparative Literature (Cambridge, Mass.: Harvard University Press, 1921). P. 127.

Mogk, Eugen. >> *Geschichte der norwegisch-isländischen Literatur* (1904). P. 895.

Möbius, Th., ed. *Analecta Norræna. Auswahl aus der isländischen und norwegischen Litteratur des Mittelalters.* 2nd. ed. (Leipzig: J.C. Hinrichs'sche Buchhandlung, 1877). P. 272.

Sverrir Tómasson. "Trúarbókmenntir í lausu máli á síðmiðöld." In Böðvar Guðmundsson, Sverrir Tómasson, Torfi H. Tulinius, and Vésteinn Ólason, ed. >> *Íslensk Bókmenntasaga* 2 (1993). Pp. 249–82, esp. p. 279.

Widding, Ole, and Hans Bekker-Nielsen. "En senmiddelalderlig legendesamling." *Mm* (1960): 105–28, esp. pp. 107 and 113–14.

– "Low German Influence on Late Icelandic Hagiography." *GR* 37 (1962): 239–62, esp. p. 248.

Zingerle, Ignaz V. *Die Oswaldlegende und ihre Beziehung zur deutschen Mythologie* (Stuttgart and Munich: Scheitlin, 1856). P. 87.

Handlist, p. 328.

PANTALEON   July 27

Two small fragments of what may be a legend of Saint Pantaleon.

Manuscript:
Odense Bys Museer, Møntergården. Two fragments (ca. 1200–1300) used
to support early seventeenth-century treasurer's office accounts in
Odense.

Literature:
Bekker-Nielsen, Hans. "Et par ord om de ældste norrøne helgensager." In
Finn Hødnebø et al., >> *Eyvindarbók* (1992). Pp. 29–33, esp. pp. 31–2.

PAUL THE APOSTLE   June 29

1. Páls saga postola I

Based chiefly on a glossed version of the *Historia Actuum Apostolorum*
now attributed to Peter of Poitiers.

Manuscripts:
AM 645 4to (ca. 1225–50) and AM 655 4to XVI (ca. 1250–1300).

Editions:
Holtsmark, Anne, ed. *A Book of Miracles: MS No. 645 4to of the Arna-
Magnæan Collection in the University Library of Copenhagen.* CCI 12
(Copenhagen: Einar Munksgaard, 1938).
Facsimile of AM 645 4to.
Unger, C.R., ed. >> *Postola sögur* (1874). Pp. 216.10–236.16.
Based on AM 645 4to with variants from AM 655 4to XVI (pp.
223.15–230.1).

English translation:
Roughton, Philip G. "AM 645 4to and AM 652/630 4to: Study and
Translation of Two Thirteenth-Century Icelandic Collections of
Apostles' and Saints' Lives." PhD dissertation, University of Colorado,
2002. Pp. 564–99.

Literature:
Battista, Simonetta. "Interpretations of the Roman Pantheon in the Old
Norse Hagiographic Sagas." In Geraldine Barnes and Margaret
Clunies Ross, ed. >> *Old Norse Myths, Literature and Society* (2000).
Pp. 24–34, esp. pp. 28–9, 31, and 34.
Bekker-Nielsen, Hans. "Paulus. Norrøn tradition." *KLNM* 13 (1968).
Cols. 153–4.
– "Et par ord om de ældste norrøne helgensagaer." In Finn Hødnebø et
al., >> *Eyvindarbók* (1992). Pp. 29–33, esp. p. 32.

Bekker-Nielsen, Hans, Thorkil Damsgaard Olsen, and Ole Widding. >> *Norrøn fortællekunst* (1965). P. 122.

Cormack, Margaret. >> *The Saints in Iceland* (1994). Pp. 145 and 244.

Finnur Jónsson. >> *Den oldnorske og oldislandske Litteraturs Historie* (1920–4). Vol. 2, p. 870.

Foote, Peter. "Saints' Lives and Sagas." In Hans Bekker-Nielsen and Birte Carlé, ed. >> *Saints and Sagas* (1994). Pp. 73–88, esp. p. 81.

Hallberg, Peter. "Imagery in Religious Old Norse Prose Literature: An Outline." *ANF* 102 (1987): 120–70, esp. p. 124.

Hofmann, Dietrich. *Die Legende von Sankt Clemens in den skandinavischen Ländern im Mittelalter*. Beiträge zur Skandinavistik 13 (Frankfurt am Main: Peter Lang, 1997). P. 142.

Jón Ma. Ásgeirsson and Þórður Ingi Guðjónsson, ed. *Frá Sýrlandi til Íslands: Arfur Tómasar postula* (Reykjavík: Háskólaútgáfan, 2007). P. 164.

Jónas Kristjánsson. "Sagas and Saints' Lives." In *Cultura Classica e Cultura Germanica Settentrionale*. Ed. Pietro Janni, Diego Poli, and Carlo Santini (Macerata: Herder, 1985). Pp. 125–43.

Kirby, Ian. >> *Biblical Quotation* (1980). Vol. 2, p. 25.

– *Bible Translation in Old Norse*. Université de Lausanne Publications de la faculté des lettres 27 (Geneva: Librairie Droz, 1986). Pp. 87–9.

– "The Bible and Biblical Interpretation in Medieval Iceland." In *Old Icelandic Literature and Society*. Ed. Margaret Clunies Ross (Cambridge: Cambridge University Press, 2000). Pp. 287–301, esp. p. 295.

Kratz, Henry. "The Language of the Old Norse Saints' Lives." *Mm* (1988): 159–73.

Mogk, Eugen. >> *Geschichte der norwegisch-isländischen Literatur* (1904). Pp. 887–8.

Roughton, Philip. "Stylistics and Sources of the *Postola sögur* in AM 645 4to and AM 652/630 4to." *Gripla* 16 (2005): 7–50.

Sverrir Tómasson. *Formálar íslenskra sagnaritara á miðöldum. Rannsókn bókmenntahefðar* (Reykjavík: Stofnun Árna Magnússonar, 1988). Pp. 268 and 351.

– "Erlendur vísdómur og forn fræði." In Guðrún Nordal, Sverrir Tómasson, and Vésteinn Ólason, ed. >> *Íslensk Bókmenntasaga* 1 (1992). Pp. 517–70, esp. p. 558.

Þórður Ingi Guðjónsson. "Apostlene i islandsk middelalderlitteratur." In *Den nordiske renessansen i høymiddelalderen*. Ed. Jón Viðar Sigurðsson and Preben Meulengracht Sørensen (Oslo: Historisk institutt, Universitetet i Oslo, 2000). Pp. 83–99, esp. p. 93.

Handlist, p. 328.

2. Páls saga postola II

Based directly or indirectly on a glossed version of the *Historia Actuum Apostolorum* now attributed to Peter of Poitiers, Pauline hagiography, and a commentary on Saint Paul's epistles.

Manuscripts:
AM 234 fol. (ca. 1340, defective), AM 236 fol. (ca. 1600, defective), AM 631 4to (ca. 1700–25), AM 655 4to XVII (ca. 1250), AM 84 8vo (ca. 1550), NRA 80 (ca. 1330), and SÁM 1 fol. (*Codex Scardensis*) (ca. 1350–75).

Editions:
Hreinn Benediktsson. *Early Icelandic Script As Illustrated in Vernacular Texts from the Twelfth and Thirteenth Centuries.* Íslenzk handrit: Icelandic Manuscripts, Series in Folio 2 (Reykjavík: The Manuscript Institute of Iceland, 1965). Plate 44.
Facsimile of AM 655 4to XVII fol. 1r.
Slay, Desmond, ed. *Codex Scardensis.* EIM 2 (Copenhagen: Rosenkilde and Bagger, 1960).
Facsimile of SÁM 1 fol.
Unger, C.R., ed. >> *Postola sögur* (1874). Pp. 236.18–283.23.
Based on AM 234 fol. (pp. 236.18–267.12 and 271.18–279.22), and AM 84 8vo (pp. 267.13– 271.18) with variants from AM 236 fol. (pp. 236.18–279.22), AM 655 4to XVII (pp. 260.25– 263.2, 271.15– 274.4, 276.17–278.30), AM 631 4to (pp. 236.18–279.22), and AM 84 8vo (pp. 236.18–267.12 and 271.19–279.22). Edition of NRA 80 (pp. 279.24–283.23).

Modern Icelandic language edition:
Ólafur Halldórsson, ed. *Sögur úr Skarðsbók* (Reykjavík: Almenna bókafélagið, 1967). Pp. 43–69.
Edition of SÁM 1 fol. (extracts only).

Literature:
Ásdís Egilsdóttir. "The Fantastic Reality: Hagiography, Miracles and Fantasy." In John McKinnell, David Ashurst, and Donata Kick, ed. >> *The Fantastic in Old Norse/Icelandic Literature* (2006). Vol. 1, pp. 63–70, esp. p. 65.
Ashurst, David. "Imagining Paradise." In John McKinnell, David Ashurst, and Donata Kick, ed. >> *The Fantastic in Old Norse/Icelandic Literature* (2006). Vol. 1, pp. 71–80, esp. pp. 75 and 77–9.
Battista, Simonetta. "Interpretations of the Roman Pantheon in the Old Norse Hagiographic Sagas." In Geraldine Barnes and Margaret

Clunies Ross, ed. >> *Old Norse Myths, Literature and Society* (2000). Pp. 24–34, esp. pp. 29 and 31.

– "The *Compilator* and Contemporary Literary Culture in Old Norse Hagiography." *Viking and Medieval Scandinavia* 1 (2005): 1–13, esp. p. 7.

Bekker-Nielsen, Hans. "Paulus. Norrøn tradition." *KLNM* 13 (1968). Cols. 153–4.

Bekker-Nielsen, Hans, Thorkil Damsgaard Olsen, and Ole Widding. >> *Norrøn fortællekunst* (1965). P. 123.

Collings, Lucy Grace. "The Codex Scardensis: Studies in Icelandic Hagiography." PhD dissertation, Cornell University, 1969. Pp. 31–52 and 208–12.

Cormack, Margaret. >> *The Saints in Iceland* (1994). Pp. 145 and 244.

Eiríkr Magnússon. "Kodex Skardensis af postulasögur." *ANF* 8 (1892): 238–45, esp. p. 241.

Finnur Jónsson. >> *Den oldnorske og oldislandske Litteraturs Historie* (1920–4). Vol. 2, p. 870.

Foote, Peter. "Postulatal." In Guðni Kolbeinsson, ed. >> *Minjar og menntir* (1976). Pp. 152–73, esp. p. 159.

Hallberg, Peter. "Imagery in Religious Old Norse Prose Literature: An Outline." *ANF* 102 (1987): 120–70, esp. pp. 131 and 149.

Hofmann, Dietrich. *Die Legende von Sankt Clemens in den skandinavischen Ländern im Mittelalter.* Beiträge zur Skandinavistik 13 (Frankfurt am Main: Peter Lang, 1997). P. 69.

Jón Ma. Ásgeirsson and Þórður Ingi Guðjónsson, ed. *Frá Sýrlandi til Íslands: Arfur Tómasar postula* (Reykjavík: Háskólaútgáfan, 2007). P. 165.

Jón Þorkelsson. "Islandske håndskrifter i England og Skotland." *ANF* 8 (1892): 199–237, esp. pp. 235–6.

Kirby, Ian. >> *Biblical Quotation* (1980). Vol. 2, pp. 25–6.

– *Bible Translation in Old Norse.* Université de Lausanne Publications de la faculté des lettres 27 (Geneva: Librairie Droz, 1986). Pp. 46 and 87–9.

– "The Bible and Biblical Interpretation in Medieval Iceland." In *Old Icelandic Literature and Society.* Ed. Margaret Clunies Ross (Cambridge: Cambridge University Press, 2000). Pp. 287–301, esp. p. 295.

Kratz, Henry. "The Language of the Old Norse Saints' Lives." *Mm* (1988): 159–73.

Mogk, Eugen. >> *Geschichte der norwegisch-isländischen Literatur* (1904). Pp. 887–8.

Ólafur Halldórsson. *Helgafellsbækur fornar*. Studia Islandica 24 (Reykjavík: Heimspekideild Háskóla Íslands and Menningarsjóður, 1966). Pp. 16–22 and 41–5.

Ólafur Halldórsson, ed. *Mattheus saga postula* (Reykjavík: Stofnun Árna Magnússonar, 1994). Pp. xli–xlviii.

Stefán Karlsson. "Islandsk bogeksport til Norge i middelalderen." *Mm* (1979): 1–17, esp. p. 6. Rpt. in *Stafkrókar: Ritgerðir eftir Stefán Karlsson gefnar út í tilefni af sjötugsafmæli hans 2. desember 1998*. Ed. Guðvarður Már Gunnlaugsson (Reykjavík: Stofnun Árna Magnússonar, 2000). Pp. 188–205, esp. p. 194.

Svanhildur Óskarsdóttir. "Universal History in Fourteenth-Century Iceland: Studies in AM 764 4to." PhD dissertation, University of London, 2000. P. 207n403.

Sverrir Tómasson. *Formálar íslenskra sagnaritara á miðöldum. Rannsókn bókmenntahefðar* (Reykjavík: Stofnun Árna Magnússonar, 1988). Pp. 232, 246–7, 257, 268, and 351.

Þórður Ingi Guðjónsson. "Apostlene i islandsk middelalderlitteratur." In *Den nordiske renessansen i høymiddelalderen*. Ed. Jón Viðar Sigurðsson and Preben Meulengracht Sørensen (Oslo: Historisk institutt, Universitetet i Oslo, 2000). Pp. 83–99, esp. p. 94.

Wolf, Kirsten. "Postola sögur." In Phillip Pulsiano and Kirsten Wolf, with Paul Acker and Donald K. Fry, ed. >> *Medieval Scandinavia* (1993). Pp. 511–12.

– "Skarðsbók." In Phillip Pulsiano and Kirsten Wolf, with Paul Acker and Donald K. Fry, ed. >> *Medieval Scandinavia* (1993). P. 596.

Handlist, p. 328.

3. Páls saga postola

An epitome of 1.

Manuscript:
AM 238 fol. XV (ca. 1450–1500).
Literature:
Cormack, Margaret. >> *The Saints in Iceland* (1994). Pp. 37n34, 145, and 244.

Sverrir Tómasson. *Formálar íslenskra sagnaritara á miðöldum. Rannsókn bókmenntahefðar* (Reykjavík: Stofnun Árna Magnússonar, 1988). P. 351.

Handlist, p. 329.

NOTE:
See also Peter the Apostle.

PAUL THE HERMIT   January 15

Páls saga eremita
A translation of *BHL* 6596 with the prologue omitted.

Manuscript:
Stock. Perg. fol. no. 2 (ca. 1425–45).
Editions:
Foote, Peter, ed. >> *Lives of Saints* (1962).
  Facsimile.
Unger, C.R., ed. >> *Heilagra manna søgur* (1877). Vol. 2, pp. 183–92.
Modern Icelandic language edition:
Sverrir Tómasson, Bragi Halldórsson, and Einar Sigurbjörnsson, ed.
  >> *Heilagra karla sögur* (2007). Pp. 135–47.
Literature:
Bekker-Nielsen, Hans. "Kyrkofäderna ock kyrkolärarna. K. i vestnordisk
  litteratur." *KLNM* 9 (1964). Cols. 690–3, esp. col. 692.
Bekker-Nielsen, Hans, Thorkil Damsgaard Olsen, and Ole Widding.
  >> *Norrøn fortællekunst* (1965). P. 125.
Boyer, Régis. >> *La vie religieuse en Islande* (1979). Pp. 160 and 197.
Carlé, Birte. >> *Jomfru-fortællingen* (1985). Pp. 40, 65, 67–8, 70–1,
  and 74.
– "Men and Women in the Saints' Sagas of *Stock. 2, fol.*" In John
  Lindow, Lars Lönnroth, and Gerd Wolfgang Weber, ed. >> *Structure
  and Meaning in Old Norse Literature* (1986). Pp. 317–46, esp. pp. 320,
  322, 324, 333, and 335–6.
Hallberg, Peter. "Imagery in Religious Old Norse Prose Literature: An
  Outline." *ANF* 102 (1987): 120–70, esp. pp. 136 and 161.
Kirby, Ian. >> *Biblical Quotation* (1980). Vol. 2, p. 47.
Lehmann, Paul. >> "Skandinaviens Anteil an der lateinischen Literatur
  und Wissenschaft des Mittelalters" (1937). P. 45.
Mogk, Eugen. >> *Geschichte der norwegisch-isländischen Literatur* (1904).
  P. 891.
Paasche, Fredrik. *Norges og Islands litteratur inntil utgangen av
  middelalderen*. Rev. ed. by Anne Holtsmark (Oslo: Aschehoug, 1947).
  Pp. 293–4.

Sverrir Tómasson. *Formálar íslenskra sagnaritara á miðöldum. Rannsókn bókmenntahefðar* (Reykjavík: Stofnun Árna Magnússonar, 1988). P. 98.
Wolf, Kirsten, ed. >> *Heilagra meyja sögur* (2003). P. x.
Handlist, p. 329.

PELAGIA THE PENITENT   October 8

Af Pelagíu

A version of the legend of Saint Pelagia incorporated into the Old Norwegian *Barlaams saga ok Jósafats*.

Manuscripts:
See Barlaam and Josaphat 1 note (p. 50).
Editions:
Keyser, R., and C.R. Unger, ed. *Barlaams ok Josaphats saga* (Christiania [Oslo]: Feilberg & Landmark, 1851). Pp. 87.24–90.2.
– ed. *Barlaams ok Josaphats saga*. Norrøne tekster 4 (Oslo: Norsk historisk kjeldeskrift-institutt, 1981). Pp. 77.3–79.23.
Modern Icelandic language edition:
Einar Ól. Sveinsson, ed. *Leit eg suður til landa. Ævintýri og helgisögur frá miðöldum.* (Reykjavík: Heimskringla, 1944). Pp. 201–2 (extract only).
Literature:
Ásdís Egilsdóttir. "Kvendýrlingar og kvenímynd trúarlegra bókmennta á Íslandi." In Inga Huld Hákonardóttir, ed. >> *Konur og kristsmenn* (1996). Pp. 93–116, esp. pp. 102–3.
Bekker-Nielsen, Hans, Thorkil Damsgaard Olsen, and Ole Widding. >> *Norrøn fortællekunst* (1965). P. 112.
Carlé, Birte. *Skøger og jomfruer i den kristne fortællekunst* (Odense: Odense Universitetsforlag, 1991). P. 28.
Haugen, Odd Einar. "Exempla in Barlaams ok Josaphats saga." In >> *Sagas and the Norwegian Experience* (1997). Pp. 227–36, esp. p. 232.
– "Forteljingane i forteljinga. Interpolasjonane i *Barlaams ok Josaphats saga*." In Karl G. Johansson and Maria Arvidsson, ed. >> *Barlaam i nord* (2009). Pp. 47–73, esp. pp. 58 and 70–1.
Mogk, Eugen. >> *Geschichte der norwegisch-isländischen Literatur* (1904). P. 872.
Wolf, Kirsten. "Klæðskiptingar í Íslendingasögunum." *Skírnir* 171 (1997): 381–400, esp. p. 383.

– "The Severed Breast: A Topos in the Legends of Female Virgin Martyr
  Saints." *ANF* 112 (1997): 97–112, esp. p. 107.
Wolf, Kirsten, ed. >> *Heilagra meyja sögur* (2003). Pp. xxxv and lvi.
Handlist, pp. 302 and 329.

PETER THE APOSTLE   June 29

1. Pétrs saga postola II

Based on a version of *BHL* 6659 with additions from *BHL* 6570, the
canonical gospels, the *Actus Apostolorum*, and other sources.

Manuscripts:
AM 629 4to (1697), AM 630 4to (ca. 1650–1700), AM 659a 4to (ca.
  1600–50), and Rask 69 (ca. 1800).
Editions:
Þorsteinn Jónsson, ed. *Hér hefjast Tíu Sögur, af þeim enum heiløgu
  Guds Postulum og pínslar vottum* (Viðeyjarklaustur: Þ. Jónsson 1836).
  Pp. 1–62.
  Based on a manuscript descended from AM 630 4to.
Unger, C.R., ed. >> *Postola sögur* (1874). Pp. 159.23–201.3.
  Edition of AM 630 4to with emendations from AM 659a 4to and
  variants from AM 655 4to XV (see 4 below; pp. 167.21–173.35). A
  section of AM 655 4to XV is edited on p. 172.23–39 (lower text).
English translation:
Roughton, Philip G. "AM 645 4to and AM 652/630 4to: Study and
  Translation of Two Thirteenth-Century Icelandic Collections of
  Apostles' and Saints' Lives." PhD dissertation, University of Colorado,
  2002. Pp. 487–559.
Literature:
Bekker-Nielsen, Hans. "Petrus. Norrøn tradition." *KLNM* 13 (1968).
  Cols. 261–3, esp. col. 262.
Carron, Helen, ed. *Clemens saga: The Life of St Clement of Rome.*
  Viking Society for Northern Research, Text Series 17 (University
  College London: Viking Society for Northern Research, 2005).
  Pp. xiii–xvi.
Cormack, Margaret. >> *The Saints in Iceland* (1994). P. 149.
Finnur Jónsson. >> *Den oldnorske og oldislandske Litteraturs Historie*
  (1920–4). Vol. 2, p. 869.

Foote, Peter, ed. *A Saga of St Peter the Apostle. Perg. 4:o nr 19 in the Royal Library, Stockholm*. EIM 19 (Copenhagen: Rosenkilde and Bagger, 1990). P. 12.

– "A Fragment of Text in AM 235 fol." In *Twenty-eight Papers Presented to Hans Bekker-Nielsen on the Occasion of His Sixtieth Birthday 28 April 1993* (Odense: Odense University Press, 1993). Pp. 237–55, esp. pp. 242–4 and 250–2.

Hallberg, Peter. "Imagery in Religious Old Norse Prose Literature: An Outline." *ANF* 102 (1987): 120–70, esp. p. 139.

Hofmann, Dietrich. *Die Legende von Sankt Clemens in den skandinavischen Ländern im Mittelalter*. Beiträge zur Skandinavistik 13 (Frankfurt am Main: Peter Lang, 1997). Pp. 69, 103–5, and 142.

Jón Ma. Ásgeirsson and Þórður Ingi Guðjónsson, ed. *Frá Sýrlandi til Íslands: Arfur Tómasar postula* (Reykjavík: Háskólaútgáfan, 2007). P. 165.

Jónas Kristjánsson. *Um Fóstbrœðra sögu* (Reykjavík: Stofnun Árna Magnússonar, 1972). P. 272.

Kirby, Ian. >> *Biblical Quotation* (1980). Vol. 2, p. 24.

– *Bible Translation in Old Norse*. Université de Lausanne Publications de la faculté des lettres 27 (Geneva: Librairie Droz, 1986). P. 86.

Mogk, Eugen. >> *Geschichte der norwegisch-isländischen Literatur* (1904). P. 887.

Ólafur Halldórsson, ed. *Mattheus saga postulà* (Reykjavík: Stofnun Árna Magnússonar, 1994). Pp. xxxvi–xli.

Roughton, Philip. "Stylistics and Sources of the *Postola sögur* in AM 645 4to and AM 652/630 4to." *Gripla* 16 (2005): 7–50.

Sverrir Jakobsson. *Við og veröldin: Heimsmynd Íslendinga 1100–1400* (Reykjavík: Háskólaútgáfan, 2005). P. 119.

Sverrir Tómasson. *Formálar íslenskra sagnaritara á miðöldum. Rannsókn bókmenntahefðar* (Reykjavík: Stofnun Árna Magnússonar, 1988). P. 351.

Þórður Ingi Guðjónsson. "Apostlene i islandsk middelalderlitteratur." In *Den nordiske renessansen i høymiddelalderen*. Ed. Jón Viðar Sigurðsson and Preben Meulengracht Sørensen (Oslo: Historisk institutt, Universitetet i Oslo, 2000). Pp. 83–99, esp. p. 93.

Vries, Jan de. >> *Altnordische Literaturgeschichte* (1964–7). Vol. 2, p. 183.

Handlist, p. 329.

2. Pétrs saga postola II

An abridged and separate recension of 1.

Manuscript:
AM 655 4to XII–XIII (ca. 1250–75).
Edition:
Unger, C.R., ed. >> *Postola sögur* (1874). Pp. 211.31–216.7.
Literature:
Bekker-Nielsen, Hans. "Petrus. Norrøn tradition." *KLNM* 13 (1968).
    Cols. 261–3, esp. col. 262.
Carron, Helen, ed. *Clemens saga: The Life of St Clement of Rome.* Viking
    Society for Northern Research, Text Series 17 (University College
    London: Viking Society for Northern Research, 2005). Pp. xiii–xv.
Cormack, Margaret. >> *The Saints in Iceland* (1994). P. 149.
Finnur Jónsson. >> *Den oldnorske og oldislandske Litteraturs Historie*
    (1920–4). Vol. 2, p. 869.
Foote, Peter. "Auðræði." In Arthur Brown and Peter Foote, ed. >> *Early
    English and Norse Studies* (1963). Pp. 62–76, esp. p. 66.
Foote, Peter, ed. *A Saga of St Peter the Apostle. Perg. 4:o nr 19 in the
    Royal Library, Stockholm.* EIM 19 (Copenhagen: Rosenkilde and
    Bagger, 1990). P. 12.
– "A Fragment of Text in AM 235 fol." In *Twenty-eight Papers Presented
    to Hans Bekker-Nielsen on the Occasion of His Sixtieth Birthday 28
    April 1993* (Odense: Odense University Press, 1993). Pp. 237–55, esp.
    pp. 242–3.
Jónas Kristjánsson. "Learned Style or Saga Style?" In Ursula Dronke,
    Guðrún P. Helgadóttir, Gerd Wolfgang Weber, and Hans Bekker-
    Nielsen, ed. >> *Specvlvm Norroenvm* (1981). Pp. 260–92.
Kirby, Ian. >> *Biblical Quotation* (1980). Vol. 2, p. 24.
Mogk, Eugen. >> *Geschichte der norwegisch-isländischen Literatur* (1904).
    P. 887.
Sverrir Jakobsson. *Við og veröldin: Heimsmynd Íslendinga 1100–1400*
    (Reykjavík: Háskólaútgáfan, 2005). P. 120.
Sverrir Tómasson. *Formálar íslenskra sagnaritara á miðöldum. Rannsókn
    bókmenntahefðar* (Reykjavík: Stofnun Árna Magnússonar, 1988).
    P. 351.
Turville-Petre, G. >> *Origins of Icelandic Literature* (1967). P. 134.
Þórður Ingi Guðjónsson. "Apostlene i islandsk middelalderlitteratur." In
    Den nordiske renessansen i høymiddelalderen. Ed. Jón Viðar Sigurðsson
    and Preben Meulengracht Sørensen (Oslo: Historisk institutt, Universi-
    tetet i Oslo, 2000). Pp. 83–99, esp. p. 95.
Vries, Jan de. >> *Altnordische Literaturgeschichte* (1964–7). Vol. 2, p. 183.
Handlist, p. 329.

3. Pétrs saga postola II

An abridged recension of 1; AM 235 fol. has insertions ultimately related
to 5.

Manuscripts:
AM 235 fol. (ca. 1400) and AM 645 4to (ca. 1220, defective).
Editions:
Foote, Peter. "A Fragment of Text in AM 235 fol." In *Twenty-eight Papers
Presented to Hans Bekker-Nielsen on the Occasion of His Sixtieth
Birthday 28 April 1993* (Odense: Odense University Press, 1993).
Pp. 237–55, esp. pp. 238–42.
Edition of fols. 13ra1–13vb18 of AM 235 fol.
Holtsmark, Anne, ed. *A Book of Miracles: MS No. 645 4to of the Arna-
Magnæan Collection in the University Library of Copenhagen.* CCI 12
(Copenhagen: Einar Munksgaard, 1938).
Facsimile of AM 645 4to.
Larsson, Ludvig, ed. *Isländska handskriften N° 645 4° i Den Ar-
namagnæanske Samlingen på Universitetsbiblioteket i København: I.
Handskriftens äldre del* (Lund: Gleerup, 1885). Pp. 74.9–90.21.
Edition of AM 645 4to.
Unger, C.R., ed. >> *Postola sögur* (1874). Pp. 181–200 and 201.5–211.29.
Edition of AM 645 4to (pp. 201.5–211.29) and edition of or variants
from AM 235 fol. in lower text (pp. 181–200).
English translation:
Roughton, Philip G. "AM 645 4to and AM 652/630 4to: Study and
Translation of Two Thirteenth-Century Icelandic Collections of
Apostles' and Saints' Lives." PhD dissertation, University of Colorado,
2002. Pp. 560–3 (extract only).
Literature:
Bekker-Nielsen, Hans. "Petrus. Norrøn tradition." *KLNM* 13 (1968).
Cols. 261–3, esp. col. 262.
– "Et par ord om de ældste norrøne helgensagaer." In Finn Hødnebø et
al., >> *Eyvindarbók* (1992). Pp. 29–33, esp. p. 32.
Bekker-Nielsen, Hans, Thorkil Damsgaard Olsen, and Ole Widding.
>> *Norrøn fortællekunst* (1965). P. 122.
Carlé, Birte. >> *Jomfru-fortællingen* (1985). P. 38.
– "Men and Women in the Saints' Sagas of *Stock. 2, fol.*" In John
Lindow, Lars Lönnroth, and Gerd Wolfgang Weber, ed. >> *Structure
and Meaning in Old Norse Literature* (1986). Pp. 317–46, esp. p. 318.

Carron, Helen, ed. *Clemens saga: The Life of St Clement of Rome*. Viking Society for Northern Research, Text Series 17 (University College London: Viking Society for Northern Research, 2005). Pp. xiii–xvii.

Cormack, Margaret. >> *The Saints in Iceland* (1994). P. 149.

Finnur Jónsson. >> *Den oldnorske og oldislandske Litteraturs Historie* (1920–4). Vol. 2, p. 869.

Foote, Peter. "Saints' Lives and Sagas." In Hans Bekker-Nielsen and Birte Carlé, ed. >> *Saints and Sagas* (1994). Pp. 73–88, esp. pp. 81–2.

Foote, Peter, ed. *A Saga of St Peter the Apostle. Perg. 4:o nr 19 in the Royal Library, Stockholm*. EIM 19 (Copenhagen: Rosenkilde and Bagger, 1990). P. 12.

Hofmann, Dietrich. *Die Legende von Sankt Clemens in den skandinavischen Ländern im Mittelalter*. Beiträge zur Skandinavistik 13 (Frankfurt am Main: Peter Lang, 1997). P. 103.

Jón Ma. Ásgeirsson and Þórður Ingi Guðjónsson, ed. *Frá Sýrlandi til Íslands: Arfur Tómasar postula* (Reykjavík: Háskólaútgáfan, 2007). P. 164.

Jónas Kristjánsson. >> *Eddas and Sagas* (1988). P. 138.

Jørgensen, Jørgen Højgaard. "Hagiography and the Icelandic Bishop Sagas." *Peritia* 1 (1982): 1–16, esp. p. 4.

Kirby, Ian. >> *Biblical Quotation* (1980). Vol. 2, p. 24.

Konráð Gíslason. *Um frum-parta íslenzkrar túngu í fornöld* (Copenhagen: Trier, 1846). P. lxiii.

Mogk, Eugen. >> *Geschichte der norwegisch-isländischen Literatur* (1904). P. 887.

Ólafur Halldórsson, ed. *Mattheus saga postula* (Reykjavík: Stofnun Árna Magnússonar, 1994). Pp. xiii–xxix.

Roughton, Philip. "Stylistics and Sources of the *Postola sögur* in AM 645 4to and AM 652/630 4to." *Gripla* 16 (2005): 7–50.

Sverrir Tómasson. *Formálar íslenskra sagnaritara á miðöldum. Rannsókn bókmenntahefðar* (Reykjavík: Stofnun Árna Magnússonar, 1988). P. 351.

Turville-Petre, G. >> *Origins of Icelandic Literature* (1967). P. 130.

Tveitane, Mattias. "Interpretatio Norroena: Norrøne og antikke gudenavn i *Clemens saga*." In >> *The Sixth International Saga Conference* (1985). Vol. 2, pp. 1067–82, esp. p. 1073.

Vries, Jan de. >> *Altnordische Literaturgeschichte* (1964–7). Vol. 2, p. 183.

Handlist, p. 329.

4. Pétrs saga postola II

A revised recension of 1.

Manuscript:
AM 655 4to XVI (ca. 1250–1300).
Editions:
Hreinn Benediktsson. *Early Icelandic Script As Illustrated in Vernacular Texts from the Twelfth and Thirteenth Centuries.* Íslenzk handrit: Icelandic Manuscripts, Series in Folio 2 (Reykjavík: The Manuscript Institute of Iceland, 1965). Plate 67 and p. xlv.
   Facsimile and text edition of fol. 2r.
Unger, C.R., ed. >> *Postola sögur* (1874). Pp. 167–73.
   Edition (pp. 172.23–39) and variants (pp. 167.21–173.25).
Literature:
Bekker-Nielsen, Hans. "Petrus. Norrøn tradition." *KLNM* 13 (1968). Cols. 261–3, esp. col. 262.
Cormack, Margaret. >> *The Saints in Iceland* (1994). P. 149.
Foote, Peter, ed. *A Saga of St Peter the Apostle. Perg. 4:o nr 19 in the Royal Library, Stockholm.* EIM 19 (Copenhagen: Rosenkilde and Bagger, 1990). P. 12.
– "A Fragment of Text in AM 235 fol." In *Twenty-eight Papers Presented to Hans Bekker-Nielsen on the Occasion of His Sixtieth Birthday 28 April 1993* (Odense: Odense University Press, 1993). Pp. 237–55, esp. pp. 242–3.
Mogk, Eugen. >> *Geschichte der norwegisch-isländischen Literatur* (1904). P. 887.
Sverrir Tómasson. *Formálar íslenskra sagnaritara á miðöldum. Rannsókn bókmenntahefðar* (Reykjavík: Stofnun Árna Magnússonar, 1988). P. 351.
Vries, Jan de. >> *Altnordische Literaturgeschichte* (1964–7). Vol. 2, p. 183.
Handlist, p. 329.

5. Pétrs saga postola I

Based on versions of *BHL* 6657, 6570, and 6668 with additional material from Peter Comestor's *Historia scholastica*, the *Actus Apostolorum*, Vincent of Beauvais' *Speculum historiale*, and other sources. Chapters 50–8 and 60–73 are derived from a text similar to *Klements saga*. See *Klements saga* 2 note (p. 79).

Manuscripts:
AM 236 fol. (ca. 1600, defective), AM 239 fol. (ca. 1350–1400), AM 239 fol. (ca. 1600–1700), AM 621 4to (ca. 1450–1500), AM 631 4to (ca. 1700–25), AM 639 4to (ca. 1450–1500), AM 658 4to I (ca. 1375–1400),

AM 658 4to II (ca. 1375–1400), AM 658 4to III (ca. 1400), AM 658 4to IV (ca. 1350–1400), AM 658 4to V (ca. 1350–1400), AM 660 4to (ca. 1475–1500, defective), SÁM 1 fol. (*Codex Scardensis*) (ca. 1350–75), and Stock. Perg. 4to no. 19 (ca. 1375–1400).

Editions:

* Carron, H.C. "A Critical Edition of Pétrs saga Postola I, Based on the Codex Scardensis." PhD dissertation, University of London, 1994.

Foote, Peter, ed. *A Saga of St Peter the Apostle. Perg. 4:o nr 19 in the Royal Library, Stockholm*. EIM 19 (Copenhagen: Rosenkilde and Bagger, 1990).
Facsimile of Stock. Perg. 4to no. 19, AM 658 4to I (3v13–27), and AM 658 4to II (3v13–27).

Slay, Desmond, ed. *Codex Scardensis*. EIM 2 (Copenhagen: Rosenkilde and Bagger, 1960).
Facsimile of SÁM 1 fol.

Unger, C.R., ed. >> *Postola sögur* (1874). Pp.1–126.16.
Based on AM 631 4to with variants from AM 639 4to, AM 239 fol. (pp. 1–106.27), Stock. Perg. 4to no. 19 (pp. 1–125.25), AM 621 4to (pp. 1–15.29, 18.3–30.30, 33.2–50.20, 52.22–85.17, 89.9–96.31, 98.29–106.17, and 108.15–126), AM 660 4to (pp. 1–2.12, 6.11–10.9, 14.6–16.5, 20.4–21.30, 25.22–27.17, 42.28–45.12, 49.27–65.12, 73.17–76.26, 78.30–90, 93.5–98.1, and 107.20–110.20), and AM 658 4to V (pp. 53.14–55.2). Edition of AM 660 4to (pp. xv–xvi, extract only).

Modern Icelandic language edition:

Ólafur Halldórsson, ed. *Sögur úr Skarðsbók* (Reykjavík: Almenna bókafélagið, 1967). Pp. 31–42.
Edition of SÁM 1 fol. (extracts only).

German translation:

Hofmann, Dietrich. *Die Legende von Sankt Clemens in den skandinavischen Ländern im Mittelalter*. Beiträge zur Skandinavistik 13 (Frankfurt am Main: Peter Lang, 1997). Pp. 286–300 (extract only).

Literature:

Battista, Simonette. "Translation or Redaction in Old Norse Hagiography." In Peter Andersen, ed. >> *Pratiques de Traduction au Moyen Age* (2004). Pp. 100–10, esp. pp. 106–8.
– "The *Compilator* and Contemporary Literary Culture in Old Norse Hagiography." *Viking and Medieval Scandinavia* 1 (2005): 1–13, esp. pp. 6–11.

Bekker-Nielsen, Hans. "Petrus. Norrøn tradition." *KLNM* 13 (1968). Cols. 261–3, esp. col. 262.

Bekker-Nielsen, Hans, Thorkil Damsgaard Olsen, and Ole Widding.
    >> *Norrøn fortællekunst* (1965). P. 123.
Carron, Helen, ed. *Clemens saga: The Life of St Clement of Rome*. Viking
    Society for Northern Research, Text Series 17 (University College
    London: Viking Society for Northern Research, 2005). Pp. xiii–xviii.
Collings, Lucy Grace. "The Codex Scardensis: Studies in Icelandic
    Hagiography." PhD dissertation, Cornell University, 1969. Pp. 83–112
    and 249–69.
Cormack, Margaret. >> *The Saints in Iceland* (1994). Pp. 90, 149, and 244.
– "Saints' Lives and Icelandic Literature in the Thirteenth and Four-
    teenth Centuries." In Hans Bekker-Nielsen and Birte Carlé, ed.
    >> *Saints and Sagas* (1994). Pp. 27–47, esp. p. 31.
Eiríkr Magnússon. "Kodex Skardensis af postulasögur." *ANF* 8 (1892):
    238–45, esp. p. 241.
Foote, Peter, "A Fragment of Text in AM 235 fol." In *Twenty-eight Papers
    Presented to Hans Bekker-Nielsen on the Occasion of His Sixtieth
    Birthday 28 April 1993* (Odense: Odense University Press, 1993).
    Pp. 237–55, esp. pp. 242–8 and 250–2.
Hallberg, Peter. "Imagery in Religious Old Norse Prose Literature: An
    Outline." *ANF* 102 (1987): 120–70, esp. pp. 130, 132–3, 137, 140, 147,
    and 154.
Jón Ma. Ásgeirsson and Þórður Ingi Guðjónsson, ed. *Frá Sýrlandi til
    Íslands: Arfur Tómasar postula* (Reykjavík: Háskólaútgáfan, 2007).
    P. 165.
Jón Þorkelsson. "Islandske håndskrifter i England og Skotland." *ANF* 8
    (1892): 199–237, esp. pp. 235–6.
Jónas Kristjánsson. *Um Fóstbræðra sögu* (Reykjavík: Stofnun Árna
    Magnússonar, 1972). P. 273.
Kirby, Ian. >> *Biblical Quotation* (1980). Vol. 2, p. 23.
– *Bible Translation in Old Norse*. Université de Lausanne Publications
    de la faculté des lettres 27 (Geneva: Librairie Droz, 1986). Pp. 46, 86,
    and 95.
McDougall, David. "Anonymous, *Pétrsdrápa* 'Drápa about S. Peter'." In
    Margaret Clunies Ross, ed. >> *Poetry on Christian Subjects* (2007).
    Vol. 2, pp. 796–844.
Mogk, Eugen. >> *Geschichte der norwegisch-isländischen Literatur* (1904).
    P. 887.
Ólafur Halldórsson. *Helgafellsbækur fornar*. Studia Islandica 24 (Reykjavík:
    Heimspekideild Háskóla Íslands and Menningarsjóður, 1966). Pp. 16–
    22 and 41–5.

Ólafur Halldórsson, ed. *Mattheus saga postula* (Reykjavík: Stofnun Árna
   Magnússonar, 1994). Pp. xli–xlviii.
Sverrir Jakobsson. *Við og veröldin: Heimsmynd Íslendinga 1100–1400*
   (Reykjavík: Háskólaútgáfan, 2005). Pp. 104 and 145.
Sverrir Tómasson. *Formálar íslenskra sagnaritara á miðöldum. Rannsókn
   bókmenntahefðar* (Reykjavík: Stofnun Árna Magnússonar, 1988).
   Pp. 12, 189, 232, and 351.
– "Kristnar trúarbókmenntir í óbundnu máli." In Guðrún Nordal,
   Sverrir Tómasson, and Vésteinn Ólason, ed. >> *Íslensk Bókmenntasaga*
   1 (1992). Pp. 419–79, esp. p. 445.
Tveitane, Mattias. "Interpretatio Norroena: Norrøne og antikke
   gudenavn i *Clemens saga*." In >> *The Sixth International Saga Confer-
   ence* (1985). Vol. 2, pp. 1067–82, esp. pp. 1070–3, 1075, and 1081.
Þórður Ingi Guðjónsson. "Apostlene i islandsk middelalderlitteratur." In
   Den nordiske renessansen i høymiddelalderen. Ed. Jón Viðar Sigurðsson
   and Preben Meulengracht Sørensen (Oslo: Historisk institutt, Universi-
   tetet i Oslo, 2000). Pp. 83–99, esp. p. 94.
Vries, Jan de. >> *Altnordische Literaturgeschichte* (1964–7). Vol. 2, p. 183.
Wolf, Kirsten. "Postola sögur." In Phillip Pulsiano and Kirsten Wolf,
   with Paul Acker and Donald K. Fry, ed. >> *Medieval Scandinavia*
   (1993). Pp. 511–12.
– "Skarðsbók." In Phillip Pulsiano and Kirsten Wolf, with Paul Acker
   and Donald K. Fry, ed. >> *Medieval Scandinavia* (1993). P. 596.
Handlist, pp. 329–30.
NOTE:
The saga includes a short tale of Saint Maternus. See the entry for this
   saint.

6. Tveggja postola saga Pétrs ok Páls

A composite text comprising a *Pétrs saga postula* similar to 1 with
chapters on Saint Paul added from a text of Paul 1.

Manuscript:
AM 656 4to I (ca. 1325–50).
Edition:
Unger, C.R., ed. >> *Postola sögur* (1874). Pp. 283.25–318.26.
Literature:
Bekker-Nielsen, Hans. "Petrus. Norrøn tradition." *KLNM* 13 (1968).
   Cols. 261–3, esp. col. 262.

Bekker-Nielsen, Hans, Thorkil Damsgaard Olsen, and Ole Widding.
>> *Norrøn fortællekunst* (1965). P. 122.
Finnur Jónsson. >> *Den oldnorske og oldislandske Litteraturs Historie*
(1920–4). Vol. 2, p. 870.
Foote, Peter. "A Fragment of Text in AM 235 fol." In *Twenty-eight Papers
Presented to Hans Bekker-Nielsen on the Occasion of His Sixtieth
Birthday 28 April 1993* (Odense: Odense University Press, 1993).
Pp. 237–55, esp. p. 242.
Hofmann, Dietrich. *Die Legende von Sankt Clemens in den skandi-
navischen Ländern im Mittelalter*. Beiträge zur Skandinavistik 13
(Frankfurt am Main: Peter Lang, 1997). Pp. 69 and 142.
Jón Ma. Ásgeirsson and Þórður Ingi Guðjónsson, ed. *Frá Sýrlandi til
Íslands: Arfur Tómasar postula* (Reykjavík: Háskólaútgáfan, 2007). P. 165.
Kirby, Ian. >> *Biblical Quotation* (1980). Vol. 2, pp. 24 and 26.
– *Bible Translation in Old Norse*. Université de Lausanne Publications de
la faculté des lettres 27 (Geneva: Librairie Droz, 1986). Pp. 87–9.
Louis-Jensen, Jonna. "To håndskrifter fra det nordvestlige Island."
Opuscula 7. Bibliotheca Arnamagnæana 34 (Copenhagen: Reitzel,
1979). Pp. 219–53, esp. pp. 221 and 252.
Mogk, Eugen. >> *Geschichte der norwegisch-isländischen Literatur* (1904).
P. 888.
Ólafur Halldórsson, ed. *Mattheus saga postula* (Reykjavík: Stofnun Árna
Magnússonar, 1994). Pp. xlix–lvii.
Sverrir Tómasson. *Formálar íslenskra sagnaritara á miðöldum. Rannsókn
bókmenntahefðar* (Reykjavík: Stofnun Árna Magnússonar, 1988).
P. 351.
Þórður Ingi Guðjónsson. "Apostlene i islandsk middelalderlitteratur." In
Den nordiske renessansen i høymiddelalderen. Ed. Jón Viðar Sigurðsson
and Preben Meulengracht Sørensen (Oslo: Historisk institutt, Universi-
tetet i Oslo, 2000). Pp. 83–99, esp. p. 94.
Handlist, p. 330.

PETER CELESTINE   May 19

Af Celestíno ok Bonifacío páfum

The direct source has not been established.

Manuscripts:
AM 624 4to (ca. 1500) and AM 657a–b 4to (ca. 1350, defective).

Edition:
Gering, Hugo, ed. >> *Islendzk æventyri* (1882–4). Vol. 1, pp. 77–83.
  Based on AM 624 4to with variants from AM 657a–b 4to.
German paraphrase:
Gering, Hugo, ed. >> *Islendzk æventyri* (1882–4). Vol. 2, pp. 65–8.
Literature:
Cormack, Margaret. >> *The Saints in Iceland* (1994). P. 35.
Wolf, Kirsten, ed. >> *Heilagra meyja sögur* (2003). P. lii.
Handlist, p. 330.

PETER MONOCULUS. O.S.B. Cist.   May 18

Af Pétro Clarevallensis

Tales of Saint Peter Monoculus incorporated into the miracles of the
Virgin Mary.

Manuscripts:
See Mary the Blessed Virgin 3 note (p. 245).
Edition:
Unger, C.R., ed. >> *Mariu saga* (1871). Pp. 493.21–499.26 and
  1152.27–1154.4.
Literature:
Heizmann, Wilhelm. "Liebe und Durst: Der Heilige Bernhard von
  Clairvaux in der altisländischen Mirakelüberlieferung." *Opuscula* 13.
  Bibliotheca Arnamagnæana 47 (Copenhagen: Museum Tusculanum
  Press, 2010). Pp. 55–118, esp. p. 109.
Handlist, pp. 324 and 330.

PHILIP THE APOSTLE   May 1

1. Filippuss saga postola I

Based on *BHL* 6814 with a homiletic prologue probably added by the
translator.

Manuscripts:
AM 629 4to (1697), AM 630 4to (ca. 1650–1700), AM 659a 4to (1600–50,
  defective), and Rask 69 (ca. 1800).

Editions:

Þorsteinn Jónsson, ed. *Hér hefjast Tíu Sögur, af þeim enum heiløgu Guds Postulum og pínslar vottum* (Viðeyjarklaustur: Þ. Jónsson, 1836). Pp. 232–6.
Based on a manuscript descended from AM 630 4to.

Unger, C.R., ed. >> *Postola sögur* (1874). Pp. 735–737.30.
Edition of AM 630 4to.

English translation:

Roughton, Philip G. "AM 645 4to and AM 652/630 4to: Study and Translation of Two Thirteenth-Century Icelandic Collections of Apostles' and Saints' Lives." PhD dissertation, University of Colorado, 2002. Pp. 743–8.

Literature:

Astås, Reidar. "Spor av teologisk tenkning og refleksjon i norsk og islandsk høymiddelalder." *CM* 6 (1993): 133–67, esp. p. 139.

Collings, Lucy Grace. "The Codex Scardensis: Studies in Icelandic Hagiography." PhD dissertation, Cornell University, 1969. Pp. 3, 63, 67–9, and 225–6.

Cormack, Margaret. >> *The Saints in Iceland* (1994). Pp. 33n14, 151, and 244.

Finnur Jónsson. >> *Den oldnorske og oldislandske Litteraturs Historie* (1920–4). Vol. 2, pp. 871–2.

Foote, Peter. "Postulatal." In Guðni Kolbeinsson, ed. >> *Minjar og menntir* (1976). Pp. 152–73, esp. p. 164.

Hallberg, Peter. "Imagery in Religious Old Norse Prose Literature: An Outline." *ANF* 102 (1987): 120–70, esp. p. 138.

Kirby, Ian. >> *Biblical Quotation* (1980). Vol. 2, p. 33.

Mogk, Eugen. >> *Geschichte der norwegisch-isländischen Literatur* (1904). P. 889.

Ólafur Halldórsson, ed. *Mattheus saga postula* (Reykjavík: Stofnun Árna Magnússonar, 1994). Pp. xxxvi–xli and lxxv–lxxxi.

Roughton, Philip. "Stylistics and Sources of the *Postola sögur* in AM 645 4to and AM 652/630 4to." *Gripla* 16 (2005): 7–50.

– "'Þá syndi hann þeim mikinn skugga': Unmasking the Fantastic in the *Postola sögur*." In John McKinnell, David Ashurst, and Donata Kick, ed. >> *The Fantastic in Old Norse/Icelandic Literature* (2006). Vol. 2, pp. 846–55, esp. p. 847.

Svanhildur Óskarsdóttir. "Universal History in Fourteenth-Century Iceland: Studies in AM 764 4to." PhD dissertation, University of London, 2000. P. 192.

Sverrir Tómasson. *Formálar íslenskra sagnaritara á miðöldum. Rannsókn
bókmenntahefðar* (Reykjavík: Stofnun Árna Magnússonar, 1988). P. 351.
Wolf, Kirsten. "Postola sögur." In Phillip Pulsiano and Kirsten Wolf,
with Paul Acker and Donald K. Fry, ed.>> *Medieval Scandinavia*
(1993). Pp. 511–12.
Handlist, p. 330.

2. Filippuss saga postola II

A close translation of *BHL* 6814 that omits the details added from
external sources in 1.

Manuscripts:
AM 238 fol. XI (ca. 1300–25), AM 628 4to (1711–12), and SÁM 1 fol.
(*Codex Scardensis*) (ca. 1350–75).
Editions:
Slay, Desmond, ed. *Codex Scardensis*. EIM 2 (Copenhagen: Rosenkilde
and Bagger, 1960).
Facsimile of SÁM 1 fol.
Unger, C.R., ed. >> *Postola sögur* (1874). Pp. 740.23–742.2.
Based on AM 628 4to with variants from AM 238 fol. XI (pp. 741.30–
742.2).
Modern Icelandic language edition:
Ólafur Halldórsson, ed. *Sögur úr Skarðsbók* (Reykjavík: Almenna
bókafélagið, 1967). Pp. 43–69.
Edition of SÁM 1 fol.
Literature:
Astås, Reidar. "Spor av teologisk tenkning og refleksjon i norsk og
islandsk høymiddelalder." *CM* 6 (1993): 133–67, esp. p. 139.
Battista, Simonetta. "Interpretations of the Roman Pantheon in the Old
Norse Hagiographic Sagas." In Geraldine Barnes and Margaret
Clunies Ross, ed. >> *Old Norse Myths, Literature and Society* (2000).
Pp. 24–34, esp. p. 29.
Bekker-Nielsen, Hans, Thorkil Damsgaard Olsen, and Ole Widding.
>> *Norrøn fortællekunst* (1965). P.123.
Collings, Lucy Grace. "The Codex Scardensis: Studies in Icelandic
Hagiography." PhD dissertation, Cornell University, 1969. Pp. 63–9
and 220–6.
Cormack, Margaret. >> *The Saints in Iceland* (1994). Pp. 37n45, 151,
and 244.

Eiríkr Magnússon. "Kodex Skardensis af postulasögur." *ANF* 8 (1892): 238–45, esp. p. 241.

Finnur Jónsson. >> *Den oldnorske og oldislandske Litteraturs Historie* (1920–4). Vol. 2, pp. 871–2.

Jón Ma. Ásgeirsson and Þórður Ingi Guðjónsson, ed. *Frá Sýrlandi til Íslands: Arfur Tómasar postula* (Reykjavík: Háskólaútgáfan, 2007). P. 165.

Jón Þorkelsson. "Islandske håndskrifter i England og Skotland." *ANF* 8 (1892): 199–237, esp. pp. 235–6.

Kirby, Ian. >> *Biblical Quotation* (1980). Vol. 2, p. 33.

Mogk, Eugen. >> *Geschichte der norwegisch-isländischen Literatur* (1904). P. 889.

Ólafur Halldórsson. *Helgafellsbækur fornar*. Studia Islandica 24 (Reykjavík: Heimspekideild Háskóla Íslands and Menningarsjóður, 1966). Pp. 16–22 and 41–5.

Ólafur Halldórsson, ed. *Mattheus saga postula* (Reykjavík: Stofnun Árna Magnússonar, 1994). Pp. xli–xlix.

Svanhildur Óskarsdóttir. "Universal History in Fourteenth-Century Iceland: Studies in AM 764 4to." PhD dissertation, University of London, 2000. Pp. 192–3.

Sverrir Tómasson. *Formálar íslenskra sagnaritara á miðöldum. Rannsókn bókmenntahefðar* (Reykjavík: Stofnun Árna Magnússonar, 1988). P. 351.

Wolf, Kirsten. "Postola sögur." In Phillip Pulsiano and Kirsten Wolf, with Paul Acker and Donald K. Fry, ed. >> *Medieval Scandinavia* (1993). Pp. 511–12.

– "Skarðsbók." In Phillip Pulsiano and Kirsten Wolf, with Paul Acker and Donald K. Fry, ed. >> *Medieval Scandinavia* (1993). P. 596.

Handlist, p. 330.

3. Filippuss saga postola

Translated from a Low German *Passionael*.

Manuscript:
AM 667 4to V (ca. 1525).
Literature:
Overgaard, Mariane, ed. *The History of the Cross-Tree Down to Christ's Passion: Icelandic Legend Versions*. Editiones Arnamagnæanæ, Ser. B, vol. 26 (Copenhagen: Munksgaard, 1968). Pp. xcix–cxix.

Sverrir Tómasson. *Formálar íslenskra sagnaritara á miðöldum. Rannsókn bókmenntahefðar* (Reykjavík: Stofnun Árna Magnússonar, 1988). P. 351.
Handlist, p. 330.

REMIGIUS   October 1

1. Remigíuss saga

The text is derived ultimately from Hincmar's *vita* (*BHL* 7152–63) supplemented from *BHL* 7150.

Manuscript:
AM 764 4to (ca. 1376–86).
Edition:
Unger, C.R., ed. >> *Heilagra manna søgur* (1877). Vol. 2, pp. 222–7.
Literature:
Bekker-Nielsen, Hans, and Ole Widding. "Legende. Norge og Island." *KLNM* 10 (1965). Cols. 421–3, esp. col. 421.
Cormack, Margaret. >> *The Saints in Iceland* (1994). P. 35.
Hallberg, Peter. "Imagery in Religious Old Norse Prose Literature: An Outline." *ANF* 102 (1987): 120–70, esp. p. 132.
Jakob Benediktsson. "Helgener." *KLNM* 21 (1977). Cols. 194–5, esp. col. 195.
Mogk, Eugen. >> *Geschichte der norwegisch-isländischen Literatur* (1904). P. 893.
Svanhildur Óskarsdóttir. "Universal History in Fourteenth-Century Iceland: Studies in AM 764 4to." PhD dissertation, University of London, 2000. Pp. 15, 58, and 240.
– "Arctic Garden of Delights: The Purpose of the Book of Reynistaður." In Kirsten Wolf and Johanna Denzin, ed. >> *Romance and Love in Late Medieval and Early Modern Iceland* (2008). Pp. 279–301, esp. pp. 292–4.
Wolf, Kirsten, ed. >> *Heilagra meyja sögur* (2003). P. li.
Handlist, p. 331.

2. Af Remigío erkibiskupi

The direct source has not been established.

Manuscript:
AM 657a–b 4to (ca. 1350, defective).
Edition:
Gering, Hugo, ed. >> *Islendzk æventyri* (1882–4). Vol. 1, p. 297.
German paraphrase:
Gering, Hugo, ed. >> *Islendzk æventyri* (1882–4). Vol. 2, p. 229.
Literature:
Cormack, Margaret. >> *The Saints in Iceland* (1994). P. 35.
Jakob Benediktsson. "Helgener." *KLNM* 21 (1977). Cols. 194–5, esp.
   col. 195.
Wolf, Kirsten, ed. >> *Heilagra meyja sögur* (2003). P. lii.
Handlist, p. 331.

ROCH   August 16

Rokuss saga

Translated from a now-lost Low German redaction that resembles the
source(s) of *Der Heiligen Leben*.

Manuscript:
Stock. Perg. fol. no. 3 (*Reykjahólabók*) (ca. 1530–40).
Edition:
Loth, Agnete, ed. >> *Reykjahólabók* (1969–70). Vol. 1, pp. 133–51.
Modern Icelandic language edition:
Sverrir Tómasson, Bragi Halldórsson, and Einar Sigurbjörnsson, ed.
   >> *Heilagra karla sögur* (2007). Pp. 207–8.
Literature:
Bekker-Nielsen, Hans, Thorkil Damsgaard Olsen, and Ole Widding.
   >> *Norrøn fortællekunst* (1965). P. 140.
Bekker-Nielsen, Hans, and Ole Widding. "Legende. Norge og Island."
   KLNM 10 (1965). Cols. 421–3, esp. col. 422.
Finnur Jónsson. >> *Den oldnorske og oldislandske Litteraturs Historie*
   (1920–4). Vol. 3, p. 141.
Kalinke, Marianne E. "Reykjahólabók: A Legendary on the Eve of the
   Reformation." *Skáldskaparmál* 2 (1992): 239–69, esp. pp. 240 and 245–6.
– >> *The Book of Reykjahólar* (1996). Pp. 28, 50, 97, 100–1, and 245.
Mogk, Eugen. >> *Geschichte der norwegisch-isländischen Literatur* (1904).
   P. 895.

Sverrir Tómasson. "Trúarbókmenntir í lausu máli á síðmiðöld." In
    Böðvar Guðmundsson, Sverrir Tómasson, Torfi H. Tulinius, and
    Vésteinn Ólason, ed. >> *Íslensk Bókmenntasaga* 2 (1993). Pp. 249–82,
    esp. p. 279.
Widding, Ole, and Hans Bekker-Nielsen. "En senmiddelalderlig
    legendesamling." *Mm* (1960): 105–28, esp. pp. 107, 114, and 127.
– "Low German Influence on Late Icelandic Hagiography." *GR* 37
    (1962): 239–62, esp. pp. 248, 255, and 259.
Handlist, p. 331.

SALINUS   January 11

A tale about the passion and miracles of Saint Salinus included in
Karlamagnúss saga. The tale is based on Vincent of Beauvais' *Speculum
historiale*.

Manuscripts:
AM 180d fol. (ca. 1700), AM 531 4to (ca. 1600–1700), and AM 657a–b
    4to (ca. 1350).

Editions:
Bjarni Vilhjálmsson, ed. *Karlamagnús saga ok kappa hans.* 3 vols. (Reykjavík:
    Íslendingasagnaútgáfan; Haukadalsútgáfan, 1950). Vol. 3, pp. 888–98.
    Normalized text based on *Karlamagnus saga ok kappa hans.*
Jakobsen, Alfred. "Er kap. 1–5 i del X af *Karlamagnus saga* lånt fra en
    samling *æfintýr?*" *Mm* (1959): 103–16, esp. pp. 106.16–111.3.
    Edition of AM 657a–b 4to.
Unger, C.R., ed., *Karlamagnus saga ok kappa hans: Fortællinger om Keiser
    Karl Magnus og hans Jævninger i norsk Bearbeidelse fra det trettende
    Aarhundrede* (Christiania [Oslo]: Jensen, 1860). Pp. 547.37–552.
    Based on AM 180d fol. with variants from AM 531 4to.

English translation:
Hieatt, Constance B., trans. *Karlamagnús saga: The Saga of Charlemagne
    and His Heroes.* 3 vols. Mediaeval Sources in Translation 13, 17, 25
    (Toronto: Pontifical Institute of Mediaeval Studies, 1975–80). Vol. 3,
    pp. 338–45.

Literature:
Cormack, Margaret. >> *The Saints in Iceland* (1994). P. 35.
Halvorsen, E.F. *The Norse Version of the Chanson de Roland.* Bibliotheca
    Arnamagnæana 19 (Copenhagen: Munksgaard, 1959). P. 47.

Jakobsen, Alfred. "Noen tillegg til 'Islendzk æventyri'." *Mm* (1960): 27–47, esp. pp. 28–9.

Louis-Jensen, Jonna. "Nogle ævintýri." *Opuscula* 5. Bibliotheca Arna- magnæana 31 (Copenhagen: Munksgaard, 1975). Pp. 263–77, esp. p. 264.

Sverrir Tómasson. *Formálar íslenskra sagnaritara á miðöldum. Rannsókn bókmenntahefðar* (Reykjavík: Stofnun Árna Magnússonar, 1988). Pp. 363–4.

Wolf, Kirsten, ed. >> *Heilagra meyja sögur* (2003). P. lii.

SEBASTIAN   January 20

1. Sebastíanuss saga

Based on *BHL* 7543.

Manuscripts:
AM 235 fol. (ca. 1400, defective), AM 238 fol. VIII (ca. 1425–50), AM 238 fol. XII (ca. 1400), and AM 238 fol. XXVIII (ca. 1275–1300).

Editions:
Foote, Peter, ed. >> *Lives of Saints* (1962).
    Facsimile of AM 238 fol. VIII, fol. 1r–v.

Loth, Agnete. "Til Sebastianus saga." *Opuscula* 5. Bibliotheca Arna- magnæana 31 (Copenhagen: Munksgaard, 1975). Pp. 103–22, esp. pp. 106–15.
    Edition of AM 238 fol. XII.

Stefán Karlsson. "Om himmel og helvede på gammelnorsk: AM 238 XXVIII fol." In *Festskrift til Ludvig Holm-Olsen på hans 70-årsdag den 9. juni 1984* (Øvre Ervik: Alvheim & Eide, 1984). Pp. 185–96, esp. pp. 188–91.
    Edition of AM 238 fol. XXVIII.

Unger, C.R., ed. >> *Heilagra manna søgur* (1877). Vol. 2, pp. 228–35.
    Based on AM 235 fol. (pp. 228–231.34 and 232.6–235) and AM 238 fol. VIII (pp. 231.35–232.5) with variants from AM 238 fol. VIII (pp. 232.5–235).

Literature:
Battista, Simonetta. "Interpretations of the Roman Pantheon in the Old Norse Hagiographic Sagas." In Geraldine Barnes and Margaret Clunies Ross, ed. >> *Old Norse Myths, Literature and Society* (2000). Pp. 24–34, esp. p. 31.

Bekker-Nielsen, Hans. "Kyrkofäderna ock kyrkolärarna. K. i vestnordisk litteratur." *KLNM* 9 (1964). Cols. 690–3, esp. cols. 690–1.
Bekker-Nielsen, Hans, Thorkil Damsgaard Olsen, and Ole Widding. >> *Norrøn fortællekunst* (1965). P. 124.
Bekker-Nielsen, Hans, and Ole Widding. "Legende. Norge og Island." *KLNM* 10 (1965). Cols. 421–3, esp. col. 421.
Carlé, Birte. >> *Jomfru-fortællingen* (1985). Pp. 37–8.
Cormack, Margaret. >> *The Saints in Iceland* (1994). Pp. 152 and 245.
Hallberg, Peter. "Imagery in Religious Old Norse Prose Literature: An Outline." *ANF* 102 (1987): 120–70, esp. pp. 124, 129, 144, and 149.
Kirby, Ian. >> *Biblical Quotation* (1980). Vol. 2, p. 284.
Lindow, John. "Norse Mythology and the Lives of the Saints." *SS* 73 (2001): 437–56, esp. p. 447.
Mogk, Eugen. >> *Geschichte der norwegisch-isländischen Literatur* (1904). P. 891.
Sverrir Tómasson. "Kristnar trúarbókmenntir í óbundnu máli." In Guðrún Nordal, Sverrir Tómasson, and Vésteinn Ólason, ed.>> *Íslensk Bókmenntasaga* 1 (1992). Pp. 419–79, esp. pp. 431 and 436–7.
Widding, Ole, and Hans Bekker-Nielsen. "Low German Influence on Late Icelandic Hagiography." *GR* 37 (1962): 239–62, esp. pp. 250 and 255.
Handlist, p. 331.

2. Sebastíanuss saga

Translated from a now-lost Low German redaction that resembles the source(s) of *Der Heiligen Leben*.

Manuscript:
Stock. Perg. fol. no. 3 (*Reykjahólabók*) (ca. 1530–40).
Edition:
Loth, Agnete, ed. >> *Reykjahólabók* (1969–70). Vol. 1, pp. 153–66.
Literature:
Bekker-Nielsen, Hans. "Kyrkofäderna ock kyrkolärarna. K. i vestnordisk litteratur." *KLNM* 9 (1964). Cols. 690–3, esp. cols. 690–1.
Bekker-Nielsen, Hans, Thorkil Damsgaard Olsen, and Ole Widding. >> *Norrøn fortællekunst* (1965). P. 141.
Dillmann, François-Xavier. "Om hedningar och hundar. Kring den fornvästnordiska sammansättningen *hundheiðinn*." *SI* 52 (2001): 17–33, esp. pp. 27–8.

Finnur Jónsson. >> *Den oldnorske og oldislandske Litteraturs Historie*
(1920–4). Vol. 3, p. 141.
Kalinke, Marianne E. "Reykjahólabók: A Legendary on the Eve of the
Reformation." *Skáldskaparmál* 2 (1992): 239–69, esp. p. 240.
– "The Cowherd and the Saint: The Grateful Lion in Icelandic Folklore
and Legend." *SS* 66 (1994): 1–22, esp. p. 10.
– >> *The Book of Reykjahólar* (1996). Pp. 28, 79, 96, 104, and 150–1.
Loth, Agnete. "Til Sebastianus saga." *Opuscula* 5. Bibliotheca Ar-
namagnæana 31 (Copenhagen: Munksgaard, 1975). Pp. 103–22, esp.
p. 122.
Widding, Ole, and Hans Bekker-Nielsen. "En senmiddelalderlig
legendesamling." *Mm* (1960): 105–28, esp. pp. 107, 115, and 127.
– "Low German Influence on Late Icelandic Hagiography." *GR* 37
(1962): 239–62, esp. pp. 250 and 255.
Handlist, p. 331.

SERVATIUS   May 13

Servasíuss saga

Translated from a now-lost Low German redaction that resembles the
source(s) of *Der Heiligen Leben*.

Manuscript:
Stock. Perg. fol. no. 3 (*Reykjahólabók*) (ca. 1530–40).
Edition:
Loth, Agnete, ed. >> *Reykjahólabók* (1969–70). Vol. 2, pp. 193–210.
Literature:
Bekker-Nielsen, Hans, and Ole Widding. "Legende. Norge og Island."
KLNM 10 (1965). Cols. 421–3, esp. col. 421.
Kalinke, Marianne E. "Reykjahólabók: A Legendary on the Eve of the
Reformation." *Skáldskaparmál* 2 (1992): 239–69, esp. pp. 240 and 245.
– >> *The Book of Reykjahólar* (1996). Pp. 28, 50, 102, and 129.
Widding, Ole, and Hans Bekker-Nielsen. "En senmiddelalderlig
legendesamling." *Mm* (1960): 105–28, esp. pp. 108 and 122–3.
– "Low German Influence on Late Icelandic Hagiography." *GR* 37
(1962): 239–62, esp. pp. 247–8.
Handlist, p. 331.

SEVEN SLEEPERS   July 27

1. Sjau sofanda saga

Based possibly on a version of *BHL* 2319.

Manuscript:
AM 623 4to (ca. 1325, defective).
Editions:
Finnur Jónsson, ed. *AM 623, 4°: Helgensagaer*. STUAGNL 52 (Copenhagen: Jørgensen, 1927). Pp. 54–9.
Unger, C.R., ed. >> *Heilagra manna søgur* (1877). Vol. 2, pp. 236–40.
Literature:
Granlund, John. "Sjusovarelegenden." *KLNM* 21 (1977). Cols. 313–14, esp. col. 314.
Konráð Gíslason. *Um frum-parta íslenzkrar túngu í fornöld* (Copenhagen: Trier, 1846). Pp. lvi–lvii.
Mogk, Eugen. >> *Geschichte der norwegisch-isländischen Literatur* (1904). Pp. 891 and 894.
Overgaard, Mariane. "AM 244, 8vo: En islandsk schwank-samling." *Opuscula* 7. Bibliotheca Arnamagnæana 34 (Copenhagen: Reitzel, 1979). Pp. 268–318, esp. p. 301.
Þórhallur Þorgilsson. "Um þýðingar og endursagnir úr ítölskum miðaldaritum." *Landsbókasafn Íslands. Árbók* 1946–7 (1948): 212–24, esp. p. 222.
Widding, Ole, and Hans Bekker-Nielsen. "Low German Influence on Late Icelandic Hagiography." *GR* 37 (1962): 239–62, esp. pp. 252–3.
Handlist, p. 331.

2. Sjau sofanda saga

Based on a now-lost Low German redaction that resembles the source(s) of *Der Heiligen Leben*.

Manuscript:
Stock. Perg. fol. no. 3 (*Reykjahólabók*) (ca. 1530–40).
Edition:
Loth, Agnete, ed. >> *Reykjahólabók* (1969–70). Vol. 1, pp. 191–212.

Literature:

Bekker-Nielsen, Hans, Thorkil Damsgaard Olsen, and Ole Widding.
>> *Norrøn fortællekunst* (1965). P. 140.

Carlé, Birte. *500–1500 – Indføring i middelalderens fortællekunst* (n.p.:
Gyldendal, 1966). Pp. 28–9.

Granlund, John. "Sjusovarelegenden." *KLNM* 21 (1977). Cols. 313–14,
esp. col. 314.

Kalinke, Marianne E. "Reykjahólabók: A Legendary on the Eve of the
Reformation." *Skáldskaparmál* 2 (1992): 239–69, esp. p. 240.

– "The Cowherd and the Saint: The Grateful Lion in Icelandic Folklore
and Legend." *SS* 66 (1994): 1–22, esp. p. 7.

– >> *The Book of Reykjahólar* (1996). Pp. 28, 50, 80, and 115.

Overgaard, Mariane. "AM 244, 8vo: En islandsk schwank-samling."
Opuscula 7. Bibliotheca Arnamagnæana 34 (Copenhagen: Reitzel,
1979). Pp. 268–318, esp. p. 301.

Widding, Ole, and Hans Bekker-Nielsen. "En senmiddelalderlig
legendesamling." *Mm* (1960): 105–28, esp. pp. 107 and 115–16.

– "Low German Influence on Late Icelandic Hagiography." *GR* 37
(1962): 239–62, esp. pp. 252–3.

Handlist, p. 331.

SILVESTER   December 31

1. Silvesters saga

A translation of texts corresponding to *BHL* 7726, 7729, 7734, 7731,
and 7732.

Manuscripts:
AM 238 fol. VII (ca. 1350–75), AM 655 4to IV (ca. 1200–25), AM 655
4to V (ca. 1200–25), and Stock. Perg. fol. no. 2 (ca. 1425–45).

Editions:
Foote, Peter, ed. >> *Lives of Saints* (1962).
Facsimile of Stock. Perg. fol. no. 2.

Hreinn Benediktsson. *Early Icelandic Script As Illustrated in Vernacular
Texts from the Twelfth and Thirteenth Centuries.* Íslenzk handrit:
Icelandic Manuscripts, Series in Folio 2 (Reykjavík: The Manuscript
Institute of Iceland, 1965). Plate 19 and pp. xiii–xv.
Facsimile and text edition of AM 655 4to IV, fol. 1v.

Morgenstern, Gustav, ed. >> *Arnamagnæanische Fragmente* (1893).
Pp. 8–14 and 22–3.
Edition of AM 655 4to IV (pp. 8–14.25) and AM 655 4to V (pp. 22.27–23).

Unger, C.R., ed. >> *Heilagra manna søgur* (1877). Vol. 2, pp. 245–86.
Based on Stock. Perg. fol. no. 2 (pp. 245–280.2) with variants from AM
238 fol. VII (pp. 261.16–266.1). Edition of AM 655 4to V (pp. 280.6–
281.7) and edition of AM 655 4to IV (pp. 281.11–286).

Modern Icelandic language edition:
Sverrir Tómasson, Bragi Halldórsson, and Einar Sigurbjörnsson, ed.
>> *Heilagra karla sögur* (2007). Pp. 63–108.

Literature:
Bekker-Nielsen, Hans, Thorkil Damsgaard Olsen, and Ole Widding.
>> *Norrøn fortællekunst* (1965). P. 23.

Bekker-Nielsen, Hans, and Ole Widding. "Legende. Norge og Island."
KLNM 10 (1965). Cols. 421–3, esp. col. 421.

Carlé, Birte. >> *Jomfru-fortællingen* (1985). Pp. 39, 54, 58–9, 67, and 105.

– "Men and Women in the Saints' Sagas of *Stock. 2, fol.*" In John
Lindow, Lars Lönnroth, and Gerd Wolfgang Weber, ed. >> *Structure
and Meaning in Old Norse Literature* (1986). Pp. 317–46, esp. pp. 320,
324, and 328–30.

Cormack, Margaret. >> *The Saints in Iceland* (1994). Pp. 33 and 152.

Finnur Jónsson. >> *Den oldnorske og oldislandske Litteraturs Historie*
(1920–4). Vol. 2, pp. 874–5.

Hallberg, Peter. "Imagery in Religious Old Norse Prose Literature: An
Outline." *ANF* 102 (1987): 120–70, esp. p. 138.

Jakob Benediktsson. "Helgener." *KLNM* 21 (1977). Cols. 194–5, esp.
col. 195.

Jón Ma. Ásgeirsson and Þórður Ingi Guðjónsson, ed. *Frá Sýrlandi til
Íslands: Arfur Tómasar postula* (Reykjavík: Háskólaútgáfan, 2007).
P. 206.

Jónas Kristjánsson. "Learned Style or Saga Style?" In Ursula Dronke,
Guðrún P. Helgadóttir, Gerd Wolfgang Weber, and Hans Bekker-
Nielsen, ed. >> *Specvlvm Norroenvm* (1981). Pp. 260–92.

– >> *Eddas and Sagas* (1988). P. 148.

Kalinke, Marianne E. >> *The Book of Reykjahólar* (1996). P. 39.

Kirby, Ian. >> *Biblical Quotation* (1980). Vol. 2, pp. 48–9.

Lehmann, Paul. >> "Skandinaviens Anteil an der lateinischen Literatur
und Wissenschaft des Mittelalters" (1937). P. 45.

Mogk, Eugen. >> *Geschichte der norwegisch-isländischen Literatur* (1904).
P. 893.

Stefán Karlsson. "Inventio Crucis, cap 1, og Veraldar saga." In *Opuscula Septentrionalia: Festskrift til Ole Widding 10.10.1977* (Copenhagen: Reitzel, 1977). Pp. 116–33, esp. pp. 127–30.
Svanhildur Óskarsdóttir. "Universal History in Fourteenth-Century Iceland: Studies in AM 764 4to." PhD dissertation, University of London, 2000. Pp. 201–2.
Widding, Ole, and Hans Bekker-Nielsen. "Low German Influence on Late Icelandic Hagiography." *GR* 37 (1962): 239–62, esp. p. 249.
Handlist, p. 332.

2. Af Konstantíno kongi

A separate version based on 1 (chapter 36). Cf. *BHL* 7734.

Manuscript:
AM 657 a–b 4to (ca. 1350).
Edition:
Gering, Hugo, ed. >> *Islendzk æventyri* (1882–4). Vol. 1, pp. 22–3.
German paraphrase:
Gering, Hugo, ed. >> *Islendzk æventyri* (1882–4). Vol. 2, p. 13.
Literature:
Cormack, Margaret. >> *The Saints in Iceland* (1994). Pp. 34n27 and 35.
Foote, Peter, ed. >> *Lives of Saints* (1962). P. 22.
Jakob Benediktsson. "Helgener." *KLNM* 21 (1977). Cols. 194–5, esp. col. 195.
Wolf, Kirsten, ed. >> *Heilagra meyja sögur* (2003). P. lii.
Handlist, p. 332.

3. Silvesters saga

Translated from a now-lost Low German redaction that resembles the source(s) of *Der Heiligen Leben*.

Manuscript:
Stock. Perg. fol. no. 3 (*Reykjahólabók*) (ca. 1530–40).
Edition:
Loth, Agnete, ed. >> *Reykjahólabók* (1969–70). Vol. 1, pp. 375–404.
Literature:
Bekker-Nielsen, Hans, Thorkil Damsgaard Olsen, and Ole Widding. >> *Norrøn fortællekunst* (1965). P. 141.
Carlé, Birte. *500–1500 – Indføring i middelalderens fortællekunst* ([n.p].: Gyldendal, 1966). Pp. 28–9.

Jakob Benediktsson. "Helgener." *KLNM* 21 (1977). Cols. 194–5, esp.
col. 195.
Kalinke, Marianne E. "Reykjahólabók: A Legendary on the Eve of the
Reformation." *Skáldskaparmál* 2 (1992): 239–69, esp. p. 240.
– >> *The Book of Reykjahólar* (1996). Pp. 28, 39, 50, 108, and 150–1.
Widding, Ole, and Hans Bekker-Nielsen. "En senmiddelalderlig
legendesamling." *Mm* (1960): 105–28, esp. pp. 107 and 118.
– "Low German Influence on Late Icelandic Hagiography." *GR* 37
(1962): 239–62, esp. pp. 249 and 255.
Handlist, p. 332.

SIMON AND JUDE   October 28

1. Tveggja postola saga Símons ok Júdass I

Based on a version of *BHL* 7751.

Manuscripts:
AM 628 4to (1711–12), AM 629 4to (1697), AM 630 4to (ca. 1650–
1700), AM 652 4to (ca. 1250–70, defective), AM 656 4to I
(ca. 1600), Rask 69 (ca. 1800), and SÁM 1 fol. (*Codex Scardensis*)
(ca. 1350–75).
Editions:
Slay, Desmond, ed. *Codex Scardensis*. EIM 2 (Copenhagen: Rosenkilde
and Bagger, 1960).
Facsimile of SÁM 1 fol.
Þorsteinn Jónsson, ed. *Hér hefjast Tíu Sögur, af þeim enum heiløgu Guds
Postulum og pínslar vottum* (Viðeyjarklaustur: Þ. Jónsson, 1836).
Pp. 176–92.
Based on a manuscript descended from AM 630 4to.
Unger, C.R., ed. >> *Postola sögur* (1874). Pp. 779–791.28.
Based on AM 630 4to (779–789.17) with variants from AM 628 4to.
Edition of AM 652 4to (pp. 789.19–791.28).
Modern Icelandic language edition:
Ólafur Halldórsson, ed. *Sögur úr Skarðsbók* (Reykjavík: Almenna
bókafélagið, 1967). Pp. 192–206.
Edition of SÁM 1 fol.
English translation:
Roughton, Philip G. "AM 645 4to and AM 652/630 4to: Study and
Translation of Two Thirteenth-Century Icelandic Collections of

Apostles' and Saints' Lives." PhD dissertation, University of
Colorado, 2002. Pp. 791–810.

Literature:

Battista, Simonetta. "Translation or Redaction in Old Norse Hagiography." In Peter Andersen, ed. >> *Pratiques de Traduction au Moyen
Age* (2004). Pp. 100–10, esp. pp. 104–5.

– "*Blámenn, djǫflar* and Other Representations of Evil in Old Norse
Literature." In John McKinnell, David Ashurst, and Donata Kick, ed.
>> *The Fantastic in Old Norse/Icelandic Literature* (2006). Vol. 1,
pp. 113–22, esp. p. 118.

Bekker-Nielsen, Hans, Thorkil Damsgaard Olsen, and Ole Widding.
>> *Norrøn fortællekunst* (1965). Pp. 122–3.

Collings, Lucy Grace. "The Codex Scardensis: Studies in Icelandic
Hagiography." PhD dissertation, Cornell University, 1969. Pp. 22–7
and 186–96.

Cormack, Margaret. >> *The Saints in Iceland* (1994). P. 152.

Eiríkr Magnússon. "Kodex Skardensis af postulasögur." *ANF* 8 (1892):
238–45, esp. p. 241.

Finnur Jónsson. >> *Den oldnorske og oldislandske Litteraturs Historie*
(1920–4). Vol. 2, p. 872.

Foote, Peter. "Postulatal." In Guðni Kolbeinsson, ed. >> *Minjar og
menntir* (1976). Pp. 152–73, esp. p. 170.

Jón Hnefill Aðalsteinsson. "Blot i forna skrifter." *SI* 47 (1996): 11–32,
esp. p. 23.

Jón Ma. Ásgeirsson and Þórður Ingi Guðjónsson, ed. *Frá Sýrlandi til
Íslands: Arfur Tómasar postula* (Reykjavík: Háskólaútgáfan, 2007).
Pp. 165 and 175.

Jón Þorkelsson. "Islandske håndskrifter i England og Skotland." *ANF* 8
(1892): 199–237, esp. pp. 235–6.

Kirby, Ian. >> *Biblical Quotation* (1980). Vol. 2, p. 35.

Magerøy, Hallvard. "Helgensoger." *KLNM* 6 (1961). Cols. 350–3, esp.
col. 351.

Mogk, Eugen. >> *Geschichte der norwegisch-isländischen Literatur* (1904).
P. 889.

Ólafur Halldórsson. *Helgafellsbækur fornar.* Studia Islandica 24 (Reykjavík: Heimspekideild Háskóla Íslands and Menningarsjóður, 1966).
Pp. 16–22 and 41–5.

Ólafur Halldórsson, ed. *Mattheus saga postula* (Reykjavík: Stofnun Árna
Magnússonar, 1994). Pp. xxix–lvii and lxxv–lxxxi.

Roughton, Philip. "Stylistics and Sources of the *Postola sögur* in AM 645
4to and AM 652/630 4to." *Gripla* 16 (2005): 7–50.

Sverrir Jakobsson. *Við og veröldin: Heimsmynd Íslendinga 1100–1400* (Reykjavík: Háskólaútgáfan, 2005). Pp. 137, 315, and 335.

Þórður Ingi Guðjónsson. "Apostlene i islandsk middelalderlitteratur." In *Den nordiske renessansen i høymiddelalderen*. Ed. Jón Viðar Sigurðsson and Preben Meulengracht Sørensen (Oslo: Historisk institutt, Universitetet i Oslo, 2000). Pp. 83–99, esp. pp. 93–4.

Wolf, Kirsten. "Postola sögur." In Phillip Pulsiano and Kirsten Wolf, with Paul Acker and Donald K. Fry, ed. >> *Medieval Scandinavia* (1993). Pp. 511–12.

– "Skarðsbók." In Phillip Pulsiano and Kirsten Wolf, with Paul Acker and Donald K. Fry, ed. >> *Medieval Scandinavia* (1993). P. 596.

Handlist, p. 332.

2. Tveggja postola saga Símons ok Júdass II

Based on a version of *BHL* 7751.

Manuscript:
AM 655 XII–XIII (ca. 1250–75).
Edition:
Unger, C.R., ed. >> *Postola sögur* (1874). Pp. 791.28–797.21.
Literature:

Battista, Simonetta. "Translation or Redaction in Old Norse Hagiography." In Peter Andersen, ed. >> *Pratiques de Traduction au Moyen Age* (2004). Pp. 100–10, esp. pp. 104–5.

Collings, Lucy Grace. "The Codex Scardensis: Studies in Icelandic Hagiography." PhD dissertation, Cornell University, 1969. Pp. 22–3.

Cormack, Margaret. >> *The Saints in Iceland* (1994). P. 152.

Finnur Jónsson. >> *Den oldnorske og oldislandske Litteraturs Historie* (1920–4). Vol. 2, p. 872.

Jón Ma. Ásgeirsson and Þórður Ingi Guðjónsson, ed. *Frá Sýrlandi til Íslands: Arfur Tómasar postula* (Reykjavík: Háskólaútgáfan, 2007). P. 165.

Jón Hnefill Aðalsteinsson. "Blot i forna skrifter." *SI* 47 (1996): 11–32, esp. pp. 23–4.

Jónas Kristjánsson. "Learned Style or Saga Style?" In Ursula Dronke, Guðrún P. Helgadóttir, Gerd Wolfgang Weber, and Hans Bekker-Nielsen, ed. >> *Specvlvm Norroenvm* (1981). Pp. 260–92.

Kirby, Ian. >> *Biblical Quotation* (1980). Vol. 2, p. 35.

Mogk, Eugen. >> *Geschichte der norwegisch-isländischen Literatur* (1904). P. 889.

Ólafur Halldórsson, ed. *Mattheus saga postula* (Reykjavík: Stofnun Árna Magnússonar, 1994). Pp. lxvi–lxxv.

Sverrir Tómasson. *Formálar íslenskra sagnaritara á miðöldum. Rannsókn bókmenntahefðar* (Reykjavík: Stofnun Árna Magnússonar, 1988). P. 352.
Þórður Ingi Guðjónsson. "Apostlene i islandsk middelalderlitteratur." In *Den nordiske renessansen i høymiddelalderen.* Ed. Jón Viðar Sigurðsson and Preben Meulengracht Sørensen (Oslo: Historisk institutt, Universitetet i Oslo, 2000). Pp. 83–99, esp. p. 95.
Handlist, p. 332.

SIXTUS II   August 6

A legend of Saint Sixtus based on *BHL* 7802 incorporated into *Lárentíuss saga erkidjákns* 1.

Manuscripts:
See Laurence of Rome 1 note (p. 199).
Editions:
Foote, Peter, ed. >> *Lives of Saints* (1962).
    Facsimile of Stock. Perg. fol. no. 2.
Unger, C.R., ed. >> *Heilagra manna søgur* (1877). Vol. 1, pp. 422–425.18.
Literature:
Cormack, Margaret. >> *The Saints in Iceland* (1994). Pp 34, 118, and 152.
Jón Hnefill Aðalsteinsson. "Blot i forna skrifter." *SI* 47 (1996): 11–32, esp. p. 28.
Mogk, Eugen. >> *Geschichte der norwegisch-isländischen Literatur* (1904). P. 891.
Sverrir Tómasson. "Kristnar trúarbókmenntir í óbundnu máli." In Guðrún Nordal, Sverrir Tómasson, and Vésteinn Ólason, ed. >> *Íslensk Bókmenntasaga* 1 (1992). Pp. 419–79, esp. p. 432.

STEPHEN THE DEACON   December 26

1. Stefáns saga

Based on the *Epistola Luciani presbyteri* and Augustine's *De Civitate Dei*.

Manuscript:
Stock. Perg. 4to no. 15 (ca. 1200).

Editions:

de Leeuw van Weenen, Andrea, ed. *The Icelandic Homily Book. Perg. 15 4° in the Royal Library, Stockholm.* Íslensk handrit / Icelandic manuscripts, Series in quarto 3 (Reykjavík: Stofnun Árna Magnússonar, 1993). Fols. 80v4–35 and 94r19– 97r34.
Facsimile and text edition.

Paasche, Fredrik, ed. *Homiliu-bók (Icelandic Sermons), Perg. 4to. No. 15 in the Royal Library, Stockholm.* CCI 8 (Copenhagen: Levin & Munksgaard, 1935).
Facsimile edition.

Wisén, Theodor, ed. *Homiliu-Bók: Isländska Homilier efter en handskrift från tolfte århundradet* (Lund: Gleerup, 1872). Pp. 175.25–176.31 and 201.3–207.

Literature:

Bekker-Nielsen, Hans. "Kyrkofäderna ock kyrkolärarna. K. i vestnordisk litteratur." *KLNM* 9 (1964). Cols. 690–3, esp. col. 691.
– "Stefan (protomartyr)." *KLNM* 17 (1972). Cols. 111–12, esp. col. 112.
– "Et par ord om de ældste norrøne helgensagaer." In Finn Hødnebø et al., >> *Eyvindarbók* (1992). Pp. 29–33, esp. p. 32.

Bekker-Nielsen, Hans, Thorkil Damsgaard Olsen, and Ole Widding. >> *Norrøn fortællekunst* (1965). Pp. 20 and 118.

Boyer, Régis. >> *La vie religieuse en Islande* (1979). P. 224.

Cormack, Margaret. >> *The Saints in Iceland* (1994). Pp. 32–3 and 153.

Finnur Jónsson. >> *Den oldnorske og oldislandske Litteraturs Historie* (1920–4). Vol. 2, p. 875.

Foote, Peter, ed. >> *Lives of Saints* (1962). P. 24.

Kalinke, Marianne E. "Reykjahólabók: A Legendary on the Eve of the Reformation." *Skáldskaparmál* 2 (1992): 239–69, esp. p. 253.
– "Stefanus saga in Reykjahólabók." *Gripla* 9 (1995): 133–87.
– >> *The Book of Reykjahólar* (1996), pp. 86–7 and 89.

Kirby, Ian. >> *Biblical Quotation* (1980). Vol. 2, p. 60.

McDougall, David. "Homilies (West Norse)." In Phillip Pulsiano and Kirsten Wolf, with Paul Acker and Donald K. Fry, ed. >> *Medieval Scandinavia* (1993). Pp. 643–4.

Sverrir Tómasson, Bragi Halldórsson, and Einar Sigurbjörnsson, ed. >> *Heilagra karla sögur* (2007). Pp. 61–2.

Vrátný, Karel. "Textkritische Nachlese zum Stockholmer Homilienbuch." *ANF* 33 (1917): 141–57, esp. p. 155.

Widding, Ole. "Et fragment af Stephanus saga (AM 655, 4° XIV B), tekst og kommentar." *APS* 21 (1952): 143–71, esp. pp. 143, 148–55, 158, and 171.

Handlist, p. 332.

2. Stefáns saga

A homiletic text somewhat abridged in relation to 1 and 5 but ultimately derived from the same translation.

Manuscript:
AM 655 4to XIV (ca. 1250–75).
Editions:
Hreinn Benediktsson. *Early Icelandic Script As Illustrated in Vernacular Texts from the Twelfth and Thirteenth Centuries.* Íslenzk handrit: Icelandic Manuscripts, Series in Folio 2 (Reykjavík: The Manuscript Institute of Iceland, 1965). Plate 43 and p. xxviii.
  Facsimile and edition of fol. 2r.
Widding, Ole. "Et fragment af Stephanus saga (AM 655, 4° XIV B), tekst og kommentar." *APS* 21 (1952): 143–71, esp. pp. 144–8.
Literature:
Bekker-Nielsen, Hans. "Stefan (protomartyr)." *KLNM* 17 (1972). Cols. 111–12, esp. col. 112.
Cormack, Margaret. >> *The Saints in Iceland* (1994). Pp. 37n45 and 153.
Foote, Peter, ed. >> *Lives of Saints* (1962). P. 24.
Kalinke, Marianne E. "Reykjahólabók: A Legendary on the Eve of the Reformation." *Skáldskaparmál* 2 (1992): 239–69, esp. pp. 252–3.
– "Stefanus saga in Reykjahólabók." *Gripla* 9 (1995): 133–87.
– >> *The Book of Reykjahólar* (1996). P. 87.
Kirby, Ian. >> *Biblical Quotation* (1980). Vol. 2, p. 106.
Sverrir Tómasson, Bragi Halldórsson, and Einar Sigurbjörnsson, ed. >> *Heilagra karla sögur* (2007). P. 62.
Handlist, p. 333.

3. Stefáns saga

A somewhat fuller version than 2 but ultimately derived from the same translation and 1, 2, and 5.

Manuscript:
AM 655 4to XXII (ca. 1250–1300).
Edition:
Hreinn Benediktsson. *Early Icelandic Script As Illustrated in Vernacular Texts from the Twelfth and Thirteenth Centuries.* Íslenzk handrit:

Icelandic Manuscripts, Series in Folio 2 (Reykjavík: The Manuscript
Institute of Iceland, 1965). Plate 68 and p. xlvi.
Facsimile and edition of fol. 2r.
Literature:
Bekker-Nielsen, Hans. "Stefan (protomartyr)." *KLNM* 17 (1972). Cols.
     111–12, esp. col. 112.
Bekker-Nielsen, Hans, and Ole Widding. "Legende. Norge og Island."
     KLNM 10 (1965). Cols. 421–3, esp. col. 421.
Cormack, Margaret. >> *The Saints in Iceland* (1994). P. 153.
Foote, Peter, ed. >> *Lives of Saints* (1962). P. 24.
Kalinke, Marianne E. "Stefanus saga in Reykjahólabók." *Gripla* 9 (1995):
     133–87.
Widding, Ole. "Et fragment af Stephanus saga (AM 655, 4° XIV B),
     tekst og kommentar." *APS* 21 (1952): 143–71, esp. pp. 148, 151–2,
     and 171.
Handlist, p. 333.

4. Stefáns saga

Fragments of a version close to 3 but independent of it and ultimately
derived from the same translation as 1, 2, 3, and 5.

Manuscript:
NRA 67 (ca. 1300–25).
Literature:
Bekker-Nielsen, Hans. "Stefan (protomartyr)." *KLNM* 17 (1972). Cols.
     111–12, esp. col. 112.
Bekker-Nielsen, Hans, and Ole Widding. "Legende. Norge og Island."
     KLNM 10 (1965). Cols. 421–3, esp. col. 421.
Cormack, Margaret. >> *The Saints in Iceland* (1994). P. 153.
Foote, Peter, ed. >> *Lives of Saints* (1962). P. 24.
Kalinke, Marianne E. "Stefanus saga in Reykjahólabók." *Gripla* 9 (1995):
     133–87.
Stefán Karlsson. "Islandsk bogeksport til Norge i middelalderen." *Mm*
     (1979): 1–17, esp. p. 6. Rpt. in *Stafkrókar: Ritgerðir eftir Stefán
     Karlsson gefnar út í tilefni af sjötugsafmæli hans 2. desember 1998*. Ed.
     Guðvarður Már Gunnlaugsson (Reykjavík: Stofnun Árna Magnússo-
     nar, 2000). Pp. 188–205, esp. p. 194.
Handlist, p. 333.

5. Stefáns saga

A composite work with material from 1, Peter Comestor's *Historica scholastica*, Honorius Augustodunensis' *Speculum ecclesiae*, the Acts of the Apostles, Augustine's *De Civitate Dei*, a fuller version of *Gyðinga saga*, and other sources.

Manuscripts:
AM 661 4to (ca. 1400–1500) and Stock. Perg. fol. no. 2 (ca. 1425–45).
Editions:
Foote, Peter, ed. >> *Lives of Saints* (1962).
   Facsimile of Stock. Perg. fol. no. 2.
Unger, C.R., ed. >> *Heilagra manna søgur* (1877). Vol. 2, pp. 287–309.
   Based on Stock. Perg. fol. no. 2 with variants from AM 661 4to.
Modern Icelandic language edition:
Sverrir Tómasson, Bragi Halldórsson, and Einar Sigurbjörnsson, ed.
   >> *Heilagra karla sögur* (2007). Pp. 33–61.
Literature:
Bekker-Nielsen, Hans. "Stefan (protomartyr)." *KLNM* 17 (1972). Cols.
   111–12, esp. col. 112.
Bekker-Nielsen, Hans, and Ole Widding. "Legende. Norge og Island."
   KLNM 10 (1965). Cols. 421–3, esp. col. 421.
Carlé, Birte. >> *Jomfru-fortællingen* (1985). Pp. 39, 41, 62, 67, and 71–2.
– "Men and Women in the Saints' Sagas of *Stock. 2, fol.*" In John
   Lindow, Lars Lönnroth, and Gerd Wolfgang Weber, ed. >> *Structure
   and Meaning in Old Norse Literature* (1986). Pp. 317–46, esp. pp. 320,
   323–4, and 336–7.
Finnur Jónsson. >> *Den oldnorske og oldislandske Litteraturs Historie*
   (1920–4). Vol. 2, pp. 874–5.
Jón Helgason. "Gyðinga saga i Trondheim." *Opuscula* 5. Bibliotheca
   Arnamagnæana 31 (Copenhagen: Munksgaard, 1975). Pp. 343–76, esp.
   pp. 370–1.
Jónas Kristjánsson. >> *Eddas and Sagas* (1988). P. 142.
Kalinke, Marianne E. "Reykjahólabók: A Legendary on the Eve of the
   Reformation." *Skáldskaparmál* 2 (1992): 239–69, esp. pp. 252–4.
– "Stefanus saga in Reykjahólabók." *Gripla* 9 (1995): 133–87.
– >> *The Book of Reykjahólar* (1996). Pp. 39, 47, 81, 86–9, 90–1, 107,
   and 118.
Kirby, Ian. >> *Biblical Quotation* (1980). Vol. 2, p. 49.

– *Bible Translation in Old Norse*. Université de Lausanne Publications de la faculté des lettres 27 (Geneva: Librairie Droz, 1986). Pp. 87 and 89–90.
– "The Bible and Biblical Interpretation in Medieval Iceland." In *Old Icelandic Literature and Society*. Ed. Margaret Clunies Ross (Cambridge: Cambridge University Press, 2000). Pp. 287–301, esp. p. 295.
Mogk, Eugen. >> *Geschichte der norwegisch-isländischen Literatur* (1904). P. 890.
Sverrir Tómasson. "Kristnar trúarbókmenntir í óbundnu máli." In Guðrún Nordal, Sverrir Tómasson, and Vésteinn Ólason, ed. >> *Íslensk Bókmenntasaga* 1 (1992). Pp. 419–79, esp. p. 439.
Widding, Ole, and Hans Bekker-Nielsen. "En senmiddelalderlig legendesamling." *Mm* (1960): 105–28, esp. p. 116.
– "Low German Influence on Late Icelandic Hagiography." *GR* 37 (1962): 239–62, esp. p. 251.
Widding, Ole. "Et fragment af Stephanus saga (AM 655, 4° XIV B), tekst og kommentar." *APS* 21 (1952): 143–71, esp. pp. 148–55, 157, and 171.
Wolf, Kirsten, ed. *Gyðinga saga* (Reykjavík: Stofnun Árna Magnússonar, 1995). Pp. lxxviii–lxxxii.
Handlist, p. 333.

6. Stefáns saga

A copy of an already existing Icelandic translation from the Latin.

Manuscript:
Stock. Perg. fol. no. 3 (*Reykjahólabók*) (ca. 1530–40).
Edition:
Loth, Agnete, ed. >> *Reykjahólabók* (1969–70). Vol. 1, pp. 213–45.
Literature:
Bekker-Nielsen, Hans. "Stefan (protomartyr)." *KLNM* 17 (1972). Cols. 111–12, esp. col. 112.
Bekker-Nielsen, Hans, Thorkil Damsgaard Olsen, and Ole Widding. >> *Norrøn fortællekunst* (1965). P. 141.
Kalinke, Marianne E. "Reykjahólabók: A Legendary on the Eve of the Reformation." *Skáldskaparmál* 2 (1992): 239–69, esp. pp. 240, 252–4, 264, and 266.
– "Stefanus saga in Reykjahólabók." *Gripla* 9 (1995): 133–87.
– >> *The Book of Reykjahólar* (1996). Pp. 28, 47, 56, 63, 80, 84, 86–9, 90–3, 95, 102–3, 106–8, 113, 117–18, 145–6, 152, 165, 239, and 241.

Sverrir Tómasson. "Trúarbókmenntir í lausu máli á síðmiðöld." In
    Böðvar Guðmundsson, Sverrir Tómasson, Torfi H. Tulinius, and
    Vésteinn Ólason, ed. >> *Íslensk Bókmenntasaga* 2 (1993). Pp. 249–82,
    esp. p. 278.
Sverrir Tómasson, Bragi Halldórsson, and Einar Sigurbjörnsson, ed.
    >> *Heilagra karla sögur* (2007). P. 62.
Widding, Ole. "Et fragment af Stephanus saga (AM 655, 4° XIV B), tekst
    og kommentar." *APS* 21 (1952): 143–71, esp. pp. 148–53, 155, and 157.
Widding, Ole, and Hans Bekker-Nielsen. "En senmiddelalderlig
    legendesamling." *Mm* (1960): 105–28, esp. pp. 107 and 116.
– "Low German Influence on Late Icelandic Hagiography." *GR* 37
    (1962): 239–62, esp. pp. 251 and 255.
Handlist, p. 333.

STEPHEN OF GRANDMONT · February 8

Af Stephano

Tales of Saint Stephen of Grandmont incorporated into the miracles of
the Virgin Mary.

Manuscripts:
See Mary the Blessed Virgin 3 note (p. 245).
Edition:
Unger, C.R., ed. >> *Mariu saga* (1871). Pp. 499.28–505.3 and 1154.6–1156.7.
Literature.
Handlist, pp. 324 and 333.

SUNNIVA AND COMPANIONS   July 8

1. Seljumanna þáttr

A version of the legend of Saint Sunniva included in the monk Oddr
Snorrason's *Óláfs saga Tryggvasonar* composed in Latin about 1190, but
now preserved only in Icelandic translation.

Manuscripts:
AM 310 4to (ca. 1250–75, defective) and Stock. Perg. 4to no. 18 (ca. 1300).

Editions:

Finnur Jónsson, ed. *Saga Óláfs Tryggvasonar af Oddr Snorrason munk*
 (Copenhagen: Gad, 1932). Pp. 96–103. Rpt. in Magnus Rindal,
 ed. *Selja – heilag stad i 1000 år* (Oslo: Universitetsforlaget, 1997).
 Pp. 299–306.
 Edition of AM 310 4to (pp. 96–101) and Stock. Perg. 4to no. 18
 (pp. 96–103).

Groth, P. *Saga Olafs konungs Tryggvasonar er ritaði Oddr muncr.* Det
 norske historiske Kildeskriftfond (Christiania [Oslo]: Grøndahl & Søn,
 1895). Pp. 49–50.
 Edition of AM 310 4to.

Guðni Jónsson, ed. *Konunga sögur.* 3 vols. ([Reykjavík]: Íslendingasagnaútgáfan, 1957). Vol. 1, pp. 80–5.
 Normalized edition based on *Saga Óláfs Tryggvasonar af Oddr Snorrason
 munk.*

Holtsmark, Anne, ed. *Olav Tryggvasons saga etter AM 310 qv.* CCN,
 Quarto serie 5 (Oslo: Selskapet til utgivelse av gamle norske hånd-
 skrifter, 1974).
 Facsimile of AM 310 4to.

Munch, P.A., ed. *Saga Olafs konungs Tryggvasunar. Kong Olaf Trygg-
 vesöns saga forfattet paa latin henimod slutningen af det tolfte aarhundrede af Odd Snorresøn* (Christiania [Oslo]: Brøgger & Christie, 1853).
 Pp. 25–6.
 Edition of AM 310 4to and Stock. Perg. 4to no. 18.

English translation:

Andersson, Theodore M., trans. *The Saga of Olaf Tryggvason.* Islandica
 52 (Ithaca: Cornell University Press, 2003). Pp. 77–9.

Norwegian translation:

Rindal, Magnus, trans. *Soga om Olav Tryggvason etter Odd munk Snor-
 resson.* Norrøne bokverk 46 (Oslo: Det Norske Samlaget, 1977).
 Pp. 76–9. Rpt. in Magnus Rindal. "Soga om seljemennene og Sunniva." In *Selja – heilag stad i 1000 år.* Ed. Magnus Rindal (Oslo:
 Universitetsforlaget, 1997). Pp. 307–10.

Literature:

Bekker-Nielsen, Hans, Thorkil Damsgaard Olsen, and Ole Widding.
 >> *Norrøn fortællekunst* (1965). Pp. 53 and 65.

Bekker-Nielsen, Hans, and Ole Widding. "Legende. Norge og Island."
 KLNM 10 (1965). Cols. 421–3, esp. col. 421.

Benson, Adolph B. "Scandinavian Saints and Legends: A Résumé." *GR*
 31 (1956): 9–22, esp. p. 13.

Bing, Just. "Sunnivalegenden." *Historisk tidsskrift* 5, Ser. 5 (1924): 533–45.

Bjarni Aðalbjarnarson. *Om de norske kongers sagaer*. Skrifter utgitt. av Det Norske Videnskaps-Akademi i Oslo, II. Hist.-filos. Kl., 1936, 4 (Oslo: Dybwad, 1937). Pp. 76–9.

Cormack, Margaret. >> *The Saints in Iceland* (1994). P. 154.

Daae, Ludvig. *Norges helgener* (Christiania [Oslo]: Malling, 1879). P. 141.

DuBois, Thomas A. "Sts Sunniva and Henrik: Scandinavian Martyr Saints in Their Hagiographic and National Contexts." In Thomas A. DuBois, ed. >> *Sanctity in the North* (2008). Pp. 65–99, esp. pp. 69–70 and 89–92.

Finnur Jónsson. >> *Den oldnorske og oldislandske Litteraturs Historie* (1920–4). Vol. 2, p. 877.

Gjerløw, Lilli. "Seljumannamessa." *KLNM* 15 (1970). Cols. 118–21, esp. col. 120.

Haki Antonsson. "Saints and Relics in Early Christian Scandinavia." *MScand* 15 (2005): 51–80, esp. p. 72.

– "The Early Cult of Saints in Scandinavia and the Conversion: A Comparative Perspective." In Haki Antonsson and Ildar H. Garipzanov, ed. >> *Saints and Their Lives on the Periphery* (2010). Pp. 17–34, esp. pp. 21 and 24.

Hommedal, Alf Tore. "Bakgrunnen for helgenanlegget på Selja og staden si rolle i den tidlege kristninga av Vest-Noreg." In *Selja – heilag stad i 1000 år*. Ed. Magnus Rindal (Oslo: Universitetsforlaget, 1997). Pp. 43–76, esp. pp. 46, 56–7, and 66.

Johnsen, Arne Odd. "Når slo Sunniva-kulten igjennom?" *Bjørgvin bispestol. Frå Selja til Bjørgvin*. Ed. Per Juvkam (Bergen: Universitetsforlaget, 1968). Pp. 40–62, esp. pp. 47–51 and 55–7.

Kratz, Henry. "Saints' Lives. 2. Iceland and Norway." In Phillip Pulsiano and Kirsten Wolf, with Paul Acker and Donald K. Fry, ed. >> *Medieval Scandinavia* (1993). Pp. 562–4.

Mogk, Eugen. >> *Geschichte der norwegisch-isländischen Literatur* (1904). P. 895.

Mundal, Else. "Legender, helgenkult og misjonsstrategi i kristningstida." In *Selja – heilag stad i 1000 år*. Ed. Magnus Rindal (Oslo: Universitetsforlaget, 1997). Pp. 77–101, esp. pp. 83 and 99.

O'Hara, Alexander. "Constructing a Saint: The Legend of St Suniva in Twelfth-Century Norway." *Viking and Medieval Scandinavia* 5 (2009): 105–21, esp. pp. 106n3 and 108.

Ommundsen, Åslaug. "The Cults of Saints in Norway before 1200." In Haki Antonsson and Ildar H. Garipzanov, ed. >> *Saints and Their Lives on the Periphery* (2010). Pp. 67–93, esp. pp. 83–9.

Rekdal, Jan Erik. "Legenden om Sunniva og Seljemenneskene." In *Selja – heilag stad i 1000 år*. Ed. Magnus Rindal (Oslo: Universitetsforlaget, 1997). Pp. 102–22, esp. pp. 105–20.

Storm, Gustav, ed. *Monumenta historia Norvegiæ: Latinske kildeskrifter til Norges historie i middelalderen* (Kristiania [Oslo]: Brøgger, 1880). Pp. xxxxi–xxxxiv and 147–52.

Turville-Petre, G. >> *Origins of Icelandic Literature* (1967). P. 192.

Widding, Ole. "Ave Maria eller Maríuvers i norrøn litteratur." *Mm* (1958): 1–7, esp. pp. 6–7.

Wolf, Kirsten, ed. >> *Heilagra meyja sögur* (2003). P. xxvii.

Young, Jean. "Legenden om den hellige Sunniva." *Historisk tidsskrift* 5, Ser. 8 (1930–3): 402–13.

Handlist, p. 333.

2. Seljumanna þáttr

A version of the legend of Saint Sunniva included in *Óláfs saga Tryggvasonar en mesta* from the early fourteenth century. The main source is Snorri Sturluson's *Heimskringla* but with additional material from other sources.

Manuscripts:
AM 53 fol. (ca. 1375–1400), AM 54 fol. (ca. 1375–1400), AM 61 fol. (ca. 1350–75), GKS 1005 fol. (*Flateyjarbók*) (ca. 1387–95), and Stock. Perg. fol. no. 1 (*Bergsbók*) (ca. 1400–25).

Editions:
Finnur Jónsson, ed. *Flateyjarbók (Codex Flateyensis: MS. No 1005 fol. in the Old Royal Collection in the Royal Library of Copenhagen)*. CCI 1 (Copenhagen: Levin & Munksgaard, 1930).
Facsimile of GKS 1005 fol.

Lindblad, Gustaf, ed. *Bergsbók: Perg. fol. nr. 1 in the Royal Library, Stockholm*. EIM 5 (Copenhagen: Rosenkilde and Bagger, 1963).
Facsimile of Stock. Perg. fol. no. 1.

Ólafur Halldórsson, ed. *Óláfs saga Tryggvasonar en mesta*. Editiones Arnamagnæanæ, Ser. A, vols. 1–2 (Copenhagen: Munksgaard, 1958–61). Vol. 1, pp. 244.9–153.11. Rpt. in In *Selja – heilag stad i 1000 år*. Ed. Magnus Rindal (Oslo: Universitetsforlaget, 1997). Pp. 313–22.
Based on AM 61 fol. with variants from AM 53 fol., AM 54 fol., Stock. Perg. fol. no. 1, and GKS 1005 fol.

– ed. *The Great Sagas of Olaf Tryggvason and Olaf the Saint: AM 61 fol.*
   EIM 14 (Copenhagen: Rosenkilde and Bagger, 1982).
   Facsimile of AM 61 fol.

Norwegian translation:

Flokenes, Kåre, trans. *Den lengste soga om Olav Tryggvason.* 3 vols.
   (Stavanger: Dreyer, 2002). Vol. 1, pp. 141–4.

Literature:

Bekker-Nielsen, Hans, Thorkil Damsgaard Olsen, and Ole Widding.
   >> *Norrøn fortællekunst* (1965). Pp. 53 and 65.

Bekker-Nielsen, Hans, and Ole Widding. "Legende. Norge og Island."
   KLNM 10 (1965). Cols. 421–3, esp. col. 421.

Benson, Adolph B. "Scandinavian Saints and Legends: A Résumé." *GR*
   31 (1956): 9–22, esp. p. 13.

Daae, Ludvig. *Norges helgener* (Christiania [Oslo]: Malling, 1879).
   P. 142.

Finnur Jónsson. >> *Den oldnorske og oldislandske Litteraturs Historie*
   (1920–4). Vol. 2, p. 877.

Gjerløw, Lilli. "Seljumannamessa." *KLNM* 15 (1970). Cols. 118–21, esp.
   col. 120.

Haki Antonsson. "Saints and Relics in Early Christian Scandinavia."
   MScand 15 (2005): 51–80, esp. p. 72.

– "The Early Cult of Saints in Scandinavia and the Conversion: A
   Comparative Perspective." In Haki Antonsson and Ildar H. Garipzanov, ed. >> *Saints and Their Lives on the Periphery* (2010). Pp. 17–34,
   esp. pp. 21 and 24.

Hommedal, Alf Tore. "Bakgrunnen for helgenanlegget på Selja og staden
   si rolle i den tidlege kristninga av Vest-Noreg." In *Selja – heilag stad i
   1000 år.* Ed. Magnus Rindal (Oslo: Universitetsforlaget, 1997). Pp. 43–
   76, esp. pp. 48, 50–1, and 56.

Johnsen, Arne Odd. "Når slo Sunniva-kulten igjennom?" *Bjørgvin
   bispestol. Frå Selja til Bjørgvin.* Ed. Per Juvkam (Bergen: Universitetsforlaget, 1968). Pp. 40–62, esp. p. 51.

Mogk, Eugen. >> *Geschichte der norwegisch-isländischen Literatur* (1904).
   P. 895.

Mundal, Else. "Legender, helgenkult og misjonsstrategi i kristningstida."
   In *Selja – heilag stad i 1000 år.* Ed. Magnus Rindal (Oslo: Universitetsforlaget, 1997). Pp. 77–101, esp. pp. 83 and 99.

O'Hara, Alexander. "Constructing a Saint: The Legend of St Suniva in
   Twelfth-Century Norway." *Viking and Medieval Scandinavia* 5 (2009):
   105–21, esp. p. 106n3.

Ommundsen, Åslaug. "The Cults of Saints in Norway before 1200." In
  Haki Antonsson and Ildar H. Garipzanov, ed. >> *Saints and Their
  Lives on the Periphery* (2010). Pp. 67–93, esp. pp. 83–9.
Rekdal, Jan Erik. "Legenden om Sunniva og Seljemenneskene." In *Selja
  – heilag stad i 1000 år*. Ed. Magnus Rindal (Oslo: Universitetsforlaget,
  1997). Pp. 102–22, esp. pp. 109–20.
Storm, Gustav, ed. *Monumenta historia Norvegiæ: Latinske kildeskrifter
  til Norges historie i middelalderen* (Kristiania [Oslo]: Brøgger,1880).
  Pp. xxxxi–xxxxiv and 147–52.
Handlist, p. 333.

3. Seljumanna þáttr

A version of the legend of Saint Sunniva included in the *Óláfs saga
Tryggvasonar* in *Flateyjarbók*.

Manuscript:
GKS 1005 fol. (*Flateyjarbók*) (ca. 1387–95).
Editions:
Finnur Jónsson, ed. *Flateyjarbók (Codex Flateyensis): MS. No. 1005 fol.
  in the Old Royal Collection in the Royal Library of Copenhagen*. CCI 1
  (Copenhagen: Levin and Munksgaard, 1930).
  Facsimile.
Guðbrandr Vigfusson and C.R. Unger, ed. *Flateyjarbók: En Samling af
  norske Konge-Sagaer med indskudte mindre Fortællinger om Begivenhe-
  der i og udenfor Norge samt Annaler*. 3 vols. (Christiania [Oslo]: Mall-
  ing, 1860–8). Vol. 1, pp. 242.9– 246.27.
Sigurður Nordal et al., ed. *Flateyjarbók*. 4 vols. (Akranes: Flateyjarútgá-
  fan, 1944–5). Vol. 1, pp. 267–71.
English translation:
Sephton, J. *The Saga of King Olaf Tryggwason Who Reigned over Norway
  A.D. 995 to A.D. 1000* (London: Nutt, 1895). Pp. 151–6.
Norwegian translation:
Mundal, Else. *Legender frå mellomalderen. Soger om heilage kvinner og
  menn* (Oslo: Det Norske Samlaget, 1995). Pp. 193–200. Rpt. in *Selja
  – heilag stad i 1000 år*. Ed. Magnus Rindal (Oslo: Universitetsforlaget,
  1997). Pp. 323–8.
Literature:
Bekker-Nielsen, Hans, Thorkil Damsgaard Olsen, and Ole Widding.
  >> *Norrøn fortællekunst* (1965). Pp. 53 and 65.

Bekker-Nielsen, Hans, and Ole Widding. "Legende. Norge og Island."
   KLNM 10 (1965). Cols. 421–3, esp. col. 421.
Benson, Adolph B. "Scandinavian Saints and Legends: A Résumé." *GR*
   31 (1956): 9–22, esp. p. 13.
Bing, Just. "Sunnivalegenden." *Historisk tidsskrift* 5, Ser. 5 (1924):
   533–45.
Daae, Ludvig. *Norges helgener* (Christiania [Oslo]: Malling, 1879).
   P. 142.
DuBois, Thomas A. "Sts Sunniva and Henrik: Scandinavian Martyr
   Saints in Their Hagiographic and National Contexts." In Thomas A.
   DuBois, ed. >> *Sanctity in the North* (2008). Pp. 65–99, esp. pp. 69–70
   and 89–92.
Finnur Jónsson. >> *Den oldnorske og oldislandske Litteraturs Historie*
   (1920–4). Vol. 2, p. 877.
Gjerløw, Lilli. "Seljumannamessa." *KLNM* 15 (1970). Cols. 118–21, esp.
   col. 120.
Haki Antonsson. "Saints and Relics in Early Christian Scandinavia."
   MScand 15 (2005): 51–80, esp. p. 72.
– "The Early Cult of Saints in Scandinavia and the Conversion: A
   Comparative Perspective." In Haki Antonsson and Ildar H. Garipzanov, ed. >> *Saints and Their Lives on the Periphery* (2010). Pp. 17–34,
   esp. pp. 21 and 24.
Hommedal, Alf Tore. "Bakgrunnen for helgenanlegget på Selja og staden
   si rolle i den tidlege kristninga av Vest-Noreg." In *Selja – heilag stad i
   1000 år*. Ed. Magnus Rindal (Oslo: Universitetsforlaget, 1997). Pp. 43–
   76, esp. pp. 48, 50–1, 56–7, and 66.
Johnsen, Arne Odd. "Når slo Sunniva-kulten igjennom?" *Bjørgvin
   bispestol. Frå Selja til Bjørgvin.* Ed. Per Juvkam (Bergen: Universitets-
   forlaget, 1968). Pp. 40–62, esp. p. 51.
Mogk, Eugen. >> *Geschichte der norwegisch-isländischen Literatur* (1904).
   P. 895.
O'Hara, Alexander. "Constructing a Saint: The Legend of St Suniva in
   Twelfth-Century Norway." *Viking and Medieval Scandinavia* 5 (2009):
   105–21, esp. p. 106n3.
Ommundsen, Åslaug. "The Cults of Saints in Norway before 1200." In
   Haki Antonsson and Ildar H. Garipzanov, ed. >> *Saints and Their
   Lives on the Periphery* (2010). Pp. 67–93, esp. pp. 83–9.
Rekdal, Jan Erik. "Legenden om Sunniva og Seljemenneskene." In *Selja
   – heilag stad i 1000 år*. Ed. Magnus Rindal (Oslo: Universitetsforlaget,
   1997). Pp. 102–22, esp. p. 109.

Storm, Gustav, ed. *Monumenta historia Norvegiæ: Latinske kildeskrifter til Norges historie i middelalderen* (Kristiania [Oslo]: Brøgger,1880). Pp. xxxxi–xxxxiv and 147–52.
Young, Jean. "Legenden om den hellige Sunniva." *Historisk tidsskrift* 5, Ser. 8 (1930–3): 402–13.
Handlist, p. 333.

4. Af Sunnivu

The last few lines of a miracle attributed to Saint Sunniva.

Manuscript:
AM 764 4to (1376–86, defective).
Literature:
Cormack, Margaret. >> *The Saints in Iceland* (1994). P. 35.
Svanhildur Óskarsdóttir. "The Book of Judith: A Medieval Icelandic Translation." *Gripla* 11 (2000): 79–123, esp. p. 84.
– "Universal History in Fourteenth-Century Iceland: Studies in AM 764 4to." PhD dissertation, University of London, 2000. Pp. 140 and 240.
– "Arctic Garden of Delights: The Purpose of the Book of Reynistaður." In Kirsten Wolf and Johanna Denzin, ed. >> *Romance and Love in Late Medieval and Early Modern Iceland* (2008). Pp. 279–301, esp. p. 292.
Wolf, Kirsten, ed. >> *Heilagra meyja sögur* (2003). P. li.

THAIS   October 8

Af Thais

A version of the legend of Saint Thais incorporated into the Old Norwegian *Barlaams saga ok Jósafats*.

Manuscripts:
See Barlaam and Josaphat note 1 (p. 50).
Editions:
Keyser, R., and C.R. Unger, ed. *Barlaams ok Josaphats saga* (Christiania [Oslo]: Feilberg & Landmark, 1851). Pp. 90.36–93.4.
Rindal, Magnus, ed. *Barlaams ok Josaphats saga*. Norrøne tekster 4 (Oslo: Norsk historisk kjeldeskrift-institutt, 1981). Pp. 80.21–82.27.

Danish translation:
Carlé, Birte. *Skøger og jomfruer i den kristne fortællekunst* (Odense: Odense Universitetsforlag, 1991). Pp. 77–9.
Literature:
Ásdís Egilsdóttir. "Kvendýrlingar og kvenímynd trúarlegra bókmennta á Íslandi." In Inga Huld Hákonardóttir, ed. >> *Konur og kristsmenn* (1996). Pp. 93–116, esp. pp. 103–4.
Bekker-Nielsen, Hans, Thorkil Damsgaard Olsen, and Ole Widding. >> *Norrøn fortællekunst* (1965). P. 112.
Haugen, Odd Einar. "Exempla in Barlaams ok Josaphats saga." In >> *Sagas and the Norwegian Experience* (1997). Pp. 227–36, esp. p. 232.
– "Forteljingane i forteljinga. Interpolasjonane i *Barlaams ok Josaphats saga.*" In Karl G. Johansson and Maria Arvidsson, ed. >> *Barlaam i nord* (2009). Pp. 47–73, esp. pp. 58 and 70–1.
Mogk, Eugen. >> *Geschichte der norwegisch-isländischen Literatur* (1904). P. 872.
Wolf, Kirsten, ed. >> *Heilagra meyja sögur* (2003). Pp. xxxiv–xxxv and lvi.
Handlist, pp. 302 and 333.

THEODORE TYRO   November 9

Theódórs saga

A translation of *BHL* 8077.

Manuscript:
AM 235 fol. (ca. 1400).
Edition:
Unger, C.R., ed. >> *Heilagra manna søgur* (1877). Vol. 2, pp. 310–14.
Literature:
Carlé, Birte. >> *Jomfru-fortællingen* (1985). P. 38.
– "Men and Women in the Saints' Sagas of *Stock. 2, fol.*" In John Lindow, Lars Lönnroth, and Gerd Wolfgang Weber, ed. >> *Structure and Meaning in Old Norse Literature* (1986). Pp. 317–46, esp. p. 319.
Jakob Benediktsson. "Helgener." *KLNM* 21 (1977). Cols. 194–5, esp. col. 195.
Kirby, Ian. >> *Biblical Quotation* (1980). Vol. 2, pp. 49–50.
Mogk, Eugen. >> *Geschichte der norwegisch-isländischen Literatur* (1904). P. 891.

Wolf, Kirsten. "The Severed Breast: A Topos in the Legends of Female
   Virgin Martyr Saints." *ANF* 112 (1997): 97–112, esp. p. 100.
Handlist, p. 333.

THOMAS THE APOSTLE   December 21

1. Thómass saga postola A

A somewhat free translation of *BHL* 8136.

Manuscripts:
AM 628 4to (1711–12), AM 629 4to (1697), AM 630 4to (ca. 1650–
   1700), AM 652 4to (ca. 1250–70, defective), BLAdd 4886 (ca. 1700–
   1800), BLAdd 11.069 (ca. 1700–1800), ÍB 165 4to (1778), ÍBR 76 8vo
   (1828), Lbs 1582 4to (1828), Lbs 1947 4to (ca. 1818), Lbs 326 8vo
   (ca. 1820), Rask 69 (ca. 1800), and SÁM 1 fol. (*Codex Scardensis*)
   (ca. 1350–75).

Editions:
Jón Ma. Ásgeirsson and Þórður Ingi Guðjónsson, ed. *Frá Sýrlandi til
   Íslands: Arfur Tómasar postula* (Reykjavík: Háskólaútgáfan, 2007).
   Pp. 293–316.
   Based on SÁM 1 fol. with variants from AM 630 4to and AM 652 4to
   (pp. 303.6–306.11).
Slay, Desmond, ed. *Codex Scardensis*. EIM 2 (Copenhagen: Rosenkilde
   and Bagger, 1960).
   Facsimile of SÁM 1 fol.
Þorsteinn Jónsson, ed. *Hér hefjast Tíu Sögur, af þeim enum heiløgu Guds
   Postulum og pínslar vottum* (Viðeyjarklaustur: Þ. Jónsson, 1836).
   Pp. 153–75.
   Based on a manuscript descended from AM 630 4to.
Unger, C.R., ed. >> *Postola sögur* (1874). Pp. 712–28.
   Based on AM 630 4to (pp. 712–727.5) with variants from AM 628 4to.
   Edition of AM 652 4to (pp. 727.7–728).
Modern Icelandic language edition:
Ólafur Halldórsson, ed. *Sögur úr Skarðsbók* (Reykjavík: Almenna
   bókafélagið, 1967). Pp. 151–69.
   Edition of SÁM 1 fol.
English translation:
Roughton, Philip G. "AM 645 4to and AM 652/630 4to: Study and
   Translation of Two Thirteenth-Century Icelandic Collections

of Apostles' and Saints' Lives." PhD dissertation, University of
Colorado, 2002. Pp. 716–42.

Literature:

Astås, Reidar. "Spor av teologisk tenkning og refleksjon i norsk og
islandsk høymiddelalder." *CM* 6 (1993): 133–67, esp. p. 137n20.

Bandlien, Bjørn. *Strategies of Passion: Love and Marriage in Medieval
Iceland and Norway*. Trans. Betsy van der Hoeck (Turnhout: Brepols,
2005). P. 76.

Bekker-Nielsen, Hans, Thorkil Damsgaard Olsen, and Ole Widding.
>> *Norrøn fortællekunst* (1965). P.122.

Collings, Lucy Grace. "The Codex Scardensis: Studies in Icelandic
Hagiography." PhD dissertation, Cornell University, 1969. Pp. 14–17
and 162–70.

Cormack, Margaret. >> *The Saints in Iceland* (1994). P. 156.

Eiríkr Magnússon. "Kodex Skardensis af postulasögur." *ANF* 8 (1892):
238–45, esp. p. 241.

Finnur Jónsson. >> *Den oldnorske og oldislandske Litteraturs Historie*
(1920–4). Vol. 2, p. 871.

Foote, Peter. "Postulatal." In Guðni Kolbeinsson, ed. >> *Minjar og
menntir* (1976). Pp. 152–73, esp. p. 165.

Hallberg, Peter. "Imagery in Religious Old Norse Prose Literature: An
Outline." *ANF* 102 (1987): 120–70, esp. p. 128.

Jón Hnefill Aðalsteinsson. "Blot i forna skrifter." *SI* 47 (1996): 11–32,
esp. pp. 21–2.

Jón Þorkelsson. "Islandske håndskrifter i England og Skotland." *ANF* 8
(1892): 199–237, esp. pp. 235–6.

Kirby, Ian. >> *Biblical Quotation* (1980). Vol. 2, p. 32.

Lehmann, Paul. >> "Skandinaviens Anteil an der lateinischen Literatur
und Wissenschaft des Mittelalters" (1937). P. 43.

Mogk, Eugen. >> *Geschichte der norwegisch-isländischen Literatur* (1904).
Pp. 888–9.

Ólafur Halldórsson. *Helgafellsbækur fornar*. Studia Islandica 24 (Reykjavík:
Heimspekideild Háskóla Íslands and Menningarsjóður, 1966). Pp. 16–
22 and 41–5.

Ólafur Halldórsson, ed. *Mattheus saga postula* (Reykjavík: Stofnun Árna
Magnússonar, 1994). Pp. xxix–xlix and lxxv–lxxxi.

Roughton, Philip. "Stylistics and Sources of the *Postola sögur* in AM 645
4to and AM 652/630 4to." *Gripla* 16 (2005): 7–50.

Sverrir Tómasson. "Kristnar trúarbókmenntir í óbundnu máli." In
Guðrún Nordal, Sverrir Tómasson, and Vésteinn Ólason, ed. >>
Íslensk Bókmenntasaga 1 (1992). Pp. 419–79, esp. pp. 446–7.

Þórður Ingi Guðjónsson. "Apostlene i islandsk middelalderlitteratur." In
Den nordiske renessansen i høymiddelalderen. Ed. Jón Viðar Sigurðsson
and Preben Meulengracht Sørensen (Oslo: Historisk institutt, Universitetet i Oslo, 2000). Pp. 83–99, esp. pp. 93–5 and 97.

Wilhelm, Friedrich. *Deutsche Legenden und Legendare: Texte und Untersuchungen zu ihrer Geschichte im Mittelalter* (Leipzig: J.C. Hinrich,
1907). P. 42.

Wolf, Kirsten. "Postola sögur." In Phillip Pulsiano and Kirsten Wolf,
with Paul Acker and Donald K. Fry, ed. >> *Medieval Scandinavia*
(1993). Pp. 511–12.

– "Skarðsbók." In Phillip Pulsiano and Kirsten Wolf, with Paul Acker
and Donald K. Fry, ed. >> *Medieval Scandinavia* (1993). P. 596.

Handlist, p. 333–4.

2. Thómass saga postola H

An almost verbatim translation of *BHL* 8136.

Manuscripts:
AM 656 4to I (ca. 1325–50) and JS fragm 8 A (ca. 1300–25).

Editions:
Jón Ma. Ásgeirsson and Þórður Ingi Guðjónsson, ed. *Frá Sýrlandi til
Íslands: Arfur Tómasar postula* (Reykjavík: Háskólaútgáfan, 2007).
Pp. 318–28.
    Edition of AM 656 4to I.

Unger, C.R., ed. >> *Postola sögur* (1874). Pp. 729–34.
    Edition of AM 656 4to I.

Literature:
Bekker-Nielsen, Hans, Thorkil Damsgaard Olsen, and Ole Widding.
    >> *Norrøn fortællekunst* (1965). P.122.

Collings, Lucy Grace. "The Codex Scardensis: Studies in Icelandic
    Hagiography." PhD dissertation, Cornell University, 1969. P. 14.

Cormack, Margaret. >> *The Saints in Iceland* (1994). P. 156.

Finnur Jónsson. >> *Den oldnorske og oldislandske Litteraturs Historie*
    (1920–4). Vol. 2, p. 871.

Foote, Peter. "Postulatal." In Guðni Kolbeinsson, ed. >> *Minjar og
    menntir* (1976). Pp. 152–73, esp. p. 165.

Kirby, Ian. >> *Biblical Quotation* (1980). Vol. 2, pp. 32–3.

Louis-Jensen, Jonna. "To håndskrifter fra det nordvestlige Island."
    Opuscula 7. Bibliotheca Arnamagnæana 34 (Copenhagen: Reitzel,
    1979). Pp. 219–53, esp. pp. 219 and 221–2.

Mogk, Eugen. >> *Geschichte der norwegisch-isländischen Literatur* (1904).
Pp. 888–9.

Ólafur Halldórsson, ed. *Mattheus saga postula* (Reykjavík: Stofnun Árna
Magnússonar, 1994). Pp. xlix–lvii.

Þórður Ingi Guðjónsson. "Apostlene i islandsk middelalderlitteratur." In
Den nordiske renessansen i høymiddelalderen. Ed. Jón Viðar Sigurðsson
and Preben Meulengracht Sørensen (Oslo: Historisk institutt, Universitetet i Oslo, 2000). Pp. 83–99, esp. pp. 94–5 and 97.

Handlist, p. 334.

3. Thómass saga postola

A translation of John 20.24–31.

Manuscript:

AM 672 4to (ca. 1400–1500).

Edition:

Kirby, Ian J. *Bible Translation in Old Norse*. Université de Lausanne
Publications de la Faculté des Lettres 27 (Geneva: Librairie Droz,
1986). P. 152.19–33.

Literature:

Carlé, Birte. "Men and Women in the Saints' Sagas of *Stock. 2, fol.*" In John
Lindow, Lars Lönnroth, and Gerd Wolfgang Weber, ed. >> *Structure and
Meaning in Old Norse Literature* (1986). Pp. 317–46, esp. p. 319.

Handlist, p. 334.

THOMAS BECKET   December 29

1. Thómass saga erkibiskups I

A somewhat free translation possibly by the (half-?) Norwegian priest Jón
Holt (d. 1312) of the so-called *Quadrilogus prior*.

Manuscripts:

AM 662b 4to (ca. 1350–1400, defective), NRA 66 (ca. 1300), and Stock.
Perg. 4to no. 17 (ca. 1300, defective).

Editions:

[Kålund, Kr., ed.] *Palæografisk Atlas: Oldnorsk-islandsk afdeling* (Copenhagen and Christiania [Oslo]: Gyldendal, 1905). No. 43.
Facsimile and text edition of Stock. Perg. 4to no. 17 (extract only).

Unger, C.R., ed. *Thomas saga erkibyskups. Fortælling om Thomas Becket erkebiskop af Canterbury* (Christiania [Oslo]: Bentzen, 1869). Pp. 1–282 and 508–19.
    Edition of Stock. Perg. 4to no. 17 (pp. 1–273.12 and 276–82), AM 662b 4to (pp. 273.12–277 and 510.38–519), and NRA 66a–c (pp. 508–510.34).

Literature:

Bekker-Nielsen, Hans. "Thómas saga erkibiskups." *KLNM* 18 (1974). Cols. 249–51, esp. cols. 249–50.

– "Et par ord om de ældste norrøne helgensager." In Finn Hødnebø et al., ed. >> *Eyvindarbók* (1992). Pp. 29–33, esp. p. 33.

Bekker-Nielsen, Hans, Thorkil Damsgaard Olsen, and Ole Widding. >> *Norrøn fortællekunst* (1965). Pp. 124 and 126.

Bekker-Nielsen, Hans, and Ole Widding. "Legende. Norge og Island." *KLNM* 10 (1965). Cols. 421–3, esp. col. 421.

Boyer, Régis. >> *La vie religieuse en Islande* (1979). Pp. 146 and 177.

Cormack, Margaret J. "Saints and Sinners: Reflections on Death in Some Icelandic Sagas." *Gripla* 8 (1993): 187–218, esp. pp. 190–1.

– >> *The Saints in Iceland* (1994). Pp. 36, 157, and 245.

Eiríkr Magnússon, ed. *Thómas saga erkibyskups: A Life of Archbishop Thomas Becket in Icelandic.* 2 vols. Rolls Series 65.2 (London: Eyre & Spottiswoode, 1875–83). Vol. 2, pp. lii and lviii–lx.

Finnur Jónsson. >> *Den oldnorske og oldislandske Litteraturs Historie* (1920–4). Vol. 2, pp. 876–7.

Foote, Peter. "On the Fragmentary Text Concerning St. Thomas Becket in Stock. Perg. Fol. Nr. 2." *Saga-Book* 15 (1961): 403–50.

Haki Antonsson: "Two Twelfth-Century Martyrs: St Thomas of Canterbury and St Magnús of Orkney." In *Sagas, Saints and Settlements*. Ed. Gareth Williams and Paul Bibire. The Northern World 2 (Leiden: Brill, 2004). Pp. 41–64.

Hallberg, Peter. *Stilsignalement och författarskap i norrön sagalitteratur. Synpunkter och exempel.* Acta Universitatis Gothoburgensis. Nordistica Gothoburgensia 3 (Gothenburg: Almqvist & Wiksell, 1968). Pp. 144–51, 153, 156, 163, and 234–5.

– "Imagery in Religious Old Norse Prose Literature: An Outline." *ANF* 102 (1987): 120–70, esp. pp. 135–6, 138, 143–4, 146, 148–9, 151–2, and 159–61.

Jakobsen, Alfred. "Et par ordformer med innskutt *a* i Thomas saga erkibiskups I." In *Sjötíu ritgerðir helgaðar Jakobi Benediktssyni 20. júlí 1977.* 2 vols. Ed. Einar G. Pétursson and Jónas Kristjánsson (Reykjavík: Stofnun Árna Magnússonar, 1977). Vol. 1, pp. 384–7.

– "Om bruken av aksenttegn i Sth. 17 qv. (Thomas saga erkibyskups)."
   Mm (1977): 89–102.
– "Thómas saga erkibiskups 1 – norsk eller islandsk oversettelse?" In
   Opuscula septentrionalia. Festskrift til Ole Widding, 10. 10. 1977. Ed.
   Bent Chr. Jacobsen et al. (Copenhagen: Reitzel, 1977). Pp. 89–99.
– "Thómas saga erkibiskups." In Phillip Pulsiano and Kirsten Wolf, with
   Paul Acker and Donald K. Fry, ed. >> *Medieval Scandinavia* (1993).
   Pp. 643–4.
Jónas Kristjánsson. *Um Fóstbrœðra sögu* (Reykjavík: Stofnun Árna
   Magnússonar, 1972). Pp. 258, 272–3, 281, 287–8, 303, and 306.
– "Learned Style or Saga Style?" In Ursula Dronke, Guðrún P. Helga-
   dóttir, Gerd Wolfgang Weber, and Hans Bekker-Nielsen, ed. >>
   Specvlvm Norroenvm (1981). Pp. 260–92.
– "The Court Style." In Régis Boyer, ed. >> *Les Sagas de Chevaliers
   (Riddarasögur)* (1985). Pp. 431–40, esp. pp. 433–4 and 437.
– >> *Eddas and Sagas* (1988). P. 143.
Kirby, Ian. >> *Biblical Quotation* (1980). Vol. 2, pp. 19 and 83.
Leach, Henry Goddard. *Angevin Britain and Scandinavia.* Harvard
   Studies in Comparative Literature (Cambridge, Mass.: Harvard
   University Press, 1921). P. 128.
Lehmann, Paul. >> "Skandinaviens Anteil an der lateinischen Literatur
   und Wissenschaft des Mittelalters" (1937). Pp. 46 and 54.
Magerøy, Hallvard. "Helgensoger." *KLNM* 6 (1961). Cols. 350–3, esp.
   col. 351.
Mogk, Eugen. >> *Geschichte der norwegisch-isländischen Literatur* (1904).
   P. 894.
Orme, Margaret. "A Reconstruction of Robert of Cricklade's Vita et
   Miracula S. Thomae Cantuariensis." *Analecta Bollandiana* 84 (1966):
   379–98.
Paasche, Fredrik. *Norges og Islands litteratur inntil utgangen av
   middelalderen.* Rev. ed. by Anne Holtsmark (Oslo: Aschehoug, 1947).
   Pp. 488 and 491.
Piebenga, G.A. "Om Marialegenden 'Fra hinum heilaga Thomase
   erkibiskupi'." *ANF* 101 (1986): 40–9.
Schier, Kurt. *Sagaliteratur.* Sammlung Metzler M78 (Stuttgart: Metzler,
   1970). Pp. 4, 67, 123, and 128.
Stefán Karlsson. "Icelandic Lives of Thomas a Becket: Questions of
   Authorship." In Peter Foote, Hermann Pálsson, and Desmond Slay, ed.
   >> *Proceedings of the First International Saga Conference* (1973).
   Pp. 212–43. Rpt. in *Stafkrókar: Ritgerðir eftir Stefán Karlsson gefnar út*

í tilefni af sjötugsafmæli hans 2. desember 1998. Ed. Guðvarður Már
Gunnlaugsson (Reykjavík: Stofnun Árna Magnússonar, 2000).
Pp. 135–52.
– "Islandsk bogeksport til Norge i middelalderen." *Mm* (1979): 1–17, esp.
pp. 6 and 10. Rpt. in *Stafkrókar: Ritgerðir eftir Stefán Karlsson gefnar
út í tilefni af sjötugsafmæli hans 2. desember 1998.* Ed. Guðvarður Már
Gunnlaugsson (Reykjavík: Stofnun Árna Magnússonar, 2000).
Pp. 188–205, esp. pp. 194 and 200.
Sverrir Tómasson. *Formálar íslenskra sagnaritara á miðöldum. Rannsókn
bókmenntahefðar* (Reykjavík: Stofnun Árna Magnússonar, 1988).
Pp. 144, 344, and 355–7.
– "Kristnar trúarbókmenntir í óbundnu máli." In Guðrún Nordal,
Sverrir Tómasson, and Vésteinn Ólason, ed. >> *Íslensk Bókmenntasaga*
1 (1992). Pp. 419–79, esp. p. 458.
Vries, Jan de. >> *Altnordische Literaturgeschichte* (1964–7). Vol. 2, p. 184.
Widding, Ole. "Conscientia i norrøne oversættelser." *Opuscula* 2.1.
Bibliotheca Arnamagnæana 25.1 (Copenhagen: Ejnar Munksgaard,
1961). Pp. 48–51, esp. p. 51.
Wolf, Kirsten, ed. "Anonymous, *Heilagra manna drápa* 'Drápa about
Holy Men'." In Margaret Clunies Ross, ed. >> *Poetry on Christian
Subjects* (2007). Vol. 2, pp. 872–90, esp. pp. 873–5.
Würth, Stefanie. "Thomas Becket: ein literarisches und politisches
Modell für die isländische Kirche im 13. Jahrhundert." In >>
Samtíðarsögur (1994). Vol. 2, pp. 878–91, esp. pp. 879–80 and 889.
Handlist, p. 334.

2. Thómass saga erkibiskups II

A composite text composed possibly by Abbot Arngrímr Brandsson
(d. 1361/2) or Bergr Sokkason (d. ca. 1370). It is based on the *Quadrilo-
gius* translation, Vincent of Beauvais' *Speculum historiale*, a translation
by Abbot Bergr Gunnsteinsson (d. 1211) of a lost Latin life of Saint
Thomas by Robert of Cricklade, and other sources.

Manuscripts:
AM 223 fol. (ca. 1700, defective), AM 224 fol. (ca. 1700, defective), AM
662a 4to I (ca. 1400), AM 662a 4to II (ca. 1350–1400), AM 662a 4to
III (ca. 1475–1500), BLAdd 5311 (ca. 1750–1800), GKS 1008 fol.
(*Tómasskinna*) (ca. 1400 and ca. 1450–1500, defective), and L.3.19–20
(ca. 1775–1800).

Editions:

Eiríkr Magnússon, ed. *Thómas saga erkibyskups: A Life of Archbishop Thomas Becket in Icelandic.* 2 vols. Rolls Series 65.2 (London: Eyre & Spottiswoode, 1875–83). Vol. 1, pp. 2–559; vol. 2, pp. 2–241 and 245–61.

Edition of GKS 1008 fol. (vol. 1, pp. 2–559 and vol. 2, pp. 2–241), AM 662a 4to I (vol. 2, pp. 245–8), AM 662a 4to II (vol. 2, pp. 248–59), and AM 662a 4to III (vol. 2, pp. 260–1).

Loth, Agnete, ed. *Thomasskinna. Gl. Kgl. Saml. 1008 fol. in The Royal Library, Copenhagen.* EIM 6 (Copenhagen: Rosenkilde and Bagger, 1964).

Facsimile of GKS 1008 fol.

Unger, C.R., ed. *Thomas saga erkibyskups. Fortælling om Thomas Becket erkebiskop af Canterbury* (Christiania [Oslo]: Bentzen, 1869). Pp. 295–504 and 520–7.

Edition of GKS 1008 fol. (pp. 295–504), AM 662a 4to I (pp. 520–521.28), AM 662a 4to II (pp. 521.30–526.17), and AM 662a 4to III (pp. 526.19–527.25).

English translation:

Eiríkr Magnússon, ed. *Thómas saga erkibyskups: A Life of Archbishop Thomas Becket in Icelandic.* 2 vols. Rolls Series 65.2 (London: Eyre & Spottiswoode, 1875–83).

Vol. 1, pp. 2–559 and vol. 2, pp. 2–241.

Norwegian translation:

Venås, Kjell. "Soga om erkebiskop Nikolas." In *Den norrøne litteraturen.* VI: *Dikt og prosa* (Oslo: Det Norske Samlaget, 1963). Pp. 181–92 (extract only).

Literature:

Ásdís Egilsdóttir. "Hrafn Sveinbjarnarson, Pilgrim and Martyr." In *Sagas, Saints and Settlements.* Ed. Gareth Williams and Paul Bibire. The Northern World 2 (Leiden: Brill, 2004). Pp. 29–39, esp. pp. 34–5.

Bekker-Nielsen, Hans. "Thómas saga erkibiskups." *KLNM* 18 (1974). Cols. 249–51, esp. col. 250.

Bekker-Nielsen, Hans, Thorkil Damsgaard Olsen, and Ole Widding. >> *Norrøn fortællekunst* (1965). Pp. 124, 126, and 128.

Bekker-Nielsen, Hans, and Ole Widding. "Legende. Norge og Island." *KLNM* 10 (1965). Cols. 421–3, esp. col. 421.

Boyer, Régis. >> *La vie religieuse en Islande* (1979). Pp. 146, 177, and 187.

Ciklamini, Marlene. "The Hand of Revision: Abbot Arngrímr's Redaction of *Guðmundar saga biskups.*" *Gripla* 8 (1993): 231–52, esp. pp. 232–3, 235–7, and 240–1.

Cormack, Margaret J. "Saints and Sinners: Reflections on Death in Some Icelandic Sagas." *Gripla* 8 (1993): 187–218, esp. pp. 190–1.

– >> *The Saints in Iceland* (1994). Pp. 36, 157, and 245.

Finnur Jónsson. >> *Den oldnorske og oldislandske Litteraturs Historie* (1920–4). Vol. 2, p. 876.

Foote, Peter. "On the Fragmentary Text Concerning St. Thomas Becket in Stock. Perg. Fol. Nr. 2." *Saga-Book* 15 (1961): 403–50.

Foote, Peter, ed. >> *Lives of Saints* (1962). P. 19.

Haki Antonsson: "Two Twelfth-Century Martyrs: St Thomas of Canterbury and St Magnús of Orkney." In *Sagas, Saints and Settlements*. Ed. Gareth Williams and Paul Bibire. The Northern World 2 (Leiden: Brill, 2004). Pp. 41–64.

– *St. Magnús of Orkney: A Scandinavian Martyr-Cult in Context*. Northern World 29 (Leiden: Brill, 2007). Pp. 43–5, 47, 50, and 52.

Hallberg, Peter. *Stilsignalement och författarskap i norrön sagalitteratur. Synpunkter och exempel*. Acta Universitatis Gothoburgensis. Nordistica Gothoburgensia 3 (Gothenburg: Almqvist & Wiksell, 1968). Pp. 144–51, 153, 157, 161, 163–4, and 234–6.

– "Jóns saga helga." In *Afmælisrit Jóns Helgasonar 30. júní 1969*. Ed. Jakob Benediktsson et al. (Reykjavík: Heimskringla, 1969). Pp. 59–79, esp. pp. 63 and 68–78.

– "Om Magnúss saga helga." In *Einarsbók: Afmæliskveðja til Einars Ól. Sveinssonar 12. desember 1969*. Ed. Bjarni Guðnason, Halldór Halldórsson, and Jónas Kristjánsson ([Reykjavík]: Nokkrir vinir, 1969). Pp. 59–70, esp. pp. 60, 66, and 69.

– "Some Observations on the Language of *Dunstanus saga*, with an Appendix on the Bible Compilation *Stjórn*." *Saga-Book* 18 (1973): 324–53, esp. pp. 326–31, 335–44, and 349.

– "Imagery in Religious Old Norse Prose Literature: An Outline." *ANF* 102 (1987): 120–70, esp. pp. 129, 131, 133, 136–7, 139–40, 144–8, 151–4, and 161–2.

– "Bergr Sokkason and Religious Icelandic Literature." In >> *Samtíðarsögur* (1994). Vol. 1, pp. 296–300, esp. p. 298.

Jakobsen, Alfred. "Thómas saga erkibiskups." In Phillip Pulsiano and Kirsten Wolf, with Paul Acker and Donald K. Fry, ed. >> *Medieval Scandinavia* (1993). Pp. 643–4.

Jón Jóhannesson. "Tímatal Gerlands í íslenzkum ritum frá þjóðveldisöld." *Skírnir* 126 (1952): 76–93, esp. p. 87.

Jónas Kristjánsson. *Um Fóstbræðra sögu* (Reykjavík: Stofnun Árna Magnússonar, 1972). Pp. 289, 303, 305, and 306.

– >> *Eddas and Sagas* (1988). P. 143.

Kirby, Ian. >> *Biblical Quotation* (1980). Vol. 2, pp. 83–4.

– *Bible Translation in Old Norse*. Université de Lausanne Publications de la faculté des lettres 27 (Geneva: Librairie Droz, 1986). Pp. 46n63, 47, and 163.

Leach, Henry Goddard. *Angevin Britain and Scandinavia*. Harvard Studies in Comparative Literature (Cambridge, Mass.: Harvard University Press, 1921). P. 128.

Lehmann, Paul. >> "Skandinaviens Anteil an der lateinischen Literatur und Wissenschaft des Mittelalters" (1937). P. 46.

Mogk, Eugen. >> *Geschichte der norwegisch-isländischen Literatur* (1904). P. 894.

Orme, Margaret. "A Reconstruction of Robert of Cricklade's Vita et Miracula S. Thomae Cantuariensis." *Analecta Bollandiana* 84 (1966): 379–98.

Paasche, Fredrik. *Norges og Islands litteratur inntil utgangen av middelalderen*. Rev. ed. by Anne Holtsmark (Oslo: Aschehoug, 1947). P. 400.

Piebenga, G.A. "Om Marialegenden 'Fra hinum heilaga Thomase erkibiskupi'." *ANF* 101(1986): 40–9.

Schier, Kurt. *Sagaliteratur*. Sammlung Metzler M78 (Stuttgart: Metzler, 1970). Pp. 4, 19, 67, 123, 125, and 128.

Stefán Karlsson. "Icelandic Lives of Thomas a Becket: Questions of Authorship." In Peter Foote, Hermann Pálsson, and Desmond Slay, ed. >> *Proceedings of the First International Saga Conference* (1973). Pp. 212–43. Rpt. in *Stafkrókar: Ritgerðir eftir Stefán Karlsson gefnar út í tilefni af sjötugsafmæli hans 2. desember 1998*. Ed. Guðvarður Már Gunnlaugsson (Reykjavík: Stofnun Árna Magnússonar, 2000). Pp. 135–52.

Sverrir Tómasson. "Norðlenski Benediktínaskólinn." In >> *The Sixth International Saga Conference* (1985). Vol. 2, pp. 1009–20, esp. pp. 1009 and 1014–19. Rpt. in Sverrir Tómasson. *Tækileg vitni: Greinar um bókmenntir gefnar út í tilefni sjötugsafmælis hans 5. apríl 2011* (Reykjavík: Stofnun Árna Magnússonar and Hið íslenska bókmenntafélag, 2011). Pp. 345–58, esp. pp. 345 and 356.

– *Formálar íslenskra sagnaritara á miðöldum. Rannsókn bókmenntahefðar* (Reykjavík: Stofnun Árna Magnússonar, 1988). Pp. 50–1, 97, 128–9, 144, 165, 251, 255–7, 304–5, 310, 344, and 355–7.

– "Kristnar trúarbókmenntir í óbundnu máli." In Guðrún Nordal, Sverrir Tómason, and Vésteinn Ólason, ed. >> *Íslensk Bókmenntasaga* 1 (1992). Pp. 419–79, esp. pp. 439, 458, and 473.

Vries, Jan de. >> *Altnordische Literaturgeschichte* (1964–7). Vol. 2, p. 184.

Wolf, Kirsten, ed. "Anonymous, *Heilagra manna drápa* 'Drápa about Holy Men'." In Margaret Clunies Ross, ed. >> *Poetry on Christian Subjects* (2007). Vol. 2, pp. 872–90, esp. pp. 873–5.

Würth, Stefanie. "Thomas Becket: ein literarisches und politisches Modell für die isländische Kirche im 13. Jahrhundert." In >> *Samtíðarsögur* (1994). Vol. 2, pp. 878–91.

Handlist, p. 334.

3. Thómass saga erkibiskups

Based on the early translation by Bergr Gunnsteinsson and joined with material perhaps from John of Salisbury's *Vita* and Benedict of Peterborough's *Miracula*.

Manuscripts:
AM 234 fol. (ca. 1340, defective), BLAdd 11.242 (ca. 1540–90, excerpts) and NRA 67 (ca. 1300–25).

Editions:
Eiríkr Magnússon, ed. *Thómas saga erkibyskups: A Life of Archbishop Thomas Becket in Icelandic.* 2 vols. Rolls Series 65.2 (London: Eyre & Spottiswoode, 1875–83). Vol. 2, pp. 262–84)
Edition of NRA 67a–d (pp. 262–9) and AM 234 fol. (pp. 270–84).

Unger, C.R., ed. *Thomas saga erkibyskups: Fortælling om Thomas Becket Erkebiskop af Canterbury* (Christiania [Oslo]: Bentzen, 1869). Pp. 528–44.
Edition of AM 234 fol. (pp. 534.9–544) and NRA 67a–d (pp. 528–534.6).

Literature:
Bekker-Nielsen, Hans. "Thómas saga erkibiskups." *KLNM* 18 (1974). Cols. 249–51, esp. col. 250.

Bekker-Nielsen, Hans, Thorkil Damsgaard Olsen, and Ole Widding. >> *Norrøn fortællekunst* (1965). Pp. 124 and 126.

Bekker-Nielsen, Hans, and Ole Widding. "Legende. Norge og Island." *KLNM* 10 (1965). Cols. 421–3, esp. col. 421.

Cormack, Margaret. >> *The Saints in Iceland* (1994). Pp. 36, 157, and 245.

Finnur Jónsson. >> *Den oldnorske og oldislandske Litteraturs Historie* (1920–4). Vol. 2, p. 876.

Foote, Peter. "On the Fragmentary Text Concerning St. Thomas Becket in Stock. Perg. Fol. Nr. 2." *Saga-Book* 15 (1961): 403–50.

– "Auðræði." In Arthur Brown and Peter Foote, ed. >> *Early English and Norse Studies* (1963). Pp. 62–76, esp. pp. 65–6.

Foote, Peter, ed. >> *Lives of Saints* (1962). P. 19.

Haki Antonsson: "Two Twelfth-Century Martyrs: St Thomas of Canterbury and St Magnús of Orkney." In *Sagas, Saints and Settlements*. Ed. Gareth Williams and Paul Bibire. The Northern World 2 (Leiden: Brill, 2004). Pp. 41–64.

Hallberg, Peter. *Stilsignalement och författarskap i norrön sagalitteratur. Synpunkter och exempel*. Acta Universitatis Gothoburgensis. Nordistica Gothoburgensia 3 (Gothenburg: Almqvist & Wiksell, 1968). Pp. 144–9, 234, and 236.

Jakobsen, Alfred. "Thómas saga erkibiskups." In Phillip Pulsiano and Kirsten Wolf, with Paul Acker and Donald K. Fry, ed. >> *Medieval Scandinavia* (1993). Pp. 643–4.

Jón Helgason. *Ritgerðakorn og ræðustúfar* (Reykjavík: Hólar, 1959). Pp. 115–17.

Jón Jóhannesson. "Tímatal Gerlands í íslenzkum ritum frá þjóðveldisöld." *Skírnir* 126 (1952): 76–93, esp. p. 87.

Jón Þorkelsson, "Islandske håndskrifter i England og Skotland." *ANF* 8 (1892): 199–237, esp. pp. 221–2.

Jónas Kristjánsson. >> *Eddas and Sagas* (1988). P. 143.

Kirby, Ian. >> *Biblical Quotation* (1980). Vol. 2, p. 84.

Lehmann, Paul. >> "Skandinaviens Anteil an der lateinischen Literatur und Wissenschaft des Mittelalters" (1937). P. 46.

Mogk, Eugen. >> *Geschichte der norwegisch-isländischen Literatur* (1904). P. 894.

Orme, Margaret. "A Reconstruction of Robert of Cricklade's Vita et Miracula S. Thomae Cantuariensis." *Analecta Bollandiana* 84 (1966): 379–98.

Paasche, Fredrik. *Norges og Islands litteratur inntil utgangen av middelalderen*. Rev. ed. by Anne Holtsmark (Oslo: Aschehoug, 1947). P. 400.

Piebenga, G.A. "Om Marialegenden 'Fra hinum heilaga Thomase erkibiskupi'." *ANF* 101 (1986): 40–9.

Schier, Kurt. *Sagaliteratur*. Sammlung Metzler M78 (Stuttgart: Metzler, 1970). Pp. 4, 67, 123, and 125.

Stefán Karlsson. "Icelandic Lives of Thomas a Becket: Questions of Authorship." In Peter Foote, Hermann Pálsson, and Desmond Slay, ed. >> *Proceedings of the First International Saga Conference* (1973). Pp. 212–43. Rpt. in *Stafkrókar: Ritgerðir eftir Stefán Karlsson gefnar út*

í tilefni af sjötugsafmæli hans 2. desember 1998. Ed. Guðvarður Már
Gunnlaugsson (Reykjavík: Stofnun Árna Magnússonar, 2000).
Pp. 135–52.
– "Islandsk bogeksport til Norge i middelalderen." *Mm* (1979): 1–17, esp.
p. 6. Rpt. in *Stafkrókar: Ritgerðir eftir Stefán Karlsson gefnar út í tilefni
af sjötugsafmæli hans 2. desember 1998.* Ed. Guðvarður Már
Gunnlaugsson (Reykjavík: Stofnun Árna Magnússonar, 2000).
Pp. 188–205, esp. p. 194.
Sverrir Tómasson. *Formálar íslenskra sagnaritara á miðöldum. Rannsókn
bókmenntahefðar* (Reykjavík: Stofnun Árna Magnússonar, 1988).
Pp. 355–7.
– "Kristnar trúarbókmenntir í óbundnu máli." In Guðrún Nordal,
Sverrir Tómasson, and Vésteinn Ólason, ed. >> *Íslensk Bókmenntasaga*
1 (1992). Pp. 419–79, esp. p. 458.
Vries, Jan de. >> *Altnordische Literaturgeschichte* (1964–7). Vol. 2,
p. 184.
Würth, Stefanie. "Thomas Becket: ein literarisches und politisches
Modell für die isländische Kirche im 13. Jahrhundert." In
>> *Samtíðarsögur* (1994). Vol. 2, pp. 878–91, esp. pp. 879–80.
Handlist, p. 334.

4. Thómass saga erkibiskups

A redaction that approximates the translation of Robert Cricklade's work
more closely than 2 and 3.

Manuscript:
Stock. Perg. fol. no. 2 (ca. 1425–45, defective).
Editions:
Foote, Peter, ed. >> *Lives of Saints* (1962).
    Facsimile.
Unger, C.R., ed. >> *Heilagra manna søgur* (1877). Vol. 2, pp. 315–20.
Literature:
Bekker-Nielsen, Hans. "Thómas saga erkibiskups." *KLNM* 18 (1974).
    Cols. 249–51, esp. col. 250.
Bekker-Nielsen, Hans, Thorkil Damsgaard Olsen, and Ole Widding.
    >> *Norrøn fortællekunst* (1965). Pp. 124 and 126.
Bekker-Nielsen, Hans, and Ole Widding. "Legende. Norge og Island."
    KLNM 10 (1965). Cols. 421–3, esp. col. 421.
Carlé, Birte. >> *Jomfru-fortællingen* (1985). Pp. 39–40, 53–5, and 67.

- "Men and Women in the Saints' Sagas of *Stock. 2, fol.*" In John
  Lindow, Lars Lönnroth, and Gerd Wolfgang Weber, ed. >> *Structure
  and Meaning in Old Norse Literature* (1986). Pp. 317–46, esp. pp. 320,
  322, 324, 328, and 331.
Cormack, Margaret. >> *The Saints in Iceland* (1994). P. 36.
Eiríkr Magnússon, ed. *Thómas saga erkibyskups: A Life of Archbishop
  Thomas Becket in Icelandic.* 2 vols. Rolls Series 65.2 (London: Eyre &
  Spottiswoode, 1875–83). Vol. 2, pp. xlix–l, lvii–lix, and clvii.
Finnur Jónsson. >> *Den oldnorske og oldislandske Litteraturs Historie*
  (1920–4). Vol. 2, p. 876.
Foote, Peter. "On the Fragmentary Text Concerning St. Thomas Becket
  in Stock. Perg. Fol. Nr. 2." *Saga-Book* 15 (1961): 403–50, esp. pp. 405–
  6, 416–22, 425, 429, 431–4, 437, 440–2, 444–6, and 450.
Haki Antonsson: "Two Twelfth-Century Martyrs: St Thomas of Canter-
  bury and St Magnús of Orkney." In *Sagas, Saints and Settlements.* Ed.
  Gareth Williams and Paul Bibire. The Northern World 2 (Leiden: Brill,
  2004). Pp. 41–64.
Jakobsen, Alfred. "Thómas saga erkibiskups." In Phillip Pulsiano and
  Kirsten Wolf, with Paul Acker and Donald K. Fry, ed. >> *Medieval
  Scandinavia* (1993). Pp. 643–4.
Jónas Kristjánsson. >> *Eddas and Sagas* (1988). P. 143.
Kirby, Ian. >> *Biblical Quotation* (1980). Vol. 2, p. 50.
Lehmann, Paul. >> "Skandinaviens Anteil an der lateinischen Literatur
  und Wissenschaft des Mittelalters" (1937). P. 46.
Mogk, Eugen. >> *Geschichte der norwegisch-isländischen Literatur* (1904).
  P. 894.
Orme, Margaret. "A Reconstruction of Robert of Cricklade's Vita et Mir-
  acula S. Thomae Cantuariensis." *Analecta Bollandiana* 84 (1966): 379–98.
Paasche, Fredrik. *Norges og Islands litteratur inntil utgangen av
  middelalderen.* Rev. ed. by Anne Holtsmark (Oslo: Aschehoug, 1947).
  P. 400.
Piebenga, G.A. "Om Marialegenden 'Fra hinum heilaga Thomase
  erkibiskupi'." *ANF* 101(1986): 40–9.
Stefán Karlsson. "Icelandic Lives of Thomas a Becket: Questions of
  Authorship." In Peter Foote, Hermann Pálsson, and Desmond Slay, ed.
  >> *Proceedings of the First International Saga Conference* (1973).
  Pp. 212–43. Rpt. in *Stafkrókar: Ritgerðir eftir Stefán Karlsson gefnar út
  í tilefni af sjötugsafmæli hans 2. desember 1998.* Ed. Guðvarður Már
  Gunnlaugsson (Reykjavík: Stofnun Árna Magnússonar, 2000).
  Pp. 135–52.

Sverrir Tómasson. *Formálar íslenskra sagnaritara á miðöldum. Rannsókn bókmenntahefðar* (Reykjavík: Stofnun Árna Magnússonar, 1988). Pp. 355–7.

– "Kristnar trúarbókmenntir í óbundnu máli." In Guðrún Nordal, Sverrir Tómasson, and Vésteinn Ólason, ed. >> *Íslensk Bókmenntasaga* 1 (1992). Pp. 419–79, esp. p. 458 and 473.

Vries, Jan de. >> *Altnordische Literaturgeschichte* (1964–7). Vol. 2, p. 184.

Würth, Stefanie. "Thomas Becket: ein literarisches und politisches Modell für die isländische Kirche im 13. Jahrhundert." In >> *Samtíðarsögur* (1994). Vol. 2, pp. 878–91, esp. pp. 879–80.

Handlist, p. 334.

5. Af Thómasi erkibiskupi

Tales of Saint Thomas Becket incorporated into the miracles of the Virgin Mary.

Manuscripts:
See Mary the Blessed Virgin 3 note (p. 245).

Editions:

Eiríkr Magnússon, ed. *Thómas saga erkibyskups: A Life of Archbishop Thomas Becket in Icelandic.* 2 vols. Rolls Series 65.2 (London: Eyre & Spottiswoode, 1875–83). Vol. 2, pp. 284–9 (first tale only).

Unger, C.R., ed. >> *Mariu saga* (1871). Pp. 198.6–203.22, 725.13–24, and 1160.6–1162.16.

Literature:

Bekker-Nielsen, Hans. "Thómas saga erkibiskups." *KLNM* 18 (1974). Cols. 249–51, esp. col. 250.

Foote, Peter. "On the Fragmentary Text Concerning St. Thomas Becket in Stock. Perg. Fol. Nr. 2." *Saga-Book* 15 (1961): 403–50, esp. pp. 407–10, 426–31, 445, 447, and 450.

Hallberg, Peter. *Stilsignalement och författarskap i norrön sagalitteratur. Synpunkter och exempel.* Acta Universitatis Gothoburgensis. Nordistica Gothoburgensia 3 (Gothenburg: Almqvist & Wiksell, 1968). Pp. 144–6.

– "Imagery in Religious Old Norse Prose Literature: An Outline." *ANF* 102 (1987): 120–70, esp. pp. 152 and 164.

Heizmann, Wilhelm. "Liebe und Durst: Der Heilige Bernhard von Clairvaux in der altisländischen Mirakelüberlieferung." *Opuscula* 13.

Bibliotheca Arnamagnæana 47 (Copenhagen: Museum Tusculanum
Press, 2010). Pp. 55–118, esp. p. 109.
Orme, Margaret. "A Reconstruction of Robert of Cricklade's Vita et
Miracula S. Thomae Cantuariensis." *Analecta Bollandiana* 84 (1966):
379–98.
Piebenga, G.A. "Om Marialegenden 'Fra hinum heilaga Thomase
erkibiskupi'." *ANF* 101 (1986): 40–9.
Sverrir Tómasson. "Kristnar trúarbókmenntir í óbundnu máli." In
Guðrún Nordal, Sverrir Tómasson, and Vésteinn Ólason, ed.
>> *Íslensk Bókmenntasaga* 1 (1992). Pp. 419–79, esp. p. 432.
Widding, Ole. "Nogle norske Marialegender." *Mm* (1969): 51–9, esp.
pp. 51 and 58.
– "Norrøne Marialegender på europæisk baggrund." *Opuscula* 10.
Bibliotheca Arnamagnæana 40 (Copenhagen: Reitzel, 1996). Pp. 1–128,
esp. p. 33.
Handlist, pp. 324 and 334.

6. Af hinum helga Thóma

An anecdote about Saint Thomas possibly composed by Abbot Arngrímr
Brandsson and based likely on the *Speculum historiale*.

Manuscript:
AM 657a–b 4to (ca. 1350).
Edition:
Gering, Hugo, ed. >> *Islendzk æventyri* (1882–3), Vol. 1, pp. 67–9.
German paraphrase:
Gering, Hugo, ed. >> *Islendzk æventyri* (1882–3). Vol. 2, pp. 57–8.
Literature:
Bekker-Nielsen, Hans. "Thómas saga erkibiskups." *KLNM* 18 (1974).
Cols. 249–51, esp. col. 250.
Cormack, Margaret. >> *The Saints in Iceland* (1994). Pp. 35, 109,
and 245.
Foote, Peter. "On the Fragmentary Text Concerning St. Thomas Becket
in Stock. Perg. Fol. Nr. 2." *Saga-Book* 15 (1961): 403–50, esp.
p. 438n78.
Stefán Karlsson. "Icelandic Lives of Thomas a Becket: Questions of
Authorship." In Peter Foote, Hermann Pálsson, and Desmond Slay,
ed. >> *Proceedings of the First International Saga Conference* (1973).

Pp. 212–43. Rpt. in *Stafkrókar: Ritgerðir eftir Stefán Karlsson gefnar út i tilefni af sjötugsafmæli hans 2. desember 1998*. Ed. Guðvarður Már Gunnlaugsson (Reykjavík: Stofnun Árna Magnússonar, 2000). Pp. 135–52.

Sverrir Tómasson. *Formálar íslenskra sagnaritara á miðöldum. Rannsókn bókmenntahefðar* (Reykjavík: Stofnun Árna Magnússonar, 1988). Pp. 355–7.

– "Kristnar trúarbókmenntir í óbundnu máli." In Guðrún Nordal, Sverrir Tómasson, and Vésteinn Ólason, ed. >> *Íslensk Bókmenntasaga* 1 (1992). Pp. 419–79, esp. p. 458.

Wolf, Kirsten, ed. >> *Heilagra meyja sögur* (2003). P. lii.

Handlist, p. 334.

THREE HOLY KINGS   January 6

Heilagra þriggja konunga saga

Translated from a now-lost Low German redaction that resembles the source(s) of *Der Heiligen Leben*.

Manuscript:
Stock. Perg. fol. no. 3 (*Reykjahólabók*) (ca. 1530–40, defective).
Edition:
Loth, Agnete, ed. >> *Reykjahólabók* (1969–70). Vol. 1, pp. 1–33.
Literature:
Carlé, Birte. *500–1500 – Indføring i middelalderens fortællekunst* ([n.p.]: Gyldendal, 1966). Pp. 28–9.

Kalinke, Marianne E. "Reykjahólabók: A Legendary on the Eve of the Reformation." *Skáldskaparmál* 2 (1992): 239–69, esp. p. 240.

– >> *The Book of Reykjahólar* (1996). Pp. 28, 49, 126, and 198.

Svanhildur Óskarsdóttir. "Universal History in Fourteenth-Century Iceland: Studies in AM 764 4to." PhD dissertation, University of London, 2000. P. 175.

Widding, Ole, and Hans Bekker-Nielsen. "En senmiddelalderlig legendesamling." *Mm* (1960): 105–28, esp. pp. 107 and 111–13.

– "Low German Influence on Late Icelandic Hagiography." *GR* 37 (1962): 239–62, esp. pp. 250 and 255.

Handlist, p. 335.

TIBURTIUS AND VALERIAN   April 14

A passion of Saints Tiburtius and Valerian included in *Ceciliu saga*.

Manuscripts:
See Cecilia note (p. 74).
Editions:
Foote, Peter, ed. >> *Lives of Saints* (1962).
  Facsimile of Stock. Perg. fol. no. 2.
Unger, C.R., ed. >> *Heilagra manna søgur* (1877). Vol. 1, pp. 285.16–
  289.
Wolf, Kirsten, ed. >> *A Female Legendary from Iceland* (2010). Pp. 107–11.
  Facsimile and text edition of AM 429 12mo.
Modern Icelandic language edition:
Wolf, Kirsten, ed. >> *Heilagra meyja sögur* (2003). Pp. 110–14.
Norwegian translation:
Mundal, Else. *Legender frå mellomalderen. Soger om heilage kvinner og
  menn* (Oslo: Det Norske Samlaget, 1995). Pp. 50–5.
Literature:
Cormack, Margaret. >> *The Saints in Iceland* (1994). P. 34.

ÞORLÁKR OF SKÁLHOLT   December 23

1. Jarteinabók Þorláks biskups in forna

The oldest of the miracle collections added to *Þorláks saga biskups C*.

Manuscripts:
AM 209 fol. (ca. 1600–1700), AM 379 4to (1654), AM 380 4to (ca.
  1600–1700), AM 383 4to IV (ca. 1370–90), and AM 645 4to (ca. 1220,
  defective).
Editions:
Ásdís Egilsdóttir, ed. *Biskupa sögur II: Hungrvaka, Þorláks saga byskups in
  elzta, Jarteinabók Þorláks byskups in forna, Þorláks saga byskups yngri,
  Jarteinabók Þorláks byskups önnur, Þorláks saga byskups C, Þorláks saga
  byskups E, Páls saga byskups, Ísleifs þáttr byskups, Latínubrot um Þorlák
  byskup.* Íslenzk fornrit 16 (Reykjavík: Hið íslenzka fornritafélag, 2002).
  Pp. 103–40.
Normalized text based on *Byskupa søgur*.

Guðni Jónsson, ed. *Byskupa sögur*. 3 vols. (Reykjavík: Íslendingasagnaútgáfan; Haukadalsútgáfan, 1948). Vol. 1, pp. 165–202.
Normalized text based on *Biskupa sögur*.

Holtsmark, Anne, ed. *A Book of Miracles: MS No. 645 4to of the Arna-
Magnæan Collection in the University Library of Copenhagen.* CCI 12
(Copenhagen: Einar Munksgaard, 1938).
Facsimile of AM 645 4to.

Jón Helgason, ed. *Byskupa sǫgur*. Editiones Arnamagnæanæ, Ser. A,
vol. 13.2 (Copenhagen: Reitzel, 1978). Pp. 121–57.
Based on AM 380 4to (pp. 121.4–8) and AM 645 4to (pp. 121.8–157)
with variants from AM 380 4to (pp. 121.8–157).

[Jón Sigurðsson and Guðbrandur Vigfússon, ed.] *Biskupa sögur*. 2 vols.
(Copenhagen: Møller, 1858–78). Vol. 1, pp. 333–56.
Based on AM 379 4to (pp. 333.1–15) and AM 645 4to (pp. 333.15–356).

[Kålund, Kr., ed.] *Palæografisk Atlas: Oldnorsk-islandsk afdeling* (Copenhagen and Christiania [Oslo]: Gyldendal, 1905). No. 13.
Facsimile and text edition of AM 645 4to, fol. 6r.

Larsson, Ludvig, ed. *Isländska handskriften N° 645 4° i Den Arnamagnæanske Samlingen på Universitetsbiblioteket i København: I. Handskriftens
äldre del* (Lund: Gleerup, 1885). Pp. 1–33.27.
Edition of AM 645 4to.

Stefán Karlsson, ed. *Sagas of Icelandic Bishops: Fragments of Eight
Manuscripts.* EIM 7 (Copenhagen: Rosenkilde and Bagger, 1967).
Facsimile of AM 383 4to IV (extract only).

Modern Icelandic language editions:

Ásdís Egilsdóttir, ed. *Þorláks saga helga. Elsta gerð Þorláks sögu helga
ásamt Jarteinabók og efni úr yngri gerðum sögunnar* (Reykjavík: Þorlákssjóður, 1989). Pp. 59–108.

Einar Ól. Sveinsson, ed. *Leit eg suður til landa. Ævintýri og helgisögur frá
miðöldum.* (Reykjavík: Heimskringla, 1944). Pp. 244–56 (extracts only).

Danish translation:

Loth, Agnete, trans. *Den gamle jærtegnsbog om biskop Thorlak* (Odense:
Odense Universitetsforlag, 1984). Pp. 25–61.

English translation:

Roughton, Philip G. "AM 645 4to and AM 652/630 4to: Study and Translation of Two Thirteenth-Century Icelandic Collections of Apostles' and
Saints' Lives." PhD dissertation, University of Colorado, 2002. Pp. 887–929.

Literature:

Ásdís Egilsdóttir. "Eru biskupasögur til?" *Skáldskaparmál* 2 (1992):
207–20, esp. p. 211.

– "Biskupa sögur." In Phillip Pulsiano and Kirsten Wolf, with Paul Acker and Donald K. Fry, ed. >> *Medieval Scandinavia* (1993). Pp. 45–6.
– "Jarteinir, líkami, sál og trúarlíf." In Ásdís Egilsdóttir and Rudolf Simek, ed. >> *Sagnaheimur* (2001). Pp. 13–19, esp. pp. 15–16.
– "St Þorlákr of Iceland: The Emergence of a Cult." *The Haskins Society Journal* 12 (2002): 121–31, esp. pp. 123 and 130–1.
– "The Fantastic Reality: Hagiography, Miracles and Fantasy." In John McKinnell, David Ashurst, and Donata Kick, ed. >> *The Fantastic in Old Norse / Icelandic Literature* (2006). Vol. 1, pp. 63–70, esp. p. 68.
– "Konur, draumar, dýrlingar." In *Bókmentaljós: Heiðursrit til Turið Sigurðardóttur*. Ed. Malan Marnersdóttir, Leyvoy Joensen, and Anfinnur Johansen (Tórshavn: Faroe University Press, 2006). Pp. 351–8, esp. pp. 355–6.
– "Orðið og bókin." In *Greppaminni: Rit til heiðurs Vésteini Ólasyni sjötugum* (Reykjavík: Hið íslenska bókmenntafélag, 2009). Pp. 43–51, esp. pp. 46–7.
Bekker-Nielsen, Hans. "Et par ord om de ældste norrøne helgensagaer." In Finn Hødnebø et al., ed. >> *Eyvindarbók* (1992). Pp. 29–33, esp. p. 32.
Bekker-Nielsen, Hans, Thorkil Damsgaard Olsen, and Ole Widding. >> *Norrøn fortællekunst* (1965). P. 40.
Bekker-Nielsen, Hans, and Ole Widding. "Legende. Norge og Island." *KLNM* 10 (1965). Cols. 421–3, esp. col. 422.
– "Religiøs prosalitteratur. Norge og Island." *KLNM* 14 (1969). Cols. 42–4, esp. col. 42.
Bibire, Paul. "Þorláks saga helga." In Phillip Pulsiano and Kirsten Wolf, with Paul Acker and Donald K. Fry, ed. >> *Medieval Scandinavia* (1993). P. 671.
Bjarni Aðalbjarnarson. "Bemerkninger om de eldste bispesagaer." *Studia Islandica* 17 (Reykjavík: Heimspekideild Háskóla Íslands; Menningarsjóður, 1959): 27–37, esp. p. 35.
Boyer, Régis. >> *La vie religieuse en Islande* (1979).
– "Les références expresses à la littérature dans les 'Sagas de contemporains'." In Gísli Sigurðsson, Guðrún Kvaran, and Sigurgeir Steingrímsson, ed. >> *Sagnaþing helgað Jónasi Kristjánssyni* (1994). Vol. 1, pp. 87–96.
Cormack, Margaret. "'Fjǫlkunnigri kono scallatu í faðm sofa': Sex and the Supernatural in Icelandic Saints' Lives." *Skáldskaparmál* 2 (1992): 221–8, esp. p. 224.
– >> *The Saints in Iceland* (1994). Pp. 27, 63, 162–3, and 193.
– "Visions, Demons and Gender in the Sagas of Icelandic Saints." *CM* 7 (1994): 185–209, esp. pp. 187 and 193–4.

- "Women and Gender in the Sagas of Icelandic Saints." In
  >> *Samtíðarsögur* (1994). Vol. 1, pp. 188–93, esp. p. 190.
- "Sagas of Saints." In *Old Icelandic Literature and Society*. Ed. Margaret
  Clunies Ross (Cambridge: Cambridge University Press, 2000).
  Pp. 302–25, esp. p. 317.
- "The Economics of Devotion: Vows and Indulgences in Medieval
  Iceland." *Viking and Medieval Scandinavia* 5 (2009): 41–63, esp.
  pp. 47–9 and 51.

Fahn, Susanne Miriam, and Gottskálk Jensson. "The Forgotten Poem:
  A Latin Panegyric for Saint Þorlákr in AM 382 4to." *Gripla* 21 (2010):
  19–60, esp. pp. 22–3, 26, 29, and 48.

Finnur Jónsson. >> *Den oldnorske og oldislandske Litteraturs Historie*
  (1920–4). Vol. 2, p. 932.

Jakob Benediktsson. "Traces of Latin Prose-Rhythm in Old Norse
  Literature." In *The Fifth Viking Congress, Tórshavn, July 1965*. Ed.
  Bjarni Niclasen (Tórshavn: Føroya Landsstýri, 1968) Pp. 17–24, esp.
  p. 23. Rpt. in Jakob Benediktsson. *Lærdómslistir. Afmælisrit 20. júlí
  1987* (Reykjavík: Mál og menning, 1987). Pp. 153–60, esp. p. 158.
- "Brot úr Þorlákslesi." In *Afmælisrit Jóns Helgasonar 30. júní 1969*. Ed.
  Jakob Benediktsson et al. (Reykjavík: Heimskringla, 1969). Pp. 98–108,
  esp. pp. 106–7.

Jón Helgason. *Norrøn Litteraturhistorie* (Copenhagen: Levin and Munksgaard, 1934). Pp. 191–2.
- "Þorláks saga helga." *KLNM* 20 (1976). Cols. 388–91, esp. cols. 388–9.

Jónas Kristjánsson. "Sagas and Saints' Lives." In *Cultura Classica e
  Cultura Germanica Settentrionale*. Ed. Pietro Janni, Diego Poli, and
  Carlo Santini (Macerata: Herder, 1985). Pp. 125–43, esp. p. 129.
- >> *Eddas and Sagas* (1988). P. 136.

Jørgensen, Jørgen Højgaard. *Bispesagaer – Laurentius saga: Studier i*
  Laurentius saga biskups, *indledt af overvejelser omkring* biskupa sǫgur
  som litterær genre. Udgivelsesudvalgets samling af studenterafhand-
  linger 12 (Odense: [n.p.], 1978). Pp. 15 and 48.

Konráð Gíslason. *Um frum-parta íslenzkrar túngu í fornöld* (Copenhagen:
  Trier, 1846). Pp. lxii–lxiii.

Kratz, Henry. "Thorlákr's Miracles." In >> *Samtíðarsögur* (1994). Vol. 2,
  pp. 480–94, esp. pp. 480–1, 483, 489, and 491–4.

Kuhn, Hans. "The Emergence of a Saint's Cult as Witnessed by the
  Jarteinabækr Þorláks byskups." *Saga-Book* 24 (1996): 240–54.

Paasche, Fredrik. *Norges og Islands litteratur inntil utgangen av middelalderen*.
  Rev. ed. by Anne Holtsmark (Oslo: Aschehoug, 1947). P. 286.

Piebenga, Gryt Anne. "Miracles, Collections of.'"In Phillip Pulsiano
and Kirsten Wolf, with Paul Acker and Donald K. Fry, ed. >>
Medieval Scandinavia (1993). Pp. 413–14.

Roughton, Philip. "Stylistics and Sources of the *Postola sögur* in AM 645
4to and AM 652/630 4to." *Gripla* 16 (2005): 7–50.

Samuelson, David Robert. "The Operation of the Bishop's Legend in
Early Medieval England and Iceland." PhD dissertation, University of
Michigan, 1977. P. 202.

Schach, Paul. *Icelandic Sagas*. Twayne's World Author Series (Boston:
Twayne, 1984). P. 64.

Seip, Didrik Arup. "Jærtegnsamlinger." *KLNM* 8 (1963). Cols. 65–8, esp.
cols. 66–7.

Sigurður Nordal. *Um íslenzkar fornsögur*. Trans. Árni Böðvarsson
(Reykjavík: Mál og menning, 1968). P. 71.

Sverrir Tómasson. "Kristnar trúarbókmenntir í óbundnu máli." In
Guðrún Nordal, Sverrir Tómasson, and Vésteinn Ólason, ed.
>> *Íslensk Bókmenntasaga* 1 (1992). Pp. 419–79, esp. p. 474.

Turville-Petre, G. >> *Origins of Icelandic Literature* (1967). Pp. 134 and 210.

Whaley, Diana. "Miracles in the Sagas of Bishops: Icelandic Variations
on an International Theme." *CM* 7 (1994): 155–84.

Wolf, Kirsten. "A Translation of the Latin Fragments Containing the Life
and Miracles of St. Þorlákr along with Collections of *Lectiones* for
Recitation on His Feast-Days." *Proceedings of the PMR Conference* 14
(1989): 261–76, esp. pp. 261–2.

– "Pride and Politics in Late-Twelfth-Century Iceland: The Sanctity of
Bishop Þorlákr Þórhallsson." In Thomas A. DuBois, ed. >> *Sanctity
in the North* (2008). Pp. 241–70, esp. p. 250.

Handlist, p. 336.

2. Þorláks saga biskups A

The so-called oldest saga of Bishop Þorlákr Þórhallsson.

Manuscripts:

AM 205 fol. (1644), AM 206 fol. (ca. 1650), AM 210 fol. (ca. 1600–1700,
defective), AM 396 fol. (1676), Kall 261 fol. (ca. 1700–1800), Stock.
Papp. fol. no. 2 (1689), and Stock. Perg. fol. no. 5 (ca. 1350–65).

Editions:

Ásdís Egilsdóttir, ed. *Biskupa sögur II: Hungrvaka, Þorláks saga byskups
in elzta, Jarteinabók Þorláks byskups in forna, Þorláks saga byskups*

yngri, Jarteinabók Þorláks byskups önnur, Þorláks saga byskups C, Þorláks saga byskups E, Páls saga byskups, Ísleifs þáttr byskups, Latínubrot um Þorlák byskup. Íslenzk fornrit 16 (Reykjavík: Hið íslenzka fornritafélag, 2002). Pp. 47–99.

Normalized text based on *Byskupa sǫgur.*

Gudbrand Vigfusson and F. York Powell, ed. and trans. *Origines Islandicae: A Collection of the More Important Sagas and Other Native Writings Relating to the Settlement and Early History of Iceland.* 2 vols. (Oxford: Clarendon, 1905; rpt. Millwood: Kraus, 1976). Vol. 1, pp. 458–92.

Based on *Biskupa sögur,* pp. 89–109.

Guðni Jónsson, ed. *Byskupa sögur.* 3 vols. (Reykjavík: Íslendingasagnaút-gáfan; Haukadalsútgáfan, 1948). Vol. 1, pp. 38–113 (pp. 77–113 upper text).

Normalized text based on *Biskupa sögur.*

Jón Helgason, ed. *Byskupa sǫgur. MS Perg. fol. No. 5 in the Royal Library of Stockholm.* CCI 19 (Copenhagen: Ejnar Munksgaard, 1950). Facsimile of Stock. Perg. fol. no. 5.

– ed. *Byskupa sǫgur.* Editiones Arnamagnæanæ, Ser. A, vol. 13.2 (Copen-hagen: Reitzel, 1978). Pp. 177–240.

Edition of Stock. Perg. fol. no. 5 with variants from the B and C versions.

[Jón Sigurðsson and Guðbrandur Vigfússon, ed.] *Biskupa sögur.* 2 vols. (Copenhagen: Møller, 1858–78). Vol. 1, pp. 89–124.

Based on Stock. Perg. fol. no. 5 with select variants from AM 205 fol. (pp. 89–114.13) and AM 206 fol. (pp. 89–114.13).

Modern Icelandic language edition:

Ásdís Egilsdóttir, ed. *Þorláks saga helga. Elsta gerð Þorláks sögu helga ásamt Jarteinabók og efni úr yngri gerðum sögunnar* (Reykjavík: Þorlákssjóður, 1989). Pp. 111–85.

English translations:

Gudbrand Vigfusson and F. York Powell, ed. and trans. *Origines Islandicae: A Collection of the More Important Sagas and Other Native Writings Relating to the Settlement and Early History of Iceland.* 2 vols. (Oxford: Clarendon, 1905; rpt. Millwood: Kraus, 1976). Vol. 1, pp. 458–92.

[Leith, Mary Charlotte Julia], trans. *Stories of the Bishops of Iceland* (London: Masters, 1895). Pp. 79–113.

Wolf, Kirsten. "Pride and Politics in Late-Twelfth-Century Iceland: The Sanctity of Bishop Þorlákr Þórhallsson." In Thomas A. DuBois, ed. >> *Sanctity in the North* (2008). Pp. 241–70, esp. pp. 251–64 (extract only).

Literature:

Ármann Jakobsson and Ásdís Egilsdóttir. "Er Oddaverjaþætti treystandi?" *Ný saga* 11 (1999): 91–100.

Ásdís Egilsdóttir. "Eru biskupasögur til?" *Skáldskaparmál* 2 (1992): 207–20, esp. pp. 211, 214, and 219–20.

– "Biskupa sögur." In Phillip Pulsiano and Kirsten Wolf, with Paul Acker and Donald K. Fry, ed. >> *Medieval Scandinavia* (1993). Pp. 45–6.

– "Mannfræði Höllu biskupsmóður." In Gísli Sigurðsson, Guðrún Kvaran, and Sigurgeir Steingrímsson, ed. >> *Sagnaþing helgað Jónasi Kristjánssyni* (1994). Vol. 1, pp. 11–18.

– "Jarteinir, líkami, sál og trúarlíf." In Ásdís Egilsdóttir and Rudolf Simek, ed. >> *Sagnaheimur* (2001). Pp. 13–19, esp. p. 15.

– "St Þorlákr of Iceland: The Emergence of a Cult." *The Haskins Society Journal* 12 (2002): 121–31, esp. pp. 123 and 126–31.

– "Konur, draumar, dýrlingar." In *Bókmentaljós: Heiðursrit til Turið Sigurðardóttur*. Ed. Malan Marnersdóttir, Leyvoy Joensen, and Anfinnur Johansen (Tórshavn: Faroe University Press, 2006). Pp. 351–8, esp. pp. 352–3 and 357.

– "Orðið og bókin." In *Greppaminni: Rit til heiðurs Vésteini Ólasyni sjötugum* (Reykjavík: Hið íslenska bókmenntafélag, 2009). Pp. 43–51, esp. pp. 47–50.

Astås, Reidar. "Spor av teologisk tenkning og refleksjon i norsk og islandsk høymiddelalder." *CM* 6 (1993): 133–67, esp. pp. 147–8.

– "Om bibelanvendelse i *Þorláks saga byskups*." *Alvíssmál* 7 (1994): 73–96.

Bandlien, Bjørn. *Strategies of Passion: Love and Marriage in Medieval Iceland and Norway*. Trans. Betsy van der Hoeck (Turnhout: Brepols, 2005). Pp. 166–7 and 173.

Bekker-Nielsen, Hans, Thorkil Damsgaard Olsen, and Ole Widding. >> *Norrøn fortællekunst* (1965). Pp. 40, 119, and 125.

Bibire, Paul. "Þorláks saga helga." In Phillip Pulsiano and Kirsten Wolf, with Paul Acker and Donald K. Fry, ed. >> *Medieval Scandinavia* (1993). P. 671.

Bjarni Aðalbjarnarson. "Bemerkninger om de eldste bispesagaer." *Studia Islandica* 17 (Reykjavík: Heimspekideild Háskóla Íslands; Menningarsjóður, 1959): 27–37, esp. pp. 29 and 32–5.

Boyer, Régis. >> *La vie religieuse en Islande* (1979).

– "Les références expresses à la littérature dans les 'Sagas de contemporains'." In Gísli Sigurðsson, Guðrún Kvaran, and Sigurgeir Steingrímsson, ed. >> *Sagnaþing helgað Jónasi Kristjánssyni* (1994). Vol. 1, pp. 87–96.

Cormack, Margaret. >> *The Saints in Iceland* (1994). Pp. 10, 49, 61, 65, 125, 129, 159, and 162.
– "Saints' Lives and Icelandic Literature in the Thirteenth and Fourteenth Centuries." In Hans Bekker-Nielsen and Birte Carlé, ed. >> *Saints and Sagas* (1994). Pp. 27–47, esp. pp. 36 and 41–2.
– "Visions, Demons and Gender in the Sagas of Icelandic Saints." *CM* 7 (1994): 185–209.
– "Sagas of Saints." In *Old Icelandic Literature and Society*. Ed. Margaret Clunies Ross (Cambridge: Cambridge University Press, 2000). Pp. 302–25, esp. pp. 308–10.
– "Christian Biography." In *A Companion to Old Norse–Icelandic Literature and Culture*. Ed. Rory McTurk (Oxford: Blackwell, 2005). Pp. 27–42, esp. pp. 30–1 and 35.
– "The Economics of Devotion: Vows and Indulgences in Medieval Iceland." *Viking and Medieval Scandinavia* 5 (2009): 41–63, esp. pp. 42 and 46.
Fahn, Susanne Miriam, and Gottskálk Jensson. "The Forgotten Poem: A Latin Panegyric for Saint Þorlákr in AM 382 4to." *Gripla* 21 (2010): 19–60, esp. pp. 21, 24–7, 29, and 43.
Finnur Jónsson. >> *Den oldnorske og oldislandske Litteraturs Historie* (1920–4). Vol. 2, pp. 563–6.
Foote, Peter. "Auðræði." In Arthur Brown and Peter Foote, ed. >> *Early English and Norse Studies* (1963). Pp. 62–76, esp. pp. 63–4.
Gottskálk Þ. Jensson. "The Latin Fragments of *Þorláks saga helga* and Their Classical Context." In Rudolf Simek and Judith Meurer, ed. >> *Scandinavia and Christian Europe in the Middle Ages* (2003). Pp. 257–67, esp. pp. 261 and 263–4.
Guðrún Nordal and Sverrir Tómasson. "Veraldleg sagnaritun 1120–1400." In Guðrún Nordal, Sverrir Tómasson, and Vésteinn Ólason, ed. >> *Íslensk Bókmenntasaga* 1 (1992). Pp. 263–418, esp. pp. 269–71, 285, 312, 345, and 348.
Gunnar F. Guðmundsson. "Latínusöngur leikra á miðöldum." In *Til heiðurs og hugbótar. Greinar um trúarkveðskap fyrri alda*. Ed. Svanhildur Óskarsdóttir and Anna Guðmundsdóttir (Reykholt: Snorrastofa, 2003). Pp. 93–112, esp. pp. 93–4.
Hallberg, Peter. "Imagery in Religious Old Norse Prose Literature: An Outline." *ANF* 102 (1987): 120–70, esp. pp. 121–2, 139, and 163.
Helga Kress. "'Grey þykir mér Freyja': Um konur, kristni og karlveldi í íslenskum fornbókmenntum." In Inga Huld Hákonardóttir, ed. >> *Konur og kristsmenn* (1996). Pp. 13–63, esp. pp. 57–8. Rpt. in Helga

Kress. *Fyrir dyrum fóstru: Konur og kynferði í íslenskum fornbók-menntum. Greinasafn* (Reykjavík: Háskóli Íslands, Rannsóknastofa í kvennafræðum, 1996). Pp. 167–219, esp. pp. 216–17.

Helgi Guðmundsson. "Þorláks saga biskups og Isidor." *Gripla* 14 (2003): 237–8.

Hermann, Pernille. "The Icelandic Sagas and the Real: Realism in *Þorláks saga*." In John McKinnell, David Ashurst, and Donata Kick, ed. >> *The Fantastic in Old Norse/Icelandic Literature* (2006). Vol. 1, pp. 372–80.

Hunt, Margaret Cushing. "A Study of Authorial Perspective in *Guðmundar saga A* and *Guðmundar saga D*: Hagiography and the Icelandic Bishop's Saga." PhD dissertation. Indiana University, 1985. Pp. 46–51.

Jakob Benediktsson. "Traces of Latin Prose-Rhythm in Old Norse Literature." In *The Fifth Viking Congress, Tórshavn, July 1965*. Ed. Bjarni Niclasen (Tórshavn: Føroya Landsstýri, 1968). Pp. 17–24, esp. p. 23. Rpt. in Jakob Benediktsson. *Lærdómslistir. Afmælisrit 20. júlí 1987* (Reykjavík: Mál og menning, 1987). Pp. 153–60, esp. p. 159.

– "Brot úr Þorlákslesi." In *Afmælisrit Jóns Helgasonar 30. júní 1969*. Ed. Jakob Benediktsson et al. (Reykjavík: Heimskringla,. 1969). Pp. 98–108, esp. pp. 103–4 and 107.

Jón Böðvarsson. "Munur eldri og yngri gerðar Þorláks sögu." *Saga* 6 (1968): 81–94.

Jón Helgason. *Norrøn Litteraturhistorie* (Copenhagen: Levin and Munks-gaard, 1934). Pp. 91 and 192–3.

– "Þorláks saga helga." *KLNM* 20 (1976). Cols. 388–91, esp. cols. 388–9.

Jónas Kristjánsson. >> *Eddas and Sagas* (1988). Pp. 181–2 and 184.

Jørgensen, Jørgen Højgaard. *Bispesagaer – Laurentius saga: Studier i* Laurentius saga biskups*, indledt af overvejelser omkring* biskupa sǫgur *som litterær genre.* Udgivelsesudvalgets samling af studenterafhand-linger 12 (Odense: [n.p.], 1978). Pp. 16–17, 29, 36–8, and 48–9.

– "Hagiography and the Icelandic Bishop Sagas." *Peritia* 1 (1982): 1–16, esp. pp. 8–16.

Kirby, Ian. >> *Biblical Quotation* (1980). Vol. 2, pp. 79–80.

– "The Bible and Biblical Interpretation in Medieval Iceland." In *Old Icelandic Literature and Society*. Ed. Margaret Clunies Ross (Cambridge: Cambridge University Press, 2000). Pp. 287–301, esp. p. 296.

Koppenberg, Peter. *Hagiographische Studien zu den Biskupa sögur: Unter besonderer Berücksichtigung der* Jóns Saga Helga. Scandia Wissenschaftliche Reihe 1 (Bochum: Scandia, 1980). Pp. 6, 14, 17, 20, 61, 66, 79, 82, 89, 94, 97–8, 131–2, 139–40, 142, 154–5, 162, 172, 178, 183–99, 220, 222, 240, 251, 253, and 255.

Kratz, Henry. "Thorlákr's Miracles." In >> *Samtíðarsögur* (1994). Vol. 2, pp. 480–94, esp. pp. 480–8.

Magnús Már Lárusson. "Biskupa sögur." *KLNM* 1 (1956). Cols. 630–1.

Martin, John Stanley. "The Function of Bishops in the Early Icelandic Church." In >> *Samtíðarsögur* (1994). Vol. 2, pp. 561–76.

McCreesh, Bernadine. "Prophetic Dreams and Visions in the Sagas of the Early Icelandic Saints." In *Verbal Encounters: Anglo-Saxon and Old Norse Studies for Roberta Frank*. Ed. Antonina Harbus and Russell Poole (Toronto: University of Toronto Press, 2005). Pp. 247–68, esp. pp. 251, 255–7, 259–60, 262, and 267.

– "Elements of the Pagan Supernatural in the Bishops' Sagas." In John McKinnell, David Ashurst, and Donata Kick, ed. >> *The Fantastic in Old Norse / Icelandic Literature* (2006). Vol. 2, pp. 671–80, esp. pp. 672 and 679.

McDougall, Ian. "Foreigners and Foreign Languages in Medieval Iceland." *Saga-Book* 22 (1986–9): 180–233, esp. p. 192.

Mogk, Eugen. >> *Geschichte der norwegisch-isländischen Literatur* (1904). Pp. 780 and 791–2.

Orri Vésteinsson. *The Christianization of Iceland: Priests, Power, and Social Change 1000–1300* (Oxford: Oxford University Press, 2000). Pp. 136, 140, 157–8, 167–8, 180, 235, and 296.

Paasche, Fredrik. *Norges og Islands litteratur inntil utgangen av middelalderen*. Rev. ed. by Anne Holtsmark (Oslo: Aschehoug, 1947). Pp. 286–7, 334, and 447.

Paul, Fritz. "Historiographische und hagiographische Tendenzen in isländischen Bischofsviten des 12. und 13. Jahrhunderts." *Skandinavistik* 9 (1979): 36–46, esp. pp. 36–8.

Roughton, Philip. "A Hagiographical Reading of *Egils saga*." In Agneta Ney, Henrik Williams, and Fredrik Charpentier Ljungqvist, ed. >> *Á austrvega: Sagas and East Scandinavia* (2009). Vol. 2, pp. 816–22, esp. pp. 816, 818, 820, and 822.

Samuelson, David Robert. "The Operation of the Bishop's Legend in Early Medieval England and Iceland." PhD dissertation, University of Michigan, 1977. Pp. 195–200.

Schach, Paul. *Icelandic Sagas*. Twayne's World Author Series (Boston: Twayne, 1984). Pp. 64–5 and 68.

Schier, Kurt. *Sagaliteratur*. Sammlung Metzler M78 (Stuttgart: Metzler, 1970). Pp. 4, 67–70, 121, 123, and 129.

Sigurður Sigurðarson. *Þorlákur helgi og samtíð hans* (Reykjavík: Skálholtsútgáfan, 1993).

Sveinbjörn Rafnsson. "The Penitential of St. Þorlákur in Its Icelandic context." *Bulletin of Medieval Canon Law* 15 (1985): 19–30, esp. pp. 21–2.

Sverrir Tómasson. *Formálar íslenskra sagnaritara á miðöldum. Rannsókn bókmenntahefðar* (Reykjavík: Stofnun Árna Magnússonar, 1988). Pp. 16, 19, 21–3, 60, 141–3, and 357–9.

– "Kristnar trúarbókmenntir í óbundnu máli." In Guðrún Nordal, Sverrir Tómasson, and Vésteinn Ólason, ed. >> *Íslensk Bókmenntasaga* 1 (1992). Pp. 419–79, esp. pp. 425, 467, 474–7 and 479.

Turville-Petre, G. >> *Origins of Icelandic Literature* (1967). Pp. 202 and 207–9.

Vries, Jan de. >> *Altnordische Literaturgeschichte* (1964–7). Vol. 1, p. 351, and vol. 2, pp. 187–8.

Whaley, Diana. "Miracles in the Sagas of Bishops: Icelandic Variations on an International Theme." *CM* 7 (1994): 155–84.

Wolf, Kirsten. "A Translation of the Latin Fragments Containing the Life and Miracles of St. Þorlákr along with Collections of *Lectiones* for Recitation on His Feast-Days." *Proceedings of the PMR Conference* 14 (1989): 261–76, esp. p. 261.

Handlist, p. 336.

3. Þorláks saga biskups B

The so-called younger saga of Bishop Þorlákr Þórhallsson, possibly composed on the occasion of the translation of the saint's relics.

Manuscripts:
AM 209 fol. (ca. 1600–1700, defective), AM 219 fol. (ca. 1370–80, defective), AM 379 4to (1654), AM 380 4to (ca. 1600–1700), AM 382 4to (ca. 1350, defective), AM 383 4to I (ca. 1250), AM 383 4to III (ca. 1400), AM 383 4to IV (ca. 1370–90), AM 388 4to (ca. 1650–1700, defective), and BLAdd 11.242 (ca. 1540–90).

Editions:
Ásdís Egilsdóttir, ed. *Biskupa sögur II: Hungrvaka, Þorláks saga byskups in elzta, Jarteinabók Þorláks byskups in forna, Þorláks saga byskups yngri, Jarteinabók Þorláks byskups önnur, Þorláks saga byskups C, Þorláks saga byskups E, Páls saga byskups, Ísleifs þáttr byskups, Latínubrot um Þorlák byskup.* Íslenzk fornrit 16 (Reykjavík: Hið íslenzka fornritafélag, 2002). Pp. 143–224.

Normalized text based on AM 382 4to and BLAdd 11242 with select variants and emendations from AM 219 fol., AM 383 4to IV, AM 380 4to, AM 379 4to, AM 383 4to III, AM 388 4to, AM 209 fol., and AM 383 4to I.

Gudbrand Vigfusson and F. York Powell, ed. and trans. *Origines Islandicae: A Collection of the More Important Sagas and Other Native Writings Relating to the Settlement and Early History of Iceland.* 2 vols. (Oxford: Clarendon, 1905; rpt. Millwood: Kraus, 1976). Vol. 1, pp. 493–502 and 569–91. Based on *Biskupa sögur*, pp. 294–301, 263, 274, and 280–93.

Guðni Jónsson, ed. *Byskupa sögur*. 3 vols. (Reykjavík: Íslendingasagnaútgáfan; Haukadalsútgáfan, 1948). Vol. 1, pp. 37–8, 77–135, and 139–61 (pp. 77–113, lower text).
Normalized text (prologue, miracle section, and *Oddaverja þáttr*) based on *Biskupa sögur*.

Hreinn Benediktsson. *Early Icelandic Script As Illustrated in Vernacular Texts from the Twelfth and Thirteenth Centuries.* Íslenzk handrit: Icelandic Manuscripts, Series in Folio 2 (Reykjavík: The Manuscript Institute of Iceland, 1965). Plate 42.
Facsimile of AM 383 4to I, fol. 2r.

Jón Helgason, ed. *Byskupa sǫgur*. Editiones Arnamagnæanæ, Ser. A, vol. 13.2 (Copenhagen: Reitzel, 1978). Pp. 175–328.
Edition of AM 382 4to (pp. 241–243.15, 244.5–9, 244.31–6, 247–253.17, 257.20–264.13, 278.6–280.15, 284.11–288.8, 289–290.6, 295.12–307.12 and 307.27–339) and BLAdd 11242 (pp. 271.17–273.21, 283.12–14, and 307.19–23) with variants from AM 382 4to. The first part of the text is presented only as variants to the A-version.

[Jón Sigurðsson and Guðbrandur Vigfússon, ed.] *Biskupa sögur*. 2 vols. (Copenhagen: Møller, 1858–78). Vol. 1, pp. 263–332.
Based on AM 379 4to (pp. 265.14–269.13, 283.33–286.8, 290.1–296.22, 297.27–299.22, 302.20–305.4, 311.12–312.6, and 313.9–315.1) and AM 382 4to (pp. 263–265.14, 269.13–283.33, 286.8–290.1, 296.22–297.27, 299.22–302.20, 305.4–311.12, 315.1–325.12, and 325.19–332), and AM 383 4to II (pp. 312.7–313.8 and 325.12–18) with variants from 383 4to II (pp. 311.12–315.7 and 322.2–326.12), AM 219 fol. (pp. 269.19–272 and 294.16–304.34), AM 383 4to IV (pp. 266.23–267.34 and 270.20–271.36), and AM 383 4to III (pp. 285.25–288.1 and 292.24–294.37).

Stefán Karlsson, ed. *Sagas of Icelandic Bishops: Fragments of Eight Manuscripts.* EIM 7 (Copenhagen: Rosenkilde and Bagger, 1967).
Facsimile of AM 219 fol.

Modern Icelandic language edition:
Ásdís Egilsdóttir, ed. *Þorláks saga helga. Elsta gerð Þorláks sögu helga
ásamt Jarteinabók og efni úr yngri gerðum sögunnar* (Reykjavík:
Þorlákssjóður, 1989). Pp. 189–220 (extract only).

English translations:
Gudbrand Vigfusson and F. York Powell, ed. and trans. *Origines Islandi-
cae: A Collection of the More Important Sagas and Other Native
Writings Relating to the Settlement and Early History of Iceland.* 2 vols.
(Oxford: Clarendon, 1905; rpt. Millwood: Kraus, 1976). Vol. 1,
pp. 493–502 and 569–91.

[Leith, Mary Charlotte Julia], trans. *Stories of the Bishops of Iceland*
(London: Masters, 1895). Pp. 115–21 (extracts only).

Simpson, Jacqueline, trans. *The Northmen Talk: A Choice of Tales from
Iceland* (London: Phoenix House; Madison: University of Wisconsin
Press, 1965). Pp. 77–84 (extracts only).

German translation:
Baetke, Walter, trans. *Islands Besiedlung und älteste Geschichte.* Neuausgabe
mit Nachwort von Dr. Rolf Heller. Thule: Altnordische Dichtung und
Prosa 23 (Düsseldorf: Eugen Diederichs, 1967). Pp. 217–33 (extract only).

Literature:
Ármann Jakobsson and Ásdís Egilsdóttir. "Er Oddaverjaþætti treystandi?" *Ný saga* 11 (1999): 91–100.

Ásdís Egilsdóttir. "Eru biskupasögur til?" *Skáldskaparmál* 2 (1992):
207–20, esp. pp. 211 and 214.

– "Biskupa sögur." In Phillip Pulsiano and Kirsten Wolf, with Paul Acker
and Donald K. Fry, ed. >> *Medieval Scandinavia* (1993). Pp. 45–6.

– "St Þorlákr of Iceland: The Emergence of a Cult." *The Haskins Society
Journal* 12 (2002): 121–31, esp. pp. 124, 127, and 130–1.

Auður G. Magnúsdóttir. "Ástir og völd. Frillulífi á Íslandi á Þjóðveldisöld." *Ný saga* 2 (1988): 4–12, esp. pp. 9–10.

– "Kvennamál Oddaverja." In *Kvennaslóðir: Rit til heiðurs Sigríði
Erlendsdóttur sagnfræðingi.* Ed. Anna Agnarsdóttir et al. (Reykjavík:
Kvennasögusafn Íslands, 2001). Pp. 46–59, esp. pp. 48–9 and 51–3.

Bekker-Nielsen, Hans, Thorkil Damsgaard Olsen, and Ole Widding.
>> *Norrøn fortællekunst* (1965). Pp. 119 and 125.

Bibire, Paul. "Þorláks saga helga." In Phillip Pulsiano and Kirsten Wolf, with
Paul Acker and Donald K. Fry, ed. >> *Medieval Scandinavia* (1993). P. 671.

Bjarni Aðalbjarnarson. "Bemerkninger om de eldste bispesagaer." *Studia
Islandica* 17 (Reykjavík: Heimspekideild Háskóla Íslands; Menningarsjóður, 1959): 27–37, esp. pp. 29 and 34.

Boyer, Régis. >> *La vie religieuse en Islande* (1979).
– "Les références expresses à la littérature dans les 'Sagas de contemporains'." In Gísli Sigurðsson, Guðrún Kvaran, and Sigurgeir Steingrímsson, ed. >> *Sagnaþing helgað Jónasi Kristjánssyni* (1994). Vol. 1, pp. 87–96.
Cormack, Margaret. "'Fjǫlkunnigri kono scallatu í faðm sofa': Sex and the Supernatural in Icelandic Saints' Lives." *Skáldskaparmál* 2 (1992): 221–8, esp. p. 224.
– "Saints and Sinners: Reflections on Death in Some Icelandic Sagas." *Gripla* (1993): 187–218, esp. p. 201.
– >> *The Saints in Iceland* (1994). Pp. 18, 63, 65, 125, 137, 162. 164, 179, 193, and 230.
– "Visions, Demons and Gender in the Sagas of Icelandic Saints." *CM* 7 (1994): 185–209.
– "Women and Gender in the Sagas of Icelandic Saints." In >> *Samtíðarsögur* (1994). Vol. 1, pp. 188–93, esp. pp. 189–90.
– "Poetry, Paganism and the Sagas of Icelandic Bishops." In *Til heiðurs og hugbótar. Greinar um trúarkveðskap fyrri alda*. Ed. Svanhildur Óskarsdóttir and Anna Guðmundsdóttir (Reykholt: Snorrastofa, 2003). Pp. 33–51, esp. p. 37.
– "Christian Biography." In *A Companion to Old Norse–Icelandic Literature and Culture*. Ed. Rory McTurk (Oxford: Blackwell, 2005). Pp. 27–42, esp. pp. 34–6.
Fahn, Susanne Miriam, and Gottskálk Jensson. "The Forgotten Poem: A Latin Panegyric for Saint Þorlákr in AM 382 4to." *Gripla* 21 (2010): 19–60.
Finnur Jónsson. >> *Den oldnorske og oldislandske Litteraturs Historie* (1920–4). Vol. 2, pp. 565–6.
Foote, Peter. "Auðræði." In Arthur Brown and Peter Foote, ed. >> *Early English and Norse Studies* (1963). Pp. 62–76, esp. pp. 63–4.
Gottskálk Þ. Jensson. "The Latin Fragments of *Þorláks saga helga* and their Classical Context." In Rudolf Simek and Judith Meurer, ed. >> *Scandinavia and Christian Europe in the Middle Ages* (2003). Pp. 257–67, esp. p. 261.
Guðrún Nordal and Sverrir Tómasson. "Veraldleg sagnaritun 1120–1400." In Guðrún Nordal, Sverrir Tómasson, and Vésteinn Ólason, ed. >> *Íslensk Bókmenntasaga* 1 (1992). Pp. 263–418, esp. pp. 319 and 345.
Hermann, Pernille. "The Icelandic Sagas and the Real: Realism in *Þorláks saga*." In John McKinnell, David Ashurst, and Donata

Kick, ed. >> *The Fantastic in Old Norse / Icelandic Literature* (2006). Vol. 1, pp. 372–80.

Hunt, Margaret Cushing. "A Study of Authorial Perspective in *Guð-mundar saga A* and *Guðmundar saga D*: Hagiography and the Icelandic Bishop's Saga." PhD dissertation, Indiana University, 1985. Pp. 51–4.

Jakob Benediktsson. "Brot úr Þorlákslesi." In *Afmælisrit Jóns Helgasonar 30. júní 1969*. Ed. Jakob Benediktsson et al. (Reykjavík: Heimskringla, 1969). Pp. 98–108, esp. pp. 103–4.

Jón Böðvarsson. "Munur eldri og yngri gerðar Þorláks sögu." *Saga* 6 (1968): 81–94.

Jón Helgason. "Þorláks saga helga." *KLNM* 20 (1976). Cols. 388–91, esp. cols. 388 and 390.

Jónas Kristjánsson. >> *Eddas and Sagas* (1988). Pp. 181–2 and 184.

Jørgensen, Jørgen Højgaard. *Bispesagaer – Laurentius saga: Studier i* Laurentius saga biskups, *indledt af overvejelser omkring* biskupa sǫgur *som litterær genre.* Udgivelsesudvalgets samling af studenterafhand-linger 12 (Odense: [n.p.], 1978). Pp. 16–17, 29, 36–8, and 48–9.

Kirby, Ian. >> *Biblical Quotation* (1980). Vol. 2, pp. 79–80.

– "The Bible and Biblical Interpretation in Medieval Iceland." In *Old Icelandic Literature and Society*. Ed. Margaret Clunies Ross (Cambridge: Cambridge University Press, 2000). Pp. 287–301, esp. p. 296.

Koppenberg, Peter. *Hagiographische Studien zu den Biskupa sögur: Unter besonderer Berücksichtigung der* Jóns Saga Helga. Scandia Wissensch-aftliche Reihe 1 (Bochum: Scandia, 1980). Pp. 7, 73, and 87.

Kratz, Henry. "Thorlákr's Miracles." In >> *Samtíðarsögur* (1994). Vol. 2, pp. 480–94, esp. pp. 480–1 and 491.

Magnús Már Lárusson. "Biskupa sögur." *KLNM* 1 (1956). Cols. 630–1.

Martin, John Stanley. "The Function of Bishops in the Early Icelandic Church." In >> *Samtíðarsögur* (1994). Vol. 2, pp. 561–76.

McCreesh, Bernadine. "Elements of the Pagan Supernatural in the Bishops' Sagas." In John McKinnell, David Asthurst, and Donata Kick, ed. >> *The Fantastic in Old Norse / Icelandic Literature* (2006). Vol. 2, pp. 671–80, esp. p. 673.

McDougall, Ian. "Foreigners and Foreign Languages in Medieval Iceland." *Saga-Book* 22 (1986–9): 180–233, esp. p. 192.

Mogk, Eugen. >> *Geschichte der norwegisch-isländischen Literatur* (1904). Pp. 791–2.

Orri Vésteinsson. *The Christianization of Iceland: Priests, Power, and Social Change 1000–1300* (Oxford: Oxford University Press, 2000).

Pp. 99–101, 112–13, 115–17, 119, 121, 123, 126, 130, 138, 140, 154, 167–9, 235, and 296.

Paasche, Fredrik. *Norges og Islands litteratur inntil utgangen av middelalderen*. Rev. ed. by Anne Holtsmark (Oslo: Aschehoug, 1947). Pp. 286–7.

Paul, Fritz. "Historiographische und hagiographische Tendenzen in isländischen Bischofsviten des 12. und 13. Jahrhunderts." *Skandinavistik* 9 (1979): 36–46, esp. pp. 36–9.

Roughton, Philip. "A Hagiographical Reading of *Egils saga*." In Agneta Ney, Henrik Williams, and Fredrik Charpentier Ljungqvist, ed. >> *Á austrvega: Sagas and East Scandinavia* (2009). Vol. 2, pp. 816–22, esp. pp. 817–18.

Samuelson, David Robert. "The Operation of the Bishop's Legend in Early Medieval England and Iceland." PhD dissertation, University of Michigan, 1977. Pp. 200–2.

Schach, Paul. *Icelandic Sagas*. Twayne's World Author Series (Boston: Twayne, 1984). Pp. 65–6 and 68.

Schier, Kurt. *Sagaliteratur*. Sammlung Metzler M78 (Stuttgart: Metzler, 1970). Pp. 4, 67–70, 121, 123, and 129.

Sigurður Sigurðarson. *Þorlákur helgi og samtíð hans* (Reykjavík: Skálholtsútgáfan, 1993).

Sveinbjörn Rafnsson. "The Penitential of St. Þorlákur in Its Icelandic Context." *Bulletin of Medieval Canon Law* 15 (1985): 19–30, esp. pp. 21–2 and 28.

Sverrir Tómasson. *Formálar íslenskra sagnaritara á miðöldum. Rannsókn bókmenntahefðar* (Reykjavík: Stofnun Árna Magnússonar, 1988). Pp. 16, 19, 50, 67, 96–7, 118–19, 122–4, 128, 131, 140–3, 145–8, 163–5, 184, 224, 227, 233, 236, 311, 315–16, 322, 324, and 357–9.

– "Kristnar trúarbókmenntir í óbundnu máli." In Guðrún Nordal, Sverrir Tómasson, and Vésteinn Ólason, ed. >> *Íslensk Bókmenntasaga* 1 (1992). Pp. 419–79, esp. pp. 467 and 474–9.

Turville-Petre, G. >> *Origins of Icelandic Literature* (1967). Pp. 82, 202 and 208–9.

Vries, Jan de. >> *Altnordische Literaturgeschichte* (1964–7). Vol. 2, pp. 187–8.

Whaley, Diana. "Miracles in the Sagas of Bishops: Icelandic Variations on an International Theme." *CM* 7 (1994): 155–84.

Wolf, Kirsten. "A Translation of the Latin Fragments Containing the Life and Miracles of St. Þorlákr along with Collections of *Lectiones* for Recitation on His Feast-Days." *Proceedings of the PMR Conference* 14 (1989): 261–76, esp. p. 261.

– "Pride and Politics in Late-Twelfth-Century Iceland: The Sanctity of
Bishop Þorlákr Þórhallsson." In Thomas A. DuBois, ed. >> *Sanctity
in the North* (2008). Pp. 241–70, esp. p. 250.
Handlist, p. 336.

4. Jarteinabók Þorláks biskups ǫnnur

A collection of miracles added to *Þorláks saga biskups C* that took place
in Bishop Páll Jónsson's time (1195–1211).

Manuscript:
AM 379 4to (1654).
Editions:
Ásdís Egilsdóttir, ed. *Biskupa sögur II: Hungrvaka, Þorláks saga byskups
in elzta, Jarteinabók Þorláks byskups in forna, Þorláks saga byskups
yngri, Jarteinabók Þorláks byskups önnur, Þorláks saga byskups C,
Þorláks saga byskups E, Páls saga byskups, Ísleifs þáttr byskups,
Latínubrot um Þorlák byskup.* Íslenzk fornrit 16 (Reykjavík: Hið
íslenzka fornritafélag, 2002). Pp. 227–50.
Normalized text based on *Byskupa sǫgur.*
Guðni Jónsson, ed. *Byskupa sögur.* 3 vols. (Reykjavík: Íslendingasagnaút-
gáfan; Haukadalsútgáfan, 1948). Vol. 1, pp. 205–32.
Normalized text based on *Biskupa sögur.*
Jón Helgason, ed. *Byskupa sǫgur.* Editiones Arnamagnæanæ, Ser. A,
vol. 13.2 (Copenhagen: Reitzel, 1978). Pp. 385–406.
[Jón Sigurðsson and Guðbrandur Vigfússon, ed.] *Biskupa sögur.* 2 vols.
(Copenhagen: Møller, 1858–78). Vol. 1, pp. 357–74.
Modern Icelandic language edition:
Einar Ól. Sveinsson, ed. *Leit eg suður til landa. Ævintýri og helgisögur frá
miðöldum.* (Reykjavík: Heimskringla, 1944). Pp. 256–63 (extracts only).
Literature:
Ásdís Egilsdóttir. "St Þorlákr of Iceland: The Emergence of a Cult." *The
Haskins Society Journal* 12 (2002): 121–31, esp. p. 130.
– "The Fantastic Reality: Hagiography, Miracles and Fantasy." In John
McKinnell, David Ashurst, and Donata Kick, ed. >> *The Fantastic in
Old Norse/Icelandic Literature* (2006). Vol. 1, pp. 63–70, esp. p. 68.
Bekker-Nielsen, Hans. "Nova Historia Sancti Ambrosii. Et tabt rimof-
ficium af Gunnlaugr Leifsson." *Mm* (1958): 8–14, esp. p. 8.
Bibire, Paul. "Þorláks saga helga." In Phillip Pulsiano and Kirsten Wolf,
with Paul Acker and Donald K. Fry, ed. >> *Medieval Scandinavia*
(1993). P. 671.

Bjarni Aðalbjarnarson. "Bemerkninger om de eldste bispesagaer." *Studia Islandica* 17 (Reykjavík: Heimspekideild Háskóla Íslands; Menningarsjóður, 1959): 27–37, esp. p. 37.

Boyer, Régis. >> *La vie religieuse en Islande* (1979).

Cormack, Margaret. "'Fjǫlkunnigri kono scallatu í faðm sofa': Sex and the Supernatural in Icelandic Saints' Lives." *Skáldskaparmál* 2 (1992): 221–8, esp. p. 224.

– >> *The Saints in Iceland* (1994). Pp. 31, 54, 62, 106, 162–3, and 185.

– "Visions, Demons and Gender in the Sagas of Icelandic Saints." *CM* 7 (1994): 185–209, esp. pp. 187, 193–6, and 202–3.

– "Women and Gender in the Sagas of Icelandic Saints." In >> *Samtíðarsögur* (1994). Vol. 1, pp. 188–93, esp. p. 191.

– "The Economics of Devotion: Vows and Indulgences in Medieval Iceland." *Viking and Medieval Scandinavia* 5 (2009): 41–63, esp. pp. 47–8.

Fahn, Susanne Miriam, and Gottskálk Jensson. "The Forgotten Poem: A Latin Panegyric for Saint Þorlákr in AM 382 4to." *Gripla* 21 (2010): 19–60, esp. pp. 29, 43, 45–8, and 54.

Finnur Jónsson. >> *Den oldnorske og oldislandske Litteraturs Historie* (1920–4). Vol. 2, p. 932.

Gunnar F. Guðmundsson. "Latínusöngur leikra á miðöldum." In *Til heiðurs og hugbótar. Greinar um trúarkveðskap fyrri alda*. Ed. Svanhildur Óskarsdóttir and Anna Guðmundsdóttir (Reykholt: Snorrastofa, 2003). Pp. 93–112, esp. p. 102.

Hallberg, Peter. "Imagery in Religious Old Norse Prose Literature: An Outline." *ANF* 102 (1987): 120–70, esp. p. 151.

Jón Jóhannesson. "Tímatal Gerlands í íslenzkum ritum frá þjóðveldisöld." *Skírnir* 126 (1952): 76–93, esp. p. 88.

Koppenberg, Peter. *Hagiographische Studien zu den Biskupa sögur: Unter besonderer Berücksichtigung der* Jóns Saga Helga. Scandia Wissenschaftliche Reihe 1 (Bochum: Scandia, 1980). Pp. 239–40.

Kratz, Henry. "Thorlákr's Miracles." In >> *Samtíðarsögur* (1994). Vol. 2, pp. 480–94, esp. pp. 480–1, 485, 489, and 492.

Kuhn, Hans. "The Emergence of a Saint's Cult As Witnessed by the *Jarteinabœkr Þorláks byskups*." *Saga-Book* 24 (1996): 240–54.

Mogk, Eugen. >> *Geschichte der norwegisch-isländischen Literatur* (1904). Pp. 791–2.

Schach, Paul. *Icelandic Sagas*. Twayne's World Author Series (Boston: Twayne, 1984). P. 64.

Sverrir Tómasson. "Kristnar trúarbókmenntir í óbundnu máli." In Guðrún Nordal, Sverrir Tómasson, and Vésteinn Ólason, ed. >> *Íslensk Bókmenntasaga* 1 (1992). Pp. 419–79, esp. p. 474.

Turville-Petre, G. >> *Origins of Icelandic Literature* (1967). Pp. 210–11.

Whaley, Diana. "Miracles in the Sagas of Bishops: Icelandic Variations on an International Theme." *CM* 7 (1994): 155–84.

Wolf, Kirsten. "A Translation of the Latin Fragments Containing the Life and Miracles of St. Þorlákr along with Collections of *Lectiones* for Recitation on His Feast-Days." *Proceedings of the PMR Conference* 14 (1989): 261–76, esp. p. 261.

– "Pride and Politics in Late-Twelfth-Century Iceland: The Sanctity of Bishop Þorlákr Þórhallsson." In Thomas A. DuBois, ed. >> *Sanctity in the North* (2008). Pp. 241–70, esp. p. 250.

Handlist, p. 336.

5. Þorláks saga biskups C

The so-called youngest saga of Bishop Þorlákr Þórhallsson. The *vita* corresponds to *B*. It is somewhat abridged, but contains material not found in *A* or *B*.

Manuscripts:

AM 209 fol. (ca. 1600–1700, defective), AM 219 fol. (ca. 1370–80, defective), AM 379 4to (1654), AM 380 4to (ca. 1600–1700), AM 383 4to III (ca. 1400), AM 383 4to IV (ca. 1370–90), AM 385 4to II (ca. 1375–1400), and AM 388 4to (ca. 1650–1700, defective).

Editions:

Ásdís Egilsdóttir, ed. *Biskupa sögur II: Hungrvaka, Þorláks saga byskups in elzta, Jarteinabók Þorláks byskups in forna, Þorláks saga byskups yngri, Jarteinabók Þorláks byskups önnur, Þorláks saga byskups C, Þorláks saga byskups E, Páls saga byskups, Ísleifs þáttr byskups, Latínubrot um Þorlák byskup.* Íslenzk fornrit 16 (Reykjavík: Hið íslenzka fornritafélag, 2002). Pp. 253–85.

Normalized text based on AM 219 fol, AM 380 4to, AM 379 4to, and AM 385 4to II. Variants from chapters 1–56 of version C are given in version B, chapters 1–70 (pp. 144–201), and C is also used to fill lacunae in B. Variants from chapters 71–106 of version C are used to fill lacunae in *Jarteinabók Þorláks biskups in forna* (pp. 103–40). Chapters 57–70 and 107–32 are printed.

Foote, Peter, ed. *A Saga of St Peter the Apostle. Perg. 4:o nr 19 in the Royal Library, Stockholm.* EIM 19 (Copenhagen: Rosenkilde and Bagger, 1990).

Facsimile of AM 385 4to II, fol. 1r10–23.

Guðni Jónsson, ed. *Byskupa sögur*. 3 vols. (Reykjavík: Íslendingasagnaút-
gáfan; Haukadalsútgáfan, 1948). Vol. 1, pp. 233–60.
Normalized text based on *Biskupa sögur*.
Jón Helgason, ed. *Byskupa sǫgur*. Editiones Arnamagnæanæ, Ser. A,
vol. 13.2 (Copenhagen: Reitzel, 1978). Pp. 343–73.
Based on AM 219 fol. (pp. 365.4–373) and AM 380 4to (pp. 343–365.4)
with variants from AM 379 4to and AM 380 4to.
[Jón Sigurðsson and Guðbrandur Vigfússon, ed.] *Biskupa sögur*. 2 vols.
(Copenhagen: Møller, 1858–78). Vol. 1, pp. 375–97.
Edition of AM 379 4to. Miracle section only; the rest of the text is
used to fill lacunae in B.

Modern Icelandic language edition:
Ásdís Egilsdóttir, ed. *Þorláks saga helga. Elsta gerð Þorláks sögu helga
ásamt Jarteinabók og efni úr yngri gerðum sögunnar* (Reykjavík:
Þorlákssjóður, 1989). Pp. 221–7 (extract only).

English translation:
Cormack, Margaret. "Better Off Dead: Approaches to Medieval Mir-
acles." In Thomas A. DuBois, ed. >> *Sanctity in the North* (2008).
Pp. 334–52, esp. p. 345 (extract only).

Literature:
Ásdís Egilsdóttir. "Eru biskupasögur til?" *Skáldskaparmál* 2 (1992):
207–20, esp. pp. 211 and 214.
– "Biskupa sögur." In Phillip Pulsiano and Kirsten Wolf, with Paul Acker
and Donald K. Fry, ed. >> *Medieval Scandinavia* (1993). Pp. 45–6.
– "St Þorlákr of Iceland: The Emergence of a Cult." *The Haskins Society
Journal* 12 (2002): 121–31, esp. pp. 124, 127, and 130.
Bekker-Nielsen, Hans, Thorkil Damsgaard Olsen, and Ole Widding.
>> *Norrøn fortællekunst* (1965). Pp. 119, and 125.
Bibire, Paul. "Þorláks saga helga." In Phillip Pulsiano and Kirsten Wolf,
with Paul Acker and Donald K. Fry, ed. >> *Medieval Scandinavia*
(1993). P. 671.
Bjarni Aðalbjarnarson. "Bemerkninger om de eldste bispesagaer." *Studia
Islandica* 17 (Reykjavík: Heimspekideild Háskóla Íslands; Menningar-
sjóður, 1959): 27–37, esp. p. 30.
Boyer, Régis. >> *La vie religieuse en Islande* (1979).
Cormack, Margaret. "'Fjǫlkunnigri kono scallatu í faðm sofa': Sex and
the Supernatural in Icelandic Saints' Lives." *Skáldskaparmál* 2 (1992):
221–8, esp. p. 224.
– >> *The Saints in Iceland* (1994). Pp. 60, 63, 67–8, 85, 106, 162–3,
and 193.

Fahn, Susanne Miriam, and Gottskálk Jensson. "The Forgotten Poem: A Latin Panegyric for Saint Þorlákr in AM 382 4to." *Gripla* 21 (2010): 19–60, esp. pp. 21, 25, 29, 43, and 45–6.

Gottskálk Þ. Jensson. "The Latin Fragments of *Þorláks saga helga* and Their Classical Context." In Rudolf Simek and Judith Meurer, ed. >> *Scandinavia and Christian Europe in the Middle Ages* (2003). Pp. 257–67, esp. p. 261.

Guðrún Nordal and Sverrir Tómasson. "Veraldleg sagnaritun 1120–1400." In Guðrún Nordal, Sverrir Tómasson, and Vésteinn Ólason, ed. >> *Íslensk Bókmenntasaga* 1 (1992). Pp. 263–418, esp. p. 345.

Gunnar F. Guðmundsson. "Latínusöngur leikra á miðöldum." In *Til heiðurs og hugbótar. Greinar um trúarkveðskap fyrri alda.* Ed. Svanhildur Óskarsdóttir and Anna Guðmundsdóttir (Reykholt: Snorrastofa, 2003). Pp. 93–112, esp. pp. 106 and 108.

Hermann, Pernille. "The Icelandic Sagas and the Real: Realism in *Þorláks saga.*" In John McKinnell, David Ashurst, and Donata Kick, ed. >> *The Fantastic in Old Norse/Icelandic Literature* (2006). Vol. 1, pp. 372–80.

Jakob Benediktsson. "Brot úr Þorlákslesi." In *Afmælisrit Jóns Helgasonar 30. júní 1969.* Ed. Jakob Benediktsson et al. (Reykjavík: Heimskringla, 1969). Pp. 98–108, esp. pp. 104–5.

Jón Helgason. "Þorláks saga helga." *KLNM* 20 (1976). Cols. 388–91, esp. cols. 388 and 390.

Jónas Kristjánsson. >> *Eddas and Sagas* (1988). Pp. 181–2 and 184.

Jørgensen, Jørgen Højgaard. *Bispesagaer – Laurentius saga: Studier i Laurentius saga biskups, indledt af overvejelser omkring biskupa sǫgur som litterær genre.* Udgivelsesudvalgets samling af studenterafhandlinger 12 (Odense: [n.p.], 1978). Pp. 16–17, 29, 36–8, and 48–9.

Kirby, Ian. >> *Biblical Quotation* (1980). Vol. 2, pp. 79–80.

Kratz, Henry. "Thorlákr's Miracles." In >> *Samtíðarsögur* (1994). Vol. 2, pp. 480–94, esp. pp. 480–1 and 490.

Kuhn, Hans. "The Emergence of a Saint's Cult as Witnessed by the *Jarteinabœkr Þorláks byskups.*" *Saga-Book* 24 (1996): 240–54.

Magnús Már Lárusson. "Biskupa sögur." *KLNM* 1 (1956). Cols. 630–1.

Mogk, Eugen. >> *Geschichte der norwegisch-isländischen Literatur* (1904). Pp. 791–2.

Orri Vésteinsson. *The Christianization of Iceland: Priests, Power, and Social Change 1000–1300* (Oxford: Oxford University Press, 2000). Pp. 99–101, 112–13, 115–17, 119, 121, 123, 126, 130, 136, 138, 140, 154, 167, 169, and 296.

Paasche, Fredrik. *Norges og Islands litteratur inntil utgangen av mid-delalderen*. Rev. ed. by Anne Holtsmark (Oslo: Aschehoug, 1947). Pp. 286–7.

Paul, Fritz. "Historiographische und hagiographische Tendenzen in isländischen Bischofsviten des 12. und 13. Jahrhunderts." *Skandinavistik* 9 (1979): 36–46, esp. pp. 36–8.

Roughton, Philip. "A Hagiographical Reading of *Egils saga*." In Agneta Ney, Henrik Williams, and Fredrik Charpentier Ljungqvist, ed. >> *Á austrvega: Sagas and East Scandinavia* (2009). Vol. 2, pp. 816–22, esp. p. 818.

Schach, Paul. *Icelandic Sagas*. Twayne's World Author Series (Boston: Twayne, 1984). Pp. 64 and 68.

Schier, Kurt. *Sagaliteratur*. Sammlung Metzler M78 (Stuttgart: Metzler, 1970). Pp. 4, 67–70, 121, 123, and 129.

Sigurður Sigurðarson. *Þorlákur helgi og samtíð hans* (Reykjavík: Skálholtsútgáfan, 1993).

Sverrir Tómasson. *Formálar íslenskra sagnaritara á miðöldum. Rannsókn bókmenntahefðar* (Reykjavík: Stofnun Árna Magnússonar, 1988). Pp. 19 and 357–9.

– "Kristnar trúarbókmenntir í óbundnu máli." In Guðrún Nordal, Sverrir Tómasson, and Vésteinn Ólason, ed. >> *Íslensk Bókmenntasaga* 1 (1992). Pp. 419–79, esp. pp. 467, 474, and 479.

Turville-Petre, G. >> *Origins of Icelandic Literature* (1967). Pp. 201 and 209.

Vries, Jan de. >> *Altnordische Literaturgeschichte* (1964–7). Vol. 2, pp. 187–8.

Whaley, Diana. "Miracles in the Sagas of Bishops: Icelandic Variations on an International Theme." *CM* 7 (1994): 155–84.

Wolf, Kirsten. "A Translation of the Latin Fragments Containing the Life and Miracles of St. Þorlákr along with Collections of *Lectiones* for Recitation on His Feast-Days." *Proceedings of the PMR Conference* 14 (1989): 261–76, esp. p. 261.

– "Pride and Politics in Late-Twelfth-Century Iceland: The Sanctity of Bishop Þorlákr Þórhallsson." In Thomas A. DuBois, ed. >> *Sanctity in the North* (2008). Pp. 241–70, esp. p. 250.

Handlist, p. 336.

6. Þorláks saga biskups D

A fragment of a miracle collection.

Manuscript:
AM 383 4to I (ca. 1250).

Editions:

Ásdís Egilsdóttir, ed. *Biskupa sögur II: Hungrvaka, Þorláks saga byskups in elzta, Jarteinabók Þorláks byskups in forna, Þorláks saga byskups yngri, Jarteinabók Þorláks byskups önnur, Þorláks saga byskups C, Þorláks saga byskups E, Páls saga byskups, Ísleifs þáttr byskups, Latínubrot um Þorlák byskup.* Íslenzk fornrit 16 (Reykjavík: Hið íslenzka fornritafélag, 2002). Pp. 158–9.
  Normalized text. Only chapter 14 printed from AM 383 4to I.

Jón Helgason, ed. *Byskupa sǫgur.* Editiones Arnamagnæanæ, Ser. A, vol. 13.2 (Copenhagen: Reitzel, 1978). Pp. 243.20–244.5
  Only a section of AM 383 4to I is printed; the rest of the text is given as variants to version B (pp. 200–3).

[Jón Sigurðsson and Guðbrandur Vigfússon, ed.] *Biskupa sögur.* 2 vols. (Copenhagen: Møller, 1858–78). Vol. 1, pp. 391–4.

Literature:

Fahn, Susanne Miriam, and Gottskálk Jensson. "The Forgotten Poem: A Latin Panegyric for Saint Þorlákr in AM 382 4to." *Gripla* 21 (2010): 19–60, esp. pp. 21, 25, and 43.

Foote, Peter. "Auðræði." In Arthur Brown and Peter Foote, ed. >> *Early English and Norse Studies* (1963). Pp. 62–76, esp. pp. 63–4.

Handlist, p. 336.

7. Þorláks saga biskups E

A fragment of a miracle collection.

Manuscript:
AM 383 4to II (ca. 1300).

Editions:

Ásdís Egilsdóttir, ed. *Biskupa sögur II: Hungrvaka, Þorláks saga byskups in elzta, Jarteinabók Þorláks byskups in forna, Þorláks saga byskups yngri, Jarteinabók Þorláks byskups önnur, Þorláks saga byskups C, Þorláks saga byskups E, Páls saga byskups, Ísleifs þáttr byskups, Latínubrot um Þorlák byskup.* Íslenzk fornrit 16 (Reykjavík: Hið íslenzka fornritafélag, 2002). Pp. 289–94.
  Normalized text based on *Byskupa sǫgur.*

Jón Helgason, ed. *Byskupa sǫgur.* Editiones Arnamagnæanæ, Ser. A, vol. 13.2 (Copenhagen: Reitzel, 1978). Pp. 377–81.

[Jón Sigurðsson and Guðbrandur Vigfússon, ed.] *Biskupa sögur*. 2 vols.
(Copenhagen: Møller, 1858–78). Vol. 1, pp. 312.7–113.8 and 325.12–18.
Variant readings from AM 383 4to II, pp. 311–315.7, 322.2–325.12,
and 325.18–326.8.

Literature:

Fahn, Susanne Miriam, and Gottskálk Jensson. "The Forgotten Poem:
A Latin Panegyric for Saint Þorlákr in AM 382 4to." *Gripla* 21 (2010):
19–60, esp. p. 21.

Jakob Benediktsson. "Brot úr Þorlákslesi." In *Afmælisrit Jóns Helgasonar
30. júní 1969*. Ed. Jakob Benediktsson et al. (Reykjavík: Heimskringla,
1969). Pp. 98–108, esp. p. 104.

Handlist, p. 336.

URSULA AND COMPANIONS   October 21

1. Af Úrsúlu

An epitome perhaps ultimately related to the *Speculum historiale*.

Manuscript:
AM 764 4to (ca. 1376–86).

Edition:
Kålund, Kr., ed. *Alfræði íslenzk. Islandsk encyklopædisk litteratur. III.
Landalýsingar m. fl.* STUAGNL 45 (Copenhagen: Møller, 1917–18).
Pp. 10.5–11.5.

Modern Icelandic language edition:
Wolf, Kirsten, ed. >> *Heilagra meyja sögur* (2003). P. xliin14.

Literature:
Cormack, Margaret. >> *The Saints in Iceland* (1994). Pp. 35 and 158.

Gjerløw, Lilli. "Ursula." *KLNM* 19 (1975). Cols. 368–70, esp. col. 370.

Svanhildur Óskarsdóttir. "The Book of Judith: A Medieval Icelandic
Translation." *Gripla* 11 (2000): 79–123, esp. p. 84.

– "Universal History in Fourteenth-Century Iceland: Studies in AM 764
4to." PhD dissertation, University of London, 2000. Pp. 15, 140, and
240.

– "Arctic Garden of Delights: The Purpose of the Book of Reynistaður."
In Kirsten Wolf and Johanna Denzin, ed. >> *Romance and Love in Late
Medieval and Early Modern Iceland* (2008). Pp. 279–301, esp. p. 292.

Handlist, p. 335

2. Af Úrsúlu

An epitome that forms part of *Breta sǫgur*, the translation of Geoffrey of Monmouth's *Historia Regum Britanniae*.

Manuscripts:
AM 544 4to (*Hauksbók*) (ca. 1302–10), AM 573 4to (ca. 1350–75, defective), Stock. Perg. fol. no. 58 (ca. 1700–1800, defective), and Trinity L.3.23 (ca. 1350, defective).

Editions:
Eiríkur Jónsson and Finnur Jónsson, ed. *Hauksbók udgiven efter de Arnamagnæanske håndskrifter no. 371, 544 og 675, 4° samt forskellige papirshåndskrifter af det kongelige nordiske Oldskrift-selskab* (Copenhagen: Thiele, 1892–6). Pp. 267.34–268.6.

Jón Helgason, ed. *Hauksbók: The Arna-Magnæan Manuscripts 371, 4to, 544, 4to and 675, 4to*. Manuscripta Islandica 5 (Copenhagen: Munksgaard, 1960).
Facsimile of AM 544 4to.

Jón Sigurðsson, ed. "Trójumanna saga ok Breta sögur." *Annaler for nordisk Oldkyndighed og Historie* (1848): 3–215, esp. p. 212.12–21; (1849): 3–145.
Based on AM 544 4to with variants from AM 573 4to.

Danish translation:
Jón Sigurðsson, ed. "Trójumanna saga ok Breta sögur." *Annaler for nordisk Oldkyndighed og Historie* (1848): 3–215, esp. p. 213.14–23; (1849): 3–145.

Literature:
Cormack, Margaret. >> *The Saints in Iceland* (1994). Pp. 35 and 158.
Gjerløw, Lilli. "Ursula." *KLNM* 19 (1975). Cols. 368–70, esp. col. 370.
Sverrir Tómasson. "Kristnar trúarbókmenntir í óbundnu máli." In Guðrún Nordal, Sverrir Tómasson, and Vésteinn Ólason, ed. >> *Íslensk Bókmenntasaga* 1 (1992). Pp. 419–79, esp. p. 432.
Wolf, Kirsten, ed. >> *Heilagra meyja sögur* (2003). P. xliin14.

VINCENT THE DEACON   January 22

1. Vincentíuss saga

An abridged translation of a form of the *passio*, *BHL* 8639.

Manuscripts:
AM 655 4to IV (ca. 1200–25) and Stock. Perg. fol. no. 2 (ca. 1425–45).
Editions:
Foote, Peter, ed. >> *Lives of Saints* (1962).
   Facsimile of Stock. Perg. fol. no. 2.
Unger, C.R., ed. >> *Heilagra manna søgur* (1877). Vol. 2, pp. 321–6
   Edition of Stock. Perg. fol. no. 2.
Literature:
Carlé, Birte. >> *Jomfru-fortællingen* (1985). Pp. 39, 41, 50, and 63–4.
– "Men and Women in the Saints' Sagas of *Stock. 2, fol.*" In John
   Lindow, Lars Lönnroth, and Gerd Wolfgang Weber, ed. >> *Structure
   and Meaning in Old Norse Literature* (1986). Pp. 317–46, esp. p. 320.
Cormack, Margaret. >> *The Saints in Iceland* (1994). P. 158.
Mogk, Eugen. >> *Geschichte der norwegisch-isländischen Literatur* (1904).
   P. 891.
Wolf, Kirsten. "The Severed Breast: A Topos in the Legends of Female
   Virgin Martyr Saints." *ANF* 112 (1997): 97–112, esp. p. 100.
Handlist, p. 335.

2. Vincentíuss saga

An epitome of the legend based on a text like that in 1.

Manuscript:
AM 238 fol. XV (ca. 1450–1500).
Literature:
Carlé, Birte. >> *Jomfru-fortællingen* (1985). P. 37.
Cormack, Margaret. >> *The Saints in Iceland* (1994). Pp. 37n45 and 158.
Foote, Peter, ed. >> *Lives of Saints* (1962). P. 24.
Handlist, p. 335.

VITAE PATRUM

Vitae Patrum (Heilagra feðra æfi)

Vitae Patrum I is a translation of *Vitae Patrum 2: Historia eremitica* (or
Historia monachorum in Aegypto). *Vitae Patrum II* corresponds to *Vitae
Patrum 3* (*Verba seniorum*) and draws also on *Vitae Patrum 5* (another
collection of *Verba seniorum*).

Manuscripts:
AM 225 fol. (ca. 1400), AM 232 fol. (ca. 1370, defective), AM 234 fol.
   (ca. 1340, defective), AM 657a–b 4to (ca. 1350), AM 668 4to (ca.
   1400–50, defective), and AM 764 4to (ca. 1376–86).

Editions:
Svanhildur Óskarsdóttir. "Universal History in Fourteenth-Century
   Iceland: Studies in AM 764 4to." PhD dissertation, University of
   London, 2000. Pp. 297–8.
   Edition of AM 764 4to.
Tveitane, Mattias. *Den lærde stil. Oversetterprosa i den norrøne versjonen
   av Vitæ Patrum.* Årbok for Universitetet i Bergen, Humanistisk Serie
   1967, No. 2 (Bergen and Oslo: Norwegian Universities Press, 1968).
   Pp. 20–1 and 23–24.9.
   Edition of AM 764 4to.
Unger, C.R., ed. >> *Heilagra manna søgur* (1877). Vol. 2, pp. 335–671.
   Based on AM 225 fol. (pp. 335–671) with variants from AM 232 fol.
   (pp. 335–374.6 and 381.7– 430.11), AM 234 fol. (pp. 335–347.2 [with
   lacunae], 356.14–365.17, 374.9–382.10 [with lacunae], and AM 392.9–
   402.6), and AM 668 4to (pp. 534.18–542.4). Edition of AM 657a–b 4to
   (pp. 632–3 lower text).

Literature:
Battista, Simonetta. "Old Norse Hagiography and the Question of the
   Latin Sources." In Rudolf Simek and Judith Meurer, ed. >> *Scandi-
   navia and Christian Europe in the Middle Ages* (2003). Pp. 26–33, esp.
   p. 32.
– "*Blámenn, djǫflar* and Other Representations of Evil in Old Norse
   Literature." In John McKinnell, David Ashurst, and Donata Kick, ed.
   >> *The Fantastic in Old Norse/Icelandic Literature* (2006). Vol. 1,
   pp. 113–22, esp. pp. 117–18 and 120.
Bekker-Nielsen, Hans. "Et brudstykke af Kongespejlet. Med be-
   mærkninger om indholdet af AM 668, 4°." *Opuscula* 1. Bibliotheca
   Arnamagnæana 20 (Copenhagen: Munksgaard, 1960). Pp. 105–12, esp.
   pp. 109–10 and 112.
– "Kyrkofäderna ock kyrkolärarna. K. i vestnordisk litteratur." *KLNM* 9
   (1964). Cols. 690–3, esp. col. 692.
Bekker-Nielsen, Hans, Thorkil Damsgaard Olsen, and Ole Widding.
   >> *Norrøn fortællekunst* (1965). P. 125.
Bekker-Nielsen, Hans, and Ole Widding. "Legende. Norge og Island."
   KLNM 10 (1965). Cols. 421–3, esp. col. 421.

– "Religiøs prosalitteratur. Norge og Island." *KLNM* 14 (1969). Cols. 42–4, esp. col. 43.

Boyer, Régis. >> *La vie religieuse en Islande* (1979). Pp. 162 and 224.

Cormack, Margaret. >> *The Saints in Iceland* (1994). P. 83.

Finnur Jónsson. >> *Den oldnorske og oldislandske Litteraturs Historie* (1920–4). Vol. 2, p. 875.

Foote, Peter. "Auðræði." In Arthur Brown and Peter Foote, ed. >> *Early English and Norse Studies* (1963). Pp. 62–76, esp. pp. 67–8.

Hallberg, Peter. "Imagery in Religious Old Norse Prose Literature: An Outline." *ANF* 102 (1987): 120–70, esp. pp. 125, 133–4, 138–40, 144, 148–9, and 159–60.

Hofmann, Dietrich. *Die Legende von Sankt Clemens in den skandinavischen Ländern im Mittelalter*. Beiträge zur Skandinavistik 13 (Frankfurt am Main: Peter Lang, 1997). P. 128.

Holm-Olsen, Ludvig. "Middelalderens litteratur i Norge." In *Norges litteratur historie* 1. Ed. Edvard Beyer (Oslo: Cappelen, 1974). Pp. 18–342, esp p. 61.

Jónas Kristjánsson. *Um Fóstbrœðra sögu* (Reykjavík: Stofnun Árna Magnússonar, 1972). Pp. 286, 288, and 290.

– "The Court Style." In Régis Boyer, ed. >> *Les Sagas de Chevaliers (Riddarasögur)* (1985). Pp. 431–40, esp. pp. 432 and 438.

– >> *Eddas and Sagas* (1988). P. 142.

Kirby, Ian. >> *Biblical Quotation* (1980). Vol. 2, pp. 20, 45, and 50–1.

– *Bible Translation in Old Norse*. Université de Lausanne Publications de la faculté des lettres 27 (Geneva: Librairie Droz, 1986). Pp. 47 and 166.

Mattsson, Ola. "Helga manna leverne." *KLNM* 6 (1961). Cols. 310–11.

Mogk, Eugen. >> *Geschichte der norwegisch-isländischen Literatur* (1904). P. 892.

Paasche, Fredrik. *Norges og Islands litteratur inntil utgangen av middelalderen*. Rev. ed. by Anne Holtsmark (Oslo: Aschehoug, 1947). P. 446.

Svanhildur Óskarsdóttir. "Prose of Christian Instruction." In *A Companion to Old Norse–Icelandic Literature*. Ed. Rory McTurk (Oxford: Blackwell, 2005). Pp. 338–53, esp. p. 341.

Sverrir Tómasson. *Formálar íslenskra sagnaritara á miðöldum. Rannsókn bókmenntahefðar* (Reykjavík: Stofnun Árna Magnússonar, 1988). Pp. 50, 62, 85–6, 92, 100–11, 116, 123, 128, 174, 183, and 206–8.

– "Trúarbókmenntir í lausu máli á síðmiðöld." In Böðvar Guðmundsson,
   Sverrir Tómasson, Torfi H. Tulinius, and Vésteinn Ólason, ed.
   >> *Íslensk Bókmenntasaga* 2 (1993). Pp. 249–82, esp. pp. 257 and 275.
Sverrir Tómasson, Bragi Halldórsson, and Einar Sigurbjörnsson, ed.
   >> *Heilagra karla sögur* (2007). Pp. xlvi and l.
Tveitane, Mattias. "Vitae Patrum." *KLNM* 20 (1976). Cols. 194–6, esp.
   col. 195.
Handlist, p. 335.

VITUS   June 15

Vítuss saga

Based on a version of *BHL* 8711 and possibly *BHL* 8714.

Manuscripts:
AM 180b fol. (ca. 1500) and Stock. Papp. 8vo no. 8 (ca. 1650–60).
Edition:
Unger, C.R., ed. >> *Heilagra manna søgur* (1877). Vol. 2, pp. 327–34.
   Edition of AM 180b fol.
Modern Icelandic language edition:
Sverrir Tómasson, Bragi Halldórsson, and Einar Sigurbjörnsson, ed.
   Heilagra karla sögur (Reykjavík: Bókmenntafræðistofnun Háskóla
   Íslands, 2007). Pp. 149–58.
Literature:
Battista, Simonetta. "Interpretations of the Roman Pantheon in the Old
   Norse Hagiographic Sagas." In Geraldine Barnes and Margaret Clunies
   Ross, ed. >> *Old Norse Myths, Literature and Society* (2000). Pp. 24–
   34, esp. p. 32.
Jakob Benediktsson. "Nödhjälparna." *KLNM* 21 (1977). Cols. 289–90,
   esp. col. 290.
Kirby, Ian. *Biblical Quotation* (1980). Vol. 2, p. 50.
Lehmann, Paul. >> "Skandinaviens Anteil an der lateinischen Literatur
   und Wissenschaft des Mittelalters" (1937). P. 49.
Lindow, John. "Norse Mythology and the Lives of the Saints." *SS* 73
   (2001): 437–56, esp. p. 447.
Mogk, Eugen. >> *Geschichte der norwegisch-isländischen Literatur* (1904).
   P. 891.

Wolf, Kirsten. "The Severed Breast: A Topos in the Legends of Female
    Virgin Martyr Saints." *ANF* 112 (1997): 97–112, esp. p. 100.
Handlist, p. 336.

WALBURGA   February 25

Valbjargar jartegnir

A translation of six of the miracles attributed to the intercession of
Saint Walburga. The sources have been identified as *BHL* 8766, 8767,
and 8768.

Manuscript:
AM 764 4to (ca. 1376–86, defective).
Edition:
Wolf, Kirsten. "A Fragmentary Excerpt on Saint Walburga in AM 764
    4to." *Gripla* 11 (2000): 209–20, esp. pp. 211–14.
Literature:
Bekker-Nielsen, Hans. "Et brudstykke af en legende i et islandsk haand-
    skrift. Hvem er W i AM 764, 4to?" *Mm* (1963): 102–5.
Cormack, Margaret. >> *The Saints in Iceland* (1994). P. 35.
Fell, Christine E. "Anglo-Saxon Saints in Old Norse Sources and Vice
    Versa." In Hans Bekker Nielsen, Peter Foote, and Olaf Olsen, ed.
    >> *Proceedings of the Eighth Viking Congress* (1981). Pp. 95–106, esp.
    pp. 97–9.
Svanhildur Óskarsdóttir. "The Book of Judith: A Medieval Icelandic
    Translation." *Gripla* 11 (2000): 79–123, esp. p. 84.
– "Universal History in Fourteenth-Century Iceland: Studies in AM 764
    4to." PhD dissertation, University College London, 2000. Pp. 60, 62,
    140, and 240.
– "Arctic Garden of Delights: The Purpose of the Book of Reynistaður."
    In Kirsten Wolf and Johanna Denzin, ed. >> *Romance and Love in
    Late Medieval and Early Modern Iceland* (2008). Pp. 279–301, esp.
    pp. 292–3.
Wolf, Kirsten, ed. >> *Heilagra meyja sögur* (2003). Pp. xxxviii, li, and lvi.
Handlist, p. 336.

Index of Manuscripts